Entertaining

Tsarist Russia

Christmas, 1999

To my favorist Russky,

Happy reading and listening.

Love,
Martha

Entertaining Tsarist Russia

Tales
Songs
Plays
Movies
Jokes
Ads
and
Images
from
Russian
Urban
Life
1779–1917

EDITED BY

James von Geldern and Louise McReynolds

INDIANA UNIVERSITY PRESS   BLOOMINGTON & INDIANAPOLIS

This book is a publication of

Indiana University Press
601 North Morton Street
Bloomington, Indiana 47404-3797 USA

http://www.indiana.edu/~iupress

Telephone orders   800-842-6796
Fax orders   812-855-7931
Orders by email   iuporder@indiana.edu

Library of Congress Cataloging-in-Publicaton Data
Entertaining tsarist Russia : tales, songs, plays, movies, jokes, ads,
    and images from Russian urban life, 1779–1917 / edited by James
    von Geldern and Louise McReynolds.
        p.   cm.—(Indiana-Michigan series in Russian and East
    European studies)
    Includes bibliographical references.
    ISBN 0-253-33407-1 (alk. paper).—ISBN 0-253-21195-6 (pbk. :
    alk. paper).—ISBN 0-253-33409-8 (compact disc)
        1. Popular culture—Russia.   2. Russia—Civilization—18th
    century.   3. Russia—Civilization—1801–1917.   4. Russian
    literature—18th century.   5. Russian literature—19th century.
    I. Von Geldern, James.   II. McReynolds, Louise, date.   III. Series.
    DK32.E6   1998
    306'.0947'09034—dc21   97-52597

    1   2   3   4   5   03   02   01   00   99   98

WE DEDICATE THIS BOOK
TO THE STUDENTS OF
MACALESTER COLLEGE AND THE UNIVERSITY OF HAWAI'I
— SEPARATED BY MOTHER NATURE,
BUT UNITED BY MOTHER RUSSIA.

Contents

Note: Performances of entries marked with an asterisk
are on the accompanying compact disk.

ACKNOWLEDGMENTS   xi

INTRODUCTION   xiii

NOTE ON TRANSLITERATION   xxvii

Part I: The Heyday of Absolutism, Late Eighteenth Century–1825

Anecdotes about Balakirev (Traditional Tales)   4

Vasily Berezaisky, *Tales of the Ancient Poshekhonians* (1798)   6

Teller of Old Moscow Tales, *The Merry Old Fellow* (1790)   10

Martin Zadek, *The Ancient and Modern Divinatory Oracle* (1821)   12

Guak, or Unbounded Devotion: A Knightly Tale (18th century)   15

The Tale of Vanka Kain (1815)   23

A. A. Shakhovskoi, *The New Sterne* (1805)   31

"Traditional Songs" (Late 18th century)*   41

Part II: Commerce Asserts Its Mediating Presence, 1825–1860

Nikolai Polevoi, *Ermak Timofeich* (1845)   49

Pavel Grigoriev, Jr., *Filatka and Miroshka the Rivals* (1833)   57

Faddei Bulgarin, *Ivan Vyzhigin* (1829)   65

Petr Ershov, *The Little Humpbacked Horse* (1834)   74

Aleksandra Ishimova, *The History of Russia Told for Children* (1838)   77

Nikolai Zriakhov, *The Battle of the Russians with the Kabardinians* (1842)   83

Etiquette Manuals (1849–1911)   93

Street Types, Illustrations by M. Pikki and K. Richau (1860)   105

Aleksei Lvov, *God Save the Tsar* (1833)*   107

Evgeny Grebenka, *Dark Eyes* (1843)*   108

N. Sokolov, *The Great Moscow Fire* (1850)*   109

Aleksandr Ammosov and O. Kh. Agrenova-Slavianskaia, *Elegy (Khas-Bulat)*
  (1858)*   111

Part III: Great Reforms and the Expansion of Civic Space, 1861–1881

Balagan Advertisements, Malafeev Theater (1883)   119

Vsevolod Krestovsky, *The Slums of Petersburg* (1864)   121

How the Russian Gave It Hot to a German (1869)   129

Fedor Ivanich Kuz'ma, *Oh Those Yaroslavites, What a Fine Folk!* (1868)   135

The Slums of the Female Heart (1870)   141

Vasily Nemirovich-Danchenko, *Correspondence from the Russo-Turkish War*
  (1876–77)   149

M. Evstigneev, *War Stories from the Present-Day War with the Turks* (1879)   154

L. A. Tikhomirov, *Where Is It Better?* (1873)   156

A Flask of Hooch (1882)   166

*Gypsy Romances**   173

Part IV: Political Stagnation vs. Rapid Industrialization, 1882–1905

B. S. Borisov and V. A. Kriger, *Scenes from a Third-Class Car* (recorded circa
  1910)*   183

M. L. Lentovsky, *Sarah Bernhardt* (1891)   186

V. P. Valentinov, *The Queen of Diamonds* (1908–1910)   198

Anecdotes (1840–1917)   203

Moscow Court Reporting, The Moscow Sheet (Early 1880s)   212

Aleksei Pazukhin, *The Terrible Wedding Night* (1883)   217

The Terrible Bandit Churkin (1885)   221

N. A. Leikin, *Where the Oranges Ripen* (1892)   230

I. I. Miasnitsky, *Messrs. Businessmen* (1890s)   239

The Diary of Maria Bashkirtseva (1889)   244

V. M. Doroshevich, *Ivanov Pavel* (1901)   250

Maxim Gorky, *Song of The Stormy Petrel* (1901)   259

M. D. Klefortov, *Light-Fingered Sonya* (1903)   261

Revolutionary Songs (Late 19th Century)*   269

Part V: The Eruption of Commercial Culture in the Interrevolutionary Years, 1906–1917

Vaudeville Skits (1905–1910)*   278

Why Was I Born into This World? Tobolsk Prison Song (1908)*   285

K[onstantin] R[omanov], *The Poor Fellow Died* (circa 1910)*   286

Marusia Poisoned Herself (1915)*   290

Olga Gridina, *Russian Sob Sister* (1910)   292

Al. Aleksandrovsky, *How the Lasses Burned a Lad in the Stove* (1911)   295

V. I. Kryzhanovskaia, *The Wrath of God* (1909)   299

Lidiia Charskaia, *The Little Siberian Girl (Sibirochka)* (1910)   306

M. N. Volkonsky, *The African Princess (Vampuka)* (1907)   316

N. N. Breshko-Breshkovsky, *Gladiators of Our Times* (1909)   323

Mikhail Artsybashev, *Sanin* (1908)   329

Anastasia Verbitskaia, *The Keys to Happiness* (1913)   333

Count Amori, *The Vanquished* (1912)   337

Petr Chardynin, *Do You Remember?* (1915)*   339

E. A. Nagrodskaia, *The Wrath of Dionysus* (1910)   341

Count Amori, *The Countess-Actress* (1916)   349

Nat Pinkerton, King of Detectives, *The Bloody Talisman* (1915)   362

The Headlands of Manchuria (1906–1908)*   377

The Heroic Feat of the Don Cossack Kuzma Firsovich Kriuchkov (1914)   379

Sergei Sokolsky, *Jackals* (1916)   383

V. V. Ramazanov, *Rasputin's Nighttime Orgies* (1917)   385

GLOSSARY   391

SELECTED BIBLIOGRAPHY   393

ACKNOWLEDGMENTS

Colleagues and friends have both helped and inspired us, for which we happily thank them. No work on Russian entertainment could begin without the godfather, Richard Stites; he offered not only invaluable suggestions but, more important, the enthusiasm that fired this project in the first place. Joan Neuberger, too, cracked wise with us, helping to keep a scholarly endeavor enjoyable.

All translations are by the editors unless otherwise noted, and we thank those who gave us materials from their own research that strengthened this collection. Hubertus Jahn and Susan Morrisey supplied stories about the First World War and student life. Albin Konechnyi provided materials about fairground entertainments, the *balagan* and the *raek,* and Tamara Mikhailova helped translate some of the most difficult. Konechnyi's own work on related topics aided us in organizing this anthology. Choices had to be made, though, and the two of us are ultimately responsible for the selections that appear here; we still have mixed feelings about what was left on the cutting-room floor.

We deeply appreciate the institutional and technical support we received at various stages. The International Research and Exchanges Board (IREX) got us to Russia to collect the materials, which we could not have done without the generous and experienced aid of bibliographers at the Saltykov-Shchedrin Public Library in St. Petersburg. Moreover, their genuine appreciation for a project such as this, so different from the usual requests made of them, reminded us of the value of the many levels of cross-cultural contact. At Macalester College, Lana Larsen of the Department of German and Russian helped with the technicalities, as did several students: Milana Berggoldt, Aleria Jensen, and Monika Krauze. At Macalester's Dewitt Wallace Library and the University of Hawai'i's Hamilton Library, Jean Beccone and Pat Polansky, respectively, tracked down numerous elusive sources. The musical selections included on the accompanying compact disk were obtained from the Library of Congress. Janet Rabinowitch of Indiana University Press recognized the inherent worth of the project from the outset and encouraged us to press forward. Jane Lyle, also at Indiana University Press, smoothed over our translations and improved the readability of the entire manuscript.

Most of all, we thank each other for the equally high levels of energy and professionalism that made collaboration a pleasure.

INTRODUCTION

In reading the histories and great literature of nineteenth-century Russia, it is easy to lose sight of ordinary Russians leading everyday lives. The people were amused as well as oppressed; the political was only one aspect of their rich and contradictory lives. Certainly the tsarist state set the overarching framework for public life: it won impressive military victories in pursuit of its imperial mission, created an unwieldy bureaucratic apparatus of supervision and control, and finally crumbled under unbearable strain. At more immediate levels of life, family structures, community relations, and economic behavior underwent gradual shifts of enormous consequence. Some of the best noble families declined into oblivion, while members of other estates rose from squalor to great wealth. An agrarian economy gave way to the commercial market. New modes of production, distribution, and consumption redrew the map of the nation, making tangible changes in daily life. Interregional and international trade sent merchants into unfamiliar places in search of business. Peasants flooded into the cities, where a whirl of impressions confronted them faster than anything they had experienced in the village. The mental landscape of ordinary Russians changed forever, a process reflected in the mass-oriented commercial culture that developed to help them cope with the new world. Created in the city, this culture was consumed by the new urban classes. It answered their needs, embodying the tastes and myths that aided their transformation into city folk.

This anthology is intended to introduce readers to imperial Russia's emerging popular and commercial urban culture, and the groups that produced and consumed it. The selections presented here illustrate in colorful detail how both the experiences and the composition of Russian society evolved over time, in response to economic, technological, and political changes. Covering a period from the late eighteenth century to 1917, when tsarist Russia was swept away by revolution, the anthology includes tales, songs, graphics, plays, skits, movie scripts, jokes, and advertisements. The materials were created for a variety of audiences: beginning with the conservative and nationalist nobility, audiences quickly expanded to include merchants and their servants, and workers and their peasant cousins. As the empire expanded, the audiences also became increasingly multi-ethnic. These diverse publics came together in many ways: reading and being read to, hearing and watching, shouting and gossiping. They gathered at homes, on fairgrounds and street corners, in circuses and taverns, and later in movie houses.

The term "culture" has so many connotations that an explanation of how it is used here is needed at the outset. At its most fundamental, culture refers to the traditional beliefs and structures that hold communities together. In this collection, culture also suggests a primary means by which Russians understood how they fit into the broad social context, and what it was that kept society glued together. Yet this culture was anything but the static traditionalist rituals of premodern communities. The materials included in this volume reflect the tremendous strains of rapid urbanization, and help today's readers comprehend how adaptations of art and literature helped people to function.

What, though, can "popular" mean under these circumstances? Cultural historians have moved in recent years beyond a class-based understanding of popular, broadening the term to include customs and conventions understood by the populace as a whole. The different social groups may diverge in how they make use of those customs, but members of this enlarged public still draw upon the same cluster of cultural referents. For example, ideas about politics and patriotism in tsarist Russia might have varied according to one's personal ambition or level of education, but all groups drew upon the same stock of symbolic tsars, Orthodox saints, and Slavic legends to create an identity as Russians.

Although certain symbols, such as the double-headed eagle of the Romanov dynasty, allowed Russians to identify themselves as members of a shared culture, they also found themselves separated along class, gender, ethnic, and even political lines. For something to be "popular," then, it had to navigate these divisions and appeal to a mix of backgrounds. The antithesis of elitism, popular artifacts of culture depended on a broad audience. In nineteenth-century Russia, this requirement put the purveyors of popular culture up against the intelligentsia, the politicized group of intellectuals who assumed for themselves the authority to define the national welfare. The intelligentsia had used culture, especially literature, as the political weapon of choice against the autocracy since the eighteenth century. Their collective reputation had such force that even writers from the boulevard had to acknowledge their fundamental axiom that literature must serve a political end. The result was an intrinsically contradictory situation in which popular writers would modify ideas and forms originating with the elites to create a hybrid culture that appealed to an increasingly pluralist society. Under these circumstances, Russian popular culture was more "middlebrow" than "lowbrow." It better suited the interests of Russians positioned between the intelligentsia and the *narod* (the catchall term for common folk), people who held the middle ground between tradition and the uncompromising elitism of the intelligentsia. "Middle" here suggests not so much a stable site where culture can be generated as a point of transition and transfer. Because social and economic circumstances changed so much during the years covered in this anthology, so did the readers and genres that constituted this middlebrow. The function of the middle as a space for negotiation, though, remained the same.

Another aspect of "culture" as used here is the role of commerce in subsidizing it, and of the market in distributing it. The commercial basis of this culture allowed for challenge and choice in ways that neither the government nor the intelligentsia permitted. The monetary self-interest of producers gave them an agenda, which they in turn passed along to consumers. This characteristic manifests itself repeatedly throughout this anthology, which traces the evolution of practices associated with consumption in modernizing Russia. Censors hovered in the background, but they were more concerned with overt political protest and sexual licentiousness than with consumption as an ethic.

Popular culture was designed for mass consumption. The intelligentsia, who failed, no less than commercial publishers, who succeeded, wanted the masses to share their opinions, but orienting a product toward the whole population meant expanding rather than reducing the common denominator. Mass-oriented culture also hinged upon making products available on a large scale. Advances in technology facilitated the dissemination of these materials; the heightened demand then stimulated further innovations. From the early-nineteenth-century fair booth that depended upon audience participation, to the movie house a hundred years later that repudiated active involvement, cultural practices underwent tremendous alterations. It would be naive to attribute an idealized political disinterest to this market-driven culture; the point is not that it reflected a non-partisan middle ground, but that it gave evidence of new values, and also offered alternative, sometimes even reactionary, solutions to mounting tensions. Culture, whether mass or elite, urban or rural, commercial or subsidized, is terrain fought over by the various groups who depend upon it to make sense of their lives.

The materials included in this anthology are arranged in rough order by chronology and by medium, divisions that reflect changing environments and social climates. They correspond to political, social, and cultural milestones: 1779–1825; 1825–1860; 1861–1881; 1882–1905; and 1906–1917. We have provided a brief introduction for each section to establish the historical context. Specific incidents, individuals, and terms are explained in numbered annotations at the foot of the page (notes with asterisks were provided by the original authors). There is a glossary at the end of the book for terms that recur throughout the collection; for readers' convenience, we have italicized these terms in the text. Also, some of the pieces here have been edited for brevity.

The first period represented in the collection opens with early signs of an urban mass-market culture and closes with the Decembrist revolt, an aborted rebellion launched by members of the politicized military elite. Although not themselves purveyors of the kind of literature included here, the Decembrists nonetheless mark the first break, because they personify the relationship between culture and sociopolitical action. They formed an embryonic public whose opinion set them apart from the state. It was in this rudimentary civic sphere that commercial culture had the opportunity to develop. The next period begins with the evolution of public opinion and ends with the momentous emancipation of the serfs in 1861. The Great Reforms, inaugurated by the emancipation, introduced so many fundamental changes into society and politics, from a relaxed censorship to an independent judiciary with ordinary Russians serving as jurors, that cultural practices also had to be adapted to provide interpretations for the new meaning of citizenship. This period includes the first two creative decades of the reform era, and concludes with the assassination of the tsar who had set it all in motion. The fourth period, 1882–1905, covers the boom in commercial culture that resulted from the state's decision to push forward with industrialization. It ends with a nationwide revolt against an obscurantist autocracy; signs of both the excitement and the stress of building a great empire are found throughout the mass-oriented culture of this period.

Readers will notice that the final section in this anthology is larger than the others, but the disproportion reflects the volume of materials produced during the dizzying interrevolutionary years, 1906–1917. The combination of political reforms and economic modernization had produced a variety of publics, and the relaxation of censorship following the 1905 revolution increased the abilities of writers, performers, and publishers to satisfy the growing diversity in tastes. The anthology ends with the Bolshevik revolution, when the players and issues took on unrecognizably different forms, although popular culture remained contested terrain. Readers interested in the Soviet period can consult the companion to this volume, *Mass Culture in Soviet Russia, 1917–1953,* edited by James von Geldern and Richard Stites.

Each chronological section breaks down further into print media, spectacles, and songs, with graphic materials interspersed throughout the volume. During the course of the nineteenth century, as new groups gathered in Russia's cities, new technologies brought them information with increasing speed. Russians learned to see, hear, and read differently. When peasant songs were replaced by urban romances, knightly tales by newspapers, and vaudevilles by movies, consumers had to relocate themselves in an expanding world and learn to process information in new ways. Readers will sense that the pieces themselves were changing—the media, their thematics and style, language and symbols—and with them, their audiences. *Lubki* (woodcut graphics with a brief text), vaudevilles, songs, newspapers, and jokes each expressed different ideas. They appealed to distinctive, though often overlapping, audiences. New narrative conventions shifted consumers' attention from the traditional structures of life to the unfolding awareness of individuals. Readers found that they had to judge more things for themselves, and do so more quickly than their parents or grandparents had.

Russian popular culture grew with the cities at the beginning of the century. The industrial age dawdled on its route east from Europe. Urban entertainment was very traditional before 1825; it consisted mostly of old songs, stories, and anecdotes—some dating back to the Western Renaissance. Affectionate tales of Peter the Great and his jester Balakirev, knightly adventures and divination books imported from the West, and a rich native lore of robber bands and wanderers were the stuff of these entertainments. Much of this culture could be classified as urban lore, passed along by word of mouth more often than by print. Many of the examples included here are simply the written renditions of long-circulating legends. They are included in this anthology for two reasons: first, most of them survived on the market until the twentieth century; second, and more significant, by the very act of printing and mass distribution, they became the foundation of urban mass-oriented culture.

Early in the eighteenth century, the popular culture of urbanites resembled the folk culture of the peasantry. Its consumers were merchants, clerks, lower-level bureaucrats, peasant cabbies, and housemen (*dvorniki*). Merchants and others read the same things from generation to generation, mostly romantic tales named for their knightly heroes, such as *Guak, Eruslan Lazarevich,* and *Bova Korolevich.* Some were of foreign origin, some Russian; some concerned upper-class life, some lower-. Distinctions were never precise. The first *lubki* were religious in content and appeared in the seventeenth century; within a century, secularism had seeped in. These inexpensive commercial prints were produced in urban specialty shops concentrated on Moscow's Nikolsky Street and distributed to the villages and towns of the empire by legions of itinerant peddlers (*ofeni*). Large-scale production of *lubki* later became possible with the switch from wood blocks to copper plates, the first of many effects that new technology would exert on commercial culture.

Several factors impeded the growth of urban popular culture in the early nineteenth century. Literacy rates and interest in literature were weak, particularly among the lower classes, and machines still exercised little influence over cultural production. Distribution systems were also crude; the people most apt to transport culture around the empire were soldiers, who brought distinctive though nonwritten songs and stories. The printing and commercial distribution of popular culture could trace its origins to 1779, when the Muscovite Matvei Komarov collected semi-factual lore about the real-life thief Vanka Kain and published it for an intended readership of shop clerks and household servants. Kain, who had terrorized the region less than a generation earlier, exemplified things to come. His life, ignored by the arbiters of taste, was written (and rewritten many times) with a disregard for literary canons that matched Kain's disregard for the law. Kain was the classic rogue; he drank, caroused, stole, and pillaged, and he spoke with a mangled grammar more modern than the idiom of his higher literary confreres.

A culture marketed to the lower and middle urban classes became fully possible only from the 1860s, after the serfs had been emancipated, print regulations had been loosened, and a lower-class population had flooded into the cities to find jobs in the new industrial sector. Defeat in the Crimean War in 1855 had forced the state to recognize the consequences of Russia's technological gap, and it launched ambitious programs to modernize the army and construct a railroad system. Peasants poured into the cities to work in factories. Thus began the process of urbanization, as this rural proletariat had to develop new coping strategies to deal with a very different outside world. Gradually they perceived that the city was no longer alien, and that their cultural needs could help to shape it. Forming the basis of a truly mass audience, they watched as a culture industry arose to meet their needs. The new print media reproduced their wares in thousands of copies, and distributed them quickly in the cities, often even to the countryside. Typesetting techniques sped up the publishing process, and pulp literature could be produced quickly and cheaply, allowing for the rapid turnover of material. It became technologically possible and economically feasible to report current events soon after they had happened.

This mini-revolution in mass communications marked another important change. Print media served the new readership, and because print workers were among the most educated of the working class, they also helped create those new readers. Journalism had traditionally been an intellectual enterprise; many of Russia's most daring and forward thinkers had been journalists who wrote for an audience of like-minded, educated people. Now suddenly the market was flooded with mass-circulation newspapers with names such as the *Voice*, the *Petersburg Gazette*, and the *Moscow Sheet*, staffed by people unencumbered by the intellectual tradition. The new breed included publishers such as Aleksei Suvorin and Ivan Sytin; editors and writers such as Vladimir Mikhnevich, Vladimir Giliarovsky, Nikolai Leikin, Nikolai Pastukhov, Aleksei Pazukhin, Vlas Doroshevich, and Aleksei Svirsky. Newspapers also provided a training ground for Anton Chekhov, Maxim Gorky, and Aleksandr Kuprin. Newspaper journalists, who often came up under hard circumstances, captured readers for whom the older journalists could no longer speak. They knew their audience, chose themes of greater sensational than didactic interest, and wrote in a muscular, compact Russian. Some made their names by exposing the blight of urban Russia; others rose from poverty to wealth as publishers, serving as models of bootstrap mobility. The style as well as the substance of newspapers affected readership and public opinion. The feuilleton, a broad-ranging sketch genre employed by the most famous reporters, ruled the daily press. Serialized fiction also stimulated daily readership. War, crime, homelessness, and disintegrating family ties caused reformers dismay and gave reporters prime material. Some writers made great careers on misfortune and disorder, from war correspondent Vasily Nemirovich-Danchenko to boulevard publisher Pastukhov, who serialized the life of Moscow bandit Vasily Churkin. In all its variety, print journalism became the focal point for a genuinely public opinion, shaping the views of readers and giving them a medium of open expression.

Newspapers brought awareness of the outside world, which in addition to nations beyond Russia's borders included other sections of the city, with their various classes and ethnic groups, as well as the other territories engulfed by the expanding empire. Foreign lands had previously had a very dim reflection in popular culture. The papers now reported on wars with the Ottoman Empire and on Paris fashions, making them topics of conversation in village taverns. Readers recognized in every bizarre urban malady evidence that their world was changing, but they often lacked the vocabulary to express the effects of change. New urban slang and rhythms slipped into the language, giving voice to readers' concerns. The shift of public discourse from the "thick" intellectual journals to the daily press also introduced sensationalism into public debate. Feuilleton writers had a nose for the relevant sensation: child prostitution, spouse beating, scofflaws, and petty thieves were spectacles that dramatized some of the great questions of the day. Public courtrooms served as theaters where juries, a novel institution in Russia, performed as the chorus, imposing their values on an often unwelcoming legal world.

Change also came to the world of theater, which gradually opened up to mass audiences. Since theater did not rely on spectators' literacy, the folk traditions of drama and spectacle, which dated back to the eighteenth century, lived on far into the nineteenth. New types of theater, visible by the 1820s, took root at large gathering points: city squares, holiday carnivals, market fairs, and smaller rural fairs. Performances were initially limited to small itinerant spectacles, of which the Petrushka puppet show was the last great representative. Gradually these shows were displaced by larger *balagany*, temporary but full-blown theaters erected for several months each holiday season. *Balagany* were run by able entrepreneurs; in the beginning, most were foreigners, but later generations were Russian. They were responsible for building the theaters, hiring the actors, writing the scenarios, and directing the plays. Most productions were spectacular, featuring stunt-filled chases, artillery barrages, and sometimes even aquatic battles.

This commercialized culture drove many educated observers to despair. They perceived a deterioration in common mores and argued that this culture had precipitated crime, family breakdowns, sexual depravity, and poverty. A close look revealed that conventional consciousness had changed, not only in values, but in its styles of interaction and perception. Traditional forms of peasant expression had been relatively unmediated, passed on from person to person in the village, and from performers who knew their audience and felt kinship with them. Now the city brought its culture to the countryside. Young villagers sang *chastushki*, satirical rhymed couplets with urban themes. They played city instruments such as the accordion, or read the *lubki* printed in the cities. This differed sharply from the intensely localized peasant culture. Each region had its own patterns and styles, and peasants perceived the culture of a neighboring region, which to outsiders seemed remarkably similar, as something alien. The new city culture was highly mobile; a rhyme originating in Petersburg could quickly make its way to Odessa. A romance of provincial workers could be sung throughout the empire, and distributed in countless "golden bouquets," as cheap song collections were called. Culture that originated in a village traveled to other villages via the city, where it was printed, performed on stage, and then brought back by migrant laborers in urbanized form. This represented not the loss of an organic Russian culture, but the creation of the first popular culture shared across much of Russia.

The educated elite who first described Russia's popular culture were hoping to control the instruction of the peasantry after emancipation, and they saw commercial products as pernicious competitors. They envisaged an impossibly homogeneous culture derived from universalisms about liberty and social harmony. Alarmed about the corruption of tastes, they could not appreciate the developing variety and unpredictability of audiences. Popular culture was as layered and mixed as an archeological dig. Merchant sons read the same knightly tales of Guak and Eruslan Lazarevich that their grandfathers had; but at night they caroused in nightclubs with gypsy singers. Peasant migrants who had been raised on traditional tales returned to the village singing urban *chastushki*.

The perception of cultural degeneration found further confirmation in bastardized versions of literary classics, especially evident in the most rapidly expanding genres, theater and narrative fiction. The classics helped transform the repertory of public theaters, which had evolved from the harlequin plays of the 1820s (imported from France through the Russian court) to the elaborately staged outdoor battle spectacles of the 1870s. After 1880, a significant part of the popular repertory consisted of Russian classics. Works by Pushkin, Gogol, and Lermontov were remade for the popular stage, but were still recognizable. Dramatic structure was taken from the originals, as was their literary Russian. When the imperial monopoly on theaters in the two capitals was abolished in 1882, an audience was ready to come indoors. Common folk who had once appeared only as characters now invaded the stalls, and their middle-class neighbors noted their unwashed clothes, their chattering during the performance, and their mad rush to get front-row seats when the doors were thrown open.

Staged performances were not limited to indoor dramatic theaters, and especially the lighter fare, such as operettas, moved into the nightclubs and entertainment gardens. Wealthy merchants viewed the plays from tables up front, while the less well-heeled could squeeze into the back rows, or even peek over the fence for free. Still-cheaper fare could be found in the variety theaters on off-streets and on the outskirts of town, where the repertory ran to musical numbers—"gypsy" songs, torrid romances, or "Russian" songs that were rarely Russian—and comic routines that relied on broad humor and a sharp sense of how society was changing. Theater penetrated deeply into popular culture. Songs first sung on the stage were later sung by midnight strollers; jokes were repeated in parlors and on factory floors. Actors also enjoyed great prestige as personalities. Their scandalous lives—often mythologized—were recounted in newspaper chronicles and retold as the latest gossip. A booming business cropped up in photographic postcards of actors and actresses, which visitors from the provinces sent home as a testament to the big-city life.

Middlebrow tastes were also reflected in fiction, where reformulations of the classics—rewrites that maintained narrative structure and some of the literary language—were a big business. The literary classics themselves also found a large audience once they had been marketed properly. Those who produced these inexpensive rip-offs for quick consumption had few qualms about authorial property, and would rewrite or even plagiarize Pushkin, Gogol, and Lermontov. They would provide a colorful cover, emphasize fantastic elements in the text, and refrain from didacticism. In later years, the classics would live yet another life in silent movies.

The desire for repackaged classics signified a change in basic cognition. To understand these works, or even to read or watch them, audiences had to have absorbed new and very different notions of the human personality, of social decorum, and of cause and effect in the public sphere. Without these ideas, many works would have seemed nonsensical. Rude resistance to authority, the predatory sexuality of golddiggers, even the sharpened ethnic consciousness of city folk were all new experiences that gave characters motives unknown in the recent past. Personality became the focus and driving engine of narrative. Individual characters, with their idiosyncrasies and desires, peopled commercial culture and moved plots in unpredictable directions. Peasant girls committed suicide or threw the local dolt in an oven; young men no longer bowed their heads to landowners, but slit their throats; the elegant lady in the opera loge turned out to be a jewel thief. Plots revolved around testing edges and penetrating barriers. Even when the story ended by confirming the value of limits, the authors and their audiences had appropriated the right to question them.

Long-term social transformations were manifest in popular culture long before political unrest erupted in 1905. By the turn of the century, the urban landscape reflected greater ethnic and gender variety, as more women and national minorities found work in the cities. These groups entered Russia's public spaces both as audiences and as creators. Born at the margin, mass-oriented commercial culture now pushed the periphery into the center. Tensions constantly interrupted the expansion. Popular culture helped to make those who consumed it increasingly cosmopolitan.

Our readers will find their expectations of audience response confirmed at times, but also confounded. Russians exhibited all the signs of modern consciousness evident in the popular culture they consumed. They were confused by contemporary life, thrilled by its opportunities yet fearful of the chaos it brought. They longed for a political freedom matching the personal autonomy that was increasingly theirs; yet they were still attached to the aura and person of their tsar. Traditional social roles were undermined by civic reform and the growth of capitalism, and the ethnic homogeneity of Russian life was disturbed by the influx of other peoples. Social and personal identities that had enjoyed a long period of stability were put to the test. Often such issues appeared in forms that made them implicit, and seemed of secondary importance to the audience. This makes them of even greater interest to us. For example, husbands and wives quarrel frequently throughout the collection, and attitudes toward spousal roles seem to change little; yet early examples of humor, which found joviality in a husband beating his wife, differ from later vaudeville portraits of fearful husbands ducking their wives en route to an assignation. The timeless disdain conceals a different power relationship and, of equal import, implies a very different audience.

Power and the powerless, community definitions of kinship and difference, solidarity and antagonism across social identities were at play in popular culture. If we expect a uniform coherence within social definitions such as "working class," which were often imposed from outside, or an altruistic solidarity between genders, classes, and ethnic groups that were oppressed by more powerful social groups, we will be disappointed. Judging by popular culture, audiences resented some of the groups responsible for their misfortunes, but they reserved their deepest resentment for the even less fortunate. Audiences that in some instances hated and struggled against power structures took pride in them in other instances. Russian xenophobes were often foreign themselves: the Great Russian patriot Bulgarin was, after all, a Pole. This anthology includes many examples of the perverse trend. A swell of patriotism aroused by the Russo-Turkish war of the late 1870s, and the concomitant hatred of Jews living in the Pale of Settlement, who suffered violence as Russian troops marched through en route to the Balkans; a pioneering woman writer, proponent of the great empire and the savage repression of Polish autonomy; or a Jewish scriptwriter, smash purveyor of sex-laden melodrama to the movie industry, writing mean-spirited pastiches of his women competitors in his spare time—all these suggest just how complex was the development of identities in a rapidly changing world, and how individuals' notions of themselves were conditioned by their contact with others.

A most influential ethnic Other figuring into the changing self-definition of many Russians was the gypsy, who was shunned in reality but was glorified in the imagination as a symbol of romantic freedom. The torrid romance songs identified as "gypsy" in spirit, if not in factual origin, reflected how popular culture not only produced and perpetuated ethnic stereotypes, but also manipulated them in ways that helped to shape Russian identity. Initially the nobles' imaginations were inflamed by fantasies of hot-blooded romance with dark-eyed beauties from Moldavia and the Caucasus, illusions generated by no less than Pushkin. Then the taste for the wild side was passed on to uninhibited sons of the staid merchant class, and anyone else who could afford the restaurants where gypsies entertained. Moscow's Strelna became in the 1880s the first tony restaurant to capitalize on gypsymania, and the star of the footlights, Vera Zorina, not a gypsy herself, tore open customers' hearts with her passionate voice. The gypsification of Nikolai Nekrasov's political poem "Peddlers" made explicit the extent to which mass culture was capable of transcending its elite inspiration. Abridged and performed by the deep-throated gypsy songstress Varya Panina, his song was transformed from a political statement into a romantic tragedy. Years later Nekrasov's poem assumed yet another role, when film director Aleksandr Khanzhonkov turned it into a silent movie in 1910.

Gypsy songs found a parallel in the lower-class genre of "cruel romance." These songs, which featured sentimental courtship, illicit love, pained rejection, and often suicide, swept the old peasant tunes out of fashion. Sung by seamstresses, janitors, metalworkers, and cabbies, they vocalized newspaper accounts of corresponding emotions on the city streets. Both the songs and the reports that had inspired them provided considerable raw material for the nascent film industry after the turn of the century.

By 1905, the year of turmoil and insurrection, the audience for mass culture differed significantly from that of fifty years earlier. Disenchantment with the status quo beset all sectors of the population, if for differing reasons. Opinions were divided about the authorities and the values they tried to propagate: the work ethic, family unity, class harmony, and loyalty to the tsar and state. Traditional values were undermined in a variety of modern and invisible ways. For example, people became increasingly conscious of fashion as a means to express personality, itself a new concept for many. Fashion mandates that value is transitory, that what was right yesterday is obsolete today. It exerted its sway over city tastes and penetrated deep into villages. Peasant boys and girls competed to show off the best kerchiefs and boots, and they insisted on dancing the latest dances, singing the latest songs. By the early twentieth century, popular culture was a creature of its place and time. Most selections in the final section of this anthology can be precisely dated by their contents, and they disappeared as quickly as they had appeared. Artifacts of pulp culture, they were designed to be consumed quickly and then jettisoned as the senses were readied for the next trend. The same flightiness could have powerful political consequences in times of upheaval, when the population was alerted to events and could respond immediately. When the old order buckled in 1905, readers knew about it the next day or week; when war broke out in 1914, news spread quickly; and when revolution swept through the country in 1917, readers could be mobilized in twenty-four hours. People could form opinions and solidarities that might have taken years in the past.

Just as high-speed presses had transformed print culture after 1870, two other new technologies, the phonograph and the movie camera, revolutionized culture at the turn of the century. At first their artistic potential went unrealized, but once it was recognized, the new media disseminated culture across the social spectrum, modifying it in the process. Russia already enjoyed a multifarious musical culture, from the opera and operetta to vaudeville, cruel romances, and gypsy songs, from which the phonograph could draw. At first, stars kept their distance from the media of mass reproduction because they feared the degradation of their talent. World-famous bass Fedor Shaliapin, however, changed his tune when he realized the astounding fees to be earned. Soon most of the luminaries of Russian music were singing into the sound horn and making fabulous money. Now all Russia could hear the voices they had only read about in newspapers. A middle-class family could afford a gramophone; the less-well-off could still visit a public gramophone parlor. Thanks to the machine, we can hear most of the songs and voices of the musical past today. This anthology is accompanied by a compact disk, featuring samples from renowned singers and vaudeville acts. Items included on the CD are marked with an asterisk in the table of contents.

The movie business, more sophisticated and also more expensive, took longer to become entrenched in urban culture. Initially Russians imported French films, short and sensational attractions. The earliest movies were simple recordings of events and enabled people to look with amazement at the world around them. The fiction and narrative structure that characterize the motion picture industry today were not a part of early films, which concentrated on documentaries and special effects. When the coronation of the tsar was filmed in 1896, most people saw the corporeal reality of this distant and semi-divine being for the first time. As the business changed, Russian studios, actors, scriptwriters, and directors matured to compete with the preferred French and Scandinavian imports. By 1908, moviegoers could view a purely Russian tale of Razin and his Persian princess, based on a song that appears in this anthology.

The politics intrinsic to commercial culture are as difficult to pin down as they are important to understand. Unlike the autocracy and the intelligentsia, who articulated their positions in no uncertain terms, the purveyors of popular culture had to negotiate between old and new, and to satisfy tastes that were in a constant state of flux. Apolitical? Hardly. The image of Russia they peddled may have seemed more monarchist than socialist at first glance, but publishers and producers held no truck with extremists at either end of the political spectrum. What did it mean that nobles were more likely to be heroes, and intellectuals to be ridiculed in this fare? Emblematic here would be sportswriter Nikolai Breshko-Breshkovsky, who renounced the radicalism of his mother, Ekaterina Breshko-Breshkovskaia, the future "Grandmother of the Russian Revolution." He and his mother crossed cultural paths in 1917, when sensationalist movie producer Aleksandr Drankov, for whom the son had written screenplays, produced a highly dramatized film biography of the mother. Although parent and child agreed on the undesirability of bolshevism, she moved toward socialism, and he toward the autocracy.

The outbreak of World War I kindled patriotic hopes for a better, stronger future.

But the cultural movements of the war, like the political, splintered among numerous competing visions of that future. When the political foundation collapsed, it brought the cultural structure down with it. The relationship of the war to the ensuing revolutions is crucial to the historiography of the end of Russia's old regime: Would the Russian political system have been able to evolve into a representative democracy had the war not strained society and the economy beyond their limits? Questions must be raised about whether pro-war, anti-socialist commercial producers were promoting political agendas that protected their financial interests first or were responding to market demands. Certainly both sentiments were at play to varying degrees.

As the pieces in this anthology demonstrate, the average Russian was intrigued by the surrounding world, though often frightened by some of its features. Many preferred the traditional entertainments of their grandparents; they read the same anecdotes and knightly adventures, and sang the same songs. Others peered at the world around them, devouring the local crime chronicles, gazing at the lights of an amusement garden, sitting at its tables—or waiting on them. As more and more consumers appeared, and from a greater variety of backgrounds, the market expanded to meet their tastes. The religious and irreverent, leftist and loyalist, modernist and traditionalist could all satisfy their desires. It would be convenient to assign each of these tastes to a specific social group, but any given reader might read Lidiia Charskaia's adventure tales in youth, and then grow up to enjoy the sexual frankness of Mikhail Artsybashev, retaining meanwhile a taste for the bandit Churkin. A more likely message, and one that signaled deeper social changes, was that Russia's mass audience showed far greater pluralism than homogeneity.

Popular culture was often formulaic, cliché-ridden, and full of prejudice and conceit. In the final analysis, however, it showed more consciousness of social change than its high-culture rivals. Russia's great nineteenth-century writers and artists were truth-tellers, prophets with a mission to save Russia from a moral abyss. Yet the truth of nineteenth-century Russia was that there was no one great truth, that the center was crumbling into smaller sectors. The vast country began the century led by a narrow caste of educated Russians, but they had lost their hegemony by the end of it. There was no one single Russian culture, no one single Russian cultural appetite. When the high priests of culture attempted to legislate a single one, the market moved in to mediate tastes, forming a vast new public space that allowed society to evolve in unanticipated or undesired directions.

Indisputably the product of a society stratified according to estates and classes, urban commercial culture belonged to all groups. It was created by nobles and highly educated people as well as the townsmen; it was distributed to and read by all classes, by country folk as well as city folk. The overlap between elite and mass culture was strong. Pushkin wrote poems and tales in an intentionally popular style, which *lubok* publishers then plagiarized and rewrote; Chekhov wrote vaudevilles and pastiched newspaper feuilletons, and was then parodied back in return. Writers crossed over, and readers sampled from across the board. The message of the culture, and thus of this anthology, is that the the modern city, which compacted and commingled cultural layers, came to dominate the sensibilities of all its inhabitants.

The ability to generate and distribute culture rapidly, and to attract new audiences, was both produced by and reflected in the contents of popular culture. *Lubki* and newspapers were peddled and mailed to remote villages; city songs were brought back to the village by migrants; and by the early twentieth century, movies were being shown there on sheets hung as temporary screens. The stories, songs, and screens brought the larger world to isolated corners, forcing its presence on even the most stubborn traditionalist.

The search for a true "Russian" consciousness, located in the nation's great works of culture, concerned many nineteenth-century thinkers. In part this was because they recognized the cultural fragmentation evident in the materials presented here, which threatened their vision of a unified Russia. Culture became an article of trade, and creators formed a new relationship with their customers. The undeniable fact of commercialization marked the final breach with the traditions of aristocratic and peasant culture. Folk culture had suppressed the urge for idiosyncratic reading, and elite culture created an ideal reader, demanding that real readers conform to the image. The marketplace responded to consumer tastes, and thus acknowledged a new reality of differing publics, and their ability to read in unique and unforeseeable ways. Seen from the outside, the new culture seemed to be one of alienation. It undermined village traditions, led young people astray, and sharpened class tensions. Yet the behavior of consumers indicated that it was traditional culture that had alienated them, with its monotony and constraints. The big world, for all the pitfalls it held, was more enticing than the village, and young peasants fled to its embrace. Any alienation they felt came from their "own" village.

We hope that readers will gain a deeper appreciation of Russian society in the era before 1917 from this anthology. The totality of mass-oriented urban culture from the late eighteenth century to the 1917 revolutions was so great that only a sampling could be included in this volume. We regret the omission of any favorite author or joke that space would not permit us to include. There is more than enough here, though, to suggest the many readerships, tastes, and values embodied by the audiences of the great Russian empire. In historical retrospect, many aspects of prerevolutionary Russia's urban commercial culture withstood the ravages of socialist realism that supplanted it. A number of the works in this anthology have returned with the overthrow of the latter, although primarily in the form of nostalgia for an imagined, and imaginary, past.

Because of space constraints, we could not include everything we would have liked in this anthology. Readers may not find all their favorites in the volume. We can provide access to many of the materials that we have been compelled to exclude. Readers are encouraged to direct their Web readers to the following address, where they will find a supplementary collection of texts and audio files.

http://www.macalester.edu/~vongelde/entertaining.html

NOTE ON TRANSLITERATION

This anthology has several intended audiences, which complicates the matter of transliteration. In the texts, we have adopted a modified version of the Library of Congress system, with concessions to pronunciation, tradition, and common sense. Thus, tsars will be Nicholas and Alexander, while in other places the names will be rendered as Nikolai and Aleksandr. Mania and Sonia, for example, will be spelled Manya and Sonya, and Berezaiskii will be Berezaisky. Readers should also note that Russians frequently use diminutives of first names. These endearments play with variations of the name, and are formed most commonly by adding -shka; for example, Foma might become Fomushka, or Mariia, Marushka. In the footnotes and bibliography, when transliterating Russian language documents, we will observe the Library of Congress system strictly. We hope this will meet the needs of all our readers.

Part I

The Heyday
of Absolutism,
Late 18th Century–1825

The eighteenth century in Russia was characterized by forced and rapid westernization. Inaugurated under Peter the Great (1682–1725) and carried through by his successors, it reached a pinnacle under Catherine the Great (1762–1796). The French Revolution, though, raised doubts about the new god of Reason and the innate benevolence of the common folk. The noble and bureaucratic classes dominated Russian cities. They favored the emotionalism offered by Romanticism, together with its implicit critique of Western culture. The Napoleonic Wars proved Russia to be the dominant power on the continent, stirring patriotic emotions among all social strata. Although history texts emphasize how this era ended with an aborted political revolution, led by westernized officers (the Decembrists, from their December 1825 revolt), the majority of St. Petersburg residents embraced nationalism with great self-confidence.

By the outset of the nineteenth century, there existed a reserve of popular culture that was distinctly urban in its origins. Songs of outlaws, soothsaying books, knightly tales, and anecdotes of the imperial court had come to life in the city, yet somehow they embodied a very traditional set of values. Passed along as oral lore rather than as written texts, they spoke of a stable social order, fantastic distant lands, and old superstitions. Indicative, though, of the odd stratification of popular culture is the fact that most of the pieces in this section maintained a mass audience until the twentieth century, transmitted then by entirely different media, and often with new values inscribed. The sole exception is the work of Prince Shakhovskoi, who seemed the most modern to his contemporaries.

Matvei Komarov stands out here as a representative of cultural transition. His popular stories of the bandit Vanka Kain were an anomaly at the onset of the nineteenth century, when self-conscious literary activity was limited mostly to members of the noble estate, writing for their peers. The literary canons of the time restricted subjects and style to informed tastes. Some satirists, for example Vasily Berezaisky with his *Tales of the Ancient Poshekhonians* and Shakhovskoi with his vaudeville *The New Sterne,* stretched the canon, but their implied audience was still upper-class, and their satires mocked ill breeding. When educated writers dealt with the lower orders, they seemed more comfortable with peasants than with townspeople (*meshchane*), whose very name implied contempt. After all, many nobles owned peasants who were, according to fashionable theories of national identity, essential to their ethnic and cultural identity as Russians.

Anecdotes about Balakirev
(Traditional Tales)

IVAN EMELIANOVICH BALAKIREV, THE BELOVED JESTER OF PETER THE GREAT, WAS NEGLECTED AND EVENTUALLY EXILED DURING THE GERMAN-INFLUENCED REIGN OF ANNA IOANNOVNA (1730– 1740). THOUGH HIS JOB WAS A MEDIEVAL ANACHRONISM IN RUSSIA'S FIRST MODERN HOUSEHOLD, BALAKIREV, AS MUCH AS HIS MASTER, CAME TO REPRESENT THE TIME AND ITS CHANGES FOR POPULAR READERS. THESE ANECDOTES WERE HANDED DOWN FOR DECADES BEFORE THEIR FIRST PUBLICATION IN THE LATE EIGHTEENTH CENTURY, AND THEY CONTINUED TO ENJOY BROAD CIRCULATION, GOING THROUGH COUNTLESS REPRINTS UP TO THE TWENTIETH CENTURY. THEY EXEMPLIFIED A POPULAR FASCINATION WITH RUSSIAN HISTORY, PARTICULARLY WITH PETER THE GREAT, AND A SYMPATHY FOR THE GREAT MONARCH, TESTING THE ASSUMPTION THAT LOWER-CLASS RUSSIANS WERE HOSTILE TO PETER'S REFORMS. MANY READERS WERE ALSO SURELY ENTERTAINED BY BALAKIREV'S MOCKERY OF FOREIGNERS, BUREAUCRATS, AND THE NOBLE ELITE.

BALAKIREV'S FAKE DEATH

Once the enraged Sovereign banished Balakirev from court and bade him never to show himself again. There was nothing he could do about it; he had no choice but to obey, and removed himself. A week passed, and then another; Balakirev still had not appeared in court, and His Majesty began to miss him. Another three weeks passed. Suddenly a rumor made the rounds that Balakirev was dead.

The Sovereign sent a messenger to find out whether the rumor was true.

Upon his return, the messenger reported that with his own eyes he had seen Balakirev laid out on a table, and that his wife was weeping for him.

"I feel sorry for him," said Peter. "He loved me and was loyal to me; I must aid his wife." He immediately sent an orderly to the supposed widow.

From *Polnye anekdoty o Balakireve, byvshem shute pri dvore Petra pervogo,* 5th ed. (Moscow: Abramov Bros., 1874), pp. 10–12, 13, 16–17, 22.

Balakirev's wife appeared in mourning, wearing the hoop skirts fashionable in that era.

Peter expressed his sympathy to her at length and then said, "I would reward the person generously who could bring Balakirev back!"

"Just how much would you give them?" asked a voice, as if from the grave.

"What does this mean? Are you really still alive, you worthless scoundrel?" shouted His Majesty.

"Nope, I'm dead!"

"You are here, you rogue. Crawl out this instant!"

"Nope, I'm not coming out. Wife, let's go home."

"Hold on!" protested Peter. "I'll give you a hundred rubles!"

The jester stuck his head out from beneath his wife's skirts.

"I promise you mercy," repeated the Sovereign.

Balakirev showed even more of himself.

"All my former privileges!"

Balakirev leaped out and fell at the feet of the Sovereign, then stood and said, "Alekseich,[1] you can keep the hundred rubles; that's for bringing me, a fool, back to life. But make sure to give me back those privileges!"

THE BROKEN STATUE

Once, as Balakirev was playing with the courtiers, he accidentally broke a statue of Jupiter. He found out what time the Sovereign was to pass through the room and, wrapped like Jupiter in a mantle, took the place of the broken statue.

Peter passed by without noticing the deception, but on the way back he saw fragments of the figure on the floor. He glanced at the pedestal and was surprised.

"Don't be surprised, Alekseich! It was I who smashed your statue, and I want to take its place."

His Majesty laughed, ordered that Her Majesty be summoned, and told her of Balakirev's latest escapade. They laughed long over the false statue.

BALDY

An official newly appointed to court was so swelled with pride that he could not endure Balakirev's barbs. Once, swept away by his fury, he said, "Are there really so many fools at court?"

"As many," answered the jester, "as there are hairs on your wise head."

The courtier was as bald as bald can be. He was forced into silence and never again mocked Balakirev.

---

1. Peter's patronymic, which only his intimates could use as an address.

FLY ON THE BROW

Many important people of various ranks, including Balakirev, were at a court assembly. Wishing to entertain the company, he approached a German and asked him, "Is it a sin, sir, to kill flies?"

"How can that be a sin?" answered the German. "I approve of killing that worthless creature wherever it might be found."

Little time had passed before a fly lit on the German's brow. Balakirev noticed it, went up to him, and, without saying a word, smacked him so hard on the head that it could be heard from every room. The guest could not help but laugh at the trick.

Tales of the Ancient Poshekhonians
Vasily Berezaisky (1798)

POSHEKHONIANS, RESIDENTS OF A REAL TOWN IN YAROSLAVL PROVINCE, WERE THE PROVERBIAL HAYSEEDS OF RUSSIAN TALES, BEGINNING WITH THE REIGN OF PETER THE GREAT. VASILY BEREZAISKY, AN ENLIGHTENED NOBLE, FINALLY RECORDED THE TALES OF THEIR IMAGINED EXPLOITS FOR THE EDIFICATION AND AMUSEMENT OF HIS COUNTRYMEN. THEY WERE REPUBLISHED MANY TIMES THROUGHOUT THE NEXT CENTURY. LAMPOONING THE PROVINCIALS WITH ALLEGORICAL NAMES (THE ORIGINAL RUSSIAN IS PROVIDED IN PARENTHESES) AND EXAGGERATED BUFFOONERY, HE HOPED HIS READERS WOULD BE SHAMED INTO MODERN MANNERS. BUT THE CONTINUED POPULARITY OF THE STORIES SUGGESTS THAT THE TYPES HE SATIRIZED CONTINUED TO THRIVE IN THE EMPIRE, AND THAT THE EDUCATIONAL IMPACT WAS MINIMAL.

From Vasilii Berezaiskii, *Anekdoty drevnykh poshekhontsev* (St. Petersburg: Meditsinskaia kollegiia, 1798), pp. 10–22.

MISSIVE THE FIRST, FROM GLIBTONGUE (SLOVOKHOT) TO LEARNINGLOVER (LIUBOVED)

Pay heed, for our fable commences

In the shire of Yaroslav, along the River Sogozha, there dwelled in days of yore a people called the Poshekhonians, who were governed in the custom of the day by a *voevoda*. Their seat to this day is situated on the very same spot and bears the same name; yet the residents themselves are no longer the same—they have so metamorphosed that not a hair resembles that of their ancestors. Whether a change in the climate or intercourse with neighboring peoples has provoked the change I cannot confirm, know though I might, for we have no need of this knowledge. That is a matter for the learned, who concern themselves with such questions. Our object is different. How cleverly inventive, how adroit and unencumbered, how sensible and quick-witted were the aforementioned ancient Poshekhonians, we will demonstrate by the following tales.

When circumstances (forced by gossip and unjust calumnies) caused the state's *voevoda* Bribelover (Vziatkoliub) to be replaced by another, named Pike (Shchuk), the worldly-wise folk considered it a duty to pay their respects to the new magistrate. So they assembled in a secluded locality, more precisely under the livestock shed, that they might not be interrupted and might think their wise thoughts as to proper procedures. For they wished not, as is said, to flop in the mud on the first try. At the end of lengthy counsel, disputation, and some slight scrimmaging, they finally resolved to dispatch several deputies to wish him welcome and pay homage to his years, intellect, experience, and knowledge of worldly discourse. They would not make so bold as to address the noble guest directly, from the front steps (for the *voevoda*'s back step served as well for such occasions).

However, to render diligence tangible, they did not wish to appear before him with empty hands. A new quandary arose over what to bring. Again they assembled in their peaceful spot, to confer, think, and contrive—how long it continued, we know not. Whether it was for a day or for yet another that they chatted, they finally resolved to grease his palm a bit. So why not? There was nothing new in this for these do-nothings. That's how things were done to keep him fat and happy. And so at their final council it was determined to offer him victuals and costly gifts from this world: more particularly, a large pot filled with enough sourdough to burst his britches, and a captured live blackbird (whether for the amusement of the *voevoda*'s offspring or for roasting, I know not).

Above and beyond that, there were as many unincubated egg-hens and coxcombs, that is fresh eggs, as there were hearths in the town. He Himself, *id est*, the alderman Deadeye (Nepromakh), was given by right of age the dough pot to wear on his head. The basket of eggs went to the delegate Fume (Ugar), and the blackbird to the *sotnik* Pluck (Khvat). They were to be followed immediately by a retinue of the elect decked out in their finest attire, as one can easily imagine. To crown it all, they agreed to greet the *voevoda* with the following speech: "Welcome, our dear benefactor and benefactress, and your itsy-bitsy babies." So as to make a more favorable and lasting impression, and not blunder in the course of the speech, they took the precaution of breaking it into three parts. The elder was, by agreement, to utter the beginning of the greeting: "Welcome, our dear benefactor," and then the delegate was to continue: "and benefactress," and the *sotnik* was to conclude: "and your itsy-bitsy babies." The gifts were prepared; the greeting was composed and committed to memory.

And so the greater part of the matter was completed—it remained for them only to go and click their heels. The cocks had already crowed the last midnight call; thick smoke billowed from the huts; the Poshekhonian horizon had stretched out and grown dark. The omens were indeed unkind—and this fabled city was seized by troubled activity. The elderly of both sexes roamed the streets like alley cats; and the young gazed upon them with empty souls. All staggered hither and thither like shadows of themselves, dumbfounded, with heads hanging. But our wise leaders paid no heed to the despair of their hamlet, and laughed inside at the superstitious rabble. Bounteous is the superiority of enlightenment over ignorance. The emissary stood ready, admiring his splendid attire, proud of his fine self and the charge entrusted to him, as was the alderman preceding him with solemn steps, balancing the dough pot on his head. The magnificent procession commenced, to the exultation of the public, toward the *voevoda*'s home, accompanied by a countless flock of spectators.

The route was not long, so the glorious procession ended anon. Our citizens had already come to the *voevoda*'s gate; the gift-bearers mounted the stoop by order of their ranks, but their path was blocked. They reported the reason for their visit, whereupon the entrance to the internal chambers was unbarred. In what manner they were greeted by the *voevoda* is unknown; one might assume that it was not unseemly. For the gifts were covered, as was customary; although the *voevoda* was a piker, *id est* a slyboots, he was no clairvoyant. So you may think whatever you please. At the very least, they were conducted in according to their virtue, which made the welcome all the finer. We hear that Deadeye, the leader and an outstanding member of the embassy, was gasping like a fish out of water as he prepared for his grand and lofty word of greeting; he tripped on the threshold and crashed full weight to the ground. Others say the cause of his hasty genuflection was that his flounce came unraveled, and that the devil made the knavish delegate step on the tail dragging along the floor. Why should this concern us? Our Deadeye ground his snout into the floor, squeaked out a groan from the depths of his heart, and blurted, "Doggone you!" The delegate had not heeded his words closely, and thinking them a compliment directed at the *voevoda*, he caught up the refrain: "And our benefactress," and the *sotnik* concluded: "and your itsy-bitsy babies."

The greeting had been spoken: only the distribution of the gifts remained. The ceremony was surely worth watching; though we did not have the opportunity to witness it, we at least heard about it. The alderman was still pummeling the floor with his nose when the pot thudded into the *voevoda*'s face and, as if they were friends, kissed him smack on the lips. The *voevoda* was unprepared for this love scene, and smashed his fist into its flank so that the aforementioned nuzzler broke into pieces, which scattered about. The delegate, wishing to perform his assignment in exactitude, made his *pas* to the fore; but, as if in retribution for his sins, he accidentally stepped on the alderman's neck, and was compelled to tumble down along with him. The basket flew from his hands and thudded onto the floor, the eggs rolling in all directions and reaching all but the *voevoda*, for he had thought to back away from the visitors. The *sotnik* Pluck, plucky not only in name but in deed, stepped up and showed his pluck. Seeing that his associates had dispensed their gifts, Pluck grasped that he had better get a move on. He stepped up to the *voevoda* as was proper, and handing him the blackbird, he released it before the *voevoda* could receive the bird. The blackbird flew off as if it had been singed, and whacked straight into the *voevoda*'s eye. Its wings squarely enlightened the crown of his head, which forced him to curtsey most deferentially. Then the bird flew furiously from the *voevoda*, back and forth between the window frames to count the panes. The glass inside and outside the chambers jangled like a *gusli*, rattling like a carriage on Millionaia Street,[1] noisy as a merchants' bathhouse. In short, there was enough racket in the house to drive away the saints themselves.

The *voevoda*'s children and their nannies fled from the visitors like mice to their holes. The *voevoda*'s wife took a notion that their home was being visited by those incorporeal beauties without whom no mill can be built,[2] and chased them hence with cross and prayer, but in vain. The master of the house was struck dumb; he stood flabbergasted, rubbing his eyes, for the sourdough had blinded him mightily—no one was concerned with his dressing gown. It is said that that very same day he ordered it boiled in onion leaf for two to three nights, to strengthen the dye. But let's drop such trivialities and return instead to our supplicants. Deadeye had yet to rise, and was spinning like cheese in butter; afore, he was covered head to toe in dough, and behind, in egg, and his face most uncommendably resembled a slaughtered ram. Flustered, he clutched the back of his head, wiped his brow, and rubbed his temples. Fume felt little better than he; he grimaced, made faces, blew for some reason on the hand that had gotten under the basket, and hid it under his robe. His German-gray *kaftan* had become pale yellow from broken eggs: his face was made up like a mummer's, so that even his own father would not have recognized him. The *sotnik* Pluck was also caught flush. To tell the mother truth, everyone got their good share. The *voevoda*, the first to snap out of his perplexity, gave his well-wishers some time to wallow and gape. He shouted, "Ho!" More so, he whistled, called—and men came running, galloping like madmen; he spoke, commanded—and they set to and put to, without discrimination or caution, whoever was nearby, some with potsherds, some with eggs, with hands and kicks, some in the nose, some on the back of the neck, some with a cudgel on the ears and the back, christening, deafening, tumbling, warming hides, boxing ears, regaling his guests, leading them from the *voevoda*'s lodgings. In short, they were so grandly entertained on that momentous day that they wended their way home without a

---

1. A street that abutted the palace in Petersburg.
2. *Rusalki*, the freshwater mermaids of Russian folklore said to lure young men to their doom.

backward glance. I leave any further description of their festivity and the rite of return procession to our deputies' home. To describe it would be to enfeeble our reader's imagination.

The Merry Old Fellow
Teller of Old Moscow Tales (1790)

THIS FOLKSY OLD FELLOW, WHOSE RHYMES WERE FIRST PRINTED IN 1790, WAS REPRINTED FREQUENTLY FOR THE NEXT FIFTY YEARS. FOR ANOTHER FIFTY BEYOND THAT, THE BOOKLET SOLD BRISKLY IN FLEA MARKET BOOKSTALLS. THE TALES BELOW PLAY ON TRADITIONAL IMAGES OF MARRIAGE AND COUNTRY LIFE. THE CONDESCENSION UNDERLYING THE TYPES OF THE WIFE AND THE PEASANT IS NOT QUESTIONED HERE; IN FACT, THE UNKNOWN AUTHOR USES THEM TO ILLUSTRATE CONVENTIONAL MORALS. YET THEY REFLECTED ISSUES THAT WERE SOON SUBJECT TO DEBATE THROUGHOUT POPULAR CULTURE, AND REMAINED SO UNTIL THE OCTOBER REVOLUTION.

ABOUT A STUPID WIFE

Here's the stupid deed of a stupid wife.
She put some portions of dinner on a plate in the stove,
And only left them there to warm,
But the tin plate melted.
She didn't know what to tell her man,
And had to blame it all on the cat.
When her husband asked for his dinner,
She took off at a run,
Shouting, "Sire, something happened:
The cat ate the meat off the plate!"
Hearing this, her husband laughed,
And guessed what he should do with her.
Fine; we'll make sure the cat won't sin again.

Starichok vesel'chak razskazyvaiushchii davnie Moskovskie byli. 3rd ed., (Moscow: V. Kirilov, 1837). 1st ed. 1790.

Watch how I make mincemeat of her.
He bound the cat to his wife's back
And whipped it hard with a length of rope.
The cat clawed her back up but good,
And she screamed, "Oh, I could die!
Do what you want with me, dear,
I admit that I wronged you."
Husband: "Don't say that, you I love;
It's the cat I'm beating for its wrongs.
It was you who said she should be beat
Because she took the meat from the plate."
And so the wife didn't fool her husband,
And brought only ruin on herself.

ABOUT THE GREAT NOBLE'S BUTLER AND A PEASANT

A butler and a peasant were sitting together,
Gabbing all sorts of gab between them,
During which the butler asked the peasant
About when peasants get together
To carouse, drink, and kick up their heels.
The peasant answered, "Sir, allow me to tell you
All that I can about the matter.
We carouse much more in the winter,
Eat, drink, amuse ourselves in sundry ways,
Once we have dispensed with all our work;
In summertime, our labors are abundant."
The butler said, "I wondered who it was that you resembled;
Your natures are most like that of the pig.
Pigs are merry when they've eaten plenty;
Their bellies bloat, they roll in the mud."
"Well, sir, you say that we are all like pigs.
And when is it that you amuse yourself?
I'd like to know that if I could,
If you'd permit yourself to tell me."
The butler answered, "We wait for spring to come.
When the beautiful weather starts,
That's when we have our fun and live it up.
Best of all for pleasure is the month of May,
There's always enough to go around for all."
Peasant: "Ain't that just the thing, sir.
My mare also has all of her fun in May.
That's when she amuses herself too,
And strolls across the fields merrily,
Snorting frequently: neigh, neigh, neigh, neigh, neigh."
Here the butler was mocking the peasant,
And was left with all the shame himself.

The Ancient and Modern Divinatory Oracle

Discovered upon the Death of the One-Hundred-and-Six-Year-Old Elder Martin Zadek, with Which He Fathomed the Destiny of Each Person through His Rings of Human Fortune and Misfortune, to Which Is Attached the Magic Mirror, or the Interpretation of Dreams; Including the Rules of Physiognomy and Palm Reading, or the Science of Ascertaining the Features, Character, and Fate of the Male and Female Species by the Contours of the Body and the Disposition of the Hand; to Which Is Appended the Same Author's Zadek's Prophecies of the Most Curious Occurrences in Europe, Confirmed by Fact; with the addition of Hocus-Pocus, or Amusing Riddles with Their Answers

(1821)

THE AGE OF SENTIMENTALISM MADE FORTUNE-TELLING FASHIONABLE AMONG YOUNG PEOPLE OF THE EDUCATED CLASSES. SOME PREFERRED OLD PEASANT CUSTOMS, SUCH AS READING WAX DRIPPINGS IN WATER; SOME READ THE "ANCIENT" DIVINATIONS OF OCCULT PROPHETS, OF WHOM ZADEK WAS THE BEST-KNOWN. BOTH SEXES INDULGED IN FORTUNE-TELLING, AS WITNESSED BY THE QUESTIONS HERE, AND BY SIGNATURES IN FORTUNE BOOKS. THESE SHORT EXCERPTS FROM ZADEK, A LEGENDARY FIGURE WHOSE PREDICTIONS FIRST APPEARED IN RUSSIA IN THE LATE EIGHTEENTH CENTURY, SHOW THAT THE PRACTICE ANSWERED CONCERNS RAISED BY THE NEW ETIQUETTE OF LOVE. AS

Drevnii i novyi vsegdashnii gadatel'nyi Orakul, naidennyi posle smerti odnogo sto-shestiletnego startsa Martina Zadeka, po kotoromu uznaval on sud'bu kazhdogo chrez krugi schast'ia i neschast'ia chelovecheskogo, s prisovokupleniem Volshebnogo Zerkala ili tolkovaniia snov: takzhe pravil Fiziognomii i Khiromantii, ili Nauk, kak uznavat' po slozheniiu tela i raspolozheniiu ruki ili chertam, svoistvam i uchast' muzheskogo i zhenskogo pola, s prilozheniem egozh Zadeka predskazaniia liubopyteneishikh v Evrope proizshestvii, sobytiem opravdannoe, s pribavleniem Fokus-Pokus, i zabavnykh zagadok s otgadkami, 3rd ed. (Moscow: Reshetnikov, 1821).

SOCIAL CONVENTIONS GOVERNING THEIR PASSIONS WERE LOOS-
ENED, YOUNG PEOPLE—BOTH MALE AND FEMALE—FOLLOWED
THE GUIDANCE OF THEIR UNPREDICTABLE AND IRRATIONAL SEN-
TIMENTS, THUS BECOMING SUBJECT TO THE WHIMS OF FORTUNE.

INSTRUCTIONS FOR THE PROPER USE OF THIS BOOK

Select a question from among those herein and, consulting the number by which it is listed, search for the corresponding Ring of Fortune. Then toss the gaming dice and mark the sum resulting from luck or providence, and search for the number key to the answer triangle on the periphery of the same figure: there, under the indicated sum, will be the provident and desired answer.

For instance, we shall take question 99, *By what means shall I end my life?* In the Ring of Fortune of that same number, with the dice providing, let us say, 7, we find *Fire;* lying across from that is 250; and under the number 250 indicated in the circle is Tamerlaine, number 7 of whose answers will be: *You will die from consumption of strong beverages.*

Questions for Bachelors[1]

1. What will my wife be like?
2. Will I marry the one I love?
3. Does the girl I love love me?
4. Would it be fitting to marry the girl of my dreams?
5. How many wives will I wed?
6. Is the person of my dreams wanton?
7. Am I pleasing to the female sex, or not?
8. Where and by what means can I find good fortune?

Questions for Unmarried Girls

9. Who will be my husband?
10. Will the man that I love take me?
11. Does my beloved love me?
12. Is the maiden of my thoughts chaste? [Trans.: *sic!*]
13. Will I soon be married?
14. Will I have a mother-in-law and brothers-in-law?
15. Will my upcoming marriage truly take place?
16. Will I marry only one husband?
17. Will I soon set eyes on my beloved?
18. Is my wedding day near or far?
19. Am I to marry the man who is courting me?

---

1. The book provides a total of 99 questions under six categories.

Questions for Married Men

20. Is my wife faithful to me? Does she love only me?
21. Is my friend master of his house?
22. What can I expect from my children?
23. How do the servants run the house in my absence?
24. Was my friend's wife chaste before her wedding?
25. Is the father of the child I know truly the man he is thought to be?
26. Is it good for such-and-such widower to marry again, or not?

Questions for Married Women

27. Is my husband faithful to me, and does he love me alone?
28. How does the woman of my acquaintance run her house?
29. Will my wife bear me a son or daughter? [Trans.: *sic!*]
30. What was the woman of my acquaintance like before her marriage?
31. Is the woman of my acquaintance with child, or not?
32. How many children will I have?
33. Will the widow of my acquaintance marry or not?

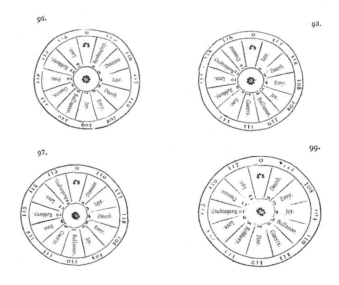

250. Tamerlaine[2]

2. Very, very much; and in that you will achieve honor and happiness.
3. That bears slight resemblance to the truth.
4. They love each other equally.

---

2. There are a total of 100 famous names in the answer lists.

5. The husband is so honest and modest that he does not even sense the horns placed on him by his wife.

6. Try it out for a while to see whether you can live here; for the people here do not tolerate pranksters.

7. You will die of consumption from strong beverages.

8. He is totally unworthy of her.

9. She is no longer free, but very much loves one individual.

10. This individual is highly industrious and obliging, but beyond that is frivolous, inconstant, and given to thievery.

11. There is no more place for you in her heart, which is occupied by many others; you will not be helped by mountains of gold.

12. Do not be hasty, but give an ambiguous answer, so that you will be able to keep your word.

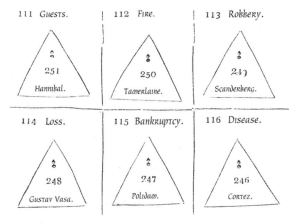

Guak, or Unbounded Devotion
A Knightly Tale
(18th Century)

THOUGH RUSSIAN HEROIC TALES DATED BACK TO THE TWELFTH CENTURY, THEY NEVER DEVELOPED THE CULTURE OF CHIVALRY THAT CHARACTERIZED WESTERN LORE. KNIGHTLY TALES OF CHIVALROUS ACTIONS AND GALLANT COMPETITION ENTERED RUSSIA FROM THE WEST, INCLUDING THE POPULAR *BOVA KORO-LEVICH* AND *ERUSLAN LAZAREVICH*. AS THEY MOVED EAST, THEY

[Author unknown] *Guak, ili nepreodolimaia vernost'. Rytsarskaia povest'* (Moscow: A. E. Gubanov, 1884).

UNDERWENT RUSSIFICATION, MAKING THEM A UNIQUE FORM OF
POPULAR LITERATURE. MOST APPEARED IN MANY VERSIONS OVER
THE YEARS, AS THEY WERE ADAPTED BY UNIDENTIFIED WRITERS
TO SUIT DIFFERENT TIMES.

THE STORY OF GUAK TAKES PLACE, ASTONISHINGLY, IN THE
PRINCEDOM OF FLORIDA. IT REVEALS RUSSIA'S PARADOXICAL
COMBINATION OF IGNORANCE ABOUT, YET FASCINATION WITH,
FOREIGN LANDS. THE VERSION BELOW WAS PUBLISHED IN 1884,
BUT IT ORIGINATED IN THE PREVIOUS CENTURY. THE POPULAR-
ITY OF THIS TYPE OF ADVENTURE SHOWS HOW RUSSIANS FANTA-
SIZED AS MUCH AS OTHERS ABOUT DERRING-DO. THE ROMANCE
OF DISPLAYING ONE'S PERSONAL BEST IN THE FACE OF TERROR
CONTAINS HINTS OF THE ATTRACTION OF INDIVIDUALISM.

Prince Zilagon, ruler of the Princedom of Florida, was a great and glorious man
who greatly expanded his territory and struck fear into the hearts of neighboring
peoples. He was gifted with an excellent mind, a handsome appearance, and unusual strength and courage. Traveling in Greece, Persia, India, China, Japan, and
Greater Bukharia, he accomplished so much that the most distinguished wise men
schooled in necromancy revered him, and he made many wizards and sorcerers
tremble. Throughout his travels, his knightly and heroic feats were praised everywhere. In the twenty-seventh year of his journeying, Zilagon returned to his fatherland and found it in a pitiful state; during his absence his father had died, and
Florida, left without a ruler, had fallen to the enemy. The whole state was destroyed.
His first action was to gather together a small band of Floridian soldiers, who let
out a joyful cry upon seeing their true leader, and decided that they would either be
victorious or die together with him. Zilagon, commanding these dedicated troops,
performed miracles of bravery; he dispersed the enemy horde, drove them from
the frontiers of his fatherland, and rid Florida completely of the enemy, daring
them to fight again.

This victorious prince was the first to enlarge the Princedom of Florida, and in
this era Florida enjoyed the flowering of prosperity that made it one of the world's
leading countries.

After his brother was killed by the enemy, Zilagon inherited the throne of the
Princedom of Florida. His first order was to revenge his brother's death, and he
raised a lethal weapon on the battlefield.

Canada was the first to feel the weight of his sword and surrendered to his mighty
power; thereafter, twelve more realms surrendered to the unconquerable and awe-
inspiring Zilagon, and after extending the borders of his domain, he married the

daughter of the king of Mexico. In the third year of their successful partnership they had a son, who was named Gualikh. Gualikh was a second Zilagon: as handsome as a day in May, as brave as Hercules, and good and generous. His six-year journey was a reflection of his glory; all trembled at the sound of his name: criminals feared his punishment, and the kindhearted praised him in their souls with tears of gratitude.

Gualikh established peace and harmony in his land, and determined to decorate his capital with a magnificent monument. He ordered that a massive amphitheater be built from white and green marble, where knightly competitions and the torture of wild animals could be held. This amphitheater was built directly across from the royal palace; inside it was so large that it could hold 50,000 spectators. Under an enormous canopy in the amphitheater were twelve places for visiting magnates. They had been gilded with pure gold, as if poured from the light of twelve suns; in the center stood the throne built for Gualikh, the decoration of which defied belief; the most precious and rare stones sparkled everywhere.

What did Gualikh still lack in his abundance? He had no wife, and his subjects implored him continually to get married so that his family lineage would not dry up. The king of Florida decided to do this. As soon as the great American landowners heard that Gualikh wanted to marry, they interrupted what they were doing and hurriedly sent ambassadors to the Princedom of Florida, offering their daughters in marriage to the king. But Gualikh did not consider glory or nobility or wealth; it was on reason and beauty that he pinned his desires. Refuda, the daughter of an African prince, one of the least well known to the European potentates, embodied all of the worthy qualifications Gualikh sought; a stunning beauty, she had an excellent mind, a generosity of spirit, and remarkable compassion. This princess had captured his heart during his travels in Europe, but at that time he was caught up in performing heroic deeds and did not think about love; when he decided to marry, Refuda was the first person to whom he turned.

Wasting no time, he sent a resplendent ambassadorial party to the African princedom to say that Gualikh, the prince of American Florida, wanted to join with the prince's bloodline and was asking for his daughter, the beautiful Refuda, in marriage. The African mogul happily agreed to this and sent his daughter, with her grand dowry, to Florida.

In the year following their wedding, Refuda gave birth to a son; she gave the region of Florida an heir, one who would occupy a principal place in history.

The birth of the prince, whom they named Guak, was celebrated in the finest manner. The prince's childhood flowed by quickly. He was scarcely out of infancy when Gualikh gave him to the care of the wisest teachers and mentors, who used every means to instill in him the knowledge necessary for an autocrat. A good memory and an exceptional comprehension shortened his studies, and he quickly finished all his courses with great success; of all his subjects, he liked knighthood the best.

Guak combined unusual courage with his natural masculinity and strength. He was still in his youth when he became a hero. Secretly, without permission from his parents, he went hunting in the woods and killed several wild animals—his bravery and courage were singular. Absolutely no one knew of these feats but an uncle, who was an eyewitness to many of them; but could they remain concealed for long? He won a stunning victory over the most horrifying crocodile, who lived at the mouth of the river that flowed into the sea, about three versts from the capital. This victory, for the people who lived along the coast, was nothing less than a gift from God, because the crocodile had killed everyone who had approached his nest, and the place was extremely dangerous not only for local inhabitants, but also for people traveling by.

The young prince killed the crocodile in the following manner: Once he was out walking alone with his uncle along the mouth of the river; suddenly one of these wriggling monsters slithered up and attacked Guak, opening its terrible jaws to devour him. Guak, seeing this dangerous adversary, drew his sword with great agility and stepped into battle with the crocodile. Luck served Guak immediately; with one blow he cut off its front legs, which prevented it from crawling any closer; then three poisonous arrows penetrated it, and with a lance his uncle had given him, he hit the open jaws hard, stabbing the crocodile to death.

As far as knightly sporting competition was concerned, the young prince was so skilled that none of the others his age could offer him any real challenge as champion, because his strength was so uncommon and his quickness and dexterity unbelievable. All Floridians said with one voice that if the young prince grew into his promise, the glory of his courage and heroism would set him apart from all others, and from that time all previous champions would have to bow before him. Although twelve men had been designated warriors, and there was no end to jousting, fighting with wild animals, or other knightly matches in Florida, this was not enough to satisfy Guak; the monotony of these activities began to bore him. He kept seeing the same faces, the same courage, the same skills, so he decided to ask his parents to sponsor a public tournament and to circulate announcements inviting the bravest knights and fighters from all corners of the world. Gualikh, who loved his son so much, could not refuse him, and he quickly sent to Europe, Africa, Asia, and America a document worded thus:

Gualikh, King of Florida and ruler of twelve lands, issues this hearty request: I inform monarchs like myself and all knights about knightly competitions and duels to be held in my capital. I invite to Florida all who wish to demonstrate their daring and courage. *Gualikh.*

When the time approached for the assemblage of great magnates and knights, the prince of Florida met with the splendid knights and heroes for three straight days, then named a day for the public games to begin. Then he gave an order for the decoration of his own place and those of the twelve visiting potentates and knights. The brave knights, strong warriors, and great lords began to gather and start their preparations; the people assembled in the streets that Gualikh would pass through and crowded into the amphitheater.

Gualikh, after greeting the potentates and knights gathered there, sat on the throne that had been prepared for him: Guak sat on his right side, and next to him people sat according to their appropriate ranks. Gualikh waved his hand, and suddenly the sound of trumpets and kettledrums rang out; when this ended, the herald of the prince of Florida stood up and in a loud voice read from the uncurled scroll the articles of Virston's proviso:

> Whosoever shall be the victor from among these knights, and whose courage will be distinguished from the others, shall be saluted by all others as a second Virston, and he will receive the most lavish rewards and the greatest honor.

As soon as the herald had read these words, a savage lion was led out in chains, the kind that can be found only in the menageries of Florida; his vicious claws could tear to pieces both anyone who dared to fight him and the attacker's horse. When the lion opened his jaws, a whole row of teeth that looked more like sickles could be seen; his fierce roar resounded throughout the amphitheater and terrified everyone.

Then the herald announced the following in a loud voice:

> If anyone from this gathering of brave men can take the bow of Nimrod, draw it, and shoot an arrow that will wound the savage lion, that archer will receive from Gualikh many precious gifts and the rank of Supreme Minister.

The herald had scarcely finished these words when an American knight suddenly appeared; he wore a gold helmet with pearly white feathers and steel armor with a black eagle pictured on it. He approached the throne of the Lord of Florida and requested permission to test his strength on the fantastic bow. Having received it, he went to the table, picked up the bow, and began to draw it. But no matter how hard he tried, how much strength he exerted, he was not able to pull it back; his movements made the crowd laugh, so he was forced to return in shame to his place. The knight who followed him was no more successful than the previous one; his strength was not enough to draw Nimrod's bow, and like the first, he had to return to his place. Many tried, expending all their strength, and although some could begin to draw it, they could not complete their actions.

Thus did the weapon of the ancient Nimrod score victories. When no one was left from the assembly to try the bow, young Guak jumped from his seat, approached the throne, and said to his father, "Dearest parent! Your burning love and your tender fatherly heart have enough power to ignite in your son your own spirit of courage and daring; permit your son to try his own strength on this weapon, with which my grandfather Zilagon expanded the borders of our fatherland, slew many enemies, and forced many distant countries to tremble before his power— the one with which you, my father, destroyed your enemies and became awesome and unconquerable."

The young prince's brave determination surprised not only Gualikh but also all the foreigners, and Guak, after receiving permission, ran up to the sword of Nimrod, where so many knights had tried before him; the people jumped up anxiously from their places and turned their gazes to the spot where Guak intended to draw the great bow, wondering how he would accomplish this difficult feat. The young hero, taking the bow in his hands, turned to the knight Velikosil[1] standing near him and said, "Don't be surprised that you were unsuccessful; one has to know how to use this bow. Because you did not understand how it works, you earned greater praise with your attempts."

With these words Guak took the arrow, put it in the bowstring, drew the bow, and let fly the arrow with all his strength, killing the beast. The air was filled with cries of surprise and admiration, and the only words that could be heard were "Glory to Guak! What knight can compete with him!"

At the end of this competition, a savage tiger was brought out in chains; the tiger was the size of a fine Persian horse, and was so wild that twelve soldiers could barely restrain him.

Seeing this most horrible beast, no one wanted to fight him; the obvious danger made even the most brave timid; not a single Floridian or foreign warrior stepped into the center of the amphitheater, where the ferocious tiger, his roar filling the air, gnawed his chains in fury, his eyes filled with blood.

Gualikh, seeing that no one wanted to go up against this savage beast, ordered his herald to announce that whoever vanquished this tiger would receive a special and extraordinary prize; but even with this announcement, no one dared to face obvious death, and when the herald raised his voice to repeat the announcement, Velikosil suddenly appeared, dressed in a suit of battle armor: in one hand he carried a huge sword, and in the other a lance inlaid with damask steel. He valiantly approached Gualikh's throne and said, "Prince of Florida! What can compare with the thrill of a hunt in the quest for glory? For him who seeks glory, everything is already decided; he disdains all else. I would not be worthy to call myself a hero or a knight if I trembled in fear like a small child in the face of danger; the greater the threat of peril, the greater the glory of the victory. Know that I am entering battle with this wild beast not because of the reward you have promised, but solely for my own self-respect."

Having said this, he lowered the visor to his helmet and went forth to challenge his vicious adversary. The tiger, catching sight of Velikosil, flew into a rage and pounced furiously upon him. The knight, though, did not allow himself to be caught, and he struck the tiger so hard with his lance that it broke into several pieces; the animal, feeling the wound, flew into an even greater frenzy. Velikosil had lost all faith in his lance, so he drew out his great warrior's sword: then the fighting between them became so intense that the audience could not tear their eyes away. A deathly quiet reigned all around, pierced only by the roar of the wounded tiger; blood poured from him in streams, and the knight continued to inflict upon him grievous wounds.

After a lengthy battle, the tiger pulled the sword from Velikosil's hands, and the warrior tried to run for a sharp dagger. But the tiger knocked him down and grasped Velikosil's neck in his teeth. No matter how much the knight twirled and

---

1. In Russian, "Velikosil" would translate as "Great Strength."

spun around, he could not counterattack, and the tiger gripped him firmly as he prepared to tear him to shreds. The audience cried out instinctively at the danger in which the courageous and fearless Velikosil found himself; the youthful Guak, seeing that the knight now had no possibility of overwhelming his opponent, threw himself like a lightning bolt into the arena where the battle was raging, and in one stroke cut the head of the tiger from its torso. Velikosil, recognizing Guak as his savior, thanked him and told him that he now had the right to all his allegiance and love.

"The last drop of my blood belongs to you, generous savior!" continued Velikosil. "I devote my whole life to serving you—command me however you want; you have the right to demand everything of me!"

Guak returned to his place, with Velikosil behind him carrying the tiger's head; the audience filled the air with applause: "Long live our young hero Guak! His glory will shine even in distant lands!"

Three days after the combat with wild animals, a day was named for a tournament featuring knightly competitions with weapons. When that day arrived, the trumpets and kettledrums summoned all the knights to gather in the amphitheater; in a short time the place filled with the majority of the knights and brave warriors; a second blaring of trumpets and drums announced the arrival of the Floridian prince Gualikh, his son Guak, and all the potentates of the princely court.

[After many duels], young Guak suddenly approached the throne of his father and said, "Beloved parent! The honor of Florida demands at least one warrior capable of defeating the strong and brave Velikosil, and I want to take up arms against this amazing adversary!"

Finishing these words, he mounted the horse that had been led to him, grabbed a steel lance inlaid with gold, and as quick as lightning rode to where Velikosil was cantering about on his horse, awaiting his next competitor. Guak, having drawn up to Velikosil, said to him, "Velikosil! Your valor and power have made timid men of all these knights and soldiers; the strongest dared to test their mettle against yours, and what happened? Shame on them, glory to you. I, seeing what an outstanding hero you are for everyone, have decided to confront you, not because I want to eclipse the glory you have already acquired, because no one could ever dispute that, but strictly because I want to show all those gathered here that I, too, can fight, and I would be flattered to test my strength against such a brave adversary. Come!"

Having said this, Guak spurred his horse and shot like an arrow away from Velikosil, across the open space of the amphitheater. These two heroes, facing each other across a sufficiently wide distance, prepared for single combat. They spurred their horses and rode at each other like two whirlwinds. When they converged, they struck each other so hard with their lances that the blow clapped like thunder and the lances broke into tiny pieces. The horses fell to their knees, and the riders could barely stay in the saddle. Thunderous applause shook the amphitheater; everywhere the air was filled with exclamations in honor of young Guak, and the brave Velikosil announced the following: "Youthful Guak! I have seen many knights, fought many duels with them, but until this time I never knew what it meant to be vanquished; now I know what it means, and I give you the full right as a hero, a brave and valorous knight, to call yourself a victor. I give you my hand as a sign of eternal and unfailing friendship, and henceforth my whole life is devoted to you as a friend and brother, and I hope that you will reward me with a reciprocal love."

Velikosil had barely finished when Guak slid nimbly off his horse and extended his arms in an embrace. The Arabian prince in the same gesture slipped off and, not saying a word, threw himself into Guak's embrace. This confirmed the unbreakable friendship and love between the two of them, and Velikosil and Guak walked arm in arm to the sound of trumpets, kettledrums, and the cries of the people, and approached Gualikh's throne.

"My dearest father," began Guak, "I present to you my friend and brother. I am firmly confident that you, loving me and being so magnanimous, will approve of my selection."

"Great Arabian prince!" said Gualikh, turning to Velikosil. "I consider myself fortunate that my son Guak has such a friend. For my part I will do all I can to show my support and gratitude for your friendship with Guak."

The tournament and competitions ended in the capital of Florida, and on the day after the great celebratory ball given by the Floridian prince, the knights began to depart, having received plentiful gifts from Gualikh. On that same evening, at sunset, an arrow flew into Guak's bedroom with news of the departure of her who had captured his heart for eternity. Try as he might, the young Prince Guak could not find out who had shot the arrow, the beautiful Amazon herself or one of her bodyguards. A note written by the Amazon was attached to the arrow. Guak opened it hurriedly and read the following:

Gentle Guak!
The way you looked at me when I was conquered by you showed me clearly the contents of your heart and soul. Oh, that flame which I saw in your eyes touched my heart. I feel that I have been completely transformed. What has become of that boldness, that intensity that I showed to men? I had only to take one look at you, and my will disappeared forever. My whole soul, beloved, is filled with you. Your precious image is constantly before my eyes. If you feel any love for me, you will try to earn the favor of my father, the Amazonian king, and then I will throw myself joyfully into your embrace. I swear to be true to you to the grave.
Veleuma, Amazonian Princess

Who can describe Guak's elation upon reading this message? He read it over a hundred times, kissed the note, laughed, cried, and behaved like a fool; everyone looked at him with incredulity, because no one had ever seen him like this before.

The letter from the beautiful Veleuma made such an impression on Guak's heart that he decided to go to the Amazonian kingdom at all costs, to earn the good graces of the king, and to become the husband of the fair Veleuma, because he realized that he could never find peace and happiness without her. Having made this decision, he went to his parents and asked for permission to set out upon his voyage. Although his mother Refuda insisted that he not go, Gualikh was not opposed to it and agreed to permit him.

Guak traveled to the Kingdom of Amazonia and married the beautiful Veleuma. When he returned home, his aged father Gualikh and mother Refuda flooded him with tears of happiness. It seemed that they now grew younger.

Guak, remaining in his fatherland with his beloved spouse, received the reins of government of the Princedom of Florida. He governed wisely and mercifully; his subjects adored him, the neighboring states loved and respected him, and his enemies trembled at his might. Guak and Veleuma lived many years in happiness and prosperity, leaving behind many descendants.

The Tale of Vanka Kain
Along with his Searches, Adventures, and Extravagant Wedding
(1815)

VANKA KAIN (IVAN OSIPOV) WAS A MOSCOW THIEF WHOSE EXPLOITS INSPIRED RUSSIA'S FIRST CONSCIOUSLY POPULAR WORK OF LITERATURE, WRITTEN IN 1779 BY THE MOSCOW TOWNSMAN MATVEI KOMAROV. THIS VERSION IS A KNOCK-OFF OF KOMAROV'S LONGER BOOK. AS IN THE WEST, PICARESQUE TALES IN RUSSIA GAVE BIRTH TO THE NOVEL — THOUGH RUSSIAN ROGUES WERE RARELY REDEEMED. OFTEN TAKEN FROM REAL LIFE, THEY DELIGHTED READERS AND IRKED OFFICIALS THROUGHOUT THE NEXT CENTURY. THOUGH CONVENTIONALIZED, PICARESQUE NOVELS OFFER A GLIMPSE INTO POPULAR LIFE AT THE END OF THE EIGHTEENTH CENTURY. THE LANGUAGE IS LOW (THIEVES EVEN SPEAK IN RHYMING *RAESHNIKI*), AND THERE IS FLAWED GRAMMAR: PRONOUNS, PUNCTUATION, REPORTED SPEECH, AND GERUNDIAL

Istoriia Van'ki Kaina, so vsemi ego syskami, rozyskami i sumazbrodnoiu svad'boiu (St. Petersburg: v imp. tip., 1815). Bound with *Kratkaia povest' o buntovshchike i razboinike Sten'ke Razine.*

VERBS (THE EFFECT IS PRESERVED IN THE TRANSLATION). READERS DID NOT NECESSARILY IDENTIFY WITH KAIN OR LIKE HIM (EXCEPT WHEN HE ROBBED A PRIEST OR GYPSIES!), BUT THEY ENJOYED HIS DODGING OF OFFICIAL CONTROL. WHEN THE TALE WAS WRITTEN, KAIN'S ADVENTURES WERE STILL CURRENT EVENTS; MOREOVER, THEY FORESHADOWED TROUBLES AWAITING URBAN AUTHORITIES IN THE NINETEENTH CENTURY.

The renowned thief named Kain was born in 1714. He had been in the service of the Moscow merchant Filatiev, in whose home he had decently performed the duties assigned him, owing to his native cleverness and dexterity, all the while committing minor thefts. But having grown weary of the services he owed his lord, he fled, absconding with a not insignificant sum of money; and upon exiting the gates he nailed to them a specially prepared broadside on which the following was written: Drink water like a goose, eat bread like a pig, but let the devil work, not me. Then joining up with another such thief, Kamchatka,[1] who was waiting for him, they went to the house of a certain priest, whom they found with only his cassock, which Kain donned. He continued on to Stone Bridge[2] in those clothes, answering each sentry that he was a priest and that he was going to serve spiritual needs. Coming in such manner to the bridge, which at that time was the normal haven for suspicious people, the rogues under the bridge first took a drink themselves, then gave some to Kain and Kamchatka; and Kain having drunk his, one hit him on the shoulder and said: Brother, you're cut from the same cloth as those of us living here, we have no lack of anything: bare skin, bare feet, our storehouses stand full of cold and hunger, we who live here have given up our peace and give alms to those who cross this bridge at night. To tell you the Mother Truth, we have nothing but dust and heat and sometimes nothing to eat. So they spent the whole night until the dawn under the bridge; and at daybreak Kain went to Kitaigorod,[3] where he was caught by a man sent by his lord Filatiev and jailed and bound near a bear. But inasmuch as the girl carrying food to the bear was indulgent toward Kain, she told him that in the house of their lord, a dead soldier had been thrown in the empty chamber. Taken before Filatiev for punishment, Kain immediately shouted the then fashionable "Treason!"[4] and was thus sent to the Privy Council, where during the interrogation, to the secretary's question "According to what article or point are you charging me with treason?" he answered, "I know not points or paints, but I will declare my case to the chief member of this place, not you." Upon the

---

1. Dunce or Back-bencher; misbehavers and slow learners sat in the back row of the schoolhouse.

2. Kamennyi most, a central Moscow thoroughfare.

3. A section of central Moscow.

4. *Slovo i delo:* word and deed, or lèse-majesté, the old Muscovite phrase that implied treason for uttering a word against the tsar. The power of the charge can be seen in the reaction of the lord.

investigation of his case it was discovered that the information he heard from the girl was true; for that he was given a passport that allowed him free residence everywhere.[5]

Having received his freedom he found his previous companion Kamchatka again and another four rogues, with whom he went to the home of a doctor and beat his manservant so that he told them how to enter the doctor's chambers; and as the indicated place was a window, Kain, the most agile of the comrades, immediately removed one pane and opening the window with his bare feet entered the bedchamber where the doctor slept with his wife. They had been stepping on a blanket that he then used to cover them, and continuing his journey about the doctor's chambers came upon the nursery where a girl lying in bed asked him sternly why he was there! But her stern demeanor in no way swayed the evil and brave spirit of Kain; silence, Kain told her, we're merchants, we've come to your house to find some things we lost. Then placing a knife to her chest, he said, "If you resist even a little bit, I'll take your life immediately"; but then he and his comrades coming in at that moment bound her mouth, tied her hands and feet and laid her on the bed between the doctor and his wife; and then emptying the rooms and taking everything in them he returned with his comrades and hid from the posse following him with the yardman of the Danilevsky Monastery.

Then in a short time one of the comrades stole into the home of a tailor and hid under the bed and letting his comrades in at night they stole a splendid sum of money and other things; and when one of the tailor's servants chased after them, letting him get close to them they tied him up and laid him in a boat which they let it go its own way down the River Yauza.

The aforementioned girl who had once met Kain had by then told him that she had available two sheds and money and a coach. And that made him so happy that he wanted that very day to check the place out. He bought a chicken and threw it into the neighboring yard, and then began knocking at the gate, wherefore the yardman came out and asked what he needed. Kain asked him to let him into the yard to catch the chicken, and the yardman not knowing of his plot allowed him in. Kain went to where the sheds were located under the guise of looking for his chicken; and when he found a place that was suitable for putting his roguish plan into action, then at night he and his comrades broke a window and harvested a splendid yield; but when a posse took off after them they were forced to throw all they had stolen into the mud and save themselves by flight. Having escaped capture, that very same night they stole a carriage and four horses from the yard of a certain gentleman. From a merchant they took a woman's frock and headdress, and then from a mill they took a female acquaintance, whom having dressed in the hat and frock and sat in the carriage, they returned to the mud into which they had thrown the stolen goods. There they removed the wheel from the axle, and halting under that pretense they dragged the things from the mud and laid them in the carriage;

---

5. All Russians were required to carry passports for purposes of identification. The use of passports helped the government to regulate the economy as well as to maintain a level of social control. Trade and taxes, for example, were regulated through passports, as was residence.

and the enlightened wench execrated them and beat them about the cheeks for lingering over their task, though it would not have been difficult to examine and repair everything at home. Having taken everything in such manner, they returned the wheel to its appropriate place and departed for Carriage Row,[6] where they took the purported lady by the arm, took the money and goods as well, and abandoned the horses and carriage.

Kain, having increased his gang to seven people, departed for the Makariev Fair;[7] there they spotted in a storehouse merchants counting money, of which one left and walked past a guard house standing nearby, where one of the rogues' society yelled Help! at him, and thus they were detained in the guardhouse; and Kain the leader of that evil enterprise told the other merchant that his comrade was in a state of distress and taken under guard; and when that merchant exited the storehouse and went to his comrade, then those rogues ignoring the fortitude of the lock broke it instantly and stole two purses and three bags with money and buried them in the sand. Inasmuch as the place was not suited to openly taking the money, Kain set up a booth selling bast wares, bought up a variety of ribbons, hung them out and pretended to be a merchant; but for what purpose he took on the guise of a merchant, all can guess for themselves; he traded from that booth only four hours, and as soon as night set, he took away all the stolen money, and left the booth and wares.

After some time, Kain, eager for theft stole from a shop a bag full of silver icon frames, was caught and beaten by the merchants, and then put in chains in the town hall. Searching for a means to liberate himself, he again shouted "Treason," and was sent to the appropriate place which in short order he left with irons removed, and although he was followed by a posse, he escaped apprehension by a fight that took place; and that very day he saw a Tatar sleeping soundly in a *kibitka*, and he noticed a trunk located at his head; he tied the Tatar to a horse standing near the *kibitka* and struck it with a stake; the horse galloped off with the Tatar, and Kain took the trunk and went to his comrades.

After a while had passed, Kain being in the city saw Filatiev's servant girl who announced that she had been handed over to the police under suspicion of helping in the robbery of her lord, and that she had been harshly interrogated as to whether she had given any consent, however she had endured the blows and insisted that she knew nothing. Wherefore after my return to my master he gave me my freedom because of those blows believing them to be unjust and she married the stableman Nelidov. Kain, wishing to show his gratitude, presented her with a case full of diamonds and gold stolen from Filatiev. Upon completion of the conversation Kain went to spend the night with her. Nelidov seeing her with another man inquired about her. She answered that he has the same master as me; and Kain answered with the following words: "I'm no burglar or thief, but I share their beliefs, however please do not doubt me. I have a certificate of discharge from the Privy Councillor's Office" taking it from his pocket and giving it to him to hold till the morning while

---

6. The section of central Moscow where carriage shops were concentrated.

7. Russia's oldest trade fair, later known the world over as the Nizhny Novgorod Fair.

he himself remained for the night. Kain though drunk could not sleep through the normal thieves' hour the hour after midnight, and climbing over the fence he made his way to the tailor's and stole three hundred forty rubles in cash from the chest, and again returned to the apartment. Nelidov hearing Kain's arrival reprimanded him for leaving the yard so early without telling him. Silence sir rider! said Kain, know thyself, and he took the stolen money from his pocket, gave it to his wife and told her the Russian saying: "Here you go, a priest's onion, peeled and ready: respect me while I'm alive, remember me when I'm dead." At daybreak thanking his host and taking his certificate he bade them farewell and returned to his apartment.

Once Kain came upon a drunken peasant transporting hay, and stopping him Kain asked where the city *voevoda* lived, and the peasant in his drunkenness instead of answering began to curse. This irked Kain. He ordered him dragged off the wagon and tied to the shaft with the reins, and the hay and manure burned, and striking a fire from the steel he carried, he lit it, and striking the horse with a club he sent it along the road, which taking fright ran off of the road, and galloped and kicked about the field until such time that the cart with the burning hay and the front axle falling off, and with the peasant tied to the shaft and with only the front wheels, ran into the village where Kain and his comrades were supposed to spend the night. But they were wary lest anyone should recognize them there, and they were compelled to walk past it to the next village, though it was late; this inhumane joke caused Kain and his comrades no dearth of merriment. They watching the horse galloping cross the field in the setting dusk with a burning wagon laughed mightily, while the poor and guiltless peasant punished by the villains barely emerged with his life.

Kain and his comrades did so much robbing that they were being sought everywhere. This forced them to switch clothing and set off for the River Volga, along which brigand boats[8] have long coursed, and on which occur frequent robberies and piracies. They had not yet reached the opposite bank of that river when six dragoons asked them who they were; and when that question caused them confusion, the dragoons recognizing them to be suspicious people began grabbing them. Kain's comrades fled in all directions. He, not knowing where to hide, dashed into the merchants' bathhouse, disrobed, threw his clothing under the bench, and then ran naked to the guardhouse, announcing to the officer in charge that the passport given to him by the Moscow magistrate had been stolen along with his clothes; thanks to which the officer sent him to the investigation section, from which after buying off a clerk and giving false testimony that he was a Moscow merchant he was freed with a two-year passport. He found his comrades again and returned with them to Moscow, where continuing his thefts he noticed once in the Greek monastery in the cell of a monk many splendid items. Looking for ways to get into there and empty the monastic trunks, he went to the cell during the mass; and inasmuch as the monk had gone off to the divine service, Kain told the remaining lay brother

---

8. *Razboinicheskie struga:* a reference to the seventeenth-century Cossack rebel and brigand Stenka Razin. See "Stenka Razin and the Princess" and "Down along the Mother Volga" in "Traditional Songs," below.

to take some wax candles to the church; for, he apprised him, his master demands them. When the poor brother left the cell with the candles and began to close the lock, Kain and his comrades tied him and beat him until he surrendered the keys to the trunk, which the villains used to abscond with many of the monastic chattels; furthermore they ordered the bound brother to inform the monk that they had purloined the chattels because he would not have given them up of his own will, and no less to save him from sin; because those who renounce the world should not accumulate property. At last this thievery brought ruin to the scoundrels, for of the things they gave to a cloth merchant to hold, a wench serving him stole two pistols and brought them to sell at the market, where the aforesaid monk took her into custody and by her evidence Kain was discovered and one other of his conspirators. But Kain's evil head and sly underhandedness found here too a means of salvation; first he bought off the sentries to let the wench and his comrade go, and then he was freed himself as innocent, for he had never confessed to theft.

This reward that befell Kain for his deeds wrought not the slightest change in his malicious spirit; and inasmuch as freedom corresponded to his intentions, he returned to his previous industry; he rejoined his comrades; he went to the city of Kashin; thence to the Frolishchev Hermitage, committing during the journey many thefts and amongst them an improbable and amusing abduction; from some gypsies riding from a village along the road he stole a covered wagon and their *sotnik,* whom they left tied on the road, and his property with the wagon and the horse they took into their care. This adventure, it seems to me, was unlikely for the reason that gypsies are more advanced in guile, perfidy, deception and adroitness than other nations; but while this is certified in Kain's unprompted confession and precisely explicated, it is hard not to find humorous the fact that the swindler deceived and swindled a true swindler.

Then Kain joined a gang composed of seventy robbers, they hatched a plan to pillage a distillery, for which purpose they dispatched an extincteur, and finally the *esaul;* and inasmuch as both were bound to a pillar by order of the distillery director, the *ataman* of that considerable band wrought an armed attack on the plant, and regardless of the stiff resistance of the director and several of his underlings; for these were seized by the bandits and locked in the storehouse. They plundered the distillery, without however committing any murders. Completing that banditry with success they rode to the River Oka, and crossing on the ferry they took by force from an officer riding with them a scarf, a badge and a sword, for which they paid him some money, and with that new purchase they arrived in Moscow, where they took residence in the coaching inns of the Pereiaslav and Rogozha cab districts, inquiring of passersby where General Shubin resided and about the holdings of his patrimonial estate; for they had conceived the notion of sacrificing it to their banditry. Waiting in such manner for a convenient moment and reconnoitering all they wished, they went to an artisans' village, but did not find General Shubin himself. However, so that their excursion might not be in vain, they robbed his house, taking with them the overseer and steward, and returned by water: though a posse followed after them, it was halted by the overseer and steward, for the bandits threatened to kill them; and when the pursuit had fallen silent, the overseer and steward received their freedom.

The *ataman* presiding over this gang of bandits was wreaking ruinous havoc wherever he went. They murdered, tormented and burned whosoever would not surrender their estates of their own volition; he turned toward Volodimer,[9] while Kain and his old comrade Kamchatka departed for Moscow to purchase arms and powder. Arriving with this purpose in Moscow, Kain made inquiries about all the robbers, thieves and swindlers in that city; he conceived the notion, whether by his own desire or by danger, to avert the cruel punishment of justice by announcing himself in the appropriate place. This intention was truly realized; he proclaimed himself a thief to one senator, related to him all his robberies and informed him that he could find many people of such status hiding in Moscow. The import of his words immediately made his wishes reality. The senator detaching a significant number of soldiers sent them with Kain to search out those he had denounced; and the dispatched party apprehended over one hundred suspicious people according to the informant's instructions.

This capture and, one could say, Kain's service to noble society suddenly altered his status, and from an irredeemable thief and true rogue and swindler he became a constable and extirpator of people of such ilk. Such a useful service was justly deserving of reward, yet Kain's evil heart infected by the poison of roguery and hidden by the mask of deceit was not worthy. But to recognize this sham was not possible! For to guess the thoughts of another, one needs to penetrate the human heart. This is not given to mortals. In such manner Kain was not only forgiven all the crimes committed by him, but the title of constable was conferred upon him and he was given a worthy party for the apprehension of thieves. Dispatching the duties laid upon him with great exactitude he apprehended more than five hundred thieves.

Arriving home late after visiting the women's convent[10] Kain saw a man running across Novodevichy Field with unusual rapidity, pursuing whom he apprehended, and perceiving blood on his hands he found him suspicious and taking him to his house and handed him over to the sentry with the intention of interrogating him well in the morn; but breaking a window at night he fled the guard and disappeared without a trace.

Meanwhile Kain turned his gaze on another object, about which I now intend to inform the reader. However much a constable he was, he performed only the duties of a thief, and he took a fancy to a girl whom he was desirous of wooing, but her stern replies proved an obstacle here; and though he employed all his eloquence to incline her in his favor, her honor kept the upper hand. He conceived the notion having become a constable of marrying her; he went to her to propose marriage, but she gave her reply immediately. He knew not what to do, yet his passion grew by the hour; for which purpose he instructed a thief being held in the constabulary

---

9. The city of Vladimir, in the old pronunciation.

10. Novodevichy (Virgin) Convent, located on the then-outskirts of Moscow.

to slander her. The thief slandered her and the innocent girl was subjected to a cruel lashing; but she could not confess of anything; for she had not committed the act of which she was accused. Kain finding the moment convenient once again repeated his proposal; but he found no success. The slander that had caused his innocent ladylove to be put under guard was so serious that she was finally subjected to corporal punishment; and when she was informed of this she was forced to seek Kain's protection, who the moment he sensed her agreement released her from bondage, though that freedom cost her several blows of the knout. After her back had healed he soon set a date for their wedding, he went with great ceremony to the wedding and wrote out a testament, as was then the custom, though it was false. The priest of the church in which he intended to be married did not wish to marry him on consideration of the false testament. It was shameful for Kain to abandon his intention; but to keep the priest from leaving the church in the sight of many people was even more shameful. He stood with his bride in the church and sent for any other priest who could be found: he rejoiced when a drunken defrocked priest was brought in, who laid the crowns on the heads of the newlyweds, led them around the pulpit seven times, saying he was adding five extra so that the newlyweds would lead long and happy lives.

After the ceremony Kain gave the priest one ruble in cash, tied his hands behind his back, hung two bottles of wine around his neck, and to the back of his cassock fastened a sheet of paper with the inscription: unbind him when the wine hanging here has been drunk up. After some time had passed the priest happened upon Kain on the street, and seeing him raised his long cassock and took to his heels, fearing that Kain might play another such joke.

Completing his wedding feast in such a manner he gave himself up once again to crime. At the request of a peasant whose son had been taken by the estate over-seer to be handed over to the army, he freed that peasant boy in the most insolent manner, and the overseer was tarred, so that he might not again surrender him willingly. He forcibly freed a thief held under guard in the commissary, and with the soldier put on duty, whom they bound with the chains taken from the thief, let him go. An acquaintance of Kain's asked him for help in freeing his ladylove; she was a nun, but having fled the nunnery she had been living with her true love, and was then caught and imprisoned in the nunnery to repent. Though the deed itself was important, the money promised was even more seductive to Kain, who donned an officer's clothing, took with him a guard's sergeant of his acquaintance and went to the nunnery where she was held. There was an easy way to put the enterprise into action; he told the mother superior to hand over the nun immediately; for he claimed she was wanted in the chancellory. It was not possible not to hand her over, seeing his stern demeanor, nor was it possible to see through his ruse. He took the nun and handed her over to her true love, promising to serve him further should he find need of yet another nun. The soldiers of the commissary office caught a certain peasant during a secret shipment of wine, who fled to Kain's protection and received the assistance he desired; for he ordered one of his band's soldiers to release the peasant, and another to latch onto the horse to take it away; and this was fulfilled with great exactitude; they freed the peasant and the horse, and the soldiers transporting the wine were left bound to the barrels. Someone informed Kain that a boat with much money was near the Moscow River gate, for which purpose he took several of his band and began trading in wheat; but rather than buying he tied the sentry on the boat and removed the money from a trunk. Soldiers of Kain's band took bills of exchange in the value of twenty thousand rubles from the pocket of a merchant; the merchant asked Kain for help, who willingly promised to show him service; he soon found that which he sought, and came by night to the merchant's mansion and concealed the bills in the attic; and next day in the morning told him where the bills were: the merchant was overjoyed and could not understand how he had divined that which the finest fortune-teller could not and he generously rewarded him for it.

Meanwhile Kain took a woman who told him of the blasphemous service of the false Messiah Andriushka,[11] and for that purpose gave him a personal message which Kain immediately took to the Chancellory, by which many people infected with that plague were discovered.

Finally Kain, performing many evil and good deeds, though splendidly practicing the former, so that much time would be needed to describe all his swindles, from which many have been omitted for lack of space, was subjected to justice and received the retribution he deserved. They soundly stroked his back with the knout, gave him a few extra nostrils, put the coat of arms on his brow and cheeks and sent him to the Baltic port to save his soul.

---

11. Popular prophets and false messiahs were a common feature of Russian popular culture which not even the reforms could completely eradicate in the countryside.

The New Sterne

A. A. Shakhovskoi (1805)

PRINCE SHAKHOVSKOI WAS BORDERLINE HIGHBROW, AND THEREFORE MIGHT BE RATHER ELITIST FOR THIS ANTHOLOGY. A CONTEMPORARY OF PUSHKIN AND KARAMZIN, HE WAS ACTIVE IN THE LITERARY POLEMICS OF HIS DAY. YET HE WAS MORE POPULAR WITH MIXED THEATER AUDIENCES THAN WITH THE INTELLIGENTSIA HE PARODIED (AND OFFENDED). DESPITE AN ARISTOCRATIC UPBRINGING, HE FOUND HIS NICHE AS DIRECTOR OF ST. PETERSBURG'S IMPERIAL THEATER; MERCHANTS FROM NEIGH-

---

From A. A. Shakhovskoi, *Komediia. Stikhotvoreniia* (Leningrad: Sovetskii pisatel', 1961), pp. 735–752.

boring *Gostinyi dvor* crowded the seats and set the tone for the most bourgeois of Russia's official theaters. Author and translator of more than 100 plays, Shakhovskoi was indispensable to the development of Russian vaudeville. He knew how to please crowds, and in so doing, he expanded the scope of the middlebrow.

The New Sterne, a takeoff on Lawrence Sterne's *Sentimental Journey,* was Shakhovskoi's first major success. Performed first in 1805, it circulated among provincial theaters for years after. The piece lampoons Karamzin, "the Russian Sterne," and the sentimentalism he made fashionable with his *Poor Liza.* Shakhovskoi re-created that classic sentimental scenario: the nobleman in love with the common girl. But no "glistening tears" need fall for the plight of his heroine. The affected Count Pronsky and his hapless manservant Ipat struggle with the effusive vocabulary of the genre, finding everything "touching" — and thus arousing the suspicion of peasant women. Shakhovskoi does not offer the trenchant social commentary of Griboedov's more famous parody of westernized nobility, *Woe from Wit,* but instead shows up the ridiculous excesses of a youthful fad.

CAST OF CHARACTERS

Count Pronsky, a sentimental voyager
Sudbin, a retired major and friend of
   Pronsky's father
Ipat, Pronsky's servant, a serf

Kuzminishna, the local miller's widow[1]
Malanya, her daughter
Foka, Malanya's fiancé

The action takes place about 500 versts from Moscow. The setting should be an attractive site, with a river and a mill in the distance, and on stage left a small hill with pine trees.

---

1. Women often took over their husbands' jobs after being widowed, as has Kuzminishna.

SCENE I

Sudbin and Ipat

IPAT: Is that really you, sir? I don't believe my eyes! You, five hundred versts from Moscow? Have you parted company with your old general?

SUDBIN: Your master's wild behavior separated me from his father!

IPAT: What, sir! So you're chasing after His Excellency?

SUDBIN: Yes! Soon it will be a month that I've been tracking you. My loyalty to old Count Pronsky has made me a traveler against my will. The father of your count wanted to marry him to a good, sweet girl, the daughter of one of our old friends; he wrote to him in Petersburg, telling him to request a leave, but in return he received a letter half the size of a book, which with great difficulty we finally understood to say that the young man feels too delicate for military service, and that his heart is too sentimental for marriage without passion, and that he's too enraptured with newfangled ideas; therefore, he's leaving the army and, not wanting to marry but desiring to publish a diary, he's decided to travel all over Russia. The old general was beset with anxiety and wanted to write to Petersburg and ask everyone about getting his son back. But I, remembering our own youth, persuaded him not to make the matter public, because that might prove ruinous for his son. Instead, I rented a carriage and set out to find the boy. I hope that I will be able to deliver your master from his delusions.

IPAT: Not likely! Every day my lord becomes more sentimental, more touching, more interesting!

SUDBIN: From what kind of silly book did you get those words?

IPAT: Oh, sir, if only I knew! The azure-pink sky, a subject of speculation, flowers of eternity, a balming influence!

SUDBIN: Enough, enough. Tell me what you two are doing here.

IPAT: Us? Depending on the weather, we're sighing, weeping, rejoicing, being touched, touching. The bright sun warms our feelings, the terrible frost fortifies our life's blood, the melody of a rolling river feeds our melancholy, a still lake forms a mirror for our sentimentalism; finally, a bucket, the wind, rain, mountains, woods, meadows, marshes, people, cows, birds, flies, mosquitoes—all influence our soul. In a word, we're sentimental voyagers! But, alas, fate willed that among the three of us geniuses, death would take one! Oh, Lady, you are no longer! Ah! Eternity!

SUDBIN: What! What do you mean? Has someone died? Who's this Lady?

IPAT: A sensitive, grateful, sentimental friend to humanity, a symbol of fidelity! Alas, the English dog that got run over by a carriage here three days ago, and to whom the count has built a monument to eternity.

SUDBIN: And that's what's keeping him here?

IPAT: Well, not completely. The death of the devoted Lady left such an emptiness in our hearts that my master wants to fill it with the daughter of the local miller.

SUDBIN: You mean Kuzminishna, at whose house I'm staying?

IPAT: Her, sir, that's her. Yesterday, when we were crying over our friend, Malanya, the touching shepherdess, was herding gentle cows, romantic sheep, and well-nourished pigs with a supple rod into a modest pen. She was singing, "Over the mountains, over the mountains." Her voice reverberated in our souls! Today I was ordered to go before dawn to find this enchantress, to tell her that a lord was asking about her. I took to my heels, approached, looked—and saw the distinguished and honorable friend of our elderly count: my heart began pounding with fear and hope.

SUDBIN: If you help me to recruit your count back among normal people, you have nothing to fear from me.

IPAT: You can count on me as on a stone wall, especially because I would like to retire from being a sentimental voyager.

SUDBIN: I just had a novel idea: I'll launch a counterfeit attack! In war, in love, and in good business, craftiness always works. And if I say that I am the father of this feminine conqueror? Ha, ha, ha. At least with this trick I can teach your artful companion a lesson. Ah, here comes my landlady now. Kuzminishna! Foka!

[*In the next three scenes, Sudbin plots with Malanya's mother and her fiancé to disguise himself as her father and discuss the marriage proposal with Count Pronsky.*]

SCENE V

Count Pronsky and Ipat

COUNT: What harmony in this landscape! What hues in Nature! (*seeing Ipat*) Simple son of Nature, exult in your mother! (*wants to embrace him*) Phoo! How he smells of vodka! How long will you disfigure Nature with that drink of folly? Have you been drinking vodka?

IPAT: Guilty. I had a tumbler in the nearby pub—for the health of Mother Nature and Your Excellency.

COUNT: You profane yourself every day with that accursed vodka, and for what?

IPAT: Oh, sir, I swear I never drink without a reason. Four days ago I drank because there was nothing else to do; three days ago I drank to help my bellyache; yesterday I drank from misery; and today I drink from happiness.

COUNT: What sort of happiness?

IPAT: Oh, sir, what kind? Joy of the soul, the heart, the imagination. As Your Excellency ordered, today I woke up before the sun and ran to the mill, but I had barely gotten down the hill when I met—whom do you think?

COUNT: My heart has guessed! You encountered . . .

IPAT: I met a kind, rust-colored cow, who was being led by her twisted horns by . . .

COUNT: Her?

IPAT: No, not exactly her, but someone like her; in a word, her sister Domna.

Dear, sharp, quick Domna! Enchantress, captivator, conqueror of faithful, clever, and agile Ipat!

COUNT: What! And so you were touched, you fell in love?

IPAT: Ah, Nature! My eyes had just caught sight of the cow and Domna when my heart began to pound, and my legs carried me to her. "Hello, pretty maiden!" "Hello yourself, young man!" "Do you know, my little queen, whose mill this is?" "How could I not know? It belongs to my father, Sidor Arkhipych." "What! It's Arkhipych's? Kiss me for that good news." "Do you really know him?" "No, but I am fervently devoted to all Sidors and am madly in love with all Arkhipyches. Tell me, was that your sister who was driving the gentle cattle yesterday?" "What a clever man! Indeed it was my sister Malanya."

COUNT: What do I hear? Her name is Melanie?[2]

IPAT: Malanya, sir.

COUNT: How crude! What ignorance! How is it possible to ruin the most interesting names? Only here do we tolerate that! Marmontel, LaHarpe, Destouches—you would turn over in your graves to hear the barbarian appellation that we give to your Melanie! Listen, if you desecrate my hearing again, then for the honor of literature and sentimentalism I'll let you feel the strength of my hand.

IPAT: I'm ready to rebaptize her if you'd like, but . . .

COUNT: Continue!

IPAT: Her sister told me that this interesting, uh, what's-her-name is getting married.

COUNT: What! Who is this lucky mortal?

IPAT: The son of the blacksmith Antip, Foka, named for the sainted Fok.

COUNT: A blacksmith's son! Foka! But Melanie must captivate all who have a heart.

IPAT: Oh, and Foka has the most passionate heart! He almost showed me his passion.

COUNT: Did you talk to her? Did you tell her sister that I . . .

IPAT: And what did you order me to say about you? You've forbidden me to call you Count Pronsky; it's been four months already, and you haven't chosen another name.

COUNT: It's true that I still haven't been able to come up with the proper name for a sentimental voyager.

IPAT: What's making you change your name, anyway?

COUNT: Everything: the desire to hide from those who probably are chasing after me, and the custom, consecrated by Sterne, who traveled under the name of Yorick.

IPAT: Yorick? That's a great name! What does it mean in their language?

COUNT: Nothing. Yorick was the jester of an English king.

IPAT: A king's jester? Perfect! Thank my brain; it's found a name for you.

---

2. *Melanie* was one of sentimentalism's early tragedies, written by Jean-François LaHarpe in 1770.

COUNT: What?

IPAT: If this Yorick was the jester of an English king, and Balakirev was the jester of a Russian tsar, then what's keeping you from calling yourself Balakirev?

COUNT: Balakir?[3] No, that sounds terrible to the ears: Balakir! What do I hear? The voice of the interesting Melanie!

SCENE VI

COUNT: What rapturous innocence! My legs are failing me; I cannot approach this angel, who has come to our earth from ethereal heights!

IPAT: I'll go for you. Good journey, pretty one! Stop, I say, my beauty.

MALANYA: Me? I thought you meant someone else.

COUNT: He called you Beauty, and that is your name.

MALANYA: Oh, sir, you're teasing. My name is Malanya.

COUNT: Modest violet! Interesting Melanie! My sentimental angel!

MALANYA: Sir, I can't speak German. (*to Ipat*) Isn't he Russian?

IPAT: Well, sort of. One or the other.

COUNT: Hear me out, my touching shepherdess.

MALANYA: What are you saying, sir? I'm not an orphan that I need to be working as a shepherdess; I've got a mother.

IPAT: And a father.

MALANYA: What? Well, yes, I guess I've got a father, too.

COUNT: Must I believe the rumor that is breaking my heart? I heard that you are going to be married.

MALANYA: Everyone knows I am marrying Foka, the blacksmith's son.

COUNT: And you have given your heart to him?

MALANYA: You're joking, sir.

COUNT: What, no knot of sympathy binds you together? You are free? It must be that mercenary parental tyranny is scorching the pale cheeks of the children with flaming tears. What! You think you must submit to your parents' will?

MALANYA: Whom do we obey if not our mothers?

COUNT (*to Ipat*): What patriarchal principles!

IPAT: Principles patriarchal!

COUNT: Thus, if only youthful servility is forcing you to become a wife, I will take it upon myself to liberate you.

MALANYA: I'm free enough.

COUNT: Angel! You are free! Ipat, are you rejoicing in this ingenuous daughter of Nature?

IPAT: I weep!

COUNT: Chaste virtue!

IPAT: Virtue chaste!

COUNT (*to Malanya*): Where are you going?

---

3. *Balakir* translates as "pot."

MALANYA: It's not nice for me to eavesdrop when others are talking.

COUNT: What integrity! How all the sophisticated beauties must blush before this peasant girl!

IPAT: The chambermaids and the ladies of the manor must blush—that is, if they can.

MALANYA: Really, this isn't what Foka says to me; he'd be beside himself. How he would screw up his face, looking at me! Oh, I'm starting to become afraid. Why aren't our people here?

COUNT: I implore you again, open to me all the curves of your heart; speak only one word; look at me, my beauty! Agnes! Violet!

MALANYA: He's been overwhelmed.

COUNT: What interesting timidity! She's like a yellow-bellied siskin, flittering away from the bird net! (*He approaches Malanya, but she ducks away, and he chases her around the stage.*) My innocent one, do not fear me—I'm no fiend!

IPAT: It's true, Malaniushka,[4] we're not dangerous; sentimental love is as pure as a dove.

COUNT (*grasping her by the arm*): Listen, listen to me! I cherish such modesty!

MALANYA: Oh, oh, what are you up to, sir? Oh, oh!

SCENE IX

Foka, Malanya, the Count, and Ipat

KUZMINISHNA: All the girls have wandered off. Malashka! Malashka!

FOKA: Cry out, but maybe Malashka has fallen into the right hands.

KUZMINISHNA: What's going on, Fokushka?

COUNT: Hear me out, good woman! This innocence, is she your daughter?

KUZMINISHNA: I gave birth to her, my benefactor.

COUNT: And you're giving her to him?

KUZMINISHNA: Yes, sire.

COUNT: You're ruining her!

KUZMINISHNA: What are you saying, sire? I'm ruining the one I gave birth to? I'm ruining my own child? What do you mean? Perhaps your kind don't take care of their children, but here we do. Come to me, Malasha. What's this gentleman been saying?

MALANYA: Heaven only knows what he's been squawking about.

FOKA: And . . . don't listen anymore.

KUZMINISHNA: No, good sir, don't start telling me that I want to ruin her; may lightning strike me if I would want to do that. I love my children! They're my only wealth, my sole treasure.

COUNT: Good woman, you touch me!

---

4. Malaniushka and (a few lines down) Malashka are diminutive forms of Malanya. See the Note on Transliteration for an explanation of diminutives.

KUZMINISHNA: What are you saying, sir? Cross yourself! I didn't touch you.

FOKA: Isn't it a sin to harass an old woman?

IPAT: Ignoramuses never understand properly. To touch doesn't mean that; to touch means—maybe that you hit someone?

COUNT: How lamentable that their sentiments are not refined. You live in a circle of ignorance.

FOKA: They don't live in a circle but in a mill!

IPAT: Oh, ignorance!

COUNT: Good mother! You have raised this modest, interesting Melanie in the bosom of Nature; she's a bud, still not cultivated by the hand of a master gardener.

FOKA: Of course not! I'm not going to give her to any gardener to work over. Now listen, baron, wouldn't it be better for you just to leave us in peace? Let's go, little mother; it's time to get started on the betrothal.

KUZMINISHNA: It really is time. Goodbye, noble master.

MALANYA: Have a good journey. (*She leaves.*)

COUNT: Angel! Stop, listen to me! They're taking her away. Ipat, stop them!

IPAT (*trying to intervene, but Foka pushes him aside*): You can see for yourself how this ruffian behaves.

COUNT: No, I won't give her up! (*He exits.*)

SCENE X

Ipat, and then Sudbin (disguised as the miller, Malanya's father)

IPAT: It's clear that my master has gone crazy. It's too bad, because he has such a good heart. Weeping authors, tearful writers! You, you have destroyed my good master; you will have to answer for this, for those little books I brought to him from the university bookshops; they've done in my poor count. Explain to me, sir, from where did that sentimental deviltry come to us?

SUDBIN: It took shape in England, deteriorated in France, got inflated in Germany, and by the time it got to us, it was in such a pitiful state that . . .

IPAT: That even the gods laugh! The pity is for those who were taken in by it.

SUDBIN: There are such lights that ruin everyone and everything they shine on. The most insane practices often have roots in worthwhile institutions. What is splendid in one regiment might not work out at all when it goes around the whole division.

[*The disguised Sudbin then tries unsuccessfully to dissuade Pronsky from marrying his "daughter."*]

SCENE XII

The Count and Ipat

COUNT: And so my lot is cast: I will become a farmer. I will take the daughter of that distinguished elder as my beloved friend, and together we will settle in a small hut. There, when the sun is rising, I will awaken the dear one in whose arms I am reposing; with her I will work our little corner of land or tend the sheep.

IPAT (*to the side*): Not very intellectually stimulating work.

COUNT: There the fruits of the earth and milk will be my food.

IPAT (*to the side*): An unenviable table.

COUNT: A soft straw mattress.

IPAT (*to the side*): Not an exceptional bed.

COUNT: Cicero, Sterne, and Young will occupy me; I will read *La Nouvelle Heloise*.[5]

IPAT (*to the side*): And your gentle spouse will yawn, or feed the pigs out of boredom.

COUNT: Ipat, I will be so happy!

IPAT: Better to say that we will both be happy.

COUNT: What do you mean?

IPAT: Your Excellency is marrying Melanie, and I her sister, Domna.

COUNT: That means you'll be . . .

IPAT: The brother-in-law of my good master.

COUNT: How dare you?

IPAT: Why are you getting angry? I, sir, have a heart. I like Domna; I will marry her, and will build a hut more modest than yours. I will drive the sheep, eat bread and milk, sleep on the straw, and on Sundays I will read *Bova Korolevich* and *Vanka Kain;* I'll enrich you with many nephews, my children; you'll be their godfather . . .

COUNT: This is too much. You're mocking me, aren't you? Impertinent fellow!

IPAT: Why are you so irate, my future brother-in-law?

COUNT: I'll teach you a lesson! But maybe this is true. Even though Ipat's a drunk, he can be Domna's husband; that would make me his relative! Oh, but we must scorn prejudices! Still, my own father . . . I will touch him with my tears; he will see Melanie and forgive his captured angel!

LAST SCENE

The village girls have surrounded Malanya and are singing; Foka leads her by one hand, Kuzminishna by the other; Sudbin is in the background, leading the other daughter.

---

5. Jean-Jacques Rousseau's *La Nouvelle Heloise* was one of the most popular of the sentimental novels.

COUNT: They lead her! Ipat, my friend, everything is decided, inhuman ones! Cease!

FOKA: Don't listen to him, he's crazy.

EVERYONE: Insane! Be careful that he doesn't bite . . .

COUNT: Distinguished elder, listen to this unhappy soul! Kuzminishna, cease! Melanie, look at me!

SUDBIN: Stop. We must hear him out.

MALANYA: Don't let him get too close to you, Mother.

KUZMINISHNA: Our place is blessed; what's to fear?

COUNT: You must know who I am; I am Count Pronsky, the son of a celebrated general.

IPAT (*to Foka*): Know who we are!

COUNT: My heart longs for happiness, that which comes not from being highborn, but from true love, sentimental friendship, ethereal bliss. Interesting Melanie has touched my heart, her father has seen my mind, and I want to belong to them forever.

IPAT: Me too. Domna is in my heart.

KUZMINISHNA: So they really want to marry my daughters.

FOKA: Aren't I the bridegroom?

SUDBIN: Master and servant, I do not approve of either of you; you cannot bring happiness to my daughters. Baron, you have a father; what will he say when he learns that you have married a peasant girl?

COUNT (*falling to his knees*): My father will approve my selection.

IPAT (*also on his knees*): My mother will bless me!

COUNT: Even though he's a prominent person, he's still a father!

IPAT: Even though she's a fine laundress, she's still a mother!

COUNT (*to Ipat*): Why don't you keep your mouth shut?

IPAT: My heart is doing the talking.

COUNT (*to Sudbin*): Distinguished elder, I will make not only your daughter happy, but your whole family; I will be a dutiful son; I will spend every minute of my life trying to satisfy you, being with you.

SUDBIN (*taking off his* kaftan, *beard, and wig*): Who can promise to be faithful to his wife's father when he has abandoned his own? Get up, Count; I am ashamed of you.

COUNT (*jumping up*): It is he!

IPAT: So it would seem.

COUNT: My God!

SUDBIN: Embrace your friend, who loves you like a son.

FOKA: What a puzzle!

KUZMINISHNA: Pay attention, it's a lesson!

SUDBIN: Today you must open your eyes: You have been insulted by this peasant girl, scorned by the others, and Ipat has almost become a relative. You must understand how the imagination of a sensitive person who has been impassioned by idiosyncratic writers can bring about his downfall. A young man born with burning emotions, a kind heart, and an ardent soul, after reading these authors who have fraudulent ideas yet write quite eloquently, can be misled for a moment. But at the first light of reason he must return to the correct path.

COUNT: I am ashamed to look at you.

SUDBIN: Your father is anxiously awaiting you.

COUNT: Oh, what have I done!

SUDBIN: The father, at the sight of his son, will forget everything but the satisfaction of embracing him. Let's go.

FOKA: Does this mean he doesn't want to get married anymore?

IPAT: You can marry both sisters if you'd like.

KUZMINISHNA: Hey, fella, what trouble are you provoking? I never!

SUDBIN: Goodbye, good people! Count, we will laugh at today's adventure.

KUZMINISHNA: Stay, Father, to observe our holiday.

SUDBIN: We will remain, Count, to share their happiness. They have done us a great favor today.

COUNT: Yes! They opened my eyes, blinded by seductive imagination. I swear to reform, and to evade all sentimental curiosities, which make us ridiculous and useless for practical work.

IPAT: No more weeping! Farewell to rivers, mountains, forests, sighs, and raptures: we, the ungrateful ones, forsake you forever.

Traditional Songs
(Late 18th Century)

MID-NINETEENTH-CENTURY DEFENDERS OF NATIONAL MUSIC FEARED THE DEATH OF RUSSIAN FOLK SONGS. PEASANT TRADITIONS WERE VANISHING IN THE FACE OF URBANIZATION, SO NATIONALIST COMPOSERS AND THEIR FOLLOWERS REVIVED FOLK SONGS AND GAVE THEM MODERN ORCHESTRATIONS. THOUGH PEASANTS RARELY SANG THEM, THEY WERE TAKEN TO REPRESENT THE "GENUINE" RUSSIAN SOUL. COMPOSERS FOUND THE SONGS NOT IN THE VILLAGES, BUT IN THE PUBLICATIONS OF INTREPID COLLECTORS WHO HAD VENTURED TO THE COUNTRYSIDE IN THE LATE EIGHTEENTH CENTURY. DESPITE THE COLLECTORS' ASSUMPTIONS, THE SONGS WERE NOT RELICS OF RURAL CULTURE,

BUT FORERUNNERS OF A LOWER-CLASS URBAN CULTURE. THEY WERE PUBLIC SONGS, SUNG AT HOLIDAY FAIRS (*GULIAN'IA*) OR ON THE WALKING PATHS OF URBAN PARKS. AS THE FOLLOWING EXAMPLES SUGGEST, A POPULAR TOPIC WAS THE NEWFOUND MOBILITY THAT BECKONED MANY TO EXPLORE THE VAST COUNTRY, AND THE OUTLAWS WHO HAD ONCE ENJOYED SUCH FREEDOM. THESE SONGS, SOME OF WHICH ARE STILL POPULAR TO THIS DAY, APPEARED IN CHEAP SONGBOOKS THROUGHOUT THE NINETEENTH CENTURY, AND WERE ADAPTED IN THE TWENTIETH CENTURY TO STAGE AND SCREEN.

STENKA RAZIN AND THE PRINCESS[1]
Traditional Song

Из за острова на стрежень,
На простор речной волны,
Выплывают расписные
Острогрудные челны.
На переднем Стенька Разин,
Обнявшись, сидит с княжной,
Нынче свадьбу он справляет—
Он—веселый и хмельной.

Позади их слышен ропот:
«Нас на бабу променял,
Только ночь с ней провозжался—

Сам на утро бабой стал.»
Этот ропот и насмешки
Слышит грозный атаман,
И он мощною рукою
Обнял ея княжий стан.

Брови черные сошлися,
Надвигается гроза,
Буйной кровью налилися
Атамановы глаза.

From behind the island harbor,
To the river's broad expanse,
Decorated ships with tapered bows
Came sailing.
At the prow was Stenka Razin,
In his arms his princess sat,
At his wedding celebration
He was cheery and was drunk.

From behind he heard the mutters:
"He's traded us in for a girl,
Here he's spent just one night with her—
And come day he's one himself."
The scowling *ataman* heard
All the heckling and laughs.
With his mighty hand he took hold
Of the girl's noble waist.

He pursed his glowering eyebrows,
And a mighty storm approached,
The wild *ataman*'s eyes
Were flooded with dark blood.

---

1. There was a rich folklore surrounding the uprising of the cossack Stenka Razin in 1670. Part of the legend was that his downfall was caused not by the tsarist army, but by a Persian princess captured in a raid.

«Все отдам, не пожалею,
Буйну голову отдам,»
Раздается голос властный
По окрестным берегам.

А она, потупя очи,
Ни жива и ни мертва,
Молча слушает хмельные,
Неразумные слова:
«Волга, Волга, мать родная,
Волга, русская река.
Не видала ль ты подарка
От донского казака?!

И чтоб не было раздора
Между вольными людьми,
Волга, Волга, мать родная,
На, красавицу возьми!
Что ж вы, черти, приуныли!
Эй, ты, Филька, шут, пляши,—
Грянем песню удалую
На помин ея души.»

Из за острова на стрежень,
На простор речной волны,
Выплывают расписные
Стеньки Разина челны.

"Take it all! I want for nothing;
You can have my wild head,"
And his powerful voice rang out
Along the river banks.

Lowering her eyes, she sat there,
Barely living, not yet dead,
And without a sound, she heeded
His intoxicated words.
"Volga, Volga, my dear mother,
Russian river, Volga dear.
Have you ever seen such presents
From a Cossack of the Don?!

So that there can be no quarrels
Flaring up between free folk,
Volga, Volga, my dear mother,
Here now, take this pretty girl!
Hey, you devils, why so downcast!
Hey there, Filka, dance your dance,—
Let us loudly sing a bold tune
To the memory of her soul."

From beyond the island harbor,
To the rivers broad expanse,
The decorated ships of Stenka Razin
Came sailing.

DOWN ALONG THE MOTHER VOLGA
Robber Ballad (recorded 1770)[2]

Внизь по матушке по Волге,
По широкому раздолью,
Разыгралася погода,
Погодушка верьховая,
Верьховая, волновая,
Ничего в волнах не видно,
Одна лодочка чернеет;
Никого в лодке не видно,
Только парусы белеют,
На гребцах шляпы чернеют,
Кушаки на них алеют;
На корме сидит хозяин.
Сам хозяин во наряде,

Down along the Mother Volga,
Down along its broad expanse,
A mighty storm came blowing,
A storm blew in from up the river,
From up the river, blew in waves,
The waves are hiding all that's in them,
One small boat shows black within;
Nobody to be seen in it,
Only its sails shine white,
Hats show black above the oars,
Scarlet sashes show on them;
The chieftain's sitting at the stern.
That same chieftain's smartly dressed,

2. This song is sometimes attributed to Vanka Kain.

Во каришневом кафтане,
Во грязетовом камзоле,
В алом шелковом платочке,
В черном бархатном картузе,
Уж как взговорит хозяин:
Мы пригрянемте ребята
Внизь по матушке по Волге,
Ко Еленину подворью,
Ко Ивановой здоровью.
Еленушка выходила,
Таки речи говорила:
Не прогневайся пожалуй,
В чем ходила, в том и вышла,
В одной тоненькой рубашке
И в кумачной телогрейке.

Dressed up in a brown *kaftan,*
In a mud-splashed camisole,
With a scarlet silken kerchief,
In a velvet cap of black,
So the chieftain tells his men:
Boys, we'll set our bearing
Down along the Mother Volga,
Down toward Elena's home,
Down a drink to Ivan's health.
His Elena came out to them,
And here is what she said:
Please do not be angry with me,
I'm wearing now what I wore then,
I'm wearing just this flimsy shirt
And a calico housecoat.

THE STEPPE IS ALL AROUND
Traditional Song (18th century)

Степь да степь кругом, путь далек лежит,
В той степи глухой замерзал ямщик.

И набравшись сил, чуя смертный час,

Он товарищу отдавал наказ:

«Ты, товарищ мой, не попомни зла,

Здесь, в степи глухой, схорони меня!

А коней моих своди к батюшке,
Передай поклон родной матушке.

А жене скажи слово прощальное,
Передай кольцо обручальное.

А еще скажи—пусть не печалится,

И кто сердцу люб, пусть обвенчается.

Про меня скажи, что я в степи замерз,
А любовь ее я с собой унес».

All around is steppe, the road lies far ahead,
In the far-off steppe a coachman froze to death.

Gathering his strength before he met his end,

He gave a final task to his trusted friend:

Comrade, when I'm gone, don't think ill of me,

Bury me right here in the distant steppe!

Lead my horses to my respected father,
And bow for me before my beloved mother.

Bid a fond farewell to my dearest wife,
Give this ring to her from our wedding day.

Let her also know that her grief will mend,

If her heart should wish, let her wed again.

Tell that I lie frozen in the steppe,
And my love for her went with me to my end.

Part II

Commerce Asserts
Its Mediating Presence,
1825–1860

The reign of Nicholas I (1825–55) is most commonly remembered in Russia's cultural history for the wedge it drove between the government and the intelligentsia. Pushkin, Gogol, and Belinsky all died young during this era, leaving profound and ambiguous legacies. But this was also a time when urban culture began to expand, embracing larger numbers and different types of audiences. The "Iron Tsar" might have been an obscurantist censor, but he was also an avid patron of the Aleksandrinsky Theater, or the "Aleksandrinka," as its mixed patronage of merchants and nobles called it. Vaudeville entertainments overshadowed the Decembrist legacy in the eyes of most patrons. Social consciousness did make an appearance in sensational literature, in addition to the responsibilities extolled by intellectuals. But it was the defeat in the Crimean War in 1855, rather than their hectoring, that paved the way for the emancipation of the serfs, as well as for an industrial revolution that promised more time for leisure, and the disposable income critical to commercial entertainments.

Urban culture in this era showed marked hostility to folk influences. The lower classes constituted a minor part of the urban population. Permanent city dwellers, the core audience of popular culture, came mostly from the state service in the first half of the nineteenth century: the military, bureaucracy, and other service classes. To them, to semi-educated merchants, and even to recent migrants from the village, peasants were bumpkins, fit only for ridicule. A key to becoming urbanized lay in identifying the peasant as the Other. Public entertainments promoted this rejection of traditional life, as in the Aleksandrinka's hit vaudeville *Filatka and Miroshka the Rivals*. When lower-class city types were introduced into culture, it was often in graphic forms, with strict typecasting that froze the images, and did not allow them to speak for themselves.

Quaint folkisms, rejected by the folk, did exert some influence—a selective influence, surely—on upper-class and noble writers, such as the great poet Aleksandr Pushkin. The cosmopolitan Pushkin, raised speaking French, boasted of the peasant nanny who taught him folk tales. He wrote verse legends that, at least in content, were based on folk models. The peasant style brought even greater success to Petr Ershov, a university student, whose *Little Humpbacked Horse* is still beloved by Russians. This tale in verse used the characters (but not the style) of traditional stories, including the renowned Ivan the Fool.

Like Komarov before him, Faddei Bulgarin stands out as a transitional figure, the writer and publisher who almost invented the popular market in the late 1820s and the 1830s. Few in Russian literature have ever attracted such opprobrium as Bulgarin, who attained record sales with his picaresque novel *Ivan Vyzhigin* and his journal the *Northern Bee* (1825–64). Bulgarin's place in Russian literary history has been as a spy for Tsar Nicholas I and a target of Pushkin's barbed epigrams. Although his grammar and his Polish accent provoked derision, Bulgarin shaped the coming age no less than the great poet. Literature, he saw, was a pursuit for the many, not the few; the lower orders appeared in his works not as the objects of aristocratic sentiment, but as actors independent of the upper classes. As a journalist, he appealed to a broad range of tastes, and chronicled urban mass-oriented culture, such as fairground theater, which was then beginning to set up its collapsible wooden booths in public places. Bulgarin's understanding of "popular" Russia did not refer to the peasant masses, but to lower bureaucrats and shop clerks with rudimentary literacy.

Bulgarin and others in the 1830s discovered several clues to market success that held true for at least a half-century. They did not set out to edify readers; their heroes, who were often from the lower classes, could be rogues as well as role models. They did not seek a specific genre or style, but satisfied a range of tastes. Perhaps most consistent were the values that expressed a Russian identity and patriotism alien to much of the intelligentsia, particularly in its attachment to the tsar. The earliest mass-oriented literature celebrated rather than criticized tsardom. The sentiment could be commissioned directly by the sovereign himself, as was the new anthem, "God Save the Tsar," but it could flow forth spontaneously, as it did in historical novels such as *Vyzhigin,* or Mikhail Zagoskin's equally fashionable *Iury Miloslavsky* (1829), and plays such as Nikolai Polevoi's *Ermak Timofeich.* Pride was felt not only in the accomplishments of the Russian people, but also in the might of the state. The following selections offer possibilities for analyzing how a confident sense of Russian identity took shape in popular consciousness.

Aleksandra Ishimova, one of Russia's first children's writers, stands apart here in several respects. Surely her patriotism was as ardent as any of her countrymen's, yet she was one of the first Russian women to participate in popular culture. If characters are counted, of course, she was not. Russian soldiers were bringing home to northern climes their exotic tales of southern conquests, both territorial and female, and the women in their popular culture usually sported dark eyes, dusky accents, and an acquiescent bearing, after they had overcome their religious and ethnic differences.

Ermak Timofeich
Nikolai Polevoi (1845)

POLEVOI (1796–1846) DISPLAYED THE VERSATILITY OF MOST WRITERS IN THE EARLY NINETEENTH CENTURY. HE WROTE FICTION OF ALL SORTS, AND WAS EDITOR AND PUBLISHER OF A "THICK" JOURNAL, THE *MOSCOW TELEGRAPH*. THE SON OF A SIBERIAN MERCHANT, HE MADE HIS WAY INTO THE CIRCLES THAT DOMINATED PRE-REFORM INTELLECTUAL LIFE. HE WON FAME FOR HIS POLEMICAL *HISTORY OF THE RUSSIAN PEOPLE*, WRITTEN IN REACTION TO KARAMZIN'S "OFFICIAL" *HISTORY OF THE RUSSIAN STATE*. HIS MERCHANT BACKGROUND AND PATRIOTIC CHAUVINISM KEPT HIM OUT OF ELITE GROUPS.

THE FOLLOWING SELECTION SHOWS HIS PATRIOTISM AND MERCHANT BIAS. IT IS THE LAST ACT OF A PLAY BASED VERY LOOSELY ON THE ADVENTURES OF THE COSSACK *ATAMAN* ERMAK, A FORMER BRIGAND HIRED BY THE STROGANOV MERCHANT CLAN IN THE 1580S TO CONQUER THE EASTERN URALS FROM THE KHAN OF SIBERIA. THE PLAY, WHICH FIFTY YEARS LATER WAS STILL POPULAR IN FAIRGROUND *BALAGANY*, FEATURES A SERIES OF MELODRAMATIC TURNS (SCORED TO NATIONALIST SONGS) AROUND THE MEMBERS OF ERMAK'S BAND. EARLY ON, STROGANOV APPEARS WITH A PROMISE OF CLEMENCY FROM IVAN THE TERRIBLE IF HE ADDS SIBERIA TO THE RUSSIAN CROWN, AND ERMAK IS GRATEFUL TO SERVE HIS TSAR. AS ACT FIVE OPENS, ANDREI, A DISINHERITED MERCHANT SCION, LANGUISHES IN PRISON, AWAITING EXECUTION. HE HAS BROKEN THE BAND'S VOWS BY MARRYING MARIA, AN ORPHAN RAISED BY COSSACKS, AND BRINGING HER INTO CAMP DISGUISED AS A MAN.

N. A. Polevoi, *Ermak Timofeich, ili Volga i Sibir'*, in *Dramaticheskoe predstavlenie v piati deistviiakh* (St. Petersburg: Tip. Karl Krai, 1845), pp. 127–144.

CAST

Ermak	Murza Alei
Andrei	Meshcheriak
Maria (Masha)	Koltso
Mitka (Mitya)	Prince Volkhovskoi
Cossacks	Tobolin

ACT V. SIBERIA, THE GOLD MINE

Scene One

The setting is a jail cell, lit by a candle. Andrei, bound, lies on a bench. Shouts and the sounds of trumpets and tambourines can be heard in the distance.

ANDREI (*alone*): Oh, God! Why have you condemned me to die? Could I have denied her, abandoned her to an orphanage? Could I not go, not give my promise? My eager heart beats heavily, bitterly—I am sick! Where are you, my dove? Has a flock of hateful blackbirds torn you to shreds? And I cannot defend or protect you! And the *ataman*—oh, let God be his judge! He was so terrible when the battle was being fought. All swords were pointed toward him. While I, Andrei, am a poor unfortunate creature, whom God has condemned to disaster after disaster!

Scene Two

MITKA (*at the window*): Hey, Andriusha,[1] is it really you?
ANDREI: Who's there?
MITKA: Don't you recognize your old army cook?
ANDREI: Mitya!
MITKA: Wait! (*He unlocks the door and enters.*)
ANDREI: Ah, Mitya!
MITKA: Yeah, Mitya. Everyone called the old cook Mitka a fool, but he's helping the smart people! What's going on? Hurry up and get off your handcuffs. (*taking off the chains*) Yeah, I can cook cabbage soup like nobody else, and make porridge. There you go, hug me in gratitude!
ANDREI: God himself has blessed you! But where is she?
MITKA: Who?
ANDREI: Masha!
MITKA: Here we go again. What do you want to do, kiss her?
ANDREI: To see her, to look at her once last time.

---

1. Andriusha is a diminutive form of Andrei. See the Note on Transliteration for an explanation of diminutives.

MITKA: So call her, she's here!

ANDREI (*throwing himself at the door*): Masha, Masha!

(*Mitka sits down to the side and starts singing to himself.*)

Scene Three

(*The same two, plus Maria*)

MARIA: Oh, Andrei!

ANDREI: My heart and soul! Only now do I understand what it means to be separated from you, how deep my love is for you. But how did you get here?

MARIA: He, Mitya, brought me to the prison.

ANDREI: Oh, savior, God will reward you!

MITKA: Not for this!

MARIA: So what do we do now?

ANDREI: Let's run away.

MITKA: Hey, brother, we can't do that.

ANDREI: Ah, Mitya. Then a terrible, agonizing, dishonorable death—and with her!

MITYA: Did the devil command you to go on a spree?

MARIA: You saved us!

MITKA: What kind of rescue is this? See why I changed my mind. There's a battle going on out there, the *ataman,* all the Cossacks. Can't you hear how it's heating up? The Siberians are holding out to the death—even blind Kuchum[2] himself has gone to fight. That's why I changed my mind. Andrei is a good fellow, and we could certainly use an extra pair of hands. Why's he just sitting there; should I let him go? I have the keys with me—I've been promoted from cook to jailor.

ANDREI: God himself sent you! Give me a sword, a harquebus![3]

MITKA: Stop for a minute—let me think. What if they kill him? I guess he'll rest with the saints. In any case, can't he be executed tomorrow? Hell, maybe he'll even do something, slick down Kuchum's cowlick for him!

ANDREI: The harquebus!

MITKA: Do you think that's okay?

ANDREI: The saber, the saber!

MITKA: In a flash! (*He runs offstage.*)

MARIA: Andrei, you're off to battle, and you're leaving me? You're heartless.

ANDREI: I will redeem my guilt with blood. Here I am a criminal, but there I will be a hero!

---

2. Kuchum, the khan of Siberia, was defeated by Ermak in 1587. He was then assassinated by his non-Muslim followers, while his son, after converting to Orthodoxy, became a titled member of Russia's nobility.

3. A harquebus was a matchlock rifle.

MARIA: It's a bloody battle—they'll kill you out there!

ANDREI: Then remember me here and rejoice, because we'll meet beyond the grave and never part.

MITKA (*running up*): Here's your harquebus, your saber, and a cap and a javelin!

ANDREI: My friends, my cherished harquebus, you, my saber, are a true comrade! (*He arms himself.*)

MARIA: Andrei, I'm going with you!

MITKA: Is fighting a woman's business? You think there won't be any work for you here? We'll stay and pray.

ANDREI: Oh pray, pray, my Maria! God will listen to you! (*He runs offstage.*)

MARIA: Andrei, Andrei! (*She hurries after him.*)

MITKA: Well, the truth is, I thought up a good plan. That's how everyone'll see it. Mitka, the idiot cook! A fool! This is terrible trouble! No! I'm no idiot, but maybe a simpleton, as in the song:

> Once there was a simpleton,
> Once there was a silly fool,
> Off went the simpleton,
> Off went the silly fool . . . (*exits*)

(*Isker[4] can be seen on the mountain. On one side is a large stone. The woods are sparse. Cannonade, gunfire, trumpets, and tambourines can be heard in the distance, but they fade gradually.*)

Scene Four

(*Ermak and several cossacks*)

ERMAK: Enough! Sound the assembly! (*trumpets*) We've done it! Glory to you, glory, Creator! You permitted me, with my sinner's hands, to be victorious. You allowed these sinful eyes to witness the monumental fall of Siberia! God! Now my energies are exhausted. Water, bring me water. (*He sits on the stone and removes his helmet.*) I'm parched, and my head is on fire. (*Someone brings him water in a helmet, which he drinks.*) Thank you; thanks, comrade! (*Soldiers begin to gather, some of them leading prisoners.*)

FIRST COSSACK: *Ataman*, Isker has surrendered!

ERMAK: Surrendered?

FIRST COSSACK: Emissaries are arriving from Isker—they're carrying the crown of Kuchum and the keys.

(*Ermak silently raises his arms to the heavens.*)

---

4. Isker was the khan's stronghold, on the slopes of the Urals.

Scene Five

(Ermak, Cossacks, Murza Alei and his retinue)

ALEI: Leader of the Russian forces, great *bogatyr!* You have defeated us; accept our surrender. Siberia is sending you this petition. Our Tsar Kuchum has run away—show mercy! Here are the keys to Isker, and here—oh, how bitter this is for me! Here is the crown of the Siberian tsar! Have pity! (*He kneels and offers two trays, with the keys and the crown.*)

ERMAK: I am a peaceful weapon of God's will: you need not render homage to me. Arise, old man, arise. Stand up as a subject of the Russian tsar! The keys to Isker. But when can you open for me the doors to God's mercy? The third tsardom[5] has surrendered, Kazan, Siberia, and Astrakhan, like three diamonds blazing in the crown of the Russian tsar! The crown of Siberia! Mighty peoples have trembled before you. What are you, destiny's anointed one? Kuchum has run away, now exiled from the tsardom. But you, are you an object of pride, envy, or fear? He who gives power is also the one who takes it away. Isker, you are utterly defeated. How paltry a man's majesty and pride seem now. We will place the Siberian crown here. Our gonfalon will fly over it. But where is our gonfalon? Where's our flag? Where's Kuzma?

SECOND COSSACK: He gave his word that he would not leave the field alive, and he kept it. He fell in battle.

ERMAK: Thank you, Kuzma! Peace and serenity to your bones. Blessed are those who fall on the battlefield for the motherland. But our flag—don't tell me that the enemy has captured it! Or have our sacred colors fallen there, on the field? Hurry, find the flag!

Scene Six

(The same people, plus Meshcheriak and Mitka)

MESHCHERIAK (*dragging Mitka*): *Ataman!* Sentence this rogue to death!

MITKA: *Ataman,* mercy!

MESHCHERIAK: This scoundrel released the prisoner!

MITKA: Clemency!

MESHCHERIAK: No mercy for you; Andrei and his wife have run away.

ERMAK (*delightedly*): They've escaped?

MESHCHERIAK: They can't get away, and we'll string Mitka up.

ERMAK: Meshcheriak, why didn't I see you on the battlefield?

MESHCHERIAK: What do you mean, you didn't see me? I was everywhere—out in front, hacking, banging, pummeling.

---

5. Polevoi uses the term "tsardom" (*tsarstvo*), but "khanate" would be more appropriate.

ERMAK: Like a carnivorous crow, you want to poison the pleasure of our victory with your malevolent croaking. Never fear, the sentence will be carried out! The criminal will not evade justice and revenge—believe me!

MESHCHERIAK (*confused*): What do you mean, won't evade? Didn't you hear that the prisoner's escaped?

Scene Seven

(The same people, plus Andrei)

ANDREI (*carrying the gonfalon in one hand, the other bound up*): *Ataman!* Hurrah! I place our holy banner at your feet—I purchased it with the blood of our enemies!

ERMAK (*grabbing the gonfalon*): Oh, our glorious gonfalon! Our banner of honor! With you, our blessing has returned! What, Meshcheriak? Can't you see that the prisoner has returned for his execution?

ANDREI (*falling*): Allow me to die at your feet, Ermak. And remember and don't forsake Maria—don't abandon . . .

ERMAK: My son! Look after that wound immediately!

(The cossacks sit Andrei down on the stone and surround him.)

ANDREI: But where's Maria? For God's sake, tell me!

Scene Eight

(The same, plus a second cossack)

SECOND COSSACK: There, *Ataman*, on the road to Moscow. See, people are coming to see us.

SECOND COSSACK: Royal boyars!

ERMAK: Boyars! That's terrible, that's wonderful! My chest is pounding! Punishment? Mercy? Oh, Ermak doesn't quiver when the enemies' swords and shots are aimed at him, when they're falling on him like rain—but he's shaking now!

Scene Nine

(The same, plus Koltso)

KOLTSO (*offstage*): Where's the tsar's *voevoda*?

ERMAK (*trembling*): The *voevoda*? Who's the tsar's *voevoda*?

(*Koltso's voice*): The prince of Siberia, Prince Ermak!

ERMAK: Oh, my friend Koltso has gone mad. What's he saying?

KOLTSO (*running in*): Mercy! Mercy! Mercy!

ERMAK: The Lord Tsar has forgiven me? Oh, thanks be to God! Remember carefully what he said: There's life and death in every word.

KOLTSO: I saw the tsar; we were dining together. Then we were praying together, with all of Moscow triumphant, when the cry went up in the Dormition Cathedral, praise, praise to Ermak!

ERMAK: In the Dormition Cathedral? Praise?

KOLTSO: The tsar has bestowed a title upon you: prince of Siberia, royal *voevoda*. Can you hear that? The boyars are coming, bringing you gifts from the tsar!

(A loud marching can be heard.)

Scene Ten

(The same people, plus Prince Volkhovskoi and Tobolin. Their retinue is carrying a suit of golden chain mail, a gold helmet, a golden goblet, and a fur coat of royal sable.)

PRINCE VOLKHOVSKOI: Royal *voevoda*, prince of Siberia, Ermak Timofeich! The Tsar and Great Prince of All of Russia, and the tsardoms of Kazan, Astrakhan, and Siberia. The Lord and Protector has commanded us to show our gratitude to you for your meritorious service, for having conquered Siberia under your mighty hand, for all the centuries to come, for as long as you shall live. He appoints you his royal *voevoda* and prince of Siberia. And he sends you this golden armor, and a golden goblet from his own table, and a sable from his own shoulders. Drink to happiness from this goblet, and wear the *shuba* in health!

ERMAK: Koltso, am I not dreaming?

PRINCE VOLKHOVSKOI: Dress Ermak Timofeich in his imperial rewards! (*They put the* shuba *and helmet on Ermak.*) Such payments are excellent!

EVERYONE: Praise to Ermak Timofeich! (*They all gather round him, weeping and kissing his hands.*)

ERMAK: Lord Tsar! I thank you. Lord! No, the wonder is not in the tsardom of Russia, but one sees it in his benevolence. Is there any wonder that the Russian tsar is great and magnanimous? That he has equal measures of majesty and mercy? That life and light shine from the throne as from heaven?

Scene Eleven

MARIA (*runs in and falls at Ermak's feet*): Ermak, Ermak! Forgive my husband Andrei! Give me my Andrei, and I'll give you my life!

PRINCE VOLKHOVSKOI: The woman is mad!

ERMAK: No, she's not crazy. Listen, brothers, and judge for yourselves. Many years ago there lived a bandit, an *ataman* of rogues. He kidnapped a boyar's daughter, took her away, the poor woman, in tears. She left him with a daughter, but the daughter disappeared. The bandit repented bitterly—often he couldn't sleep nights. He wept bloody tears. He searched everywhere for his dear daughter, but couldn't find her. But finally, when he had paid his debt, the Lord blessed him and he found her. God and the tsar have forgiven him, and sent him mercy from on high. But his daughter was condemned to death—her only crime was that she loved a daredevil and refused to leave him, a fellow who served God and tsar mightily with his blood. I am that bandit, and the daughter—there she is! And in front of God and tsar, Ermak, who has never gone to his knees for anyone, I bow before you now, friends, brothers! (*falling to his knees*) Forgive my daughter and my son-in-law! Return my son and daughter to me! This is not Ermak the prince and *voevoda* who beseeches you, but a father who asks you!

EVERYONE: Prince Ermak! We forgive them! Arise in health!

ERMAK (*getting up*): Andrei, Maria! Son, daughter!

ANDREI AND MARIA: Father, father!

ERMAK: My heart is full. It beats in joy, like waves on a shore!

MESHCHERIAK: Well, Prince of Siberia, I congratulate you, but my account is not yet closed. Let's finish it now. (*He tosses Ermak a sword. Many jump up to shield Ermak.*)

PRINCE VOLKHOVSKOI: Stop! Hold him!

MESHCHERIAK: So it didn't turn out right? It will now—to the devil with you. What are you waiting for? There's only one ending! (*He braces himself.*)

ERMAK: Poor fellow. He never understood the secrets of repentance, neither of this world nor of God's. Oh, glory to God on high! Rejoice, brothers! Give me the royal goblet—long live the tsar! God grant him health, eliminate his sorrows, and give him many years on this earth!

PRINCE VOLKHOVSKOI: Hurry to Moscow. Honor, salutations, and a place in the boyar duma[6] next to the tsar await you!

ERMAK (*thoughtfully*): No, no, don't send me back to Holy Russia. It's not for me to see gold-domed Moscow, not for me to be gladdened by the tsar's speeches, or to fall under the gaze of our little father, the tsar. Siberia, you will receive Ermak's bones! The mighty waves of the Irtysh will prepare a wet grave for me. God's will be done. The feat is completed. Oh eagle of Russia, you are flying over Siberia, the tsardom of Kuchum, now a province of the Russian tsar. And who gave the tsar this Siberian pride? Who made a present of this territory to Holy Russia? The disreputable Cossacks! Ermak, take no personal conceit in this: God's will directed you. The mountains fell, the dense woods separated, and the rivers' waves parted like the sea in Israel. It's all shriveling up before you—the wretchedness, the slick surfaces, the hordes of enemies—they're all defeated. Oh, my heart rejoices with so many pleasures! But what about me now? Time is disappearing—I see my fate clearly before my eyes! Beyond Siberia, to the distant seas, Russians continue forward. A new world is located there—the sea is white with ships' sails. Wealthy India, brilliant mountains. The eagle's wing touches—another rests on the ocean's icy breast. Golden waves flow from the depths and shores of Siberia: Bashkirians, Persians, Mongolians, Indians, Chinese—they are all carrying tribute to us. Oh, how

---

6. The boyar duma was a rudimentary council of advisors to the tsar.

bright and clear I see your fate, Mother Russia. It radiates like a Russian mind; it burns as a candle does before an icon, an eternal flame! And there, on the banks of the Tobol, my image is chiseled in granite. It stands tall and powerful. A shining star flies over Siberia, the shadow of Ermak, and says to his descendants: "It was Ermak who gave Siberia to Holy Russia!"

THE END

Filatka and Miroshka the Rivals; or, Four Suitors for One Girl
A Vaudeville in One Act, by the Actor Pavel Grigoriev, Jr.
(1833)

VAUDEVILLES WERE A MAINSTAY OF PETERSBURG'S ALEKSAN-DRINSKY THEATER, THE JEWEL OF IMPERIAL CULTURAL PATRON-AGE. EDUCATED OBSERVERS CLAIMED THAT CLERKS FROM THE NEARBY *GOSTINY DVOR* MADE UP MOST OF THE AUDIENCE, BUT NICHOLAS I FREQUENTED THE SHOWS AS WELL. THIS PIECE, WHICH ENJOYED FIFTEEN YEARS OF SUCCESS, PLAYED TO MANY SPECTATORS WITH ITS EVOCATIONS OF NAIVE TSARISM AND PA-TRIARCHAL ORDER. PEASANT MEN SPEAK IN DIALECT, WHILE THEIR WOMEN SPEAK THE SENTIMENTAL RUSSIAN OF KARAM-ZIN'S POOR LIZA; AND UNSCHOOLED CHARACTERS REMAIN UN-CONSCIOUS OF THEIR OWN SILLINESS. THOUGH OVERSEERS ABUSE MILITARY RECRUITMENT, AND HUSBANDS BEAT THEIR WIVES, JUSTICE IS ULTIMATELY REINSTATED BY A BENEVOLENT NOBLE.

STARRING GRIGORIEV HIMSELF AND THE RENOWNED PROV SA-DOVSKY IN THE ORIGINAL PRODUCTION, THIS VAUDEVILLE SPAWNED SEVERAL SEQUELS, AND FOUND NEW AUDIENCES LONG AFTER LEAVING THE ALEKSANDRINKA. IN HIS SIBERIAN PRISON,

P. Grigor'ev, mlad., akter. *Filatka i Miroshka soperniki, ili chetyre zhenikha i odna nevesta. Vodevil' v odnom deistvii* (St. Petersburg: v tip. vdovy Baikovoi, 1833).

Dostoevsky saw it performed by criminal prisoners, some in drag. Their uproarious laughter suggests that the humor was not confined to nobles and clerks.

THE CAST[1]

Count Lidin	Sidorich, the village *starshina*
The countess, his wife	Gavrilich, the miller
Vasily (Vasya), the count's batman	Kuzminishna, the poor widow
Zabiraev, clerk of the Land Court	Grusha, her daughter
Pakhomich, his scribe	Petr, her son
Filatka	Guests of the count, men and women
Miroshka	peasants

The theater is set as a village. To the right stands a table and bench; to the left are a hollow old tree trunk and a bush.

ACT II. FILATKA AND MIROSHKA

MIROSHKA: Filatka!

FILATKA: What's your hankerin'?

MIROSHKA: Let's go play.

FILATKA: Don't sound so good.

MIROSHKA: Why's that?

FILATKA: Paw got his dander up; he tells me, "Filatka! Don't be tossin' them knucklebones; git yourself over and make up to your sweetheart." And how ya gonna make to her? I'd of moseyed over there yesterday, and had a notion to give her a cuff: but her eyes bugged out so you'd a thought that hell froze over!

MIROSHKA: And just who might your sweetheart be?

FILATKA: Didn't ya know? It's Grusha Kuzminishnaia.

MIROSHKA: You don't say! But her brother's tryin' to hitch her to me!

FILATKA: No kiddin'. Well, you might be courtin' her, but I'll be marryin' her.

MIROSHKA: We'll both get married!

FILATKA: Nope, brother; my paw says, "Get married by yourself, and don't share your wife with no one!"

MIROSHKA: But it wouldn' be for nothin'! I'll git you a pound of spice cake.

FILATKA: Well, ain't you a clever one? Grusha's a heap sweeter'n cakes.

---

1. Village society consisted of the noble landowner, who is primarily a presence behind the action rather than a central character; the local official Zabiraev; and serfs, the elite of whom included the steward (not represented here), the count's servants, and the miller.

Nope, I ain't so dumb that I'd
Share my wife with you,
My sweetheart's finger-lickin' good:
I thinks that I'll git married.
She's the only one I loves,
And I thinks heaps of her!
So for cakes I ain't gonna give
You my lovely sweetheart.

MIROSHKA: Where'd ya git this hankerin' to marry?

FILATKA: Whaddaya mean where? I sees her whenever I sleeps.

MIROSHKA: You're pullin' the wool over muh eyes. You don't see nothin' when ya sleep.

FILATKA: Uh-uh, brother, I sees her; honest, I sees her.

MIROSHKA: How's that?

FILATKA: Jus' like that; when I wakes up, I sees like she's draggin' me by the hair.

MIROSHKA: Oh, brother, that ain't no good.

FILATKA: Paw says, "Let her kick up her heels till the weddin', then you can pull in the reins."

MIROSHKA: What an oaf your paw is! How ya gonna rule the roost? That Gruniakha's a sturdy girl! Let's marry together, brother, and I'll help; maybe the both of us can crack the whip.

FILATKA: Whatcha pesterin' me for? What if she don't want the both of us?

MIROSHKA: Why'd she wanna be like that?

FILATKA: Why? Stupid, ya recollect that hand that your and muh paws hired? Why didn' he wanna?

MIROSHKA: He said he didn't like doin' the work o' two fellers.

FILATKA: Well, that's what she'll say: she don' like workin' on two.

MIROSHKA: Button your lip! Here she comes with her maw. Let's duck beyond them bushes and lissen to what they says.

FILATKA: Well, why not. (*Filatka hides in a hollow, and Miroshka in the bushes.*)

ACT III

The same characters, plus Grusha and Kuzminishna, her mother.

KUZMINISHNA: Enough moonin', Grusha, honey child!—you know Vasily is comin' home soon; you remember that One-Eyed Senka came home from Piter and said, "The master's retired, got himself married, and will soon be here with the young mistress."

GRUSHA: Here it's been two years I've waited for him day and night: perhaps he's forgotten me!

FILATKA (*from the hollow*): Ya hear, Miroshka, she's waitin' for Vasily, not you.

MIROSHKA (*from the bushes*): Don't git all het up; she ain't waitin' for you neither.

KUZMINISHNA: There, there, silly goose; how could he forget you? You grew up together, played together. When I remember your dances and joys, my heart goes pitter-patter.

GRUSHA:

> But without Vasily, I have no joy.
> All my comforts and my pleasures,
> You've taken, darling, far away,
> While I, a forlorn young girl,
> Ceaselessly pour streams of tears.
> Woe is my unhappy fate!
> They're wedding me to a man I loathe!
> The sun is setting on my youth:
> No longer will I see my sweetheart!

My happy days have passed me by! Our elder keeps pestering me to marry Tarasich Zabiraev.

MIROSHKA: Hear dat, brother? Tarasich also got a hankerin' to get hitched! It's like he's crazy!

GRUSHA: And if I don't marry him, he threatens to have brother Petr enlisted.[2]

FILATKA: What a bad business! He always itchin' fer a scrap.

KUZMINISHNA: That's what afflicts me, my little one! It's wartime now, and we have paid our soul tax, so can misfortune be far away? Oh, my.

GRUSHA: Don't be sad, Mother; we'll manage to get by somehow!

KUZMINISHNA: Oh, child! We'd get by if only you'd listen to me and marry Filatka Terentiev, anybody but Tarasich.

GRUSHA: No, Mother, whatever you wish, but I won't marry such a fool!

MIROSHKA (laughs): Hear that, brother Filatka? Take a bow!

KUZMINISHNA: Well, child, if that groom is unthinkable, then there's another: the miller Gavrilich is proposing Miroshka Andreianov; you yourself know that Andreianov is a well-off peasant. If ever we have need of money, he won't turn us down.

MIROSHKA: How could that be! No, brother, Paw won't give a kopeck!

GRUSHA: No, Mother! What help can we expect from Andreian? Don't you know that he's as stingy as a Jew?

FILATKA (laughs): Hear that, brother Miroshka? Take a bow!

MIROSHKA: No, brother, she's foolin': he's no Jew, he's muh paw.

KUZMINISHNA: Well, Grusha, there's no pleasing you: one's not handsome, the other's no good! Where are you going to find all these sweeties?

FILATKA: If I'm not good-lookin' 'nuff for ya, then you can go bury yourself! See if you can find a better rooster.

---

2. Each village in pre-reform Russia was responsible for providing a levy of recruits for the army. These recruits were taken for twenty-five-year hitches, which essentially removed them from village society. Only by paying a "recruit tax" could draftees avoid this disaster.

GRUSHA: I will wait for my Vasily, and I won't marry anyone but him.

KUZMINISHNA: All right, child, do what you like. Look, here comes Eremei Tarasievich. Tarry a bit with him; maybe you'll take a liking to him. (*She leaves.*)

MIROSHKA: How could anybody! He's uglier than a scarecrow!

ACT IV

The same characters, plus Zabiraev.

ZABIRAEV (*approaching Grusha*): I wish you long life, my treasure! Apple of my eye! My . . .

GRUSHA: Hello, Eremei Tarasievich.

FILATKA: Heh-heh, he's so dumb he don't know she's a pear and not an apple.[3]

ZABIRAEV: Why so sad, my beauty? Have you been offended in any way by your neighbors? You can announce in my name: we'll deal with him. He'll be registered in the protocol and whipped for dishonor!

GRUSHA: No, Eremei Tarasievich, they're all really agreeable; you're the only one offending me.

ZABIRAEV: What! I offend you? Is it because I love you more than bribes from petitioners? Is it because I have withered like the grass in the fields for you? That you are the thorn in my flesh? Oh, Grusha, that's enough stubbornness: you'll live the good life with me!

MIROSHKA: Clever, he's already slippin' the butter under her nose! But if she married me, I'd respect her even if she was cuckoo.

ZABIRAEV (*sings*):

> My passion for you flames within me,
> I swear my love alone to you:
> If, tender friend, you shan't believe me,
> I shall confirm it with a vow!
> That I, enraptured by your gaze,
> Am an obedient slave in all:
> You shall be my magistrate;
> And I your secretary.

GRUSHA: I believe you, Eremei Tarasievich; but I won't marry you. My Vasya will remain in my heart forever.

ZABIRAEV: Your Vasya? And in what respect is he yours? Know this, my beauty: you will be my wife; and if you resist me further, I will, by the power invested in me by the enlistment decree, draft your brother Petrushka.

GRUSHA: You think you can scare me into it? Just you try! God will not permit you to destroy a poor family. Farewell, evil man! (*She leaves.*)

---

3. The name Grusha also means "pear" in Russian.

ZABIRAEV: Evil man! How fickle these young girls are! They curse us until they get married, and after they marry us, they can't praise us enough.

MIROSHKA: You're lying, Tarasievich! My maw married my paw, and she don't say nothin' good 'bout him, she just swears at 'im. . . .

ACT VII

VASILY: Here I am home again. Good thing the master decided to get married and retire, or else I would have had to wait even longer to see my Grusha. My? And how do I know that she's still mine? Could not two years apart have changed her, could she not have found another as foolish as I to fall in love with her? Devil take it! How strange! Somebody's coming. It sounds like Grusha's voice; and it's our old clerk with her. Let me listen in; what tune is he singing to her! (*He hides in the bushes.*)

ACT VIII

Vasily, Zabiraev, and Grusha.

ZABIRAEV: Stop resisting me, my beauty; don't say no, or you'll cause your brother's destruction.

GRUSHA: Why don't you leave me alone?

ZABIRAEV: Don't be angry, my little chickadee.

VASILY (*aside*): If she's a little chickadee, then you're an old crow.

GRUSHA: Didn't I say that I would not marry such a monster?

ZABIRAEV: If that's so, then from this moment, your brother is enlisted as a recruit.

VASILY (*aside*): Just you wait, you worthless old fool! I'll go tell the master everything: and then you'll be unmasked. (*He leaves.*)

ACT IX

Zabiraev, Grusha, Kuzminishna, and Petr.

ZABIRAEV (*to Kuzminishna*): Hey, tell your daughter that she should say yes again, or else it will be too late!

KUZMINISHNA: Eremei Tarasievich! Can I force her to do it?

Petr: Force her? Who? Not my sister? No, Mother, don't do that; it would be a sin before God and a shame before people. And why should you have to force her, and I not be of service here? Am I not a Russian? Would I not willingly die for our sire the tsar and for our motherland, Holy Russia?

> I chose to go into the service,
> Serving holds nothing to fear:

I came into the world a Russian,
And a Russian I will leave.
I have only one desire,
And I have one thing to say:
May God give Health to Our Father,
Nicholas—the Glorious Tsar!

How could a real Russian fear serving his tsar!

ZABIRAEV: Just you wait, buddy boy; as soon as they shave your head, you'll talk differently.

PETR: Never!

GRUSHA: Oh! Here comes the elder with the recruiters.

ACT X

The same characters, plus the elder, Gavrilich, Miroshka, and the peasant men.

ELDER: God save, good people!

ZABIRAEV: Greetings, Faddei Sidorovich. (*to the peasants*) I beg your attention, sirs! (*He takes out a paper.*)

FILATKA: Hey, brother Miroshka, didn't he see us? What's with this here sirs?

ZABIRAEV (*reads*): "By the powers invested in me . . ."

He takes out his snuff box and takes a pinch of tobacco; at that moment, the elder approaches Kuzminishna and says quietly:

ELDER: Hey, old woman, come to your senses. The man told you: give him the hand of your daughter; take this opportunity.

ZABIRAEV (*coughs*): "By the power invested in me . . ." (*He glances at Kuzminishna.*)

MIROSHKA: Tarasievich! Ya keep hummin' the same bar: powers and powers; but what's your order? Cat got your tongue?

GAVRILICH: Hush, Miroshka, it's none of your business.

ZABIRAEV: "By the powers invested in me, I hereby decree the following to the widow Afrosinia Kuzmina: In light of the fact that she, the aforementioned widow Kuzmina, has not settled the soul tax and recruit obligations for the past year, her son Petr must be given up to the army."

FILATKA: And Grusha to me!

ACT XII

The same characters, plus Vasily, the count, the countess, and guests.

COUNT: And here, my friends, is where my estate ends and the civil district begins.

ALL THE PEASANTS: Good health, Your Excellency!

ELDER: Our congratulations, dear sir, on your lawful wedlock.

COUNT: I thank you, good people. Aha, Vasily, you're here! Will you show us your sweetheart?

VASILY (*leading Grusha over*): Here she is, Your Excellency!

COUNT: My, what a pretty girl! (*to his wife*) Am I not right?

COUNTESS: Yes, very nice.

COUNT: Well, Vasily, I praise your choice.

FILATKA: Hey, master, why don't ya say nothin' good 'bout me; I cotton to her too.

COUNT (*laughing*): Do you really want praise so much?

FILATKA: Master, that's a stupid question! It's plumb better than gettin' a lickin'.

COUNT: He doesn't stand on ceremony.

ELDER: Your Excellency, forgive that fool.

FILATKA: Hey, Mr. Elder, don't go swearin' at me; lissen up here.

COUNT: Well, Vasily, where is your rival?

VASILY: Here he is, Your Excellency.

COUNT (*to Zabiraev*): I regret, good man, that you were not able to earn the affection of Grusha; my Vasily captured her heart before you could. As for your knavery, I could treat you very poorly; however, I forgive you—and I myself will pay the recruit tax.

PEASANTS: Long live the count!

PETR AND KUZMINISHNA: Our humble gratitude, Your Excellency!

VASILY AND GRUSHA: We shall never forget your kindness.

MIROSHKA (*to the miller*): Uncle Elizar! Looks right sure that Vaska's up an' married; and whaddabout me?

GAVRILICH: You should get married too.

MIROSHKA: You too! But who? I knows that Vaska won't give Grusha up; and another girl'd be wors'n you.

GAVRILICH: Why not ask the master? Maybe he'll give you a wife from his own village; each girl there is prettier than the next.

MIROSHKA: Yes indeedy. (*to the count*) Master!

COUNT: What would you like?

MIROSHKA: Whadda I needs? A wife.

COUNT: A wife?

MIROSHKA: Your Vaska stole muh girl, so give me another. Uncle Elizar knowed your girls is plumb purty, so's you can give me at least one.

COUNT: So be it.

GAVRILICH: Did you hear, Miroshka? Now bow.

MIROSHKA: Why not bow: Count! Uncle Elizar bow ta ya.

FILATKA: Here Miroshka gots a wife, and I still don't. Let me go ask the master. Master!

COUNT: Yes?

FILATKA: Would you have a wife for my hand too?

COUNT: You're fine as it is.

FILATKA: If ya wants to, fine, and iff'n ya don't wants to, fine.

ELDER: Vasily, let's all make up; a bad peace is better than a good war.

COUNT: How true, my friends; my advice is to always hold to that saying. (*to his guests*) Let us go, gentlemen!

ELDER: Stay, sire, and watch our games. Today is our parish holiday.

COUNT: I would fulfill your desire with pleasure, but alas I cannot; my own peasants have also prepared a celebration for our arrival, and we would cause them offense if we remained here.

ELDER: Well, as you wish, sire.

MIROSHKA: Master! Since you're here for the holiday, Filatka and I'll stomp a dance out for ya.

COUNT: It will be my pleasure.

FILATKA: Well, brother, happy or not, give me that bride!

COUNT: Well, farewell, good people. (*He leaves.*)

EVERYONE: Farewell, Your Excellency!

ELDER: Now, fellows, it's time to set to dancing.

MIROSHKA: Filatka, you and I is buddies.

ELDER: Let the festivities begin!

Ivan Vyzhigin

Faddei Bulgarin (1829)

BULGARIN (1789–1859) ENJOYED THE DUBIOUS DISTINCTION OF BEING ONE OF NICHOLAS I'S FAVORITE WRITERS. THE SON OF A POLISH REBEL, HE ROAMED AS A SOLDIER OF FORTUNE BEFORE SETTLING INTO WRITING. HE IS BEST KNOWN IN HISTORY AS AN ULTRACONSERVATIVE JOURNALIST; IN FACT, HIS POLITICS HAVE OVERSHADOWED HIS LIVELY PROSE. BULGARIN'S READERSHIP SPREAD WELL BEYOND RUSSIA; *VYZHIGIN* QUICKLY SOLD OUT THREE EDITIONS AND WAS TRANSLATED INTO FRENCH, GERMAN, AND ENGLISH.

VYZHIGIN WAS RUSSIA'S EQUIVALENT TO TOM JONES. THE PICARESQUE HERO GREW UP AN ORPHAN, FINDING HIS MOTHER ONLY IN THE SECOND VOLUME OF HIS ADVENTURES. VYZHIGIN TRAVELS ALL OVER THE EMPIRE, INCLUDING THE BORDERLAND

From Faddei Bulgarin, *Ivan Vyzhigin,* adapted here from an English version by an unidentified translator. (Philadelphia: Carey and Lea, 1832), pp. 67–79.

STEPPES AND KIRGHIZIA, ALLOWING THE AUTHOR TO DESCRIBE A GREAT VARIETY OF PEOPLES AND PLACES. IN THE PASSAGE BELOW, HE BECOMES INVOLVED WITH AN ACTRESS, ALTHOUGH BY THE STORY'S END HE HAS A WIFE AND CHILDREN. (THE UNFORTUNATE GRUNYA DIES IN PARIS.) FOR ALL OF HIS WEAKNESSES, VYZHIGIN CONCLUDES THAT "ALL THE EVIL IN THE WORLD PROCEEDS FROM AN INSUFFICIENCY OF MORAL EDUCATION, AND ALL THE GOOD FROM REAL, SOUND KNOWLEDGE." MOREOVER, BULGARIN PROVIDED A POSITIVE IMAGE OF MANY SOCIAL TYPES, INCLUDING MERCHANTS, AND THUS DISTANCED HIS WORK FROM THE DISDAIN FOR THE RUSSIAN CHARACTER THAT DISTINGUISHED INTELLIGENTSIA WRITING.

CHAPTER XXV. THE HISTORY OF GRUNYA: INTIMACY WITH A CLEVER ACTRESS, OR THE SHORTEST, SUREST, AND PLEASANTEST ROAD TO RUIN

I showed up for dinner. Grunya received me with open arms, laughing, weeping, and repeating a thousand times that there was not a happier being in the world than she, now that she was reestablished in my affections. During dinner, I briefly recounted to her my adventures in the Kirghizian steppe. After dinner we sat down on a divan, and Grunya began her narrative.

"My father, as you know, left behind him considerable property; but my mother, to whose management it was entrusted until I came of age, squandered it, in addition to incurring large debts. You saw how we lived. Our house was a gathering place for card-players, amateurs and professionals alike. All that my mother gained as a result of her partnership with the professional gamblers, she lost in trying her luck against them, plus some money of her own. To make matters worse, she fell in love with a young ne'er-do-well, who promised to marry her, borrowed a large sum of money from her, and then married another. Our condition before setting off for Orenburg was quite desperate: the house was mortgaged, not a kopeck of our capital remained, and our debt was more than twice the value of the whole property. At that time my uncle died, and we hastened to Orenburg to claim what he had left, hoping that everything would go in our favor.

"I had hardly left the boarding school, where I had accomplished the usual goals—good posture and fluency in conversational French—when my mother decided to finish my education herself, by teaching me coquetry, so that I might draw rich young men to the house with my beauty and fascinating ways. You have heard how I used to pick out cards for a hot-blooded *ponteur,* advising him to wager large sums on my good fortune. I always chose for this purpose players who could not maintain their composure in the presence of my charms, and willingly submitted to me. I need hardly add that the card I chose always lost, as the gamblers whispered into my ear which one to pick. This was a disagreeable role to perform, but I was obliged to obey, and had, besides, to dispense kind looks and friendly smiles, and listen to the amorous speeches of all the players who were in love with me, and to flatter them with the hopes of reciprocal affection. I give you my word of honor that I coquetted with the greatest aversion before I knew you.

"I was ordered to lure you to the house. This was an extremely pleasant task. From the time that I left the boarding school, I had no occasion for pretense, for I loved you sincerely. As you will recall, not only did I not draw you into the play, I even made a practice of withdrawing you from it. My mother often scolded me for that; but I resolutely declared to her that if I did not have to involve you, I would decoy anyone else she wanted. So she left me alone.

"In Orenburg another misfortune befell us. The court had scarcely resolved to turn possession of my uncle's property over to us when other claimants appeared—half a dozen *elevées* [schoolgirls], with a will properly drawn up and witnessed. The property had been acquired by my uncle himself; thus it would have been a vain endeavor at best to attempt to have the will set aside, and even more so in this case, when the claimants were good-looking girls with strong patronage. My frustrated mother opened a gaming house, wrote to Moscow for some experts, and appointed me to play the role of siren again, to lure ill-fated adventurers on the sea of fortune to our Scylla and Charybdis.

"Business went very badly for us till winter. We practically lived on credit. Particularly at first, we were in desperate need of money. At this time there arrived in Orenburg, on government business, the adjutant of Petersburg general, Captain Count Lovkov, an agreeable young man from a wealthy family, with a cheerful disposition and fascinating manners. He saw me on the promenade, fell in love with me, introduced himself at our house, and became a daily visitor. My mother, under threats of her curse, ordered me to use all my powers to make a prize of Count Lovkov. The game of love is much more dangerous than any game of cards, and it often happens that the loser is the side that sets all its snares to capture the other. Count Lovkov lost money in our house, but as compensation he asserted his rights over me, unknowingly catching me in the very same trap that I had prepared for him. Listening patiently to his declarations of love, and becoming so accustomed to them that I felt uneasy when I did not hear them, at last, in order to continue this agreeable amusement, and keep the count hanging around, I acknowledged that I liked him. The count was a man of the world, and experienced beyond his years in affairs of this kind. We soon formed a close friendship and familiarity, of which you were a witness.

"You still lived in my heart, but I confess that your respectful, timid love seemed but child's play compared with the fiery, impetuous passion of the count. When he learned from Vorovatin that you had come to Orenburg looking for me, he swore that he would kill you; and in order to save you from danger, I thought it best to keep you at a distance, and even to abuse you. It is true the medicine was rather harsh, but at the time I thought that I was doing the right thing. Your sudden appearance put me into such a state of agitation that I was beside myself. I do not know what I said. Your attempt to debase me in the eyes of the count put me into a rage. My dear Vanya, forgive me!"

Grunya wept, and I solemnly swore that I forgave her completely, and did not harbor even a trace of displeasure for anything that had happened. "Be assured, Grunya," said I: "All is forgotten, all is forgiven: I love you more than ever!"

"I wanted to find out what had become of you," said Grunya. "I was told that you had been taken ill; that the next day Vorovatin had found other lodging; that someone had come for you in a cart, to take you to your new accommodations, but that the landlord of this other place had not seen you. A few days later, Vorovatin left Orenburg without saying goodbye, and I did not know what had become of you. A secret voice within me reproached me for my behavior toward you. Shocking dreams frequently disturbed my sleep. I saw you dying, saw your spirit threatening me with vengeance. I thought that you were dead; I wept, I prayed: at last my spirit began to grow calmer, and while I did not forget you altogether, I did think about you less often.

"My dear friend! Allow me to omit the more particular details of my adventures, mixed up as they are with transgressions, the enormity of which I feel to its fullest extent, and of which I repent from the bottom of my soul. The count, having artfully represented to me my unfortunate situation in the gaming house, and promising to marry me after the death of his old and sickly father, persuaded me to elope secretly to Kiev, where his regiment was quartered, and to which he had been ordered, on having given up the designation of adjutant. It was not long before I saw my error. The count was amiable, tender, and respectful, like all lovers till such time as their objectives are attained; thereafter he was rude, capricious, and cold, and seemed anxious to rid himself of his gullible victim. Not a day passed without quarreling, mutual abuse, and tears. The contempt with which I was showered cut me to the quick, and the fickleness of the count, who amused himself with other liaisons, drove me to desperation. At last he declared to me that his father was dead, and that he was obliged to leave immediately for Petersburg. I reminded him of his promise: he was silent. I asked him to take me with him: he said that it was impossible. At last he departed, and in a month I learned that his father was alive, and that my lover was married to a rich young lady from an illustrious family.

"You can imagine my despair. I thought of returning to my mother, who had moved back to Moscow; but in answer to my letter, I received the news that my mother was dead. I was an orphan, cast out into the wide world without a protector, without money, and without my good name!

"The count appointed one of his friends to settle things with me, and offered me an annuity, on condition that I would leave him in peace. I spurned his offer and wrote his wife a letter in which I exhausted my indignation at the source of my unhappiness. For a while I was not sure whether I wanted to live or to throw myself into the water. My youth at last overcame my despair: I began to feel calmer, but I did not know how I would be able to support myself. I thought of hiring myself out as a servant. At the time there chanced to be in Kiev a troupe of strolling players, composed of undereducated schoolboys, expelled students, semi-literate actresses, and serfs who had been given their liberty, or were allowed by their masters to live on passports. The thought suddenly struck me that I should become an actress. The manager of this group, an aging prompter, having evaluated my abilities for the theater, was so pleased with me that he immediately installed me in his troupe as first singer, first tragic and comic actress, and first dancer. I declined to perform in Kiev, where the officer knew me. We set off for the Malorussian[1] fair, where I garnered acclaim and drew crowds to the booths in which we performed. I was the main draw of the company, and for that I was looked up to by all, more than even the manager himself. Even though I had moved ahead of them, the women loved me, too, because I did not interfere in their affairs; I conducted myself modestly and kept admirers at a distance, even getting a reputation for being hard-hearted. I had no rest from suitors: some of the small country gentry offered me their hands, but I preferred a free life, and did not choose to bury myself alive in the pens of any of these sheep-shearers. Applause became a necessity of life for me; I thought of nothing but fame!

"Wherever we went, want of money followed us like a guilty conscience. When we arrived in a town, we usually lived on credit till we could collect enough money to pay our debts and defray our expenses to another place. We clothed ourselves from the proceeds of our benefits, and boarded or lodged at the expense of the common stock or the manager. The division of the profits was regularly arranged on our arrival at each fair, but at the end it seemed that there was never anything to divide. However, we lived—if not in wealth, then at least in cheerfulness, not caring for the future, and consoling ourselves with the present.

"On one occasion, as we passed through a small market town, the manager announced to us that our funds were so depleted that we could move no further without a fresh supply. We stopped at a tavern, erected a shed in the yard for a theater, made chandeliers out of cask hoop, created our own paper scenery, and plastered every street corner with written advertisements. Some days passed, and we had not a single spectator. At this time there chanced to alight at the tavern a rich gentleman, who was on his way from Petersburg to his estate in the country. Reading in our advertisements that our company intended to perform Sumarokov's tragedy of *Demetrius the Pretender* and the opera of *The Miller,* and that all we needed was an audience to show off our splendid abilities, the traveling gentleman, for his own entertainment, ordered a performance for himself, and at the cost of a fifty-ruble note, he entered the theater alone, with his poodle. Notwithstanding that the poodle interrupted our performance, barking prodigiously as soon as our Demetrius the Pretender fell into a rage; notwithstanding that some of the candles attached to the hanging hoops went out, and some fell on the actors' heads; notwithstanding that there was not an unbroken fiddle in the whole orchestra, we went through the performance with *éclat,* and the rich gentleman observed in me an

---

1. Ukrainian.

ability which he was pleased to call great talent. Out of pure generosity he made me a present of two hundred rubles to pay my expenses to the government town, where a dilettante of the drama was entertaining a theatrical company. I followed his advice, left my companions, and on my arrival at the government town, made myself known to the proprietor of the theater. After my debut, I was allowed a benefit performance on condition that I would perform a certain number of times with all profit going to the theater. My benefit went splendidly, for the elections of provincial magistrates and the public hunt were happening at that time. With the money that I had acquired, and letters of recommendation, I set off for Moscow, introduced myself to one of the actresses belonging to the theater here, and you, having seen me in my first appearance on the Moscow boards, can form your own idea of my small abilities and of the success that I am likely to attain in the career that lies before me in this metropolis."

"Dear Grunya," said I, "you see nothing but flowers in the path that you have chosen. You forget to take into account the chance of meeting with reverses. Listen to my advice: Give up the theater; I will marry you; we will settle down in some country town, and I will either enter into trade or take up agriculture. Hearts that are happy together have little need of material pleasures!"

Grunya mused a little, then, placing her hand on my shoulder and with a look of tenderness, she said, "Vyzhigin! Your country castles would do for a vaudeville, but not for real life. Is it possible that fame can turn your heart cold? Is it possible that the splendid success of your Grunya does not move you? Vanya, dear Vanya! If you only knew the pleasure I get from public applause, from seeing my name in print, from reading my praises in the newspapers, if you loved me, you not only would not wish to take me away from my profession, you would be doubly happy in the enjoyment of my love and my good fortune! No, Vyzhigin, I cannot leave the theater at the very moment when it is resounding with applause for me, when it provides me both the means of existence and the highest pleasure, and reconciles me with the world, from which, I may say, I deserted. Wait a little while; allow me to indulge my present enjoyment, and then I am yours forever."

I wished to disagree, to argue the matter, but Grunya begged me to end my discourse. "Fame and love!" she exclaimed. "That is the watchword of a good actress. Accept things as they are, or I will be unhappy!"

It was my duty to submit, or rather it was not my duty but I thought it better to submit and held my peace. A month passed: Grunya became an object of adoration for all the lovers of the fair sex and of the drama, and the envy of all coquettes. She triumphed: I suffered and was silent. A small society gradually formed in my house—patrons of the theater; humble and officious servants of actresses, the kind who follow in the wake of any of their sisters who bears the bell, in hopes of acquiring a cast-off admirer or of getting some benefit tickets; and some of the official people connected with the theater, who are as necessary for the success of an actress as the wooden stands are for the scenery. But Grunya behaved admirably. Toward the rich and noble dilettantes she behaved with respectful pride; she received them only on fixed days and at fixed hours, always in the presence of other females, and did not allow the smallest freedom in either word or behavior. The officers[2] of the theater she knew how to treat in such a way that they invariably anticipated her wishes. Grunya passed for a paragon of wit and virtue. In the higher circles, nothing was talked of but the beautiful Russian actress, who spoke French admirably. Upon learning of this last circumstance, the hoary admirers of the fair sex were beside themselves. "A Russian actress speak French?—C'est charmant! C'est charmant!" replied the old gallants. "What a pity that she is virtuous! Virtue in an actress is an extravagance that ought not to be tolerated!" So the gallants reasoned, but Grunya smiled and loved me alone.

One day I found Grunya quite melancholy; her eyes were red, her cheeks pale— it appeared that she had been crying. I was perplexed. "Dear Grunya, what has happened to you? For God's sake, tell me!" "Ah, Vyzhigin, what an unfortunate creature I am! They have given me the leading role in the new opera, to gratify the malice of that foolish, faded Maskina, who takes all her pride in having access to the property of Count Zhilkin, and appearing on-stage in a blaze of gold and diamonds. She will perform the second part in that opera; that was my doing in spite of all the intrigues of the count's party. I did, however, have to put up with a most silly declaration of love from an ass of an employee behind the scenes. Don't be afraid, Vanya; I see your eyes growing big, and you are losing heart already: I only heard the declaration, and have now quite forgotten it. Be that as it may, the principal part is mine! Now what does that spiteful Maskina think to do? She will be playing my rival, a rich old widow; and so she has ordered a sumptuous dress embroidered with pure gold upon velvet, and intends to appear dripping with diamonds beside me, who will be in false gold and glass pearls!" Grunya wept. "But there are ways and means to remedy that," said I, stammering. "Don't cry; let's discuss this calmly." "What is there to discuss? Out of a hundred old debauchees, I might be able to find one who is agreeable and who would be ready to spend all his money on me. But I couldn't make up to one of those men for all the money in the world. Every woman has her own way of thinking; but I could never say "I love you" to a man to whom *memento mori* would be more fitting. Young beauties are either as poor as church mice or so preoccupied with themselves that they believe their looks to be prettier and more valuable than diamonds. What conscience there, Vanya? I love you alone, and would rather sink and burn for shame than be false to you." I kissed Grunya's hand and said, "My dear Grunya! Your performance will eclipse the splendor of Maskina's dress." "How can I perform well when I have that ostentatious doll before my eyes?" "What would a dress cost?" "Fifteen hundred." "Fifteen hundred is not much, but the diamonds . . ." "The diamonds could be borrowed; only a deposit would have to be made for them. For my own use I want only a decent pair of diamond earrings and a pearl clasp: the rest could be borrowed. But let's drop the subject; sit down beside me, Vanya, and we will talk about something else." "Excuse me, Grunya, but I must go now. I have but one request: do not torment

---

2. In Russia, the theater, like the church, is part of the state [trans.].

yourself, and don't commit yourself to anything before dinnertime. I will come and dine with you, and we will put our heads together. Who knows; perhaps even Vyzhigin can do something for you!"

In a state of strong agitation, I left Grunya. She loves me, thought I—she disdains all other suitors because of her love for me, and for my sake she even sacrifices female vanity and self-love. O my priceless Grunya! I ought to compensate you for your affection, and return to you a portion of the pleasure that I enjoy from your love. With these thoughts, I flew home, took my bank receipts, went with them to the Board of Guardians, borrowed ten thousand rubles, and went immediately to a jeweler. I selected a beautiful pair of earrings and a pearl *femoir*, for six thousand rubles, then borrowed a tiara necklace, and bracelet, valued at twenty-five thousand rubles, leaving the rest of the money as collateral. I then returned to Grunya, who was just sitting down to dinner, supposing that I would not come. She received me tenderly but with a melancholy countenance. "You know, Grunya that I have a superstitious fear of dreams?" "What do you mean?" "I dreamed last night that something happened to you during dinner: put my mind at ease, my dear, by seeing if all is right in the kitchen. Did you hear that a cook recently sprinkled a tart with what she thought was sugar, but which was actually arsenic that had been placed in a cupboard to kill rats?" "My God what strange thoughts fill your head!" said Grunya, and she went out of the room. While she was gone, I took the jewelry from my bag and placed it on a table, along with a couple thousand rubles for a dress. When she came back into the room, I was waiting for her at the door. Taking her by the hand, I led her up to the table, saying, "Begone, dull care; I pray you begone from Grunya." She looked at the things, then gave me a look that almost melted me on the spot; she threw herself screaming into my arms and fainted.

After carrying her to a sofa and calling to the maid, I quickly sprinkled her with water and perfumes, at last managing to bring her around. "Vanya," she said, "I don't know how to convey the gratitude that this heart, which belongs to you, feels, but my tongue is too weak to express."

Grunya, in the spring tide of spirits that had replaced her depression, was in such glee that I feared she would lose her senses. She screamed, laughed, and sang, trying on first the tiara, then the necklace, and then the bracelets, one after the other. I made her sit down at the table, but every minute she jumped up from her chair to take a look in the mirror and adjust her ornaments to suit her fancy. "Grunya," said I, "you who are so wise! Surely these splendid toys cannot be of such value in your eyes as to absorb all your thoughts." "No, my friend," she replied: "it is not the things that I care for, but the triumph over my haughty rival—a triumph which she does not anticipate, and which I will value the more because it was your doing!"

As the day of the performance approached, Grunya informed me that the friends of Count Zhilkin were hatching a plot against her. "Dear Vanya," Grunya said to me, "the world is not aware of our intimacy, and so you must organize a party in my favor. I could easily do it myself, but I do not wish to excite your jealousy or wound your feelings. Take a few dozen tickets, tell your friends that you won them in a wager, and distribute them gratis. Treat some of the most hot-headed, noisy, and daring bullies to dinner or *dejeuner*, and instruct them to support the right cause, to encourage me with their applause, and to call me to come forward, while they hiss Maskina." I tried to object, but Grunya covered my mouth with her fair hand, kissed me, and demolished with a smile my entire philosophic battery. I was obliged—or should I say, inclined—to submit.

At last the day of the performance arrived. I hosted a dinner in a tavern near the theater for a party of friends—bullies, that is to say; and when they were all half-drunk, I asked them to go to the theater and support the right side, distributing at the same time the tickets. We all went to the theater together, and my friends only waited for my signal to hiss or clap their hands. In the meantime, Grunya remained in her dressing room till it was her turn to come upon the stage. When she made her appearance, Maskina was disconcerted at the sight of the diamonds and of the magnificent dress that Grunya wore; and the entire faculty behind the scenes made it clear that it was impossible to be better or more beautifully dressed than Grunya. She was beside herself with joy, and her mood had such a powerful effect upon her acting that she surpassed all expectations; while Maskina, in despair at her rival's triumph, forgot her part and bungled her performance. Count Zhilkin's friends did what they could to support his mistress, but the hisses of our party drowned their feeble plaudits, and Grunya, who was showered with applause throughout the performance, was summoned for a curtain call after its conclusion, while Maskina, covered with shame and ridicule, abused Grunya behind the scenes, and on her return home quarreled with the count.

Grunya met me with open arms. She had a party of guests to supper, but I was so unsettled by the conflicting emotions of the day that I felt unwell and went home.

Considering Grunya's success in her dramatic career, and considering the extent of her fame, it was only fitting that she should dress better than, or at least as well as, other actresses, that she should have a better apartment and keep her own carriage; there was no way I could allow Grunya to look to others to supply her wants, so I did what was needed. She had no shawls, but never asked me for any; when I would ask her to take a walk with me, or to put on her diamonds of an evening, she would refuse with a smile because she had no shawl, and without one, it would be quite foolish to go for a stroll or wear fancy dresses. So of course I had to buy her a few shawls—what I had brought with me from the steppe having been sold.

In the course of the year, three new performances, two changes of lodging, the purchase of a wardrobe and winter clothing, the setting up of her carriage, one celebration of her name day, and one of her birthday cost me forty thousand rubles, and put me ten thousand rubles in debt. I repeat that she never asked me for anything, and I had not the slightest inclination to purchase the love or the good graces of anyone. Neither I nor Grunya had any idea at the time that so much money was being spent. She wanted certain objects, and my money was the natural and obvious means to be used to acquire those objects for her. Left out of the calculation was the fact that the one had to be parted with before the other could be procured! I was left without a kopeck in the world, without any means of procuring more money, and obliged to maintain my poor mother.

Reflecting upon my situation made me desperate, but I didn't have the heart to tell Grunya of my misfortune. I thought of shooting myself, thought of running away to the Kirghizian steppe, but my mother's condition stopped me. Some days I did not dare to appear before Grunya, and sat shut up in my room, thinking how I might decently keep my head above water. I told my mother that I was unwell. I could not come up with a plan, and only fifty rubles remained in my purse. I had already written to Arsalan Sultan by way of Orenburg, but had received no answer. I now again wrote to Arsalan and the Kirghizian elders, informing them of my place of residence, and begging them to send me the remainder of the money I was owed from the sale of the booty. The silence of my friends of the steppe was not a good omen. In the meantime, I feared lest my friends, patronesses, and creditors should hear of my ruin. A thousand projects were born and died within my head. Then suddenly, on the evening of the sixth day, the door to my room flew open, and in came Grunya.

The Little Humpbacked Horse
Petr Ershov (1834)

ERSHOV (1815–1869) WROTE THIS ENCHANTING TALE IN VERSE WHILE A STUDENT AT PETERSBURG UNIVERSITY. MORE FOLKISH THAN THE FOLK, IT WAS AN INSTANT CLASSIC. THE POEM WAS WRITTEN AT A TURNING POINT FOR RUSSIAN CULTURE, WHEN EDUCATED RUSSIANS WERE BEGINNING TO SEE FOLK CULTURE AS A SOURCE OF NATIONAL IDENTITY. THOUGH INSPIRED MORE BY GERMAN PHILOSOPHERS THAN BY RUSSIAN SERFS, THE FOLK IN-FLUENCE YIELDED UNEXPECTED BENEFITS. THIS POEM, ALONG WITH SIMILAR WORKS BY PUSHKIN, BECAME A CLASSIC OF CHIL-DREN'S LITERATURE, REPLACING DIDACTIC TALES AND TRANSLA-TIONS FROM FOREIGN LANGUAGES. IT RAN INTO COUNTLESS EDI-TIONS, AND WAS ADAPTED FOR THE RUSSIAN IMPERIAL BALLET IN 1864.

ETHNOGRAPHERS WERE BEGINNING TO COLLECT PEASANT TALES WHEN ERSHOV WROTE HIS POEM, AND HE DREW ON TRADI-TIONAL FIGURES SUCH AS THE FIREBIRD AND IVAN THE FOOL,

Pyotr Yershov, *The Little Humpbacked Horse* [*Konek-Gorbunok*], trans. Louis Zellikoff (Moscow: Raduga, 1957), pp. 100–104.

A SCORNED SIMPLETON WHO TRIUMPHS OVER SLYER FOLK. THIS EXCERPT IS THE CONCLUSION OF THE TALE, WHEN IVAN, PREPARED BY THE HUMPBACKED HORSE, TRIUMPHS IN HIS ORDEAL AGAINST THE OLD TSAR, AND WEDS THE YOUNG TSARITSA.

All the Tsar did was to say
That his groom come straightaway.
"Are you sending me once more,"
Cried Ivan, "off to the shore?
No, Your Majesty—not if
I can help it—I'm still stiff
As it is—no, I won't go!"
"No," the Tsar said "No, no no
Listen, now tomorrow morn
On the palace court-yard lawn
I will have three cauldrons filled:
One will have cold water, chilled;
In the second cauldron pot
There'll be water, boiling hot;
While with milk I'll fill the last,
Heating it till it boils fast.
You, Ivan, must do your best
These three cauldrons you must test
First bathe in the milk, my son,
Then the waters, one by one."
"Listen to his blarney," said
Vanya, and he shook his head.
"Chickens, pigs, and turkeys—yes—
People scald them, I confess;
I'm no pig or turkey, though,
Nor a chicken, as you know.
Now, a cold bath—why that's quite
Diff'rent and, I'll say, all right;
As to being boiled alive
You can't tempt me—don't you strive;
But enough, Your Majesty
Don't you make a fool of me."
Wrathfully, the Tsar's beard shook
"What—me argue with you? Look!
If my bidding be not done
With the rising of the sun,
I will have you drawn and quartered,
Tortured on the wheels and slaughtered!
Off with you, you wretched plague, you!"

Shivering as with the ague,
Vanya to the hayloft crept,
Where his little humpback slept.
"Why, Ivanushka, so sad?
Why so downcast, then, my lad?
Has our bridegroom found another
Task for you, my little brother?"
Said his horse. Ivan, in tears,
Kissed his little horse's ears,
Held his neck in close embrace
As the tears rolled down his face.
"Woe is me, my horse," sobbed he,
"He will be the death of me;
Now I've got to bathe, undressed,
In three cauldrons, for a test;
In the first, there's water, chilled;
Next, with boiling water's filled;
In the third milk, scathing hot."
"Yes that is a task you've got,"
Said his horse. "For this, you need
All my friendship, yes, indeed;
Your misfortunes are the price
Of refusing my advice;
Thank that evil feather for
All your woes and sorrows sore.
But, God bless you—do not cry,
We will manage, you and I.
I would sooner perish, than
Leave you in the lurch, Ivan.
Listen, lad—tomorrow morn,
When you strip there on the lawn,
Say: "Your Gracious Majesty!
Please to send my horse to me
So that I can say good-bye
To my horse before I die."
Now, I know he will agree
And he'll send a groom for me.
I will wave my tail about,
In each cauldron, dip my snout;

Then I'll squirt upon you, twice,
Whistle long and loudly thrice;
You be sure to look alive,
In the milk then quickly dive,
Then in waters hot and cold
Dive, just as you have been told.
Now, my lad, go, say your prayers,
Sleep in peace, forget your cares."

Dawn had scarce begun to peep,
Humpback roused Ivan from sleep:
"Hey, my lad, stop snoring, do!
Up! Your duty's calling you!"
So Vanyusha scratched his head,
Yawned, and scrambled out of bed,
Crossed himself and said a prayer,
Sauntered to the court-yard, where,
Near the cauldrons, in a row,
Sat the servants, high and low
Princes, dukes, and lords and pages,
Cooks and coachmen, fools and sages
Sat and whispered with a smile
And discussed Ivan, the while
Logs were fed on to the fire
So that it should not expire.

Then the portals opened wide
And the Tsar, with his young bride,
Came to watch there, with the rest,
How Ivan would stand the test.
And the Tsar called out: "Ivan,
Now, undress yourself, my man
Dive, and bathe without delay
In those cauldrons there, I say!"
Vanya stripped—no word said he,
And the young Tsaritsa, she
Veiled herself right then and there
So as not to see him bare.
To the cauldrons Vanya sped,
Peered inside, and scratched his head.
While the Tsar said: "Now, Ivan
Come on do your duty, man!"
Said Ivan: "Your Majesty,
Please do send my horse to me
So that I can say good-bye
To my horse, before I die."
Pondering o'er this request,
Graciously he acquiesced,

And the Tsar was pleased to send
For Vanyusha's faithful friend,
And Ivan then said adieu
To his humpbacked horse so true.

Humpback waved his tail about,
In each cauldron dipped his snout,
Then he squirted on him twice,
Whistled long and loudly thrice;
Vanya gave his horse one look,
Then a deep, long breath he took,
After which, as he was told,
In each cauldron dived, full bold.
In and out he dived, and when
He emerged—no words nor pen
Could describe him—he was so
Handsome, I should have you know.
Then he dried himself, and dressed,
To the Tsar-Maid bowed his best,
Glanced around with haughty air,
No prince handsomer, you'd swear.
"What a wonder did you ever?"
Cried the crowd, and "Well I never!"
Hastily the Tsar undressed,
Twice and thrice he crossed his breast,
Dived into the cauldron pot
And was boiled there on the spot!
Here the Tsar-Maid stood up, and
Called for silence with her hand;
Then, unveiling her fair face,
Thus addressed the populace:
"Listen, now! The Tsar is dead
Will you have me in his stead?
Am I pleasing in your eyes?
Speak! If so, then recognise
As the lord of all the land,
My beloved husband" and,
Pointing to Ivan, she placed
Her fair arm around his waist.

"We are willing!" all replied
"We would die for you!" they cried
"For the sake of your sweet eyes,
Tsar Ivan we'll recognise."

Hand in hand, the Royal pair
Tsar, and young Tsaritsa fair
To the holy altar sped,

And in God's church they were wed.
Cannons from the castle flashed,
Trumpets blared and cymbals crashed;
From the cellars, then and there,
Casks were rolled with vintage rare.
And all night the drunken throng
Shouted out in merry song:
"Long live Tsar Ivan!" they cried,
"And the Fair Tsar-Maid, his bride!"

In the palace, mirth held sway,
Wines like water flowed that day,
And before the groaning boards
Princes drank with Dukes and Lords.
'Twas a pleasure! I was there,
Mead and wine I drank, I swear;
Though my whiskers bathed in wine,
Nothing passed these lips of mine.

THE END

The History of Russia Told for Children
Aleksandra Ishimova (1838)

FEW WORKS OF LITERATURE IN THE NINETEENTH CENTURY WERE WRITTEN ESPECIALLY FOR CHILDREN. FOLK TALES, TOLD BY PEASANTS, AND BY THE PEASANT NANNIES OF WELL-OFF FAMILIES, PLAYED A PROMINENT ROLE IN THE CULTURE OF CHILDHOOD. STARTING IN THE 1830s, WORKS AIMED AT YOUNG MINDS BEGAN TO APPEAR. MANY OF THEM SUGGESTED A FAINT UNDERSTANDING OF CHILD PSYCHOLOGY.

ISHIMOVA (1804–1881), THE DAUGHTER OF AN EXILED BUREAUCRAT, WROTE THE FIRST HISTORY PRIMER TO GAIN BROAD POPULARITY. FORCED FROM AGE TWENTY TO EARN HER OWN LIVING, SHE WAS INTRIGUED BY THE SPECIAL STORIES READ BY THE CHILDREN OF SOME ENGLISH ACQUAINTANCES. SHE RESOLVED TO CREATE HER OWN, IMBUED WITH A RUSSIAN SPIRIT AND PATRIOTISM. ENCOURAGED IN HER LABORS BY NO LESS THAN PUSHKIN, ISHIMOVA WAS PRAISED BY CRITICS FROM THE LEFT AND THE RIGHT, AND HER WORK WAS REVISED AND REPRINTED THROUGH THE 1890s (AND IS RETURNING TO PRINT AT THE PRESENT). AL-

Aleksandra Ishimova, *Istoriia Rossii v razskazakh dlia detei,* 5th ed., revised and expanded (St. Petersburg: Iakov Trei, 1862).

THOUGH IT WAS DESIGNED FOR CHILDREN, ITS LANGUAGE AND
IDEAS DIFFER LITTLE FROM ADULT TEXTS. THIS EXCERPT, CON-
CERNING THE POLISH UPRISING OF 1792–93 (SIMILAR TO THOSE
THAT FLARED UP IN 1830 AND 1863), INTRODUCED CHILDREN TO
THE IMPERIAL VIEWPOINT, IN WHICH THE ENLIGHTENED RUS-
SIAN AUTOCRACY GUARANTEED THE WELFARE AND HAPPINESS OF
SUBJECT PEOPLES, THREATENED ONLY BY THE HORRORS OF
REVOLT.

POLAND FROM 1792 TO 1795[1]

While Russia was flourishing under the salutary protection of its autocratic government, enjoying all the fruits of happiness and glory that its renowned sovereign
could provide, almost all the other kingdoms of Europe were far from enjoying
those fruits. They were gripped by horrible disorders, whose common source was
France. The residents of that unfortunate country, always famous for their volubility
and unreliability, brought untold calamities upon their fatherland. It started with
the American war between England and the North American colonies; many
Frenchmen who had taken part in it returned to Europe with frivolous dreams of
independence and the irrational desire to change their government. That wish,
which was baseless and counter to all the principles that had maintained the fortune
of their fatherland over the course of entire centuries, led the French to immense
civil disorders. The disorder grew with almost every day, and in less than three years
had attained horrifying proportions. Following new, willful fashions in thought,
they ceased to consider their sovereign's power *sacred*—power established by God's
law. Was it surprising, then, that they gradually ceased to fear God himself? A man
who has come to such a piteous condition, a man who has had the misfortune to
forget his own merciful Creator—what will he not do, what foul deeds will he not
commit? This was proved fully by those latter-day Frenchmen. How quickly their
unbridled willfulness led them to neglect their God; all crimes seemed permissible
to them, and all conceivable misfortunes were sent down upon the godless by the
righteousness of heaven. Their virtuous king Louis XVI was the first victim of the
terrible overthrow that took place then in France: the madmen preaching freedom
began by depriving their legal ruler of that selfsame freedom. As if that were not
enough, they deprived him of his life! You are horrified, my dear readers? His entire

---

1. Poland was first partitioned in 1772, by Russia, Austria, and Prussia. Though smaller, the country
recovered in the subsequent two decades, and in 1792 it adopted a constitution on the American model.
This was intolerable to the partitioning monarchs, and Catherine invaded Poland in 1793, destroying
the reforms, and partitioning the country further. A popular rebellion, led by Tadeusz Kosciuszko, hero
of the American Revolution, was eventually crushed by Russian forces led by Aleksandr Suvorov, and
Poland disappeared from the map of Europe until 1918.

family and everyone who showed the slightest attachment to him or to the old order was subject to the same fate. It is terrible to write of it, and impossible to describe all the horrors that took place then in France: suffice it to say that for more than a year, blood flowed in rivers; evil deeds previously unheard of were committed daily in the name of justice. But God punished the evildoers: as if by providence, some of them tried to exterminate the others. All the states of Europe watched the piteous events in France indignantly. Many of them broke off all relations, with which Russia, guided by its wise sovereign, could not but concur. Russia did even more: it offered refuge to several French princes, unfortunate relatives of Louis XVI. Catherine[2] even conceived the magnanimous intention of sending troops to tame France's horrible anarchy, but before that charitable thought could be executed—which under the conditions reigning at that time in Europe would have been difficult— the madness of the French created a new evil: followers of their godless principles were found in many other states, and one can imagine the new horrors that could be anticipated from that.

Of those states, the one closest to Russia in both its situation and its location was Poland. Several zealous adherents of the French innovations appeared, and they, at the instigation of their leader, Ignacy Potocki, decided to make important changes in their government. They appointed the prince of Saxony to replace their king, Stanislaw Poniatowski, and made the Polish throne his hereditary domain; and in place of laws approved by Catherine, they wrote a new constitution. The Russian sovereigness could not stanch these whims at their advent; her armies were occupied at that time on the borders with Turkey and Sweden. But upon the conclusion of peace with those countries, she considered it her obligation to uproot that evil whose consequences had been so pernicious and had become so widespread in the neighborhood of her kingdom. The king of Prussia, who in this instance was of much the same reasoning as Catherine, had already experienced the dangers of bordering on states infected with the mad French principles, and entered into a friendly alliance with the Russian empress to pacify the Polish mutineers. In a short time, their troops compelled the Poles to repeal their new constitution and return the state to its previous order. A consequence of the victory of the Prussians and Russians was the second partition of Poland between those two states. Russia recovered regions that had belonged to it several centuries earlier and had been seized by Lithuanian princes. These regions were Minsk, Podolsk, and parts of Volynia and Lithuania, in total approaching 4,000 square miles. Prussia received Danzig, Torun, Plotsk, Poznan, and Kalisz, i.e., part of northwest Poland comprising 1,000 square miles. This took place in September 1793.

And so calm was reestablished in Poland, which, still stretching 4,000 square miles and having 3,600,000 residents, could remain in the ranks of the European states and, having discovered from experience the harm that an insubordinate spirit causes a nation, now learned to value the patronage of the mighty Russian sovereign. The Poles could have formed a separate state under that strong patronage,

---

2. Catherine the Great, whose youthful enthusiasm for freethinking had cooled by then.

but Providence intended for them to unite with their fellow tribesmen; they were to return to their original state of national unity, to unite their destiny and ancient glory with the destiny and glory of that nation. But before that unification could take place, both nations were to experience the woeful consequences of their quarrels. No more than six months had passed since their pacification—an incomplete pacification at best, because the Russian army stayed behind to preserve calm in Warsaw and its environs—when Krakow was gripped by a new "revolution,"* accompanied by horrors that resembled the horrors of the French Revolution. The main participants and directors contrived at a certain day and hour to launch unexpected attacks on all Russians whereever our armies were located. The terrible conspiracy enjoyed complete success, and almost all the Russians located in Poland suffered an unexpected death! Catherine was horrified when she received the news, and seeing the necessity of crushing the Polish mutineers with greater firmness than before, she dispatched Count Suvorov. The name alone of the great general ensured the success of the matter and filled the hearts of the leading conspirators against the Russians with fear.

The count, as commander-in-chief of forces situated in the provinces of Ekaterinoslav and Tauride, and the newly acquired region of Ochakov, lived at the time in Kherson and was working on the fortification of the border with Turkey. Suvorov, who passionately loved wartime activity, called this work idleness, and was gladdened by the assignment given him by the empress. He had long listened to terrible stories of the French Revolution with disgust and horror, and then about its pernicious influence on other states, for which he had long wished to demand satisfaction from the French. Frequently, as if having a presentiment of all the evil that could be anticipated from the disorders in France, he told the empress with impatient agitation, "Send me against the French!" Before the count's ardent wish could be granted, the Polish revolution and the traitorous destruction of the Russian garrison took place. The empress chose Suvorov to take vengeance for the innocent blood spilled by their compatriots. Austria and the Prussian king sided with Russia, and the latter had already begun the siege of Warsaw with General Fersen. Suvorov was approaching rapidly with an army corps 12,000 strong when he was surprised to discover that the Prussian king had been forced to lift the siege on the Polish frontier in order to rush off and suppress a mutiny in his own territories bordering with Poland. General Fersen, deprived of the troops to continue his siege, followed his example and also retreated.

Such a sudden change of circumstances would have stopped any other commander—but not Suvorov. With a small detachment of his own, which was extraordinarily reduced by its encounters with and victories over the enemy, Suvorov decided to storm the capital of the rebels, where a single outlying town held 30,000 soldiers. When he first conceived the attack, he ordered all the Russian troops dispersed around Poland to gather in one spot—around his own detachment. And

---

*This was what the French called their terrible overthrow of their government, and what all popular disturbances are subsequently called.

even that unified army consisted of no more than 22,000 men. Suvorov considered that number sufficient for the subjugation of Warsaw and the strongly fortified suburb of Prague.

One of his best assistants in this renowned campaign was General Fersen. Hurrying to join his corps to the count's, he was met on the way by the chief general of the Poles—the famous Kosciuszko, who wished to impede that unification. Knowing all the harm the Russians would suffer in the event that Kosciuszko managed to fulfill his desire, Fersen not only prepared a courageous defense against the attack, he also decided to attack first. His daring was fully rewarded: Kosciuszko was crushed, losing 6,000 men dead, 1,600 taken prisoner, and his entire artillery. Worst of all, he fell prisoner himself.

After this glorious battle, which plunged Poles into despair, particularly the capture of the most important of the commanders leading their revolution, Fersen hurried to link up with Suvorov; another Russian general located in Poland, Derfelden, did the same with his troops, so that by the 22nd of October a corps 22,000 strong had gathered under the leadership of Suvorov.

Not one to do tomorrow what could be done today, the count marshaled his troops after a two-day rest, marched to the walls of Prague, and the next day, the 25th of October, at five o'clock in the morning, began to attack the suburb, which was so large as to be a separate city. Despair from one side and inexhaustible, one might say incomparable, bravery on the other—both were equally astounding; yet in the end, the former had to yield to the mighty exertions of the latter, and after four hours of battle, Prague, despite its numerous troops, its strong fortifications, its evident invincibility, fell before Russia's incomparable hero. The finest historians to have described that amazing happening say that the chronicles of war have rarely recorded an undertaking so daring in plan, so skillful in execution, and so important in its consequences. The last is particularly just: the taking of Prague extinguished in one day the entire horrible flame of the Polish Revolution, and at the price of spilled blood, the reestablishment of social calm. That price was dear for the Poles: 13,000 of their men died on the field of battle, 2,000 men drowned in the Vistula River, and more than 14,000 were taken prisoner.

Such an absolute defeat horrified the leading mutineers. From the walls of their capital, they looked sorrowfully on Suvorov's brilliant victory and recognized immediately the necessity of submitting to his invincible strength. However, negotiations continued for another three days concerning the conditions for surrendering Warsaw to the Russian army. At last, the count dictated the following terms: (1) All Poles must lay down their arms. (2) Leave only 600 infantry soldiers and 400 cavalry soldiers for the king's guard. (3) Render the king all due honors deprived him by the mad mutineers. (4) Dispatch all arms, all artillery, and all other military apparatus to Prague. (5) Immediately free all Russians taken prisoner. And lastly, (6) by the 8th of November, resurrect the destroyed bridge over the Vistula for the victors' ceremonial entry into Warsaw.

The Poles were compelled to agree to all the proposed terms and to fulfill them exactly. The horrors of revolution had taught them to fully value the peace that had been established, and the 8th of November seemed to be a joyous day for them:

they met the Russians with all tokens of submission and even zeal. Peaceful citizens, who usually suffer the most during rebellions, threw themselves at the count's feet, calling him their savior, and shouted, "Long live Catherine! Long live Suvorov!" Most solemn of all was the moment at the very entrance to Warsaw when Suvorov was greeted by its magistrate, who presented him the keys to the city. The pious hero accepted them with reverence and delight, kissed them, and, raising them to the heavens, spoke in a moved voice: "Almighty God! I thank You that these keys did not cost as much . . ." Tears prevented him from continuing, and only his gaze pointed toward unfortunate Prague.

The measures he took to crush the remaining rebels scattered about Poland were so well planned and so skillfully executed that the social tranquility was not violated by any more disturbances, and the Poles willingly submitted to a new and final partition of their state. Their consent was speeded by the fact that their king, weary of the deprivations closely associated for several years with the Polish throne, refused to occupy it. Catherine did not avail herself of her victor's right—a right by which she could have become the absolute sovereign of a country she had conquered without the assistance of the allies. But on the contrary, wishing to reconcile Poland's interests with the necessity of eliminating its separate existence among the European states, she proposed to the king and the allies that the Sejm[3] be convened in the city of Grodno. Here at the Sejm the fate of all Poles was resolved for the final time, and the kingdom was divided among Russia, Austria, and Prussia. The first received Vilnius, Grodno, the remaining part of Volynia, Samogitia, Troki, Brest, and Chelm, totaling in expanse 2,030 square miles, and in residents 1,176,590 people.

Austria received Krakow, the district of Sandomierz, Lublin, parts of Chelm, Podolia, and Mazovia, totaling 834 square miles and 1,037,732 residents.

Prussia was given Warsaw, Bialystok, the Augustow district, parts of Mazovia, Radom, Plock, and Troki, totaling 997 square miles and 939,297 residents.

Stanislaw August [Poniatowski], renouncing the throne, was assigned a yearly pension of 200,000 gold rubles by Russia and Prussia. Long enjoying the patronage of Catherine, he hoped to finish his days peacefully in her dominion rather than elsewhere, and thus soon after the conclusion of the Sejm he departed for Grodno, and then to Petersburg, where he subsequently passed away.

Thus was destroyed the mutinous Polish kingdom, and thus the restless Poles were the cause of their own destruction. The hero who had subdued them remained another year in Warsaw and the new Russian territories; when everything needed for security and calm was in place, he, too, finally left for Petersburg. There awaited him new honors and awards from the generous sovereign; but he had already received the most flattering of all a year previously, for the glorious taking of Prague: the rank of field marshal. The details of this conferral are curious. The count, having won an unprecedented victory, preserved his wonted modesty, and his report to the empress this time was briefer than ever. He wrote only "Hurrah,

---

3. The Polish national congress.

Prague!" The empress, even wittier and enthralled by the celebrated victory, answered just as briefly: "Hurrah, Field Marshal!"

Before we finish our story, my readers should know that, along with the newly acquired regions of Poland, Russia received another new dominion: Courland, a Polish suzerainty since the time of its Count Ketlers.[4] Courland did not want to recognize the authority of a collapsing state, and before its fate could be decided at the Grodno Sejm, it offered itself to the Russian empress as a possession in perpetuity.

And so Russia, extended in all directions, elevated to the heights of glory, was enjoying complete good fortune when fate struck it a sudden and terrible blow, the demise of Catherine in 1796.

---

4. Gothard Ketlers, last master of the Livonian Order of Knights, which disintegrated in 1561. It was replaced by the Duchy of Courland, whose first duke he became.

The Battle of the Russians with the Kabardinians
Or, The Pretty Muslim Woman Who Died at Her Husband's Grave: A Russian Story
Nikolai Zriakhov (1842)

RUSSIA'S CONQUEST OF THE CAUCASUS IN THE FIRST HALF OF THE NINETEENTH CENTURY WAS FOLLOWED BY ADVANCES INTO CENTRAL ASIA AND EASTWARD. AS THE EMPIRE GREW, IT ENCOMPASSED TRIBES AND ETHNIC GROUPS WHO, IN THE EYES OF THE CENTRAL GOVERNMENT, NEEDED TO BE RUSSIFIED TO JOIN THE CIVILIZED WORLD. AMONG THEM WERE BRAVE TRIBESMEN CAPABLE OF CONVERTING TO FIT IN, WHO ENCOUNTERED MAGNANIMOUS RUSSIANS WHO BAPTIZED THEM WITH LAWS AND RELIGION, ALONG WITH THE SWORD. ALL THESE CHARACTERS ARE PRESENT IN THE FOLLOWING STORY, WHICH, DESPITE ITS TRAGIC DENOUEMENT, OFFERS OPTIMISM FOR THE FUTURE OF CONQUEST.

I. Zriakhov, *Bitva russkikh s kabardintsami* (1866), in *Lubochnaia kniga* (Moscow, 1990).

IT IS A VALUABLE GLIMPSE INTO RUSSIA'S NINETEENTH-CENTURY ORIENTALISM. THIS TALE IS ALSO A BOWDLERIZED VERSION OF PUSHKIN'S "PRISONER OF THE CAUCASUS," AND ORTHODOXY PLAYS A MORE PIVOTAL ROLE IN THIS TELLING.

THE ACTION TAKES PLACE DURING THE REIGN OF TSAR ALEXANDER I (1801–1825). EXCERPTS HAVE BEEN COMBINED FROM A MUCH LONGER ORIGINAL, WHICH CAME OUT IN VARIOUS VERSIONS OVER A SPAN OF SIXTY YEARS.

The Kabardinians,[1] who live just beyond the Terek River, which serves as the frontier between them and the Caucasus Province, maintain permanent dwellings in the mountains and canyons. This is an especially strong and impressive people, extremely brave, and well known for the excellence of their horses, which are famous everywhere for their strength, beauty, and agility in races. They also produce very substantial armaments, for example, sabers, daggers, spears, arrows, guns, pistols, and remarkably light chain mail. This so-called three-ringed chain mail weighs only six pounds, and if you hold it in your hands it resembles a fine mesh; but when you put it on, it works like steel, and only a very powerful soldier can tear through it with his bayonet. Bullets will not puncture it, and our sabers slide off it without doing any harm. Only Cossack javelins penetrate between the rings to injure or kill the enemy. The Kabardinians handle their weapons expertly; they fire pistols very accurately, their arrows and spears cause terrible harm, and their sharpest daggers, when tossed in hand-to-hand combat, inflict incurable wounds. Many Kabardinians also cover up to half of their horses in chain mail during battle. They fight without formation, and their attacks are extremely dangerous. Especially courageous armored troops often ride into our camps and, after inciting much damage and confusion, ride out during the intervals in our shooting, winding like snakes with their spears, and disappearing in the blink of an eye from our bullets and buckshot. Their wives and daughters are as attractive and gallant as the men; they often do battle to revenge the loss of fathers, brothers, husbands, and children.

According to several historians, the Kabardinians are descendants of the intrepid Amazons, because they have settled their former lands; others suggest that they are newcomers to this area. But let the historians who know this territory better than I research this question; we will now return to our description of this remarkable people.

In general, all Kabardinians are Muslims. Looking at how they live, we know that each man may have up to seven wives, the eldest of whom enjoys supremacy. Muslim women are dominated by their men. Each must respond immediately to the wishes

---

1. A Muslim Caucasian tribe inhabiting the northern slopes of the Caucasus Mountains, who, along with many other Caucasus ethnic groups, resisted the imposition of Russian rule.

of her lord and master; his tender gaze or smile induces rapture, but the slightest woe or harsh look makes her tremble. They love their husbands passionately and fear them as the masters who control their lives.

[*This portrait of the tribe is followed by a description of a battle between conquering Russian troops and the forces of Prince Uzbek.*]

The brave Cossack leader Pobedonostsev, scornful of the multitudinous enemy, like a true Russian hero struck them on all sides with his heavy sword; all of the Kabardinians whom he stabbed with his lightning blows fell from their horses, either dead or seriously wounded. But he fought alone. His Cossacks were engaged with the armored horsemen, who were preventing them from uniting with their commander, surrounded on all sides by Kabardinians.

This extraordinary hero did not want to retreat a single step from the battle, and he asserted his courage alone against the enemy. He already had three wounds in his side from Kabardinian spears. Suddenly a striking young Kabardinets on an exceptional horse appeared, the visor on his helmet raised. He motioned the other soldiers aside and began a duel with our hero. Their sabers met; sparks flew. The young Kabardinets took his time, then stabbed our hero furiously in the chest with his sword. The latter, ignoring his terrible wound, drove his sword with astonishing strength into the chest of his foe, piercing the armor and thrusting him from his horse. At this moment Pobedonostsev suffered a severe wound to his right hand. Blood poured from the wounds on his hands, his knightly strength was exhausted, and the sword dropped from his powerful clasp. His valiant body slumped forward onto his horse's head. He was about to fall to the ground when Prince Uzbek, who respected knightly valor more than anything else in the world, and was impressed by the unusual strength and courage of the young hero Pobedonostsev, grabbed him and ordered his entourage to take him from his horse. He ordered them to use every means possible to save him, without the slightest delay. "Tell my daughter Selima especially to care for this brave warrior as she would her own father, and to teach him our religion."

Having said this, Prince Uzbek dressed Pobedonostsev's wounds with remarkable skill and then added, "Tell my doctor Brazin to treat him himself, and to use all means possible, everything he knows, on these wounds. Go! Allah guard your way! Tell them that I, praise to our prophet, am alive and well and hope to see them soon!" Four muscular soldiers placed the still-unconscious Pobedonostsev on four shields tied together and covered by a rug that had been woven by Uzbek's beautiful daughter Selima. Raising him to their shoulders, they quickly carried him away.

Delivering the wounded man to the beautiful princess, they bowed low as they stepped backward out of the *kibitka* toward the door, because Muslims consider it impolite, even criminal, to turn their backs on their superiors or their owners.

After they exited, the lovely Selima, reflecting on her father's orders, felt a tremor in her heart and wanted to explore the lines of the wounded man's face.

At this moment the sun's rays were shining directly through the windows of the *kibitka* and onto his face. Approaching Pobedonostsev, Selima suddenly became terribly upset when she found herself looking at this most handsome of men. Dark brown curls shaded his proud face and thin eyebrows; thick, curly eyelashes proved to be hiding beautiful eyes. A flush emphasized the cheekbones of his white face, which was otherwise covered with a deathly pallor. The lips of his small mouth, still arguing with death, were crimson. Wide shoulders, a high chest, a slender waist, and his above-average height made him appear a conqueror before her. She sighed languidly; tears trickled from her exquisite eyes at the thought that he might die. This first spark of chaste love, this embryo that steals imperceptibly into our hearts, had already begun to grow for our hero in Selima's delicate soul.

"Oh, my father, how right you are!" she exclaimed softly and ran to fetch Brazin for the injured soldier. Soon she returned with Brazin, who examined the sick man and treated him according to the customs of his land. Here we can interject and say this about Asian peoples, that their rudimentary medicines and the adhesives they make return the wounded and the ill to health as well as European ones.

In just a few minutes, thanks to Brazin's proficiency, Pobedonostsev regained consciousness. He opened his big, dark eyes, quickly took in everything around him, and with great surprise quietly exclaimed, "Oh, God, where am I?"

Selima, quivering from joy, and knowing a few words of our language, answered demurely, "You are with friends, who are taking care of you."

Selima's gentle statement, although not quite grammatically correct, prompted him to turn his gaze on her; Pobedonostsev, struck by the beauty of this Kabardinian princess, suddenly felt a flame in his chest; his heart began beating faster than normal, and a bright blush covered his cheeks.

"Where am I?" he asked again. "And who are you, who appear before me and call yourself my friend?"

"I am Selima, the daughter of the Kabardinian Prince Uzbek," the young princess answered directly and simply. "You were wounded and fell prisoner to him. But seeing your unbelievable bravery, he saved your precious life and sent you to us, his people, and ordered us to tend your wounds and treat you like his son." (She reddened.) "Dr. Brazin and I were specifically directed to care for you."

Pobedonostsev, agitated by a variety of emotions, said softly to himself, "A prisoner of the Kabardinians. Hence the hand that carried my steel sword betrayed me." (He stared at his right hand, tried to lift it, but could not.) "Now I understand why I'm here! Thus, I'm separated, maybe forever, from my parents, from my compatriots my comrades—and what's more important, from the glory of the laurel wreaths that crown their heads. I, an unhappy prisoner, must suffer here in the shackles of captivity! Oh, this is dreadful!" (With his left hand he wiped away his tears.)

Selima (softly and compassionately): "Christian fellow, do your heroes weep? Aren't you ashamed! Didn't I tell you that you were among friends? Don't you believe me?"

Pobedonostsev (moved): "Yes, I believe you with all my heart, most beautiful princess. But I am a Russian warrior, and how can I not be bitter to be imprisoned at a time when my compatriots are spilling their blood for tsar and fatherland!"

Selima: "Yes, and you've already spilled much of your own for them. You have five deep wounds, and your hand took the lives of twenty of my brave compatriots in battle; that's certainly enough to testify to your courage and to cover you with glory!"

Pobedonostsev (quietly, noticeably weakened by the strain of conversing with the princess): "Thank you, most beautiful princess, for your kind opinion of me! You have cheered me up."

Brazin (speaking in their language, Circassian, to Selima): "For the sake of Allah be silent, most serene one! Your conversation is placing this handsome and sympathetic soldier in a most dangerous position. This is very bad for his severe wounds, which are now inflamed and can bring on an even more dangerous disease, from which death would be inevitable; the blame would be entirely yours, and not our spears or arrows. Retreat from here for at least an hour, and let him grow strong from the medicine I am preparing; maybe not even this can save him."

Pobedonostsev, not taking his eyes from the lovely princess during this conversation, and understanding their language as well as his own, watched her face change greatly from fear of the words that Brazin had spoken. Elated by her emotions and sensing that his bliss lay in a future with her, he said to Selima in Russian: "Beautiful princess, remain here. Your absence would increase my pain and suffering. Your presence gives me new life and relieves my spiritual and physical burdens." (Then he turned to Brazin and said in their language): "Respected doctor! Don't worry so much about my condition. I am a Russian soldier and have the strength and fortitude to survive the severity of my illness. I implore you, don't send the lovely princess away; her presence is mandatory for my recovery. Moreover, she is fulfilling her father's orders. I give you my word that I will refrain from long conversations. Give me your medicine, if you consider it necessary. Selima (wringing her hands ecstatically): "Oh, Allah! He speaks our language! What happiness for Selima!"

During their conversation, Brazin (who understood no Russian) prepared his medicine for the wounded man. Selima observed him curiously, because she knew his strength, and also because she feared for the wounded one; she knew her fellow countrymen well, and their hatred for Christians, and especially for Russians. Brazin administered to Pobedonostsev the red elixir he had prepared. Its magical power overcame him, and he fell into a deep sleep.

[*Brazin has been bribed to kill Pobedonostsev by the Kabardinian prince to whom Uzbek has promised his daughter, but Selima, sensing something like this, threatens the doctor. Preferring his life to the money, Brazin restores the Russian's health.*]

Recovering his senses and staring raptly at Selima, Pobedonostsev said, "Oh, whoever you are, a mortal or a heavenly creature, your appearance has calmed my heart. I implore you, don't go away; stay here, if only for a few more minutes. I feel that your presence relieves my suffering, and that having looked upon you, I could cheerfully close my eyes forever."

Selima: "Good soldier! I'm no apparition, but a mortal just like you. I likewise mistook you for a heavenly creature, as you did me. We were both mistaken. If my presence pleases you, I am happy to give you my time—not so that you can close your eyes, but rather for all the happiness you bring. Your features are deeply etched in my heart, and only death can end the burning passion I have for you. From first glance I knew that I would surrender my whole being to you, but I fear that you will reject my love." (She lowered her eyes.)

Pobedonostsev: "What do I hear? Do my ears deceive me? What soothing words! Repeat them; tell me again what you just said! My darling, you have brought me back to life. Your love promises to enrich me with all joys; to refuse your love would be to refuse all that is most precious in the world to me. One would have to have lost all human feelings and have a heart of stone to do so. No, I love you so much that I cannot believe my own euphoria; even now I fear that your declaration of love was a jest!"

After three days, Pobedonostsev felt much better. Selima came to him with the sunlight; approaching his bed, she sat cross-legged in the Asiatic fashion and gazed at him tenderly, lovingly.

Pobedonostsev: "My dear, my darling one. I believe you have something special you want to tell me."

Selima: "How did you guess, Andrei (for that was his name)! Yes, I want to very badly, but if I have mistaken your feelings, I will die forever."

Pobedonostsev: "Beloved Selima! What is this secret, what does this mean? For heaven's sake, tell me quickly. I see how you're trembling. Speak!"

Selima: "All right, I'll confess. Listen, and then answer me with complete honesty. When my father saved you, horribly wounded, from certain death and sent you to our village for treatment, through his envoy he ordered me to care for you as I would for him, and also to begin to teach you our religion. Of course he was so impressed with your looks and great courage that he wanted to bring us together. But I cannot become your wife as long as our different faiths create an impenetrable obstacle between us. Now tell me, do you wish to fulfill my desire, to accept our laws and religion and belong to me only, inseparable unto the grave?"

Pobedonostsev (grown pale): "Dear Selima! I love you more than my own life and am prepared at this moment to sacrifice everything for you, but to renounce the Orthodox faith of my ancestors and parents, to become a traitor to the vows I made to Christ the Savior, to my tsar and fatherland, who would cast me out and make my name hated among my countrymen, wipe out the renown and honor of my elderly and generous parents, whose only son I am and heir to a wealthy estate: no, most beautiful Selima, no! I cannot, and not even the most agonizing death could change my mind, because honor and glory are dearer to me than anything else on earth. That, beautiful princess, is my candid answer. It is decisive and made with my whole heart and soul and loyalty to the Russian throne. But I swear to heaven that despite the differences in our religion, I will adore you forever, and if fate separates us for eternity, I will die a bachelor and, carrying your divine image in my heart, I will be faithful to you till the grave!"

Selima (horrified): "All is decided. I must die!"

Pobedonostsev (with dread): "What are you saying, Selima? Your words frighten me! What! With your bright mind, you are still capable of succumbing to such despair! I beseech you, wipe the terrible thought from your mind that can destroy our hopes and future, which have not yet disappeared, which can still be realized. Be patient, dear Selima! Happiness still shines like a bright star for us; fate will make you mine, and I will thrill to hold you to my heart. Oh, if only you knew my law and religion, dear Selima, you would love my God with your whole heart, the great Christian God and his mother, the Blessed Virgin Mary, who protects all that is good and leads sinners to the path of righteousness! What heavenly joy our Orthodox Christian faith fills us with, the teachings of our Christ, who came down from heaven to redeem us from eternal suffering with his blood and death on the cross!"

Selima listened attentively to Pobedonostsev and sat for a while confused, pondering his words. "I understand from what you've said that your faith is greatly superior to ours, and how magnificent the religious ceremonies must be. Oh, if I had the power, I would go with you to your fatherland, which must be prettier than our wild mountains and canyons, which are filled with predatory animals and carnivorous birds."

When Selima left, Pobedonostsev was beside himself with joy. Now he understood completely the beautiful princess's emotions. They inspired him with the exciting thought of converting her to Christianity and convincing her to run away with him to the fatherland. These plans and sweet dreams for the future filled his soul with bliss, and aided his speedy recovery.

Selima, returning to her room, was also happy, because she realized how tenderly and passionately Pobedonostsev loved her. Andrei's hot kiss still burned on her crimson lips. But despite this joy, an inexplicable sorrow weighed heavily on her soul when she recalled Brazin's words, that Pobedonostsev would blossom again, but for the grave, not for this world. "Whatever happens to him and me, I have already decided that I belong to this handsome youth. Let one blow shorten our lives!"

[*Selima began to study Orthodoxy; Uzbek learned of this and became very upset that Pobedonostsev was not the one converting.*]

Pobedonostsev: "Honorable prince! To change religions is probably the most important step we can take in our lives. Maybe another man would gladly accept your proposition, relishing both Selima's beauty and your wealth. But I was solidly instructed in the Christian law and the faith of my ancestors, and I consider it sacred. But because I do not want to appear ungrateful to you, I will study your Koran and then, comparing the two, will give you my final answer about my opinion and intentions. I know your language very well; I can read and write it, and this will help my studies. But there will be places in your Koran that will require explanation, that to me will seem cryptic and incomprehensible. Who will be my tutor?"

My readers might think at this point that our hero has been tempted by the beauty of the Kabardinian princess or her father's wealth, and he feels passionate love toward the one and allegiance and friendship toward the other, and they have caught him in a net. Or perhaps the Koran contains exquisite rewards for Muslims. But these readers are mistaken. My hero, ingenious and intelligent, and raised firmly in the laws of Christianity, realized that the best way to undermine the teachings of Mohammed was through reasoned argument, and he guessed correctly that Selima would be his tutor. He knew that her presence was necessary, and by showing her the false prophecies of Mohammed, he wanted to turn her to our faith.

Selima (ecstatically): "My father has blessed us! I'll be your teacher! How wonderful this is for me, Andrei. Isn't it true that my father is a good man? He loves you as he did his son, Ramir."

Pobedonostsev (dazed): "Whom I killed, whom I deprived of all life's goodness, struck down in the prime of his life, took away from my benefactor forever . . ."

Selima (with horror): "Who told you this?"

Pobedonostsev: "Your father himself. After this I can never be your husband; I am your brother's murderer! His blood still streams from the wound on my hand! Oh, Selima! We must part forever!" (He sighs.)

Selima (decisively, in desperation): "Part! You cruel, pitiless, insensitive boy! One victim isn't enough for you! See how another is ready! (She pointed a sharp dagger at her heart.) Andrei, you still don't understand how Muslims love and die. Watch and enjoy my blood, my death!"

[*She tries to stab herself. He intervenes and is cut in the process. He agrees to marry her despite having slain her brother. Then his religious lessons begin.*]

Through both hard evidence and articles of faith, Pobedonostsev swayed Selima to prefer his religion to hers. She herself saw the errors in the teachings of Mohammed and with all her heart began to love our Savior, and became so firmly attached to our religion that she was barely able to conceal her feelings of heavenly Christian love from her family. In their presence, she performed her duties for the sake of appearance, all the while thinking about our Christ with all the love and modesty in her captivating soul. Pobedonostsev, delighted with the success of his strategic plan, soon taught her to read and write Russian. That made it even easier for him to confirm her in our faith.

Thus did six weeks pass like six minutes. The Kabardinians, defeated in many battles with Russian troops, sensing the inability to continue the war any longer, selected an ambassador from among their wealthiest, most renowned, and reasonable men, which included Prince Uzbek. Because of his experience, he was selected to head the delegation sent to the commander of the Caucasian corps, with a valuable tribute, to ask for mercy and peace. Thus did the battle between the Russians and the Kabardinians end, with both sides suffering bloodshed and the deaths of many of their finest warriors.

[*Andrei returned home, but without Selima, whose father forbade her to go. He is out in camp again with his troops when a soldier is caught sneaking into camp in disguise.*]

Pobedonostsev and the solder entered his tent, where a wax candle was burning. He told his orderly to put on the teakettle immediately and to bring out a bottle of the best wine. "Now you can take off your armor without any danger, and rest from your journey."

The soldier (I presume that you readers have already figured out that it was Princess Selima) pulled off her helmet and armor, put down her spear, shield, and saber, and laid them alongside Pobedonostsev's arms. With tears of ecstasy she turned into the embrace of her beloved, trembling from happiness.

Selima: "Now do you see how much I love you, Andrei? Did you believe that your Selima was living peacefully after you left? No, without you, there was an awful void in our home; I shed tears on the pillow and bed where you lay when you were with us. Every little corner and back road where I walked with you is covered with my tears. Only Mother Nature witnessed my woes in silence. An unfamiliar melancholy pulled at my heart, my soul was despondent, and then I made up my mind to unite with you and never again part. But we must do this as quickly as possible—tomorrow I will be baptized, and then the marriage ceremony. Otherwise my father will come here and snatch me back, destroying our plans. A parent's authority is absolute, but if we are already married, then it will be too late to separate us. Do you agree?"

Pobedonostsev (showering her hands with kisses): "Darling, extraordinary Selima! Our union will fill my soul with heavenly bliss and make me the happiest man on earth! Everything will be prepared in the course of the next few minutes, my dearest one. But first a glass of the finest Rhine wine; it will bolster you."

Selima: "Have you forgotten, Andrei, that Muslims don't drink wine?"

Pobedonostsev: "Let Muslims do what they will, but Christians always toast to an engagement!"

Selima: "I surrender! To the health of my dear friend and the happiness of our union! (She drinks.) Oh, this is strong! I'll get drunk."

Pobedonostsev: "No shame in that! The sooner you fall asleep, the better. I'll sit with you a while. Don't you want anything to eat? I have a wonderful pilaf with chicken, which I prepared in memory of you, when you took care of me. I wasn't expecting such a precious guest."

Selima (kissing him): "Now you know how Muslim women love!"

[*She is baptized and changes her name to Sophia; then they are wed in the cathedral. Prince Uzbek learns only that Andrei has married, and he brings him a generous tribute.*]

Uzbek (wiping his eyes): "Oh, Allah, what do I see? My daughter Selima! Why are you here?"

Andrei and Sophia fall to their knees before Uzbek.

Sophia (with a pleading look and tears): "Oh, my parent, forgive me! I could not live without this man, and now he is my husband. Separation from him would end my life. (She kisses her father's hands.) Forgive your daughter and bless our union!"

Uzbek (wiping his tears): "Unworthy daughter, but still dear to my heart! How could you take such a daring and dangerous step, you who were so quiet and innocent! Oh, cruel, ungrateful daughter, you didn't think about the shame with which you were covering your father's head, digging a path to his grave!" (His tears flow.)

Pobedonostsev: "My father! My benefactor! Forgive your blameless daughter and pour your wrath out on me: it was I who filled her with the first sensations of love and turned her subtly toward Christianity. We took an oath before God, at Ramir's grave, that we belonged to each other until death. Isolated from me, your daughter decided in desperation to marry me. She accepted our law, our faith, and now she is my legal wife. Forgive us and bless us!" (He throws his arms around Uzbek's knees, kissing his hands, weeping.)

Uzbek: "Stand and embrace me. You will always be dear to my heart."

At the end of their first year of marriage, Sophia gave birth to a beautiful son. She did not want to entrust him to another, this first pledge of their love and union, so she fed him from her own breast. This deepened the tender love of her husband, who could not get enough of watching his wife and son.

Five months after the birth of Arkady, as they named him, our young couple were enjoying their well-being and good health, when suddenly one midnight Andrei became grievously ill. He felt a terrible pressure in his chest. He began coughing up blood, and our hero felt all his strength leave him. The deep wounds in his chest and right hand had disappeared; they had undoubtedly been cured. Doctors were called in, and they consulted with others. The shadow of death hung over our young hero, and all their skills were for naught. Sophia, carrying in her heart the dread and horror of her beloved husband's dangerous situation, wrote to her father immediately and asked him to send Brazin as soon as possible.

Brazin's arrival, with gifts and letters, gave both the invalid and Sophia some kind of hope, but they now worried about her father's health, too. This doctor, examining the patient, grew white, shook his head doubtfully, and sighed heavily. He could not conceal this from Sophia's scrutinizing gaze, and she sobbed bitterly. Brazin's medicine allowed him to live several days longer, and he felt a little better. When he told his wonderful spouse this, it filled her with elation, which lasted but a short while. Inexorable fate took the life of the best soldier, the truest friend, the most handsome man, the most passionate and tender husband, and a true son and respected servant of the throne and fatherland, so horrible to the enemy, with his giant's strength, skills, and courage in battle.

[*Sophia does not believe that she can live without him.*]

Andrei's mother: "Sophia! Look how your son, his eyes filled with tears, clings to your hands. How can you leave him an orphan? Doesn't the weeping of your innocent son strengthen pity and reason in you?"

Sophia: "No, no, I cannot live without him, without the precious love of my life, lying in his grave without breathing! The Angel of Death has already stabbed me with his sword. Forgive me!"

As she walked to her spouse's grave, Arkady let out a pitiful cry and followed behind her. She turned to him, kissed him tenderly, wiped the bitter tears from his eyes with her hand, blessed him, and in a voice choked with grief said, "Calm down, my son. God is watching over you. Your mother leaves you in the best of hands. Your Guardian Angel is watching over you!"

Kissing him again, she hurried toward her husband's grave. Climbing to the last step, drawing up to these remains so beloved to her, she said loudly, "Precious husband! I am coming to you," and fell on his coffin. Sophia's beautiful soul was carried up to heaven with a peaceful sigh.

Etiquette Manuals
(1849–1911)

A SURE INDICATOR OF SO-
CIAL TRANSFORMATION CAN
BE FOUND IN ETIQUETTE
MANUALS, FIRST PUBLISHED
IN RUSSIA IN THE EIGH-
TEENTH CENTURY, WHEN PE-
TER THE GREAT INTRODUCED
THEM AS YET ANOTHER EU-
ROPEAN IMPORT TO "CIVI-
LIZE" RUSSIANS. ADVICE ON BEHAVIOR REFLECTED THE FACT
THAT MORE AND DIFFERENT TYPES OF PEOPLE HAD TO LEARN TO
INTERACT. RUSSIA'S ADVICE BOOKS REVEAL HOW ATTEMPTS TO
IMPOSE GOOD MANNERS CAMOUFLAGED IMPLICIT SOCIAL TEN-
SIONS. THE FIRST OF RUSSIA'S "CLEVER CAVALIERS" (AS MANUALS
DUBBED THEM) WERE TOLD NOT TO PICK THEIR NOSES WITH
KNIVES. TWENTIETH-CENTURY READERS STILL NEEDED ADVICE
ON TABLE MANNERS AND POLITE CONVERSATION. THAT THESE
TEXTS INITIALLY PAID LITTLE ATTENTION TO HOW WOMEN BE-
HAVED PROBABLY SUGGESTS MORE ABOUT INDIFFERENCE TO
GENDER THAN ABOUT PERPETUALLY FINE FEMININE MANNERS. A
NUMBER OF BOOKS ON "GOOD FORM" ADDRESSED BOTH SEXES.
THE FACT THAT BY 1910 ADVICE ADDRESSED PREGNANCY AND

DIVORCE SPEAKS AS ELOQUENTLY AS ANY STATISTICS COULD ON
SOCIAL CHANGE.

BELOW ARE SAMPLES OF ADVICE FROM THREE ETIQUETTE MAN-
UALS, SPANNING THE PERIOD FROM BEFORE THE GREAT REFORMS
TO POST-1905 SOCIETY.

A HANDBOOK FOR YOUNG AND OLD
OF BOTH SEXES (1849)*

*Before the 1860s, when industrialization and Alexander II's reforms made social
change inescapable, many Russians of even noble estate had little idea of how to conduct themselves in public. The following passage reflects a keen interest in advance-
ment up the social ladder, and the business positions that would accompany such
a rise.*

MAINTAINING PROPRIETY IN CONVERSATION

The most attractive face, one that is the greatest pleasure to look upon, can become unpleasant and lose all its charm if, when its mouth opens, it speaks stupidly
or impolitely. There is nothing more ludicrous than to mix crude expressions, collo-
quialisms, or words used improperly from foreign languages. Of course, with today's
elementary instruction of young people in the native tongue, such sins are committed less frequently. Yet there remain a number of people who continue to employ
French and Latin phrases, thinking that they can thus show off their education.

It is so very disagreeable to listen to platitudes, hackneyed sayings, pretentious
expressions, and incomprehensible words. The former show that the speaker is not
well educated, and the latter that he wants to hide his intellectual deficiencies with
bombast and artificial phraseology. The devotee of novels often lapses into affectation, because the imagination suppresses the sharp and critical mind, filling it instead with fanciful daydreams.

Often a story about an insignificant subject, when the telling is lively, takes on an
exceptional fascination and inspires an especially entertaining conversation. This is
an art derived from natural abilities, and those who lack it but still want to lead a
spirited conversation must avoid being long-winded at all costs, as this brings only
boredom and drowsiness to the listener. It is imperative that the educated person
master elegance of expression and the facility to inflect words with the appropriate
tone if he wants listeners in society to give him their attention.

---

*Ruchnaia i vspomogatel'naia kniga dlia molodykh i pozhilykh osob oboego pola, soderzhashchaiai v sebe pravila
priatnogo obrashcheniia s litsami znatnogo klassa i s damami pri vizitakh* (Moscow: V. Got'e, 1849), pp. 15–20,
60–65.

Expressions must be natural, unstrained; the more clear and sonorous the voice, the more pleasing the speeches being made. It is quite unattractive and impolite to mutter through clenched teeth, or to speak through one's nose, or to try to shout one another down. Light banter does not hurt pretty lips; in fact, it often makes them more appealing.

Crudity and double entendres should not be encountered in educated speech. By the same token, one must avoid frequent exclamations or insinuations, as these can tire listeners and obscure the thrust of the conversation. A story must be cheerful and lively if it is about lighthearted topics, but filled with deep emotion if it touches upon misfortune or suffering. Careful reading of exemplary authors can provide guidance on this point. The rare gift of being able to tell an entertaining story can be realized by frequent attendance at the best dramatic productions, as well as by interaction with people who can speak intelligently and pleasantly about the most ordinary subjects. Boredom is the principal enemy of any circle. Nothing is more tedious than the continued repetition and detailed description of mundane and irrelevant topics. And if these are recounted in a listless voice or a long-winded fashion, the speaker waits in vain for the listeners' attention.

DEPORTMENT IN THE COMPANY OF FEMALES

Young people, and even older ones, are in grievous error when they overstep the bounds of common courtesy in female company. Women do not like it when men feign sensitivity or flatter excessively. Nor do they like it when men toss languid glances their way or use pretentious phrases. At first women will tolerate this to amuse themselves, then they will ridicule it, and then eventually such men will not be accepted in their company. Women demand from men a superior education, tender feelings, and modesty, but not at the expense of masculinity, steadfastness, and strength of character. The man must be the anchor that can moor a woman during life's stormy days; she can rely with confidence on only such a man as this. An effeminate weakling is incapable of securing her future; she will look on him as a toy, a doll.

Behavior in female company must be like that in any educated circle, but here it must manifest even greater sensitivity and refined taste. Every profane word, every immodest and impolite action is felt doubly here and punished by contempt. Amusing jokes, compassion without the slightest attempt to flaunt erudition, and a minimum of that exhausting chatter about business and politics—this is what is considered polite in those circles where beauty and a sharp mind reign. Ambiguity, defamation, swearing, dirty jokes, inappropriate flattery, and in general anything that sullies tender feelings must be banished. It is also imperative to refrain from judgments about physical inadequacies or comeliness; it is quite possible that one of the ladies in attendance will lack exactly the sort of beauty that is the subject of conversation, and our opinion will therefore offend her. Given the diversity in topics of conversation, it is easy to avoid discussing human weaknesses and deficiencies. It is incomparably better to show attention to all women and to use every possible means to help them pass the time agreeably.

If sometimes women appear to be less interested than decorum says they should be, if they try to force others to take notice of their jurisdiction in the home or the versatility of their knowledge of housekeeping, if they try to show off their learning or exhibit the desire to attract or even to break a heart, then at such times they are behaving completely contrary to the rules of civility. They are positively mocking etiquette by breaching it. The entire feminine sex is bound together by a single chain, and when one woman behaves discourteously, all feel equally outraged.

It is even more inconsiderate to pay special attention to a single woman in a group; if a man does this as a joke, the women consider him dangerous. In any case, the others feel insulted by him. Talent and beauty must be given their due respect, but at the same time it is rude to embarrass others in a circle by showering excessive praise on a single individual.

LIFE IN SOCIETY, AT HOME, AND AT COURT (1890)*

Almost fifty years later, the Russian social world had become increasingly complicated, with three designated spheres requiring different styles of conduct. The section in this manual on the court does not, as it might appear, make an elitist identification of those socializing with the royal family. Rather, it reflects an expansion of court activities, an extension of the overlap of social and political circles.

The following passage suggests that the grandchildren of those counseled in the previous selection enjoyed more opportunities to step out together, but that propriety still limited their fun.

SOCIAL RELATIONS BETWEEN MEN AND WOMEN

There are many degrees and shades in the rules of etiquette and social relations that society has established. There are differences between how we relate to strangers, or at least to people with whom we have only a superficial acquaintance, the intimate relations we have with our friends, and lastly our families. But all of these gradations are subject to the same general rule that incorporates the indispensable maintenance of civility, courtesy, and tact, and an absence of egoism. Guided by these principles, it is easy to follow the true path.

First and foremost, you must conduct yourself with the same restraint with friends and family as you would in society; you must pay strict attention to your dress, manners, and expressions, with the difference that here you may show more warmth, emotion, and constancy, and less discrimination or pride.

Zhizn' v svete, doma i pri dvore (St. Petersburg, 1890), pp. 23–31.

The difference between the sexes mandates that a distance always be observed between husband and wife, brother and sister, uncle and niece, and cousins of the opposite sex. On the one hand, modesty and reserve are required, and on the other, respect and consideration. A man becomes crude and feral as soon as he stops being polite and attentive. Therefore familiarity and complete freedom can exist only in friendship between members of the same sex; it is unthinkable between a man and a woman. We must add that it is precisely this modesty and restraint that confers a special charm on their mutual relations.

Men make friends, often fleeting, that they do not introduce to their families; these are business acquaintances, or casual ones, struck up in a cafe, on the street, or at the theater. Of course, businessmen have many associates whom they cannot introduce to their families because this would be unproductive, a waste of time on both sides, and would widen their circle of friends too greatly. All of these are perfectly respectable reasons, but there are others which completely preclude more intimate contact: if you suspect someone of doing wrong, or if he is someone you cannot esteem, you must not call upon him or maintain any association. You must be open about all your acquaintances. Only a person with nothing to hide, who has no reason to blush before anyone, may be called proper.

The prudent married man does not have friends beyond his family circle; he does not need them, and he knows that they can draw him into situations adverse to family life. Nevertheless, all men stubbornly consider it their right to have friends whom they do not bring home. However, serious unpleasantness and even disasters often arise from these relationships.

Now we will go into detailed accounts, discussing step by step various predicaments and circumstances in which any person might find himself or herself.

When attending the theater, people who have taken a box and invited their friends to sit with them must give these friends the front seats. If two of the invited guests are unacquainted with each other, they must both sit in the front, but if they are members of the same family, then only one may take advantage of this courtesy, and the other must decline decisively. The front seats must always be offered to women, regardless of the age of the men accompanying them. However, there are occasions where the social position of the man requires him to behave uncivilly. For example, a minister will sit in front of a lady-in-waiting; etiquette demands this.

When you see your friends in the theater, it is impolite to gesture to them, and even worse to call out to them; you should only nod slightly, without getting up. If it is an especially important person, then you should stand and bow deferentially. During the intermission, men may visit with women they know, regardless of where they are sitting. These conversations, however, must not be long; that would be considered indelicate because it would prevent them from visiting with other friends. In the subsequent intermissions, you may return to these women only by their invitation.

If a woman is without an escort, then you may offer to accompany her into the foyer, or even to aid her departure. If she declines, you must not insist. You must never invite women with whom you are not acquainted, or to whom you are not related, out for entertainment. By the same token, women must not accept invitations from men they hardly know. But if a man escorts a woman to the theater, he must invite her for ice cream, cool drinks, or candy; it is up to her to accept or reject the offer.

It stands to reason that if a man takes a woman out, be she wife, relative, or friend, he must not leave her to go and converse with other women or to offer them his services. If he wants to go out during intermission, but she prefers to remain seated, then he may leave for a few minutes to chat with a friend in the foyer, but he does not have the right to visit with female acquaintances, unless they happen to be friends of the woman he is accompanying, or unless the latter herself has dispatched him to another woman.

If other men appear in his box to speak with his escort, then he may take advantage of this situation to depart and chat with some of his friends. He must return before the other men have left, though, so that his escort will not be left alone. But if she is left with a single caller, under no circumstances should he let her out of his sight: A woman is considered to have lost her position in society the moment that she enters into a dishonorable relationship with a man. A bow, any hint of acknowledgment, even a fixed stare from a man accompanying a decent woman is enough to be considered the gravest insult to her; if her companion forgets himself, she must immediately withdraw from him. A proper woman pretends not to notice a man she has met earlier in risqué company, and must never make any allusion to it in his presence; for her, the earlier meeting never took place.

It is permissible to look freely through one's lorgnette at the stage. However, it is better for young women to look primarily at the actresses, and they should avoid watching the love scenes or looking at low-cut gowns. Moreover, they should refrain from looking frequently around the hall through their lorgnettes; their role is to stimulate delight and admiration. In fact, the majority of women envy them this role, and that is why they are watching others through their lorgnettes! Men and women alike should equally refrain from looking around at the audience during the performance; this is considered showing off, because it attracts attention to oneself.

In the theater, as on the street, one must refrain from gesticulations, loud conversations, pointing fingers at acquaintances, and very obvious dissatisfaction with actors' performances. It is permissible to judge their talents, but decorum prohibits reproaching them directly in person.

Applause must be moderate, although when men are moved by an exceptional performance, they may express their admiration loudly. Men and women who occupy a high place in society must applaud very quietly; a slight gesture connotes approval from them. . . .

In general it is quite risky for men to pay attention to women escorted by other men. Such attentions might arouse jealousy, and can have unexpected and unhappy results. Some husbands do not even permit compliments to be directed to their wives, and more than once we have witnessed a very unpleasant scene when this has happened.

Misconceived politesse and helpfulness to strangers are both imprudent and can precipitate a shameful situation. Once a young couple, husband and wife, not yet experienced in the ways of the world, gave much attention and assistance to a charming but unknown woman, one who seemed to them so simple-hearted, honest, and grateful that this inexperienced pair was completely taken with her. She turned out to be a woman from the demimonde who subjected the young woman who was assisting her to much anguish, and compromised her completely with another of her acquaintances. Therefore it is necessary to beware not only of women who have already lost their reputations, but even more so of those who conceal a degenerate heart and morals behind a deceptive facade. We have also seen a young man, traveling with his invalid mother, who could not tolerate drafts, nonetheless open the window of their train car in order to please another woman suffering from a migraine and asking for fresh air. The desire to flatter our own conceit by showing ourselves to be extremely helpful and attentive must never allow us to forget those obligations prescribed to us by honor and duty.

A man must not fear being overly considerate and accommodating. He is obliged to rescue women from every form of inconvenience and fatigue. It is appalling to see a man walking with empty arms next to his wife, who is carrying packages or a child, as we observe so often among the poorer classes. It is by no means disreputable to see a husband carrying his child or pushing it in a buggy, if he cannot afford a servant for this; it is considerably more commendable than to see him put all this on his wife.

Many people are now discussing introducing in the near future the English custom of bowing, where the women bow first. We cannot understand this. A bow is a sign of not familiarity but of respect. It is well understood that a man's offering his hand to a woman can be objectionable to her because this is a sign of friendship, or at least of equality. The same may be said about approaching a woman in a public place or at a party. But a bow may come from someone lower on the social order or a slight acquaintance; there is nothing compromising in this.

We are often asked the following question: If a woman is walking arm in arm with her escort, is it permissible for another man to bow to her, or must he await a signal of permission from her? Is it not possible that she does not wish to acknowledge their acquaintance? There are exceptional cases in which this is possible, but in general it is insulting both to her and to oneself to meet a woman in a public place and not bow. Such an action either marks a man as compromised, a member of a disreputable crowd, or suggests to others that he does not consider this woman worthy of recognition. This could lead to members of her group asking him to account for his actions.

In exceptional personal circumstances, this can be a matter of tact, delicacy, and mutual understanding. Dandyism is such a fatal stumbling block for men and often propels them to commit any number of stupidities. For example, a man meets a woman on the arm of her husband, and he is not acquainted with the latter; he immediately assumes that if he were to acknowledge the wife, he would enkindle jealousy, because his vanity tells him that she has hidden their past relationship. On the contrary, the poor woman has told her husband all, and now the dandy insults them both by walking past without a sign because of something that happened only in his imagination.

All depends upon good sense and tact, but there are many women who, for various reasons, out of either compulsion or apprehension, keep everything secret. But we know of one young lady who lives openly, looks everyone in the eye, and blazes up in anger, considering herself insulted, if a man says, "I did not bow because you were with another man." And she is completely in the right. In their relationships with men, women must maintain the utmost discretion, but not at the expense of mincing words.

A woman must avoid meeting social acquaintances in her bedroom; a young lady cannot do this under any circumstances. Only the doctor, a close elderly relative, or a priest—and the latter only if she is too sick to arise—may enter the bedroom. A woman must never ask a man first about his health; only after he has already asked about hers may she pose the same question, but only casually. She must eschew scandalous and flippant discussions. All conversations about sensations are forbidden between young people, and between girls and older women; by the same token, they should not discuss medical matters.

We must now address one of the most ticklish questions, raised by one of our correspondents, whose husband works for a banker who also manages an important commercial firm. The role of his hostess is played by a very kind and courteous person, but nevertheless one whom society will not receive. The banker constantly invites people to his home, and always insists that those who work for him bring their wives! This is understandable; having wealth and power, on general principle, he strives for that which he does not have: social respect and esteem. Not wanting to throw stones at anyone, our correspondent continues, we feel justified in considering it offensive that we female slaves must bear, and bear often, the very heavy burden of bowing before someone who has given her life to whimsy and caprice. Yet not to go to the boss's party would insult him.

Not excusing weakness and passion, we could tell our correspondent only that the lives of these women, which might appear whimsical, and to which society has attached its contempt, is far from being as carefree and jolly as it seems, that many thorns and sharp pieces of flint have been strewn along the path!

This banker obviously does not realize that he is putting both himself and his friends in an awkward situation. If she cannot decline because of illness, she may attend with her husband, but never under any circumstances should she take her daughter. Moreover, she must not affect a disdainful, tense, or cold mien; on the contrary, she must be especially courteous so that others may view and appraise her deference. It would be absurd to accept money from this man and at the same time express contempt for him. If a woman is too inflexible by nature to submit to circumstances, then her husband should look for another job.

GOOD MANNERS: A COMPILATION OF RULES, DIRECTIONS, AND ADVICE ON HOW TO BEHAVE IN VARIOUS CIRCUMSTANCES OF HOME AND SOCIAL LIFE (1911)*

Daughters discouraged from visiting the banker's less-than-respectable home with their mothers may well have gone anyway; by the time they were seeking guidance on comportment, a number of the rules had changed. Booklets now let newlyweds study the biology and psychology of their situation, and even etiquette manuals acknowledged awkward questions of adoption, divorce, and second marriages. Socially mixed marriages also appeared to be on the rise.

This 1911 edition of Good Manners *offers instruction not only on appropriate public behavior, but also on the fundamentals of furnishing one's home, using good table manners, and identifying the appropriate wines. These telling differences reveal the omnipresence of new money and the expansion of what had been called "polite society" a century earlier.*

THE RIGHTS AND OBLIGATIONS OF SPOUSES

The husband imparts to his wife, if she is of a lower rank than he, all the rights and privileges that accompany his rank, title, or status. The wife does not lose any rights thus acquired, even if he is deprived in court of all rights associated with his status. The opposite holds true if the husband is of a lower rank than his wife; she does not transfer privileges to him, but neither does she lose hers. Thus a hereditary noblewoman who marries a peasant will retain her nobility, while her husband remains a peasant. The couple must live together; unless the husband permits otherwise, the wife may not live separately. The husband is obligated to love his wife, to live with her in harmony, to defend her, and to provide her with sustenance and support appropriate to his means. The wife must submit to her husband, and abide with him in love, respect, and absolute obedience. Each spouse may own property separately from the other; the dowry always remains the wife's property.

ATTENDING THE THEATER, CONCERTS, AND VISITING MUSEUMS

Opinions differ on what to wear to the theater and concerts. One may wear what one would at home or at work to the theater, as long as it is neat and proper. Only those who are sitting in the boxes and the first rows must dress up.

When going to the theater, concert, or any sort of public gathering, do not wear too much perfume. By the same token, it is unpleasant to be in the company of men

---

*A. Komfil'do, *Khoroshii ton. Sbornik pravil, nastavlenii i sovetov, kak sleduet vesti sebia v raznykh sluchiiakh domashnei i obshchestvennoi zhizni, s risunkami* (Moscow: Konovalov, 1911), pp. 69–71, 169–173, 181.

who smell of tobacco, wine, or beer. Hats with feathers, or large female headwear in general, are not permissible in theaters.

Those who come late, after the performance has begun, must wait until a propitious moment to take their seats, so as not to disturb those already seated.

Before visiting a gallery or museum, it is useful to read a catalogue or guidebook in order to acquaint oneself with the collections and learn which of the different works of art merit the closest attention.

TABLE MANNERS

In order to behave properly at the table, to eat and drink appropriately and freely, without tension, without making a special effort, and with the grace and movement that marks the well-raised individual, it is essential to eat soup and other hot dishes slowly and quietly, without slurping or emitting sounds such as "gulp! gulp!" with every spoonful.

Unfold your napkin and place it on your knees; do not tuck it into your vest or your collar, as this will indicate slovenliness even before you have even begun to eat.

Cut your food without visible signs of effort. Showing exertion while cutting will make others fear that the plate will shatter.

Drink slowly, with small swallows, considerately, without sounding like a stream or waterfall. And do not raise your elbows.

Never cut bread with a knife, but break it with your fingers. Always hold your fork in your left hand and your knife in your right, and never put your knife in your mouth.

The rules of good table manners prohibit speaking with your mouth full, chomping, chewing with your mouth open, and clicking your tongue; staring at other people's faces or looking at a neighbor's mouth or plate is not advisable.

When making a speech at the table, as when giving a toast to a woman's health, it is necessary to stand. The guests then go individually to the person being honored in order to clink glasses. For subsequent toasts, it is permissible to remain seated and to clink only with those close by; one may respond to those far away by raising one's glass and looking directly at them.

A gentleman must pay as much attention as possible to the woman he is escorting.

When the hostess suggests that everyone get up from the table, offer your arm to the woman next to you and lead her into the drawing room. There, bow to her, and if the gentleman is feeling especially nimble and wants to be extremely courteous, he may draw the woman's fingers toward his lips, and she will raise her hand lightly in assent.

In the smoking room, men may speak freely and easily. If young people want to demonstrate their good breeding, however, they should observe certain customs in regard to their elders.

In society, one may smoke only when one is offered cigars or cigarettes; in the company of women, one must ask their permission first.

When playing cards, the guest displays deficiencies in manners and upbringing when he tries too hard to win. The well-bred person plays with discretion, making it appear that he would prefer for others to win.

LIFESTYLE

The correct lifestyle is the best means for keeping one's health into old age. This is especially important for those who sit hunched over for long hours, such as clerks or seamstresses. It is generally thought that physical labor is healthier than mental, but this supposition is entirely erroneous; most factory labor is terribly harmful for workers.

The correct lifestyle consists of routine and balance, of preserving harmony among all the body's primary functions: sleeping, eating, working, resting, and entertainment. Normally, every workday should be divided into three nearly equal parts: one for sleep, another for work, and the third for rest and eating.

Concerning sleep, either too much or too little has the worst possible effect on the nervous system and quickly exhausts the organism. Sleep must last not less than six and not more than eight hours. This may include a nap either before or after dinner, but one should take recourse to this only in exceptional circumstances. It is very important to be able to sleep in a timely manner: to go to bed at night before midnight and arise sufficiently early in the morning. Evening work, especially if it is mental, shortens the life to the same degree as evening entertainment, which might include going to clubs, bars, and other public places in order to carouse or to play cards.

Eating should normally take no longer than one and one-half to two hours a day; only people who are celebrating should spend a prolonged time at it.

The character of the occupation of the workday depends upon the profession, of which there is extraordinary variety, even among intellectuals, not to mention the purely physical labor of factory and agricultural workers. In general, among non-physical jobs, the longer one sits or stands hunched over, the worse it is for one's health. It is likewise harmful to have to inhale gases. On the whole, the workday should last no longer than eight hours; only those occupations that do not require continuous and monotonous work should be excluded from this rule.

As far as rest and entertainment are concerned, they must correspond to the character of the occupation; they must supplement it. Thus, people who spend most of their day sitting or hunched over—bureaucrats, clerks, students, etc.—must spend their free time in motion, doing some sort of physical activity—gymnastics, bicycling, billiards, playing skittles. Hunting is also a fitting enterprise for those who lead a sedentary life. For the latter, playing cards is the worst, because it often results in hemorrhoids, problems with digestion, or headaches. The opposite is true for people who have very physical occupations; playing cards or reading is a very hygienic activity for them.

Street Types

Illustrations by M. Pikki and K. Richau (1860)

"Physiologies," which depicted the lower-class types populating various corners of Russia's great cities, gained popularity in the 1840s, reaching their peak in the 1860s. Initially a high-literary movement, physiologies quickly found their way into journalism and popular graphics. Below are some illustrations from a middlebrow publication; similar pictures could be found on cheap postcards and in morocco-bound albums.

Street Beggar

Peasant Migrants

A. Golitsynskii, *Ulichnye tipy.* Text by A. Golitsynskii with 20 drawings by M. Pikki (Moscow: tip. V. Got'e, 1860).

Organ Grinder

Hack Cabbie

Servants

Peasant Nanny

Flea Market Rag Lady

Beat Cop

God Save the Tsar

Aleksei Lvov (1833)

Upon hearing "God Save the King" on a visit to England, Tsar Nicholas I commanded a member of his traveling retinue, General Aleksei Lvov, to compose something at least as good for Russia. The general, who had composed church music and operas, some set to words by the poet Vasily Zhukovsky, came up with a composition that delighted the tsar. Nicholas gave immediate orders that the song be adopted by the army, and be performed at all important concerts and theater presentations. It was played at all high state functions, and in many other places, until it was replaced by Grechanin's "Hymn of Free Russia" after the February 1917 revolution.

Боже, царя храни!
Сильный, державный,
Царствуй на славу,
На славу нам.

God save our Noble Tsar!
Great be his glory!
Growing in power
And majesty.

Боже, царя храни!
Сильный, державный,
Царствуй на славу,
На славу нам.

God save our Noble Tsar!
Great be his glory!
Growing in power
And majesty.

Царствуй на страх врагам,
Царь православный;
Боже, царя
Царя храни.

Tsar! May good fortune be
Showered on thee;
God save thee still,
Our Noble Tsar!

Царствуй на страх врагам,
Царь православный;
Боже, царя
Царя храни.

Tsar! May good fortune be
Showered on thee;
God save thee still,
Our Noble Tsar!

Translated by Florence Attenborough, in *The National Anthems of the Allies* (New York: G. Schirmer, 1917). The final stanza is more properly translated: "Rule to the bane of our enemies / Orthodox Tsar; / God, Save our Tsar / The Tsar."

Dark Eyes
Evgeny Grebenka (1843)

V. I. Vavich

GREBENKA (1812–1848), OR JEV-
HEN HREBINKA IN HIS NATIVE
UKRAINIAN, WAS INSTRUMENTAL
TO THE ROMANTIC DISCOVERY OF
HIS HOMELAND'S CULTURE. HIS
OWN POEMS AND STORIES, ALONG
WITH THOSE OF HIS PEER, THE
FREED SERF TARAS SHEVCHENKO,
ESTABLISHED THE CLAIM OF THE
"LITTLE RUSSIANS" TO THEIR OWN
LEGITIMATE CULTURE. THOUGH HIS FAME CAME FROM HIS
UKRAINIAN WORKS, WITH THEIR FOLKLORIC CAST, GREBENKA
ALSO WROTE IN RUSSIAN. HIS STORIES WERE CLOSE TO THE
"PHYSIOLOGICAL" SCHOOL, AS LITERARY WORKS FROM THE
1830S AND 1840S DETAILING THE LIVES OF LOWER-CLASS FOLK
WERE OFTEN CALLED. THEY SHOWED A STRONG SOCIAL CON-
SCIENCE AND STAKED THE LOWER-CLASS'S CLAIM TO SOCIAL AT-
TENTION. HIS RUSSIAN LYRICAL WORKS, SUCH AS THIS SONG,
HAD A UKRAINIAN TINGE TO THEM. IN ITS RENOWN, THIS POEM
OUTGREW HIS ORIGINAL INTENT. IT WAS SET TO MUSIC AND — IN
A SIGN OF THE COMPLEX POLITICS OF ETHNICITY — BECAME A
PART OF THE "GYPSY" REPERTOIRE, WHERE IT HAS RETAINED ITS
IMMENSE POPULARITY FOR A CENTURY AND A HALF. ON THE AC-
COMPANYING CD IT IS PERFORMED BY M. I. VAVICH, OPERETTA
STAR AND ROMANTIC LEAD FROM THE TURN OF THE CENTURY.

From *Russkii romans,* ed. Vadim Rabinovich (Moscow: Pravda, 1987), pp. 429–430.

Очи черные, очи страстные!
Очи жгучие и прекрасные!
Как люблю я вас! Как боюсь я вас!
Знать, увидел вас я в недобрый час!

Ох, недаром вы глубины темней!
Вижу траур в вас по душе моей,
Вижу пламя в вас я победное:
Сожжено на нем сердце бедное.

Но не грустен я, не печален я,
Утешительна мне судьба моя:
Все, что лучшего в жизни Бог дал нам,
В жертву отдал я огневым глазам!

Oh, your dark black eyes, eyes so
  passionate,
Eyes that burn through me, eyes so
  beautiful.
How I love you so, and I fear you so.
When I saw you first, was my fatal hour!

Oh, you're darker than the sea's darkest
  depths!
Within them I see my dear soul's
  demise.
In them I can see the flame of defeat,
It's been burned into my poor suffering
  heart.

But I am not sad, and I feel no grief,
I draw comfort from my own destiny:
Everything fine in life that God gave to
  us,
I have sacrificed to your fiery eyes.

The Great Moscow Fire
N. Sokolov (1850)

THE NAPOLEONIC WARS, WHICH ENDED IN VICTORY, GLORY, AND
A SURGE OF PATRIOTISM FOR RUSSIANS OF ALL CLASSES, LEFT A
DEEP IMPRINT IN POPULAR CULTURE. THIS SONG WAS WRITTEN
BY A MINOR POET LONG AFTER THE FACT, YET IT GAINED RAPID
POPULARITY AND WAS SUNG IN MANY VERSIONS FOR THE NEXT
SEVENTY YEARS. THE AUTHOR'S NAME HAD BEEN LOST AND THE
LYRICS HAD BEEN POLISHED BY THE TIME THEY REACHED THE
REPERTOIRE OF THE FAMED SINGER NADEZHDA PLEVITSKAIA IN
THE 1900S. ALREADY HUGELY FAMOUS, SHE BECAME EVEN MORE
SO WITH THIS SONG. IT REPEATS TRADITIONAL MOTIFS OF POPU-
LAR CULTURE, MOST CURIOUSLY A FASCINATION WITH NAPO-

From *Russkii romans,* ed. Vadim Rabinovich (Moscow: Pravda, 1987), pp. 429–430.

Шумел, гремел пожар московский,	Moscow burned with noise and thunder,
Дым расстилался по реке.	Fire spread along the river bank.
А на стенах высот кремлёвских	Atop a mighty Kremlin tower,
Стоял он в сером сюртуке.	He stood in his uniform of gray.
И призадумался великий,	The great man stood in contemplation,
Скрестивши руки на груди.	And crossed his hands upon his chest.
Он видел огненное море,	He saw below a sea of fire,
Он видел гибель впереди.	And saw death awaiting him ahead.
И, притаив свои мечтанья,	And, keeping all his dreams inside him,
Свой взор на пламя устремил	He turned his gaze toward the flames,
И тихим голосом сознанья	Whispering in recognition,
Он сам с собою говорил:	He softly uttered to himself:
«Зачем я шел к тебе, Россия,	"Why did I come to take you, Russia,
Европу всю держа в руках?	When Europe was already mine?
Теперь с поникшей головою	And now I stand here with my head
Стою на крепостных стенах.	bowed,
	High up here on the fortress walls.
«Войска все, созданные мною,	"All the soldiers I have summoned
Погибнут здесь среди снегов,	Will die here, buried in the snow,
В полях истлеют наши кости	Our bones will bleach white in the
Без погребенья, без гробов».	fields,
	Without a coffin or a grave.
Судьба играет человеком,	"Man is but the plaything of his Fate,
Она изменчива всегда,	And she is fickle to the end,
То вознесет его высоко,	Raising him unto his zenith,
То бросит в бездну без стыда!	Then casting him down without shame."

From *Russkii romans,* ed. Vadim Rabinovich (Moscow: Pravda, 1987), pp. 450–452.

Elegy (Khas-Bulat)

Aleksandr Ammosov and O. Kh. Agrenova–Slavianskaia (1858)

KHAZ-BULAT (FLASHING SWORD), A CHECHEN TRIBESMAN, EM-
BODIED RUSSIANS' LONG IMPERIAL ADVENTURE AND THEIR FAS-
CINATION WITH EASTERN PEOPLES. TRIBES ON THE PERIPHERY
OF THE EXPANDING EMPIRE PROVIDED RUSSIAN CULTURE WITH
THE COLOR THAT OTHER IMPERIAL CULTURES FOUND IN THE NA-
TIVES OF AFRICA, ASIA, AND AMERICA. EXOTIC WORDS SPICED
THE LITERATURE, AND PASSIONATE TRYSTS FILLED THE FANTA-
SIES OF RUSSIAN NOBLEMEN FROM PUSHKIN TO TOLSTOI. FOR-
BIDDEN IN PROPER SOCIETY, THESE WILD THINGS PROVIDED A
MARGIN IN WHICH THE VALUES AND IDENTITY OF RUSSIAN SOCI-
ETY COULD BE TESTED. IN THIS SONG, WHERE A PRINCE CON-
FRONTS AND IS CONFOUNDED BY CHECHEN MORES, THE ARISTO-
CRATIC ADVENTURE IS ASSIMILATED BY POPULAR CULTURE.

«Хас-Булат удалой!
Бедна сакля твоя;
Золотою казной
Я осыплю тебя.

Саклю пышно твою
Разукрашу кругом,
Стены в ней обобью
Я персидским ковром.

Галуном твой бешмет
Разошью по краям
И тебе пистолет
Мой заветный отдам.

Дам старее тебя
Тебе шашку с клеймом,
Дам лихого коня
С кабардинским тавром.

"Khas-Bulat, bold and brave!
How your *saklya*[1] is poor.
I will shower you with
All the gold in my vaults.

I will furnish your hut
In full luxury.
I will hang on its walls
A rich Persian rug.

Finest lace will be sewn
To your old *beshmet*[2] hems,
And I'll make you a gift
Of my favorite gun.

And my saber is yours,
It is older than you,
And my spirited steed,
Kabardinian-bred.

From *Russkii romans,* ed. Vadim Rabinovich (Moscow: Pravda, 1987), pp. 450–452.
1. Caucasian mountain hut.
2. A quilted native coat.

Дам винтовку мою,
Дам кинжал Базалай,—
Лишь за это свою
Ты жену мне отдай.

Ты уж стар, ты уж сед,
Ей с тобою не житье,
На заре юных лет
Ты погубишь ее.

Тяжело без любви
Ей тебе отвечать
И морщины твои
Не любя целовать.

Под чинарой густой
Мы сидели вдвоем,
Месяц плыл золотой,
Все молчало кругом.

И играла река
Перекатной волной,
И скользила рука
По груди молодой.

Мне она отдалась
До последнего дня
И аллахом клялась,
Что не любит тебя!»

Крепко шашки сжимал
Хас-Булат рукоять
И, схватясь за кинжал,
Стал ему отвечать:

«Князь! рассказ длинный твой
Ты напрасно мне рек,
Я с женой молодой
Вас вчера подстерег.

Береги, князь, казну
И владей ею сам,
За неверность жену
Тебе даром отдам.

Ты невестой своей
Полюбуйся поди,—
Она в сакле моей
Спит с кинжалом в груди.

Here's my rifle, it's yours,
And my Bazalai knife.
For all that, I but ask
That you give me your wife.

You are old, you are gray,
With you she has no life,
At the dawn of her youth
You are ruining her.

It is hard without love
To respond to your kiss,
And your old wrinkled brow
She will kiss but not love.

In the plane tree's deep shade,
We two sat all alone,
Moonshine shone gold above,
Silence reigned all around.

In the river below,
Water played in a wave,
And a hand slipped across
Her young breast.

She surrendered to me
Till the end of her days,
And to Allah she swore
That she doesn't love you!"

Khas-Bulat firmly gripped
The hilt of his sword,
As he reached for his knife,
He began his response:

"Prince! It has been all in vain
That you told your long tale,
As you met with my wife
I was lying in wait.

You can keep your vaults closed
And hold on to your wealth,
For her faithlessness you
Can have my wife for free.

You can go feast your eyes
On your newlywed bride,
She's asleep in my hut
With my knife in her breast.

Я глаза ей закрыл,
Утопая в слезах,
Поцелуй мой застыл
У нее на губах».

Голос смолк старика,
Дремлет берег крутой,
И играет река
Перекатной волной.

I have dimmed her eyes' light
As I drowned in my tears.
And my kiss has grown cold,
As it lay on her lips."

The old man ceased to speak
As the river bank slept.
In the river below,
Water played in a wave.

Part III

Great Reforms
and the Expansion
of Civic Space,
1861–1881

The "Tsar Liberator," Alexander II, embarked upon a series of reforms in the 1860s and 1870s designed to turn Russia into a modern state capable of competing as a Great Power. The peasants were liberated; municipal reforms increased middle-class participation in government; economic reforms sparked an industrial boom. Although neither Alexander II nor his two successors could ever synthesize economic industrialization with political autocracy, the social changes wrought by the reforms—which increased education as they relaxed censorship—stimulated demands for new forms of entertainment. The pivotal imperial event of the era was the war against the Ottoman Empire in 1877, a war won on the battlefield but then lost on the negotiating tables of the Congress of Berlin. The repercussions of the reforms were played out in various aspects of this war: fought by independent conscripts, reported via new lines of communication, and inflamed by Pan-Slavic public opinion, the war brought ordinary Russians into the outside world as never before, and sparked a revolution in newspaper reading. Russia's first true war correspondents journeyed to the front and reported back in a fact-laden style new to journalism that helped readers imagine themselves at the scene. Factual objectivity has never prevented journalists from taking sides, though, and Russians from all walks of life sympathized intensely with their Serbian and Bulgarian brothers, taking to heart the old Slavophile myth of Slavic fraternity.

Other protagonists of newspaper dramas included Cossacks and stage stars, pickpockets and murderers. Readers discussed the news avidly; they retold it, embellished it, even created anecdotes around it. New types of mass-oriented entertainments, inspired by a new readership, new production technologies, and new modes of communication and transport, answered the demand for current news and fresh gossip. Modern though they were, the new media often perpetuated attitudes from older entertainments, particularly the fairground *balagan* theaters and Petrushka puppet booths. The world they recorded was much broader, and the events they reported more recent, yet they reflected audience confusion about modernity and the world outside Russia's borders. Curiosity about foreign lands abided alongside derisive images of Turks and Germans, who served as generic representatives of eastern and western nations, respectively. Newspapers were instrumental not only in informing the Russian public about the great outside world, but in fanning a virulent anti-Semitism, which assumed "modern" forms as a secondary result of the war coverage.

Other aspects of the modern world also evoked ambivalence. A fascination with female sexuality did not soften the harsh tone in which willful women were described (unless they were exotic gypsies); and the allure of city life did not quell the fears it aroused. The pathologies of urban life and modern individuality permeating common experience caused the educated public great anxiety. They saw unenlightened folk swarming into urban territory they had once considered "theirs." Their concern created a voracious audience for Vsevolod Krestovsky's best-selling novel *The Slums of Petersburg*, which sketched a panorama of common Petersburg for educated readers throughout the empire. Featuring beggars, con artists, child prostitutes and prisoners, and enough fallen members of high society to act as stand-in observers for educated readers, the novel exposed eyesores that had festered for decades.

Some intellectuals took pains to direct the activities of the lower classes as they were incorporated into civil society (*obshchestvo*). Often they were driven by the belief that common folk could not cope with the modern world: they would be either swamped by secular sin or overwhelmed by modernity. They needed enlightenment: the light of God, as provided by the church; the light of order, as provided by the army and state; or the light of reason, as provided by intellectuals. Each of these estates generated materials intended to lead the "dark" people into the promised future. The church, as always, published saints' lives, religious calendars, and other materials; the army introduced the very successful *Readings for Soldiers* series. This enterprise, exemplified here by *A Flask of Hooch,* continued for decades, and proved that didactic readings could find a popular audience.

The attempts of educated society, moving from right to left across the political spectrum, to dictate common tastes met with little success. Ambivalence about the people, who needed education but conspired to avoid it, clouded their agendas. By the end of the 1860s, intellectuals were frustrated by their alienation from the people. A new generation, the *narodniki* (populists), decided to go directly to the people. Dressing as peasants, they ventured to villages and factory towns to meet, listen to, and educate people about their plight and the means to alleviate it. They distributed literature written in an intentionally folkish style and language. Stories such as "Where Is It Better?" presented Russia's misfortunes in stark, if allegoric, terms, and blamed them on the tsar himself. Later political activists such as the young Vladimir Lenin would concentrate on more urban sectors of the lower class, who they anticipated would be politicized by circumstances to the point of demanding revolutionary change.

Balagan Advertisements
The Malafeev Theater (1883)

BALAGANY WERE TEMPORARY THEATERS BUILT FOR THE YULETIDE AND LENTEN FESTIVALS. PRICES WERE LOW, PERFORMANCES FAST BUT PROFICIENT; POTENTIAL AUDIENCES, WHO CAME FROM THE LOWER TO MIDDLE CLASSES, WERE REGALED BY A BARKER (PICTURED HERE)—CALLED "GRANDPA" IN THE LOCAL SLANG. HE STOOD ON THE BALCONY AND SHOUTED RHYMES, WHOSE CONTENT VARIED ACCORDING TO HOW CLOSE THE POLICE WERE. BALAGANY HAD A DISTINCT STYLE STRESSING COLOR AND MOVEMENT; AND SKILLFUL STAGECRAFT PACKED PLENTY OF ACTION INTO THE FIFTEEN TO THIRTY MINUTES ALLOTTED FOR EACH PERFORMANCE.

BELOW ARE TWO ADVERTISEMENTS FOR THE MALAFEEV THEATER, ERECTED IN THE "FIRST ROW" OF PETERSBURG'S ADMIRALTY SQUARE. THE FIRST IS A CLASSIC BARKER'S CHANT, THE SECOND A NEW-STYLE FLYER. MALAFEEV, RARE AMONG BALAGAN OWNERS, WAS A RUSSIAN, AND PLACEMENT IN THE FIRST OF FOUR ROWS WAS TESTAMENT TO THE HIGH QUALITY AND PRICE OF HIS PRODUCTIONS. TROUPE MEMBERS WORE MANY HATS: MALAFEEV WAS OWNER, DIRECTOR, AND ANYTHING ELSE NEEDED FOR THE SHOW; THE PLAYWRIGHT, N. MUSHINSKY, ALSO WROTE AD COPY. IN FACT, THIS AD TAKES A SWIPE AT CRITICS OF ANOTHER OF HIS PLAYS, WHICH WAS RUNNING NEXT DOOR AT THE BERG THEATER. WHATEVER CRITICS FELT, THIS PLAY FIT AUDIENCE TASTES. TAKEN FROM THE PRIMARY CHRONICLES, IT CATERED TO POPULAR PATRIOTISM THAT SAW THE CONTEMPORARY TURKISH WAR AS A RIGHTFUL CAMPAIGN FOR THE RUSSIAN "TSARGRAD."

BARKER'S CHANT*

Oh, my wife is a pretty one. She has ruddy cheeks, her snot leaks. Along Nevsky she rides, and mud flies to the sides.

Her name is Sophie, wasted three years on the stove loafing. When I took her down, she bowed to the ground, and then fell in pieces. What could I do! I took some bast, sewed her fast, fit to last for three years.

I sent her to market, to buy a brisket, she got a whole basket, but only gristle. There the dogcatchers killed her, and irked me till my tears flowed, though back I wouldn't go. The lice dripped from her head, she fought with three hens, until I broke it up.

Off I went to Haymarket Square, to spend a pence on her pair, and a cat to boot. The pence was for the cat, the wife was thrown in for free, God forbid she should eat.

FLYER FOR THEATER NO. 2, V. MALAFEEV**

A big dramatic picture from Russian history, with chorus and ballet, in eight scenes.

"Oleg the Seer, Prince of Kiev, by the walls of Tsargrad"[1]

The play is about a famous hero of our Russian history, Oleg the Seer, who was proclaimed prince of Kiev, but was unaccustomed to inactivity from his youth and wished to immortalize his name in the memory of his descendants by some unusual deed. He conceived the notion of attacking Tsargrad (the present Constantinople), which was a Greek city in that era, and was an impregnable fortress. The mighty Oleg decided to conquer it. Marrying his nephew Igor to the princess Olga, he left him behind to rule Kiev and set sail along the Dniepr for Tsargrad in his barques,[2] directing the foot soldiers and cavalry along the riverbank. During the march he met a sorcerer in the woods, who foretold complete victory, which inspired the enterprising Oleg even more. When the Greek tsars discovered that Oleg was advancing with his troops, they gave orders to block the aquatic route through the Bosporus. They built an underwater fortress of iron chains so that Oleg's barques could not pass through to the bay, and dispatched an embassy to inform him, so that he might not expend himself in vain and would turn back. "You Greeks are cunning, but you won't outsmart the Russians!" Oleg told the embassy, and immedi-

---

*From A. Kel'siev, "Peterburgskie balagannye pribautki, zapisannye V. I. Kel'sievym," *Trudy etnograficheskogo obshchestva liubitelei estestvoznaniia, antropologii i etnografii*, IX. *Sbornik svedenii dlia izucheniia byta krest'ianskogo naseleniia Rossii (obychnoe pravo, obriady, verovaniia i pr.)* (Moscow, 1889), pp. 114–115.

**Blin. *Maslianichnyi balagurnyi listok* (St. Petersburg: N. Mushinskii, 1883), p. 3.

1. Russian tsars, particularly Catherine the Great, had at various times conceived a claim to Constantinople—Istanbul. The name Tsargrad, which dated back to Kievan days when the "caesar" lived there, invoked this claim implicitly.

2. The plot for this spectacle was drawn from an incident in the eleventh-century Primary Chronicle, which depicted a successful incursion of Russian forces into Byzantine territory.

ately ordered that the barques be dragged onshore, their rudders and oars be removed, and wheels be attached in their place. "Let us erect masts, raise the sails, and take our barques by land to Tsargrad!" The embassy communicated all they had heard to their tsars, who, knowing of his valor, believed it all, and lost spirit. They were saved from peril by the princess Helena, daughter of the Greek Tsar Leo; she volunteered to go with the embassy to Oleg's camp and ask him personally to accept the ransom and to return home without harming Tsargrad. Oleg was astonished, seeing the maiden among the emissaries. With tears in her eyes, the princess begged him to have mercy on the city. "Mighty Oleg, if you want to conquer Tsargrad, then enter it without shedding blood; enter not as a destroyer but as a friend, as a brother to Tsar Leo! Is it not true that all tsars are brothers to each other?!" she said to him. Oleg was deeply touched by the tears and exhortations of the Greek princess, and immediately promised to fulfill her request. The joyful princess was sent back to her father with great honor, for the man whom no power and no weapon could subdue had been subdued by her tender words and tears. In the finale of the play, Oleg and his army approach the city, where the gates are thrown open to him and he is met with great honor by the Greek tsars, with whom he concludes a peace treaty that will last for centuries. To memorialize his conquest of Tsargrad, he orders his shield attached to the city gates. The splendid decorations and the historical accuracy of the weapons and costumes will give the play the necessary color that every properly staged Russian popular play must have. As regards the playwrighting, its merits or defects, I have no right to say anything about myself. If critics see fit to admonish me, so be it! For it is far more pleasant to hear a sensible rebuke than unearned praise.

The Slums of Petersburg: A Book about the Well-Fed and the Hungry
Vsevolod Krestovsky (1864)

KRESTOVSKY (1840–1895) ENJOYED A REPUTATION THAT CIRCU-
LATED ALMOST AS WIDELY AS THAT OF HIS CONTEMPORARIES
DOSTOEVSKY AND TOLSTOI IN THE ESTIMATION OF THE RUSSIAN
READING PUBLIC. HIS BEST-SELLING NOVEL *THE SLUMS OF PE-
TERSBURG* INTRODUCED THEM TO THE UNDERBELLY OF RUSSIA'S
CITIES. A RADICAL IN HIS YOUTH, KRESTOVSKY WAS ON THE WAY

V. V. Krestovskii, *Peterburgskie trushchoby (kniga o sytykh i golodnykh)* (St. Petersburg: Khudozhestvennaia literatura, 1993), 1:235–244.

TO BECOMING AN ARDENT CONSERVATIVE WHEN HE WROTE THIS
NOVEL. HE INTERSPERSED SYMPATHETIC DESCRIPTIONS OF THE
POOR WITH PICTURES OF PATHOLOGY AND DEBASEMENT THAT
DROVE PUBLIC DEBATE FOR A DECADE. CHILD PROSTITUTES,
HEREDITARY THIEVES, CHILDREN RENTED OUT AS BEGGING
PROPS — SUCH HORRORS RIVALED THOSE THAT FRENCH READERS
HAD DISCOVERED WITH HUGO AND SUE, AND ENGLISH READERS
WITH DICKENS. IN GRAPHIC DETAIL, KRESTOVSKY DEPICTED THE
BASEMENTS AND PRISONS OF PETERSBURG, IN PARTICULAR OF
THE HAYMARKET (DESCRIBED IN THIS EXCERPT), WHERE THE
POOR AND MIGRANT POPULATIONS CONGREGATED. THE NOVEL
WAS TAKEN MORE AS ETHNOGRAPHY THAN AS FICTION. IT AC-
QUAINTED READERS WITH THE RICH CULTURE AND SLANG OF
CRIMINALS, AND WITH THE FLOPHOUSES AND BASEMENT SNACK
COUNTERS THAT WERE THEIR MEETING SPOTS. KRESTOVSKY'S
FAME DID NOT GUARANTEE SUCCESS FOR HIS LATER WRITINGS,
BUT HE WAS ABLE TO SUPPLEMENT HIS INCOME WITH TOURS OF
THE HAYMARKET FOR RUSSIANS WHO WISHED TO WITNESS THIS
EXOTIC SEGMENT OF NATIONAL LIFE.

It was getting to be nine o'clock.

An armed sentry paced the guardhouse platform, wrapped up in his mantle.
Across the street a motley crowd of beggars stood soaked and shivering on the portico of Our Savior of the Haymarket.[1] The church service was just ending. A respectable number of beggars had gathered that day: tomorrow would be the Day of the
Dead, which meant that vespers this evening would attract an abundance of merchants and other worshippers who wished to dole out generous alms in memory of
their parents and kin.[2]

Here stood a group of bareheaded, barefooted boys and girls, ages five to twelve,
dressed in rags, with rolled-up sleeves inside which they warmed their numb
hands—or rather hand, since while the left was being warmed, the right would be

---

1. The Church of the Assumption of the Holy Mother of God on Haymarket Square, nicknamed Our
Savior of the Haymarket (Spas na Sennoi), was built in 1826 as one of the wealthiest churches in Petersburg. But its location on the Haymarket made it the site of begging, and not rarely of theft.

2. *Roditel'skaia subbota,* a day of remembrance for the dead at the end of October.

stretched out for alms. Drops fell along their faces, either tears from their eyes or extraneous drops from the nose. The way these people stood on the cold stone porch was inhuman, for while one foot was performing its natural function, the other, racked by convulsive shivers, tried to warm itself in the loosely hanging rags. Barely would a worshipper exit the church when a throng of little beggars would mob him. The pack, ignoring the painful jabs and kicks of the adult beggars, would surround him in front and behind, tugging at his clothes and stretching up their little blue hands, pleading for "a kopeck for the love of Christ" in a tiresome, squeaky monotone. The throng would block his path, accompanying him from the portico stairs for as much as twenty steps, persecuting their victim in the vain hope of a kopeck's alms. A kopeck came their way only rarely, and the whole throng raced back to the portico to occupy the most advantageous spots in expectation of new worshippers. This was the most pitiful of all the species of the beggars' fraternity. None of them had done time in a house of corrections, from which minor beggars are released into the custody of people who have contracts with the grown-up beggars who exploit them. These little boys and girls, doomed from the crib, are the future victims of vice and crime. They are candidates for prison and Siberia, or for the spoils of debauchery, which reaches them very early, provided that death does not get them first. It happens that a beggar girl of the dark Haymarket slums, barely twelve years old, sometimes even younger, starts giving herself up to vice for the most insignificant sums.

The grown-up beggars conducted themselves a bit more decorously than the minors. If a worshipper passes by without offering anything, the adults greet him with naught but an outstretched hand and a head bowed in supplication. But just let him show an inclination to perform the rite of Christian charity, and they cluster round the benevolent giver. With loud entreaties, dozens of wrinkled, dirty hands stretch greedily toward him through gaps and cracks in the throng, wherever a set of dexterous fingers can squeeze through. After such a maneuver on the part of the beggars' fraternity, a benevolent giver often arrives home to discover his handkerchief, wallet, or pocketwatch missing. These mob scenes happen primarily at vespers or midnight matins, when the early murk of the winter evening conceals the beggars' fraternity from the sharp eye of the beat cop, who is wont to pack them off to the clink. True poverty is rarely found among the yard and portico cadgers (that is, cadgers who stand on church porticoes[3]). True poverty and indigence are first and foremost virtuous, shy, and timid; they keep to themselves, and if they approach passersby with an entreaty, it rings with physiological hunger and real need.

First among the adult beggars stood the older women. They had the same sort of clothing as the children, the same rags sewn together at random, the same scraps falling apart at the seams, the same standard begging chant, memorized like a song. They held babies bundled up in rags; whoever lacked her own could always rent

----

3. *Pritvornye:* Krestovsky's parenthetical explanation stresses the fact that the Russian word also means "dissemblers."

one. There stood two hideous, noseless hags, unspared by vile disease but spared by death, which allowed them to cross the age barrier that divides the vice trade from the begging trade in the Haymarket. They had not managed to rent a baby, and thus each had wrapped a log in rags and was soothing it like a baby. Nobody could see in the dark, and besides, who would take a close look at what the old women were holding?

The spots farthest back, on the portico itself, had been won by the beggars' aristocracy, who always had some mark of distinction, usually a deformity. There, huddling and shivering in the darkest, gloomiest corner, was an emaciated old woman with a long pointed nose, and sunken eyes that were scouting their quarry; a tuft of black and gray hair poked out from under the damp kerchief on her forehead and gave an even more disheveled look to an already disheveled physiognomy. She also had something muffled up in rags, but it was not a child or a log—it was a deformed old idiot dwarf woman, whom she was holding like a baby to attract people's compassion. The idiot woman was tiny and terribly emaciated. The tangled gray clumps of her hair obscured her dull, staring eyes. Frightened, fitful grimaces accompanied the idiot's every glance, and whenever she found a peaceful moment, she sucked on the fringe of her nanny's kerchief, along with a tuft of her own hair, or she would suck with gusto on a lump of plaster she had knocked loose from the damp, clammy wall. The old beggar lady with her odd bundle feared being visible at all times; she hid in the dark corner away from the stares of people and, at times, of the police. But her hiding made her even more vigilant for quarry. The moment a benevolent giver would appear in the portals, the beggar woman and idiot would leap into the crowd of beggars with the speed and agility of a wild cat and, clawing their way forward, stretch out an emaciated, withered hand. No sooner would the wrinkled hand sense a kopeck's charity on the shriveled skin of its palm than the hag would return with equal haste to the darkness of her customary place, from which she pounced as greedily as a spider from its web.

By the inner doors of the church stood not a man, but the likeness of a man, or else the hint of a human organism. He presented himself joylessly to the gaze as a deformed, hunchbacked, legless being, holding himself on wooden stocks attached to what had been his haunches, and were now stumps cut off above the knees. He moved with the help of his arms, which he used instead of his hands. His figure bore an extraordinary likeness to a hedgehog or porcupine, and in his small, deeply recessed eyes, which the creature moved from side to side, shone something mouse-like. "Lord Jesus Christ, Our Lady of Mercy," he muttered mindlessly, with an odd whistle in his falsetto voice, and his right hand bobbed with unusual quickness, as if rushing to trace as many signs of the cross as it could. "For the love of Christ, alms for Old Man Kasian," he chanted in a quivering voice, struggling to extend his hand above the others. As a result of his advantageous position, the greater part of the alms fell in Old Man Kasian's palm before the others. Old Man Kasian would never have occupied the best begging spot if he had not had powerful and close support. That support appeared in the form of his neighbor and comrade, who was known as Foma the Blessed. A red-haired stocky man about thirty-five years old, of above average height, broad-shouldered and thickset he offered such a pitiful being as Old Man Kasian a reliable and imposing bulwark. Fomushka[4] never washed or cut his hair. A brownish velvet skullcap like a monk's covered part of his tangled mane of wiry red hair. His puffy, meaty cheeks and his swollen, cranberry red nose were the outstanding features of his goggle-eyed, piggish physiognomy; his visage was decorated by a reddish bristle instead of whiskers and by untidy tufts of beard, which grew as isolated clumps in various directions. The blessed one used a steel hoop in place of a belt to gird the waist of his black robe, which was also meant to resemble a monk's cossack. The hem of his robe, hanging in tattered clumps, was covered with a layer of street grime that, since it was never washed off, had matted into several layers, lumps, and incrustations. Fomushka and his clothes permeated the air for three paces around with an intolerable stench. But the stench and grime gave him particular pleasure, and his admirers put it all down to zealotry and asceticism. Foma stood by himself on his own spot, spry and independent, scratching his head every minute, and breathing so heavily through his nose that it was audible to the entire portico. The whole brotherhood respected his imposing fist, which was truly unpleasant to meet in an isolated and deserted place.

A wrynecked woman across from the hedgehog Kasian offered a complete contrast to Foma the Blessed, a woman of more than forty years with pious humility etched on her yellowed face. A large black scarf cascaded from her head, and the rest of her clothing, distinguished by its neatness, was something between a nun's costume and the semi-secular clothing of the lay women pilgrims who wander from cloister to cloister. Like Fomushka the Blessed, whose patronage she enjoyed no less than Old Man Kasian, this personage enjoyed particular authority and was known by the name of Makrida the Pilgrim. She stood distinct from the rest of the brotherhood, and could not truly be reckoned part of them. Makrida stood with a book—it seemed that her job was collecting voluntary contributions for the construction of a temple.[5] She said it had something to do with a dream vision. Makrida the Pilgrim worked together with Fomushka the Blessed and Old Man Kasian as a family, pursuing a common goal. . . .

The service was over; people streamed from the church.

A pious upholder of the law walked out of the church, and a crowd of beggar children, spotting the approach of their enemy from afar, scattered to dark corners in the vicinity of the church before he reached them. Meanwhile the adult beggars pretended that they were not beggars, but were just leaving the church. The upholder of the law slipped into the murk, and the porch assembly took up their former posts.

A consumptive merchant came out and put a grosh (a penny) into the hand of Old Man Kasian.

---

4. Fomushka is a diminutive form of Foma. See the Note on Transliteration for an explanation of diminutives.

5. One of the most common devices of Russian beggars was to collect money for the reconstruction of a local church.

"Don't be a cheapskate." Fomushka poked him in the head with his finger and stretched out his broad paw to the almsgiver. Makrida also stretched her hand out with a book, on the cover of which lay several coppers, "for *blezir*."* At that moment a tall, gaunt old man in a robe, taking advantage of the crush around the giver, inconspicuously slipped a grosh from Makrida's book and, sticking it in his pocket with spasmodic rapidity, stretched out his hand from under the elbows of a beggar in hopes that the charitable merchant would mistake the two separate hands as the hands of two people, and would put a coin in each. The emaciated old man could occasionally get away with the trick, but it also drew the endless scolding and mockery of the beggars. When Fomushka the Blessed turned up behind the merchant, his heavy paw gave the old man a light whack in the back of the head.

"What are you doing, you old devil? Playing two-handed again?**" he wheezed to him in a whisper. The old man just snapped, bared his teeth, blinked rapidly from fury, and worked his way to a spot far from the blessed man.

Out came a young merchant woman who loved to distribute alms, and the same process was repeated on the portico. The old man, standing apart from Fomushka, played two-handed again.

Another merchant woman, chubby, elderly, drowsy, with a piously dull-witted expression of cowed apathy on her face glistening with sweat, came out and gave Makrida a friendly greeting, as if they were friends: "Hello, Makridushka; hello, darling!" she said in a half-plaintive singsong. "Come tomorrow night for some *bliny*, to remember our ancestors. Don't say no! And make sure to have the blessed one come too."

At the appearance of this person, a stupid and unthinking smile instantly crossed Fomushka's face, a sign that he was now playing the role of the holy fool.[6]

"Stepanida, servant of the Lord!" he muttered, crossing himself. "The angels rejoice, the church bells of Moscow ring out. Bring out the oaken tables, bake the *kulyebyaka* pies and the *bliny:* I will praise them to the heavens, Stepanida, servant of the Lord."

"Give praise, Fomushka; give praise, blessed one!" the low-browed fat woman pleaded in tears. She had heard only the sound of the holy fool's last phrase, without catching the meaning, and placed a five-kopeck piece in his hand.

Fomushka, encouraged, finished his thoughts in a singsong. "I will give praise, oh mother mine, I will give praise; may all the saints rest in peace, may there be blessed Easter eggs with their crowns of red, and may a kopeck for Fomushka rattle in each, so that Foma can go rap-rap with his little hammer."

When he spoke the phrase about resting in peace and the little hammer, the fat woman's expression turned to senseless, sheep-like terror. Noticing it, Makrida gave her friend Fomushka an elbow in the side and crooked her eyebrows at him.

"Do not grieve, servant, do not grieve!" the blessed man muttered again. "Go

---

*In thieves' argot, *blezir* means "appearance's sake."

**Dvurushnichat' means to put out two hands at once.

6. The tradition of considering some manifestations of insanity to be signs of holiness persisted into the nineteenth century in Russia.

thou to thy home in peace; thy husband lies in drunkenness, and chances are he will beat you. But thou, servant of the lord Stepanida, shall live a century."

Stepanida, servant of the lord, calmed down and heaved a sigh.

"You see all, my dear, and speak through the will of God," she spoke in a minor key. "You are right, he surely will beat me, most likely because the liquor has turned his head and he can't find the samovar. Oh, tut-tut! What a life we have!"

"The blessed one, mother, is seeing the divine light!" Makrida explained to her piously. "Darkness too can come upon him, and then he lies as if dead. That means that his soul is talking with God."

"For the love of God, give a kopeck to Old Man Kasian," interrupted the legless man's quivering tenor.

The merchant's wife, repeating the invitation for the *bliny*, distinguished Makrida and Kasian with her coins and continued her portly procession, with the same delegation from the brotherhood. The emaciated old man, keeping a sharp eye on Fomushka, stuck his long hands out from behind someone's back.

Almost everyone had left the church when a meaty older man of medium height, apparently a retired soldier, stepped out on the portico in a gray uniform coat and a cockaded cap of military cut. A sense of ambition and self-satisfaction animated the old man's figure, an unusual combination that was revealed in his piggish eyes and dyed corkscrew mustache.

"Osip Zakharych, my deepest bow!" he turned unexpectedly to the emaciated old man. "What have you been doing, dear sir?"

"Well, see . . . I'm suffering . . . piles . . . ," the old man uttered in a muffled, witless, sickened tone, visibly confused by the unexpected and unwanted encounter. "Stepped out for a prayer," he continued, trying to avert his eyes in an unspecified direction. "Majesty—the temple . . . to tell the truth . . ."

"But why are you wearing such light clothes? And when you're sick? You're not taking care of yourself," the retired army man scolded him, shaking his head with concern.

The old man threw a glance at the hem of his robe and became completely confused.

"I . . . it's . . . nothing . . . worry thee not, it is said . . . hurrying to the prayer vigil . . . no time . . ."

"Right! He was in a hurry!" some of the old beggar women denounced him in a scolding voice, babbling all at once. "Go on, he put it on on purpose!"

"Some moneybags; it's like he don't have no good clothes."

"Miser, that's what he is."

"In a hurry! And here he has the time to play two-hands with our folks—he's just taking bread away from the orphans!"

"Why not go and count up his wealth! His trunks are bursting. And that's all been taken from orphans too!"

"What can you say? King Midas himself!"

As the stream of denunciations began, the old man gave the retired army man a hurried bow and, trying not to look at anyone, ran down the steps to the square.

"What's this, ladies? Why are you standing around? Why don't you take your babies home? They're all frozen stiff—march home! Lively now!" said the self-satisfied retired military man, turning with a peremptory voice to two women carrying babies.

"Petr Kuzmich! Mister Spitz! Our gracious major!" the women begged in pleading voices. "Please consider our situations; let us keep the babies till tomorrow! After the mass—for love of Christ—we'll bring them."

"Enough, enough! No more talk! This is nonsense, it can't be done!" Mister Spitz cut them off curtly.

"Why can't it be done? We never do your renting wrong, we always respect it . . ."

"Take them home, I said!" the major interrupted, tapping his foot imperiously. "You can give them to the lady, my wife, and tell her to feed them. You unfeeling beasts! You rely on us to feed the babies, or else you'd starve them yourself!"

"We'd only keep them till early service tomorrow, and then we could stand through the late service. The handouts are real skimpy nowadays: you can barely get a coin even if you stand for the whole mass."

"You're lying, you old hags! Tomorrow is the Day of the Dead; there'll be plenty of handouts, so the rent will be forty kopecks per child, whoever wants one," Major Spitz announced decisively to everyone within earshot.

"Why so much? That's way too expensive! It's always fifteen, and even twenty was as much as you took, and now just look! Forty!" the dissatisfied beggar women objected.

"So stand without a baby if you want; I don't care," concluded the major, indicating his intention to leave.

"Why, sire, are you being so obstinate with your little babies?" remarked a crooked-eyed and bent-armed old slobberer. "Your goods don't even fit our girls very well. Your tykes have spotless little faces, and the ones we have to hold have their faces eaten up by ulcers. For an ulcer-face on the Day of the Dead you can get thirty-five kopecks, and yours ain't worth more than twenty-five!" The major answered the slobberer with naught but a squinting glance of lofty disdain.

"Mavra can't get her baby to bawl very loud," explained one of the women interested in the matter.

"So, what of it?!" objected the dissatisfied major. "Give the little bastard a pinch, real light, or else give a little prick with a pin—then it'll cry for you all you want."

"So then take twenty-five apiece, Petr Kuzmich!" the women pleaded.

"Thirty-five kopecks, not one kopeck less!" the major determined.

"We'll add a bit, just let us have them—you understand, it's a matter of business, between friends. How 'bout thirty with a half-bottle thrown in?"

The major wavered. The vodka was enticing.

"Well, okay, you devils! You really are devils!" agreed Petr Kuzmich, waving his hand. "I'll be losing money on the deal. Cough it up for the vodka and take the kids to the lady. Tell her I'll be there soon—I met a friend, and stopped by for a bit of tea."

The drummer at the sentry post beat out the signal for the evening watch. The portico crowd came and wandered off in various directions, mostly toward the tavern of the Poltoratsky building and the grubby cellars of the Haymarket.

How the Russian Gave It Hot
to a German
(1869)

RUSSIAN POPULAR NATIONALISM, WHICH TOOK NEW FORMS IN
POST-EMANCIPATION DECADES, WAS VERY DIFFERENT FROM THE
UPPER-CLASS IDENTITY FORMED IN OPPOSITION TO THE CUL-
TURED WEST. POPULAR NATIONALISM WAS FORMED AGAINST THE
BACKGROUND OF NATIONALITIES POPULATING THE RUSSIAN EM-
PIRE: THE CAUCASIAN PEOPLES, TATARS, JEWS, AND GERMANS. IN
THIS PIECE, THE CONNECTIONS BETWEEN MODERN NATIONALISM
AND OLD FOLK TALES ARE VISIBLE. RUSSIANS SHOW ARROGANT
GERMANS THE SAME FALSE SUBMISSION THAT PEASANTS HAD
ONCE SHOWN THEIR MASTERS; AND BY DOING SO, THEY TOO
DUPE THE SUPERCILIOUS OUTSIDER. ROOTS IN THE PETRUSHKA
PUPPET PLAYS ARE EVIDENT IN THE FACT THAT THE NARRATOR
AND CHARACTERS SPEAK IN *RAESHNIK* VERSE (WHICH HAS NOT
BEEN TRANSLATED HERE), AND TAKE MALICIOUS PLEASURE IN
THEIR ANTAGONISTS' DOWNFALL.

Once upon a time there lived a Russian *muzhik* named Timofei and a sly German
by the name of Friedrich Schmertz. Although Timofei was not much to look at, he
always had plenty of money. Winter and summer, year-round, he never ran out of
money. As for Schmertz, a German from overseas,[1] except for his good looks, his
goatee, and a coat that pinched, he didn't have a cent to his name. In a word,
Friedrich Schmertz was a pauper's pauper, though he looked as sharp as a rooster.

Schmertz was sitting and thinking deep thoughts about how to make a buck and
build up some capital; and who doesn't know that Germans are quick with a
scheme? It's not for nothing they say that monkeys were invented by a German.

Schmertz thought a while and hit upon a scheme as sly as they come.

Friedrich Schmertz knew that Timofei had all the money he needed, and that he
had a secret money-box known only to him. A tidy pile of rubles was hidden away
in the box, so Schmertz figured he could handle his expenses if he could finagle

---

Skazka o tom, kak russkii nemtsu zadal pertsu (St. Petersburg: V. Spiridonov, 1869), pp. 3–6, 7–11, 18–32.

1. In folk and popular culture, "German" meant a foreigner of any sort. Though Schmertz in this tale
is actually a German, he is still referred to as a German "from overseas."

those rubles of Timofei's into his pocket. Thinking up a scheme, Schmertz went to visit Timofei.

"Mine reshpects, Herr Timofei, how do yours do, are yours making a goot liffing?" began the German.

The peasant smiled and said, "I'm getting along; we don't have too much, but not too little either!" And he thinks to himself, "I know you, you sly German, you overseas bird. I know you didn't come for nothing. Well, brother, you won't outsmart me. I'm no blockhead, I'm no fool; you won't get the better of us—we'll give it to you hot in the end."

Meanwhile the German was hatching a plan to sneak up on the peasant and climb into his pocket unnoticed.

"Herr Timofei," the German remarked, "you must become a mershant, dress up in zoot, and zen mine vill be useful to you."

"Thanks for the advice," Timofei answered. "We'll live just fine without the suit, and manage to earn a thing or two."

"Still, mine herr, it vouldn't be bad to get some capital and become a mershant."

"Who says it would be! Even you wouldn't turn down money, would you Schmertz?"

"Oh, mine vill be rich. I alone know a zekret zat vill make ze monies come on zeir own. Do you vant to go fifty-fifties? Mine loves you, only zen tell me vat to do."

"Well, brother, I see that you're no simpleton," said Timofei. Schmertz didn't understand that the peasant was mocking him. He just stroked his beard, put his hands in his pockets, strutted about the hut, and made up to Timofei.

"I tell yours," he said, "my zekret is zo goot zat I vill not take vun hundred rubles for it, I vill tell it to nobody."

"Really, not to anyone?"

"Not for any money in ze world."

"So, what sort of secret is it?"

"Ze secret is zat I can sew boots mitout any needle, or thread, or leazer. Understand, zat copplers must buy zese things vit money, and I can make boots vitout them. Und zese boots can fit anyone."

"Aha!" spoke Timofei. "I can see that you're a total slyboots. Let's sit down and talk about it a bit."

Hearing these words, the German was even happier than before, and he was already counting Timofei's money, stuffing it into his pockets, without understanding that the peasant was making fun of him. Schmertz couldn't stop bragging, while the peasant was figuring out how to trick the German. . . .

"Well, Schmertz, I can see straight off that you're a German from overseas: you live in Russia but don't know Russian. I'll say it simple: Let's get a drink of vodka and a bit of pie, and then we can talk business."

"Oh, mine love schnapps!" shouted Friedrich Schmertz. "Mine can trink a whole barrel."

"A barrel? Well, we'll see."

Timofei began giving the German vodka, and we know that Germans can't compete with Russians in these matters. Schmertz was getting drunk and animated,

and Timofei didn't slow down, pouring more and more vodka into his glass.

Finally Schmertz got so groggy that he could barely move his tongue. His feet were dragging, and his arms flapped around.

"I'm . . . I'm," he mumbled drunkenly, "mine Friedrich Schmertz, ze famous boot-maker." He couldn't say anything more, collapsing under the table and emitting a heroic snore. Timofei looked at him and said, "You German, you overseas slyboots, I can see that cheap Russian vodka is no match for German schnapps." He grabbed him, tied him up hand and foot, put a dunce cap on him, pasted an oakum mustache on him, and bound him to a post in the yard.

Peasant men and women walked by, saw Schmertz tied to the post, and said to each other, "Look here, they put a scarecrow from overseas out in the yard."

By morning a crowd had gathered round, making fun and laughing at him. They crammed dead sparrows and jackdaws in his pockets and put torn shoes in his hands, but Schmertz felt nothing and slept the sleep of the mighty. Finally the German came to, looking around himself and understanding nothing. . . .

Timofei was happy that Schmertz didn't remember that he had collapsed under the bench in Timofei's hut, and set to assuring him: "You know, Schmertz, a poltergeist played a joke on you."

"O, I know zat der Russian polterghost is angry, he don't like us Germans."

"Well . . . he really gave it to you hot."

"You are truth, Timofei, zat Russian polterghost is big joker. Ven he don't like someone, he does his hocus-pocus to him."

"There you go! Just make sure you don't get him mad." Schmertz left the peasant with complete confidence that nobody else but a poltergeist had tied him to the pillory.

Schmertz figured that since things had gone badly and he hadn't been able to trick Timofei, he should find another fool. The sly German heard of a rich merchant who needed a mechanic—the merchant was leasing a small factory. He thought and thought and finally came up with a scheme.

"Vy," he reflected, "shouldn't I be a mechanic? I have a goatee, a nice coat—in a vord, everything I need."

Schmertz reported to the merchant as a German mechanic; he assured the merchant that he was truly a trained mechanic, came to terms with him, and gave him a deposit.

"So," thought Schmertz, "I can't miss now, I be living vell in no time. A machine isn't a man, it von't find me out, it von't guess that I'm a German peasant and not a trained mechanic."

Our Schmertz set up his new life, dressed himself like a baron, strutted around his machine, and looked at the cogwheels, just like some famous mechanic.

If only nothing had gone wrong, the sly German might have gotten himself a pile of money. But as if on purpose, to his misfortune, a fire spout broke, and the boss ordered the German summoned to him.

"Well," he said to him, "my dearest Schmertz, show us your art, fix the spout; I want to watch how you work. They say that we Russians have a long way to go before we catch you Germans."

Schmertz saw that catastrophe was inevitable. He went over to the spout, looked at it from the side, crawled under it, then climbed on top of it.

The merchant saw that the German was playing a sly game.

"What, my Schmertz?" he shouted to him. "Is it fixed yet?"

"Just a second, boss, everything will be ready!" He started turning a screw, kept turning till it was so tight that the spout fell to pieces. Schmertz burst into tears and didn't know how to repair his woe. The boss grasped that the German understood nothing, that he was just swindling him. He called for the blacksmith, a simple Russian peasant.

The blacksmith came, looked at the spout, shook his head, and said, "Oh, you educated German, I see that you don't know the first thing. Better you be a ditchdigger than a trained mechanic." With those words the blacksmith set to work; he quickly fixed the spout, then pointed the hose at him.

When the boss saw that, he shouted, "Spray some water on him! Pump it lively! Let him know that a Russian gave it hot to a German."

Schmertz stood there shaking all over, and they kept hosing him, giving him water for free.

"Oh, weh mir, good boss, do not perish me, do not make me die badly."

The merchant answered him: "Oh, you worthless German, good-for-nothing Schmertz, ask my pardon, and I'll forgive you and let you go free."

The German begged his pardon even harder than before. The merchant took pity and ordered that he be driven from the factory in shame.

Schmertz grew thinner and older from this disaster. He didn't have a cent to his name. Wherever he spent the day and night, his stomach was empty; yet he still dressed like an aristocrat, and he couldn't stop thinking about how to get himself some money and build up some capital.

———

Schmertz was walking along the street once with his nose hanging, when he saw a beauty walking down the sidewalk dressed all in silk and velvet.

"Must be rich!" thought the German. "I should get married—being a husband is a lot better than vorking as a mechanic. First, though, you have to know how to cut a dash, and then things can progress from there."

He fell in step with the young lady, glanced in her eyes, and flashed a smile; the young lady kept silent, saying nothing to him.

"Your face is familiar to mine," he began.

"And yours is not to me!" the beauty replied.

"I am Baron Schmertz; I haf vealthy holdinks and own a big castle." Hearing these words, the maiden smiled, because day and night she dreamed of marrying some baron or prince, though she was the daughter of a wealthy merchant.

"Well, Mr. Baron," she replied, "Glad to meet you."

"Mine is very happy! I vant to luf you, to ask your hand."

Hearing these words, Schmertz's young lady invited him to her home and promised to marry him if her father would give his permission.

In the servants' quarters of the merchant lived our acquaintance, the peasant Timofei. He was sitting by the gate and looking around when he saw the young lady walking with an admirer.

He looked and couldn't believe his eyes.

"But that's our Schmertz!" Timofei said to himself. "Only I can't figure out where the young lady picked him up. Just you wait, German, I'll teach you again how to think straight; this time you won't forget 'how a Russian gave it hot to a German.'"

Hearing that Schmertz had called himself a baron and promised the father to marry his daughter, Timofei told the father the whole story.

The merchant was furious at the sly German Schmertz for his affront.

"Just you wait, you filthy kraut! I'll teach you how to think straight. You'll remember how a Russian gave it hot to a German."

The merchant went into the parlor and promised his daughter's hand to the German. They discussed it for a while and decided that the wedding would be in three days.

Schmertz was so happy, he couldn't feel the ground beneath him. "Now," he thought, "I can live like a gentleman, vith a young vife, thanks to her father's fat purse."

The wedding day arrived, and Schmertz drove up in a white tie, dressed to the nines.

"Well," said the merchant, "let's go take a look at the dowry, my most gracious Schmertz. And call the bride here!" he yelled to Timofei.

The German ran on tiptoe. They went into the study, and the merchant locked the door.

The German saw a pockmarked old woman standing in the corner in a white dress. Two sacks lay in the middle of the room.

"Well," said the merchant, "untie the sacks, German, your dowry is inside."

Schmertz untied them and went "Ah!" In one there were rags, in the other woodchips.

He stood silently, without saying a word.

"And here's your bride!" the merchant added, pointing to the old woman. "Go get married, and in the future don't pretend to be a baron, don't go where you don't belong, and remember how a Russian gave it hot to a German. If you resist, I'll have your hands bound tight and put you, you imposter, in prison."

There was nothing to be done, Schmertz married the old woman, and she turned out to be a nasty one. Instead of a menial, now she had a German. He chopped wood, stoked the stove, and still couldn't please her. She tormented him, tyrannized him, so he had no life.

Once he met up with a comrade, Fedor Spitz.

"How do you do, my Schmertz?" he asked.

"Badly, badly! That Russian gave it so hot to me, a German, that I want to flee home from my wife."

"Me too."

"Let's flee together."

"Let's flee, my friend."

They decided to leave for their homeland.

The whole city was sleeping. Only Spitz and Schmertz were awake, waiting for their wives to fall asleep.

The clock struck twelve; the friends crawled out of bed as quietly as mice and set off.

The met in an agreed-upon spot.

"Is that you, Schmertz?" asked Spitz.

"It's me. Is that you, Spitz?"

"It's me! Let's get out of here." They wanted to get going, when they suddenly heard behind them: "Stop! Stop! I'll get you, German!"

They turned around, and before them stood their wives.

They grabbed their husbands by the scruffs of their necks and dragged them home, and gave them such a treat that even today the men repeat: "Oh, oh, you won't ever forget 'how a Russian gave it hot to a German.'"

Oh Those Yaroslavites, What a Fine Folk!
A True Story of How a Yaroslavite Walked to Piter, Duped the Devil, Fooled the German, Became a Bartender, and Married the Village Elder's Daughter.

Fedor Ivanich Kuz'ma (1868)

THE EMANCIPATION OF THE SERFS IN 1861 TRIGGERED A WAVE OF URBAN MIGRATION. YAROSLAV PEASANTS FLOCKED TO PETERSBURG, WHERE AN INFORMAL SYSTEM OF MUTUAL AID (*ZEMLIACHESTVO*) HELPED THEM THRIVE. BY THE END OF THE DECADE, THESE NEW CONSUMERS HAD CREATED A MARKET FOR SIMPLE STORY BOOKS (*LUBKI*), WHICH WERE OFTEN CHARACTERIZED BY CONSERVATIVE VALUES AND RESPECT FOR HARD WORK. THE LITERATURE ALSO BETRAYED AN AMBIVALENCE TO CITY LIFE THAT LASTED MANY DECADES.

Ai, da iaroslavtsy! Vot tak narodets! Pravdivyi razskaz o tom, kak odin iaroslavets prishel peshkom v Piter, nadul cherta, odurachil nemtsa, sdelalsia bufetchikom i zhenilsia na starostikhinoi dochke, published by Kuz'ma Fedor Ivanich (St. Petersburg, 1868). Translated by Jeffrey Brooks.

I

Ah! Life is tough! It is nighttime in such a blizzard that you can't see your hand in front of your face. Head bowed, a young fellow of twenty-two or twenty-three trudges along a country road with a knapsack on his back. He looks up occasionally, but only to see if a village or post house where he could toast his benumbed feet and rest a bit hasn't appeared by chance. It is getting dark, now pitch black, and still there's not a dwelling in sight.

Our hapless fellow can barely drag his legs through the deep snow. He glances around just to see that he hasn't strayed from the path. Suddenly something shows up black against the snow right under his feet. He bends, looks, and sees that it's a shawl, and something is wrapped in it. He picks it up, unties his find, and sets off a merrier fellow, for in the shawl is a ten spot.

"Great," the fellow thinks. "Now things are going my way. Here's money for the iron horse. If I can get to the tracks, I'll be in Piter in a day. Wait! There's a twinkle of light. It must be a roadhouse."

And, sure enough, off to the side of the road a light shone. In a quarter of an hour the shivering fellow stepped into a warm, spacious room filled with various travelers.

"God bless and keep you, good fellow! Where are you headed?" asked the proprietor.

"I'm on my way to Piter. May I spend the night?"

"Take off your duds and stretch out on the bench, or if you want, over the stove. And maybe you would like a bite of something? There's noodles, cabbage soup, kasha . . ."

"Thanks, I'll warm up a bit first."

The fellow took off his knapsack and sat down on a bench. Just then he noticed an old woman in a dark corner of the room weeping bitterly over something.

"Granny, what's your trouble? Why so sad?" he asked her.

The proprietor answered, "Well, this is her trouble. She says she lost her money." The fellow winced.

"Yes, my dear. I sold the cow. . . . Akh, then I lost all the money. Now there is nothing for me to do but finish myself off. Oy! Woe is me! In the shawl. Oy!"

"Keep it or give it back?" thought the fellow.

All night he tossed and turned. He couldn't sleep—his windfall wouldn't let him. All night long the old lady sniveled, and the devil kept whispering in his ear, "Keep it, and you'll ride the iron horse."

The fellow wrestled with himself for a long time. Finally, just before dawn, his conscience won out. He rose quietly, crossed himself, and said in a whisper, "Granny. Hey, granny!"

"What is it, my dear? Akh, my sins!"

"Granny, I found your money. Here it is."

"Oh! My provider! Dearheart!" The old lady dropped to the floor like a shot, raised herself on her knees, kissed the earth, and carried on like a madwoman. "My savior! I'll pray to God forever for you. By my word, the Heavenly Tsar will reward you for your honesty. Believe me—you'll be rich and happy. Mark my words!"

II

When a person does a good deed, his soul is light and things go his way. Andrei (so our fellow was named) got up about eight o'clock, washed, prayed wholeheartedly to God in thanks that He did not let the devil lead him astray, and strode off cheerfully down the road. The morning was freezing, but the storm had quieted and the going was much easier. Andrei thought about how God would see him to Piter, and he also thought about the village where he had left his sweetheart. A fine girl, that Aksiutka, the village elder's daughter, and she loved him. But the elder was a terribly proud fellow, and the whole village had a laugh on Andrei when he sent for the matchmaker. Poor Aksiutka got plenty of grief, too. How could she think of marrying a nothing like Andriukha Kunavin? So Andrei, the laughingstock of the village lads and girls, decided to take himself to Piter to seek his fortune. Only Aksiutka didn't laugh at the poor fellow, and warmly kissed him goodbye at night behind her father's house, and swore to him that she would have no other.

III

God didn't forsake Andrei. He walked past two or three stations along the rails, and even managed to ride a bit. Here he helped the stoker, there he carried bags for some fat landowner from the station to the *tarantas,* and earned his way a whole stop, or even two.

One day (he was already in the province of Novgorod), Andrei noticed a dog lying motionless on the tracks. Coming closer, he saw that her back leg had been crushed by the train. The poor animal was bleeding, and whether from pain or from long hunger, she couldn't move off the tracks.

Andrei was seized with pity.

"Hey, sweetheart! . . . You're lying there with your head right on the tracks, and here comes a train!!"

The train rushed down on them so fast that Andrei barely managed to pull the dog to the side of the tracks. After the train flew by, Andrei looked at his foundling and examined her wound.

"Oh, my dear. What am I going to do with you? It would be a pity to leave you like this," he said, stroking the dog. "Look at how your ribs stick out! You must not have eaten for three days."

Andrei was a good fellow, and he knew that God commanded us to be kind to animals. He took off his knapsack, pulled out a slab of stale bread, broke off a soft bit, and raised it to the dog's mouth. The poor animal grabbed the offering out of Andrei's hand and gulped down piece after piece, almost choking. Her rescuer tore a piece of calico from his neckerchief, and began to bind the foot of his foundling.

IV

Morning. Seventy versts or so down the line from Petersburg, a young fellow sauntered along boldly and gaily, smoking a nosewarmer[1] and playing with a three-legged dog that ran after him. It was our Andrei with his Blackie, whose health had completely recovered.

"Hey! My good fellow!" a voice sounded behind Andrei.

Andrei looked around. A gentleman of some kind sat in a small carriage.

"My man. Where did you get your dog?"

"This dog? She latched onto me, sir. I found her on the road, I mean . . ."

"And do you want to sell her? That's a hunting dog, a setter."

"I think so too, sir, she's a hunter. She must have got left behind by her master on a hunt. But I won't sell."

"And what if I give you a ten spot?"

"I wouldn't take even a hundred rubles, sir."

"Oho! And what is she, a performer? Trained?"

"That's right. The only thing she can't do is talk."

In fact, Andrei had discovered that his Blackie had many talents. She had a great sense of smell, and could fetch things from several versts away, and in general she was excellently trained.

The gentleman continued to ride alongside Andrei.

"Going to Piter?" he asked.

"Yes, sir."

"Well, climb on, and I'll take you as far as Ushakov."

Andrei got in, and Blackie jumped up without ceremony.

"A splendid dog!" said the gentleman. "It's a shame that she's missing a foot."

"That doesn't matter, sir. She can run faster on three legs than another can on four."

"And what tricks does she do?" asked the gentleman.

"All kinds, sir."

"For example?"

"Well, what can I say? Here's an example. I can take an item, bury it on the road so she can't see it, and then we ride off for ten versts or so. When I send her off to find it, she'll bring it back."

---

1. A short pipe.

"Is that so?!"

"I'm telling you the truth—she'll bring it."

"And if she doesn't?"

"She will."

"Well, let's make a bet. I say that she won't," insisted the gentleman.

"She'll bring it, sir," repeated Andrei.

"Well, is it a bet?"

"With pleasure, except, sir, the only money I have is twenty kopecks—and I earned that here at the station."

"It doesn't matter. If you lose, you can buy us each a beer, and if you win, I'll stand for two dozen."

"All right, sir."

"Here, I'll give you a silver ruble. Bury it by the road."

The gentleman gave Andrei a silver ruble. Andrei spat on the coin, rubbed it against the dog's nose several times, and then took a kerchief, blindfolded Blackie, went a bit away from the road, and buried the ruble in the already thawing ground.

When they had gone eight versts, the gentleman got impatient. "OK, send your Blackie. We'll see."

"Blackie! Fetch! Lost! Find it! Back there—behind! Fetch!"

Andrei pointed back. Blackie leapt down onto the road like a mad dog, raced around several times, and at last vanished from sight.

V

Andrei and the gentleman went bumping along. Andrei kept looking behind, because it was already time for Blackie to be running back. The gentleman was splitting his sides, laughing at Andrei.

"Well, brother, it looks like you'll have to stand us a couple of beers. Ha ha ha!!"

"And maybe it'll be you, sir. My Blackie will come. This is not her first time."

"We'll see! Ha ha ha!!"

They fed the horse, rested, and went on, but still no Blackie. Andrei became gloomy and worried. He wasn't sorry to lose the bet, but to lose a smart dog.

They arrived in a village late in the evening. Poor Andrei paid for the beers, but he didn't touch his own. The hapless fellow didn't sleep a wink. He bade the gentleman goodbye in the morning, and trudged off on the road to Piter, lonely as an orphan.

He went about five versts, all the time looking back, and then sat down on a big stone by the road and wept bitterly.

VI

Let's have a look now at what Blackie was up to during this time.

When Andrei bet the gentleman and sent her to fetch the ruble, she ran off. She ran about eight versts, and sniffed out the place where Andrei had gotten off the cart by the side of the road. Once she'd picked up the scent, finding the spot where the ruble was buried was easy. She hit on it and began to dig.

Just then some kind of German[2] in a two-wheeled gig came by. Seeing the dog digging up the ground, he climbed out and went up to Blackie and began to lure her with some bread. Blackie gave a growl, and the German ran for it. He got a hunk of sausage from the gig, and this time went up to her more bravely. Blackie had run many versts and was famished, and she began to eat the sausage. In the meantime, the German saw his chance, and dug up the ground. To his astonishment, he saw a silver ruble.

"Oho!! Vat a sveet dog! You are smarter than my vife!!"

The German put the ruble in his trouser pocket, and then took a cord and tied Blackie to the gig.

"Oh, zis is a very best dog! I'll bring her home on my vife."

Toward nightfall the German came to an inn, ate some sausage, drank some beer, had another round of beer and sausage, and lay down to sleep. He put his breeches under his head, and tied Blackie to his foot. When the German fell asleep, she gnawed through the cord. She had noticed in the morning that the German put the ruble in his trousers, and she very quietly pulled them out from under his head, opened the door with her paws, and ran down the road.

When she met the train, hundreds of passengers stuck their heads out to see what it was that the dog had in her mouth. No one could imagine that it was breeches, and German breeches at that!

VII

Andrei had a little wandering left to do. By the evening of the day after he lost Blackie, he was in Kolpin. Stopping not far from the station to rest a bit and to suck his pipe, he was startled out of his dreaming by the cries of peasants crowded around the station.

"There, look at that, boys! That dog's got something in her teeth! What is it, a bird?"

"That's it, a bird!"

Andrei jumped headlong onto the railroad platform. Blackie ran up quick as a flash, panting, wet, and dirty.

She threw herself on Andrei with a yelp, put her paws on his chest, and held up her burden. Andrei took the German's breeches with

---

2. A generic term used for all Western European foreigners.

amazement. He poked his head into the pocket and brought out a silver ruble and then a purse, which turned out to have seven hundred rubles in it.

Poor German! Why couldn't he mind his own business! Now he is left with no money and no pants. Very shameful!

VIII

Three months later, a troika came roaring down the steep hills onto the main street of a big village in one of the districts of the province of Yaroslavl. In the troika sat Mr. Bartender of a Petersburg hotel, the Horn of Plenty, Andrei Parfenovich Kunavin. At his feet sat Blackie.

"Watch out! Take it easy down the hills!"

"Nothing to worry about, sir," answered the driver.

"Straight to the elder's house!"

The troika quickly drew up to the elder's house.

"Well!! Andrei Parvenich![3] My deepest respects! It seems like ages since we've seen you!" exclaimed the elder.

"Is Aksinia Fedotovna alive and well?"

"Praise the Lord, praise the Lord!"

"Fedor Antipich, I . . . as you know, I request the marriage of your daughter's hand; I mean—"

"I bless you! May God keep you both."

Dear Aksiutka darted out of the sitting room and threw herself on Andrei's neck, sobbing for joy.

Ands so, you see, the old woman spoke the truth.

---

3. The elder is addressing Andrei in the polite form, rather than the familiar.

The Slums of the Female Heart
Scenes from the Dark Corners of Hearts of the Gentle Sex
(1870)

ONCE-TABOO IDEAS ENTERED POPULAR CULTURE UNDER THE IN-
FLUENCE OF CITY LIFE AND THE GROWTH OF SENSATIONALIST
JOURNALISM. JUST AS KRESTOVSKY HAD DESCRIBED THE LOWER-

Zhenskie trushchoby (*iz zhizni temnykh ugolkov serdtsa prekrasnogo pola*) (St. Petersburg: Spiridonov, 1870), pp. 3–32.

CLASS "SLUMS" (*TRUSHCHOBY*) *FOR HIS EDUCATED READERS,*
THIS LUBOK TALE, PRICED FOR A POORER AUDIENCE, DESCRIBED
"SLUMS" OF ANOTHER SORT. IT PLAYED UP THE ISSUES OF FEMALE
SEXUALITY, SOCIAL MOBILITY, AND HIGH-SOCIETY VENALITY,
WHICH HAD BECOME CONSTANT THEMES OF THE POPULAR IMAG-
INATION. MANY RUSSIANS, BOTH FROM THE EDUCATED CLASSES
AND FROM THE LOWER ORDERS, ASSOCIATED SUCH MORAL COR-
RUPTION WITH THE CITY, AND THE "DARK CORNERS" OF THE UR-
BAN LANDSCAPE.

I

Every woman has a weak string (*corde sensible*) to be plucked; there is a dark corner in the heart of each of these beautiful creations—a slum, so to speak. Seek out
that dark corner, pluck a woman's weak string, and she will change from your sovereign to your slave; to attain the object of your desires from a woman, you must
locate the dark corners of her heart precisely and learn them to the smallest
detail. With that knowledge you can do what you want with her; but woe to him
who strikes a false chord on that string, for he will be fatally diminished in the eyes
of his lady!

All women love presents; the gifts given to them must vary in accordance with
their characters and idiosyncrasies. The best gift for one woman might be a tightly
packed purse, perhaps a bit worn and battered. But give the same thing to a dreamy,
sentimental woman, and she will consider it an insult. A splendid bouquet would
be a different matter. She will admire it with the innocence of a child and become
softer than wax.

For the edification of my readers, I will tell a short tale of two ladies: Olga Aleksandrovna and Anna Pavlovna.

Olga Aleksandrovna and Anna Pavlovna grew up together and went to the same
boarding school. They were friends; that is, in the ancient tradition of boarding
schools, Mlle Olga adored Annette, and Mlle Annette adored Olga. The friendship
of the two girls ended with the completion of their schooling, ended because they
set out along two entirely different paths.

Olga, as the daughter of a rich tax-farmer, quickly succeeded in making herself
a career—she married the elderly holder of a high office. Annette also made a
career for herself, but along another path; leaving the boarding school, she found
work as a governess in the home of an old widower, who was also a powerful man,
and soon in her own turn she was transformed from governess to the master of his
heart. In the character and habits of the two former friends there was much in
common, but also much that was different. Both loved gifts in the same measure.
Olga loved flowers, bouquets, and expensive things, while Annette, as a selective

woman, saw the value of a gift in its cost. Both had dreams: Olga dreamed of romantic love, and Annette of wealth. Finally, both loved going to clubs and playing the card game loo:[1] Olga played with passion whether she was winning or losing, while Annette was her complete opposite. She would quit playing as soon as she began losing; she loved not the game but the winning. Olga did not love her husband, but she feared him; Annette for her part did not love her admirer, but rather than fearing him, she controlled him.

If it had not been for the club, perhaps the former boarding school friends would never have met each other again.

Once on a fine summer's eve, which did not stop it from being unlucky for her, Olga Aleksandrovna got up from the card table, having lost all the money she had brought in her purse. She went to the club library with the thought of getting a cash loan. However, as if on purpose, none of her acquaintances was there. She was debating whether to pawn her bracelet when she spotted a lady leafing through a book. The face seemed familiar. The lady's toilette said clearly that she was rich, "and thus she might help me in my misfortune" flickered through Olga's head. She began to recall why her physiognomy was familiar. "Mais, mon Dieu, c'est . . . c'est Annette!" she exclaimed.

"Mon Dieu, est ce toi, Olga!" responded Anna Pavlovna, who had long ago recognized her friend.

They rushed into each other's arms. But however ecstatic the meeting was, Olga thought, "They say she's an easy woman . . . but . . . but she might make me a loan today," while Annette in turn said to herself, "True, she's empty and stupid, I know that, but . . . but she has a position in society; her acquaintance will do me honor."

"Ah, Annette!" said Olga. "How happy I am that I met you; we have not seen each other for so long. I hope, chère amie, you will visit me. Let's go walk through the garden; it's stuffy in here." So they went outside.

"You know, Olga," said Annette, spotting an arbor, "let's sit down and talk."

"Sure."

They took a seat in the shade of the trees, taking care to strike graceful poses.

"Do you play loo, Annette?" asked Olga.

"Yes, and you?"

"Me? Oh I love playing; and imagine this— I owe meeting you today to loo."

"And how is that?"

"Simple: Imagine, my luck today was just

---

1. Full name Lanterloo, or in Russian *muskka:* a five-card contract game associated with gambling, which thrived in many variations in many countries from the sixteenth to the late nineteenth century.

horrid, I was an utter failure; so I was looking for a friend to borrow money from till tomorrow. I entered the library and saw you!"

"You of course will keep playing?"

"No . . . no! My friend has probably left already, and I don't have any more . . ."

"In that case, chère Olga, my purse is at your disposal!"

"Annette!"

"I beg you not to stand on ceremony; take as much as you need." Anna Pavlovna handed Olga an elegant enamel purse; she understood that by that service she was acquiring the right to visit Olga, and thus entrance to the evening gatherings at her house.

"Merci, merci, let's go play!"

And the women left the garden to return to the card table.

From that day Annette became Olga's permanent club banker; she gave money to her in fairly large sums and did not regret it, because in compensation she could attend balls arm in arm with a grande dame, and sit in the same box with her in the theater. In a word, Annette found the dark corner in the heart of her friend and touched it.

II

Misha and Vasya were good friends despite the fact that Misha was rich and Vasya was poor; their characters were similar: they both looked at life pragmatically and did not waste their time on learning or romance.

"But Misha, we've got to make careers!" said Vasya.

"Right! As for me, I don't need money, but a rank and medals."

"I, on the other hand, need money."

"That's right. Do you know who I'm going to turn to?"

"Who?"

"To Anna Pavlovna; I already have a plan of action."

"What sort?"

"You see, she's a well-placed woman."

"Yes, I know!"

"Well, she's due to give birth any day now. I've ordered a mother-of-pearl box for her as a gift; but what's important is not the box but the two thousand that will be put in it. I'm sure that it will get me a position."

"Excellent plan, but mine isn't bad either."

"What's your plan of action? It too involves a woman, of course?"

"Of course. You found a dark corner in the heart of Anna Pavlovna, and I, as your friend, discovered the slum in the heart of her friend."

"Bravo! Olga Aleksandrovna's?"

"Yes; you see how well it all came out: you're rich, and can choose a path that requires money, while I'm poor, and must choose a path that's not as expensive. My place won't cost me more than a pot of flowers and five rubles."

"Flowers?"

"Sure! You see, there are two slums in Olga Aleksandrovna's heart: one is taken by her passion for card playing, and the other by her passion for flowers."

"And then?"

"And then, then by bad luck; so to make her happy, I'll lose a couple hands to her, and she'll be in ecstasy. Then I'll touch the second dark corner, and incidentally tell her that I saw a rare flower at the home of one of my friends. I'll volunteer to get it for her, get it, and she'll be in ecstasy. Add on a few sentimental phrases, and the position will be mine."

"Bravo, bravo! You're a real psychologist!"

"So in a week we can congratulate each other on our new careers."

III

On her birthday, Anna Pavlovna was seated at her dressing table in morning ne-gligé. She was weighing a very important decision: Should she do her hair à la chinoise or à la Margot? Meanwhile several well-wishers seeking her patronage had gathered in the reception hall, among whom was Misha.

"Well, let's see," said Anna Pavlovna, primping in the mirror. "Let's see if my protégés can amuse me with something today; if only they'd spare me the bouquets, the albums, and all that worthless junk. Ridiculous people, they still don't under-stand that only solid, valuable presents are significant in my eyes. Isn't that right, Masha?" she added, turning to her maid.

"Of course, ma'am. Ain't that like all men; just the other day it was my birthday, and so's my Ivan up and brings me a pie, says he coughed up three rubles for it, and he didn't even think that it weren't worth nothin' that way, and he shoulda just gived me five rubles. Nope, he did it all in his head, like he was runnin' a tab or somethin'."

Anna Pavlovna smiled in reply to the words of her maid and made her entrance into the hall.

"Bonjour, mes amis!" she told her visitors, who were for the most part underlings of her admirer.

"Allow us to wish you a happy birthday, Anna Pavlovna," said Misha, stepping forward and presenting her with an elegant box. "Please don't refuse this little trifle."

"Merci for remembering!" Accepting the gifts and good wishes, Anna Pavlovna invited her guests in to breakfast, and under the pretext of attending to household affairs, she stepped into the dressing room to look at the gifts that the obliging Misha had brought. There were silver toiletries, a paperweight, and bracelets.

"All that stuff is so-so," she said, "but let's look at the box." With those words she opened it, and her eyes beheld a packet of rainbow-colored bills. "Bravo!" she exclaimed. "Good going, Michel, an even two thousand rubles. I can guess that he needs something, and I promise in advance to fulfill his wish. We'll have to invite him to a soirée."

"You have very sophisticated tastes," Anna Pavlovna remarked to him at breakfast. "Your box is just darling, and I even looked inside it."

"Pshaw, it was nothing!"

"Don't forget, we'll expect you here this evening."

"Much obliged."

When Misha entered Anna Pavlovna's richly illuminated ballroom that evening, it was already full of guests; with all the splendid clothes and the military uniforms and medals flickering by, it was easier to take the party for an aristocratic ball than for a dinner given by a lady of the demimonde.

"Ah, Monsieur Michel!" she greeted him. "Merci for remembering; I will dance the first quadrille with you!"

"Thank you, thank you!"

The music was struck up, and the quadrille began.

"Why aren't you in the service?" Anna Pavlovna asked Misha.

"I wouldn't be against the service, but until I have found a solid position, I don't want to take just anything."

"Is that so? People like you are needed these days."

"True, but you also need protection."

"Oh, on that count I can help you."

"Would you be so kind?"

"And right away."

"Is that possible?"

When the quadrille was over, she recommended Misha to Ivan Fedorovich; the latter, as befitting an important dignitary, shook the young man's hand and exchanged a few cordial phrases with him.

Gradually the guests began to leave, and Anna Pavlovna remained tête-à-tête with Ivan Fedorovich.

"Well, my pussycat," said the dignitary, caressing Annette, "you look like an angel today, my treasure!"

"Jean!" said Annette, embracing him, "I have a favor to ask of you today; promise you'll do it!"

"Please, my dearest, anything you want; just kiss me."

"Please!" And she kissed the old man as he melted.

"You see," continued Anna Pavlovna, "there's a young man who gave me a darling gift today, and I gave him my word that I'd get him a position."

"Well, pussycat, I can do that!"

"Do you have any vacancies?"

"We'll find one. Who's your protégé?"

"That young man whom I introduced to you today."

"Ah!"

"But you have to give him a solid position."

"Of course; send him to me. How could I not indulge you, my pussycat?"

IV

While Misha's career was being decided with the assistance of Anna Pavlovna, Vasya in his own turn was not napping, and he carried out the plan he had formulated. Arriving at the club, he took in the players with a glance, and noticing Olga Aleksandrovna, he seated himself at the table vis-à-vis her. When he had lost almost ten silver rubles, he got up from the table and went out into the garden, smiling inwardly at the result of his policy. Vasya easily noticed that Olga Aleksandrovna was ecstatic over her winnings—her face glowed with unfeigned ecstasy. When Olga finished the game, got up from the table, and went out to the garden, everything seemed rosy to her: she was happy, as happy as only a gambler can be who has won back a fortune that was lost, or a person who wins 200,000 silver rubles in the lottery.

"He," thought Olga, "is a most attractive young man! The woman who becomes his wife will be very happy; we should invite him to visit more often." Olga found herself face to face with Vasya.

"Ah, Olga Aleksandrovna!"

"Yes," she answered like a schoolgirl caught playing a prank by a strict mistress. "Yes, I stepped out for a breath of fresh air. I love nature—it's my passion."

"You and I have similar tastes! I also love flowers and nature madly."

"Oh, flowers, I wouldn't trade them for any jewels in the world."

"That proves that you have a kind heart."

"Apparently! Tell me, what flowers do you love most?"

"Me—roses!"

"Me too. Roses are charming; how much grace and life they have!"

"Especially a nice one!"

"I have a wonderful collection of roses; I can show it to you."

"I'm already sure that you haven't the rarest sort; I saw it only once in Petersburg, at a friend's."

"Really?"

"I assure you."

"Then I must get one of that sort for myself, whatever it takes."

"I can assure you that you won't get this sort for any amount of money; it's imported from abroad. But if you will permit me, I can get one . . ."

"You? But really, I'd be ashamed to trouble you!"

"On the contrary, I'd be glad to give you pleasure."

"Oh, merci! Merci! My husband will be ecstatic—he's also a passionate lover of flowers."

"The flower will be in your house the day after tomorrow."

"Merci! And again, in anticipation! Apropos, why do you visit us so rarely? Come dine with us without ceremony, without an invitation."

"Much obliged; were I not looking for a position, I would have been a visitor long ago."

"Are you entering the service?"

"For the time being I'm only looking—these days good positions are so hard to find."

"Isn't that wonderful, you can work for my husband."

"I could desire nothing more, but . . ."

"No buts. I'll expect you for dinner the day after tomorrow; for better or worse, I'll get you a position with my husband. And so, till the day after tomorrow!"

"I'll consider it my duty to be there."

Olga Aleksandrovna gave Vasya a friendly shake of the hand and went home.

V

The next day, after dinner, Olga Aleksandrovna, seated at the table with her husband and caressing her little son, said with a tender smile on her lips, "Paul! Do you remember Danshin [Vasya's surname]?"

"Certainly I remember! A little man, but not to be sneezed at!"

"Imagine, I met him at the club; he's a passionate lover of flowers."

"Really?"

"Yes, and he promised to bring us a new type of rose tomorrow, a rare one."

"Is that so?"

"Surely."

"Oh my, he is a nice young man! Does he serve anywhere?"

"No, he's looking for a position."

"Let me take him in at my office."

Within a week, Vasya and Misha had received news that they were to begin service.

After hearing my story, none of my readers will dispute me, and all will agree with me, that knowing the dark corners of the female heart is one of the great sciences of life, and that with its help you can achieve the highest and most important goal of your life, which is to make yourself a career.

Correspondence from the Russo-Turkish War

Vasily Nemirovich-Danchenko (1876–77)

IN 1877, RUSSIA FOUND ITSELF AT WAR AGAIN WITH THE OTTO-
MAN EMPIRE. MUCH ABOUT RUSSIA HAD CHANGED, THOUGH,
SINCE THE CRIMEAN DISASTER OF 1855. POLITICAL REFORMS
HAD KINDLED HOPES FOR A MEANINGFUL SENSE OF CITIZENSHIP,
AND AN ARMY CONSCRIPTED FROM ALL SOCIAL ESTATES FOR A
LIMITED TERM WAS A MORE NATIONAL INSTITUTION THAN IT
HAD BEEN. MOREOVER, THE PRESS HAD CHANGED, AS A RESULT
OF BOTH WEAKER CENSORSHIP AND HIGH-SPEED PRESSES. RUS-
SIA'S TWO MOST INFLUENTIAL PUBLISHERS, A. S. SUVORIN AND
I. D. SYTIN, GOT THEIR STARTS BY RECOGNIZING READER INTER-
EST IN THE WAR. NOT SURPRISINGLY, RUSSIA'S FIRST STAR RE-
PORTER ALSO EMERGED FROM THE BATTLEFIELDS.

NEMIROVICH-DANCHENKO (1844–1936) STARTED THE WAR
WITH A MODEST REPUTATION — WHICH WAS WHY HE LANDED
THE UNPRESTIGIOUS WAR BEAT. A SPECIALIST IN ETHNOGRAPHIC
STUDIES, HE HAD NO INTELLECTUAL OR EDITORIAL PRETEN-
SIONS. HENCE HE WAS POSITIONED FOR THE JOURNALISTIC REVO-
LUTION THAT MADE OBJECTIVITY PARAMOUNT. HE RECOGNIZED
NEWSPAPERS' IMMEDIACY, AND HIS EYEWITNESS ACCOUNTS OF
THE ACTION HELPED IGNITE INTEREST IN HIS STORIES AND HIS
OWN CAREER. DURING THE RUSSO-JAPANESE WAR AND WORLD
WAR I, HIS INFLUENCE WAS SO GREAT THAT HE ENJOYED PER-
SONAL ACCESS TO COMMANDERS.

THE FOLLOWING EXCERPTS ARE FROM THE BATTLE OF THE
SHIPKA PASS (SUMMER 1877), ONE OF THE COSTLIEST OF THE
CONFLICT. THEY CONVEY THE INTIMACY HE CREATED THROUGH
CAREFUL ATTENTION TO DETAIL. THEY ALSO ILLUSTRATE THE

V. I. Nemirovich-Danchenko, *God voiny* (*dnevnik russkogo korrespondenta*) *1877–1878* (St. Petersburg:
B. I. Likhachev and A. S. Suvorin, 1878), pp. 27–56.

ATROCITIES THAT INFLAMED EUROPEAN PUBLIC OPINION SO
HEAVILY AGAINST THE TURKS.

Having just arrived in Tyrnovo, I was settling in for what I hoped would be three or four days when I suddenly heard that the Turks had launched an attack from the south, and massive numbers of their troops were racing toward the Shipka Pass. The sultan had ordered pashas Suleiman and Reif to recapture this pass from the Russians at all costs, and then the rest of the mountains and gorges, which he referred to as "my heart." The Turks' movements had been so secretive that we were not even aware of them on the eve of the attack. On the contrary, General Boreisha (who was in Elena) suddenly telegraphed that he saw hordes of Turks before him, Suleiman's army, and that he needed help. From his position on the heights, he could see that the Turkish army was moving, but he could not make out in which direction. He was denied full backup support, but Dragomirov's brigade and a quarter brigade of gunners were dispatched to Elena, where 3,000 men from Orlov's division and a Bulgarian detachment were being overrun in a desolate hollow by 60,000 of Suleiman's and Reif's troops. It was understood three days prior that Radetsky's corps, the closest to Shipka, could not be refused even the slightest aid. Our soldiers, supported by only two batteries, had to fight against heavily superior odds, one against twenty. These three days will live forever as those of our greatest glory, although for the meager detachment at Shipka they became a martyrology, an obituary.

In all the towns they passed through, the Turks had been ordered by the pasha to confiscate Bulgarian clothing and take it with them. Then we understood the intent of this command: it allowed the Turks to orient themselves better when we were marching in the dark. Prisoners reported a goodly number of Europeans among Suleiman's and Reif's troops, mostly deserters and scouts, but also fifteen Englishmen who, through interpreters, were advising the sultan. That was the information I gathered at Tyrnovo. I stayed there five days. The constant talk of the town was:

"The troops will soon be moving out. Those who just returned from Elena won't even have a chance to rest."

"The situation is very serious—we've got to hurry."

"Dragomirov is leaving tonight. Radetsky has already gone."

"The battle has been raging all day. I think that by now only eight more companies from Orlov's regiment have joined the seven already there with the five Bulgarian regiments. The artillery's nothing exceptional. They've already launched twenty attacks. The population in Gabrovo could hear cannon fire yesterday. Our troops don't have enough supplies or arms to hold out . . ."

A few hours ago the Briansky regiment was dispatched to Shipka, and General Dragomirov's brigade will advance tonight—the Zhitomirsky and Podolsky regiments, General Tsvetsinsky's infantry brigade, which consists of the 13th, 14th, 15th, and 16th battalions, a platoon of one mountain and two field batteries.

The gravity of the situation became manifest when most of the citizens of Ga-brovo evacuated to Tyrnovo. That city and the entire road south were overwhelmed with refugees. Frightened by stories of Turkish atrocities, the populations of the neighboring towns and villages lying to the south toward the mountain range scur-ried for safety in Tyrnovo. There they intermingled with the natives of Eska-Zagra and of other villages lying in the Tundzha Valley and Maritsa. The streets of Tyrnovo are spilling over with them. In several spots it was difficult to fight your way forward. The local administration of Balkan Bulgarians, spared from the swords of the bashi-buzukis[1] and the Circassians, was being quartered in houses that the Turks had abandoned. They permitted the refugees to harvest Turkish fields and appropriate Turkish vineyards and gardens. Moreover, Mr. Naryshin and Mr. Khomiakov, repre-sentatives from the Slavic Benevolent Committee,[2] gave them financial aid. But that was only a drop in the ocean. The hapless refugees streamed forward, loaded down with what remained of their oxen, horses, and whatever they could grab from their houses before the onslaught of the merciless destroyers of the Bulgarian people. You could distinguish the city people from the villagers because the former had carriages, and through the wheels you could see flashes of bright carpets and red and yellow pillows. The old people sat on the horses or in the carriages, holding small children. The profusion of children was amazing. Often the horse or donkey would be lumbering slowly forward, almost doubled over from the weight of the load, and in the middle of the animal's back, between the packs, a two-year-old child would be sleeping, its olive face in the hot sunlight. You could see rugged Bulgarians everywhere. One obviously very tired man was carrying a little boy piggy-back, and also carrying his small daughter. Behind him, almost delirious, on the verge of total exhaustion, walked his wife, nursing a baby. Sometimes these families have nothing at all—no donkey, no horse, no oxen. Obviously they escaped with only what they had on. Abandoned children wander, crying. Their parents simply left some of them, the Turks slaughtered the mothers and fathers of others, and some saved themselves and are now helpless, unable to do anything with their tiny hands.

We were shown a child whom they had started to slice up and then for some reason changed their minds. The poor girl was left with no ear. A bit farther on we met a mother who had gone mad. She had a husband and six children. The Turks had killed them all in front of her eyes. How and why she had saved herself, God only knows . . . She smiled at everyone, laughing until she spotted a baby, at the sight of which she would tremble and beat her head against a wall. Several childless Bulgarians took in abandoned children. The most common facial expression is one of dull melancholy and pain. Sometimes you would see a soldier carrying a kid, an old woman hobbling alongside. She was plainly fatigued, and a Fedor Gavrilov would help her, having stopped down the road in a wretched village and found a tiny baby. Once we came upon a Bulgarian officer riding with one child under

---

1. The elite and deadly Turkish regiments.
2. A private society formed to support the war effort, associated with the Pan-Slavic movement.

each arm, and their mother clutching the stirrup. The contrast between the stern, bearded, suntanned face and the two innocent little heads was striking. Caravans had settled for a rest on both sides of the road. Oxen tried in vain to graze on the already dried grass, campfires smoked, horses snorted, and whole groups of women and children gathered around hastily assembled basins with all kinds of dishes in their hands. The men gathered either around the fires or with the oxen. Occasionally you would be surrounded by a crowd asking not for money but for bread. If you offer them money, they'll turn you down, because there's nowhere to buy anything. It is heartbreaking to see these mothers' pain.

Many of the Bulgarian refugees are armed. All have knives tucked in their belts, and some even have pistols. They say that the Turks would not even permit them to carry knives, not to mention other weapons. In general, the population lived under house arrest. In the cities where Turks and Bulgarians lived together, the Christians did not have the right to take walks in the evenings, when the air had cooled, because the various khans would be out strolling with their harems, enjoying the fresh air. Bulgarian refugees constantly follow our troops. They eat with the soldiers, who especially pity the children. They even sleep between the tents. "Hey, brother," they call out, "give us a crust."

An unbearable heat set in on August 11, worse than the first two days, but the troops had gotten some rest and began to cheer up. There were only six incidents of sunstroke. Gabrovo flashed by as if in a dream. The population greeted us happily along the narrow streets. Women held out their babies to us and threw flowers; old men blessed the soldiers from a distance; young boys sang the Bulgarian anthem and brought wine and water. From behind the iron grilles in the windows of the light blue houses, people stared fixedly at the troops marching by, only now feeling able to breathe freely. In the shade between the tall stone buildings a cold stream flowed, splashing out onto flagstones. The soldiers crowded together there, everyone hurrying to scoop up some water and have a drink. Half an hour later the city had already blinked past, with its bright eastern colors, its hustle and bustle, and cheerful crowds.

"Hurrah!" burst out from a group of soldiers.

"What's going on?" asked those standing by.

"There it is!"

High in the blue sky, beyond the forest ridge, stretching upward, we saw the steep crest of Mount St. Nicholas. It was shrouded by smoke. The frequent thunder of guns sounded from there.

"Hurrah!" joined in the new troops, and the cheer echoed through the glen and ravines, along all sides of the Balkan foothills.

Songs broke out and died away. The soldiers were obviously sincerely happy; nothing was affected. Only here could you truly understand the military camaraderie among them. From morning you heard everywhere: "Faster, faster; they're dying up there; they're thinking of surrendering; we won't arrive in time. . . ." A bend in the road, and again St. Nicholas hid behind the neighboring mountains, only to appear a few minutes later, bigger and more threatening. The heart pumped quickly, wanting to get there now, to join forces with those detachments now dying, having held out for three days, one man against twenty. They wanted to cry out to them: "Hold on; three more hours and we'll be with you." A feverish impatience gripped the soldiers.

It is impossible not to acknowledge, however, that we created many of the problems at Shipka for ourselves. If the pass had been fortified in time, if the heights had been dressed with artillery, if garrisons had been stationed at the most vulnerable points, Suleiman would not even have thought about penetrating here. Now, despite the heroic defense of the ravines and roads, the outlet to the Kazanlyk valley is in the hands of the Turks, and only three-quarters of the pass is under our command. The surrounding mountains are also in Turkish hands, and we must defend a long and torturous position surrounded everywhere but the north by enemy detachments. Suleiman's movements following the retreat from Gurko were patently obvious. We should have fortified the slope of the mountain into the valley, taken the hills, and then controlled the villages around Shipka. Then the Turks would have occupied the valley, and our trenches would have loomed over them from the heights. Even the most superficial strategic planning should have forced Suleiman to retreat behind the lower Balkans or fortify them. Besides, in winter, as early as October, the Shipka Pass is difficult to cross—there are storms, blizzards, avalanches. Having captured the Shipka gorge, the Turks could not be stopped from taking Gabrovo, Travna, and Drenovo. With these positions, it was easy to capture Tyrnovo. This made our position on St. Nicholas all the more profound, and the tenacity of its defense unparalleled during those first three days, August 9–11. . . .

After three days of continual fighting, the Shibinsky detachment could rest. Only sporadic shots rang out, but after the recent battle, the quiet seemed deathly. Our batteries fell silent, having used up all their ammunition.

At the end of the battle, from high on Mount St. Nicholas, the triumphant "hurrah" rang out, traveled down the crest below, and froze in the hollow at the aid stations, only to start up again. It was repeated three times before Radetsky ordered it stopped.

"Why stop them now?"

"The soldiers are extremely nervous right now. If they don't calm down before they go to bed, they won't sleep well. They'll dream about Turks and shout out, startling the sentries."

And truly, the next day I was an eyewitness to some of those nighttime anxieties.

War Stories from the Present-Day War with the Turks

Compiled by M. Evstigneev (1879)

THE LAST SELECTION ILLUSTRATED CHANGES IN THE WORLD OF JOURNALISM WROUGHT BY THE RUSSO-TURKISH WAR. THE TOPIC DID NOT ESCAPE *LUBOK* WRITERS SUCH AS MISHA EVSTIGNEEV, WHO HAD BEEN A BEST-SELLING AUTHOR IN THE 1860s AND EARLY 1870s. RUMORED TO BE AN ALCOHOLIC BY THIS TIME, EVSTIGNEEV MADE HIS LIVING BY COLLECTING ANECDOTES AND PUBLISHING THEM UNDER HIS OWN NAME. HE HAD A SHARP SENSE FOR FASHIONABLE SUBJECTS, AND HERE HE CATERS TO THE PATRIOTISM THAT SURGED AMONG MOST CLASSES DURING THE CONFLICT. HE PLAYED ON THE STANDARD IMAGE OF THE COWARDLY TURK, AND USED A SIMILAR IMAGE FOR SHTETL JEWS, WHOSE PALE OF SETTLEMENT LAY ALONG THE RUSSIAN MARCH ROUTE TO THE BALKANS. AFTER THEIR DEFEAT, THE TURKS NO LONGER POSED A SUBSTANTIVE EXTERNAL THREAT. HATRED FOCUSED EVEN MORE INTENSELY ON THE IMAGINED ENEMY WITHIN, ESPECIALLY THE JEWS, WHO THREATENED THE INTEGRITY OF THE EMPIRE WITH THEIR CLAIMS TO A SEPARATE IDENTITY.

THE COSSACKS AND THE WOUNDED PRUSSIAN

When our forces entered Mitau, our soldiers combed the city, asking if the enemy was hiding anywhere.

A Jew led two Cossacks to the pastor's house with spiteful glee and announced that a Prussian officer was hidden there.

The Cossacks burst into the house and into a room in which they found a seriously wounded Prussian who, although near death, rose from the bed as they entered. The Cossacks stood stunned. One of them told the wounded man, "Nicht furcht Prussian, Cossack nicht scoundrel!" and gave him his hand, trying somehow

---

M. Evstigneev, *Voennye ankedoty i epizody iz sovremennoi voiny s turkami* (Moscow: Manukhin, 1879).

to convince him that he had nothing to fear. Then both Cossacks fell upon the Jew and drove him out of the house with their *nagaiki*[1] for thinking them capable of killing a poor, defenseless enemy.

MITROFAN KOLOKOLTSEV'S ANSWER

"Which noncom will be supervising the work?" General Skobolev[2] asked Melnitsky.

"Mitrofan Kolokoltsev will."

"Show him to me."

A handsome sapper was led up to the general.

"Was that you, old sport, digging that trench under fire yesterday?"

"Yes, your excellency."

"Well, my fine fellow, if you finish digging in the battery by tomorrow night and dig a small bunker in front of our left flank, I'll present you with a St. George's Cross."

"I'll do my best, sir."

"Don't forget, soldier."

"As long as I'm not killed, I'll do it."

"If they kill you, you'll die with honor, for the motherland."

"Yes, sir."

DO WHAT YOU MUST

Mukhtar Pasha[3] was extraordinarily fond of quoting famous military leaders.

Before the battle at Deve Boinu, he summoned his chief of staff and asked, "What did Henry IV say before the Battle of Ivry.[4]

The chief of staff answered, "Henry IV told his soldiers, 'I am your king, you are Frenchmen, there is the enemy. Now do what you must!'"

Mukhtar Pasha wrote this down, and when the moment came, he rode out before his troops.

"I am your commander," he said, "you are Turks, there is the enemy. Now do what you must!"

The Turks fled.

---

1. *Nagaiki* are whips with metal pieces added to the tips in order to inflict greater damage.
2. Russian commander of the war effort.
3. Mukhtar Pasha (Ghazee Ahmed; 1837–?): a Turkish general in the Balkan and Russian campaigns.
4. Ivry-sur-Bataille: a village where Henry IV won a stirring victory over Catholic League in 1590.

Where Is It Better?

L. A. Tikhomirov (1873)

HOPES AROUSED BY THE EMANCIPATION OF THE SERFS IN 1861 WERE SOON QUASHED. UNFAIR LAND ALLOTMENTS AND LOW LEVELS OF EDUCATION MADE INTEGRATION OF THE PEASANTS INTO CIVIL SOCIETY A TOUGH TASK. OVER THE NEXT TWO DECADES, EDUCATED SOCIETY DEVISED MANY PLANS TO AID THE COMMON FOLK, MOST OF WHICH INVOLVED EDUCATING THEM AND ALERTING THEM TO THEIR NEEDS. IDEAS CAME FROM THE RIGHT AND LEFT, FROM THE CHURCH, THE MILITARY, THE LIBERALS, AND, AS IN THE FOLLOWING PIECE, FROM RADICAL POPULISTS. IN THE SUMMER OF 1873, POPULIST STUDENTS WENT "TO THE PEOPLE" IN VILLAGES. THOUGH THEY EXPRESSED THEIR IDEAS IN TRADITIONAL FORMS SUCH AS THE FOLKTALE, THEIR LITERATURE WAS "FOR THE PEOPLE," NOT "BY THE PEOPLE." HERE, LEV TIKHOMIROV (WHO LATER BECAME A CONSERVATIVE) REVISES A FOLKTALE FROM POSHEKHONIA TO CRITICIZE POST-REFORM LAND PARTITION AND INSTITUTIONS SUCH AS THE NOBILITY AND CHURCH. TIKHOMIROV FOLLOWED A RULE THAT OTHER POPULISTS WOULD LEARN ONLY LATER: CRITICIZE THE ELITE, BUT NEVER THE TSAR. FOR A NUMBER OF REASONS, THE POPULISTS FAILED TO SWAY VILLAGE FOLK, AND WITHIN A YEAR MOST WERE ON TRIAL—THOUGH MANY WERE ACQUITTED BY JURIES.

Excerpted from *Agitatsionnaia literatura russkikh revoliutsionnykh narodnikov. Potaennye proizvedeniia 1873–1875 gg.* (Leningrad: Nauka, 1970).

IN THE FOREST

Once upon a time not too long ago, nobody knows quite when, and nobody knows quite where (though they say it was in Mother Russia), there were four brothers, Ivan, Stepan, Demian, and Luka. They lived deep in the forest from the day they were born to their maturity, never seeing another human face. How they got into the forest in the first place, I have to admit I never heard.

The four brothers lived together heart and soul; they loved each other, helped each other in all things, and each would rather have starved than go without feeding his brothers. They built themselves a cabin in the woods, and every day, while one brother stayed home to take care of the housekeeping, the others went into the woods to hunt. So living together in harmony, the brothers knew neither want nor grief; and while they also knew no luxury, that did not seem to bother them.

The brothers had lived in the forest from their earliest years, and so they didn't know that there were people on earth besides themselves. They supposed that there were, but they didn't know how they lived, and they didn't even think about it.

One day the brothers were out hunting and they met a bear. They saw that Misha[1] had a splendid coat. Why, they asked, shouldn't they kill the beast? The bear took to his heels, with the brothers right after him, and they chased him like that for almost the whole day; the damned beast just wouldn't give up. Finally they reached a tall mountain; the bear climbed to the top and hid in the woods, since the mountain was completely overgrown by trees. The brothers saw that they were too tired to follow him up the hill. They moaned and groaned a bit for having let the beast get away, but there was nothing to be done, and since it was getting dark, it was time to get home.

All the brothers wanted to do was get home, but none of them knew which direction to turn. They had gotten lost chasing the bear all day. The brothers thought a while, then sent Ivan up the mountain, so that he could climb up to the very top and spot the road, because things are more visible from high up. Ivan didn't refuse; he went to the mountain and in a minute was hidden by the forest.

The brothers waited and waited, but Ivan didn't return. The brothers started to worry whether something had happened, and they sent Stepan to the mountain to look for their brother and find the road. Demian stayed below. He waited an hour, then another; still no brothers. Demian got scared and climbed up the mountain himself.

He climbed up to the top, but no brothers. So he started shouting and calling them—nope, it was as if they'd been swallowed up. Demian burst into tears and climbed a tree to find the way home. He looked from on high, and he saw a wondrous thing. On the other side of the hill the forest ended, and beyond it stretched a broad plain, so huge that there was no edge in sight. Several villages and hamlets stood on the plain; farms and meadows could be seen, cattle were grazing in the fields, wagons were rolling along the roads, and people were walking. Demian saw a great multitude of people. In the distance a city was barely visible, with white-

---

1. Just as American bears would soon become "Teddy," Russian bears were all called Misha.

stone three-story buildings, with tall churches whose golden cupolas gleamed in the bright sunshine. This was what Demian saw from the top of the tree. He had never seen so many people, so many villages and hamlets; he had never seen such beautiful white buildings and gold-domed churches. It all surprised him greatly, and he stayed there and watched until the sun set and evening fell.

"Miraculous," he muttered.

"Truly wondrous," someone answered from another treetop.

"Verily, it's wondrous!" someone said from a third tree.

Demian looked and saw his brothers in the trees. As it turns out, they had been so enthralled by the spectacle that they hadn't heard him yelling and calling them. The brothers rejoiced and left for home, because they could see the road clearly from the treetops.

As the brothers walked, they discussed what they had seen from the mountain.

"Here, brothers," said Ivan, "must be the place where people live in paradise. There were lots of them, and they could master any labor. Whether cleaning the forest, drying up the swamp, extending the road, building white-stone palaces— they could do it all, because there were many of them living together, and their strength was great. Since we live the four of us alone, what can we do? Nothing. We live little better than some bear. That's the truth, by God. And if someone gets sick, there's lots of them, somebody will always be healthy; and with us, remember how it was when the bear winged me, and Luka was sick with a fever? We all almost dropped from hunger. What can you say? What could be better than a lot of people living together, with everyone happier and more satisfied?

"So, brothers," said Stepan, "should we walk out of the forest, take a look at the people, and show ourselves? What a life we'll lead! We'll live off the fat of the land."

"So let's go," agreed the brothers.

They arrived home and told their younger brother about everything they had seen, and decided to leave the forest the next day.

It was no sooner said than done. They put on their best clothes, took enough provisions for several days, bowed to all four points of the compass, and left their native forest. In two days they had made their way to the plain and were walking along a country road; their path was flanked by rustling rye fields, and the brothers' hearts were light and cheery.

Suddenly they heard the sound of wheels. It was a squalid cart hitched to a wretched nag, carrying a pale, skinny, raggedy peasant.

"Hello, good man," said the brothers.

"Hello," he answered. "Where has the Lord brought you from?"

The brothers told him where they were from and why they had come. The peasant bobbed his beard up and down and said, "You came for no good reason, friends. If you had stayed put in the forest, you would never run into the landlord or constable. You will go through much grief now."

The brothers took fright. "Tell us, grandpa, why would it have been easier to stay in the forest?"

"Why should I go around scaring people? I've got no time to explain things to you, friends. I'll just say: Go back to the forest. It'll be better there."

On that note, the old man left. The brothers stopped and tried to figure out whether the old man had been telling the truth or lying. They thought and thought and decided that he must have been lying, because what could possibly make life bad here? There was lots of land and lots of folks, and if life was so bad, then why had people built palaces that could be seen even from the mountains? Nope, the old man must have lied.

The brothers set off again. They saw a pilgrim walking along and singing a song, a song that was so plaintive that the brothers stopped to listen:

> I walk through the meadows; the wind whistles there:
> > It's cold, pilgrim, cold;
> > It's cold, my friend, cold;
> I walk through the grain—why so thin, grain?
> > It's cold, pilgrim, cold;
> > It's cold, my friend, cold;
> I get to a village—do you live warmly, peasant?
> > It's cold, pilgrim, cold;
> > It's cold, my friend, cold . . .
> I traveled all of Russia: the peasant moans and howls,
> > He moans from the cold,
> > He howls from the hunger.

The pilgrim passed, but the brothers continued to stand there, feeling their hearts sinking as they listened to his song.

"Well, brothers, you have to think that people don't sing songs like that when life is good. It seems that the old man was speaking the truth."

"It seems that he wasn't lying," said Stepan.

"What should we do now?" asked the third brother.

"Go find where it's better," said the fourth.

And the brothers decided to go find out where life was better. One would go north, another south, a third east, and the fourth west. Then they would get back together and decide which way they should go. The brothers said their farewells and went their separate ways.

[*The adventures of Ivan in the north, Stepan in the south, and Demian in the east have been omitted here. They all have encounters with the authorities, after which they are sentenced to Siberia.*]

IN THE WEST

The youngest brother, Luka, went west. Whether he walked for a long time and saw many places, I don't know. I know only that he saw plenty of peasant woe. He saw how the lords and authorities fleeced the working people; he saw how oppressed the poor folk were; he saw the unjust judges; he saw how the poor and those oppressed by ignorance and cowardice endured overwhelming grievances, and still resigned themselves, moaning, like a dog that is beaten by its master.

Luka saw enough of that. He began to hate both the greed of the rich and the cowardice of the poor.

Once while walking along the road, he suddenly saw a monastery in the distance. The monastery stood on a hill, overlooking a river, and it was surrounded by gardens. White walls, green roofs, and golden cupolas peeked gaily out from the thick foliage of trees. Throngs of pilgrims were entering and leaving the monastery. A hushed bell tolled from the tower, summoning the faithful to prayer.

"I'll go to the monastery," thought Luka. "Holy men live there—they serve the Lord God, they pray and do good deeds; there is no contention among them or bloody battle. I'll go to the monastery and relax from the lawlessness of the world."

He went to the monastery and entered the church. It was packed with people. It was quiet and nice in the church: the monks piously sang the prayers; candles burned, brightly illuminating the icons. The icons glittered with silver, gold, and precious stones. The air smelled of incense. It was wonderful!

"It's as fine as heaven here," thought Luka. "I'll stay in the monastery."

After the service he approached the Father Superior and asked, "Permit me, Father, to stay in the monastery. I will do any labor for you, and perhaps the Lord will reward me with a monk's habit."

Well, the Father Superior agreed. Luka was assigned to clean cells. He was overjoyed and went to his spot, his feet barely touching the ground. He saw two monks sitting in the corner and arguing heatedly.

"They gave me more money!" yelled one of them. "Why should I give it to you!"

"Damned liar, you dog!" yelled the other. "You know we agreed to split things evenly. You cheat! If I'd gotten more than you, I would have shared."

It seemed shameful to Luka that the holy fathers were cursing at each other. "It doesn't befit them," he thought. He asked a servant what they were arguing about.

"You see, there's this here wonder-working icon, and some relics too. Some pilgrims can't push their way through the crowds, so they pass money to the monks so they'll light a candle or put it down. So's these two monks made a deal that one'd take money for icons and the other'd take it for the relics, and then they'd split it even-steven. So now ya sees that brother Irenei collected more, and so he don't want to split it. And brother Germogen got less. And so they're fighting."

Luka was horrified to hear that the monks were robbing the sanctuary. He stood petrified as the monks argued, argued so violently that they grabbed each other's beards. Lord—a fight broke out! Brother Germogen was a bit stronger; he crushed Brother Irenei, took his money, and ran. Brother Irenei leapt up, grabbed a rock, and threw it at brother Germogen, almost breaking his skull. He let out a string of swear words.

Luka ran to the Father Superior. "Holy Father," he said, "these are the sorts of things that are happening in the monastery." He told him the whole story.

The Father Superior frowned. "My son," he said, "how can you bother me with such trifles? I'm tired and want to rest. Get out of here!"

Luka left with his head down. "Are such things really considered trifles here?"

All the same, the Father Superior summoned Irenei and Germogen and chewed them out.

"You idiots," he said. "You know the old saying: Steal all you like, just don't get caught. You're giving the monastery a bad reputation and driving away the pilgrims. You can die yourselves then from hunger. Go, idiots, and don't forget that if I hear that you've done something like that again, I'll give you a good thrashing! You can take the money, just don't make a lot of noise about it!"

When Irenei and Germogen left the Father Superior, they were very angry. They met Luka and confronted him. "Hold on!" they said. "You so-and-so, if we get our hands on you, you'd better watch out! You won't ever forget it."

Luka went to clean the cells in the evening. The corridor was long and straight, with the cells arranged along both sides. As Luka walked down the corridor, he heard a noise in the cells—by God what a noise! In one there was singing, in another cursing, in a third fighting. Luka looked into one cell through a crack in the door and saw monks and nuns sitting with vodka and snacks on the table. A monk holding a guitar was dancing a *trepak* and singing, "Oh, my sweetheart, how beautiful you are!" The other monks sang along loudly. The nuns sat drunk and flushed from the wine.

Luka could only spit.

Early the next day, Luka went to the church and began praying to the miracle-working icon of the Virgin Mary, asking her to punish the impious monks and to save him and confirm his faith. There wasn't another soul in the church. Luka prayed ardently to the icon, which was renowned in all Russia. It shed tears, healed the sick, and worked many miracles.

The Father Superior entered with another monk. They didn't notice Luka. The Father Superior approached the icon and pushed down on the candlestick before it.

"What's this, Brother Filaret—there aren't any tears on our icon! Is the machine broken?"

"Father Superior, did you push the candlestick good?"

"Good and hard, and still no tears! What a turn of events!"

They took the icon from the wall and began examining it. Luka saw that the wood had been carved out from behind the eyes, tiny holes had been poked in the eyes, and a wet sponge and been put in the hole. The sponge was covered over with a small board, which had a string connecting it to the candlestick. When you pushed on the candlestick, the string stretched tight and the board squeezed the sponge, pouring water from the eyes like tears. And that was the whole mechanism! Seemingly simple, yet it brought the monks a lot of money. The Father Superior looked over the icon and saw that the string was weak and couldn't press the sponge, so no tears were flowing.

"It should be fixed," said the Father Superior.

They went to get some string and tools, and locking the door to keep everyone out. Luka was left alone. "So that's what kind of wonder-working icon it is!" he said.

"A monkish trick and nothing more! And here I was praying to that painted board!" He spat straight in the icon's eyes. "Wait," he thought. "I'll take another look at the relics."

He went to the holy relics and opened them. He looked—it was a body like any other. He touched it, and the body felt a bit hard. When he scratched it, he scratched off some of the body. When he looked, it was wax, pure wax, just painted over. He snapped a finger off the holy man and brought it to the flame: the whole finger melted. Luka spat on the relics. At that moment the Father Superior and the monk walked in. Luka barely managed to hide, and they began fixing the icon: string, a hammer, nails—they had brought everything. They finished the work. The Father Superior pushed down on the candlestick: tears streamed from the icon. "Well, now, that's better!" they said. They left the church, but Luka waited until the service had begun to leave with everyone else. He had seen enough of the monastery's holy places!

After that Luka wanted to leave the monastery, but then he had a thought. "Let's take a look," he said, "at how they work those miracles. A chunk of wood, a chunk of wax—how can they heal people? Must be some mechanism again." And so he stayed.

Once he went out for a stroll. He walked along the bank of the river and saw a monk walking along gathering opaque pebbles.

"What are you doing?" asked Luka.

"Gathering pebbles."

"What do you need them for?"

The monk started laughing. "You're about to find out a lot of things," he said. "You'll soon be much older."

He left without saying anything.

The next day Luka went to the church and saw the same monk sitting by the doors surrounded by a crowd of people. Everyone was listening to him say "When the Lord Jesus was crucified on Golgotha, his virgin Mother stood by him and wept bitter tears. Her purest tears fell on the dry earth. Here the Lord worked a great miracle: these tears turned to stone, and they are still on Mount Golgotha to this day. When I, a sinful monk, was honored to be in the holy city of Jerusalem, I went to Mount Golgotha and gathered the tears of the Holy Virgin. The tears will preserve you from many sorrows and illnesses. Buy them, pious people!"

The people crossed themselves, and each wanted to take a look at the wondrous tears. Many bought them for five kopecks, a hefty sum. When Luka looked, he saw that the monk was selling the same pebbles that he had been gathering on the river. "Well," he thought, "some tears. These monks really know how to fool people."

Almost six months passed. The annual celebration of the wonder-working icon arrived. On that day, ten times the usual number of people came to the monastery. A couple days before the holiday, Luka happened to be cleaning the Father Superior's room. Next door the Father was sitting with Filaret, and the door was open, so that everything could be heard.

"So," asked Filaret, "what sort of miracle will happen this year? We can't get by without a miracle."

"How can you ask?" answered the Father Superior. "Of course there will be a miracle. I've already hired a boy. He'll be possessed. Clever boy, he's so good at being possessed that it's a pleasure to watch!"

"Was he expensive?" asked Filaret.

"Almost free: ten rubles. After the holidays he's heading off for Solovki:[2] he can heal himself there. We'll send him there ourselves to make sure that the affair gets sewn up."

The Father Superior called for the boy, who came in.

"Hey, Senka, let's see you do God's work!" said the Father Superior.

Senka strained and turned blue; he yelled with a voice not his own, and fell to the ground in contortions. He began foaming at the mouth, wild cries tore from his chest, and his arms and legs writhed. The boy was horrible to look at.

"Nice job," Filaret praised him.

"Enough, or you'll tire yourself out," said the Father Superior. Senka got up as if nothing had happened.

On the day of the celebration, crowds of people flooded to the monastery. They couldn't all fit into the church, so most stood outside. Senka wandered among the crowds. Suddenly he screamed and went into his contortions. The people surged back a few steps and began genuflecting: "Good Lord, what is this?" Senka played his comedy for half an hour before getting tired and stopping. And then he said, "Pious folk, my fate is bitter. I never prayed to God, I never gave money to the honest monks, and for my sins a demon entered me. He torments me sorely. Help me, pious people; is the wonder-working icon nearby? Only she, the Holy Mother, can save me. I'm not from around here; I don't know where to find the holy icon."

The worshippers led him into the monastery and told the Father Superior. He looked at Senka as if he were seeing him for the first time, and began the prayer service. And Senka's possession started up again. He screamed and shouted. Finally the Father Superior said to him, "Be gone, impious spirit, from God's slave Simeon. By the almighty power of God, I exorcise you!"

As he said it, he pressed down on the candlestick. Tears poured from the icon's eyes.

"She took pity, Holy Mother of God, she took mercy," whispered the people. Senka instantly leapt up as if he had been healthy forever, and began praying to the icon to thank it for his healing. The people fell to their knees and praised God for the great miracle.

Luka couldn't stand it any longer: he stepped forward and said, "Orthodox brethren, the monks put the boy up to pretending to be possessed! They're duping you. The icons also . . ."

One of the monks threw himself on Luka and covered his mouth. "Silence, blasphemer!" he shouted. Other monks came running up, tied up Luka, and led him off to the cellar. Then they took him to the authorities. The authorities put him on trial, found him guilty of blasphemy, and exiled him to Siberia.

---

2. A region in the far north famous for both its monastery and, in Soviet times, its harsh-regime prisons.

WHERE IS THE PLACE FOR THE POOR?

Oh, you, the glorious Vladimir Highway! You twist for many versts, long and broad, and you lead straight from Mother Russia to Stepmother Siberia. The Vladimir Highway has been beaten down and trampled, and dust floats above it like a fog. The road is trampled by the feet of convicts, but the dust is lifted by government-issue boots. So much grief passes along that glorious road, so many tears pour out upon it, so many moans and curses are heard on it. The unfortunate go along it day and night in their leg irons, under guard; countless numbers of them go, and they will be going for long still. Pious folk, does the merciful Lord truly not see these burning tears, does he not hear the pitiful moans, and will he not be merciful to these "unfortunates"?[3]

A group of convicts walked quietly along the road; the convicts rattled their chains, and the soldiers' rifles gleamed. The group approached the far end of Mother Russia. A tall pillar stood there, and on that pillar was a plaque: on one side it read "Russia," on the other "Siberia." There ended Mother Russia! Howls and moans rose up from the "unfortunates"; everyone was wailing, saying farewell to their homeland; they kissed the earth, chanting, "Farewell, farewell, our mother: you nourished us, fostered us and raised us, but these evil men wouldn't allow us good fortune, and we misfortunates are now heading for cursed Siberia, to hard labor, to a joyless life!"

Only one convict did not cry, did not sob, did not bid his homeland farewell! He stood silently, crestfallen; his eagle eyes grew dim, and his black thoughts were sad. It was Ivan, the elder brother, thinking about his beloved brothers.

A column of dust twisted up over the road in the distance: it was a second group of "unfortunates." The convicts rattled their chains, and the soldiers shook their rifles. Among the unfortunates walked Stepan, the middle brother, thin, pale, exhausted, bound up in chains, with a brand on his forehead. The new group approached, and they stopped to rest with the others. The brothers saw each other and burst into tears. They began talking about their adventures, and their convict tales were sad.

"Life in the north is good," said the elder brother. "Life is good for the rich, life is good for the landowner, life is good for the factory owner—but there's no place for the poor! They're enslaved by the rich, they go about in ragged clothing, and God alone knows what they eat and drink. There's no place for the poor in the north!"

"There's no place for the poor in the south," said Stepan, the middle brother.

Again a column of dust rose over the highway: a third group of convicts was walking, among them Demian, rattling his chains. The new group walked up, and the brothers threw themselves around each other's necks, wailing and telling each other of their adventures. Demian told his brothers, "There's no place for the poor in the east." The brothers sank crestfallen into thought at this point. "Where is there a place for the poor?" they thought. And then they saw: a new group was

---

3. In popular speech, convicts were sympathetically deemed "unfortunates" rather than criminals.

coming, and in that group was Luka, the youngest brother. And Luka told his brothers, "There's no place for the poor in the west!"

Their thoughts grew even sadder, and only the elder brother did not give in to the melancholy. "So, brothers," he said wisely, "it seems that there's no place for the poor; it seems that the rich have taken all the places. We've covered all of Mother Russia, and we saw the same thing everywhere: the rich plunder the poor, the people are crushed by the village bloodsuckers, and the nobles, and the factory owners, and the masters! They hold the working people in bondage, strip them of their last thread, and then they puff themselves up and fool the stupid *muzhiki*. And the authorities and the tsar think only of their own good and don't care about the poor; they stand up only for the rich, defend the cruel robbers, and they wrote their laws so as to bind the poor hand and foot and hand them over to the robbers. And the people! Your heart moans when you think how obediently they bear their oppression; they submit to all manner of scum and don't recognize their own strength. The people are stupid, dear brothers; the pious folk are cowards, and they slumber in eternal sleep, like the enchanted knight in the tale. Like tiny lice and bedbugs, the village bloodsuckers suck them dry, but the people are asleep and don't feel a thing. Still, dear brothers, the end of this lawlessness is coming. The terrible hour will strike; the people will awake, they will feel their mighty power, their unconquerable strength, and then they will crush their plunderers, their merciless tormentors; they will shed rivers of blood in their anger and take brutal vengeance on their tyrants. The tsar with his ministers and boyars, the factory and land owners, the two-faced monks and tormentors of the people—all will pay for their terrible sins; the people will wipe them all from the face of the earth and then live off the fat of the land.

"Oh, that will be a happy time, when there will be no evil on earth, no falsehood, no oppression, and no violence. The fertile Mother Earth, the ancient sleeping forests, and the green meadow—all this will belong to the peasants. In the cities, all the factories will become the property of the workers. And then there will be no tsar, no landowners, no masters, no bosses; nobody will be drafted as a soldier, nobody will demand taxes, nobody will be exiled to Siberia. And the free peasants and workers will live in plenitude and joy, without constraint, in full freedom.

"Oh, my dear brothers, are we really going to a Siberian prison, are we really going to work for the state treasury? No cell can hold a mighty eagle; no prison can hold a brave man! We will escape to Mother Russia, brothers; we will go awake the pious people. Arise, arise, honest peasants; abandon your foolish timidity, feel your mighty power. Arise, pious people, like the wrath of God, and destroy your enemies!"

Right then and there the brothers forgot their grief, and they began to sing a hearty song. They seized their opportunity on the first night and escaped from the guards to freedom.

From that time on, they have walked the Russian land; they wake up peasants everywhere and call them to the bloody feast. They travel in the south, in the north, in the east, in the west; nobody knows them, but all heed their powerful voices. Peasants draw strength from their voices; they lift their lowered heads, their blood begins to boil, and they are ready to fight for their freedom, for their land, and for the good of the peasants. And when they have enlightened all peasants, Mother Russia will hum and roar, as if the blue sea had risen and inundated all their cruel enemies with its powerful waves.

A Flask of Hooch
A Tale
(1882)

Soldier culture constituted a special part of Russian popular culture. The poor training of Russia's recruits, revealed first by the Crimean fiasco of 1856, inspired self-examination and eventually, in 1874, military reforms. The twenty-five-year enlistment was rescinded, and military authorities devoted less time to drill and more to education. Soldiers became more literate as the term of service was shortened in proportion to their level of education. Series such as the army-produced *Readings for Soldiers,* of which the following was part, were meant to satisfy soldiers' needs without inflaming their political consciousness. They preached the values of loyalty, obedience, and sobriety.

This anonymous morality tale embodies two common themes: it demonstrates graphically the dangers of alchohol (a barrier to military preparedness), and it offers a peek, albeit skewed, into the ways of the Islamic peoples with whom the army found itself in frequent conflict.

Fliazhka romanei (*skazka*), with 4 drawings (St. Petersburg: Chtenie dlia soldat, 1882).

Crimea, a rich and fertile land, is now one of the southernmost regions of the Russian Empire; but in the distant past, Crimea was ruled by the Tatars. Crimea was called a khanate: there was a khan, which means tsar in their language, and he had a strong army, which he sent many a time to pillage our Mother Russia. He had commanders for that army, his pashas and *esauly*. My story is about the great Tatar pasha Ali-Khanym, who was mirza prince to his khan: that means he was the biggest pasha in the Tatar khanate.

The day was so hot that you could bake rusk bread under the sun; there wasn't a soul to be seen on the streets, and even the bazaar was shut up. Only the shoemakers were at their benches, with their armyaks[1] off and their warm caps on. They were stitching soles onto morocco-leather shoes, while an occasional weary camel pulled a dray loaded with wheat down the street.

Ali-Khanym was stretched out on the sofa, contemplating how he might fall asleep, motionless, without so much as twitching a hand or foot. The Tatars are like us: if you don't have anything to do, then it's best to sleep. Ali-Khanym was beginning to feel sleepy.

The mirza had napped for a bit when suddenly someone shook him awake. The mirza came to, squinted, and looked: before him stood his favorite servant, who was called Khamysh.

"Well, what do you want?" asked the mirza, not rubbing his eyes but only pointing to the pipe that he smoked before and after sleep. Khamysh handed Ali-Khanym the pipe.

"Speak," said the mirza. "I'm listening."

"Russian merchants have arrived in our Guesleve* from beyond the Dnepr River and ask permission to appear before you and then trade in our city."

"You mean they have come with their wares?"

"That's right," answered Khamysh.

"And what wares did they bring?"

"Silk, satin, pearls, morocco, and cloth."

"Well, good; but first let them show me their goods, and then I'll tell the merchants if they can do business in our city."

The mirza dressed, set his fur-trimmed cap over his brow, and sat down on the same couch he had been lying on a minute before. The merchants entered; behind them at the door stood sentinels: two Tatars with clubs. Next to the mirza stood his interpreter.

"Ask them," said Ali Khanym, turning to the interpreter, "what they need." The answer was the same as earlier.

"That's fine," replied the mirza, "but I would like to view your wares."

Each of the merchants—there were three in all—bowed low and began unfolding his supply of wares before the mirza, offering him the gift of his choice.

---

1. A padded jacket worn by peasants and artisans.
*The old name of the ancient Tatar city now called Kozlov or Yevpatoria.

The merchants before Ali Khanym

Ali-Khanym surveyed the wares with an air of importance, occasionally nodding and ordering something that he liked to be set off to the side.

"Well," he concluded, "you may trade in our city for three days. But wait!" he added, spying the flask hidden behind the belt of one merchant. "What's that?"

The merchant explained that it was hooch—a drink that gladdens the heart, and banishes woe and grief.

"A glorious drink!" observed the mirza. "If I ever become bored, I'll take a gulp. Leave me the flask." There was no way around it; the trader had to leave his flask. The mirza looked at his gifts closely once more, kicked at a bundle of scarlet-red cloth that did not please him, and stood in contemplation before the flask.

"What an odd thing," he thought. "It gladdens and banishes woe? How can it do that? Maybe it's worth trying. Perhaps I really might feel happier?"

Ali-Khanym took the flask, looked it over, and, standing in the middle of the room, carefully uncorked it. The first swallow seemed so pleasant to the mirza that, pressing the flask to his heart, he began peering around: was anyone watching? He said with a sly smile, "It tastes good, for sure, and it smells of honey—like it was made by the bee itself! Why not have some fun? If the flask has enough fun in it for a full week, then I'll sample its pleasure for a single day!"

The mirza, who in accordance with Islamic law had never drunk anything but *kumiss,** took a few more swallows. And he truly felt a bit happier; but at the same time, like other drunks, he began to think sinful thoughts. Kind Ali-Khanym

---

*Kumiss is a [fermented] drink made from mare's milk.

The mirza violates Islamic law

now looked about dourly; true, he smiled, but as if he were taking pleasure from another's woe. He staggered around the room without even recognizing things that were long familiar. He was even ready to cut up the couch with his saber. At that moment, a pale and worried Khamysh ran in.

"Noble mirza!" shouted the servant.

"Yes?" was the only answer Ali-Khanym could muster, lowering himself exhausted onto the couch.

"The khan himself, with his entire household, has arrived in our city, and he demands that you appear before him."

"So what . . . hold me up and I'll make it to the khan's," replied Ali-Khanym. "Did you notice how happy I am? The merchants brought an amazing drink."

The khan met his mirza sternly and menacingly. But Ali-Khanym fell at the touch of his master and, following Tatar custom, kissed his shoes several times. The khan took pity on the old man. He stretched out his hand, which Ali-Khanym kissed with respect.

"Be seated," the khan said to him.

The mirza pulled up a bench and took a seat at the khan's feet.

"What's new with you?" asked the khan.

"All, by the grace of Allah, lives and prospers for the pleasure of my master," answered the mirza. "By the by, I beg to report that Russian merchants have arrived with wares and ask to be allowed to trade in our city."

"And for that did you get anything for the khan's treasury?"

Ali-Khanym was feeling so merry, and had so forgotten himself, that he paused before answering: "I received many treasures, master."

"Now that's good," continued the khan. "So tell me a story; I'd like to take a nap."

The mirza was like a flour sack—no matter how much you shake it, it still gives off dust. The mirza cleared his throat and began telling the khan a tale of old:

"The great Turkish padishah [sultan], Mahmud, once became seriously ill. His retinue sobbed and wept for him; they wept as if he were already in the grave. The mirza alone—obviously a good man—did not weep, but pondered: How could he aid the padishah, to save him from his sickness and suffering? He remembered a time when a sick man had been cured by putting on the shirt of a happy man. The mirza advised the padishah to try the same remedy. People were sent immediately to find a happy man, but even the padishah's retainers, his favorites, lavished with all his attentions, could not say that they were happy. One called himself unhappy because he had not received from the padishah a gift that he had wanted very much; another confided that his happiness was not complete because he had not yet accumulated enough money. In short, the emissaries could not find a happy man among all the sultan's subjects. They were on their way back to the padishah to tell him that in his whole kingdom there was not a single happy man, when suddenly they saw by the road a country bumpkin walking briskly and singing a merry song at full voice.

"Halt!" the emissaries told him. "You, it seems, are unacquainted with woe, you seem so happy."

"Yes, I am," answered the poor man, "because I have nothing to weep for. Glory to Allah: my family is well fed, as am I; I have plenty of work, and my house is filled with all that a man could need."

"Does that mean you're happy?" the emissaries asked him.

"Absolutely!" responded the poor man.

The emissaries were overjoyed when they heard that answer; they seated the peasant in the cart and transported him to the padishah's palace.

"Here is a truly happy man," they told the sultan. "Take his shirt!" They undressed the poor man. But what happened? They could not find what they were looking for on him. That happy man who was so satisfied with life was not even wearing a shirt.

"All right," said the khan when Ali-Khanym had finished his story, "we will tell the truth and say that true happiness is not in gold and honors, but in that modest satisfaction that seeks nothing extra for itself and thanks God for those little things by which it lives. Thank you, Ali-Khanym, I had a pleasant doze from your tale. I'd even like a full nap. But don't leave yet—I'd like to reward you, and you will soon receive your gift. Farewell."

The khan exited. Ali-Khanym was left alone. His head was spinning from the hooch and from exultation. He fell into deep thought about what the khan wanted to give him.

"That's right," he thought, "the khan's gift won't be some cheap bauble: he won't just give me an old shoe. And even if he did give me that, I'd accept it with gratitude."

At that moment the mirza was joined in the room by a woman covered with a chadra [veil]: it was Kubegulia, the oldest and ugliest of the khan's wives.

"Ali-Khanym!" she said, approaching the mirza.

"Here I am," responded the mirza. "What have you to say, most beautiful daughter of our steppes, you as bright as the summer lightning, as eternally young as the newborn moon?"

"The khan has promised you a gift befitting such a noble and favored mirza."

"He did," responded Ali-Khanym, "and he was standing in that spot when he did. He also told me that he would give me a treasure."

"Here it is."

"Where?" shouted the overjoyed mirza. "Oh, most beautiful of wives," he continued, "show me that treasure."

Kubegulia opened her veil. "The khan has given me to you," she said.

The khan's gift

When he saw Kubegulia's old face, Ali-Khanym hopped away like a popped cork; but then he slowly approached the khan's wife, leaned on his sword, and, peering at Kubegulia's face, could only whisper, "Surely I have received this bounty for my sins."

"And what do you have to say?" asked Kubegulia.

"What can I say?" responded Ali-Khanym. "In my opinion, the khan is very generous if he has given me a treasure that he himself kept for a full fifty years."

"But mirza, your services to the khan are too great."

"That's true! And for that the reward is so dear! I am not worth such favor and refuse the gift."

"How can you?" asked the astounded Kubegulia.

"This is how, my treasure. You go back to the khan's harem."

Ali-Khanym would never have dared refuse a gift of the khan; he would even have been scared of such an audacious thought, had he not sampled the hooch. But now he was feeling very brave.

"Beautiful Kubegulia," he said, "you will find it hard to live with me: I am capricious and spiteful."

"My caresses will make you tamer than a lamb."

"You mean turn me straight into a sheep? Most obliged. Surely my life won't be any happier from all this."

"I can sing our native songs to you," continued Kubegulia.

"Much obliged, but after all, I'm a bit deaf," answered Ali-Khanym.

"I can dance for you, whenever you desire!"

"Just what I need!" thought the vexed mirza. "Incidentally," he continued, "I won't hide from you that I am supposed to die any day: a smart fortune-teller told me so."

"Oh, don't worry," added Kubegulia. "I will weep at your funeral."

That answer utterly infuriated the mirza; he had already stopped thinking about the fact that the old woman, offended by his rejection, would throw herself at the khan's feet, break out in tears, and complain to his master about him.

"I have no need for you—go back to where you came from!" shouted Ali-Khanym. Solemnly donning his cap askew, he scrambled, helped by two of the khan's servants, into the saddle, then, holding onto the mane, rode off to his chambers.

The goblet is a dangerous thing, especially for those who think that it makes us happy or drives away life's woe. And the merchants had told the mirza that hooch gladdens the heart and banishes woe and grief. On top of that, it seemed to Ali-Khanym this first time that the intoxicating drink gave him a special courage.

"So what?" he thought, pacing his mud house. "I don't think I did anything stupid by rejecting Kubegulia. Of course, the khan might get angry, but fury also makes for mercy!"

Smiling at the last thought, Ali-Khanym glanced at the flask. It seemed that he owed such a jolly thought to the flask.

"So what if I drink just a bit more?" thought the mirza. "The khan's ire probably won't frighten me."

With those words, the mirza took a swallow from the flask, smiled, and drained it to the bottom.

Ali-Khanym's head began spinning. He could barely stay on his feet: the room spun before his eyes, the windows grew to twice their size, the doors seemed to hop off their hinges and come at him, and his beloved servant seemed to walk by him on six feet.

"What is all this?" thought the mirza, dropping heavily to the couch. "They said that hooch would make me happy, but to the contrary, it's as dull as a deathbed and as horrible as a hanging. My head is on fire, my feet feel like they were cast from lead, and my hands . . . There . . . I can't see, I feel so bad. Help me!"

And with those words, Ali-Khanym fell to the couch and began snoring.

The mirza saw dreams, each more horrible than the last. First he dreamed that he had been turned into a donkey with such a heavy load that he was almost falling; then he dreamed that he was at the khan's feast, that he was terribly thirsty, that everyone was drinking, but that the khan refused him *kumiss*.

After five hours of sleep, Ali-Khanym came to in a state of terror. He heart beat wildly, his hands were shaking, and his head hurt.

"Allah, Allah!" thought the mirza. "What happened to me?" He had forgotten the hooch, and about his many indiscretions of the day before.

At that moment, an officer of the khan's guard entered the mud house, followed by two Tatars armed with clubs who took position by the door.

"Ah! Khairatan! What do you have to say?" asked the mirza, who was feeling more awake.

"The khan, our great master, announces to you his displeasure," said the commander of the khan's guard.

"Why? What did I do?" muttered Ali-Khanym, turning pale.

"Merchants were here yesterday who did trade in our city. Though you received gifts from them, you contributed nothing to the khan's treasury."

"You're right!" shouted the mirza, who had come to his senses. "I remember it now—I promised the khan to take our due from them. Where are they?"

"The merchants have already departed. The khan himself sent for them, but could not catch them; they're already on the other side of the Dnepr."

"Damned drink!" shouted Ali-Khanym.

"You did something even worse, mirza; you angered the khan by rejecting his gift."

"Damned drink!" repeated the mirza, looking at the flask with hatred. "Poison, a real poison! My senses abandoned me yesterday, and my mind, and my thinking. What a terrible poison that wine is! If not for that hooch, I wouldn't have done what I did for any treasure in the world! I'm doomed."

The mirza's ire

"Yes, mirza, hand over your saber, and these people will take you to the khan's court, where you will receive either mercy or chastisement from the khan."

Almost staggering, Ali-Khanym crossed the room. His heart moaned from regret and repentance. But still he didn't blame himself—he blamed the flask for everything. And we believe the same thing as that Tatar: it's not the drunk who is guilty, but the glass!

The mirza stared long at the flask, cursed it, and finally threw it to the floor with bitterness.

"Here!" he shouted, turning to the two attendants. "Punish it, punish it hard!"

The two Tatars began clubbing the innocent flask and smashed it to smithereens.

"Now you can take me to my execution!" said Ali-Khanym. "As that flask died, now let me die too!"

Gypsy Romances

GYPSY SONGS (*TSYGANSHCHINA*), MELANCHOLIC, SENSUAL, AND EVOCATIVE OF AN IMAGINED LIFE OF FREEDOM CELEBRATED AROUND DISTANT CAMPFIRES, WERE LONG A STAPLE IN RUSSIAN CULTURE. THE ROMANTIC POETS PUSHKIN AND LERMONTOV THRILLED TO THEM. LEV TOLSTOI FANCIED THEM. AND NO NIGHTCLUB COULD AFFORD NOT TO OFFER AT LEAST THE OCCASIONAL GYPSY CHORUS AMONG ITS ATTRACTIONS. MOST OF THE POPULAR SINGERS INCLUDED THESE ROMANCES IN THEIR REPERTOIRE: VERA ZORINA, ALEKSANDR DAVYDOV, ANASTASIA VYAL-

TSEVA, AND THE GYPSY HERSELF, VARVARA PANINA. LISTENERS COULD USUALLY EXPECT SHARP RISES AND FALLS IN TEMPO, ELABORATE FLOURISHES, AND AN UNFETTERED SPONTANEITY THAT MATCHED THEIR MOOD. THEY COULD ALSO READ IN THE NEWSPAPERS ABOUT THE SINGERS, WHO LIVED THE LIVES DESCRIBED IN THEIR SONGS, FILLED WITH CHAMPAGNE, FREE-SPENDING, AND NIGHTS OF LOVE. THE CULTURAL REVOLUTION OF THE 1920s COULD NOT EXTINGUISH THEIR POPULARITY, AND GYPSY CHORUSES RETURNED WITH PRIVATE RESTAURANTS IN THE 1990s.

RASPOSHEL*
A Gypsy Romance

This song was a standard of the repertory. The refrain of the song was written in a mix of Romany and Russian, not fully comprehensible (and thus not fully translated here), but suggestive of unfettered passion and spontaneity. Sung here by Davydov, the song featured the intensifying rhythm and the innuendo of the genre, which won it a broad audience for decades.

Черные очи, белая грудь,
До самой зари покоя не дают,
  Эх, распашел тум-ро
  Сиво грай пошел,
  Ах, да распашел,
  Ты хорошая моя!
Налейте, налейте бокалы вина,

Забудем невзгоды, коль выпьем до дна,

  Эх, распашел тум-ро
  Сиво грай пошел,
  Ах, да распашел,
  Ты хорошая моя!

Darkest of eyes and whitest of breasts,
Till break of day they give me no rest.
  Hey, raspashel tum-ro
  Sivo grai poshel,
  Hey, da raspashel
  You pretty one of mine.
Pour out, oh pour out the goblets of wine,
Drink to the bottom and life will seem fine.
  Hey, raspashel tum-ro
  Sivo grai poshel,
  Hey, da raspashel
  You pretty one of mine.

*Zonophone, Sbornik libretto dlia plastinok Zonofon: opery, operetki, romansy, piesni, razskazy i pr. (Vilna: I. I. Pirozhnikov, 1910–12), 1: 137.

KOROBEINIKI (THE PEDDLERS)*
Nikolai Nekrasov (1861)

This song is an excerpt from a longer poem by Nikolai Nekrasov, Russia's greatest civic poet of the nineteenth century. A masterful wordsmith, Nekrasov focused on the lives of poor Russians, for whom he evoked considerable sympathy. "Peddlers" was a collage of rural Russia after the emancipation, and a strong political statement. Yet this extract, sung with throbbing passion by Varya Panina of Moscow's Yar Restaurant, suggested very different intentions.

Не тростник в поле колышется,
Не дубравушка шумит,
Молодецкая поступь слышится,
Коробейники идут.

Ой, полна, полна коробушка,
Есть и ситцы и парча.
Пожалей, душа зазнобушка,
Молодецкого плеча!

Выди, выди в рожь высокую!
Там до ночки погожу,
А завижу черноокую—
Все товары разложу.

Are the reeds in the fields rustling,
Or the leaves moving in the breeze?
No, that's the jaunty step of a young man,
As the peddlers come to town.

Hey! My box, my box is brimming,
I've got cottons and brocades!
Hey there, sweetheart, take some pity
On a young man's aching back.

Step out with me into the tall rye,
I'll wait there for you till dark,
When I catch sight of your dark eyes,
I'll lay out my goods for you.

Moscow's Yar Restaurant, home of gypsy music and Varya Panina

*Varya Panina, "Korobeiniki," Beka Record G76119. Text in Zonophone, *Sbornik*, 1:58.

Разузнала ночка темная,	Oh, the dark night saw it all there,
Как поладили они,	How the two of them came to terms,
Разпрямись ты, рожь высокая,	Straighten up your stalks there, tall rye,
Тайну свято сохрани.	Keep your sacred secret safe.

TROIKA*
Performed by Anastasia Vyaltseva

Troikas, the famous three-horse sleighs whose bells jingled through the Russian countryside, represented the freedom and expanse of outdoor Russia. In many gypsy songs, troikas dashed toward waiting lovers, so that the very mention of the vehicle set the imagination running. The song is performed here by Anastasia Vyaltseva, whose beauty and extravagance were renowned. By the time of this performance, she was the wife of an officer, who died later in the First World War.

Anastasia Vyaltseva

Тройка мчится, тройка скачет,	The troika hurries, the troika gallops,
Вьется пыль из под копыт.	Clouds of dust come from their hooves.
Колокольчик звонко плачет,	The sleighbells' jingling is plaintive,
Колокольчик так звонит: Ах!	The sleighbells ring out in this way: Akh!
Едет, едет, едет к ней,	He's driving, driving, driving to see her,
Едет к милушке своей.	Driving to see his sweetheart.
Кто сей путник и отколе,	Who's that wayfarer, and whence
И далек ли путь его?	Has he journeyed from afar?
Поневоле иль по воле,	Is it by his will he comes
Мчится он в ночную тьму? Ах!	Rushing through the nighttime dark? Akh!
Едет, едет, едет к ней,	He's driving, driving, driving to see her,
Едет к милушке своей.	Driving to see his sweetheart.

---

*Zonophone, *Sbornik,* 1:241.

Динь, динь, динь, и тройка встала,
Тпру! ямщик спрыгнул с облучка.
Красна девка подбежала
И целует ямщика. Ах!

Едет, едет, едет к ней,
Едет к милушке своей.

Ding, ding, ding, the troika pulls up,
Whoa! He hops down from his seat.
A pretty girl races to him,
And she kisses the coachman. Akh!

He's driving, driving, driving to see her,
Driving to see his sweetheart.

The Aerial Journeys of Madame Garnerin with a Russian Lady in Moscow, 8 and 15 May 1804. This woodcut commemorates the first balloon flight in Russia. Aerial ascents captured the public imagination and were featured in scientific experiments and fairground spectacles alike. The text praises the fearlessness of the women who ascended during a violent thunderstorm. Early nineteenth century. Pushkin Museum of Fine Arts, Moscow.

(ABOVE) *Universal Cosmorama.* The peepshow or *raek* featured exotic pictures on a carousel rotated by the vender, who accompanied each with a rhyming caption. Sensationalism enlivened such commentaries. Here a bearded Brazilian woman, contemporary sex scandals, and the Crimean War are described in oblique terms. 1858. Saltykov-Shchedrin Public Library, St. Petersburg.

(OPPOSITE TOP) *A Cossack Goes Fishing for Frenchies.* This patriotic woodcut, printed during the Napoleonic invasion, embodies popular sentiment toward the heroic Russian defenders and their foreign foes. Circa 1812. Originally collected by Dmitry Rovinsky and printed in his *Russkie narodnye kartinki* (St. Petersburg, 1881).

(OPPOSITE BOTTOM) *A Yaroslavl Man Returns Home.* Peasant migrants, many from the Yaroslavl region of Central Russia, flooded big cities during the mid-nineteenth century. The text describes typical experiences and the stereotypes of the migrants. "The Yaroslavl man lived several years in the big cities as a restaurant waiter without bothering to send any money home. Then his father refused to send him his passport, and he had to return home; when he arrived, everyone was amazed at his stoutness. His father asked him if he had brought any money, but he answered only by rubbing his belly. 'Father, I could barely feed myself. Things were bad; I couldn't scrape up any money for you.'" 1857–58. Pushkin Museum of Fine Arts, Moscow.

Pantiushka and Sidorka See the Sights of Moscow. Pantiushka and Sidorka, like their peers Gavriukha and Kiriukha, were the standard hicks targeted by urban popular audiences. In this routine, depicted here in a woodcut and relived in countless vaudeville acts and print forms, the two villagers gape at such big-city sights as the Kremlin, Red Square, and the Bolshoi Theater. 1879. Russian Museum, St. Petersburg.

(OPPOSITE TOP) *The Pleasant Dream of a Moneylender.* Popular hatreds were reflected in this *lubok* depicting a moneylender who dreams that he has befriended the devil. His new friend provides him the services of his demons, who count his money, put it into bags, and enter it into his ledger, fulfilling his fondest wishes. 1858. Historical Museum, Moscow.

(OPPOSITE BOTTOM) *Down along the Mother Volga.* The sustained popularity of this and other historical ballads is suggested by this *lubok.* Such song sheets were best-sellers for publishers and fed the growing tastes of the public for Russian music, both contemporary and traditional. 1870. Saltykov-Shchedrin Public Library, St. Petersburg.

Yermak Timofeevich, Conqueror of Siberia. The Cossack *ataman*
Yermak was one of many Russian military heroes who were
glorified in popular culture. Commissioned by the
Stroganovs, Yermak extended Russian power to Siberia by
subduing native peoples. He died in 1584 in battle with the
Siberian khan Kuchum. 1868. Russian Museum, St.
Petersburg.

The Types of Russia: Gypsies and Little Russians. As the Russian empire subsumed ever more diverse populations, ethnic stereotypes, both benign and hostile, circulated ever more widely. These postcards depict common stereotypes of Gypsies and Ukrainians in "typical" clothing and poses. 1896–1905. From Anne Goulzadian, *L'Empire du dernier tsar: 410 cartes postales, 1896–1917* (Paris, 1982).

Advertisements. Veneration of great figures from the Russian past became a part of popular patriotism and yielded unexpected applications. Here, Nikolai Gogol is used to sell caramels, and Generalissimo Aleksandr Suvorov represents a brand of cigarettes. State Historical Museum, Moscow.

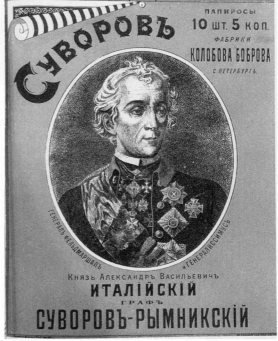

Sylvan Poses. Middle-class families visited photography studios to record their lives for friends and for posterity. Striking poses against highly staged backdrops, they said more about their fantasies than about their everyday lives. Early twentieth century.

The Chains of Love. The lush passions evoked in this sheet music by V. Ya. Radomsky were celebrated in many popular songs and often played out in the scandalous lives of their celebrity performers.

Bobrov and Kurashov: The Original and Only Knife-Sharpener Motorists—Parodies of the Lives of Common People. Mockery of peasant culture was a stock item in the vaudeville that flourished during the early twentieth century.

ТАНГО

9

Испол. артистами
ОФЕЛЬ-БЕЦКОЙ и АНДРЕЕВЫМЪ.

The Tango and the Dance of Death.
Danced by Ofel-Betskaia and
Andreev and Elsa Kruger and her
partner Mack respectively.
Combining the wild popularity of
new dance styles and the fin de
siècle themes of death and
seduction, these photographs
feature two of the more celebrated
dance teams that toured Russia
and introduced sophisticates and
provincials to the latest fashions
from around the world.

Pilot Garro's Heroic Deed. The exploit of one of Russia's earliest air heroes is celebrated in this World War I poster. 1905–1906.

Our Constitution: Please Don't Blow Too Hard. This skeptical caricature depicts Count Witte, prime minister and author of the 17 October 1905 manifesto promising liberal reforms, attempting to create a new constitution. 1905. *Al'bom revoliutsionnoi satiry* (1926).

Сегодня ты.

А завтра я.

"Nikolai II: You Today, Me Tomorrow" and *"Moscow on the Barricades."* Resentment against the ruling regime became so strong and widespread in 1905 that it manifested itself even in postcards. 1905–1906. *Al'bom revoliutsionnoi satiry* (1926) and Anne Goulzadian, *L'Empire du dernier tsar: 410 cartes postales* (Paris, 1982).

The King of Paris. This poster advertises one of the last great dramas of the pre-revolutionary cinema. Produced by Khanzhankov and directed by Evgeny Bauer, it was designed by a little-known young studio employee named Lev Kuleshov, who would soon become one of Soviet cinema's great innovators. 1917. N. I. Baburina, *Russkii plakat: vtoraia polovina XIX–nachalo XX veka* (Leningrad, 1988).

Diary of a Female Model. N. Breshko-Breshkovsky, whose writing is represented in this anthology by selections from *Gladiators of Our Time,* made his literary fortune as a purveyor of lurid tales of sex and high society. The images he evoked by innuendo in his prose are made more explicit on this cover to another of his novels. 1914.

The Keys to Happiness. Manya with Jan in the 1913 movie based on the Verbitskaia novel. Produced by the team of Yakov Protazanov and Viktor Gardin, the film broke all box-office records. 1913.

A Bourgeois Tragedy. In this movie poster, Vera Kholodnaia, the reigning starlet of pre-revolutionary Russian cinema, who was best known for her deep eyes and wan beauty, advertises one of the many melodramas of high-society life and passion that she made into box-office hits.

УЧАСТВ: В. ХОЛОДНАЯ
А. СМИРНОВ И. ХУДОЛѢЕВ.

МѢЩАНСКАЯ
ТРАГЕДІЯ

по ром. Л. Цукколи.

постановка В. К. Висковскаго

дскор. А. А. Уткина.

ДРАМА ВЪ 5ТН ЧАСТ.   операт. В. Ф. Сиверсенъ

ФАБРИКА КИНЕМАТОГРАФИЧЕСКИХЪ КАРТИНЪ Д. И. ХАРИТОНОВА. МОСКВА. ЛѢСНАЯ с. д. ТЕЛ. 3-91-97 и 5-81-40.

Part IV

Political Stagnation vs. Rapid Industrialization, 1882–1905

Marked by violence at both ends—the assassination of Alexander II at one and a sweeping political revolution at the other—this era witnessed the rapid industrialization of the empire. The grandest achievement, the laying of the Trans-Siberian Railroad, united the country more symbolically, though, than technologically. In the world of urban entertainments, the most significant achievement came with the end of the government's monopoly over theaters in the the two capitals in 1882. Social change could be found in the clientele at the growing number of nightclubs, restaurants, and other forms of public space that catered to the new money. Fan magazines circulated photos for emulation and stoked the fires of celebrity with mild gossip. Middle-class men began organizing into athletic clubs, and a bicycle race between St. Petersburg and Moscow left one contestant dead from the grueling ordeal. The paradoxical thrills and dangers of urbanization appeared in the "yellow" press and vaudeville skits.

To a certain extent the new literature revealed a growing cosmopolitanism, however unrefined. The national character could be the object of gentle satire, as was the merchant family the Ivanovs in Leikin's account of travels abroad, or the object of chauvinistic defense, as in many pieces by Vlas Doroshevich, the most famous journalist of the time. Merchants began to frequent shows written with their specific interests in mind. They enjoyed the farces of I. I. Miasnitsky, in which they were the main characters. When they really wanted a night on the town, they went outside it, to gypsy restaurants or suburban nightclubs. The stage entrepreneur cut a new figure on the cultural horizon, represented here by the flamboyant Mikhail Lentovsky. A daring and frequently bankrupt impresario, Lentovsky had considerable ambitions for the idea of public theater, and such notables as Konstantin Stanislavsky and Anton Chekhov remembered him affectionately. Whatever his pretensions for the people, Lentovsky made his reputation as a producer of variety shows in entertainment gardens. His stagings always showcased the latest fashions, which he spoofed for a mixed audience.

As diverse as the people to whom it catered, commercial entertainment often captured their most un-civil attitudes. Everywhere critics looked, they imagined philistines like the merchants of Leikin and Miasnitsky, immune to enlightenment. Even the lightest entertainment, which intellectuals found most appalling (and the stiffest competition for their own work), showed the changes that culture and the human personality were undergoing. Uncouth merchants trampling the hallowed grounds of Italy, or merchant wives bullying their husbands into tickets to Sarah Bernhardt were objects of mindless entertainment; but they alerted viewers to the presence of newly assertive women and merchants. For many social groups, the public display of personality was remarkable, and still a bit disreputable; yet the taboo made such outbursts fodder for entertainment. Uncultured peasants on the railroad, or refined if petulant young ladies such as Marie Bashkirtseva expressed themselves to a variety of audiences, who were often mortified, but just as often felt empowered to make similar displays.

The dangers of lower-class individualism, which included an upsurge in crime and promiscuity, alarmed many people. The great novelist Count Lev Tolstoi moved from writing brilliant novels of upper-class manners to composing Christian morality tales under the rubric *Tales for the People*. Maxim Gorky, who had himself lived a difficult life in several cities, chose the more optimistic route of inspiration. His stories and poems, represented here by "Song of the Stormy Petrel," romanticized revolutionary struggle and personalized it, making the abstractions of revolutionary ideology accessible. In addition, songs that inspired revolution had the capacity to develop independent of their authors, changing according to the variables of each performance. Anthems such as the "Varsovienne" and the socialist "Internationale," whose driving melodies were ideal for bringing people together, often drew them into illicit activities when they might otherwise have hesitated.

The unpredictable interaction of individual personality and social structure was most graphically represented by the huge readership of crime literature, both factual and fictional (a line that was not always clear). The public sphere reserved for celebrity was broadened to accommodate a new class of bold and daring thieves, exemplified by Vasily Churkin, the factory worker and bandit. The real Churkin, who terrorized villages around Moscow in the early 1880s, was eventually captured; the Churkin fictionalized by N. I. Pastukhov, however, was serialized over months and more than a thousand pages, eluding capture through a series of ingenious escapes. He continued Kain's tradition, which became feminized with Light-Fingered Sonya, the Odessa girl who toured the great cities of Russia and Europe, paying her way by high-stakes pilfering. She was eventually captured and exiled to the prison colony on Sakhalin Island, where her celebrity survived, as reporters journeyed east to interview her. Future technological innovations, the still and moving cameras, enhanced her notoriety in postcards and Russia's first movie serial.

Scenes from a Third-Class Car

B. S. Borisov and V. A. Kriger, actors of the Korsh Theater
(recorded circa 1910)

NEWLY BUILT RAILROADS BROUGHT A FLOOD OF PEASANT MIGRANTS INTO RUSSIAN CITIES IN THE 1880S AND 1890S. RIDING THIRD-CLASS, OR "HARD-CLASS," THESE MIGRANTS ARRIVED IGNORANT OF BIG-CITY ETIQUETTE. THEY WERE MOCKED, AND BECAME STAPLE FIGURES OF JOKES AND VAUDEVILLE, BUT THEY ALSO AROUSED ANXIETY.

THE FOLLOWING VAUDEVILLE SKIT, FIRST HEARD IN THE 1880S, AND PERFORMED HERE BY THE MOSCOW (KORSH THEATER) COMEDY TEAM OF BORISOV AND KRIGER, USES ALL THE STANDARDS OF THE GENRE. GAVRIUKHA AND KIRIUKHA (COMMON PEASANT NICKNAMES FOR GABRIEL AND CYRIL) ASSAULT THE SENSIBILITIES OF A NEURASTHENIC SOCIETY LADY. THEY SPEAK SUBSTANDARD RUSSIAN, SING UNCOUTH DITTIES, AND IGNORE CLASS ETIQUETTE. HOWEVER, THE TWO PEASANTS, LIKE SO MANY OF THEIR REAL-LIFE BROTHERS, DISPLAY A SLY KNOWLEDGE OF THE RULES, PARTICULARLY HOW THEY CAN BE USED TO ADVANTAGE.

ГАВРЮХА: Кирюха!

KIRIUKHA: Huh!

ГАВРЮХА: Скучно, брат!

KIRIUKHA: That's for sure!

ГАВРЮХА: А что, гармошку захватил?

КИРЮХА: А? Чаво?

КИРЮХА: Известно, скучно!

GAVRIUKHA: Kiriukha!

KIRIUKHA: Huh?

GAVRIUKHA: Dull, ain't it, brother!

KIRIUKHA: That's for sure!

GAVRIUKHA: Hey, did'ja bring yer accordion?

КИРЮХА: Захватить-да захватил-то. Да что толку-то в этом? Вишь, барыня!

ГАВРЮХА: Вишь. Барыня! Коли значит, мы билет по таксе взяли, да за гармошку заплатили, стало

KIRIUKHA: Sure, I brung da accordion. But what's da point? Don't you see there's a lady?

GAVRIUKHA: A lady! So what, we gots our tickets, we paid for da

---

This skit was transcribed from a recording. There is no written source available.

быть, нам играть слободно! Качай, режь, смоли, Кирюха.

КИРЮХА: Качай.

> Барыня, да барыня,
> Сударыня-барыня,
> Барыня, барыня
> Сударыня-барыня.

БАРЫНЯ: Ох, ох! Господа, господа. Я больной человек. Я не выношу такой музыки.

КИРЮХА: Гаврюха. А? Слышь? Ну? Барыня больная и музыки не любит.

ГАВРЮХА: Ишь, не любит. Коль значит, мы билет по таксе взяли, за гармошку рупь с пятаком заплатили—так нам играть слободно! Качай, режь, смоли, Кирюха.

> Ежели едет развалился
> Это значит на чужих.
> Барыня, барыня,
> Сударыня, барыня...

БАРЫНЯ: Ах! Господа! Господа! У меня нервы.

КИРЮХА: Гаврюха! Ты слышь? У барыни, стало-быть, того, маневры!

ГАВРЮХА: Маневры.

КИРЮХА: Значит, играть нельзя.

ГАВРЮХА: Маневры, врешь ты! Коли значит мы билет по таксе взяли, за гармошку заплатили, значит нам и играть слободно. Качай, режь, смоли.

> Ежели едет развалился
> Это значит на чужих.
> Барыня, барыня,
> Сударыня, барыня...

accordion, so's we can play if we want! Hit it, Kiriukha.

Kiriukha: Hit it.

> Lady, oh lady fine,
> Mistress, oh lady fine,
> Lady, oh lady fine,
> Mistress, oh lady fine,

LADY: Oh, oh! Gentlemen, gentlemen. I'm not well, and I can't stand that music.

KIRIUKHA: Gavriukha. Ya hear? Da lady's sick and don't like our music.

GAVRIUKHA: So what if she doesn't like it. Our ticket's still good, and we paid good money for the accordion, so's we can play all's we want! Hit it, Kiriukha.

> A wagon's ridin', busted up,
> So's that means it's leavin' home.
> Lady, oh lady fine,
> Mistress, oh lady fine . . .

LADY: Gentlemen, gentlemen, my nerves!

KIRIUKHA: Gavriukha! Ya hear? Da lady's got, ya know, maneuvers!

GAVRIUKHA: Maneuvers.

KIRIUKHA: I guess we can't play.

GAVRIUKHA: Maneuvers? No way! So what, we gots our tickets, we paid for da accordion, so's we can play if we want! Hit it, Kiriukha.

> A wagon's ridin', busted up,
> Sos that means it's leavin' home.
> Lady, oh lady fine,
> Mistress, oh lady fine . . .

БАРЫНЯ: Кондуктор, кондуктор, кондуктор.

КОНДУКТОР: Господа, господа. Здесь вагон для некурящих! Что ж вы здесь безобразие делаете?

ГАВРЮХА: Господин кондуктор, мы ведь не курим, а значит, так на гармошке симфонию жарим для услаждения. Потому билет по таксе взяли, за гармошку заплатили. Значит, нам играть слободно! Жарь!

> Барыня, барыня,
> Сударыня, барыня...

КОНДУКТОР: Ах, так вот как? Отдайте гармонь!

ГАВРЮХА: Что ж вы? Господин кондуктор! Что вы, гармошку-то, выбросили? Ведь ж деньги стоит. Зачем же, господин кондуктор. Эх, брат, Кирюха, это дело дрянь. Кирюха!

КИРЮХА: Чаво?

ГАВРЮХА: Скучно, брат!

КИРЮХА: Известно, скучно. Эх, ты, барыня-то, с маневрами. Эх-ты, анафемская душа твоя.

ГАВРЮХА: Кирюха!

КИРЮХА: Чаво?

ГАВРЮХА: А ну-ка, сыграй на губах!

КИРЮХА: На губах? Для барыни? Специально?

ГАВРЮХА: Специально!

КИРЮХА: Вали.

ГАВРЮХА: Ну что-ж валяй (поет)

БАРЫНЯ: Господа, господа, я умоляю вас, умру же от вашей песни.

ГАВРЮХА: Не умрешь! Не умрешь!

БАРЫНЯ: Господа! Кондуктор! Кондуктор!

LADY: Conductor! Conductor! Conductor!

CONDUCTOR: Gentlemen, gentlemen. This is a no-smoking car! Don't you know how to behave?

GAVRIUKHA: Mr. Conductor, we's not smoking, we's just cooking something up for your delectation on this here accordion. Since we bought the ticket, and paid for the accordion, we can play all we wants. Hit it!

> Lady, oh lady fine,
> Mistress, oh lady fine . . .

CONDUCTOR: So that's how it is? Give me that accordion!

GAVRIUKHA: How can you? Mr. Conductor! Whatcha throwing the accordion out for? It cost us money. Why, Mr. Conductor. Brother, Kiriukha, this stinks. Kiriukha!

KIRIUKHA: Huh?

GAVRIUKHA: Dull, ain't it, brother!

KIRIUKHA: That's for sure! And the lady gots maneuvers. Oh, you and your black heart.

GAVRIUKHA: Kiriukha!

KIRIUKHA: Huh?

GAVRIUKHA: Play it on your lips, ok?

KIRIUKHA: On my lips? Specially for the lady?

GAVRIUKHA: Specially for the lady!

KIRIUKHA: Let's hear it.

GAVRIUKHA: Let's hear it. (*He sings.*)

LADY: Gentlemen, gentlemen, I beg you; your singing will be the death of me.

GAVRIUKHA: You're not gonna die! You're not gonna die!

LADY: Gentlemen! Conductor! Conductor!

| КОНДУКТОР: Замолчите! Замолчите, вам говорят. А то выкину вас вон! | CONDUCTOR: Silence! Silence, I tell you. Or else I'll throw you out of here! |
| ГАВРЮХА: Нет, врешь! Этого инструмента не выкинешь. | GAVRIUKHA: Nope, youre wrong! You can't throw *that* instrument out a window! |

Sarah Bernhardt
or, Loge No. 2 in the Dress Circle
M. L. Lentovsky (1891)

LENTOVSKY WAS IMPRESARIO EXTRAORDINAIRE FOR THE OPER-
ETTAS, VAUDEVILLES, AND SUMMER GARDEN THEATERS FRE-
QUENTED BY THE BOURGEOISIE. HE WAS ALSO A CONSUMMATE
PERFORMER, SINGING, ACTING, WRITING, DIRECTING, AND PRO-
DUCING FOR THE *ESTRADA*, THE "SMALL STAGE" THAT FUNC-
TIONED AS THE RUSSIAN EQUIVALENT OF THE AMERICAN VAUDE-
VILLE OR THE ENGLISH MUSIC HALL. DISCOVERED BY THE GREAT
SERF ACTOR MIKHAIL SHCHEPKIN JUST MONTHS BEFORE THE
LATTER'S DEATH, LENTOVSKY SKIRTED BACK INTO THE HIGH-
BROW WHEN HE HIRED THE THEN-UNKNOWN BARITONE FEDOR
SHALIAPIN FOR HIS HERMITAGE THEATER. NEVERTHELESS, LEN-
TOVSKY SEEMED CONTENT TO ENTERTAIN RATHER THAN EN-
LIGHTEN.

THE FOLLOWING SKETCH BURLESQUES THE HOOPLA SUR-
ROUNDING THE SECOND OF SARAH BERNHARDT'S THREE RUS-
SIAN TOURS. THE CHARACTERS' MANY ASIDES TO THE AUDIENCE
ARE TYPICAL LENTOVSKY. THIS SKETCH WAS CO-AUTHORED BY L.
GULIAEV, WHO HELPED WITH THE SHORT DITTIES PUT TO MUSIC.

M. Lentovskii, L. Guliaev, *Sarra Bernard, ili bel'etazh No. 2. Vodevil' v dvukh otdeleniiakh* (Moscow: Lito-grafiia Kommissionera Obshchestva Russkikh Dramaticheskikh Pisatelei S. F. Razsokhina, 1891).

CAST

Viktor Semenovich Panin, a barrister
Anna Lvovna, his wife
Luka Ilich Ptichkin, a minor bureaucrat
Sophia Pavlovna, his wife and a former
    actress
Petya Lidin, a young dandy of
    undetermined means and a friend of
    Panin's

Schlecht, a musician
Kriukov, the manager of the building
    where the Panins live
Mikhail Nikolaevich Ashmetkin, a
    retired general
Various servants

The action takes place in Moscow, in the Panins' apartment. Between the first two acts, an hour passes.

ACT 1: "GUILTY WITHOUT GUILT"[1]

The kitchen in the apartment. The clock strikes noon. Luka Ilich and Sophia Pavlovna enter.

LUKA ILICH (*he begins to sing*):

> What a dinner they prepared,
> What a wine they served,
> I'm already . . .

SOPHIA PAVLOVNA: Luka Ilich!
LUKA ILICH: Sorry, Sonka. I'm just excited.
SOPHIA PAVLOVNA: *Silenzio!*
SOPHIA PAVLOVNA (*wringing her hands*): It's noon. The master isn't home, the mistress is still dressing. And on such a momentous day, such dreadful *desordre!*
LUKA ILICH: Well, maybe . . .
SOPHIA PETROVNA: Don't interrupt! No, the words from Tolstoi's tragedy do not describe this household: "The Russian land is big and wide, but still there's order in it."[2]
LUKA ILICH: Sonka, Tolstoi never said that.
SOPHIA PAVLOVNA: Luka Ilich, don't try to argue with me. You like the "tra-la-la," but I was raised on the classics.
LUKA ILICH (*to the audience*): Don't believe her. She's definitely a fan of the classics, but she's forgotten everything she learned. She gets everything muddled.

----

1. The title of a popular play by Nikolai Ostrovsky, a mainstay of the Russian repertory.
2. Originally, "The Russian land is big and wide, but still there's no order in it," from the eleventh-century Nestorian Chronicle, and more recently the epigraph of A. K. Tolstoi's satirical poem "The History of the Russian State from Gostosmysla to Timashev" (1868).

SOPHIA PAVLOVNA (*sitting down in the armchair, posing, speaking dreamily*): Oh, yes, today is one of the great days of my life. Sarah Bernhardt's arrival has invigorated me—I can sense how completely her artistic temperament is like mine. This realization inspires me, gives me strength . . . she has resurrected my talents. I am painting again. (*tenderly*) Luka! Mon petit Luka, tell me, was that portrait of you I did this morning so bad? Wasn't the likeness stunning?

LUKA ILICH (*to the audience*): Likeness, yes, but to a stray dog, not to me.

SOPHIA PAVLOVNA: She has reminded me of my debut. Oh, how delightfully successful it was. I made my entrance . . . I was playing the role of Ophelia in *Mary Stuart.*

LUKA ILICH (*to the audience*): What did I tell you about her disorientation?

SOPHIA PAVLOVNA: Imagine . . . (*she stands*) The theater was packed with the cream of society. The stage had been turned into a dark forest, mountains on the left, bushes on the right, a river in the distance, moonlight. A young girl, stunningly beautiful, enters from the wings. Me. (*She reenacts the scene.*) Eyes lowered, I walk to the footlights and, plucking a flower, begin to sing softly,

> He was a stocky fellow in a helmet with a sword,
> Old father Danny, he drank beer with gusto.

LUKA ILICH (*to the audience*): She's gone completely crazy.

SOPHIA PAVLOVNA: When I walked off the stage, I collapsed. I was beside myself with joy. The applause and encores didn't stop.

> Even the chief of police
> Sent a carriage for me.

LUKA ILICH (*to the audience*): She's right about that. Everywhere she debuted, the local government paid for a coach to get her out of town.

(*Anna Lvovna enters.*)

ANNA LVOVNA: Hello, my dear aunt and uncle. Sorry I made you wait.

SOPHIA PAVLOVNA: *Silenzio!* Listen, Anya, this momentous day is passing quickly, and you have such *desordre* here!

ANNA LVOVNA: So what, Auntie? I overslept, and then it took me forever to get dressed.

SOPHIA PAVLOVNA: You cannot tease your way out of this one, my good woman.

ANNA LVOVNA: Oh, what's your problem, Auntie? Let's have breakfast, please.

LUKA ILICH: Breakfast, good idea. Ah, tongue, stuffed chicken, caviar—

> Ah, the smell, the taste of chicken,
> Oh, how it entices me . . .

SOPHIA PAVLOVNA: Luka!

LUKA ILICH: It's from "The Little Creole Girl."[3]

ANNA LVOVNA: A little vodka, Uncle?

LUKA ILICH: If I might.

ANNA LVOVNA (*pouring*): You not only might, you must. (*A servant enters.*)

ANNA LVOVNA: What do you want?

SERVANT: Kriukov, the new building manager, is here to see you.

ANNA LVOVNA: Ask him to return when the master is home.

SERVANT: Certainly. (*exits*)

SOPHIA PAVLOVNA: Don't tell me you're changing apartments again. You're such spendthrifts!

ANNA LVOVNA: It's not that, Auntie. Yesterday I was at the Petrovskys', and I met our new manager. He told me that he needs this apartment and suggested another, more comfortable one, in another wing. At first I agreed, but then I thought it over and talked to Viktor. I sent him a note this morning asking him to discuss it with my husband.

(Luka Ilich is stuffing his face, coughing, in general eating like a pig.)

SOPHIA PAVLOVNA: He'll be the death of me.

ANNA LVOVNA: So, Auntie, today is the day of days, wonder of wonders, miracle of miracles.

SOPHIA PAVLOVNA (*excitedly*): Aniushka! I never thought I'd see this day.

ANNA LVOVNA: Neither did I! Just imagine, the theater will be full, only the best people there, and we'll walk into loge number two.

SOPHIA PAVLOVNA: Will we really have that place? It's still unbelievable.

ANNA LVOVNA: Believe it. Loge two, left side. I saw Viktor's tickets myself.

SOPHIA PAVLOVNA: Heaven. So close to the stage.

ANNA LVOVNA: I'll be all decked out, in the latest fashion.

SOPHIA PAVLOVNA: Me too.

ANNA LVOVNA: During the intermission they won't be able to take their binoculars off me.

SOPHIA PAVLOVNA: Me neither.

ANNA LVOVNA: Then suddenly in the aisles I hear "What an ugly face!"

SOPHIA PAVLOVNA (*threateningly*): They aren't talking about me?

ANNA LVOVNA: Of course not—about Ashmetkin.

LUKA ILICH: Is he coming with us?

ANNA LVOVNA: Of course. You know how it is with Ashmetkin. Today he is sending a letter of recommendation on your behalf to an important person, and you'll get the position you wanted.

(Panin enters.)

---

3. A very popular contemporary song.

ANNA LVOVNA (*kissing him*): Hello, homeless one!

PANIN (*disturbed*): Is that anything to say, dear? Auntie, Uncle!

ANNA LVOVNA (*anxiously*): Is anything wrong?

PANIN: No, of course not. (*quietly to Luka Ilich*) Uncle, I have to speak with you in private.

ANNA LVOVNA (*turning to her aunt and uncle*): Today he left at ten and gets home at two. What have you been up to?

PANIN: Business. . . .

ANNA LVOVNA: Maybe you think I'm lonely without you. Not so. Yesterday I was at the Petrovskys', and we had such a wonderful time. I met a wonderful young man there, Kriukov. Educated, interesting . . . He was after me all evening—such eyes! Wavy hair, rosy lips, black mustache—so handsome, much more so than you. He invited me to see Sarah Bernhardt this evening.

PANIN (*angrily*): This is intolerable! (*He tries to leave.*)

ANNA LVOVNA: Where are you going? I won't let you!

PANIN: I can't endure this stupid comedy any longer.

ANNA LVOVNA (*kissing him*): Oh no, my dear, my darling. You're angry, I'm sorry. There, there. . . .

(*Someone approaches offstage.*)

SOPHIA PAVLOVNA (*poking her head outside*): Aniutochka! Someone's here from Madame Schlecht.

PANIN (*frightened*): What? What's Madame Schlecht doing here?

SOPHIA LVOVNA: She's a seamstress and sent over a dress.

ANNA LVOVNA: What's the matter with you, Viktor? What are you so scared of? Your face is white.

PANIN (*pulling himself together*): Nothing, nothing at all. I was just thinking about something else, and then your aunt screamed.

ANNA LVOVNA: Are you okay?

PANIN: I'm fine. It's just that all this Sarah Bernhardt business is wearing on my nerves. Now you two leave. I have to speak with your uncle.

(*The women leave.*)

PANIN (*pacing nervously*): I'm going nuts! Schlecht! Paulina Fedorovna Schlecht, my wife's seamstress! I'm dead!

LUKA ILICH: Good Lord, Viktor, should I send for a doctor?

PANIN: I don't need a doctor, I need a rope! Do you think we're going to the theater this evening?

LUKA ILICH: Of course. Loge number two, left side.

PANIN: Do you have the tickets?

LUKA ILICH: No, you do.

PANIN: I did, but I gave them away. With my own hands. To Paulina Fedorovna Schlecht.

LUKA ILICH: The seamstress? How?

PANIN: Here's how. When Petya Lidin gave me the tickets, it was in exchange for my promise to spend all yesterday evening, his birthday, with him—celebrating like bachelors, if you catch my drift. We ended up with a lot of people, quite drunk. Somebody suggested a masquerade.[4] Why not? We arrived and started in on more champagne. I don't even remember who brought the woman to our table. She was wearing a mask. We started talking. She knew everything about me—my wife's name, the servants, what my apartment looked like. I was drunk, and I didn't believe that she could know all of this, so I challenged her to a game of truth or dare. Of course I lost.

LUKA ILICH: How much? A hundred, two hundred rubles?

PANIN: That would've been nothing. She insisted on the tickets to loge number two that she knew I was holding.

LUKA ILICH: And you gave them to her?

PANIN: My buddies kept pressing me, telling me it would be dishonorable not to. My head was pounding something fierce. I've spent all day searching the city for tickets for loge number two, right side. Money won't buy those tickets. When my wife finds out that I gave her seamstress the ticket—she's flame, and I'm ash. . . .

(Anna Lvovna enters.)

PANIN (*tenderly*): What do you say, Anya, let's not go to the theater this evening.

ANNA LVOVNA: What do you mean, not go, when you've already got the tickets?

PANIN (*decisively*): What if I lost the tickets, or gave them away?

ANNA LVOVNA: Then I'd be mad at you for the rest of my life. I'd hate you. I don't know what I'd do if I couldn't see Sarah Bernhardt.

> If I don't see Bernhardt,
> You can kiss my love goodbye,
> My friend, I'll learn to hate you,
> And fall in love with another.

PANIN: Anya, what are you saying?

ANNA LVOVNA: I'm answering a joke with a joke.

(The servant announces Lidin and Ashmetkin. They enter, exchange greetings, kiss Anna Lvovna's hand. Ashmetkin sits next to her.)

ASHMETKIN: I congratulate you, Anna Lvovna, on this glorious day—at last you will get to see Sarah Bernhardt.

---

4. Masquerades were quite popular in turn-of-the-century Russia; they were often public rather than private parties, and organizers charged admission.

LIDIN: Congratulate me also. Something "superfine delicatesse" happened to me today, too. Just think, an hour ago I was given a ticket to one of the loges to see Sarah Bernhardt! Free! There's a woman who's in love with me, and she invited me.

PANIN: Loge seats! I'm saved!

ASHMETKIN: Merci, Anna Lvovna, merci for letting me sit in the loge with you. Honestly, I'm not much of a fan of the theater. But to see Sarah Bernhardt! In fact, my rank pretty much obligates me to go. I'm retired, but still, for a general not to have seen Sarah Bernhardt?!

PANIN (*aside, to Lidin*): I hope you'll give me your tickets.

LIDIN: Not for anything!

PANIN: Save me from a fight with my wife!

LIDIN: On the contrary, I'll start the fight. When she learns that you don't have the tickets, she'll make a scene. Then I'll step in and offer her mine to the loge. You understand. She'll be *very* grateful, and that'll increase my chances with her.

PANIN: That's dishonorable.

LIDIN: I'm not an honorable guy. . . .

(Luka Ilich enters. He greets everyone and pulls Panin aside.)

LUKA ILICH: We're dead. You don't know the latest scandal. I went to Madame Schlecht to beg her for the tickets. She insisted she didn't have them. Lies. I got on my knees. Suddenly the door opened and a man walked in. He turned out to be her husband, and how do you think he reacted to a man on his knees in front of his wife? That German started screaming. I still don't know how I got out of there.

(Schlecht enters.)

SCHLECHT: 'Scuse me, gentlemen, but I'm lookink for zombody. . . . (*He sees Luka Ilich, hiding behind the chair.*) You tought I vouldn't find you, but you left your coat ven you ran away. You insulted my vife, down dere on your knees.

ANNA LVOVNA (*runs to Panin*): What's going on?

PANIN: For God's sake, leave, go to your room.

ANNA LVOVNA: Let me go. I want to know everything.

ASHMETKIN: What's going on?

SCHLECHT: Your Excellency, I didn't know you vere here. You're my benefactor. You helped me, and now you can help my vife. I'll start from ze beginnink. Last night I had to vork at a masquerade. I play the trombone. I took my vife vit me. She sat down at a table vit some guy (*looking closely now at Panin*) — hey, dat's him! He played a game vit my vife, and she won from him a ticket, loge number two, left side.

ANNA LVOVNA: What! You went to a masquerade and lost my ticket? You were drinking and flirting, and gave away my seat! I'll never forgive you! I'm going to see Sarah Bernhardt. I must tell Kriukov to wait for me.

PANIN: I won't allow it.

ANNA LVOVNA: What?! After what you've done? I'll do whatever I want. You're a monster, a brute. I hate you! I'm so unhappy.

ASHMETKIN (*to Luka Ilich*): And what kind of a man are you? I'm going to fire you from the position I just arranged for you.

LUKA ILICH: I'm found guilty without being guilty!

PANIN (*to Schlecht*): Do you have the tickets with you?

SCHLECHT: I'm goink to sell it, cheap. I didn't do anytink to earn, got it free from a fool.

PANIN: How much?

SCHLECHT: Ask Paulina Fedorovna.

ASHMETKIN: I see now what a laugh you've had on my account. Invite me, and then not take me.

PANIN (*to Lidin*): Get out of here or I'll kill you!

ANNA LVOVNA (*taking Lidin's arm*): Don't go yet; you can accompany me out. (*to Panin*) Now I understand why you were so upset all day. You were afraid of being found out. I'll get my revenge, I'll get my revenge. . . . (*to Sophia Pavlovna*) Auntie, our husbands have betrayed us. They've swapped us for the seamstress, given her loge number two, right side.

SOPHIA PAVLOVNA: Does this mean I don't get to see Sarah Bernhardt? Oh, Luka! I'll make you answer for everything! Where is he? I'll get him, kill him, and toss his ashes far away!

ANNA LVOVNA (*exiting*): Leave me alone! I never want to see you again!

ACT TWO: "OH, YES, SARAH BERNHARDT!"

(*Kriukov is onstage with the doorman.*)

KRIUKOV: Where have they all gone? They left the apartment empty like that? Are you sure you aren't drunk?

DOORMAN: I never touch the stuff, sir. And it wasn't vodka that upset them either, but St. Bernard.

KRIUKOV: A dog?

DOORMAN: Is St. Bernard a dog? Whatta ya know.

(*The doorman exits, and Panin enters.*)

PANIN (*to himself*): I barely got her to go home. Now she's locked herself in her room and is talking about revenge, about how she's going to go see Sarah Bernhardt with her brunette. If I see him . . . (*sees Kriukov*) Who's that?

KRIUKOV (*bowing to him*): Excuse me for bothering you . . .

PANIN (*to the audience*): A brunette, with a mustache. Could this be Kriukov?

KRIUKOV (*to the audience*): Why's he looking at me so strangely? (*to Panin*) Allow me to introduce myself.

PANIN: Don't bother. I know you. Kriukov, isn't it?

KRIUKOV: Yes. So Anna Lvovna's told you all about me. She's already agreed, but wanted to talk it over with you.

PANIN (*unhappily*): If she's already given her consent, I won't stand in the way of your happiness. Take her.[5]

KRIUKOV: I didn't think you'd agree so quickly. I'd heard you really like her a lot.

PANIN (*bitterly*): Like her, don't like her—until today I never thought I'd part with her. But when I learned that others, like you, were after her . . .

KRIUKOV: Me? No, I don't want her for myself. Another man saw her and simply fell in love with her. But this is all secret. If I take her for myself, it won't be for long. I don't really like her that much. Besides, I couldn't afford her for long. . . . When will you let me have her?

PANIN: Go to hell! I won't give her up!

KRIUKOV (*to the audience*): What a strange guy! (*to Panin*) What are you so upset about? If it's too much trouble, just tell me and I'll find another, better than yours. I have to leave now.

PANIN: Where are you off to? We need to talk.

KRIUKOV: No, I've got to get ready for the theater. Sarah Bernhardt.

PANIN: Who are you going with?

KRIUKOV: Certainly not alone. Who needs to know?

PANIN: Don't be so naive.

KRIUKOV (*to the audience*): He certainly is strange. (*exiting*) I really do have to go now.

PANIN (*following him off*): Now the bird is in the cage. My dear, I'm going to make sure that you remember Sarah Bernhardt!

(*Lidin enters and sings about jealousy. Then Panin returns.*)

PANIN: I've locked him in the pantry. He can sit in the dark all evening thinking about Sarah Bernhardt. (*to Lidin*) What are you doing here? Snake! Vampire! Get out!

(*Panin exits. Luka Ilich and Sophia Pavlovna enter.*)

SOPHIA PAVLOVNA: I won't agree to your plan. Do you think I'm so simpleminded that I'll immediately believe in my husband's innocence? Frailty, thy name is man. . . .

---

5. The Russian word for apartment, *kvartira*, is feminine. From this point, both Kriukov and Panin are using the pronoun "her," but Kriukov is referring to the apartment, while Panin thinks he's referring to Anna Lvovna.

LIDIN: Sophia Pavlovna, listen to reason. If Luka Ilich gets the position he wants, that means a nice salary, and you'll be able to live quite well. You can go to the theater and see Sarah Bernhardt whenever you want to. In fact, you'll have such a nice apartment that you can live like an aristocrat, and will be able to develop your own artistic talents. You can draw, paint—charming! You'll live such an exotic life. I'm sure that in ten or fifteen years, with the proper advertisments, you too will be an international celebrity, just like Sarah Bernhardt!

SOPHIA PAVLOVNA (*ecstatically*): Thank you, thank you! Young man, you're right. In fifteen years I'll be a marvelous actress again. I'll agree to your scheme. (*extending one hand to each man*) Gentlemen, escort this genius to her dressing room!

(They exit. Then Lidin returns with Ashmetkin, who is drunk.)

ASHMETKIN: God, I'm drunk, and you got me this way. I know why. I've been serving thirty years. You want me to write a letter of recommendation. I can't recommend a man who cheats on his wife! God, I'm drunk.

LIDIN: That's no crime. All of Russia drinks.

ASHMETKIN: Okay, listen. I'm smashed, but I haven't forgotten your promise to show me Sarah Bernhardt. Panin promised me a loge seat, but it turned out he was making fun of me.

LIDIN: I promise, this is no joke. That was a misunderstanding.

ASHMETKIN: I still can't figure out what she's doing here.

LIDIN: It's a secret. Turns out that Sarah Bernhardt needed a good lawyer, and someone recommended Panin. She's here consulting with him. (*to the audience*) Now you've got the joke! (*to Ashmetkin*) See how well I take care of you? And just last week you refused to give me money. (*exits*)

ASHMETKIN (*alone*): Boy oh boy. I'm going to get to talk to Sarah Bernhardt! Oh my God, what language? My French is terrible! Let's see, I know the words for boots—*bottes;* collar—*collier;* shoes—*chaussures.* . . . Here she comes! I hope I don't faint!

(Sophia Pavlovna enters, moving dramatically. She walks upstage.)

SOPHIA PAVLOVNA (*to the audience*): Don't you think I look remarkably like Sarah Bernhardt?

ASHMETKIN: Madame, you are Sarah Bernhardt?

SOPHIA PAVLOVNA: Oui.

ASHMETKIN (*ecstatically*): I'm talking to Sarah Bernhardt!

SOPHIA PAVLOVNA: *Vous parlez français?*

ASHMETKIN: *Bottes, chaussures, collier, farine*—flour.

SOPHIA PAVLOVNA: *O, il est beau joli.*

ASHMETKIN: Do you speak Russian?

SOPHIA PAVLOVNA: Yes. The Russians are such a good people. (*beckoning to him*) *Venez ici.*

ASHMETKIN (*to the audience*): Oi, oi. Her eccentric personality is beginning to show.

SOPHIA PAVLOVNA: Are you coming to the theater this evening?

ASHMETKIN: I can't, I don't have a ticket.

SOPHIA PAVLOVNA: *C'est dommage.* Never mind. I'll recite a monologue for you here. You'll be my Armand.[6] (*She begins a nonsensical recitation, mixing French with Russian, that mentions Hamlet and Romeo and Juliet.*) *Mon général! Je l'adore. Baise main, baise main!*

(*Luka Ilich, Anna Lvovna, and Lidin enter.*)

LUKA ILICH: What is this! Your Excellency, what are you doing on your knees?

ASHMETKIN: What's so surprising about me on my knees? Sarah Bernhardt wanted to recite a monologue, and I was playing Armand.

EVERYONE TOGETHER: Huh? What Sarah Bernhardt?

ASHMETKIN (*pointing to Sophia Pavlovna*): There she is!

(*Everyone starts laughing.*)

LUKA ILICH: What kind of Sarah Bernhardt is that? That's my wife!

ASHMETKIN (*to Lidin*): Thanks a lot. You told me it was Sarah Bernhardt. (*to Sophia Pavlovna*) Why did you trick me?

SOPHIA PAVLOVNA: You mistook me for her, and I, because I am such a great actress, played her for you.

LUKA ILICH: Well I won't stand for this. You were trying to seduce my wife, to destroy my family. You were on your knees, kissing her hand. I have witnesses, and I'm taking you to court. All Moscow will find out about this!

ASHMETKIN: But it's all a mistake!

LIDIN: Come on, Luka Ilich, forgive him. What if he gives you that letter of recommendation?

LUKA ILICH: Not for you, not for anything! (*softening and taking the letter*) Okay, give it to me. Let's shake hands. Now you must ask my wife for her forgiveness.

(*Panin enters.*)

ANNA LVOVNA (*throwing herself at him*): Viktor, you terrible, evil man! How could you have played such a dirty trick on me?

PANIN: Huh? What are you talking about?

LIDIN: See how he continues with the joke. Only a very talented actor could show such surprise. Enough already. I've explained the joke to Anna Lvovna, how we

---

6. The young lover in Sarah Bernhardt's most famous role, *La Dame aux Caméllias.*

plotted the whole thing about the masquerade with Schlecht. (*He gives him the tickets.*)

PANIN: Now what about this brunette you were writing to?

ANNA LVOVNA: Kriukov, our building manager. I wrote him to discuss the business of changing apartments with you.

PANIN: The apartment? (*to Lidin*) Please let him out of the closet I locked him up in. You're my savior. I'm so grateful to you. Now, where did you get these tickets?

LIDIN: From Schlecht, the woman who's in love with me.

ANNA LVOVNA: Oh, Auntie, it's time to start dressing for Sarah Bernhardt.

PANIN: We're certainly all going to remember her!

ANNA LVOVNA: I will for the trick that was played on me.

ASHMETKIN: And I for how I was fooled.

LUKA ILICH: And I for the letter I got.

LIDIN (*to the audience*): I found out because of her that Madame Schlecht conducts herself *sehr schlecht* [very disreputably].

SOPHIA PAVLOVNA: And I because she gave me the opportunity to dust off my talents.

ANNA LVOVNA: Now everyone is satisfied.

LIDIN: No, not everyone. (*points to the audience*) Some of them are still in doubt.

ANNA LVOVNA:

> Now the actors stand before you,
> We have a custom in the theater,
> To sing a couplet at the end.
> We're in the terrible position
> Of not knowing your opinion,
> Was it so bad? Tell us truthfully,
> We want to know your honest answer,

(pointing to the actors assembled onstage)

> Look at us here,
> Did you enjoy it or not?

CURTAIN

The Queen of Diamonds
A Comic Opera in Three Acts
V. P. Valentinov (1908–1910)

VALENTINOV WAS A KEY FIGURE IN THE RUS-
SIAN OPERETTA, WHERE HE WAS BEST KNOWN
FOR SHOWS SUCH AS *MOSCOW AT NIGHT, SE-
CRETS OF THE HAREM,* AND *THE QUEEN OF
DIAMONDS.* VALENTINOV, LIKE MANY OPER-
ETTA COMPOSERS, DID EVERYTHING FROM
PERFORMING TO DIRECTING AND PRODUC-
ING. HIS MOST POPULAR TALENT WAS WRIT-
ING "OPERATIC MOSAICS," MEDLEYS OF SONG AND DANCE WOVEN
TOGETHER BY SLENDER STORYLINES, AND FEATURING PRETTY
GIRLS, LIVELY MUSIC, AND SLIGHTLY RISQUÉ SITUATIONS. THE
POPULARITY OF JACQUES OFFENBACH AND FRANZ LEHAR
THROUGHOUT RUSSIA SUGGESTED THE NEED FOR A NATIVE COM-
POSER. ALTHOUGH VALENTINOV DID NOT ENJOY SUCCESS
ABROAD, HE SATISFIED RUSSIAN TASTES. RUSSIA EVENTUALLY
BRED ITS OWN (SMALL) GALAXY OF OPERETTA STARS, WHO AP-
PEARED AT SUCH THEATERS AS THE BOUFFE AND THE HERMIT-
AGE: HANDSOME LEADING MAN MIKHAIL VAVICH, CHARACTER
ACTOR NIKOLAI MOKHANOV, AND VERA SHUVALOVA, WHO
TRAINED IN THE PETERSBURG CONSERVATORY BUT PREFERRED
THE VARIETY STAGE.

WE PROVIDE HERE A SYNOPSIS OF *THE QUEEN OF DIAMONDS,*
FOLLOWED BY TRANSLATIONS OF SEVERAL REPRESENTATIVE
SONGS. THE SHEET MUSIC IS ALSO INCLUDED.

CAST

Oleg Zimin, a poet
Tatiana, his sister
Romashkin, his friend and a petty
   bureaucrat

Zina, Romashkin's wife
Baron Talin, Romashkin's boss
Vera, his wife

Snezhkov, a capitalist   Chorus
Fredi, a Neapolitan singer

SYNOPSIS

Act One: Oleg opens by singing his poetry in ballad form to Tatiana, who is appreciative of her brother's talents, but wishes he could earn money with them. Their friends the Romashkins join them, which results in much drinking, singing, and dancing. Zina, Tatiana, and Romashkin celebrate the "golden liquid in their goblets" until Tatiana passes out, unaccustomed to such heady refreshment. When she comes to, she recounts a dream, in which her brother ruled as tsar and she at last enjoyed great wealth. Oleg, who has not joined their revelry, ends the first act coaxing her back to sleep, as only in dreamland could her fantasies come true.

Act Two: The curtain rises on dancing and singing "in the whirlwind of a waltz." Various romantic intrigues are made known at this point: Romashkin and his boss's wife, Vera, are carrying on with each other, as are their respective spouses—all unbeknownst to each other. The spouse-swapping is really nothing more than light-hearted flirtation. Baron Talin, while chasing "Zizi," as he calls Zina, promises the group a big surprise, which turns out to be an appearance by Tatiana, who now reigns on the concert stage as the "Queen of Diamonds." She too has found illicit amour, with the aging capitalist Snezhkov. Why they conceal their relationship is unclear: perhaps because Talin also seems interested in Tatiana? All the characters but Oleg, who seems somewhat smitten with Vera, have the opportunity to sing about true love in this act. However, age flows as an undercurrent in the refrain that "love is given to spring and youth," and all these people are well beyond their first blush.

Act Three: Youth enters in the figure of Fredi, the Neapolitan singer who appears among them without explanation. Touched by his romance, the group cries for more, until Tatiana intervenes and tells them that he must protect his voice. Quickly it becomes clear that he and Tatiana are in love and plan to run away together. Snezhkov lashes out in a jealous rage; Tatiana tells him that she never loved him, only his money. He announces that he has been her lover, which surprises everyone. Fredi challenges him to a duel to protect her honor, but to spare Fredi, Tatiana admits the truth. Their friends are stunned, but she shocks their sensibilities even more with her determination to pursue "wealth and a place where there is no need for tears." Oleg begs her to listen to honor and reason, but she cannot surrender her crown. Tatiana vows never to return "anywhere that people suffer," and Oleg "damns her to eternity." The play ends as the first act did, with Oleg's lament to his sister to go to sleep, because only there can her dreams come true.

SELECTED SONGS

Fill Your Goblet with Golden Liquid
(from Act One, sung in three parts: Zina, Tatiana, Romashkin)

Zina
Among life's petty skirmishes, and woes, and cares,
Wine is the only spring of divine blessing.
It gives us everything—youth, courage, and passion,
Even the old folks regain their former zeal.
It's confusing: of course, there's a debate
About whether wine is the source of strength!

Tatiana
I've put rouge on my cheeks, my eyes burn like fire,
Sadness and troubles are forgotten,
Bewitching dreams beckon to us in the unknown distance,
One and then another goblet calls, no need to press,
It's easy for us to recognize love and the sweetness of a kiss.

Romashkin
Words of love cannot intoxicate,
They contain eternal lies and betrayal,
There is only one path to the truth, given to us by heaven.
Flowers, sighs, the moon, a poet's mournful delirium,
In the light mist, look for victory in wine!

Chorus
Fill your goblet with a golden liquid,
Drink it boldly and nimbly,
This is our life's ideal,
In it is solace and forgetfulness!
(*Repeat chorus.*)

In the Whirlwind of a Waltz
(opens Act Two, danced and sung by the chorus)

We throw ourselves into the whirlwind of a waltz,
We sing songs and rollick without a care;
The waltz enchants, it stirs our blood,
We are ready to dance all night.
La la, la la, la la, la la, la la, la la, la la, la la!

The waltz gives happiness to everyone,
It beckons tenderly in the distance,
How many sweet moments and marvelous sounds it has given us,
How many sweet moments and marvelous sounds it has given us!
La la, la la, la la, la la, la la, la la, la la, la la!

I can give up the whole world,
I can give up the whole world,
I can forget everything, everything, everything,
In order to live in the waltz.
I can forget everything, everything, everything,
In order to live in the waltz.

We throw ourselves into the whirlwind of a waltz,
We sing songs and rollick without a care;
The waltz enchants, it stirs our blood,
We are all ready to dance all night.

Everything That Is Beautiful
(from Act Two, sung by Tatiana and Zina)

Tatiana
When lilac buds are growing and the sun warms happily,
When the flowers are blooming and the nightingale singing,

Zina
Then there are no boring, sad stories,
The soul is completely filled with ecstasy,
With sweet, sweet daydreams,
In those days when spring reigns!

Tatiana
The silver brooks babble and roses give off their aroma,

Zina
When spring sings its song, don't let these days slip away!

Tatiana (*sings the refrain alone*)
All that is beautiful, all that is beautiful,
Only golden spring gives to us,
All that is beautiful, all that is beautiful,
Only golden spring gives to us!
Autumn comes, everything dies, or else it flies away,
Autumn comes, everything dies, or else it flies away!

Tatiana
When the heart beats fast,
And anger flares from love and passion
When fire burns in the blood,

Zina
Then give yourself over to your feelings courageously,
Only in them is the source of happiness,
Don't let it hide from you completely
In these days when youth reigns.

Tatiana

Love, ardent kisses, don't wait for autumn's somber days.

Zina

Love is filled with beauty in these days when youth reigns!

Tatiana

All that is beautiful, all that is beautiful,
Only golden youth gives to us,
All that is beautiful, all that is beautiful,
Only golden youth gives to us!
Old age comes, everything dies, or else it flies away,
Old age comes, everything dies, or else it flies away!

(Then Zina and Tatiana sing the refrain together.)

Potpourri with Dances
(one of the novelty numbers from Act Three, this one sung by Tatiana, and then Romashkin and Zina join her in the chorus as they sing and dance together)

Here is a map of hot southern countries,
A Negro, black as coal, goes into a seedy nightclub,
He thirsts for intense caresses
From a completely respectable Negress,
He gulps whiskey and starts up a ruckus!
Having drunk a great deal, he can no longer distinguish race,
At that moment he sidles up to the white beauties,
Waving his arms in bizarre and wild ecstasy,
He dances his favorite dance right there with two of them!

Tatiana, Zina, Romaskin (dancing)
He thirsts for intense caresses
From a completely respectable Negress,
He gulps whiskey and starts up a ruckus!

Tatiana, What I Saw Now
(Oleg's final lament)

Sleep, go to sleep,
You will see radiant Paradise in your dreams,
Where fresh roses bloom,
And beautiful May shines eternally!
Sleep, go to sleep,
Sleep, go to sleep!

Anecdotes

(1840–1917)

ANECDOTES, A PRODUCT OF THE CITY, ENTERED POPULAR CUL-
TURE SOMETIME AFTER THE EMANCIPATION OF THE SERFS. THEY
REFLECTED THE EXPERIENCE OF CITY DWELLERS, MOST PROMI-
NENTLY THEIR RELATIONS WITH PEASANTS AND ETHNIC MINORI-
TIES. MANY ANECDOTES ORIGINATED ON THE STAGE, AND IN-
CLUDED HERE IS ONE FROM THE ACKNOWLEDGED MASTER OF THE
GENRE, IVAN GORBUNOV, WHO REGALED PETERSBURG AUDI-
ENCES UP TO THE 1880S WITH TALES WHOSE HUMOR SEEMS
TRAGIC TODAY. MANY OF THE ANECDOTES WERE DEVOID OF
STANDARD PUNCHLINES, OR EVEN THE STRUCTURES OF HUMOR.
YET AUDIENCES FOUND THE VERY MENTION OF ETHNIC OR PEAS-
ANT ECCENTRICITY FUNNY. SINCE ETHNOGRAPHIC DETAILS, IN-
CLUDING LANGUAGE, WERE AN ESSENTIAL FEATURE OF HUMOR,
THE ORIGINAL RUSSIAN IS INCLUDED WHERE APPROPRIATE.

Two cabbies were arguing about which is more harmful to drink: vodka or beer.

First: Listen, brother Serega, it's time to quit hard liquor; the docs say that it's bad for the stomach. They say that beer, even though it's alcoholic, is usefuller for human beans.

Second: No way, Uncle Faddei, I'll never give up hard liquor. Beer is just fine, I have nothing agin it, but there's a special little place in my belly for vodka.

Два извощика спорили о том, что вреднее пить: водку, или пиво.

1-й извощик. Послушай брат Серега, пора нам отстать от трехпробного: дохтура бают, что дескать вредно оно для желудка. Вот пиво, примером сказать, хотя и хмельное, но уж гораздо пользительнее для человека.

2-й извощик. Нет! дудки, шутишь, дядя заддей, никогда не отстану от спиртуозного; пиво то пивом, от него не прочь, но для водки у меня есть особое местечко в брюхе.[1]

---

1. K. G., ed., *Al'bom balagura* (St. Petersburg: Shtab Voenno-uchebnykh zavedenii, 1851), p. 321.

IN THE VILLAGE

"Hey Ivan, you back from the city?"	—А, Иван, ты из города?
"Yup."	—Из города.
"Ya ride back?"	—Приехал?
"Nope."	—Нет.
"Walk?"	—Так пришел?
"Nope, didn't walk either."	—Нет, и не пришел.
"Then how'd ya git here?"	—Так как-же.
"Brought muh cow back."	—А привел назад корову.[2]

Evening. Some bricklayers from an artel are walking home from work past the big municipal public hospital. Glancing at the huge building, one of the workers turns to his comrades and says:

"Now there, guys, is a real place!"

"How's that?"

"That's where they make corpses. Two of my buddies died there, and a third is dying now."[3]

"How many people died?" asked the infirmary doctor.

"Nine."

"How did that happen? I prescribed medicine to ten patients."

"That's right, but one refused to take it."[4]

"What a disgrace! I had to walk to the city to look for work! There's life in Russia for you!"

"What, didn't you have your passport with you?"

"Of course! I even had two, and both of them new!"[5]

OUR SERVANTS

Lady: You, dearie, are truly impertinent!

Cook: What, five rubles a month and you expect compliments too?[6]

"Vaniukha, Vaniukha [a peasant name]! Did you cut off a length of board?"

"Sure I cut it, but it came out too short!"

"By very much?"

"Just a straw."

"Well, that's all right; it can be stretched with a nail."

---

2. Aleksandr Nevskii, ed., *Nashi zuboskaly. Razskazy, stseny iz russkogo, evreiskogo, armianskogo i drug. bytov* (St. Petersburg, 1879), p. 6.

3. Aleksandr Nevskii, *Poteshnik. Iumoristicheskii al'bom* (St. Petersburg, 1876), p. 13.

4. *Smekhotvor ili shuty gorokhovye*. izd. Krakovskogo (St. Petersburg, 1880), p. 35.

5. Graf Lapotochkin. *Sovremennye Ivany. Komicheskii sbornik narodnykh russkikh kupletov, duetov i pesen dlia peniia pod balalaiku* (Moscow: Konovalov, 1913), p. 4.

6. *Sovremennye Ivany*, p. 24.

"It can't be stretched."

"How come?"

"Because I also cut the board it fits against, a straw too short."[7]

MISERY

A Scene from Folk Life, told by I. F. Gorbunov

A peasant is sitting on the porch, hanging his head. Another peasant approaches; the first is fairly drunk.

First: Now I'm a lost man!

Second: How?

First: Just buried my wife.

Second: So what? We're all born to die.

First: But she was my only wife, the onliest of 'em all.

Second: God's will be done.

First: But she was my onliest wife.

Second: Well, ya can't have ten—only Tatars can have lots of 'em!

First: And here I had only one.

Second: You can get married again.

First: That won't happen soon.

Second: Why not? There's lotsa girls in the village.

First: You go and find a match for my dear departed wife. I could give her a thrashing, give her a thrashing that not even a pillow would slow down, and she wouldn't even think of hitting back with an oven fork or nothin', she'd just cry.

Second: Why'd ya wanna beat her in the first place? Was she really so hard to handle?

First: A real witch, not to speak ill of the dead.

Second: Ya gotta avoid a wife like that like the plague.

First: Well, I'm not nice when I'm drunk, I can be mean. . . . I love order and obedience: I'd smack her right in the face the second anything happened—sometimes with a stick. And there you take a wife like Protasikha: her husband hits her, and she hits right back with a rolling pin or oven fork—she almost knocked his brains out; that's plenty, thanks! Now, that's the sort of wife ya gotta avoid![8]

"Vodka is your worst enemy!" said the preacher to a peasant who loved a stiff drink or two.

"That's right," answered the peasant. "But sir, doesn't the Holy Gospel tell us to 'Love thy enemy'"?[9]

---

7. Reginald E. Zelnik, ed. and trans., *A Radical Worker in Tsarist Russia: The Autobiography of Semen Ivanovich Kanatchikov* (Stanford: Stanford University Press, 1986), p. 22.

8. *Poteshnik*, p. 3.

9. *Novyi smekhotvor. Iumoristicheskii al'bom s karritaturami*, pt. 1 (St. Petersburg: R. Golike, 1876), p. 7.

A wealthy landowner kept two orangutans, which he dressed up for fancy-dress balls. They were standing by the entrance when a peasant from the neighboring estate brought a basket of peaches and pears. When the peasant reached the porch, the fruit-loving animals threw themselves at his basket and gobbled up the fruit.

The peasant, who was seeing such animals for the first time in his life and mistook them for people, respectfully doffed his cap, put the basket on the steps, and watched them casually, as if this were how things were done.

When the monkeys had eaten their fill, the peasant picked up the empty basket and went into the owner's room to give him a note from the neighbor.

"Where is the fruit, my fellow?" asked the landowner.

"Your children were pleased to eat it, sir," was the answer.[10]

ETHNIC HUMOR

Ethnic tensions grew after the 1860s, as the minorities of the empire came to the big Russian cities. Anecdotes, which reflected the tensions, were marked by outright bigotry. Told with odd accents (which are conveyed weakly in these translations), such jokes poked fun at ethnic types such as penny-pinching Armenians and avaricious Jews. Anecdotes could also be backhanded praise to certain ethnic attributes, and at times, they even mocked or subverted common stereotypes.

IN THE CLUB

An eastern (Armenian) type approaches a young girl in a club.

Armenian (in a singsong): Miss! Would you dance the French quadrille with us?

Girl: With pleasure.

Armenian: And might one sit next to you?

Girl: Why not? Please sit.

Armenian (sits down next to the girl and stares into her eyes, as if trying to find a conversational topic there. A short pause): Miss, why are you so white, and your cheeks so red?

Girl (embarrassed): I don't know.

Armenian: You don't know? Do you come here often?

Girl: No, not often.

Armenian: So, then, miss, you must have a papa?

Girl: Yes, I do.

Armenian: And do you have a mama?

Girl: Yes.

Armenian: Hmm. You know, we have two parents too.[11]

---

10. M. Evstigneev, ed., *Kha! Kha! Kha! Sobranie iumoristicheskikh anekdotov* (Moscow: Frum, 1876), p. 5.
11. *Poteshnik*, p. 4.

HONESTY

A scene from Jewish life

A gentleman newly arrived in Berdichev, who was staying in a Jewish hotel, was being served by a ten-year-old Jewish boy named Itzko. Serving the gentleman his tea, Itzko asked:

"Meester, maybe you lose someting today?"

"Why? Did you find something?"

"I finds a zilver piece by your door. It must be yours?"

"Good boy. Keep the silver piece as a reward for your honesty."

"Tank you," said the overjoyed Itzko.

Several days later, the same gentleman lost the gold key to his watch.

"Itzko, did you find my gold watch key?"

"Certainly, sir, I find it even yesterday in de hallvay."

"Then why haven't you given it to me?"

"Sorry, sir, I kipt it as a revard for my honesty."[12]

THE CONVERT

A young Jew was baptized. One day he was walking along the street and met another Jew, who had not converted.

Convert: Hello!

Unbaptized: Hello!? You fraud!

Convert: Why fraud?

Unbaptized: What do you mean, why? Didn't you do anything?

Convert: So what did I do?

Unbaptized: Didn't you convert to Christianity?

Convert: So what?

Unbaptized: So what? What about your father, who died three years ago? He's probably turning over in his grave.

Convert: That's all right. In two weeks my little brother is converting, too, and then he can turn back over again![13]

TURKISH MANNERS

Even Turks know how to be polite. For instance—

Conversing with the Turkish ambassador, a pretty lady belonging to high society

---

12. *Nashi zuboskaly,* p. 4.

13. Pavel Veinberg. *Stseny iz evreiskogo i armianskogo byta Pavla Veinberga.* 6th ed., greatly expanded (St. Petersburg: Remezov, 1878), pp. 180–181.

expressed her dissatisfaction with the Islamic Koran, which allows Turks to have many wives. "Why should that be?" she asked.

"Madam, it is because we can find many women with the rare qualities and beauty that are so happily united in your person."[14]

A Jew was boasting about his great deeds:

"With one stroke of my saber, I cut both feet off a Turk," he said.

"His feet? Why not his head?" asked his listener.

"Someone had cut it off already."[15]

THE TAKING OF BRAILA

A Scene from Jewish Life, told by Pavel Veinberg

After the fortresses of Shumla and Varna had been taken,[16] folks began debating whether the Russians would take the fortress of Braila. A Jew was asked:

"What do you think, Shmuel—will they take Braila Fortress?"

"Who?"

"The Russian army."

"Russian soldiers?"

"Right."

"Of course they'll take it. They'll take it all. When they came through our town, whatever they saw, they took! Pots, pans, geese—they took it all! Whatever they lay their eyes on, they'll take; don't you worry!!!"[17]

A [Russian] lawyer wanted to make fun of an Armenian.

"Jafar, have you heard the old saying "An Armenian is worse than a Yid"?

"Good saying. And what will be worse than an Armenian?"

"What could be worse? The plague, maybe? Ha, ha, ha!"

"That's correct. Well, there's another saying, you know: 'A lawyer is worse than the plague.' And look how it comes out, my good lawyer: an Armenian's worse than a Jew, the plague is worse than an Armenian, and a lawyer's worse than the plague. How do you like that saying, my good man?"[18]

---

14. *Nashi zuboskaly,* p. 11.

15. *Veselaia strunka. Sredstvo ot melankholii i khandry vsiakogo roda* (Moscow: I. I. Rodzevich, 1879), p. 23.

16. Both towns were located in Bulgaria, and were taken by the Russian army during the 1878 Turkish campaign.

17. *Poteshnik,* p. 4.

18. *Veselaia strunka,* p. 67.

STUDENT JOKES

Student subculture was marked by shenanigans familiar to other countries. Students were one of the most radical sectors of the population, and their anecdotes (as well as their songs and tales) were more overtly political than those from other sectors of Russian culture.

Tsar Alexander III dies and goes to heaven. He approaches the gates of paradise and knocks.

"What strange forest creature comes to us so early in the morning?" asks the Apostle Peter from behind the gates.

"It is I, His Imperial Highness, Emperor of All the Russias, King of Poland, Grand Duke of Finland, etc., etc."

"We can't accept such a big herd of people all at once. Come back one at a time, and make it a little later, when the heavenly powers have had their tea," Peter angrily replies.

There is nothing he can do. So the tsar-peacemaker walks away, sits down, and begins to cry bitter tears. Then a smuggler comes up to him and asks:

"Why are you crying, Alex?"

"They won't let me into heaven."

"Well, tell you what," says the smuggler. "If you promise not to be stingy with me, I'll help put an end to your misery."

So they reached an understanding.

Now, who should step up to the gates of paradise just then but some kind of foreigner. He knocks. The keys jingle, and again the grumbling voice of Peter asks:

"Who's there?"

"It's me, Carnot, president of the Republic of France."

Again the jingling of keys. This time the gates open wide. The smuggler takes a sack and says to the tsar, "Climb into it." At first Alexander III refuses, pointing out his origins and his services to the Russian people, whose benefactor he so recently was, having provided them with land captains and village policemen, and having restored the birch rod to the peasants, who longed for it so much, by permitting them to be flogged in the township administrative offices.

However, even these indisputable services fail to move the unrelenting smuggler:

"You'll go to the devil's furnace, no more, no less, if you don't climb into the sack. Just remember, you too wanted to maintain a high moral tone. But I'm sure when you were drunk like a pig, you didn't observe all the . . . ," the smuggler declares forcefully.

After hearing such convincing arguments, the tsar climbs into the sack. The smuggler slowly straps it up, bends his knee to the ground, and, barely managing to hoist it to his shoulder, carries it to the gates of paradise.

"Who's there?" Peter asks once again.

"It's President Carnot's baggage."

The gates open wide, and the smuggler is allowed into paradise.[19]

Professor: What is the average lifespan for a human being?

Student: For us, professor, until you meet your first patriotic demonstration.[20]

Professor: Which diseases known to man are unconditionally terminal?

Student: Judaism and intellectualism, sir.[21]

Everything is upside down nowadays: once Lomonosov[22] walked to the university from Arkhangelsk, and now they're sending all the Lomonosovs from the universities to Arkhangelsk.[23]

—Why are all those people crowding around the bookstore window; are the police doing a search?

—No, some student is actually buying textbooks![24]

AT A MEDICAL SCHOOL POSTMORTEM

—Hey, listen, how did you sew up that body? It has two right legs!

—Yeah, there's something fishy going on. The corpse I sewed over on *that* table has two *left* legs. I don't get it![25]

Rumor has it that third-year students of the women's medical school asked a lecturer to give them a talk on the differential diagnosis of *herpes labialis* and *herpes nasalis*. It's nice to see the girls paying such close attention to the subject.[26]

OUR STUDENT DICTIONARY

Alcoholic: a man who drinks vodka on only two occasions: when he has herring, and when he doesn't have herring.

---

19. Kanatchikov, pp. 140–141.

20. *Strely,* no. 6 (1905).

21. *Strely,* no. 3 (1905).

22. Mikhail Lomonosov (1711–1765), Russia's first great scientist and writer, was born a peasant in the northern Arkhangelsk region. He walked south from there to the capital cities to find a higher education.

23. Sasha Chernyi, *Maski,* no. 5 (1905).

24. *Satirikon,* no. 25 (28 Sept. 1908): 3. Special student issue.

25. Ibid., p. 4.

26. *Bal'naia gazeta,* no. 3 (November 1912).

Autonomy: a word that cannot be translated into Russian.

Fashion: the art of dressing to be undressed later.

Sausage: the appetizer, main course, and dessert at a student dinner.

University: a building which is entered rarely by students, and periodically by police.[27]

ANECDOTES FROM 1917

"Papa," Nicholas Romanov was asked by his son Aleksei, "is *autocrat* spelled with a capital letter?"

"It's not spelled at all."

"How about 'Tsar of Poland' or 'Grand Duke of Finland,' are they spelled with capitals?"

"They're not spelled at all anymore."[28]

Protopopov[29] says, "Rasputin's spirit has left me, and there's no point in keeping me in prison."

He is told, "We can let you go only when your *own* spirit leaves you."[30]

Nicholas II, strolling around the courtyard of his prison, exclaimed: "Now I understand how the Jews felt in the Pale of Settlement!"[31]

An "old-regime" statesman says, "Russians need a big stick over their heads to make them live right."

An anarchist asks him, "Do you consider yourself a Russian?"

"Indubitably."

So the anarchist picks up his cane and cracks him on the skull.[32]

---

27. Excerpted from *Studencheskii sbornik «Gaudeamus»* [Kharkov], no. 1 (5.XI.1913).

28. *Anekdoty pro tsaria Nikolia dikaria* (Petrograd, 1918).

29. Aleksandr Protopopov (1866–1917) was a failed newspaper publisher, the last tsarist minister of the interior, a confidant of the empress after Rasputin's death, and an object of mob hatred after the February Revolution. He was eventually executed by the Bolsheviks.

30. *Sovetskie anekdoty* (Berlin: Chuzhbina [1928–1932]), p. 3.

31. *Sovetskie anekdoty*, p. 7.

32. *Sovetskie anekdoty*, p. 13.

Moscow Court Reporting

The Moscow Sheet (Early 1880s)

THE JUDICIAL REFORMS OF 1864 INTRODUCED TRIAL BY JURY TO
RUSSIA. INITIAL FEARS THAT THE LOWER CLASSES WOULD NOT
TAKE THE DUTY SERIOUSLY WERE UNFOUNDED; BUT JURIES DID
OFTEN CONFOUND THE AUTHORITIES BY ELEVATING "EMO-
TIONAL" CONSIDERATIONS ABOVE STRICT LEGALITY. THE JURY
TRIAL MADE ITS WAY INTO POPULAR CULTURE, FEATURING A
CAST OF CHARACTERS SUCH AS THE AUTHORITATIVE, IF BEWIL-
DERED, JUSTICE OF THE PEACE; THE SKILLED ADVOCATE, WHO
WAS OFTEN AN UNDERGROUND PROFESSIONAL, AND NOT ALWAYS
ETHICAL; AND A MOTLEY THRONG OF DEFENDANTS AND WIT-
NESSES FROM ALL CLASSES, WHOSE CLAMOROUS DESIRES WERE
UNCHECKED BY THE LAW. TRIALS WERE POPULAR NOT ONLY FOR
THEIR DRAMA BUT FOR THE INSIGHTS THEY PROVIDED INTO POP-
ULAR PSYCHOLOGY. A JUICY CASE COULD DRAW WIDESPREAD AT-
TENTION IF IT WAS COVERED BY THE MASS-CIRCULATION PRESS,
AND MANY WERE THE SUBJECT OF GOSSIP IN ALL CORNERS OF
THE CITY. AS SPORTS OR ROYAL LOVE AFFAIRS WOULD IN OTHER
ERAS, COURT COVERAGE PROVIDED AN INCREASINGLY SEG-
MENTED SOCIETY WITH COMMON CONVERSATIONAL TOPICS AND
CURRENT SYMBOLS THAT ADDRESSED IMPORTANT SOCIAL QUES-
TIONS.

A FAMILY AFFAIR

The Presnensky District Court tried the following curious case. The judge summoned Mr. and Mrs. Elizarov, who approached the bench: a seemingly ill man and
a woman in high spirits. The justice of the peace read the petition of the plaintiff,

Collected in Semen Kaftyrev, ed., *Vot ona, nasha matushka Moskva! Sbornik dedushki Posiseia. Poteshnye
ocherki, razskazy, stikhotvoreniia i sudebnye razbiratel'stva iz zhizni proletariev. Iazvy nashego vremeni i tipy shantaz-
histov-literatorov, Kit Kitychei s shirokoi naturoiu i moshchnym kulakom i proch.*, izd. "Novogo znakomogo" (Moscow: E. I. Pogodin, 1883), pp. 108–109, 143–146, 155–158.

from which it was evident that Mr. Elizarov treated her cruelly, beat her, and threatened to tear off her head and hang it with the pots.

Justice: It would be better for you to reconcile.

Elizarova: I cannot! He has become loathsome to me. I have no wish to see him; let him give me my passport.

Justice: That is not in my power. Ask your husband for that. Do you, Mr. Elizarov, admit your guilt?

Elizarov: No way, sir. She found herself another man, and anyways everyone knows she doesn't like me. She's been gone for two months.—Tell me, ma'am, says the defendant to his wife, why don't you like me?

Elizarova: You reek of corpses, and your breath stinks of scurvy.

Justice: Mr. Elizarov, what is your occupation?

Elizarov: I read the psalter for the dead; when I leave for work, she goes to her lover.

The justice calls the witness Konov.

Justice: Tell us what you know about the case and what happened between the Elizarovs.

Konov: She, Your Honor, you see, was drunk, and her husband wasn't home. She packs up her belongings, has them taken away, and then she grabs the psalter. And you see, he can no more work without his psalter than I can without my han'strument: so, they get in a fight and that's all.

Elizarova: The witness is giving false testimony, since my husband read the psalter for his grandmother for free.

Konov: Nope, for two rubles; I wouldn't lower myself to that.

Justice: That's not relevant to the case. Would you like to reconcile?

Elizarova: No, sir, let him give me back my passport.

Elizarov: She's got another husband, a cobbler.

Elizarova: He'll be better and cleaner than you.

A second witness gave similar testimony. The justice acquitted Elizarov.

In the vestibule, Elizarov pleaded with his wife to come to the apartment.

"Is this what you want?" she asked, sticking the fig[1] in his face and leaving with a young man in boots and jacket. Elizarov, hanging his head, left in the other direction.

THE BATTLE OF THE HEREDITARY HONORARY CITIZEN KORZINKIN AND THE NONCOMMISSIONED OFFICER KHOTILIN AT THE RACE TRACK

The justice of the peace of the Presnensky District heard a case that vividly illustrates the mores of our distinguished merchants. The case involved a fistfight insti-

---

1. A gesture of derision, consisting of clenched fist and thumb extended through the middle and index fingers.

gated by the Hereditary Honorary Citizen[2] Korzinkin while he was drunk in a public place, the race track at Khodynka Field.

From the police report read in court, it is evident that Mr. Korzinkin rode to the horse races with a troika of thoroughbreds; but at the stairway entrance by the main gate, the doorkeeper Khotilin dared, by the strength of his position, to ask His Excellency for an entry ticket, without, of course, knowing that it would be considered a great impertinence.

"You insignificant nothing, don't you know me?" thundered His Grace.

"I know you, sir, but please show me your ticket," was the doorkeeper's answer.

"My ticket!" shouted Mr. Korzinkin. "Here, take it!" Mr. Korzinkin then swung his arm and struck the chest of Khotilin, who was staggered by the powerful blow and fell.

Seeing this, His Grace wanted to go home, but thanks to the chief of police, Colonel Paul, he was handed over to the justice of the peace. Mr. Korzinkin did not appear in court, but his lawyer, Mr. Kotliarov, did appear.

Here are the main points of the investigation:

Justice: Khotilin, tell us what happened and why Mr. Korzinkin hit you.

Khotilin: Your Honor, I ask nothing of him; we've made peace. Aleksei Ivanovich—God grant him health—gave me three hundred rubles.

Justice: That is irrelevant to this court—tell me what happened.

Khotilin: I'm standing by the entrance, sir, when a team of four delivers Mr. Korzinkin and some ladies. They go straight upstairs, and I say, "Mister, your ticket please." So he answers me, "Don't you know nothing?" and knocks on my chest with his fist. "I know you, sir, Your Grace, but I have orders not to let anyone in without a ticket," I answer him humbly, and he spits in that ham of a fist and, gathering all his strength, swings from the shoulder, though we're not allowed to engage in fisticuffs, and whacks me in the ear so hard I hear ringing in both ears. Colonel Paul heard about it and ordered a police report written up.

Justice: Was Korzinkin drunk?

Khotilin: He'd had a bit.

The doorkeeper Filipov confirmed Khotilin's testimony.

Police deputy Bebikhov arrested Korzinkin, since a fine has no real meaning for a millionaire, and won't prevent him from fistfighting in public in the future.

Mr. Korzinkin's lawyer, the barrister Kotliarov, contending that there was no noise made, and that a blow to the face does not constitute a disturbance of the peace, declared that in addition Korzinkin suffers from a heart defect, and that he was in a state of irritation. Inasmuch as the victim had been generously compensated, the barrister asked that his client be acquitted.

The justice of the peace, declaring Korzinkin guilty of public fighting in a drunken state, resolved to fine him a sum of twenty-five rubles.

---

2. "Honorary Citizen" was a special social category created by Nicholas I in 1832 to reward persons, usually merchants, who had made important contributions to some area of national development, but were not members of the hereditary nobility.

Korzinkin's lawyer was most satisfied with the sentence and immediately paid the fine for his client.

— N-Kaftyr

THE CASE OF THE MERCHANT MIKHAIL DMITRIEVICH SOROKOUMOVSKY AND HIS HOUSEKEEPER SVISHCHEVA CONCERNING THE ORDER OF A COTTON SKIRT AND OTHER ITEMS

Interesting cases that characterize the customs and mores of our millionaire merchants often appear in the Moscow courts. A case that was recently tried in the chambers of the Aleksandrovsky District justice of the peace can be numbered among them. This case, though it was not as bellicose as the above case of Mr. Korzinkin, was nonetheless distinguished by its own kind of piquancy, and thus aroused the considerable interest of Muscovites, particularly those of the merchant estate. It arose from the complaint of one Anna Ivanovna Svishcheva, and was directed against the well-known merchant Mikhail Dmitrievich Sorokoumovsky, who owns a fur store on the Ilinka. Svishcheva's request, or rather her complaint, demanded that Sorokoumovsky hand over all belongings of hers that Mr. Sorokoumovsky had thought fit to convert for his own use. The crux of the case was stated thus: Three and a half years ago, Miss Svishcheva made the acquaintance of Mr. Sorokoumovsky while horseback riding in the Moscow riding school located on Bronnaia Street. He suggested that she come and share his apartment, which at that time was in the Kuznetsov house on the fourth block of the Tverskaia section of Nikitskaia Street. More than three years passed; Mikhail Dmitrievich was contemplating marriage, and he asked Miss Svishcheva to leave him in peace and move to another apartment, which of course Miss Svishcheva did. But she left her things in Mr. Sorokoumovsky's apartment for the time being. Soon after her departure to the other apartment, Miss Svishcheva made several requests, both verbally during their meetings and even by letter, for him to return the things she had left with him. But Mr. Sorokoumovsky neglected her requests. Losing patience, Miss Svishcheva was forced to file a complaint with the justice of the peace.

Despite the fact that the case was being scheduled for the second time (it had first been scheduled several days previously), Mr. Sorokoumovsky for some reason did not appear this time either. Perhaps his conscience would not let him appear before the court and the public; the justice decreed a judgment by default in the case, which declared the following: "Mikhail Dmitrievich Sorokoumovsky is ordered to return to Miss Svishcheva all the things left in his apartment by her, including the cotton skirt."

OH, THOSE LAWYERS!

A summons was issued to the Hereditary Honorary Citizen Skorokhvatova, who was accused of failing to observe a police order. Some character wearing a long *chuika* approached the bench and presented his credentials.

Justice: Your last name is Shalygin? Are you the lawyer of Skorokhvatova?

Shalygin: Precisely, Your Honor, her solicitor.

Justice: Do you have a certificate for your right to petition?

Shalygin: I have a deferment from the police station, because my passport is no longer valid, and they're so strict about that nowadays!

Justice: Give me the signed statement. Now, what objections have you to the police indictment?

Shalygin: I cannot say.

Justice: But there was a sentence in abstentia according to which your client was fined fifteen rubles for refusing to clean her latrine. You submitted an opinion requesting a review of the case, and so I have summoned the witnesses. Would you like me to question them?

Shalygin: Please don't trouble yourself; I'm most satisfied, sir.

Justice: So do you admit that the police indictment was properly written?

Shalygin: Right as rain!

Justice: Then why did you request a review of the decision, when, in your own words, the police made legal demands: the garbage was not cleaned, and Miss Skorokhvatova admits that this is all correct. You must understand this, as a man who pursues the lawyer's trade.

Shalygin: It's my fault, sir; I don't do slanderous cases, but you see her spouse ordered me to come to Your Grace. I'm a tradesman myself—I burned two rubles on this here case; I do more hack work for gravediggers. I couldn't not do it; they'da canned me—they're big landowners.

The justice determined that the decision in this case should stand.

THE CASE OF THE DEMONS

The justice of the peace of the Arbat District was trying a curious case, in which Zinovy Karpov Mednikov, a peasant of the Tarussky District, was charged with selling beverages mixed with harmful substances.

The justice summoned Mednikov and Tikhonov.

Two characters approached the bench and bowed low. Tikhonov was a hunchbacked peasant dwarf, and Mednikov was a chubby figure with an overgrown belly, bald with lumps on his head.

Justice: Tikhonov, tell us in good conscience what happened.

Tikhonov: I go to him, Mr. Justice of the Peace, Your Honor, and I natters: "Happy holiday, pops!" It was Easter then, and he says, "Howdy, nephew of the devil; have a drink of vodka for the holiday." And he says, "You'll overindulge." How can a Christian soul overindulge? So he runs over to the tavern and brings back some red stuff. I drink it down and thank him, then go home, and I'm all tied up in knots; my innards are burning like they're on fire. It's time to give up the ghost, I think. But thank the Lord, I got better.

Justice: Mednikov, what can you say, is that how it happened? Do you offer or sell vodka cut with fuchsin?

Mednikov (waving his hands): Mr. Judge, he went around drunk for two weeks, with his tongue hanging out. He was seeing demons, and do you have any idea, Mr. Judge, how much them kikes in our neighborhood charge for wine? Solomoshka the Jew is a butcher, and I ain't no damned socialist—but I got no bone to pick with him, even if he ain't my kin, and I don't stand to inherit no money from him. Well, off he goes drunk, and the devils start tormenting him, and everyone knows that devil put a saddle on drunks, and his master is just a real bad sort, a despot; the hens start cackling. So she calls the doctor, and he turns out to be a human being after all. This doctor goes up and says, "Who gave you the vodka, he poured out way too much, because like everyone knows, the devil made him do it."

Justice: What are you saying, what devils?

Mednikov: That's absolutely right; they get inside you when you're drunk. Demons tormented a policeman in our village with wine for two weeks—he kept going at everyone—and then there was another they hid under the Stone Bridge *(laughter among the spectators)*.

Tikhonov: You're slandering me for nothing; my soul is Christian, not Jewish—what demons could get to me?

The justice acquitted Mednikov for lack of evidence. As they were leaving the chamber, Mednikov tried to give Tikhonov some advice: "My dear dunderhead, go to mass, or else the demons will torment you to death. Once Satan saddles you, you won't get away easy."

Tikhonov muttered something, spat, waved his hand, and left.

—N. Dobrokhotov

The Terrible Wedding Night
Aleksei Pazukhin (1883)

PAZUKHIN (1851–1919) HAD FEW EQUALS AMONG THE WRITERS CHURNING OUT SERIAL DRAMAS FOR RUSSIA'S "YELLOW" PRESS. A RURAL SCHOOLTEACHER FROM YAROSLAVL PROVINCE, HE PULLED HIMSELF OUT OF THAT HARD LIFE WHEN HE JOINED THE STAFF OF *MOSKOVSKII LISTOK* IN THE MID-1870S. PAZUKHIN'S SUCCESSFUL LITERARY FORMULA BROUGHT HEROES AND HEROINES ALIKE FROM THE UNDERCLASSES AND TOOK THEM THROUGH NUMEROUS ADVENTURES, ALLOWING THEM TO EXPERIENCE

A. M. Pazukhin, *Zloba dnia: Sbornik razskazov, ocherkov, stsenok i kartinok* (Moscow: A. Gattsuk, 1883).

BOTH SERENDIPITOUS AND ILL-FATED COMBINATIONS OF
WEALTH AND ROMANCE BEFORE PULLING IT ALL TOGETHER IN A
HAPPY ENDING. THE TITLES OF HIS SERIALS CONVEY THEIR AL-
LURE: *THE LIONHEARTED ATAMAN, DRAMA ON THE VOLGA, THE
COMING FORCE,* AND *THE TEMPEST IN STAGNANT WATERS.* THE
SHORT STORY PUBLISHED BELOW, WRITTEN IN HIS CHARACTERIS-
TICALLY COMPACT AND THRILLING PROSE, ILLUSTRATES HIS
ABILITY TO GENERATE DRAMATIC TENSION ON AN EPISODIC
BASIS.

I loved her passionately, my dear, sweet Liza! I waited a long time to propose to
her. She was so good, so charming, to say nothing of so wealthy, that I, an unassum-
ing teacher who was far from rich, could not be a very attractive suitor for her. But
I knew she loved me, and so I proposed. She accepted, and I became the proprietor
of my goddess, my dear, dear beauty, Liza!

We celebrated our wedding modestly, inviting only our closest friends to the ceremony, which was held in one of Moscow's churches. Oh, how lovely Liza looked in
her wedding dress, her long veil cascading to the floor in feathery pleats, as if her
graceful, elegant figure were enveloped in a light cloud. She was gloriously fine, and
I was deeply happy. I loved her so, and thanked fate for bringing me such happiness.

After the service, we went to Liza's mother's house. In the company of our closest
relatives and friends, we drank a bottle of champagne, and then had tea before we
said our goodbyes and headed off for the Kursk railroad station. We wanted to catch
the first train to Kursk so that we could spend our first married days with one of
Liza's aunts there.

Everyone who had been at the wedding accompanied us, and at the station we
downed another bottle of champagne. At last we found our seats in a first-class car.

The third bell rang, the steam whistle sounded shrilly, the wheels of the cars
rumbled, and the train moved out, almost touching the crowd gathered on the
platform.

Alone at last.

"My dear, my darling!" I whispered passionately, embracing the slender figure of
my young wife, planting my burning lips on her mouth. She blushed all over; her
radiant eyes looked at me languorously; her lips whispered a tender word.

I was inexpressibly ecstatic at that moment.

Then I sat my dear wife down on the divan. I sat at her feet, held her hands
tightly, and talked for a long, long time. I spoke to her about happiness, about the
delights of family life, and about working together. I swore my eternal love.

Liza listened to me attentively, pressed my hand understandingly, leaned over
often, and kissed me shyly, but I could see a veiled sadness on her sweet face. A
musing of some sort was clouding her eyes.

"What's the matter, my dear?" I asked. "You're unhappy about something. I can see that something heavy is weighing on your heart. Do you miss your mother?"

"Oh, no, darling!" she answered. "I love Mama very much. But with you . . . no, I'm not homesick, my dear."

"Then what's making you so sad?"

"I don't know. But something is making me inescapably unhappy. A kind of inexplicable, uninvited melancholy has seized me. It's as if a terrible sorrow will befall us."

"Enough, dear! It's simply that you are lonely for your home, your relatives, and I can understand this. Calm down, darling, and drive away those depressing thoughts. We'll make jokes, talk, make plans for our future life together!"

I tried to amuse my Liza, told her some funny stories, related a few of my more comical adventures, and then caught her up on the latest gossip. Then I told her all about my ideas and shared my plans with her.

We were so caught up in our conversation that we didn't notice time passing, that the stations were flashing past us one after the other.

"And if I should die, where will you bury me?" Liza suddenly interrupted my cheerful chatter.

The question gave me chills, and I felt sick at heart.

"Liza!" I reproached her. "It's sinful to talk about death on a night like this, at a moment like this. Just today you tied the knot, and now you're talking about death?"

Liza leaned her head toward me, and hot tears fell on my face.

"Forgive me, my dear! I let the question slip out. . . . I . . . I . . . for some reason I think I'm going to die!"

In a burst of profound despair I arose, took Liza into my arms, and covered her face with kisses, involuntarily trembling.

"Liza, my dearest Liza! What's the matter with you? Where did these words come from? These thoughts? We're going to live, to be so happy!"

I wanted to sit down on the divan and put her on my knees, but the train lurched and I reeled, barely able to maintain my balance. Then there was another lurch, this one stronger. Then a crash, and the silent night was shattered by an awful heart-rending shriek. The floor of the car began to shake beneath our feet, the light in the lamps blinked off momentarily, and we began to sink into what seemed like an abyss. Then the scream sounded again, louder and more horrifying.

Clods of falling dirt began to rumble on the roof of our car. Inside it became as dark as a tomb and as stifling as a grave. Death had arrived. What had happened, I didn't know, but I could feel Death's hot breath.

Feeling all around me with my hands, I could tell that the car was on its side, that the walls were under me. There was my Liza. She was alive. Her body was warm, but she was breathing heavily.

"Liza, Liza!" I called out, but my bride was quiet.

I lifted her head and covered it with kisses.

"Liza, my life! What's happening to us? Where are we? Answer me, my happiness," I whispered.

"I can't breathe! It's terribly stuffy!" Liza could barely speak, and I could feel her heart beating beneath my hand. Standing up, I pushed my chest and hands against the walls with inhuman strength. I could feel the planks giving way, cracking under my hands. But then they would move no farther; the earth was holding them down.

"We're buried, buried alive!" I shouted as loudly as I could, but my voice was scarcely audible. Sounds cannot be heard in a grave.

I leaned over Liza again. She was already breathing more quietly, and her body had begun to grow cold.

"Liza, Liza! Why this hideous accident? We're buried alive. We're in a grave!"

My bride lay silent. I fell on her breast and sobbed, sobbed without tears.

The chill of the grave began to seep in. It was growing more difficult to breathe. I could feel pressure in my chest, and my lungs were about to burst. There was less and less air. The cold of the ground began to freeze my blood.

"Air! Air!" Liza whispered and began tossing about. I bent over her again. she was completely cold. Life was abandoning her. "There . . . above us . . . windows . . . break them," she whispered.

I jumped up and, reaching out, I groped around above me to find the glass in the windows. I found where they were broken, with my cut hands; hot streams of blood flowed down my palms from where I had sliced my hands on the glass.

Yes, the glass was broken, but not a single breath of air was coming through it. Instead of air, something horrible began pouring through the broken windows: wet, cold mud.

It was all over. Death was approaching with rapid steps.

Goodbye, everyone, goodbye!

I could feel my legs giving way, my strength evaporating. I fell on the body of my Liza, already grown cold.

Rivulets of wet muck gushed forth. There it was, that curious mud, beginning to crush my chest, now touching my face.

In a burst of agony in my death struggle, I screamed out in harrowing desperation and woke up.

The rays from the bright summer sun shone through the car window. The train sped quickly along past the flashes of woods, forests, and fields covered with ricks of freshly harvested grain. My sweet young wife was sleeping soundly; a delightful smile played on her rosy face.

I sighed deeply, deeply, and thanked God that it had been only a terrible nightmare, brought on by thoughts about a recent accident on this same rail line.

The whistle sounded. The train pulled into Kursk, and I awakened my dear wife with passionate kisses.

———

I heard this story from a friend, and hope from the bottom of my soul that nothing like it should ever happen to you readers. With that, I end this tale.

The Terrible Bandit Churkin

His Adventures in Jail and at the Penal Colony, His Escape from Siberia, His Life in the Cities, and the Macabre End to His Despicable Life

(1885)

VASILY CHURKIN WAS A REAL-LIFE THIEF WHO TERRORIZED PEAS-
ANTS AND TRAVELERS IN MOSCOW PROVINCE IN THE 1870S. NO
ROBIN HOOD HE, BUT A RUFFIAN WHOSE BIOGRAPHY FIT THE
FACTS OF THE STORY HERE: A DRUNK, A FACTORY WORKER, AND
A CONVICT IN SIBERIAN EXILE. BUT HE BECAME AN ANTI-HERO.
PASTUKHOV, PUBLISHER OF *MOSKOVSKII LISTOK*, DESCRIBED HIS
ADVENTURES IN ONE OF THE NEWSPAPER'S MOST POPULAR SE-
RIAL NOVELS. THE CHURKIN FAD GARNERED SUCH ACCLAIM
THAT ALARMED CENSORS FORCED PASTUKHOV TO KILL HIS CHAR-
ACTER OFF, THUS ENDING THE SERIAL. THE PUBLISHER DID THE
ROGUE IN WITH A TREE BRANCH, WHILE IN REAL LIFE HE WAS
MURDERED BY EITHER HIS ESTRANGED WIFE OR ANGRY VIL-
LAGERS.

BELOW IS ONE OF THE MANY IMITATIONS OF PASTUKHOV'S SE-
RIAL; THE UNKNOWN AUTHOR WAS CASHING IN ON THE SCOUN-
DREL'S POPULARITY (THE ILLUSTRATION IS FROM THE PASTU-
KHOV ORIGINAL). DESPITE THE TANTALIZING TITLE, CHURKIN
GETS ONLY AS FAR AS HARD LABOR IN SIBERIA IN THIS PARTICU-
LAR ADVENTURE.

CHAPTER I

Not so far away from Moscow, in Bogorodsky County, in the village of Barsky, an honest father and mother gave birth to a son. This baby was Vasily Churkin, who went on to become a bandit and murderer who wreaked fear and terror with his crimes in all the villages of Bogorodsky county, and then in other areas. From earli-

---

Strashnyi razboinik Churkin. Prikliucheniia ego v ostroge, na katorge, v rudnikakh, ego begstvo iz Sibiri, zhizn' ego v gorodakh i strashnyi konets ego uzhasnoi zhizni (Moscow: V. V. Ponamarev, 1885).

est childhood, Churkin exhibited his stubborn and evil character, so much so that his father truly did not know what measures to take to discipline his son. The future bandit did not fear the birch rod, the leather strap, or the lash; he was afraid of nothing. Sometimes his father would grab the delinquent by the hair and lash him with a strap for some brash shenanigan; he would beat and beat until he was exhausted, but Vaska would sit there like a corpse, not uttering a sound, as if he had not been flogged.

"Damned kid!" his angry father would cry, striking out at his son. But Vaska would sit in the shop, scratching his back, smiling craftily and chanting, "Auntie buy me gingerbread; I was ill and you beat me well."

These pranks got Churkin to thinking about himself in relation to his family and the other villagers, and he decided that he was an unusual fellow. Some of the elders even thought that an evil spirit had possessed him.

When Churkin was sixteen, he was sent to work in the merchant Savotin's factory. There, Vasily got drunk often and began to behave so disgracefully that one day a delegation of thirty other workers went to the director to complain about him.

"Karl Adamych," the workers addressed the German director, "we came to ask you to spare us from Churkin."

"What's going on?" asked the director.

"It's impossible to get along with him. He hits everyone, curses, gets drunk, and corrupts others."

The director ordered Churkin sent to him. When the latter arrived, he asked, "What did you do to the others to make them denounce you?"

"Your honor, good sir director, I'll tell you the whole truth," said Churkin. "I bought half a bucket of vodka and gave each of them a glass, but they said that that wasn't enough and asked for more."

"He's lying! Speaking nonsense," said the workers. "There wasn't any vodka, and we don't even want to hang out with him."

"This is just the first time," said the director, and he warned Churkin sternly to start behaving.

But only a few days later, the director heard rumors that Churkin was drinking and acting up again. This time he issued an order expelling Churkin from the factory.

"One bad apple can spoil the whole bunch," he told Churkin.

"I beg your pardon," bowed Churkin, and as he walked out, he boxed the ears of one of his former co-workers so hard that the latter dropped to the ground like a dead man.

"Don't complain anymore!" said Churkin.

Witnessing this scene, several other workers pounced upon the tough guy, but he pulled a pistol out of his pocket and said, "I'll kill the first one who touches me!"

The frightened workers scattered. Some even went to report him to the police, but Churkin had vanished. Returning to the village, he told his father straightaway that he had been fired from the factory.

"Oh, you're a cold one," said his father. "What am I going to do with you?"

"Don't be such a miserable old biddy; I'll earn even more money," answered Vasily.

"What can a bum like you do in this place?"

"That's my business. I'll get you money."

That summer Churkin went to an outdoor fair in a neighboring village and noticed the local beauty, who was named Arina. Churkin fell in love at first sight and could not take his eyes off her. The girl frequently returned his gaze, because he was a handsome lad—tall, broad-shouldered, his striking face framed by a thin, dark beard. Curls hung over his eyes, which shone with audacity and brazen resolve. A blue cotton *kaftan* was draped around his body, and his legs, in shiny boots, were slender and attractive. In general, he had a nice body, and the other guys looked at him with envy. On his way home that evening, he met the lovely Arisha.[1] He took her by the hands and said, "Tell me from the bottom of your heart, Arisha, do you love me or not?"

The girl said nothing.

"You're quiet. That means you don't love me. In that case, forgive my being so forward. We won't see each other again," said Churkin.

"Where are you going?" Arina stopped Churkin.

"Wherever my eyes can see. It's a big world, and maybe I'll get only to the first grove before they put a noose around my neck."

To tell the truth, when he said these words, Churkin was prepared to fulfill them, because it was already clear that he had no morals and was not certain what would become of him.

Arina grew pale and began to tremble. She grasped the lad's hand and said quietly, "Vasya, my dear, you love me truly, don't you?"

Churkin embraced her, and they kissed. It was a quiet, moonlit night. Only the sound of the land rails calling in the fields, and the cries of other night birds, could be heard. On that night Churkin told Arina that she would be his wife, that he would marry no other.

"I'm not sure they'll give me to you," said the girl. "Bad stories are already circulating about you."

Churkin did not say anything to this. Then he suddenly bolted. "I spit on whatever they're saying about me."

The matchmakers approached Arina's father to talk to him about Churkin.

"No, I won't give my daughter to Vasily Churkin."

---

1. Arisha is a diminutive form of Arina. See the Note on Transliteration for an explanation of diminutives.

"What's the problem?"

"He's a hopeless scoundrel who scoffs at everything."

This time the matchmakers walked away empty-handed. Churkin, however, did not abandon his plan to marry Arina. To show himself in the best possible light, he got a job at a factory and in no time was able to present himself as a good, industrious worker. In the meantime, Arina's father had found another suitor from a neighboring village for his daughter, a kind, modest, hardworking fellow. Learning of this, Churkin confronted Ivan (the fellow's name) and asked him, "Is it true that you want to marry Arina Antipova?"

"It's true," Ivan answered.

"Well, let me tell you," Churkin continued. "If you marry her, I'll kill you like a dog. I myself love and plan to marry her."

The guy lost his nerve.

"What's gotten into you, Vasily?" he muttered.

"Swear to me that you won't marry her!" insisted Churkin.

"Is this some kind of joke?"

"If that's what you think, you'd better start praying to God," said Churkin, pulling out a long knife.

The young man fell to his knees and swore that he would not marry Arina.

"That's better," said Churkin, and he walked quietly away.

Ivan married another village girl. Arina's father, seeing how Churkin had reformed himself, gave his daughter to him. Churkin's wedding was celebrated in great style. A lot of money was spent on the refreshments—where it came from, no one knew.

At the beginning he lived properly, worked at the factory, did not drink, and did not offend anyone. The first year passed thus, and then one day he went to his wife and told her, "Goodbye, Arina, I'm leaving."

"Where are you going?"

"Far away, but I'll be back soon."

"Tell me where," she started insisting like an old woman.

"It's none of your business," answered Churkin, and he left for who knew where.

CHAPTER II

Three weeks passed and Churkin did not return, which greatly upset his wife. One evening she was sitting in her hut, spinning, and thinking about her good-natured husband.

Knock! Knock! sounded at the window.

Arina shuddered and then went to it.

"Who's there? We are protected by the power of God!" she added quietly, wondering who could be knocking in the dead of night.

"Open up, it's me!" rang out from the street.

"My fathers, it's Vasya!" the young woman cried and ran to the door. Our friend

Churkin really was standing there. He entered the hut, sat silently at the table, and lit up a pipe.

"Vasya, dear, where did you come from?" asked his wife.

"Far away," answered Churkin. "Where was I? I was . . . I'll tell you later; for now, get me some vodka."

"Dear, we don't have a drop."

"Then go to the tavern."

Arina knew that it was impossible to protest, so she dressed quickly and went to the bar.

"A bottle of vodka," she said, putting her money on the counter.

"It's awfully late, Arina Ivanovna, to be ordering vodka," observed the barman.

"I have to now because early in the morning my godfather is coming in from Gorok," explained Arina.

Having gotten the vodka, she returned to her husband.

"Here's a little something to eat, and vodka!"

"The tavernkeeper didn't say anything?"

"He said it was late to be buying vodka."

"To hell with him," interrupted Churkin. He poured himself a glass, which he drained in a gulp.

"That's bad vodka," he said, taking a bite of pickle and then spitting to the side.

"I'm sorry, Vasily Vasilevich," said Arina.

"It's nothing. Soon I'll buy some good stuff. I have money." With this, Churkin pulled a billfold out of the top of his boot and tossed it open onto the table.

Arina glanced with surprise at the billfold lying there, fairly glowing with hundred-ruble notes.

"Oh, that's a lot," she said.

"Soon it'll be exactly five hundred thousand rubles," said Churkin.

"Yes, well, where . . . uh, did you . . ."

"Get them?"

"Yes," said Arina.

"I didn't get them anywhere," said Churkin, downing another shot.

"Did you earn them?"

"I earned them, Arina, I earned them."

"Who were you living with?"

"I was staying with a tailor," he said, preparing his new fur coat and beaver hat to leave.

Arina listened but did not understand.

"Does this mean you're going to live here with me now and not leave again?" she asked.

"I'm leaving, because there's no work for me here."

"Huh?"

"The police don't care for tailors like me."

"Vasya, I don't get it."

"Now do you understand?" he said, pulling a knife and a revolver out of his belt.

"Oh, some breadwinner you are!" cried Arina, stepping aside.

"Here's my needle and thread."

Arina finally figured out her husband's business.

"Well, what if they catch you?" she said.

"They won't get me," answered the bandit, and he drained another glass of vodka. A tune popped into his head, and he lit his pipe and began to sing:

> Dear Vanya, the most daring of chaps,
> How much farther are you going from me!
> You are my world,
> Sta—ay—ay!
> With whom will I spend the winter,
> Or walk with in the beautiful summer!?

Churkin sang, then cocked his head to the side and said, "This is my goodbye!" He finished packing. Arina looked at him, still in love.

"Oh, my darling," she whispered, "what are you thinking? What's spinning around in your reckless mind? You certainly were born for no good."

Early in the morning Churkin awakened, quickly poured himself the last of the vodka, and said to his wife, "Goodbye, Arina—but I'll be back soon."

"Do you have to go?" asked Arina, on the verge of tears.

"I'm leaving."

"Where to?"

"I have to."

And Churkin did leave. Traveling about seven miles from his native village, he found himself in a thick woods, where he began to whistle loudly and steadily. Soon he heard a similar whistle in response. Churkin lay on the grass and smoked his pipe. Not five minutes had passed before another fellow appeared beside him, a large man with the look of a wild animal. He had a rifle on his shoulders and a club in his hands. This was the prisoner Osip, who had escaped from Siberia five times and had killed at least a hundred people in his day. Osip was Churkin's *esaul* and right-hand man, and he loved him like no one else. He followed Churkin everywhere, like a dog after its master.

"Vasily Vasilevich!" said the convict, bowing and sitting down next to the *ataman*.

"Hi, Osip. How's things?" said Churkin.

"Not so good."

"What do you mean?"

"The Mitrokhinskoi shepherd turned us into the cops."

"Sidorka Bespalyi?" Churkin cried angrily.

"Himself."

"Oh, the devil. I'll bury him!" continued Churkin. His face became distorted, his eyes filled with blood. "I'll shoot him this minute!"

"Churkin, get up!" said the convict.

"Listen, Osip, where can we catch him?"

"He's got to be in the pasture with his flock."

"Let's go!"

The bandits went to the field, where they indeed saw the Mitrokhinskoi shepherd. Churkin stole up to him and grabbed him by the throat.

"Now I've got you, stepson of the devil!" cried the bandit.

"Churkin!" uttered the frightened shepherd.

"That's who I am. Tell me, dog, who did you tell about us?"

"No one, Uncle!"

"Don't lie! I'll kill you!"

"I told our village elder."

"What?"

"That you were near our village."

"And what did the elder do?"

"He went to the local chief."

"What do you know!" cried Churkin as he plunged his knife into the unlucky shepherd's chest.

"Nicely done," said Osip.

"It served him right!"

"What are we going to do now?"

"Let's go to the main highway. A merchant is on it today."

"Which merchant?"

"From the city of Bogorodsk."

"Not Ivan Zakharov!"

"That's the one."

"Well?"

"Fool," said Churkin, "don't you get it? He has money, and we need money."

"We need it very badly," agreed Osip.

"Let's go!"

The bandits set off for the highway.

"Hear it?" said Churkin, hiding behind a bush.

"What?"

"The jingling."

"Yes, yes, jingling! That has to be the merchant," answered Osip, taking his rifle from his shoulder.

The carriage appeared. An old man sat in the driver's seat, barely able to control the horses. The merchant was seated in the back. He was about forty years old, of average appearance. Churkin whistled.

"God be with us!" the merchant made the sign of the cross and began to whip earnestly.

At that moment Churkin and Osip jumped out from the bush. The latter grabbed the horse's bridle, and the former approached the merchant and said, "Our respects, good merchant."

"What kind of people are you? What do you want?" cried out the frightened merchant.

"Your Honor," began Churkin, "our heads ache from a hangover. Would you be so kind as to give us something to make it better?"

"You're out of your mind. I have no money!"

"You're lying, merchant; yes you do."

"How can you stop my horse like that?"

"What can we do, merchant?"

"You can go away. I don't have any money."

"You want this?" said Churkin, putting his pistol right into the merchant's nose. The latter grew white and began to shake.

"Thief, what are you doing?" he cried out.

"I'm not doing anything yet," answered Churkin, "but I'll certainly do something if you don't give me the money."

"How much do you need?"

"Give me the whole billfold."

"You're nuts."

"You should know."

"Take a hundred."

"Five thousand."

"I don't have that kind of money."

"You lie. I know that you're carrying ten thousand."

"Who are you?"

"Churkin."

The merchant grew frightened. "Take five hundred rubles," he said, "and prepare your soul for repentance."

"To hell with you. Give me three thousand."

"One and a half."

"Three."

"Will you take two?"

"If we're going to bargain over this, merchant, I'll put a bullet in your forehead," said Churkin, cocking the gun.

"Oh, have mercy, take twenty-five hundred," said the merchant.

"Say your prayers!"

"Okay, okay, take the whole three."

The merchant pulled out his billfold and gave Churkin thirty bright bills.

"Thank you, merchant," said Churkin.

"Thanks," added Osip.

The poor driver sat so motionless, you couldn't tell if he was dead or alive. The merchant crossed himself and said, "Now let me go."

"Leave, but don't say a word about us to anyone," said Churkin.

The merchant set off, saying to himself the whole way, "That turned out well; he could've killed me, the murderer."

CHAPTER III

Churkin and Osip headed straight for the tavern in the next village. No one knew them there yet, so they could drink their vodka in peace.

"Are you good people from far away?" asked the innkeeper.

"We're from Kazan Province," answered Churkin.

"What do you do?"

"We work with wool."

"Could you make me a pair of *valenki*?" asked the innkeeper.

"We can," said Churkin.

"How much will they cost?"

"Not much."

"And this is your assistant?"

"Yes," said Osip.

"Do you have a place where we can spend the night?" asked Churkin.

"We're always happy to have guests."

As soon as they had lain down, Churkin whispered softly to Osip, "You get the old woman, and I'll take the innkeeper."

"His wife, and anyone else?" asked the convict.

"His elderly mother-in-law."

"Okay, they're mine."

That night Churkin and Osip did indeed kill the innkeeper, his wife, and his mother-in-law, then stole everything and left.

"How much did we get?" Osip asked when they were on the road.

"We took about a thousand," answered Churkin.

"Now we're rich men!" said Osip.

They came to the woods and lay down to sleep.

"Get them!" the cry rang out.

The bandits jumped up and saw that they were surrounded on all sides by men with cudgels in their hands.

"Give up, sweethearts!" they cried.

Churkin grabbed his revolver and fired, but he shot a blank. The convict waved his knife, but they captured them anyway.

"Now you won't get away," the peasants said.

"Let us go, Orthodox brothers," said Churkin.

"Yeah, you'll be in jail."

"I'll give you money."

"You can't bribe us," answered the Orthodox peasants.

And that's how Churkin and Osip landed in the city jail.

CHAPTER IV

In prison Churkin pretended to be submissive, and the police did not guard him very closely. Once Osip sneaked into his cell and whispered, "Bad news for us, Vasily Vasilevich!"

"What do you mean?"

"They want to send us to Siberia."

"We'll break out."

"How?"

"Idiot, this isn't your first time."

"Yeah, but it'll be difficult."

"Shut up. I know what I'm doing."

In the meantime Arina had learned that her husband was in jail, and she devised a clever plan. She baked a pie, but instead of the normal filling, she put in a saw. Then she took this pie to her husband. Churkin spied the saw. "Oh, what a woman I've got! Now I'll be free."

He quickly sawed his way through the bars, then freed Osip, and they ran.

"I have a clever wife," said Churkin, and Osip agreed.

Arriving in Moscow, they began to rob and steal. Once they were sitting in a beer hall when suddenly the door opened and five detectives entered.

"Churkin, you're ours!" said one of them.

"I certainly am," answered Churkin.

They tied up him and the convict and led them under armed guard back to prison. In a short time, Churkin and Osip were sentenced to hard labor in Siberia.

"Let's go on a spree, Osip," said Churkin to his *esaul*.

"We can run away again," answered the convict.

Churkin remained at hard labor for more than five years and at last was able to escape, but he was captured again and sent back to Siberia, where he remains to this day.

There is no end to the stories about this bandit; much continues to be heard about him.

Where the Oranges Ripen
A Humorous Account of the Travels of Nikolai Ivanovich and Glafira Semenovna Ivanov along the Riviera and in Italy
N. A. Leikin (1892)

LEIKIN WAS BORN INTO ONE OF PETERSBURG'S OLDEST MER-
CHANT FAMILIES, ALTHOUGH HE TOOK GREATER PRIDE IN A
PEASANT ANCESTOR WHO SOLD PIES IN THE STREET. HE WAS OF A
GENERATION THAT CHALLENGED TRADITION, AND HAD A BROAD

N. A. Leikin, *Gde apel'siny zreiut. Iumoristicheskoe opisanie puteshestviia suprugov Nikolaiia Ivanovicha i Glafiry Semonovny Ivanovykh po Riv'ere i Italii* (St. Petersburg: Khudekov, 1892).

READERSHIP AMONG A GROWING BOURGEOISIE COMFORTABLE WITH ITS OWN FOIBLES. GROWING UP AROUND HIS FATHER'S SHOP, HE BEGAN HIS CAREER BY PASSING ALONG GOSSIP TO THE LOCAL "BOULEVARD" PRESS. ALTHOUGH HIS LASTING CLAIM TO FAME WAS BRINGING THE YOUNG CHEKHOV TO THE PUBLIC, LEIKIN'S CONTEMPORARIES LOVED THE DRY WIT WITH WHICH HE DESCRIBED THEIR NEIGHBORS' LIVES.

FOR THIRTY-THREE YEARS, LEIKIN CONTRIBUTED FEUILLETONS TO THE *PETERSBURG GAZETTE*. THE FOLLOWING EXCERPTS RECOUNT THE MISADVENTURES OF RUSSIAN MERCHANTS TOURING THE CONTINENT FOR A TASTE OF "CULTURE." NATIONALISM AND PROVINCIALISM RUN HIGH IN THEIR MUSINGS; THE AUTHOR AT TIMES BETRAYS SIMILAR LESS-THAN-LIBERAL INCLINATIONS. LEIKIN'S WIT RELIES ON SUBTLE IRONY, DRAWN FROM DETAILS OF PHYSICAL SURROUNDINGS AND CASUAL CONVERSATIONS. UNLIKE THE NEWSPAPER'S SERIAL NOVELS, HIS FEUILLETONS DRONED ON QUIETLY, HUMOROUSLY, LIKE THE HUMAN COMEDY THEY PORTRAYED.

It was about eleven o'clock in the evening. Three Russians sat in the Marseilles train station buffet, waiting for the midnight train to Nice: a Petersburg merchant, Nikolai Ivanovich Ivanov, heavyset, with a round belly; his wife, Glafira Semenovna, a young full-figured woman; and their traveling companion, another Petersburg merchant, Ivan Kondratevich Konurin. The travelers were all dressed in the latest fashion; the men were even shaved in the French manner. Still, their Russian merchant mentality shone right though. They sat at a table, the dishes and remains of dinner not yet cleared away, drinking red wine. Their hand luggage lay on the floor beside them; particularly noticeable was a large pillow in a red calico case strapped to a parcel. The men did not look happy, even though three empty bottles of wine and half a carafe of cognac stood on the table before them. Yawning and chatting, they were exhausted by the long trip from Paris to Marseilles.

The woman was yawning, too. Peeling an orange, she said, "As soon as we get to Italy, I'm going to go to an orchard, find myself a branch filled with oranges, and pack it and take it back to Petersburg, so that I can show everyone that we were in the land of oranges."

"Oranges grow in Italy?" asked Ivan Kondratevich, sipping his wine and breathing heavily.

"What?" laughed Nikolai Ivanovich. "You're a fruit seller yourself. You run a huge fruit stand in Petersburg, but you don't know where oranges grow? What a hayseed!"

"Yeah, well how am I supposed to know that? We buy the oranges for our stand in crates from a German, Karl Bogdanych. I thought oranges grew in a place called Orangeland."

"I think there's some kind of Orangeland in Italy—a province or a district maybe," said Nikolai Ivanovich.

"I can't stand your foolishness any longer!" cried out Glafira Semenovna. "There isn't any Orange Province, and there never has been any kind of Orange District. Oranges grow only in Italy."

"Then please explain why we sell Jerusalem oranges," objected Ivan Kondratevich.

"Those are some sort of kike oranges, from Jerusalem nobility."

"On the contrary. They're considered the best."

"I don't know anything about that. The main thing is that oranges grow in Italy, and therefore Italy is called the country of oranges."

"Okay, okay. Orangeland no longer exists, but there is an Orange District," chimed in Nikolai Ivanovich.

"Why are you arguing with me? Nikolai Ivanovich, there is not and never has been an Orangeland. I studied geography in boarding school, and I know there isn't one."

"You always did have a book in your hands. As a matter of fact, I don't care. I was in the Commercial Institute only two years. We studied geography, but hadn't gotten to the southern countries yet when my father pulled me out and put me to work in the business."

"There you go. And you're the one who's arguing."

There was a short pause. Konurin smacked his lips.

"I wonder what my wife's doing. She's already pigged out at dinner and gone to bed," he said.

"What do you mean, gone to bed?" laughed Glafira Semenovna. "I'd have to say just the opposite."

"What do you mean, the opposite? What can she do at home all by herself at this hour? She's already put the kids to bed and turned in," answered Konurin.

"And what time do you think it is in Petersburg now?"

"What do you mean, what time is it? It's night, midnight."

"No, you've got it backwards. Now we're in the south. And when it's night in the south, it's day in Petersburg. So your wife hasn't gone to bed."

Konurin's jaw dropped in surprise.

"You don't say, Glafira Semenovna," he murmured.

"It's true, it's true. Don't argue with her. It's so," declared Nikolai Ivanovich. "She knows. They taught her at boarding school. I myself read it in the newspapers. Now we're in the south, and everything's backwards in Petersburg because it's in the north."

"It must be a gag!" marveled Konurin. "I never realized the mechanics of all this. Abroad! So, Glafira Semenovna, according to your system, what time is it now in Petersburg?"

Glafira Semenovna started pondering the situation.

"The hour? I don't know. I'd have to look at the calendar, but I think it's three o'clock in the afternoon," she made a random guess.

"Three o'clock. Mercy me," Konurin shook his head. "Three o'clock. That means that the wife has already had dinner and is now preparing tea. This is terrible!" he sighed. "Heavens, where have we traveled to? Even the time is the opposite—that's the kind of place we've come to. If someone had said to me a month ago, 'Ivan Kondratevich, you're going to be on French and German soil,' I wouldn't't've believed him. I'd've spat at him."

"This is the second time we've gone gadding about the continent," said Nikolai Ivanovich. "The first time we went to the Paris exhibition. It was frightening—we didn't understand any of the foreign rules. But the second time, as you yourself have seen, we are very comfortable with travel. We learned some words at home, from our conversation books. But the first time we toured, I knew only the words for liquor, and she knew them only for the hotel rooms. We didn't know any of the vocabulary for railroad travel, not one word. Glasha, remember how the first time we were going to Berlin but ended up someplace else and had to go back and even pay a fine?"

"How could I forget! It's been the same this time. Trying to get from Berlin to Cologne, we almost ended up in Hamburg. You . . . you don't know any words, but you still try to make conversation with the French and Germans."

"No. This time I studied. Judge for yourself. How could I have gone into Paris without you, with only Ivan Kondratevich, and bought a hat and coat for myself, a jacket for him, shoes, pants, a vest, ties, and even gone to a barbershop and had my hair and beard trimmed in the French style? They understood me perfectly everywhere."

"Sure, understood perfectly. That's why they turned Ivan Kondratevich into Napoleon instead of giving him a normal shave."

"That was a simple mistake. I told the Frenchman, 'en pe, but only français po frantsystee.' But the barber was obviously deaf. Zap! Zap! with the scissors, and suddenly his cheeks were bare. While that one there just sat silently. He only knows one word, 'mussour.'"

"What do you mean, I just sat there?!" cried out Konurin. "I even grabbed the scissors, and he cut my finger. But it was too late. My beard had already been cut. He was working so feverishly that it was gone in an instant. I glanced in the mirror—no longer a Russian sitting there, but a Frenchman. Yeah, brother, I feel real sorry for that beard. I'll never forget it," he sighed.

"Napoleon! You look just like Napoleon," chortled Glafira Semenovna.

"You shouldn't be laughing, Glafira Semenovna, but crying for the shame of it," said Konurin. "It's all your fault, Nikolai Ivanich. Time will never forgive you. You dragged me into the barbershop, saying, 'Your beard doesn't look proper for someone abroad.' What was improper about it? A beard is a beard. Not this one, which looks like a spade."

"All right already! Shut up! Why are we still talking about this beard? In the name of Franco-Russian solidarity, you can walk around with a Napoleonic beard," said Nikolai Ivanovich.

"Solidarity . . . Napoleonic . . . I look like a goat."

"A true patriot of his own fatherland and a man sensitive to Franco-Russian friendship could never complain of looking like a goat."

"Easy for you to say. You're sitting here with your wife, while mine's in Piter. How can I show up back home looking like a goat? She might not even believe that it was an accident. She'll say, 'You were steppin' out, drunk, and some mamzelle decided to play a trick on you and had you shaved bald.' What are you laughing at? She didn't see it. She can imagine anything, and she's a very suspicious woman."

"Don't be so nervous; your beard'll grow back in no time. We're on our way to Italy, and it'll grow quickly there. They say that in Italy hair grows faster than grass," Nikolai Ivanovich said, still laughing.

At that moment the railroad conductor appeared and rang the bell, announcing that it was time to board the train. Everyone started bustling about, grabbing their hand luggage.

"Garçon! Payez? Combien do we owe?" shouted Nikolai Ivanovich to the waiter, trying to pay for what they'd eaten and drunk.

[*The tourists are now in Italy, where they have met up with other Russians, another merchant, Grablin, and a Russian painter, Perekhvatov. Russian artists, like others seeking the imprimatur of "culture," were required to make a pilgrimage to Italy.*]

Everything they ordered in the restaurant was served exquisitely. The food was fresh, prepared deliciously and in large portions. The restaurant made a marvelous impression on them, even though Glafira Semenovna did not touch the bouillabaisse or the oleapatrida, because she generally did not eat fish dishes abroad for fear that they would add "something like snakes." She truly enjoyed only steak and ice cream. The men, though, found the bouillabaisse, which was spicy and heavily peppered, better than Russian fish soup (*selianka*). They quacked with delight as they ate it, allowing themselves the smallest glasses of cognac. The oleapatrida, too, was not a bad hors d'oeuvres to go with cognac, although Konurin fished out several suspicious bits and, examining them, observed, "A German could eat this, but not a Russian. A German loves his forshmak[1] even though he doesn't know what's mashed up in it. Try to figure out what's in it? Not on his life. Could be hare, could be crocodile."

"Crocodile? You don't say!" smiled Nikolai Ivanovich.

"Why not? They'll eat absolutely anything here."

"Listen, you're ruining the appetites of those around you," Glafira Semenovna remarked squeamishly to Konurin.

---

1. A dish made of herring or meat mashed with potatoes.

"Not to worry. They don't eat crocodiles in Italy. They don't even have them here," said the artist, Perekhvatov. "They don't have hares, either; that's northern food. Just rabbits."

"Pshaw! That's even better!" spat Konurin.

"Eat, eat! Stop taking your food apart," Nikolai Ivanovich nodded at him. "When you return to Piter after being abroad, you'll bless your food regardless."

"I don't understand why you ordered that food in the first place," muttered Glafira Semenovna.

"To live like real Italians. I must admit, for the most part the food was prepared deliciously, and nothing goes better with cognac than those hors d'oeuvres. Whadda ya say, fellas, maybe one more little cognac for the road?" suggested Nikolai Ivanovich.

The bottle on the table was emptied into their glasses; they were having a wonderful time. Three bottles of sparkling wine added to their enjoyment.

"Gentlemen! Let's go to the San Carlo Theater!" proposed the artist Perekhvatov. "It's right across from us. We only have to cross the square. One cannot go to Naples without visiting the famous San Carlo Theater. It's considered the largest theater in the world."

"What kind of shows do they have?" asked Grablin.

"Opera, opera! Oh, ignorance! Young singers from all over the world come here and consider it a special honor if they are allowed to debut at the San Carlo. This stage makes singing careers."

"Really? Why so important? And we only have to move ourselves across the square," answered Nikolai Ivanovich. "Listening to opera is always nice."

"What's this talk of opera? 'Yes, opera is very necessary,'" grimaced Grablin. "Maybe they're presenting a funereal opera. After cognac and sparkling wine, is it really necessary to talk about opera? Let's go to one of the local hotspots. Rafael and I have already been to three nightclubs, and they say there's a fourth 'den of iniquity.' The local girls aren't much—they couldn't hold a candle to the ones in Paris—but what the devil. Maybe in this fourth den something worthwhile will turn up."

Glafira Semenovna caught fire.

"Listen, Grigory Averianych, you've forgotten that you're sitting here with family people!" she said sharply to Grablin.

The latter caught himself abruptly, slapping his hand to his mouth.

"Pardon, madame! Please, please forgive me!" he exclaimed. "I had completely forgotten that you are a real lady. Since I left Petersburg, I haven't seen any real ladies, or even any signs of them. In the three weeks that I've been hanging out abroad, you're the first married woman I've seen. Again, pardon. In order to smooth over my faux pas, I'm prepared to take you to the San Carlo or to any funereal opera you'd like to hear."

"Yes, of course we'll go the San Carlo," chimed in Perekhvatov. "It would be a shame to be in Naples and not see the San Carlo. We'll hear the opera and then go home early, so that we can get up early tomorrow morning to travel to Pompeii and see the ancient ruins."

"Silence, Paintbrush! Paint over your mouth! I'll go to the San Carlo. Not for you, but for the madame," interrupted Grablin. "Would you like that, Madame?"

"Positively!" nodded Glafira Semenovna. "Pay, Nikolai Ivanych, and let's be off," she said to her husband.

"A rose for my gaffe," continued Grablin, then exclaiming, "Ah, a bouquet! You delightful rascal, come here!"

He waved the flower seller over, bought a bouquet of roses, and handed them to Glafira Semenovna. In five minutes the group had paid its bill and crossed the square, walking toward the theater. A swarm of peddlers selling a variety of trinkets followed them out of the restaurant, chasing them across the square, trying to thrust flowers, vases, albums with scenes of Naples, coral, shells, little mosaics, photographs of singers, opera librettos, etc. into their hands.

"Get outta here!" cried Konurin, trying to brush them away, but they continued to follow behind, boasting about their goods.

A two-act opera and a short ballet were being performed in the theater that evening. The San Carlo astonished everyone with its huge size.

"Brother! You could put the whole Mariinsky Theater, including the roof, in this hall!" marveled Nikolai Ivanovich.

They were also impressed by the cheap prices. They bought seats in the sixth row for practically nothing.

"Good God! What kind of opera do we have in Piter?" said Konurin. "We've got great seats in the sixth row, and we would've paid more than twice as much to be chased into the farthest rows of the Mariinsky. And we would've had to bribe the cashier, too!"

They were also surprised by the unusually short intermission. The curtain was lowered, and five minutes later it was raised again. The ballet consisted of six scenes, and they changed the sets instantaneously, at the sound of a bell. The speed with which the scenery was moved and the dancers changed costumes was surprising. The performance was over by ten.

"Listen, Madame, abroad it's not at all unusual for a married woman to be in a nightclub," Grablin said to Glafira Semenovna as they stood in the theater entrance. "Let's all go out to one together."

"No, no, we're going home. We have our tea. We'll try to drink it and then go to bed. Tomorrow we have to get up early to go to Pompeii. We've already decided that," answered Glafira Semenovna.

"What's this Pompeii business? Why do we have to leave so early for Pompeii? We can always go later. Come on, Madame, let's go out and have some fun."

"You can go to the nightclub alone, with your translator."

"Alone? I'm tired of hanging out with Raphael. Here's what we'll do: We'll all accompany you back to your hotel and leave you there, and your husband can come out with us."

"You've lost your mind!" Glafira Semenovna's eyes blazed angrily.

Grablin had to resign himself. They all went back to the hotel. But when they got there, Grablin could not hold back any longer. He was already out of the carriage and headed to his room when he stopped, thought it over, jumped back in, and cried out to the artist Perekhvatov, "Raphael! Get in! Just the two of us can go and rate the nightclub monasteries. It's too early to go home! There's nothing for us to do there. Our kids aren't crying for us at home!"

Perekhvatov shrugged his shoulders and obeyed.

As it was suggested, so it was done. The Ivanovs arose early the next morning, before seven. Glafira Semenovna got out of bed first, opened the window, raised the blinds, and sighed blissfully. A spectacular panorama of Naples spread out before her; she had a bird's-eye view. The hotel was built on a steep mountain, and the entire city was visible from the window. The sea and the blue beyond lay in the distance. Black dots of barges with sterns like tie pins moved across the water, and white sails on boats, and Vesuvius loomed on the left, its cone smoking. Below, terrace-lined streets slid down to the sea. The roofs, cupolas, and spires of buildings, mixed in with the greenery of the gardens, sparkled with all the colors of the rainbow in the morning sun. A warm, bracing breeze blew in the open window, eliciting spontaneous sighs.

"My God, what beauty! To have such a lovely morning in March!" she exclaimed. "Nikolai Ivanych, get up! Why are you still wallowing around? Look at this bewitching view!"

Nikolai Ivanovich got up and, together, without even dressing, they took in the stunning view for a long time. Half an hour later, just as they had sat down to coffee, Konurin entered.

"I just wrote a letter to my wife," he said. "I told her that when I was in Rome, the pope invited me to tea. So when we arrive in Petersburg, please don't say anything when she asks me about the pope. I'm going to tell everyone in Petersburg that I was his guest at the Vatican."

"Didn't you say anything to your wife about Mrs. Pope?" asked Glafira Semenovna.

"You mean the contortionist? What am I supposed to say about her? We haven't met so many shrill representatives of the female sex on this trip, have we? Actually, that gal was very peculiar, but that's nothing to write the wife about."

"Yeah, I'll write your wife about that gal. I'll write about how you were her guest after the show in the Orpheum. You think I didn't notice how you quietly sneaked away from us."

Konurin flushed. "Why would you write about something that never happened?"

"It happened, it happened."

"Okay, write what you want. My wife is completely fearless. We don't end up with battle scars because of her migraines. Really, she'll make a sour face when I meet her at the station, but I'll sweeten her up with the lace scarf and all the silk and the dress I bought her in Paris. My wife is a mild-mannered woman."

"Oh, God forgive you. I won't write anything. Sit down and have some coffee with us before we set off for Pompeii. Where's that playboy Grablin and his friend?"

"Passed out. I knocked on the door, but heard only lowing."

"Go again, and tell them that if they don't get up right now, we're going to Pompeii without them."

"Maybe a little cup of coffee for the slugs."

Konurin had a lot of trouble awakening Grablin and Perekhvatov. Only much later, after Glafira Semenovna had become angry about the long wait, did Konurin bring them in. Their faces were puffy, their voices hoarse, their eyes red.

"Pardon, pardon, Madame," Grablin excused himself. "We made the mistake of drinking a sweet wine last night. Raphael, what was it called?

"Lachryma Christi."

"There, there. We made a terrible mistake. I've already poured two pitchers of water into me, and I still can't make sense of anything. Listen to my voice. The only thing it's good for is another octave in the church choir. But the Spanish girl I met in the club—what a ripe little raspberry she was! 'Cara mia, cara mia!' Raphael taught me how to speak to her. Raphael, was she Spanish or from some other estate?"

"Stop! Please don't tell me any more about your nighttime adventures with women!" interrupted Glafira Semenovna.

"Pardon, I beg your pardon. Truly, I forgot that you are a married woman," recollected Grablin. "So, how are we getting to this excavated city? A little breeze will seem like nothing to me after yesterday's inebriation."

"We're ready. We've only been waiting for you. Now drink your coffee and let's get going."

"I can't. On the morning after such a binge, I can only put seltzer in my mouth. Really. Raphael, what kind of a scoundrel are you, going after somebody else's rolls and butter?" Grablin hollered at Perekhvatov. "Jeez, whatta pig."

"Gimme a cup of coffee. I can't travel today; I'm not myself."

"I simply cannot understand how a person can consume anything after a spree like yesterday's." Grablin slapped his thighs.

"Yeah, well, you were the one overdoing it last night, not I," answered Perekhvatov.

"Well, you weren't sitting at St. Anthony's table."

"I was only drinking in moderation and trying to protect you. It's not good to tell everything that happened. Imagine sliding into the orchestra pit and deciding that you want to play the Turkish drum with the musicians. Needless to say, you punched a hole in the skin. I had to make a deal with them—they took twenty lira."

"What's twenty lira in comparison to the crazy Spanish girl, who yesterday . . ."

Glafira Semenovna flared up again. "Gentlemen! If you don't stop . . . !"

"Pardon, pardon! It's just so hard to get used to a married woman after three weeks of partying with female firecrackers!"

"Let's go, let's go, guys—on to Pompeii." Glafira Semenovna hurried the group along. Five minutes later, they were out of the hotel.

"Raphael, hire a driver and be our guide!" Grablin hollered at Perekhvatov. "What else did I bring him to Italy for? He's been bragging to me about how he knows Italy like the back of his hand."

"Yes, I know Italy, but only from the books. I studied the books thoroughly. Sit, people, get in the carriage. We've got to get to the railroad station. It's a half-hour trip from Naples to Pompeii. Hurry, hurry. We don't want to miss the morning train and then have to wait three hours for the next one."

"That's very important, but if we're late," answered Grablin, "I can order my breakfast at the station. Something a little sour, a little salty, maybe a little cognac—'the hair of the dog that bit me'—we'll pour on some lacquer, a little red wine, and then the next train'll get us to Pompeii. Raphael, what was that spicy stuff we ate called in Italian?"

"Hurry up, Grigory Averianych! I don't want to wait in the station for the next train!" Glafira Semenovna shouted at Grablin.

"I'm coming, cara mia, mia cara. Ah, at two or three in the morning, last night's Spaniard was teaching me her language," muttered Grablin, taking a seat in the carriage in front of the Ivanovs.

"You can't call me that! Since when am I your cara mia?!" snapped Glafira Semenovna.

"Please. . . . Anyway, it's not a swear word! Really . . ."

"What? Now you're calling me profanities!"

"'Cara mia' means 'my dear'—what else would I be calling the Spanish girl?"

"I cannot possibly remind you of your Spanish girl. Anyway, what kind of a horse is this without a bridle?"

The carriage was moving down the mountain; the drivers braked the wheels as they drove through filthy alleys. At the food stands in these alleys, dirty Italians breakfasted on pasta and boiled beans, stuffing their mouths with their hands, which were even dirtier. Barefoot Italians stood drinking from clay and tin mugs. The carriage made it down to the sea. The dust was unimaginable. It flew in the nose, in the mouth; it stung the eyes. But everywhere they could see through the dust poles, and drying on these poles, like laundry, was pasta.

At last they arrived at the train station.

"I'm still thinking," said Grablin. "In this excavated city, I don't think we're going to find any excavations where we can have a little something to eat and drink."

The Ivanovs did not answer him. Perekhvatov ran up to the carriage.

"Hurry, hurry! The train leaves in five minutes," he said.

The group ran to the ticket window.

Messrs. Businessmen

Sketches by I. I. Miasnitsky (Baryshev) (1890s)

MIASNITSKY ENJOYED POPULARITY AS THE "MOSCOW LEIKIN," AND MATCHED HIS NAMESAKE IN PRODUCTIVITY. THE ADOPTED

From *Prokazniki. Iumoristicheskie ocherki, stsenki, kartinki i fotograficheskie snimki s natury dobrodushnogo iumorista*, 4th ed. (Moscow: D. P. Efimov, 1904), pp. 302–310. The Hermitage was one of Moscow's tonier night spots. It combined in several halls, indoors and out, restaurants, dancing, and two theaters—a small one that featured novelty acts, and the main one, which showcased headliners.

(AND PROBABLY ILLEGITIMATE) SON OF PUBLISHER K. T. SOLDA-
TENKOV, HE KEPT HIS BENEFACTOR AFLOAT AS BOTH BOOK-
KEEPER AND BESTSELLING AUTHOR. MIASNITSKY CHURNED OUT
FEUILLETONS FOR THE *MOSKOVSKII LISTOK*, AS WELL AS AT
LEAST EIGHTEEN NOVELS AND SHORT-STORY COLLECTIONS. HE
CHRONICLED THE EVOLUTION OF RUSSIA'S MIDDLE CLASSES, BE-
GINNING WITH HIS OWN ESTATE, THE MERCHANTRY. AT TIMES,
MIASNITSKY PUT A SERIOUS PEN TO THE PROBLEMS OF MER-
CHANT FAMILIES CAUGHT UP IN SOCIAL CHANGE, AS IN HIS
NOVEL *THE MERCHANTS AT GOSTINYI DVOR*. BUT THE FOLLOW-
ING VIGNETTE OF MERCHANTS DINING AT A POPULAR MOSCOW
RESTAURANT EMPHASIZES HIS MORE POPULAR HUMOROUS SIDE.

MIASNITSKY WAS ALSO A SUCCESSFUL FARCE WRITER, SUPPLY-
ING THEATER OWNER F. A. KORSH WITH ENOUGH MATERIAL TO
UNDERWRITE MORE AMBITIOUS PRODUCTIONS, SUCH AS THE
FIRST STAGING OF CHEKHOV'S *IVANOV* IN 1887. INTERESTED
READERS CAN ALSO FIND *LONG LIVE FREEDOM!*, A ONE-ACT DO-
MESTIC COMEDY WRITTEN IN 1908, ON THE INDIANA UNIVER-
SITY PRESS WEB SITE. THIS THEATER PIECE SHOWS THE LIGHTER
SIDE OF RUSSIA'S INTERREVOLUTIONARY PERIOD, WITH STAN-
DARD MOTHER-IN-LAW CLICHÉS TOLD IN THE IMAGERY OF 1905.

AT THE HERMITAGE

The garden at the Hermitage. Everyone already knows what it looks like. It is
evening. The "women from the demimonde" are easy to separate out from the
crowd wandering around the garden. These night birds are patiently lying in wait
for some "fledglings."

"My stars! Goodness, so much passion here," an elderly merchant in a peaked
cap said delightedly to himself, guiding his wife by her elbow. "Dunya, oh, Dunya!
You'd better go home, Mother. So much commotion, things are gonna happen
here, you'll see."

"I'm not going to let you make a fool out of me," she cut him off. "I see your
scheme, you old goat. You're getting all heated up, staring at them. Stop slobbering,
you bald sinner!"

"Shhh!" The "sinner" waved her off. "How she misinterprets me. I give her advice
from the heart, and she reads it just the opposite."

"You've been fooling me with those faces for twenty years now," said the wife, refusing to calm down. "It's time to get to down to brass tacks. I'm surprised at how you're staring, with those disgusting walleyes of yours. You look like something the cat drug in."

"To think that this woman drove a car, and in public. Let's sit down, better than sinning . . . Hey, garçon!" The merchant waved a finger at the waiter. "Are you gonna get us a table or not? Wanna guzzle some tea?" He tried to take care of his wife.

"You know I will. I'm not gonna run all over the garden, like your eyes are doin'."

"Stop being such a sourpuss. Hey, be a nice guy, garçon. Bring us a little tea first, and then look over here when they start ringing the gong for the next courses . . ."

"There's not going to be anything else for you," the wife said. "Besides, I wanna go outside to drink. But it can be bad to drink out in the fresh air."

"Oh, gulp it down. I don't care how much; what am I complaining about? Good lord! It doesn't take much to get you upset—this time over a little tea."

"Well, I dunno. Getting upset . . . Stop! Where are you going?"

"To the buffet. Don't get so excited—I'll be back in no time."

"Aren't there enough waiters to send? Find another one. Listen, you; hey, watch the coattails!"

"You idiot! It's not easy for even the most demanding merchant to get a glass of vodka from the other side of the garden."

"Yeah, well, I'm staying with you, if not . . ."

The merchant spat and plopped down on the stool next to his wife, glaring malevolently at her.

Some distance from this couple, a group of bearded merchants sat around a table set with bottles and tea service, "refreshing themselves." Two of them wore top hats, pushed to the backs of their heads, two were in feather caps, and one wore a visored cap. These men, to use the technical term, were "in their cups."

"What a great guy the deceased was," said the oldest top hat, emptying the remains of the carafe of vodka into his glass. "So smooth."

"What can I get you?" A waiter flew up to them.

"See, it's dry, and grass doesn't grow in a drought. Pour! Grisha, wake up!" He turned to the one in the visored cap.

"I thank you most kindly," that one answered. "And furthermore, I propose . . ."

"What are you, huh? Think you're in my shop doing business? You came in from Zakolounaev, and now you're trying to become such a righteous individual. With those rules of yours, you couldn't get into our monastery."

"We understand that all too well, Akim Nikitich, but if that there riffraff gets into . . ."

"What do you mean, gets into?"

"God Almighty!"

"Stop!" the top hat's eyebrows began moving. "Grigory Vasilych! Can't you show some respect for a Moscow merchant of the first guild, Akim Zapivovalov?" he asked, leaning over in his chair.

"Always."

"Okay, drink! To us, brothers—get into trouble and don't leave sober. Oooo, bitch!" he turned to the "fairy"[1] walking by. "That kind goes straight for our pockets—what a piece of meat," he snorted to the guy in the visored cap.

"Excellent items, Akim Nikitich."

"A crow, without a mark," continued the top hat. "It's been almost three months since I've known her. The shrew. Caramels—how she could sing, that diabolical soul; you give her all your cash, and then more. Her specialty is to say nonchalantly, 'Mama, I want to get married.' The whole time you're thinking it's you she wants to marry. Then the final slap—you're just giving a hand, only trying to help her take it off—right there in front of God! They're so good at everything, especially working out the ending. Trash—and to think that they could have descended from the good-natured merchantry! These are our 'eligible girls.' Just begin them with a score of 30 and then start whittling them down, use a little grease, and why? Because our 'eligible biddies' are stumps, nothing more. No one else would walk into the embrace of a hundred-year-old log. . . . But these others have a completely different philosophy. She'll smack you on your bald spot, you look back, and she's already in another room, cackling. . . . A dream—just one word! Let's raise our glasses! Jeez, look at how that little devil is scampering around our table. It's obvious that now she's looking for a merchant meal ticket. When I first met her, I invited her to tea. 'Don't you want to take care that it doesn't all boil away?' I asked. 'I know what you mean about boiling over—you start off steaming, but you're ice by the end,' she says. And now, meet her anywhere, and you'd hear, 'Hey, Papa, are you gonna get me drunk on tea?'"

The guys started laughing. On a bench under a billowing awning sat two married couples.

"Isn't it our turn now?" said the husbands, getting up.

"We're afraid to sit here alone!" exclaimed the wives. "There are some suspicious types hanging around. They'll sit next to anyone and start picking their teeth."

"You just keep quiet," advised the husbands.

"And what if it's an officer? That would be flattering."

"Come on, end this already. What are you babbling on about now?"

"Oh yeah? What about the officer who sat down next to Anna Petrovna? They started chatting, and the next thing you know she was inviting him to drop by when her husband wasn't home. Boom, the next day the officer came by; her husband caught him, and boxed her ears. That's the kind of conversations you have here."

"You fool, you would have made a date like that, too."

"Well, we aren't taught how to make polite conversation. We mess things up when we're just trying to be nice, and something damaging comes out. We'll just try to keep our mouths shut in those situations."

"Enough already. Hey, you there, Seryozha!"

"Petya, Petya, wait! What am I supposed to do if an officer asks if he can sit next to me?"

---

1. This term referred to a beautiful woman.

"Just say that the place is taken, that the others are on their way back. That's all you need to say."

"Seryozha, Seryozha, wait! What if the officer starts talking about something like the weather?"

The husbands waved them off and disappeared into the crowd.

In one of the side booths tied off by an awning, two elderly friends sat conversing over a bottle of Chateau Lafitte.

"Oh, how she loved me. Don't punish me, Lord," confessed one to the other, draining the wine. "Not a day went by that she wouldn't send me a little note. 'My outrageous little fatty,' she would write, 'I get so bored without you, without your health to worry about'—that's the kind of thing she thought about. Oh, I'd bring her a bracelet, earrings . . . Then she'd burst into tears—'You've lost interest in me?' Jealousy consumed her. She was jealous of everyone, of the coachman, of Trofim. 'He's a rascal,' she'd say. 'He's always around you, but I only get to see you in the evenings.' Once she even tried to rip off my goatee. And it started with such a petty incident. She'd hired a new cook, and I, fool that I am, complimented her for it. That's all. The witch burst into flames! Sleep and food ended this romance. And boy did I invest a lot of money—there was no end to the spending. It wasn't only presents, as far as that goes, it was everything, and I felt so flattered! The wife would get one dress, Anfiska two. The wife would get nothing special, but for Anfiska, a surprise package. Oh, sometimes she'd start howling. She'd sound so plaintive. I'd purse my lips—'Just tell me if you've stopped loving me. I'll infect myself with smallpox and die, or maybe I'll get a bottle of vinegar and drink it. I'm Traviata and you're Alfred.' . . ."

"Did she die?" asked his companion.

"Don't I wish! I ran into her not long ago—I wanted to break her face."

"That's some Traviata."

"A *sterviata*[2] she was, not Traviata. There I was, in a lover's ecstacy, until I got a note one day telling me that my Traviata was being visited regularly by a troubador from the telegraph office, who plays a guitar. What kind of absurdity is that? I wondered. Exchange Alfred for a guitar? What kind of instrument is that, a guitar?!"

"It's a terrible instrument," agreed his companion.

"It wouldn't have been so bad if she'd gone for a drummer. At least he'd show some style when he played. Look at me now—my heart's in my throat and my skin's clammy. A guitar! Wood chips, a noise maker. I could spit on it. Dammit to hell!"

The first bell sounded, and the crowd rose and began moving into the theater.

---

2. Here he plays on the Russian word *sterva*, calling her *sterviata*, which can mean either "carcass" or "little stinker" (or worse!).

The Diary of Maria Bashkirtseva
(1889)

A Jewish fortune-teller promised the mother of Maria (1861–1884) that her daughter would be a star, and from her earliest memory, the child committed her destiny to grandeur. Of noble blood, the pretty girl grew up indulged and with a decidedly artistic temperament. Ill health plagued her, however, and she lived most of her life in Europe, where she studied painting.

Obsessed with the likelihood of an early death, Bashkirtseva feared that she would go before making her mark. She began her diary at age twelve, noting when death was imminent that "if I die young, I wish my journal to be published." Multilingual, she kept her diary in French, but it was translated into her native Russian in 1889, and into English not long after she died. This literary sensation went through many editions in all three languages over the next three decades.

The diary's appeal to later readers lies in its author's self-confident tone, her frankness, and her ability to re-create herself through her moods and surroundings. Part travelogue, part confessional, this intimate self-portrait became the rage in late imperial Russia because of its gossipy tone and the soap-opera ending of a heroine dying young. Though Maria had only a veneer of social or political consciousness, she was taken as a prototype for the liberated woman.

From *The Complete Journal of Marie Bashkirtseff,* translated from the French by A. D. Hall (Chicago and New York: Rand, McNally and Co., 1889, 1913).

1879

Saturday, March 18th.—I have not had an instant alone with A—, and it annoys me. I love to hear him tell me that he loves me. Since he has told me so, I spend much of my time, with my head in my hands, thinking, thinking! Perhaps I am in love. It is when I am tired out, and half asleep that I think that I love Pietro. Why am I vain? Why am I ambitious? Why am I sensible? I am incapable of sacrificing for an instant's pleasure whole years of magnificence and satisfied vanity.

"Yes," say the writers of romance, "but that instant's pleasure is enough to brighten, with its beams, a whole lifetime." Oh, no, I do not believe it! Now I am cold and I love: tomorrow I shall be warm and I shall not love. See, how the changes in temperature affect the destinies of men.

When he went away, A— said: "Good evening," and took my hand and held it in his, asking me a dozen questions to defer our parting.

I immediately told all this to mamma; I tell her everything.

March 20th.—I behaved horribly this evening.

I spoke in a low tone to the scapegrace, and gave everybody reason to believe things which will never come to pass. With other people about, he does not amuse me; when we are alone, he speaks to me of love and marriage. The son of a priest is jealous—furiously jealous; and of whom? Of everybody.

I listen to his rhapsodies, laughing with cold indifference, and at the same time let him take my hand. I also take his hand, in a manner almost maternal, and if he has not entirely lost his wits through his *passion* for me, as he says, he must see that, while driving him away with my words, I detain him with my eyes.

I tell him that I shall never love him, but I do love him, or at least, I act as if I did. I say all sorts of silly things to him. Another man (an older man) would be contented; but he tears a napkin, breaks two pencils, or rips a curtain!

All these actions permit me to take him by the hand and to tell him he is an idiot.

Then he looks at me with fixed fury, and his black eyes are plunged in my gray ones. I say to him; perfectly gravely: "Make up a face for me," and he laughs and I pretend to be vexed.

"Then you don't love me?"

"No."

"I ought not to have hoped it."

"Good heavens! yes; one must always hope; hope is a part of man's nature, but— as far as I am concerned, why—I will not give it to you."

And as I spoke laughingly, he went away passably satisfied.

Wednesday, May 24th.—This evening, when retiring, I kissed mamma.

"She kisses like Pietro," she said, laughing.

"Has he ever kissed you?"

"He has kissed *you*," said Dina, with a laugh, thinking that she was saying the most awful thing, and causing me keen regret, almost shame.

"Oh, Dina!" said I, with such an air that both mamma and my aunt cast on her a look of reproach and displeasure.

"Marie kissed by a man! Marie, the proud, the reserved, the haughty! Marie, who has made such fine speeches on that subject!"

This caused me great inward shame.

Indeed, why was I false to my principles? I will not admit that it was through weakness, through passion. If I admitted that, I should no longer respect myself. I cannot say that it was through love. It is enough to be thought unapproachable. People are so accustomed to see me so, that they would not believe anything else, even if they saw it with their own eyes, and I have said so many severe things in regard to the proprieties of life, that I would not believe it myself if it were not for this journal.

Moreover, a girl should allow herself to be *approached* only by a man of whose love she is certain for he will not betray her; while, with men who are simply flirting, she must be covered with quills, like a porcupine.

Be free with a serious, loving man; but be severe with a man of free manners!

Heavens! how glad I am that I have written exactly what I think.

Friday, December 27th.—This week has been lost to me for the studio. For the last three days I have wanted to write down certain reflections, I don't know just what. But distracted by the singing of the young lady in the second story, I began to read over my life in Italy, and then I was disturbed, and I lost the thread of my ideas, and that feeling of melancholy which it is so pleasant to indulge in.

What surprises me is to see what grandiloquent words I employed to describe simple adventures.

But my mind was full of lofty sentiments, and I was vexed at not having anything astonishing to relate—any tremendous, romantic sensations, and I *interpreted* my sentiments; artists will understand me. All that is very well; but how was it possible that a girl, who pretended to be intelligent, did not better understand the value of men and events? I say this because the thought has come to me that my relatives ought to have enlightened me on such subjects, and told me, for instance, that A— was not an earnest man, nor a man for whom I should have suffered one moment of pain. It is true they spoke to me, but in a wrong way, my mother having even less experience of the world than I; but, after all, that is of minor importance, and since I had such a high opinion of my own intelligence, I should have known better, and treated him like the others; instead of bestowing so much attention upon him, both in this journal and elsewhere.

But I burned with impatience to record something romantic, and fool that I am! There might have been more romance if I had been more patient. In short, I was young and inexperienced, notwithstanding my foolish boasting. I must acknowledge that, whatever it costs me to do so.

There! it seems to me that I hear someone say: A strong-minded woman, like you, should never be obliged to retract her words.

Sunday, December 29th.—Last night I laid my head down on the sofa and slept soundly until 8 o'clock this morning. It is amusing to sleep like that outside of your beds.

Art has lost its hold on me and I cannot interest myself in anything else. My books are packed up, I am forgetting my Latin and my classics, and I seem quite stupid to myself. The sight of a temple, of a column, of an Italian landscape makes me feel a horror of Paris, so dry, so learned, so experienced, so refined. The men here are ugly. This city, which is a paradise for superior natures, is nothing to me. Oh! I have deceived myself; I am neither wise nor happy. I want to go to Italy, to travel, to see mountains, lakes, trees, seas—with my family, with bundles, recriminations, tribulation, daily little quarrels? Ah, no, a hundred times no! To really enjoy the delights of travel, I must wait—and time passes. Well, so much the worse! I can always marry an Italian prince whenever I wish; then let them possess my soul in patience.

But you see, if I took an Italian prince, I could work, since the money would be mine; but I should have to give him some. In the meantime I will remain here, and work at paintings.

Saturday, they found my sketch, done in two days, not bad. You understand that it is only with an Italian that I could live as I wished, and where I wished in France, or in Italy; what a beautiful life it would be! I should divide my time between Paris and Italy.

1880

Saturday, January 3d.—I cough continually; but, by a miracle, instead of it making me unattractive, it gives me an air of languor which suits me.

Saturday, January 31st.—Tonight, Saturday, we went to the concert and ball given under the patronage of Queen Isabella, for the benefit of those who suffered by the floods in Murcia. The Queen was present at the concert, and afterward came into the ballroom and stayed an hour.

I do not altogether like dancing. It is not amusing to feel one's self in the arms of a man. In short, it is a matter of indifference to me; for I have never understood those troubles caused by waltzing, of which novels speak.

In dancing, I think only of the lookers-on.

Thursday, June 8th.—It is after 4 o'clock, it is broad daylight; I close the blinds hermetically to create an artificial night while the blue blouses of the workmen are passing in the street, going to their work already. Poor people! It is before 5 o'clock in the morning, and it rains; these unfortunates suffer, and we whimper over our misfortunes in laces from Doucet's. Look at me writing a common-place phrase, a banality. Each one in his own sphere suffers and complains, and each one has good reason for it. I, at the present moment, do not complain of anything; for, if I have no talent it is nobody's fault. I only complain of unjust, unnatural, detestable things, like much in the past, and in the present also, although this isolation may be a blessing which, perhaps, will bring me to fame. Happy Carolus Duran, who is celebrated and believes himself the most sublime artist of all time!

I wish to go to Brittany and work there.

Wednesday, June 20th.—Well! nothing new. A few calls exchanged and painting—and Spain. Ah, Spain! A volume of Théophile Gautier is the cause of all this. Is it possible? What! Have I passed through Toledo, Burgos, Cordova, Seville, Granada? Granada! I have run through those places whose names, even, it is an excitement to pronounce! It is a fever! Oh, to return there! To see those marvels again! To return alone or with people who can sympathize with me! I suffered enough when I went there with my family! Oh, poetry! Oh, painting! Oh, Spain! Ah! how short life is! Ah! how unhappy we are to live so little! For to live in Paris is only the point of departure for everything. But to make these sublime, artistic journeys! Six months in Spain, in Italy! Italy, sacred soil; divine, incomparable Rome! it takes away my reason.

Ah! how women are to be pitied; men are free, at least. They have absolute independence in ordinary life, liberty to come and go, to start out, to dine at a restaurant or at home, to go on foot to the Bois or to a cafe; that liberty is the half of talent and three-quarters of ordinary happiness.

But, you will say, superior woman that you are, give yourself that liberty!

It is impossible for the woman who emancipates herself thus—the young and pretty woman, be it understood—almost has the finger pointed at her, she becomes singular, commented on, insulted, and consequently still less free than before she shocked idiotic custom.

So there is nothing to do but deplore my sex and return to dreams of Italy and Spain. Granada! gigantic Arabs; pure sky, brooks, rose laurels, sun, shadow, peace, calm, harmony, and poetry!

Saturday, December 1st.—Have I made a mistake in my vocation? Who will give me back the best years of my life, which have been, perhaps, expended in pursuit of a will-o'-the-wisp?

But there is an excellent answer to these doubts of my worst self, and that is that I have really nothing better to do; if I had taken a different course and lived like other people, I should have had to suffer too much. But then I should not have attained this mental development which has given me a superiority so burdensome to myself. Stendhal knew at least one or two beings who were capable of understanding him while I am in a frightful position; everybody seems to me dull and flat, and those I once took to be people of intelligence now appear to me stupid. Have I become what is called a misunderstood being? No; but still it seems to me that I am not to be surprised and discontented when people believe of me things of which I am incapable, and which attack my dignity, my delicacy, and even my position in society.

You see I want someone who would thoroughly understand me, to whom I could tell everything, and in whose words I would recognize the reflection of my own thoughts. Well, my dear little girl, that would be love.

1884

Monday, May 26th.—This is better. Instead of stupidly waiting, I am now indignant, and that is a sentiment which need not be concealed; it is almost refreshing.

Twenty-six third class medals were awarded yesterday, and there are six more to be awarded to-day. M— has a medal for the portrait of Julian.

Why is it that I have received no medal? For medals have been awarded to pictures comparatively bad.

Injustice? I don't care much for that excuse. It is the one most pleaded by people without brains.

They may admire my picture or not, as they please; but the fact remains that it contains seven children, grouped together, and with a background that also has some merit. Everyone whose opinion is worth anything thinks it good or even very good; there are some who say that I could not have painted it all by myself. Even the elder Robert-Fleury, without knowing who the artist was, thought it very good. And Boulanger said to people who did not know me that he did not care for that style of painting, but nevertheless he thought this particular picture very well done and very interesting.

What, then, can it mean?

Pictures with no merit whatever have been awarded medals; I know that this has been the rule. But, on the other hand, there is no artist of talent who has not had his medals. So that there are "daubers" decorated with medals, but no man of genius without one, What then? What then? I also have eyes; my picture is a *composition*.

Suppose I had dressed those urchins in the costume of the middle ages, and painted them in a studio (which is much easier than in the open air) with a background of old tapestry?

I should then have an historical painting which would be much appreciated in Russia.

What can I believe?

Here is another request for reproduction—from Baschet, the great publisher.

It is the fifth that I have signed. What of it?

Tuesday, May 27th.—It is over. I have no medal. But it is frightfully provoking. I did not give up hope until this morning. And if you knew the things to which they have given medals!

Why am I not discouraged? Because I am so astonished perhaps. If my picture is good, why did it not receive a prize?

Intrigues, they will say.

That is all very well; but still, if my picture is good, why did it not receive a prize? I do not wish to set myself up as a guileless child, who does not know there are such things as intrigues; but yet when a picture is good—

Then it must have been bad? No, that can not be.

I have eyes, even in judging my own works—and then the others! And the forty newspapers!

Thursday, May 29th.—I have had a fever all night, and I am frightfully irritated and wildly nervous. It is not the medal alone, but that combined with a sleepless night.

I am so unhappy! I long to believe in God. Is it not natural to seek for some miraculous porter that can help you, when all is wretchedness and misery, and there is no loop-hole of escape anywhere?

One tries to believe in an Omnipotent Being, Whom one has only to appeal to, to be heard, and Whom one can address without fear of humiliation or coldness. Then one has resort to prayer. The doctors are powerless, and we ask for a miracle, which does not happen; but while we are asking and expecting it, we are somewhat caroled. It does not amount to much. God can be only a just God; but if He is just, why does He allow things to be as they are? A second's reflection, alas! is all that is required to destroy our belief. What is the use of living? What is the use of dragging on such a miserable existence? Death presents this advantage, at least—it is a means of finding what this famous future life really is; that is, if there is any future life at all.

Ivanov Pavel
(Dedicated to His Parents)
V. M. Doroshevich (1901)

VLAS DOROSHEVICH, "KING OF FEUILLETONISTS," WAS TSARIST RUSSIA'S PREMIER NEWSPAPER COLUMNIST. HIS WORK RANGED FROM SOBER REPORTING TO AESOPIAN FABLES, AND FEATURED A DRY WIT THAT DISSECTED OFFICIAL OBSCURANTISM. DOROSHEVICH PREFERRED THE SIMPLE SENTENCES CONSONANT WITH JOURNALISTIC OBJECTIVITY THAT ALLOWED STORIES TO TELL THEMSELVES, ALTHOUGH HE WOULD OFTEN ADD A FILLIP. HE TOOK GREAT PRIDE IN HIS STATUS AS A POPULAR INTELLECTUAL FIGURE DESPITE A MINIMAL EDUCATION; RUSSIAN SCHOOLS HAD SIMPLY BORED HIM INTO DROPPING OUT EARLY.

THE FOLLOWING PASSAGE PRESENTS A POPULAR RUSSIAN CHARACTER, THE DAYDREAMING SCHOOLBOY "IVANOV PAVEL," WHOSE IMAGINATION SOARED ONLY OUTSIDE THE CLASSROOM. THE LINEAGE OF IVANOV PAVEL IS OBSCURE, BUT HE WAS NOT ORIGINAL TO DOROSHEVICH. THE JOURNALIST MADE THE SCHOOLBOY THE HERO OF MANY FEUILLETONS, TAKING LICENSE

V. M. Doroshevich, *Ivanov Pavel* (Paris: "Ocharovannyi *Strannik*," 1927).

TO CRITIQUE THE EDUCATIONAL SYSTEM THAT HAD EXPELLED
SO MANY BRIGHT CHILDREN LIKE HIMSELF.

Ivanov Pavel,[1] a student in the second grade at Gymnasium no. 4, walked out of his house one wet, gloomy autumn morning. This was not Ivanov Pavel, but the express train from Petersburg to Orel, traveling at the speed of eighty miles an hour. The countryside flashed by, and charging out of the gate past the posts, Ivanov Pavel gave two warning whistles so as not to run into the delivery man's water barrel. Ivanov Pavel, hissing and puffing steam, moving like lightning from turn to turn, amazed at his own artistry, crossed the street. In the winter he had been a pathfinder, studying tracks in the snow very closely, finding in them many secret, suspicious, and alarming things that compelled him to hoot like an owl.

But in the autumn, while memories of his trip to the village were still fresh, he was the express train that left for Orel Province every morning at eight o'clock.

Coming up to Shestopalov's shop, Ivanov Pavel whistled and steamed as the train stopped. "The engineer is out to lunch." Ivanov Pavel entered the shop, put the five-kopeck piece he had received at breakfast down on the counter, and said, "Give me a 'National' chocolate bar, the one with nuts. If you don't have any, give me your best roll . . . or, well, I don't need a roll—make it a bar of halvah. The best."

He left Shestopalov's shop slowly, absorbed in chewing the halvah. The bar was chewy, like a piece of rubber. It got stuck in his teeth, often so hard that he could not move his jaw and had to put his fingers in his mouth. He liked that. "These are real battle rations. The Indians didn't eat at all. And Cook was so hungry that he ate his moccasins!"

He arrived at the gymnasium right before the bell, and his heart was suddenly full of anxiety. He had wanted to cram before school this morning, but now there was no time. He was filled with a terrible uneasiness. Everyone around him sensed his fear and apprehension. They ran around, playing and shouting, but nervously, as if they hoped that the noise would muffle the inner uneasy voice. Some of his friends ran up to Ivanov Pavel and cried, "What's with you, Devet?[2] Why are you so late? We had a battle without you. Go see Kruger."[3]

Ivanov Pavel shouted back irritably, "Get the hell away from me! You're a fool, not Kruger."

"So, and you're not Devet!" answered the insulted Kruger.

The others began to shout, "Hey guys, guys! Ivanov is no longer Devet!"

Kruger hit him in the side with his fist, and Ivanov Pavel kicked him with his heel. Just then the bell rang.

"First class. Russian. Please don't call on me."

---

1. Ivanov Pavel, with the family name listed before the given name, was how the student would have been listed on a class roster and addressed in the formal classroom.

2. General Devet, a Boer who enjoyed many victories over the British during the Boer War.

3. S. J. Kruger, president of the Transvaal Republic during the Boer War.

But Nikolai Ivanovich, the Russian teacher, entered the classroom and after the prayer announced: "Dictation!"

Ivanov Pavel's heart sank. Dictation lasted the whole hour. When the bell rang and the first recess began, the other kids flew up to Ivanov Pavel: "Why did you kick Kostiukov like that? You know that isn't allowed. It's against the rules!"

"Gentlemen! I've got to cram for Latin now!" declared Ivanov Pavel. But the others began hollering, "Coward! Coward!"

Mozgov Ignaty shouted, "Aren't you supposed to be the second-strongest guy in the class?"

It was now a question of self-respect. Ivanov Pavel moved out from behind the desk and said, "Stand there. I'll use my left hand. How many of you are ready?"

"Don't kick! Kicking isn't allowed!" the others cried.

The strongest boy in the class stood nearby, prepared to enter the fray at any moment. Mozgov hopped around from front to side, but Ivanov Pavel hit him every time and had easily pinned him to the desk when the bell rang. They all rushed back to their places.

The slow, measured steps of the Czech who taught Latin resounded through the corridor. Ivanov Pavel's whole body suddenly began to itch.

"Rise!" the Czech Latinist gestured with his hand. All rose. "Sit!" declared the Czech Latinist, dropping his hand. All sat.

"Rise!" again said the Czech Latinist. Again all stood.

"Sit!" the Czech Latinist said again. Again all sat. He did this four times, then sat down in his chair, made a note of who was absent, announced the next lesson, and picked up his notebook.

"Lord, not me! Not me!" whispered Ivanov Pavel, and he began to cross himself repeatedly under his desk.

The Czech Latinist moved his finger down his notebook, then exclaimed, "Mozgov!"

"Not me! Not me!" Ivanov Pavel's spirits soared. He sat very low in his seat, hunched over the desk, and kicked the tall boy sitting in front of him, Veretennikov.

"Sit up! You've got to sit higher so that he won't see me."

"I'll sit as high as I can," whispered Veretennikov in reply, putting two books under himself and stretching up to attention.

"Higher, I tell you, higher! So that he can't see me!" Ivanov Pavel hit him beneath the desk.

"I can't go any higher!" snapped back Veretennikov.

"Weretennokov Nikwai! What are you sayink back dere?" The Czech's voice suddenly rang out. "With whom? Kum here!"

He stared fixedly at Ivanov Pavel, flat against his desk. Ivanov Pavel could feel the blood pounding in his head and burning in his ears. He sat stooped over, unable to look at the Czech, but conscious of his penetrating gaze. The whole class sat hushed; a deathly silence reigned.

"Call on someone! Call!" thought Ivanov Pavel to himself, and as if in a death struggle he slid beneath his desk.

The voice rang out from the rostrum: "Vere are you? Stind!"

Ivanov froze. Another excruciating, interminable minute passed. The Czech moved his finger down his book. At last,

"Iwanov, Poivel!"

Ivanov Pavel felt his legs weaken as he walked to the blackboard.

"You had a '2' last time,"[4] the Czech began slowly and spoke carefully. "You must do bitter. Bitter!"

Ivanov Pavel blinked, shook, blushed, paled.

"Please allow me to explain, Oskar Viktorovich . . . "

"Spik!" declared the Czech. "Spik! You said you have somethink to say. Ve are vaiting, Iwanov Poivel!"

"Please let me tell you, Oskar Viktorovich . . . " Ivanov Pavel began to whimper.

"Don't veep! It is not necessary to veep," the Czech interrupted him. "How to form the plural in Latin?"

Ivanov Pavel stood helplessly in front of the class. The best student, jug-eared Patrikeev Nikolai, sat in the first row, his eyes imploring the Czech through his glasses, "Call on me, Oskar Viktorovich! Ask me how to form the plural!"

Postinkov Aleksei had already raised his hand to show where he had stained his palm with ink; he was prepared to jump up at any moment and start a commotion. Mozgov stuck his tongue out at Ivanov. Kostiukov made a sign in the air, as if to say, "Just you wait."

"They're all bastards; I'm glad that I don't know," thought Ivanov, and he suddenly felt so hurt, so small, so unhappy, that tears began to trickle from his eyes. "I don't . . . don't know anything about the plural."

"Iwanov Poivel doesn't know any Latin plurals!" the Czech exclaimed abruptly, feigning surprise, and in such a loud voice that it echoed down the corridor.

The class giggled.

"Your ears, Iwanov Poivel; will you tell about the Latin plural or not?"

The class sat at attention, anticipating a scene. Ivanov Pavel began to hiccup with sobs.

"Aanser!"

"I don't know!" Ivanov Pavel muttered timorously.

The class snorted and burst out laughing. Ivanov Pavel looked like a trapped animal.

"Iwanov Poivel niver saw his own ears," declared the Czech Latinist.

The class strained, sobbed, rolled with laughter.

"Siddown."

"Oskar Viktorovich, my head . . . " Ivanov Pavel took a step forward.

"Every person hass a head," declared the Czech, taking his notebook and dipping his pen in the inkwell.

"Oskar Viktorovich!" cried out Ivanov Pavel in desperation.

"Siddown," said the Latinist, writing all over the page. The whole class pointed at Ivanov Pavel.

---

4. The Russian grading system goes from 5, which is excellent, to 2, which is unsatisfactory.

But Patrikeev Nikolai began to whisper, "Sit down already!" Then he raised his hand. "I know the Latin plural, Oskar Viktorovich."

Ivanov Pavel returned to his seat, beginning to howl even louder.

"Iwanov Poivel veeps," said the Czech. "Let him leaf and stind and veep there."

Ivanov Pavel left the room and stood in the hallway. The class could still hear his sobs. From time to time he would appear in the door, his face red, wet, smeared with ink, and say, "Os . . . Os . . . Oskar . . . Vik . . . Vik . . . Viktorovich . . . "

Each time the Czech would answer calmly, "Stind in the hallvay," and then continue quizzing the other students.

Thus the lesson ended. Next class was with the priest.

"Ivanov Pavel, why the tears? Why are you sobbing inconsolably, like an abused child?" asked the priest.

"Oskar Viktorovich . . . out there . . . made me stand . . . there," sniffled Ivanov Pavel.

"You must study your lessons with diligence, not with tears, Ivanov Pavel!" responded the priest. "Now, go and wash up. You look like a scarecrow."

Ivanov Pavel cleaned up and returned to the classroom. He asked his neighbor for his notebook and began copying everything from the past two weeks. He decided that from this moment on, he would learn all of his assignments by heart. This decision soothed him and kindled hope in his heart. "Maybe I can be forgiven. In the future I'll study very hard."

He sat and daydreamed: "I'll be the best student. I'll get 5's on all my homework. Mama will let me do gymnastics in the house."

But remembering his mother, he began to sob again. Terrible apprehension seized his heart. He became somber, anxious, agitated. As soon as the bell rang, he flew out the door at breakneck speed, knocking down everyone in his way.

The main recess had begun. The students were playing noisily below. From behind the door to the teachers' room, he could hear conversations and laughter. Two students stood at this door: Ivanov Pavel and another boy, also from the second grade, but a different section. He was the weakest boy in the class.

"Who do you want to see?" asked the weak boy.

"Oskar Viktorovich. He made me stand in the hall. You?"

"The German," answered the weak boy. "He threw me out for making noise."

They both started crying. They stood there crying for about five minutes, and then the most feeble boy in the class, his voice broken by sobs, said, "Would you like to trade an old Napoleonic feather pen for a new eighty-six one?"

"I've already got an eighty-six, one with a screw top," answered the whimpering Ivanov Pavel. "What if I give you some India rubber for your old Napoleonic pen?"

"Whadda ya mean?" responded the weak boy with more animation. "What do I need with your old rubber? I already have my own."

With that he pulled a piece of black rubber out of his mouth.

"So that's what you've been chewing on. Well, mine was boiled in kerosene," answered the weeping Ivanov Pavel. "I could smack you. You want me to hit you in the head?"

Ivanov Pavel kicked the feeble boy with the back of his heel. Just then the door to the teachers' room opened, and the Czech Latinist walked out.

"Fighting here? Agin, Iwanov Poivel? Stind aginst the vall. Stind there an hour!"

"Oskar Viktorovich!" Ivanov Pavel threw himself at the Czech and grabbed his coattails. "Oskar Viktorovich!"

"Stind!"

"Oskar Viktorovich! I'll study very hard!"

The Latinist walked down the stairs.

"Who's out here screaming? Are you the one screaming?" the director's loud voice rang out as he exited the teachers' room.

Everything went suddenly quiet. Not even the sobbing could be heard. He sat there, sighing, repeating passively to himself, "What can I do? What can I do?"

Then he was struck by a thought that made him writhe and wriggle, until he successfully expelled the idea: What if there were no future?

He calmed down a little in French class. Although he played with a feather under his desk, he did not enjoy it. Right before the end of the last class, arithmetic, the supervisor came into class and announced, "Ivanov Pavel is ordered to stay after school for one hour."

Ivanov froze on the spot. His whole body shuddered, and then his spirit finally collapsed.

The students left the gymnasium noisily. It was empty, except for the nine students, including Ivanov Pavel, forced to stay after. The older ones whispered among themselves and laughed; the younger ones cried. The supervisor on duty was writing notes to their parents.

"Ivanov Pavel!" He gave Ivanov a note: "Ivanov Pavel, student in the first section of the second grade, for flunking Latin and for noise and fighting during the main recess, remained after class for one hour. Assistant to the School Preceptor A. Pokrovsky."

Ivanov Pavel—who had sat there the whole time thinking about how he could turn over a new leaf once and for all, and who in his daydreams had already received a letter of commendation and books from the director himself—took the note and started to howl: "What do you mean, noise? I didn't make any noise! I was only fighting."

"Bring it back tomorrow with your parents' signature," announced the supervisor, and at three-thirty he said, "Rise!"

It was depressing and creepy to walk out of the school through the empty, quiet halls. It was weird to see his gray coat hanging in the middle of all the empty hooks. And it was a bleak and eerie walk through the large empty courtyard.

"If you want, Ivanov, I'll walk you home and then you can walk me home," suggested a student from the third grade, also kept after for "persistent disobedience to the class preceptor."

"Get outta here!" Ivanov answered spitefully and unhappily. But rather than going straight home, he visited several churches. He first entered a chapel to the Mother of God, then went to another, then to a third, then into one dedicated to the Redeemer. In all of them he prayed long and passionately, bowing low to the ground sometimes and kissing it. He felt better, peaceful, calmer, as though a weight had been lifted from his soul. Even when a kid from a shop ran after him crying "Blue meat! red trousers!" Ivanov Pavel did not turn around and swear at him. Instead, he thought to himself, "The Lord commanded us to forgive everyone. God, forgive him his transgression."

He was terribly afraid of angering God. He swore upon his soul, "I'll be so good, so good. Please just don't let them beat me today." Suddenly he remembered how on Saturday he had run away from vespers so that he could fight with some boys in the churchyard. Fear gripped him. He crossed himself subtly, so that passersby would not notice, and said, "I will always, always go to vespers now. Just don't let them beat me today."

He entered Kazan Cathedral[5] and knelt before the icons. He spent an especially long time at one in particular. He always prayed before this icon; in fact, he had learned to pray here. It was necessary to kneel down, lean backward a little, and speak in a whisper, so that your voice was as deep as possible and you could feel your insides tremble.

"Lord, Lord! God help me, that today . . . that today . . . they don't beat me!" he said quietly, ashamed before God with such a request. He crossed himself earnestly, making a big cross, holding his fingers together tightly, and bowing to the ground, remaining for a long time with his forehead on the cold floor.

He prayed thus for so long that a familiar sensation began to overtake him: his heart began to rise in his chest, his throat tightened, large tears dropped from his eyes, and a calm settled in his soul. "This means they won't beat me," he decided, comforted by the familiar sensation.

Suddenly, though, he became frightened by his own presumption. He began crossing himself hastily. "God, forgive me, forgive me!" Standing up, he genuflected before the icon, crossed himself three times, and exited the cathedral. He stopped again at the doors and began making the sign of the cross: They won't beat me!

Dusk had set in. He was extremely hungry. Ivanov Pavel headed home. The closer he got to home, the more despondent he became.

"If a woman walks out from behind that corner, I'll get beaten. But if it's a man, I won't."

A woman came out.

"No! No! It can't be! If it takes me an even number of steps to reach that post, no beating. Odd number—beating."

He started counting, taking giant steps, then tiny ones, but then a man passing by nearly knocked him off his feet, and the number of steps came out odd.

Arriving home, he took off his coat, stood in the hallway, and started to bawl.

"Come, come here!" said his mother. "You're a night owl, not coming home till midnight! Come here. What's going on?"

---

5. The main Petersburg cathedral, on Nevsky Prospect. Site of many important demonstrations.

No sooner had he crossed the threshold into the living room than she boxed his ears.

"Mommy, I won't! I won't!" Ivanov Pavel began to howl.

"Okay, okay. We'll talk about this later. What are you so happy about? What've you brought?"

"Oh, Mommy, it's not true . . . "

"Give me the note now!"

His mother read the note, pursed her lips, looked at Ivanov Pavel as though he were a vile creature, stood silently for a moment, and then asked, "What do you want me to do with you? Eh?"

"Mommy, I won't . . . "

"What do you want me to do with you?"

Ivanov Pavel felt his ears burning. His head began to spin, and he crumpled like bark in a flame.

"Okay, okay. We'll discuss it later. Then . . . ," Mama said ominously.

"Later!" he thought to himself. "At least not now." His spirits lightened.

"Go to the kitchen and wash your ugly face. Who do you look like?"

Ivanov Pavel went into the kitchen to wash up. The cook Aksinia busied herself at the stove, heating up his dinner.

"So, who beat you up?"

Ivanov silently washed his face.

"Why didn't you do your dictation?" the cook insisted on pestering him.

"It wasn't dictation but Latin. Fool! You idiot!"

"Don't you go calling your elders names! I'll hold you down while your mama beats you. I'll hold you down, I will," teased the cook.

Ivanov Pavel wanted to go after her with his fists, but he held back. He wanted to say, "Aksiniushka, please, don't hold me down for long." Again he resisted. "Let them kill me. It'll be better." Gulping down his cold food, tears still flowing, Ivanov Pavel imagined that he had been whipped to death. Everyone was sitting around eating at the funeral dinner; his mother was tearing out her hair, screaming, "It was I, I who killed him! Wake up, Pasha, come to your senses, my darling, my precious!" She was sobbing as she had when he had scarlet fever. Ivanov Pavel began to feel sorry for himself, for his mother, for all the others, and he began to weep bitterly.

"Ah, haven't you finished dinner yet? Well?" his mother's voice could be heard.

Ivanov Pavel jumped up. "Mommy, Mommy! I'm starting my homework!"

"Okay, okay. Start your assignments."

Ivanov Pavel sat down to work and began copying. He learned everything there was to learn. He skipped taking a break for tea. Finally there was nothing more to copy, nothing more to read. His back and chest ached. Ivanov Pavel stood up and began pacing around the room.

"Madame wants to know if you've finished." A maid appeared at the door.

"No, no!" muttered the frightened Ivanov Pavel. He sat down again and started to work on translations. Then he started fantasizing that his entire house was engulfed in flames. No. It was that the enemy had attacked the city, and everyone was locked in his house. Like an ancient Greek warrior, he directed the enemy to a secret path along a dark staircase. They were slaughtering everyone. He alone was ahead of the enemy . . . and he was massacring them all, every one of them. They were throwing themselves at his feet, begging for mercy. But he was unrelenting. What tortures he was dreaming up! Even he began to shudder and feel sorry for them. He would simply order them killed. Except for Mama. "I'll spare Mama."

Ivanov Pavel knelt down before his mother, who had just entered the room.

"Mama, dearest, not now! I have to say my prayers."

"One last breath before dying?" smiled his mother. "Pray, pray! You have to take your clothes off anyway."

But Ivanov Pavel did not undress. He knelt for a long time before the icon, bending to the ground, and whispering as loudly as possible, so that his voice could be heard in the next room.

"Lord have mercy on my dear mama. Lord, save her, defend her, have mercy on my dearest mother!" Can she hear how I'm praying for her? wondered Ivanov Pavel, and he raised his voice even louder.

Aksinia stood in the door to the children's room and pronounced his sentence: "Better start turning somersaults, brother! It's about to begin."

The maid walked in and said loudly, on purpose, "Where are the birch rods? Such good ones!"

Ivanov Pavel couldn't bear this. He jumped up. Mama entered the room. "Take off your clothes and lie down."

"Mommy!" wailed Ivanov Pavel. "Mommy, I won't! You'll see, I won't!"

"Take off your clothes and lie down."

"Mommy!" Ivanov Pavel slid before her on his knees, grabbed her dress, kissed it, but tried not to get so close that she could lock his head between her knees. He knew this method and hated it most of all. Ivanov Pavel was ready.

"Lie down!"

"Mommy, please don't hurt me, please don't do it for long!" he said breathlessly, trying to hold up his arm, which she was getting ready to whip.

"There's nothing to it. You can't talk me out of it. Now lie down."

"Mommy?"

"Shall I lay you down?"

"I'll do it myself, Mommy."

"Aksinia!"

"Mommy, it isn't necessary to have Aksinia hold me down. I'll stay down."

"Aksinia!"

He felt Aksinia grab his thin legs, and then the burning whip. "Oooww!" screeched the boy, pinned down, feeling the burning lashes on his hands, trying to twist away. They pinned him again, and again he tried to yank free.

"Glasha! hold his hands!"

"A-a-a-h!" the boy screamed like a wounded animal, completely defenseless.

"Study! Study! Study!" repeated his mother.

"Mommy, I won't! I won't!" howled Ivanov Pavel.

"Don't be a troublemaker! Don't make noise! Be quiet! Quiet!"

"Mommy, I wasn't making noise! I wasn't making any noise!" He felt like he was dying. The bed smelled of fresh birch leaves. The red lamp flickered before the icon. Sobs could be heard in the darkened room. Ivanov Pavel's breast was filled with tears. His body ached, smarted. But his soul was calm.

"It's over. It happened, and now it's over. There's nothing more to fear."

Quietly whimpering, the poor boy fell asleep. He dreamed that he was chief of the Comanches, and that they were scalping all the white people . . .

Why perform such an outrage against the human body, against such a young human soul?

Song of the Stormy Petrel
Maxim Gorky (1901)

GORKY (1868–1936) WAS BORN IN THE CITY OF NIZHNY NOV-GOROD, WHICH WAS RENAMED GORKY IN HIS HONOR MUCH LATER, AFTER HE HAD BEEN DESIGNATED PATRON SAINT OF SO-VIET LITERATURE. HE ALWAYS ENJOYED POPULARITY, THOUGH, FROM HIS DEBUT IN 1892, RIVALING THE FAME OF THE GREAT LEV TOLSTOI. HE CAME TO HIS EMINENCE THROUGH ADVERSITY; ORPHANED EARLY, HE EMBARKED ON HIS MANY JOBS AND WAN-DERINGS AT THE AGE OF ELEVEN, ACQUIRING THE ROUGH EDUCA-TION THAT WOULD ANIMATE HIS WRITINGS. HIS LASTING FAME IN RUSSIA AND ABROAD CAME FROM HIS WRITINGS ABOUT MIS-FITS AND OUTCASTS.

GORKY WAS SUCCESSFUL WITH NEWSPAPER COLUMNS, PLAYS, NOVELS, AND MANY OTHER GENRES. BELOW IS ONE OF HIS RO-MANTIC PROSE POEMS, WHICH ADDRESSES THE THEME OF REVO-LUTION IN AN ALLEGORICAL FORM DESIGNED TO STYMIE CENSOR-SHIP. DESPITE HIS DIFFICULT LIFE, GORKY COULD BE VERY OPTIMISTIC AND INSPIRATIONAL. HE ROMANTICIZED REVOLU-TIONARY STRUGGLE AND PERSONALIZED IT, MAKING REVOLU-

Translated by M. Wettlin in Maksim Gorky, *Selected Short Stories* (New York: F. Ungar, 1959), pp. 160–161.

O'er the silver plain of ocean winds are gathering the storm-clouds, and between the clouds and ocean proudly wheels the Stormy Petrel, like a streak of sable lightning.

Now his wing the wave caresses, now he rises like an arrow, cleaving clouds and crying fiercely, while the clouds detect a rapture in the bird's courageous crying.

In that crying sounds a craving for the tempest! Sounds the flaming of his passion, of his anger, of his confidence in triumph.

The gulls are moaning in their terror—moaning, darting o'er the waters, and would gladly hide their horror in the inky depths of ocean.

And the grebes are also moaning. Not for them the nameless rapture of the struggle. They are frightened by the crashing of the thunder.

And the foolish penguins cower in the crevices of rocks, while alone the Stormy Petrel proudly wheels above the ocean, o'er the silver-frothing waters!

Ever lower, ever blacker, sink the storm-clouds to the sea, and the singing waves are mounting in their yearning toward the thunder.

Strikes the thunder. Now the waters fiercely battle with the winds. And the winds in fury seize them in unbreakable embrace, hurling down the emerald masses to be shattered on the cliffs.

Like a streak of sable lightning wheels and cries the Stormy Petrel, piercing storm-clouds like an arrow, cutting swiftly through the waters.

He is coursing like a Demon, the black Demon of the tempest, ever laughing, ever sobbing—he is laughing at the storm-clouds, he is sobbing with his rapture.

In the crashing of the thunder the wise Demon hears a murmur of exhaustion. He is certain that the clouds will not obliterate the sun; that the storm-clouds never, never, will obliterate the sun.

The waters roar . . . The thunder crashes . . .

Livid lightning flares in storm clouds o'er the vast expanse of ocean, and the flaming darts are captured and extinguished by the waters, while the serpentine reflections writhe, expiring, in the deep.

The storm! The storm will soon be breaking!

Still the valiant Stormy Petrel proudly wheels among the lightning, o'er the roaring, raging ocean, and his cry resounds exultant, like a prophecy of triumph—

Let it break in all its fury!

Light-Fingered Sonya
The Adventures of the Infamous Thief and Murderess, and Her Imprisonment on Sakhalin
M. D. Klefortov (1903)

SOPHIA (SONYA) BLIUVSHTEIN WAS ONE OF RUSSIA'S MOST COL-
ORFUL CRIMINALS. PICKPOCKET, SUSPECTED MURDERESS, OPERA-
TOR OF AN ILLEGAL STILL ON THE PRISON ISLAND OF SAKHALIN,
SHE CAPTURED THE IMAGINATIONS OF MILLIONS WITH HER ESCA-
PADES. HER RUSSIAN NICKNAME, "ZOLOTAIA RUCHKA," TRANS-
LATES LITERALLY AS "THE GOLDEN HAND," AND SHE USED WHAT
WAS APPARENTLY A GOLDEN BODY AS WELL TO GET HER WAY.
POPULAR JOURNALIST VLAS DOROSHEVICH, WHO INTERVIEWED
HER ON SAKHALIN, NOTED THAT POSTCARDS OF HER IN CHAINS
WERE THE MOST SOUGHT AFTER OF PRISON SOUVENIRS. TABLOID
READERS FOLLOWED HER EXPLOITS, AND FICTIONAL PORTRAITS
SUCH AS THIS ONE BY KLEFORTOV EMBELLISHED HER LIFE. HER
CROWNING MOMENT CAME IN 1914 WHEN ALEKSANDR DRANKOV
TURNED HER ADVENTURES INTO RUSSIA'S FIRST MOVIE SERIAL.
(THE ACTRESS PLAYING HER, NINA GOFMAN, NEARLY MATCHED
SONYA'S LIGHT-FINGERED SKILLS, LIFTING A WATCH FROM AN
UNAWARE ACTOR WITH THE CAMERAS ROLLING.) TOO ELASTIC
FOR STEREOTYPES, SONYA WAS NEITHER HEROINE NOR VILLAIN-
ESS. SHE PERSONIFIED BOTH THE THRILL AND THE PRICE OF MA-
NEUVERING BEYOND THE LAW.

SONYA'S FIRST APPEARANCE AND HER ACQUAINTANCE WITH THE MERCHANT B.

It had been ages since the theater was as crowded as it was the evening of 3
February 18—. The opera *Demon* was playing, and a famous actor who had never
appeared on our stage was singing the title role. The bright electric lights seemed

---

M. D. Klefortov, *Son'ka "Zolotaia ruchka." Pokhozhdeniia znamenitoi vorovki–ubiitsy i eia prebyvanie na Sakha-
line,* ed. S. S. Poliatus (Odessa: Poriadok, 1903).

to flow into the diamonds and finery of the ladies seated in the box seats and loges. At last the curtain lifted, and the orchestra struck up the prelude. The audience watched the stage intently.

Little by little, however, binoculars and lorgnettes in the loges were turned to one side of the theater. A number of people who had been following the opera realized that the attention of many others was not on the stage, but on a loge close to it. Many seated in the upper rows became annoyed when a noisy whispering disrupted their beloved opera. During the intermission, all the talk was about the beautiful woman in the theater; everyone had forgotten the famous actor.

"Who is that marvelous beauty?" people asked theater regulars. But no one could answer. Some said she was an Italian who had come with the actor, perhaps his fiancée. Others thought her the daughter of a wealthy marquis. No one knew the truth.

The son of the merchant B. sat in the loge opposite hers, and he could not tear his eyes away.

"Who is that beautiful lady?" he asked his uncle, the moneylender A., seated next to him. "You must've heard of her. You know everyone in the financial world, so you must somehow know her."

The moneylender A., as if awakened from a reverie, did not answer his nephew immediately.

"I know her very well. She's the daughter of a trader I'm holding a lot of pawn tickets for," said A. "I've proposed to her several times, but she's turned me down cold. I'm still hopeful, though. I'll squeeze him some more, and then boom! She won't escape me."

"Anyway, Uncle, please introduce me to her."

"It would be useless, my friend. Besides, she's poor."

"Why would I need wealth from her when she herself is gold?"

"Oh, you're still young, Nephew, or you wouldn't think like that."

Despite his uncle's refusal, the nephew met both the girl and her parents, who never left their daughter's side. The elegant and reasonably handsome young merchant tried from the beginning to make a favorable impression on the beauty, "Sophie." He trembled before her, and her dark, burning eyes penetrated him, smiling ironically.

The curtain went up for a second time, and "Demon" sang his famous aria to "Tamara": "You will be queen of the world." The audience, enthralled by the beautiful woman, did not applaud him, but instead began shouting "Encore!" to her. The actor, not expecting such ingratitude from the audience, stopped on the last note, on the verge of tears. "Tamara" was speechless, unsure whether they were cheering her or the beauty.

Despite an excellent performance, the audience paid little attention to her all evening. At the end of the performance, B. invited the beauty and her parents to ride home in his carriage. They in turn invited him to visit.

B. began to court Sonya. Her parents considered the young merchant a suitable fiancé for their daughter, and they persuaded her to take advantage of the situation, not to drive him away. Sophia had many suitors whose hand she had refused. So it would have been no surprise if she had turned him down, too, as her parents feared. Sophia had a very strong will; she did not like to be pressured. She was not especially tall, but had a stunning figure. Her dark eyes burned with fire and shot glances like arrows. Her skin was a bit dull, but thick black hair poured over her neck like a lion's mane. When she walked, she called to mind a tigress.

"How happy I am, kissing your golden hands," said B., on his knees before her. "Promise me that you will belong to no one but me, that you will be my queen!"

"If I am to be your queen, then you must be my Demon," Sophia answered. In a few months they were married. There was a flurry of rumors about the most beautiful woman ever seen and about how she had engrossed the audience that evening. B. took great pride in his queen, and they spent the first few months of married life abroad. She was stared at everywhere, like a supernatural creature.

After six months abroad, Sonya began to grow melancholy. She stopped going out for walks. Her husband could not understand the reasons for her depression. She made excuses, told him that she was feeling the first pains of pregnancy, and that it was difficult for her to go out, even in a carriage. Fearing illness, or perhaps that she was homesick for her parents, B. took her back to Odessa.

THE STRANGER; SONYA DISAPPEARS

Not long after she returned to Odessa, Sonya gave birth to a daughter. But, she was still unhappy. No joy could chase away her blues. One lovely May evening, while out walking with her husband, she passed a stranger; at the sight of him, Sonya grew pale and flinched. The stranger disappeared into the crowd. Something about this person who had caused his wife to almost faint bothered B. But she would tell him nothing. However, he began to grow suspicious at heart, even though she had been a faithful wife until that point. He lay awake all night, thinking about the incident. He was being torn apart. The next day he was sick with depression, but refused to discuss his anxieties with his wife. Sonya understood what was tormenting her husband, and, not wanting to bring any more suspicions upon herself, she decided to complete her plans immediately. Agents in Warsaw were awaiting the arrival of their new patroness. Therefore she had to leave quickly. But what pretext could she use to travel alone, without a husband? Unable to think up an excuse, she stole away in secret. By evening her trail was cold.

THE "GOLDEN HAND" COMMITS BURGLARIES IN WARSAW, MOSCOW, AND PETERSBURG; HER HUSBAND'S PURSUIT

Searches were conducted all over the city, but no one could find her. Her husband was puzzled by her disappearance. He informed the police, but in vain—she had vanished without a trace. He sent her description to every city in Russia, but no one had any information.

In the meantime Sonya, disguised as a marquise, and her gang were committing very successful robberies in stores, theaters, clubs, and banks. Emptying the pockets of many rich men, the incognito Sonya stayed at the most elegant hotels. Before leaving town, she would inform the agents of her new destination. In Warsaw she successfully drew the attentions of an aging Polish count, who declared his love for her at first sight: "Oh, my dear, please let me kiss your golden hands!" She swindled him out of more than 20,000 rubles. Her husband arrived in town the very day that she slipped away.

In Moscow, her agents met the "Golden Hand" in great style. She arranged several robberies there, and even took part in a murder. Then she moved on to Petersburg.

The "Golden Hand" appeared in Petersburg in her guise as a marquise. The elegant apartments she occupied were so appropriate to her masquerade, no one would suspect that the marquise was a cunning thief. In just a few days she conquered the hearts of many society gentlemen, who, when parting with her, also parted with their gold, their diamonds, and even a few tightly packed wallets.

Her agents arranged for the "Golden Hand" to meet only the wealthiest men; without money, no man could court her. She organized many thefts in Petersburg before slipping away from the police. How was she able to escape undetected when the whole force was searching for the clever crook? Quite simply: In each city, just before leaving, she would disguise herself in a new way. Sometimes she was a beggar, at other times a nun or a pilgrim. Most often, though, she donned men's clothes and melted into the background by traveling through villages as a peddler. Her husband followed her trail until at last he caught up with her in Petersburg. Here she came up with a way to elude him forever. But this involved a compromise: her husband, exhausted from the road and tormented by his constant suffering, had just awakened when he heard a knock on his hotel door. Dressing hurriedly, he opened the door and met a well-dressed gentleman. The man excused himself, asking for a few minutes of the husband's time, emphasizing urgency, and promising that he would be able to put him on the right track.

"Please, come in! I'm at your service," said the husband B. excitedly.

"Here's the story," began the stranger. "Yesterday I met a woman claiming to be a marquise who had just arrived from Switzerland. When I was leaving, I realized that my billfold, which held about 10,000 rubles, had disappeared. I went right back to her hotel, but she had already left. At that time I learned from some other people there that you were looking for your wife, who resembled the marquise. Please forgive me for speaking so harshly about your wife. I'd like to offer you my services, so that you can get your wife back, and I can get my 10,000 rubles. Otherwise I'll have to go to the police. I don't want this affair to turn into such a scandal that your wife gets put in jail, thus ruining forever the life of the husband who loves her so much. I have learned that she is staying in a hotel in Paris. You can take her by surprise there and insist on taking her home. Tell her that if she doesn't return my money, I will make her pay. Hurry! Remember, she's using the name Marquise B. If you ask for anyone else, you'll ruin everything."

B. went to the hotel and asked for Marquise B. When she let him in, he went crazy with happiness because at last he stood face to face with his wife. He fell to his knees, begging for sympathy. But Sophia wrung his emotions dry, and convinced him that she would never give in to his wishes. Sitting him on the divan, she hypnotized him with passionate embraces and explanations. When he went under, she fled with all the money he had left. By the time he awoke, her trail had grown cold. He finally realized that the whole thing had been a set-up, and that he must stop fantasizing that his wife would return. Thus the "Golden Hand" escaped her husband forever.

THE "GOLDEN HAND" GOES ABROAD AND MEETS FAILURE

Eluding her husband made her all the bolder. Like a bird of prey, she swooped down on grandeur, hoping to feed upon gold. But after a series of failures, she suffered an unpleasant incident. While riding around the city in a coach attended by a footman, she decided to visit the jewelry stores. Chicly dressed and drenched in diamonds, she entered one store and demanded to see the finest diamond rings. They showed her a large selection of jewels, which she examined attentively. When a beggar came in asking for a handout, she, a rich woman, could not refuse to do her part.

Not able to find just the right ring, she returned them to the merchant and turned to leave. Just then the merchant noticed that three of the most valuable were missing. (And it was evident that she knew her diamonds.) Not intimidated by the wealthy customer, he demanded a search. Upset, her eyes flaming, the "Golden Hand" at last gave into his demands, but to his great surprise, he found nothing on her. She threatened to take him to court for slander. You readers have no doubt already guessed that the beggar was one of her gang, and that the missing rings were passed to him as alms.

From Paris she traveled around the world, visiting every capital, resort, and exhibition, as well as other places where the public gathered. She considered it her duty to visit Monte Carlo, where the gold on the roulette tables shone brighter than sunlight. In Rome she visited St. Peter's for the first time on Palm Sunday, where she cleaned out the pockets of the wealthiest pilgrims, stuffing the goods into her own secret pockets. In the church, she stole a gold and diamond cross from around the neck of an abbot. In London she was caught after her first caper and brought to trial. But here the "Golden Hand" used her beauty to beguile; despite all the direct evidence, she was able to charm the judge and get off scot-free. Even when she was traveling, she did not waste the time spent on the train. She would mesmerize a passenger and pick him clean, then jump off at the station, change her make-up, and continue on. She went from London to Antwerp and Hamburg, generating quite a commotion over her colossal thefts. She barely escaped to America, disguised as a poor immigrant. From there she went to Turkey, Jerusalem, Haifa, Cairo, and Constantinople, where she used her feminine wiles to steal from the wealthy Turks, who are known to have a weakness for such pretty women. Then it was on to Serbia, Bulgaria, Romania, and then Berlin, where she was caught following a major robbery. By this time the whole world knew about the cunning thief, and that she was a Russian citizen. The Germans were returning her to Russia under armed guard, but she escaped at the border.

THE "GOLDEN HAND" RETURNS TO RUSSIA: CAPTURE AND TRIAL

The "Golden Hand" grew homesick and decided to return to Russia. Her return, however, was not a happy one. She landed in N–skoi prison. One of the guards fell in love with her, so she was easily able to escape by seducing him and stealing his uniform. But from that time on she suffered many failures and ended up in various prisons. Although she had several more great successes, at last her fortunes changed. She was arrested for the murder of a wealthy merchant on a train. This time the court treated her very severely, and she was sentenced to hard labor at the prison on Sakhalin Island. She never fainted, showing her bravado throughout the trial. On a table lay the evidence against her—a mound of rings, bracelets, and watches. The judge asked one of her victims to pick out the things that had been stolen from her. The woman, her hands shaking, began to sort through the pile. The sarcastic voice of the "Golden Hand" rang out from the defendant's table: "Don't worry, lady, those diamonds are fakes."

The crowd applauded her boldness loudly. The evidence showed that she had committed more than five hundred significant robberies, to the tune of about a million rubles.

THE "GOLDEN HAND'S" FIRST VENTURES

After reading about so many thefts, you readers must be asking yourselves: Why did she continue such a dangerous life when she already enjoyed enormous wealth, knowing that on the morrow she might be forced to pay a high price?

It is difficult to see into the soul of such a human animal. But I can tell you briefly about her life from her first days as a thief, and you will understand how a person traveling the wrong path can little by little become accustomed to evil and begin to think it the reason for existence. As you know, the "Golden Hand" was the only daughter of poor merchants. Her parents were unable to give her a good education, despite the fact that she picked up all the European languages immediately. She started off at a fourth-rate boarding school but did not graduate because she was caught stealing books, an act that foreshadowed her future career. After this incident, her parents would not allow her out of their sight, unless she was visiting her only friend. One time some people appeared at this friend's house, and they asked Sophia to leave. But she could not understand the problem. After a heated conversation with her friend, Sophia learned their secret: the friend's parents and these mysterious guests were involved in shady deals, of which the friend disapproved. The secret consumed Sophia's soul; she thought about it day and night. Fantasies of wealth and elegance suggested an ideal life for such a pretty girl. But how could she move freely? Her parents would not let her out of their sight! She did not want to run away, because she loved her parents very much. However, at her friend's house, she met a man who became her mentor. In the beginning, she would secretly elude her parents and walk around stores, stealing small items. But the young thief was soon apprehended and put back in her parents' custody. From that time she did not have a free minute, until the evening at the theater. Nevertheless, her association with suspicious characters continued, despite her parents' strict control. They wanted to save their only, but disgraced, daughter, and they hoped that the right husband might put her back on the right path with his love. Sophia would never have agreed to tie the knot with someone who would deprive her of freedom if she had not been so devoted to her parents. Maybe she could have become an honest woman, but the people with whom she had been involved continued to follow her. The man she met on the boulevard asked for her final decision: "Yes or no?" He threatened death if she refused. The thirst for life overcame her love for her parents. She made her decision. Leaving everything behind, she abandoned herself to the passion for easy profit.

However, sometimes she showed signs of humanity. Once on a train she made the acquaintance of a bureaucrat's widow traveling to St. Petersburg to petition for support for her many children, who had been left penniless. The unhappy widow had received a one-time allocation of 5,000 rubles. The "Golden Hand" smelled the money lying nearby, and with no pity for the widow, she stole it and disappeared. Soon a notice appeared in the paper: "Several days ago a widow with small children was robbed of 5,000 rubles, and now she and her family are left with no means of support. She is seeking information about the thief." The "Golden Hand" was moved to tears reading this. She immediately put the money in an envelope with the following letter: "M. G. I read about your misfortune in the paper. Because of my thoughtlessness and passion for money, I caused you grief. I am returning your money, with some advice: in the future, hide it deeper in your bag. Again, I ask your pardon and that of your poor orphaned children. N. N."

The "Golden Hand" also spent huge sums of money on a school in England, exclusively for the children of her gang members, where they could study thievery.

THE "GOLDEN HAND" ON SAKHALIN

After her life of luxury, the damp prison did not suit her. The talk in all the cells was about the new prisoner. But the "Golden Hand" managed to win the love of even the most hardened murderers, those who intimidated new arrivals. Still, her life at hard labor, especially at the beginning, was very unpleasant. She had to work with all the other prisoners, and this tortured her both physically and mentally. But she faced her punishment with the steadfastness of a gladiator going to battle. Once she tried to take off her irons and run away. She was caught and sentenced to a whipping. The most violent prisoner was chosen to carry it out—a murderer, who was ordered to beat the beautiful Sonya, or "Goldhand," as they called her. A crowd of the curious gathered. Cries began from all sides: "Ivan, beat her harder!" "Show

Light-Fingered Sonya in Sakhalin

no pity!" "There's no blood!" "Don't be timid! She's a strong woman. She can stand it!" The executioner Ivan, encouraged by the ruthless crowd, upped the heat. Her body shook with every blow, and stifled cries arose from her breast. She finally passed out. And this was not her only beating. The whole prison took pride in Sonya for her courage in standing up to the authorities. They might not have loved her, but they respected her, and considered her the top woman. Nothing could break this criminal personality—not hard labor, not solitary confinement, not chains, not a bullet or the lash of a whip. Only nature could break her. In her final years, she grew very homesick. She dreamed of returning to Russia, for at least a glimpse of her home region. Whenever she met anyone from Odessa, she showered him with questions about her native city, where she had spent so many happy days. She asked about her daughter, who undoubtedly did not want to know anything about the existence of a mother who had disgraced her and the family so . . .

During her final attempt to escape, she collapsed before she had gone a mile. She was found and taken to the hospital, where the doctor worked a long time to bring her back to consciousness. When she came to, blood poured from her throat, and a fever set in. She was delirious for several days, her rantings terrifying the other patients. It was as if her eyes had left their sockets; her pupils darted to every corner of the room. They had tied her to her cot, and she tried to tear herself free, thinking that she was back in irons.

"Take off these chains! Why are you torturing me so? Let me go to my beloved daughter!" cried the "Golden Hand" in the throes of death. "You, Bogdanov, why are you looking at me like that? You want to hold me down and drink my blood?

No, no! I won't allow any more persecution. I paid for my sin. Now, enough already! Let me repent and cleanse my sinful soul. Don't touch me again with those hands, stained with human blood!"

Thus ended the life of a person who had chosen the wrong path in life. In her final minutes, the same specters appeared before her that had surrounded her in life. Far from the city, in a deserted spot lies a wooden cross that the wind has blown away from the grave. A hand picks it up, someone no less sinful than she, but a still a caring person who watches over the remains of the unhappy victim of passion, the "Golden Hand."

Revolutionary Songs
(Late 19th Century)

REVOLUTIONARY SONGS PROVIDED WORKERS AND LEFTISTS WITH A SIGN OF SOLIDARITY AT TIMES WHEN PUBLIC EXPRESSION WAS PROSCRIBED. THEY COULD BE SUNG AT MEETINGS, DURING FUNERAL PROCESSIONS, AND WHENEVER LARGE GROUPS OF PEOPLE NEEDED TO BE BROUGHT TOGETHER. THERE WAS AN INTERNATIONAL FLAVOR TO RUSSIAN FAVORITES. ONE OF THE MOST FAMOUS SONGS, THE "VARSHAVIANKA" (ORIGINALLY "VARSOVIENNE"), TOOK ITS TUNE FROM AN OLD FRENCH MILITARY MARCH AND ITS WORDS FROM A POLISH UNDERGROUND SONG. IT WAS TRANSLATED IN 1897 BY LENIN'S COMRADE, GLEB KRZHIZHANOVSKY, FROM HIS PRISON CELL. ITS APPEAL STEMMED FROM THE RELENTLESS MARCHING BEAT AND THE PATHOS OF THE WORDS. A FAVORITE PROTEST SONG BEFORE THE REVOLUTION, USED BY MANY PARTIES AND GROUPS, IT LATER BECAME A STANDARD IN SOVIET FILMS ABOUT THE LABOR MOVEMENT. THE "INTERNATIONALE," THE ANTHEM OF THE SECOND INTERNATIONAL, WAS COMPOSED BY THE FRENCHMAN FELIX DEGEYTER. FREELY TRANSLATED INTO MANY LANGUAGES, IT BECAME A POPULAR ANTHEM AROUND THE WORLD. IT HAD A THOROUGHLY RUSSIAN HISTORY OF ITS OWN. LENIN'S FAVORITE ANTHEM, IT SERVED AS

THE SOVIET NATIONAL ANTHEM UNTIL 1943, AND WAS EVEN THE
TUNE PLAYED BY THE KREMLIN BELL TOWER.

VARSOVIENNE
(1897)

Вихри враждебные воют над нами,
Темные силы нас злобно гнетут,
В бой роковой мы вступили с врагами,
Нас еще судьбы безвестные ждут.

Но мы подымем гордо и смело
Знамя борьбы за рабочее дело,
Знамя великой борьбы всех народов
За лучший мир, за святую свободу.

Припев:
На бой кровавый, святой и правый,
Марш, марш вперед, рабочий народ!
На бой кровавый, святой и правый,
Марш, марш вперед, рабочий народ!

Мрет в наши дни с голодухи рабочий,
Станем ли, братья, мы дольше молчать?
Наших сподвижников юные очи
Может ли вид эшафота пугать.

В битве великой не сгинут бесследно
Павшие с честью во имя идей,
Их имена с нашей песней победной
Станут священны мильонам людей.

Припев.

Нам ненавистны тиранов короны,
Цепи народа-страдальца мы чтим,
Кровью народной залитые троны
Кровью мы наших врагов обагрим.

The enemy whirlwind is blowing above
us,
The forces of darkness and evil oppress,
The enemy's started our fatal battle,
Our unknown fate awaits us ahead.

But we shall raise up, proudly and
bravely
The banner of struggle for worker's
rights,
The banner of every nation's great
battle
For holy freedom, and a better life.

Refrain:
To bloody battle, holy and righteous,
March, forward march, working class!
To bloody battle, holy and righteous,
March, forward march, working class!

The worker today is dying from hunger,
Will we, brothers, keep silent anymore?
Can the scaffold continue to frighten
The young eyes of our comrades-in-war?

They who have fallen with honor in
battle
For the ideal will not die in vain.
The song of our triumph sung by the
millions
Will sanctify their immortal names.

Refrain.

We despise the crowns of the tyrants,
And honor the people's chains of woe.
Thrones drenched in the blood of the
people
Will become red with the blood of our
foes.

Месть беспощадная всем супостатам,
Всем паразитам трудящихся масс,
Мщенье и смерть всем царям-
    плутократам,
Близок победы торжественный час.

Merciless vengeance to our oppressors,
And to the parasites of the working
    mass,
Death and vengeance to all the
    plutocrats
When our triumphant hour comes at
    last.

Припев.

Refrain.

THE INTERNATIONAL
Felix Degeyter (1888)

Вставай, проклятьем заклейменный,
Весь мир голодных и рабов!
Кипит наш разум возмущенный
И в смертный бой вести готов.
Весь мир насилья мы разрушим
До основанья, а затем
Мы наш, мы новый мир построим:
Кто был ничем, тот станет всем.

Arise ye prisoners of starvation,
Arise ye wretched of the earth,
For justice thunders condemnation,
A better world's in birth.
No more tradition's chains shall bind
    us.
No more shall force hold us in thrall.
The world shall rise on new
    foundations.
We have been naught, we shall be all.

Припев:
Это есть наш последний и решительный
    бой,
С Интернационалом воспрянет род
    людской!
Это есть наш последний и решительный
    бой,
С Интернационалом воспрянет род
    людской!

Refrain:
'Tis the final conflict, let each stand in
    his place.
The international party shall be the
    human race.
'Tis the final conflict, let each stand in
    his place.
The international party shall be the
    human race.

Никто не даст нам избавленья—
Ни бог, ни царь и не герой.
Добьемся мы освобожденья
Своею собственной рукой.
Чтоб свергнуть гнет рукой умелой,
Отвоевать свое добро,
Вздувайте горн и куйте смело,
Пока железо горячо!

We want no condescending saviors
To rule us from a judgment hall,
We workers ask not for their favors,
Let us consult for all!
To make the thief disgorge his booty,
To free the spirit from its cell,
We must ourselves decide our duty,
We must decide and do it well.

Припев.

Refrain.

Лишь мы, работники всемирной,
Великой армии труда,

Toilers from shops and fields united,
The union of all we who work;

Владеть землей имеем право,
Но паразиты—никогда!
И если гром великий грянет
Над сворой псов и палачей,
Для нас все так же солнце станет
Сиять огнем своих лучей.

Припев.

The earth belongs to us, the workers,
No room here for a shirk.
How many on our flesh have fattened,
But if some noisome birds of prey
Shall vanish from the sky some morning
The blessed sunlight still will stay.

Refrain.

Part V

The Eruption
of Commercial Culture
in the
Interrevolutionary Years,
1906–1917

Urban culture virtually exploded between the revolutions of 1905 and 1917. Censorship and other forms of authority revived after the first two exhilarating years of liberty, but the failure of the 1905 revolution to achieve all its goals hardly denoted a return to the past. The great themes of this era explored individual freedom, which answered the needs of a rapidly growing audience. The invention of moving pictures changed the cultural landscape forever. On the eve of war in 1914, Moscow alone boasted twenty private theaters. Western hegemony threatened once again, as Russian producers scrambled to produce films that could compete with the flood of foreign imports. Singers and sports figures earned exorbitant salaries and celebrity status. At the same time, the images and vocabulary of revolution worked their way into popular literature and theater. They did not so much threaten as serve as a reminder that political dissatisfaction was still a measure of everyday life.

Cities of the Russian empire were increasingly multi-ethnic, filled with peoples of the east and west: Central Asians and other Muslim peoples, Poles, Germans, Jews, Balts, and others. In the streets one might encounter a bewildering array of costumes, smells, habits, and etiquettes. For many Russians, particularly those living in the villages or newly arrived in the cities, being conscious of one's own nationality, not to mention differences from others, was a relatively new experience. Merchants grew accustomed to dealing with other nationalities; their business often brought them into contact with eastern groups such as Armenians, Persians, and Tatars who frequented the great summertime mercantile fair of Nizhny Novgorod. Among the most significant of these multiple ethnicities were the gypsies, especially through the vicarious thrill associated with their music. They were the romantics' gypsies, who swirled around the fringes of empire with the allure of danger and sexual license. The popularity of "gypsy" romances, though, said less about ethnicity than about the presumed freedom and spontaneity of darker southern peoples. The most renowned singer of this genre, Varya Panina of Moscow's Yar Restaurant, was among the few real gypsies to achieve legitimate star status.

Other ethnic and racial groups also made a useful scapegoat for the anxieties that derived from the building of a great empire. Nat Pinkerton, one of several western pulp fiction heroes to find himself in Russian serial literature, found himself up against a loathsome, cunning, and pernicious "yellow peril" in *The Bloody Talisman*. Yet Japanese success in the Russo-Japanese War also inspired respect, as illustrated by other crime series featuring the Oriental Pinkertons Oka-Shima and Kio-Hako, local rather than imported heroes. Anti-semitism, a stock in trade for humor, drew from stereotypes common since the Middle Ages—avarice, cowardice. Yet it nonetheless kept pace with change. Jews of the earlier jokes were shtetl Jews, isolated from the rest of the empire within the Pale of Settlement, the circumscribed area of southwestern Russia to which they had been restricted since late in the eighteenth century. Jews of later jokes were urban, shaped by contact with their Russian compatriots. Although still the butt of some jokes, Jews now fought back with their own brand of humor on vaudeville stages. In hoary punch lines, gypsies, Armenians, and women continued to be ridiculed, yet ways were also found to turn the humor back on the jokers.

The Eruption of Commercial Culture in the Interrevolutionary Years   275

In the years after 1905, discontent with the status quo was evident in popular culture no less than in specifically political arenas. Modernity continued its assault on traditional values. Sex and sexuality, once controlled by custom and law, assumed a place of prominence. The action often took place on the margins of society: prostitutes and actresses, philosophers and perverts, Jews and wrestlers. Blunt sex talk was common on the vaudeville stage, with men and women employing the same semi-veiled language. The tabloid press covered prostitutes sympathetically, depicted here in an interview of the *Kopeck Gazette*'s Olga Gridina. Sex could be portrayed at its most cynical, as when Breshko-Breshkovsky peddled the affairs of brawny wrestlers and languorous ladies, or when Count Amori's "countess-actress" ventured to upper-class orgies. It could deliver powerful political messages, as in Mikhail Artsybashev's *Sanin,* whose Nietzschean title character dreams of seducing his sister, or in Evdokia Nagrodskaia's *Wrath of Dionysus,* with its open discussion of homosexuality, and above all in Anastasia Verbitskaia's *The Keys to Happiness,* whose heroine struggles with social norms and turbulent desires in her quest for independence.

The disorientation implicit in change, accented by sexual emancipation and growing personal freedom, precipitated imagined utopias of many sorts. Utopianism had deep roots in peasant culture, and utopian fiction reached a mass market by the 1900s, expressing a wide range of philosophic views. V. I. Kryzhanovskaia and her occult mysticism offered competing versions of the past and future, but played to one large audience. Nikolai Fedorov, whose *One Evening in the Year 2217* is mounted on our Web site, offered scientific optimism for the future. His confidence in a more rational future shared much, and competed, with the socialist utopia *Red Star* (1908), written by the Bolshevik Aleksandr Bogdanov.

Visionaries confronted a harsh reality, however, when the Great War exploded in 1914. Fighting the Huns generated a wave of patriotic fervor that, though short-lived, had deep foundations in the culture. The anti-German images and sentiments of propaganda were familiar: the heroism of the Don Cossack Kuzma Kriuchkov and the plaint of "The Headlands of Manchuria" relied on older expressions for their emotional power. The clown Sergei Sokolsky castigated war profiteers (and thus, implicitly, Jews) from the circus arena.

Cinema blossomed during the war, when foreign supplies were cut off and an audience desperate for entertainment created favorable business conditions. Directors shot war adventures (featuring brave Russian soldiers and barbarous Germans), romantic melodramas, costume dramas, adaptations of literary classics, and others. They attracted huge audiences and made stars of many directors and actors. Ivan Mozzhukhin, a former operetta singer whose rich baritone was useless in silent films, became famous for his expressive eyes, and the dark-eyed Vera Kholodnaia (Vera the Cold) recalled gypsy songstresses with her cool sensuality. Most of these people fled the country after the October Revolution, many continuing successful careers with the burgeoning Western cinema.

The question of the relationship between popular opinion and commercial culture sharpened throughout 1917. After the February Revolution had toppled both autocracy and censorship, the sexual adventures of Grigory Rasputin and the tsarina were recounted in countless stage revues and periodicals. Although moderate socialists were presented sympathetically, Bolsheviks appeared primarily as objects of distaste, scheming outsiders, and demonic subversives. On this score, those who produced popular culture were more prescient than their intellectual counterparts, who felt relief at watching the market for culture dismantled after the Bolsheviks took power. A philistine corruption of tastes was perhaps not what they should have feared most.

Vaudeville Skits

(1905–1910)

VAUDEVILLE MADE ITS MARK IN RUSSIA AFTER 1880, FLOUR-
ISHING IN THE EARLY YEARS OF THE TWENTIETH CENTURY.
THOUGH MANY VAUDEVILLE WRITERS WERE ANONYMOUS, CHE-
KHOV AND MIASNITSKY GOT THEIR STARTS THERE. THEATERS
RAN THE GAMUT FROM MOSCOW'S CLASSY KORSH THEATER TO
ENTERTAINMENT GARDENS. VAUDEVILLE WAS CONSIDERED THE
LIGHTEST OF ENTERTAINMENTS, WHICH WORKED TO ITS ADVAN-
TAGE AFTER 1907 AND DURING WARTIME, WHEN ARTISTS COULD
FLIRT WITH THE OUTSKIRTS OF PROPRIETY. RISQUÉ SKITS DEAL-
ING WITH SEXUALITY AND ETHNIC MINORITIES TITILLATED THE
ORIGINAL AUDIENCES, BUT THEY ALSO INTRODUCED INTO THE
PUBLIC SPHERE NOTIONS THAT WERE TABOO IN HIGHER AND
MORE "LEGITIMATE" ENTERTAINMENTS. HERE WE SEE EXAMPLES
OF THE COUPLET SINGERS AND COMICS WHO DOMINATED VAUDE-
VILLE. THEY RANGE FROM THE RENOWNED, SUCH AS THE COU-
PLET SINGER SARMATOV, TO THE OBSCURE. THEIR WORDS ARE
TRANSCRIBED HERE FROM WAX-CYLINDER RECORDINGS MADE BY
A DEUTSCHE GRAMOPHONE EXPEDITION, AND OFFER A LIVING
GLIMPSE INTO THE PAST OF RUSSIAN ENTERTAINMENT.

S. F. Sarmatov (1907)

WORK AND PLAY*
Couplets, Sung by S. Sarmatov (1905–1910)

Каждый день гулять в Пассаже
Иль на дамской распродаже
Модным франтом нарядившись
И отчаянно завившись
И пленять девиц дородных
И старух к любви голодных
Заводить романы смело
Это дело, только дело.

Но пленить красотку-швейку
Целовать ей груди, шейку
Завести ее в берлогу
Уверять: «Ведь все могу.»
Обещать на ней жениться
Надругавшись удалиться
Причинив ей огорчения—
Это будет развлечение!

Встретить недруга лихого
Обругать его сурово
Ухватить его за горло
Так, чтоб дух прохвоста сперло
Нос ему разбить всей силой
Так, чтоб кровью все залило,
В синяках чтоб было тело—
Это дело, только дело!

Но гуляя с дамой сердца
Кредитора встретить перца
И когда он к вам пристанет
И срамить при даме станет
И начнет жужжать как муха,
Залепить ему раз в ухо
Чтоб оставил попеченье—
Это будет развлечение!

Каждый день с своей женою,
С бабой жирною такою,
По ее лишь мановенью,
Предаваться наслаждению.
Как машина энергична,
И вполне автоматична

Every day go to Passage,[1] or
To a sale of ladies' things,
You put on your foppish finest
And put your hair up in curls,
To enchant the well-fed girls,
And old women starved for love,
Striking up romances freely—
Now, that's a job, that's just a job.

But to charm a pretty seamstress
And to kiss her breasts and neck,
Luring her up to your home lair,
Swearing, "I can do it all."
Promising that you'll get married,
That's before you quarrel and scram,
Having only done her wrong—
Now, that's what I call fun!

Then you meet a foe so jaunty
That you chew him out but good,
Then you grab him by the throat, so
That it takes the scoundrel's breath.
Then you smash his nose so hard
That's he's drenched in his own blood,
And his body's bruised all over—
That's a job, that's just a job!

But to walk with your heart's mistress,
And to meet a creditor,
When he starts to badger you,
Shaming you before your girl,
And he buzzes like a housefly,
Then you smack him in the ear
To get him to leave you alone—
Now that's what I call fun!

Every day with your own wife,
A wench so fat and plump,
Giving yourself up to pleasure
When she makes the slightest gesture.
Like machines, you're energetic
And you're just as automatic,

---

*Transcribed from S. Sarmatov, *Delo i razvlechenie, kuplety,* Favorit Record no. 1-77116.
1. A fashionable department store on Petersburg's main thoroughfare, Nevsky Prospect.

The Eruption of Commercial Culture in the Interrevolutionary Years   279

Сильно, степенно, умело—
Это дело, только дело!

Но с полезной бледнолицей,
И с шантанною девицей
Провести годок в тумане
На воздушном океане.
В жгучих глазках утопиться
А потом начать поститься
И приняться за леченье—
Это будет развлечение!

Strong and steady, ever able—
That's a job, that's just a job.

But with a white-complexioned
Little *café-chantant* girl,
Spend a whole year in the fog
On an ocean of the air.
In her fiery eyes you will drown,
Then go off to make a fast,
Or you leave to take a rest cure—
Now, that's what I call fun!

THREE HUSBANDS*
Varya Zimina

Была я, ей-ей-ей, женою трех мужей.
Как женщина у них у всех
Имела я успех!

Супруг мой первый Гер
Был славный гренадер
И надо мною, господа,
Командовал всегда.
Не молчал, все ворчал,
Все кричал...
Есть все новое просил,
Вечно все меня учил
Ой-ей-ей-ей-ей!

Он меня ворочал вправо
То налево, то направо.
То глаза я строю многим,
То не так я ставлю ноги,
То как пыж я вечно пыжусь,
И не так как нужно вижу.

Второй муж, например,
Был ярый землемер.
Так этот, каждый материал
По-своему смерял.
То меряет в длину
То вширь, то в глубину
Всегда внимательно следил
Всегда одно твердил:

I've been, oy-oy-oy, the wife of several
    men.
As a woman with them all
I enjoyed success.

My first spouse was named Herr,
A handsome soldier boy.
And with me always, gentlemen,
He was in command.
Never silent, always growling,
Always shouting . . .
Always asking for new dishes,
Always teaching me new tricks,
Oy-oy-oy-oy-oy!

He would roll me to the right,
First to the left and then the right.
First I'm making eyes at men,
Or I can't put my feet right,
Or I'm puffed up like a wad,
Or else I'm not seeing right.

Husband Number Two
Was hot on surveying.
He would take materials
And measure them around.
First he'd measure them for length,
Then for width and depth.
He'd keep a close check on the job,
Repeating constantly:

---

*Varia Zimina (russkaia kupletistka and shansonetka), *Tri muzha*, Beka Record no. 56859.

«Миллиметр
Километр
Сантиметр»
Ой-ей-ей
И меня не без угроз
Всю измерил до волос!
Ой-ей-ей-ей-ей!

На меня чуть глазом кинет
Измеритель он свой вынет.
И потом приступит к делу,
И начнет водить по телу
Спереди, с боков и зад
Руки, голову, до пят.
Надоел он меня со своим рвением
С очень частым измерением.

А третий муж был врач
Безжалостный палач.
Он химию свою вполне
Всю изучил на мне.
В жару или в мороз
Все ставит диагноз,
Среди ночи и среди белого дня
Отщупывал меня.
То садись,
То ложись,
То нагнись...
А не то положит вниз
Взяв при этом в руки шприц
Ой-ей-ей
И колол меня он часто
Я лежала в виде пласта
Без движении, словно пухла
От уколов вся распухла
Ой-ей-ей-ей-ей.

И теперь скажу вам прямо
Что законченная я дама.
И теперь вот мне на ужин
Муж четвертый очень нужен!

"Millimeter,
Kilometer,
Centimeter."
Oy-oy-oy.
He measured me from head to foot,
And not without some threats!
Oy-oy-oy-oy-oy!

He couldn't cast a glance at me
Without whipping out his ruler.
He'd get right to the task at hand,
Across my body laying it,
From the front, the sides and back,
The hands and head, down to my feet,
He bored me stiff with all his efforts,
With his frequent measurings.

A doctor was the third,
A pitiless butcher.
He tried out all his chemistry
Completely on me.
In a heat wave or a frost
He could always diagnose,
In dark of night or bright of day,
He would probe me in and out,
First sit down,
Then lay down,
Then bend over . . .
Or then he'd lay me out flat,
Grabbing his syringe at that,
Oy-oy-oy.
He would prick me frequently
As I lay there like a sheet.
Motionless and all puffed up,
Swelling up from all his shots,
Oy-oy-oy-oy-oy.

I can say straightforwardly
That I am a finished lady.
And now for my evening snack,
I really need a fourth husband!

BUM-TA-RA-TA-TA*
Alek. Nazar. Kondratenko and S. E. Komisarov; recorded circa 1910

Попрошу тебя Сережа
Куплетики сыграй,
А чтоб вышло веселее
Громче подпевай.
Нам для публики стараться
Надо петь в стихах.
А припев какой возьмем мы?
—Какой хочешь?
А припев какой возьмем мы?
— Бум-та-ра-та-та!
А припев какой возьмем мы?
— Бум-та-ра-та-та!

Do me a favor Sergei,
Strike those couplets up,
And to make it even more fun,
Sing them with me loud.
Give our best stuff to the public,
And let's sing in verse.
But what should the refrain be?
—What do you want?
But what should the refrain be?
Bum-ta-ra-ta-ta!
But what should the refrain be?
Bum-ta-ra-ta-ta!

Раз в каком-то ресторане
Сашка закутил,
Налимонившись изрядно
Но не заплатил.
Чтобы было Вам понятно
Верьте господа,
Да уж! Там лакеи его знатно,
Бум-та-ра-та-та!

One day in a restaurant
Sasha went on a binge,
He drank a lot of liquor
But didn't pay the bill.
Let me say it so you'll get it,
Believe me, gentlemen,
Enough! The lackeys worked him over
Bum-ta-ra-ta-ta!

Вот чудак один женился,
Взял красавицу жену.
Но вдруг гневом растворился
Да сказала та ему:
«Ты напрасно, думал, милый,
Будто-б я честна.»
Да она говорит откровенно:
«Видишь-ли, я давно уж,
Муж желанный,
Бум-та-ра-та-та!»

An oddball once got married,
Took himself a pretty wife,
But then fury overtook him,
When she said to him:
"Sweetheart, you were wrong to think
That I've been virtuous."
And then she told him candidly:
"See here, husband dear,
For a long time now I have been
Bum-ta-ra-ta-ta-ed!"

Вот певицу угощает
Один господин
И все ей подливает
Крема фрикасин,
Ей знакомая гадает,
Ведь-то не спроста,
Да видно он меня желает,
Бум-та-ра-та-та!

Here's a songstress being hosted
By a gentleman.
He leans over and keeps pouring
Her *crème fricassée*.
Then a girlfriend told her fortune,
It was off the cuff,
So it seems that he wants me to
Bum-ta-ra-ta-ta!

---

*Transcribed from Alek. Nazar. Kondratenko and S. E. Komisarov, *Bum-ta-ra-ta-ta*, kom. duet, Beka Grand Record no. 56433.

Шансонетку в лоб ласкает
Один музыкант.
И уж очень восхваляет
Он ее талант.
Ты поет и ты ламшана,
Вот вам и звезда.
А сам мерзавец думает
Как бы ее даром
Бум-та-ра-та-та!

Then a music man was petting
A songstress on the head.
And he had the highest praises
For her great talent.
He sings sweet nothings to her,
Here's a star for you.
While the lecher's only thinking
How to get for no cost
Bum-ta-ra-ta-ta-ed!

THE MODEST DESIRE OF FOUR NATIONS*
A. V. Stepanov (1905–1910)

Спрашивают у немца:

— Что бы Вы желали иметь в жизни?

— Что я желаль? Я желаль и сколько есть чернил на белой свет—булл один большой чернило. И сколько есть перо у белой свет—булл один большой перо. И сколько есть бумага на белой свет—булл один большой бумага. И сколько можно-же, это перо в эту чернилу на эта бумага написать деньги—булл мой деньги. Больше я ничего не желаю.

Спрашивают грека:

— Ну-с, а Вы что желаете?

— И что греческой человеко желать? Греческой человеко желает и сколько есть пшеничико на белом свете, эта пшеничико будет наша. Мы из этой пшеничико сделаете мука и положите туда песочеку, песочеку, песочеку, и посылайте эта мука во время компахия на война—мы корошие деньги зарабо-таете. Больше мы ничего не желаете.

Спрашивают армянина:

— Ну-с, а Вы что желаете?

— Что мы желаем? Мы желаем да,

A German is asked:
—What do you want in life?
—Vat do I vant? I vant all ze ink in ze vorld; one big ink. And as many pens as zere are in ze world; one big pen. And as much paper as zere is in ze vorld; one big paper. And take ze ink and pens and paper, and draw as much money as you can on it. And so zat all ze money vas mine. And I vant nothing more.

A Greek is asked:
—What do you want in life?
—What could a Greek want? A Greek wants only as much wheat as there is in the world, and that it could be ours. And to make flour from the wheat, and to sprinkle some sand in the flour, and then during the war campaign to sell the wheat and make good money from it. And we want nothing more.

An Armenian is asked:
—What do you want in life?
—What do we want? We want all the

---

*Transcribed from A. V. Stepanov, performer at the Petersburg Theater, *Skromnoe zhelanie 4-x natsii. Dilizhans*, Beka Record no. 56536. The acts were performed in a variety of thick ethnic accents, and with grammatical idiosyncrasies, similar to the sort ascribed to the German here.

сколько есть бирюза-фирюза на белый свет, мы был да хозяин этой бирюза, сколько есть халва, рахат-лакум, бишмала, лакум-шиптала, курага, сколько нет на белый свет—мы был да хозяин этой. Больше мы ничего не желаем.

В конце-концов спрашивают еврея:
— Ну-с, а Вы что желаете?
— Что мне желать? Один себе хочет чтоб у него все деньги были? Нехай себе будут. Другой хочет чтобы все коммерческие обстоятельства на война из мукой сделать?—а-а-а- нехай себе делает. Третий хочет и писташки и мисташки и балаза—нехай себе на здоровье имеет. Я себе одного прошу и желаю. Чтоб они в один день все трое с холером подохли и чтоб я после них единственный наследник остался.

А больше я себе ничего не желаю.

turquoise-schmurquoise in the world, and that we owned it, and all the *khalva,* all the *rakhat-lakum* [Turkish delight], all the *bishmala,* all the *lakum-shiptala,* all the apricots there are in the world—and that it was all ours. And we want nothing more.

Finally a Jew is asked:
—What do you want in life?
—What do I want? One guy wants all the money? Let him have it. Another wants to do big business selling flour to the army? Let him do it. The third wants pistachios and mustachios and *balaza?* Let him have it all for his good health. I only want one thing for myself. I hope that one fine day all three get the cholera and croak, and leave me as the sole heir.

And I don't need anything else for myself.

STAGECOACH
A. V. Stepanov[2]

Из Житомира в Киев шел дилижанс, наполненный пассажирами. Налетает шайка грабителей. Атаман командует: «Стой! Ни с места! Руки вверх!»

Все пассажиры покорно вышли из дилижанса и подняли вверх руки. Один из тбпассажиров обращается к атаману: «Господин начальник! Через две минуты вы все равно у нас все заберете. Позвольте мне на минуточки с одной рукой слазить в карман. Мне надо что-нибудь отдать своему соседу!»

A stagecoach full of passengers was traveling from Zhitomir to Kiev when a band of robbers attacked. The *ataman* commanded, "Halt! Nobody move! Hands up!"

All the passengers obediently climbed out of the stagecoach and put their hands up in the air. One of them turned to the *ataman:* "Mr. Chief! You're gonna take everything from us in a couple minutes. Let me go into my pocket with one hand for a moment. I have to give something to the guy standing next to me."

---

2. The victims in this sketch are recognizably Jewish, by name, by accent, and by the location of Zhitomir inside the Pale of Settlement.

«Ну, скорей!» Направляет на него дуло револьвера.

Пассажир лезет в карман, достает оттуда сто рублей и, обращаясь к своему соседу, говорит: «Соломон! Я таки-тебе был должен сто рублей. Так на, получи. И умей в виду, что я тебе теперь больше ничего не должен.»

"Hurry it up!" He pointed the barrel of his revolver at him.

The passenger went into his pocket, took out one hundred rubles, and turning to his neighbor, said: "Solomon! Didn't I owe you a hundred rubles? Here, take it. And keep in mind that we're even now."

Why Was I Born into This World?
Tobolsk Prison Song (1908)

To a tradition that encompassed Dostoevsky, Krestovsky, Chekhov, and Doroshevich, among others, the prisons of Siberia were a troubling and intriguing second face of Russia. Prisoners were deemed "misfortunates," less to be hated than pitied. For Dostoevsky, they were the best and worst of the nation: strong but predatory, chained and yet free. Thriving on the geographic and social margin, the songs and argot of convict culture offered fresh and frightening alternatives.

In 1908, V. N. Hartveeld journeyed to the camps to collect convict songs, which, since instruments were banned in prison, were performed *a cappella*. He brought the songs, including this one, back to the capital, where a chorus performed them to packed auditoriums that included the cultural elect. Their unfettered emotionalism and open discussion of matters left unsaid in the years of backlash, made them a permanent feature of popular culture.

Pesni katorgi, ed. V. N. Gartevel'd (Moscow: Pol'za, 1913), p. 16.

Зачем я, мальчик, уродился,	Why was I born into this world,
Зачем тебя я полюбил?	Why did I fall in love with you?
Ведь мне назначено судьбою	You know that destiny has sent me
Итти в Сибирские края!	Far off into Siberia!
В Сибирь жестокую далеко	Sentenced to a cruel exile,
Судом я в ссылку осужден,	The court has sent me far away,
Где монумент за покоренье	Where they erected a monument
В честь Ермака сооружен.	To the conqueror Ermak.
Придет цирюльник с вострой бритвой,	A barber will take up his sharp razor
Обреет правый мой висок,	And shave my right temple clean,[1]
И буду вид иметь ужасный	My appearance will be horrible
От головы до самых ног.	From my head down to my toes.
Пройдет весна—настанет лето,	The spring will pass; it will be summer,
В садах цветочки расцветут,	And outside all the flowers will bloom,
А мне несчастному за это	But I, misfortunate, for all of that
Железом ноги закуют.	Will have my legs chained up in iron.
Но там, в Сибири, в час полночный,	But then, some midnight in Siberia,
Свяжусь я вновь с чужим добром,	Again I'll get my hands on loot,
И одинокий и несчастный	Alone again and still misfortunate,
Пойду урманами тайком.	I'll sneak across the broad *urman*.*
Дойду до русской я границы,	I'll walk to the Russian border,
Урядник спросит: «Чей такой?»	The guard will ask me, "Who goes there?"
Я назову себя бродягой,	I'll say that I am but a wanderer,
Не помня родины своей.	Who has forgotten where he's from!

---

1. To make them recognizable and prevent their escape, exiled prisoners had their heads shaved.
*Urman: the taiga.

The Poor Fellow Died
A Folk Song
K(onstantin) R(omanov) (circa 1910)

THE CRYPTIC INITIALS K. R. STOOD FOR KONSTANTIN KONSTAN-
TINOVICH ROMANOV (1858–1915), GRAND DUKE, PRESIDENT OF
THE IMPERIAL ACADEMY OF SCIENCES, AND A POET WITH HIS

Marus'ia otravilas'. Noveishii sbornik russkikh pesen (Moscow: I. D. Sytin, 1915), pp. 3–4.

FINGER ON THE PULSE OF POPULAR RUSSIA. TCHAIKOVSKY SET KONSTANTIN KONSTANTINOVICH'S LYRICS TO MUSIC, AND FOLK-LORISTS FOUND THEM BEING SUNG IN THE COUNTRYSIDE. HIS SONGS, POEMS, AND PLAYS WERE DISTINGUISHED BY A SENTIMEN-TAL POPULISM THAT PASSED FOR LIBERALISM, AND HE WAS ONE OF THE FEW RUSSIAN POETS WHO ATTRACTED AN AUDIENCE ACROSS CLASS LINES — THOUGH NOT ACROSS ETHNIC LINES. AF-FECTION FOR THE SIMPLE RUSSIAN PEOPLE, WHO SUFFERED, FOUGHT, AND ENDURED WITHOUT LOSING THEIR TRADITIONAL LOYALTIES, WAS A HALLMARK OF K. R., AND DEMAND FOR HIS WORKS NEVER FLAGGED IN THE YEARS OF WAR AND UPHEAVAL. THIS SONG OF A PEASANT PATRIOT STRUCK A SYMPATHETIC CHORD WITH MANY LISTENERS, PARTICULARLY THE LOWER CLASSES. IT WAS ORIGINALLY WRITTEN IN 1885, AND LATER UP-DATED, REACHING THE PINNACLE OF ITS FAME AS PERFORMED BY THE GREAT NADEZHDA PLEVITSKAIA. DURING THE FIRST WORLD WAR, THE SKOBELEV COMMISSION, WHICH ORGANIZED PATRI-OTIC PROPAGANDA, PRODUCED A MOVIE BASED ON THE SONG IN AN UNSUCCESSFUL ATTEMPT TO SHORE UP THE WAR EFFORT.

Умер, бедняга! В больнице военной
  Долго, родимый, лежал;

Эту солдатскую жизнь постепенно
  Тяжкий недуг доконал...

Рано его от семьи оторвали:
  Горько плакала мать,—
Всю глубину материнской печали
  Трудно пером описать!

С невыразимой тоскою во взоре
  Мужа жена обняла:

Полную чашу великого горя
  Рано она испила.

The poor fellow died! He lay, the dear man,
  In the infirmary long;
The life of this soldier was gradually ended
  By his fatal disease . . .

He was wrenched from his family early,
  His mother shed bitter tears.
My pen is not up to describing the full depths
  Of her motherly grief!

With an ineffable sadness filling her eyes,
  The wife hugged her husband goodbye.

Early in her life she'd had to imbibe this
  Abundant cup of great woe.

И протянул к нему с плачем ручонки
　　Мальчик, малютка грудной...

Из виду скрылись родные избенки
　　Край он покинул родной.

В гвардию был он назначен, в пехоту,
　　В полк наш, по долгом пути;

Сдали его в государеву роту
　　Царскую службу нести.

С виду пригожий он был новобранец,
　　Стройный и рослый такой,
Кровь с молоком, во всю щеку румянец,
　　Бойкий, смышленный, живой;

С еле заметным пушком над губами,
　　С честным открытым лицом,
Волосом рус, с голубыми глазами,—
　　Ну, молодец–молодцом!

Был у ефрейтора он на поруке,
　　К участи новой привык,

Приноровился к военной науке,—
　　Сметливый был ученик.

Старым его уж его считали солдатом,
　　Стал он любимцем полка;
В этом измайловце щеголеватом
　　Кто бы узнал мужика!

Он безупречно во всяком наряде
　　Службу свою отбывал,

А по стрельбе скоро в первом разряде
　　Ротный его записал.

Мы бы в учебной команде зимою
　　Стали его обучать,

И подготовленный, он бы весною,
　　В роту вернулся опять;

And hands were extended to him by a
　　sobbing
　　Boy, still an infant in arms . . .
Then he lost sight of the huts of his
　　birthplace,
　　As he abandoned his home.
He was assigned to the infantry
　　guardsmen,
　　To our regiment, for the long haul;
Then he was placed in His Majesty's
　　garrison,
　　Assigned to serve the tsar.
A comely recruit he was in appearance,
　　Tall and well-built he was,
A healthy complexion, cheeks full and
　　ruddy,
　　Lively, and clever and spry;
With barely visible fuzz on his top lip,
　　And an honest, open face.
Light brown of hair, his eyes were the
　　bluest.
　　As handsome as they might come!
He was put under the care of the
　　corporal,
　　Which helped him get used to his
　　lot,
He showed a knack for being a
　　soldier,—
　　He was a fast learner.
He was already a seasoned soldier,
　　The regiment's favorite guy.
Who would have noticed yesterday's
　　peasant,
　　In this Izmailov Guard dandy!
Whatever his costume, he did his
　　duty
　　Without a fault to be found.
The company leader gave him the
　　ranking
　　Of first on the shooting range.
Once the winter set in, we would have
　　put him
　　In the training brigade.
Trained and prepared, he would have
　　returned
　　To our company in the spring.

Славным со временем был бы он
  взводным...
    Но не сбылися мечты!
Кончились лагери. Ветром холодным
    Желтые сдуло листы,

Серый спустился туман на столицу,
    аьются дожди без конца...
В осень ненастную сдали в больницу
    Нашего мы молодца.

Таял он, словно свеча, понемногу,
    В нашем суровом краю;
Кротко, безропотно Господу Богу
    Отдал он душу свою.

Цынгу, все болезни, и холод и голод
    Русский солдат испытал,

Все ж под конец, перед самою смертью,
    Он Порт-Артур вспоминал:

«Крепость-то, крепость была
    неприступная,
    Но все же пришлось нам отдать,
Долго в засаде сидели голодными,
    Нечем нам было стрелять»...
Умер вдали от родного селенья,
    Умер в разлуке с семьей,
Без материнского благословенья
    Этот солдат молодой.
Ласковой, нежной рукою закрыты
    Не были эти глаза,
И ни одна о той жизни прожитой
    Не пролилася слеза!
Полк о кончине его известили,—
    Хлопоты с мертвым пошли;

В старый одели мундир, положили
    В гроб и в часовню снесли.

К выносу тела, к военной больнице
    Взвод был от нас наряжен...

По небу тучи неслись вереницей
    В утро его похорон.

What a sergeant he would have made—
    But such dreams could not be.

Camp life had ended. A cold autumn
    wind blew
    Yellow leaves from the trees.
A gray fog descended over the capital,
    Rain pouring down endlessly . . .
We sent our young fellow off to the
    hospital
    During that foul-weathered fall.
Like a candle he melted little by little
    In our harsh northern clime;
He surrendered with meekness and
    resignation
    His soul to his Lord God.
Scurvy, diseases, the cold and the
    hunger
    This Russian solder had seen,
Still at the end, as he stood before his
    death,
    Port Arthur came to his mind:
"The fortress, that fortress seemed
    impregnable,
    But still, surrender we did,
Hungry, we sat in that ambush forever,
    But we had nothing to shoot . . ."
He died far from his home village,
    Away from his family he died,
Without the blessing of his dear mother,
    The young soldier died.
His dying eyes would never be shut
    By a loving, tender hand,
Nobody shed any tears for the passing
    Of the life that he'd lived.
When the regiment heard that he'd
    passed on,
    They took care of the corpse.
They dressed him up in an old coat and
    laid him
    In the chapel for the wake.
To the hospital we assigned a
    detachment
    To carry the coffin . . .
A row of storm clouds filled the horizon
    On the morn of his funeral day.

Выла и плакала снежная вьюга, 　С жалобным воплем таким Плача об участи нашего друга, 　Словно рыдая над ним! Вынесли гроб, привязали на дроги, 　И по худой мостовой	Outside a blizzard lamented and wailed, 　With such a mournful moan, Crying about the lot of our good friend, 　As if it were sobbing for him! They took out the coffin, secured it in 　the hearse, 　And along a worn-out road
Старая кляча знакомой дорогой 　Их потащила рысцой. Сзади и мы побрели за ворота, 　Чтоб до угла хоть дойти:	An old nag, on a route long familiar, 　Dragged them along at a trot. We followed them out beyond the 　gateway, 　Reaching the bend in the road:
Взводу до первого лишь поворота 　Надо за гробом идти.	The soldiers had only to make the first 　corner, 　To take the dead to their rest.
Дрогам вослед мы глядели-глядели 　Долго с печалью немой...	We followed the hearse with lingering 　glances 　And a mute sadness for long . . .
Перекрестилися, шапки надели 　И воротились домой...	We crossed ourselves, put our hats on 　our heads, 　And then returned to our homes . . .
Люди чужие солдата зароют 　В мерзлой земле глубоко, Там, за заставой, где ветры лишь воют 　Где-то в глуши, далеко.	Deep in the frozen dirt, strangers will 　Dig the soldier a grave, There where the winds howl, outside 　the city, 　Far away in the woods.
Спи же, товарищ, ты наш одиноко 　Спи же, покойся себе.	Sleep on, dear comrade, sleep on, our 　lonely one, 　Sleep on, you've earned your rest.
В этой могиле сырой и глубокой, 　Вечная память тебе.	May your memory live for eternity 　In your grave, dank and deep.

Marusia Poisoned Herself
A New Song From Saratov
(1915)

"TEAR-JERKERS" (*NADRYVNYE PESNI*) WERE FAVORITE SONGS FOR
ALMOST A CENTURY AFTER THE EMANCIPATION. POPULAR SONG-

Marus'ia otravilas'. Noveishii sbornik russkikh pesen (Moscow: I. D. Sytin, 1915), pp. 3–4.

SMITHS THRIVED ON THE SALE OF SHEET MUSIC, AND ROYALTIES WERE AUGMENTED BY RECORDING TECHNOLOGY AT THE TURN OF THE CENTURY. THIS PARTICULAR SONG, OF UNKNOWN ORIGIN, WAS FOUND AMONG SARATOV WORKERS SOMETIME IN THE 1910S, AND WAS SOON SUNG THROUGHOUT RUSSIA IN MANY VERSIONS.

HIGHLY CONVENTIONALIZED AND SENTIMENTAL, ROMANCES WERE A SENSITIVE INDICATOR OF SOCIAL CHANGE. CRITICAL ISSUES TOUCHED UPON IN THIS SONG INCLUDE THE OPPORTUNITIES AND SEXUAL MORES CONFRONTING MIGRANT LABORERS, AND THE RASH OF SUICIDES AMONG ALL CLASSES AFTER THE FAILURE OF 1905.

Вечер вечереет,
Наборщицы идут.
«Маруся отравилась, —
В больницу повезут».
  В больницу привозили
  И клали на кровать
  Два доктора, сестрицы
  Старались жизнь спасать.
«Спасайте—не спасайте.
Мне жизнь не дорога.
Я милого любила —
Такого подлеца».
  Давали ей лекарства —
  Она их не пила;
  Давали ей пилюли —
  Она их не брала.

Подруги приходили
Марусю навестить,
А доктор отвечает:
«Без памяти лежит».
  Приходит мать родная
  Свою дочь навестить,
  А доктор отвечает,
  Что при смерти лежит.
Пришел ея любезный, —
Хотел он навестить, —
А доктор отвечает:
«В часовенке лежит».
  «Маруся, ты, Маруся!

The eveningtide is falling,
The typesetter girls go home.
"Marusia drank some poison—
The ambulance took her away."
  They got her to the hospital
  And laid her on the bed;
  Two doctors and some nurses
  Tried to save her life.
"You can save me or not save me,
My life means nothing to me.
I found myself a sweetheart—
But he turned out to be no good."
  Some medicine was brought in—
  But she wouldn't drink it down;
  And then they brought some
   tablets—
  But she wouldn't swallow a one.
Her girlfriends went to the hospital
To sit with Marusia a bit,
But the doctor told them,
"Marusia is unconscious."
  Her mother came to the hospital
  To see her daughter dear,
  But the doctor told her that
  She's lying close to death.
Her beloved came to the hospital,
He wanted to see her again—
But the doctor told him,
"In the chapel she lies."
  "Marusia, oh, Marusia!

<table>
<tr>
<td>

Открой свои глаза!»
А сторож отвечает:
«Давно уж умерла».
Кого-то полюбила.
Чего-то испила;
Любовь тем доказала:
От яду умерла.

</td>
<td>

Please open up your eyes!"
But the watchman told him,
"She died a long time ago."
She fell in love with someone,
And then she drank something down;
By taking that poison,
She proved her love to him.

</td>
</tr>
</table>

Russian Sob Sister
Olga Gridina (1910)

ALTHOUGH NO BIOGRAPHICAL INFORMATION IS AVAILABLE ON GRIDINA, HER PERSONA AFFORDS HER A PLACE IN HISTORY. GRIDINA'S COLUMN APPEARED IN RUSSIA'S FIRST TABLOID, *GAZETA KOPEIKA* (THE KOPECK GAZETTE), IN 1910, AND CONTINUED UNTIL THE FIRST WORLD WAR OVERSHADOWED HUMAN INTEREST STORIES. ALTHOUGH WOMEN HAD LONG WORKED AS REPORTERS, GRIDINA WAS THE FIRST TO HAVE HER OWN BYLINE. SHE WROTE PRIMARILY FOR *KOPEIKA*'S FEMALE READERS, ESCHEWING "FEMINISM" WHILE TALKING TO AND ABOUT WOMEN. SHE WAS THE RUSSIAN VARIANT OF THE "SOB SISTER," LICENSED TO USE EMOTIONAL REPORTING TO EVOKE TEARS. THESE FEMALE REPORTERS COULD EXPLOIT SENSATIONALISM, SINCE EXPRESSING EMOTIONS WAS DEEMED NATURAL TO THE FAIR SEX, AND THUS GAIN ACCESS TO A PARTICULAR SPHERE OF INFLUENCE. LIKE THE DOMESTICITY THAT GAVE WOMEN POWER IN THE HOME, THE SOB SISTER'S AUTHORITY WAS RESTRICTED TO SPECIFIC SPACES. SHE NONETHELESS ENJOYED UNPRECEDENTED OPPORTUNITY TO BRING WOMEN INTO THE LARGER PUBLIC WORLD REPRESENTED BY THE NEWSPAPER.

From *Gazeta kopeika*, 6 October 1910, no. 795, p. 2.

"THERE IS A LIFE, WHICH . . . "

This is Liza's story.[1]

It was one o'clock in the morning. I was returning home from the opera, completely absorbed by the marvelous melodies. At the Anichkov Bridge I heard some cries and a whistle coming from the Fontanka Canal. Several women threw themselves almost directly in front of my driver and then quickly ran forward. They were stylishly dressed, but their silk petticoats were dragging in the mud, and their large hats were knocked askew.

One of the runners suddenly fell right in front of my carriage. At that very same moment, a hefty guy with a badge who had been chasing her grabbed her by the shoulder and, losing his patience, began shaking her:

"You're down, get up!"

The woman raised her head, and I recognized Liza. I recognized her by her eyes, still so kind and alert, as before. But only pathetic traces of her former beauty remained.

Her cheeks, clumsily made up, were sunken, and she had only two teeth left of a smile that had been pearly white.

The man with the badge yanked her to her feet.

"Get up, you piece of garbage. I don't have time to play around with you."

I immediately jumped down from the carriage.

"What are you planning to do with this woman?"

"What am I gonna do? Take the scum to jail, that's what."

"Why are you swearing in public? Don't you know it's against the law? And what are you accusing this woman of?"

"Vagrancy."

"Nothing else?"

"What more do you want? She's a vagrant."

"Do me a favor, please. I know this woman. Let me take her."

"For a little something to buy myself tea."

Something round and shiny brought a satisfactory end to our conversation, which could have continued much longer. I sat Liza in the carriage, the driver picked up the reins, and we drove on.

"Where do you live, Liza? Can we take you home?"

Liza grabbed my hand, and before I could pull it away, she began kissing it.

"Thank you, ma'am, thank you! But why bother? I can't go home. The landlady will beat me. I have no place to go."

"How can she beat you?"

"Whose permission does she need? She wants to, so she beats me."

"You could complain."

"Who to? I'm a vagrant. The laws weren't written for us."

"What are you saying, Liza? Go to the justice of the peace tomorrow."

---

1. Gridina probably uses the name Liza in reference to Karamzin's sentimental classic *Poor Liza*. See Shakhovskoi's *The New Sterne* in this volume.

"Okay. Let's say I turn her in. And then where will I go? No landlady will take me in, and I'll roam the streets like a dog."

"And it's impossible to live without a landlady?"

"Oh, ma'am, ma'am! You don't understand our accursed life! I don't even know how it all worked out this way. Remember when I told you 'I might sell myself, but I don't consider myself trash. We all sell what we have. Honor—that's the net profit!' Do you remember?"

"Yes, I haven't fogotten that encounter."

"Well, it was all baloney. I don't even remember when I started to wallow in this pit. They're bastards—not those who simply use your body, but those who degrade it. Did you notice? My teeth have been knocked out. That's what life's become. They've beaten my soul out. With boots and grubby mitts, they knocked the soul right out of me. I'm worse off than a dog now. 'I sell only my body.' Ha ha ha. You can peddle what you've done with your hands or your brain. That's human. But God made humans, and you shouldn't sell what God made. No, ma'am, you don't understand me."

"Keep talking, Liza. I'm listening. Unburden yourself."

"Soon I'm going to unburden myself completely. Soon. Today you saved me from fists and humiliation for the moment, but now what? You saved me today, but the same thing will happen tomorrow. I have nowhere to go, except into the canal! Everything that I said then . . . And I wasn't paying attention to how my landlady was squeezing me. Suddenly I found myself her slave, spilling my blood—everything went to her, and I wasn't bringing in any money. A merciless battle. I was up to my ears in debt to her. We're all in bondage to that harpy, and my heart is on fire because they've driven out everything in me that is human—and what's human, God . . . God . . . "

Liza began to weep softly, her body quivering from restrained sobs.

"Do you want to throw all this away? Do you want to work again, be a servant?"

"It's too late."

"It's not too late, Liza. I, others, we can help you."

"It's too late, ma'am. I don't have the heart to go on. Now I can either drink myself into unconsciousness, or get beaten into unconsiousness, or work the whole problem out with ammonium chloride. I'm not fit for anything else."

"Don't despair, Liza. If you really wanted to . . . "

"No, ma'am, no! I would need great strength to be able to pull myself up again, but I . . . There's only one road open to me. Either with the acid, or under a tram. Thank you for the kind words. They're enough. Enough. Driver, stop!"

Liza jumped out of the carriage.

"My poor thing, where are you going?"

"Nowhere, ma'am, nowhere! Where can I go from the streets? I gave myself to them, and they swallowed me. There's only one possible ending."

"Promise me that you won't hurt yourself."

I said this reflexively, and then the falseness of these words struck me—"won't hurt yourself"? And what else was left for this exhausted, disfigured, accursed soul?

Liza began to laugh softly and continued forward. She stopped for a moment, turned, and cried back to me:

"Not today, but maybe tomorrow . . . "

She disappeared into the darkness.

And every day now I read the chronicle of suicides with terrible pain, afraid that I will see a familiar name. The feeling is even worse when I convince myself that she hasn't done it yet.

Because there is a life that is worse than death.

How the Lasses Burned a Lad in the Stove
A Christmas Tale
Al. Aleksandrovsky (1911)

ALEKSANDROVSKY WAS ONE OF THE MOST SUCCESSFUL *LUBOK* WRITERS OF THE POST-1905 ERA. LURID STORIES OF SEXUAL DEVIANCE, SUCH AS *THE WEDDING NIGHT OF A FATHER AND DAUGHTER* (1910), OR OF VIOLENCE IN THE COUNTRYSIDE MADE HIM A FAVORITE. THE SENSATIONALISM OF HIS TALES BROUGHT HOME TO READERS THE RADICAL CULTURAL CHANGES RUSSIA WAS UNDERGOING IN THE YEARS OF POLITICAL REACTION, AND OFTEN EXPRESSED FEARS OF THE "DARK MASSES" THAT WERE FELT KEENLY BY ALL LEVELS OF SOCIETY AFTER THE 1905 REVOLUTION.

In the dark corners of our vast Russia, the peasant folk still hold to the customs of times long past. Prejudice and superstition reign undisturbed among the dark masses. Such was the tiny village, lost in the forest, where an extraordinary event once took place.

I would now like to tell you this story. It happened in winter, on the eve of the Feast of St. Basil—that is, on New Year's Eve, during Christmastide.

Al. Aleksandrovskii, *Kak devki sozhgli parnia v pechke: sviatochnyi rasskaz* (Moscow: A. S. Balashov, 1911), pp. iii–xvi.

Starting with the second day of Christmas, girls would gather every evening at each other's houses. They'd sit and spin, and sing some songs; then the boys would find them, and the young people would make merry long past midnight. They would tell jokes and stories. From time to time, someone made up such a whopper that you'd stick your fingers in your ears. No matter, the simple-hearted girls would just laugh.

But not all the girls were visited by the boys. No surprise: you find flies where there's honey. Some girls were so homely that nobody was interested in them. They had their own gatherings, and their talk wasn't so lively and merry. They would sit and crack sunflower seeds. All the songs they sang were sad, and merry laughter was never heard. They envied the pretty girls who were enjoying themselves. Just about every one of them was betrothed, and many would get married after Twelfth-night.

The unattractive girls would gather every evening in the hut of a poor old peasant woman, who had a twenty-year-old daughter named Akulina. Not one decent boy dropped in on them during the whole Christmas season. They sat fuming, wishing all sorts of misfortunes on the lucky girls.

A peculiar boy named Yashka, the laughingstock of the whole village, was the only one who visited them. Every evening as the fire was lit, Yashka's ice-caked bast shoes would scrape along the porch. He'd open the low door slowly, letting the cold air in from outside.

"Hey, shut the door, you jerk. It isn't summer anymore. What the hell brought you here? Who ever saw such an eyesore. Why did you come here, scarecrow?"

"Not for rye, not for wheat, but for a pretty girl to meet," drawled Yashka in his sleepy voice.

"Go to hell, idiot."

But Yashka stepped forward and sat on a bench, ignoring the greeting. He was a squat fellow of twenty, clumsy as a bear; his sheepskin coat was torn and patched all over. His white-blond head looked like a worn-out rag, and his unwashed face was grimy. Yashka would sit silently and make goggle eyes at snub-nosed, pockmarked Akulina, daughter of the house. But Akulka[1] just made fun of him and called him unholy names.

The other girls also teased poor Yashka. "Hey, Yashka, stand up," one of them said.

Yashka stood up, and the girl stuck a needle in the wood. "Okay, you can sit down again, scarecrow."

"Ouch, ouch!" howled Yashka, clutching his backside, and spinning like a top in his pain.

The girls snickered, and soon Yashka sat back down carefully in his old place. And then another girl said, "Hey, girls, let's play blindman's buff."

---

1. Akulka is a diminutive form of Akulina. See the Note on Transliteration for an explanation of diminutives.

They all got into a circle and counted off to see who was It. They cheated Yashka on the count and blindfolded him with a dirty black rag, which they had smeared with soot from the stovepipe when the fool wasn't looking.

Yashka caught one of the girls, who on purpose didn't get away, and took off the blindfold. Loud laughter rang out: Yashka's face was all smeared with soot. But the boy didn't understand why everyone was laughing, because he couldn't look into a mirror. There was a stupid grin on his face as he looked at the others.

"Hey, girls, let's do something else," said one of the girls.

"I know a real fun trick," said snub-nosed Akulka, "Hoo boy, take a looky here."

She had already thought up a prank, and when they covered Yashka's eyes, she put a big pitcher of cold water on top of the stove shelf.

When they finished playing blindman's buff, Akulka climbed up on the stove.

Everyone watched to see what would happen next, including the idiot.

"Yashka, give me the rag you tied up your mug with, and get those scissors from the wall. Get cracking, you devil!"

Yashka gave her the rag and scissors.

Suddenly Akulka dropped the scissors on the floor, as if by accident.

"Pick it up, Yashka!"

Yashka bent over to get the scissors.

Right at that moment, Akulina dumped the cold water on the simpleton.

"Yikes, that's hot . . . cold . . . " Yashka cursed like one possessed, while dirty streams of water ran from his disheveled hair onto his coat, washing the soot from his face.

And so it would go every night. Each time, they would come up with some new scheme to drive Yashka away.

But Yashka would endure these pranks with stoic equanimity, and even joined the girls in laughing at himself. His heart ached for the snub-nosed, pockmarked Akulka.

He would never go home before midnight.

One night before New Year's Eve, the girls met at Akulka's; her old mother went out just before Yashka arrived. Akulka shouted: "Ladies, if you only knew how sick I am of that disgusting Yashka. God help him if he comes tonight . . . "

"Who wouldn't be sick of that scarecrow!" said the other girls. "We've had it up to here with him ourselves."

"How can we get rid of that plague?"

"We'll think of a way," said Akulka. "Just you come a bit early on St. Basil's Eve; Mom won't be in—she's leaving to spend the night with her brother in the village of Khatovka, and I'll be alone. Then we can think up something good for Yashka."

Yashka kept coming to chew the fat every night without suspecting anything.

Early in the morning on the day before New Year's, the old widow left to visit Khatovka for about three days. The girls met at Akulka's after dinner, close to noontime.

"I thought up a trick for Yashka," said Akulka. "We'll get rid of him forever." And she told the girls about her hellish plan. They all agreed to it.

The Eruption of Commercial Culture in the Interrevolutionary Years   297

She brought in an armful of stakes and an axe. Work went fast under the strong hands of the healthy girl. She sharpened about ten stakes, then opened the cellar trap near the front door. Work was completed in half an hour: the girls buried the stakes with the points up and shut the trapdoor.

Meanwhile twilight was falling, and soon it was completely dark. The fire was lit, and the door was put on the latch. The girls sat quietly, and they didn't even sing their sad songs. Everyone felt a little uneasy.

The latch on the porch door rattled, and steps crunched outside. They instantly put out the fire.

"Who's there?" Akulka asked through the locked door to make certain that it was really Yashka.

"It's me-e," he drawled in answer.

"Why'd you come here, idiot?'

"Not for rye, not for wheat, but for a pretty girl to meet."

"But we don't even have a fire going: we're telling fortunes. Well, alright, come on in!" Akulka mumbled in a quivering voice as she threw back the latch. At the same moment, she lifted the trap by its ring and jumped aside into the front corner. The door opened, and Yashka, crossing over the threshold, stepped forward out of the shadows.

"Eeek! Yi-i-ikes . . . I'm dy-dy-ing," the poor man moaned in a barely audible voice, and soon fell quiet.

Akulka quickly slammed the trap shut and lit the fire. Everyone was as pale as a ghost. Horror and the consciousness of an irreparable sin bound their tongues.

"What're we going to do with him now?" one girl said timidly.

"Let's burn him up in the stove, and no one will be the wiser," answered Akulka. "We'll just need more wood. It's still early, though; we'll wait so that nobody can guess. We'll stoke the fire near midnight, and then pile the wood high!"

Everyone raced outside and grabbed an armful of wood. They laid it in the stove and soaked it with kerosene. After midnight, they opened the trapdoor and together dragged the dead body from the cellar. His sheepskin was drenched in blood; a bloody hole yawned where his right eye had once been.

The girls staggered back in horror when they saw the disfigured corpse of the dead man; but conquering their fear, they lifted it and with great effort stuffed it in the stove. Immediately, they lit the firewood. . . .

Aunt Matryona always stoked the stove early, around three in the morning. That morning, rising at the usual hour, she went out for wood. Stepping outside, she sniffed the air.

Something strange was up, she thought—something's on fire somewhere; she smelled burning. She threw back the gate latch and stepped out on the roadway. It was frosty. The moon shone as bright as day.

She saw thick, black smoke billowing from the chimney of the neighbor widow. The smoke stank so bad you couldn't breathe.

"Lord save them from burning down," thought Matryona, and she knocked on the neighbor's door.

Akulka unlocked the door and nimbly positioned herself in front of the stove. The girls were sitting in the front corner.

"Ladies, you need a good spanking for staying up so late."

"We were telling fortunes, Aunt Matryona."

"Who was visiting you, girls? Your chimney smoke stinks like you haven't cleaned it in a while. Watch out it doesn't catch catch fire."

"But looky here, we just cleaned it," Akulka said, confused, avoiding Matryona's glance.

But Matryona continued to poke around in the stove, and managed to find out what was burning in there.

"Ivan, Ivan!" Running into the hut, she shook her husband as strongly as she could. "Wake up! They're burning a body at the widow's."

"Huh? Whad'ya . . . " mumbled Ivan, rubbing his eyes.

"Wake up, I say; they're burning someone at the widow's."

The man's head cleared of his holiday hangover instantly.

"Go get the neighbors, quick; wake everyone up!" he said in a rush, dragging his sheepskin and boots from atop the stove.

In the morning, the village elder and marshal rode off posthaste to the county seat, and the authorities arrived in the village after noon.

The next day, the seven girls were taken to the city under armed guard.

The Wrath of God
A Novel of the Occult
V. I. Kryzhanovskaia (1909)

KRYZHANOVSKAIA TAPPED INTO A FASHION FOR THE SUPER-
NATURAL WITH A SERIES OF OCCULT NOVELS SET IN MYSTIC LO-
CALES IN ANCIENT EGYPT AND MEDIEVAL EUROPE. HER PEN
NAME, "I. W. ROCHESTER," DISGUISED HER GENDER, BUT ONCE
SHE BEGAN TO SELL, SHE USED BOTH NAMES ON HER WORKS.
RUSSIA'S CRITICS REFUSED TO TREAT HER SERIOUSLY, BUT AFTER
SHE WAS NAMED TO THE FRENCH ACADEMY OF ARTS, THE RUS-
SIAN ACADEMY OF SCIENCES GAVE HER HONORABLE MENTION. A
1917 FILM VERSION OF ONE OF HER NOVELS, *THE COBRA CHOIR*,

V. I. Kryzhanovskaia (Rochester), *Gnev bozhii. Okkul'tnyi roman* (St.-Petersburg: Sfinks, 1909), pp. 69–83.

SUBTITLED *THE SNAKEWOMAN,* ANTICIPATED MARIA MONTEZ'S
1944 CULT CLASSIC *COBRA WOMAN.*

ASSOCIATED WITH THE FAMED THEOSOPHIST MME BLAVATS-
KAIA, KRYZHANOVSKAIA CAPITALIZED ON RUSSIA'S ORIENTAL-
ISM: THE CENTER OF HER OCCULT LIES IN THE HIMALAYAS, THE
SERVANTS ARE "HINDUS," AND MOST CHARACTERS SPORT NAMES
THAT SOUND INDIAN. THEY TRAVEL THROUGH SEVERAL NOVELS,
BACK AND FORTH ACROSS CONTINENTS AND CENTURIES, SEEKING
A PERFECT UNION OF GOD AND SCIENCE. THOUGH SUCCESSES IN
ONE AREA ARE MATCHED BY DISAPPOINTMENTS IN ANOTHER,
THEIR CREATOR BELIEVED THAT THE TWO WOULD MERGE IN
THE FUTURE.

THE FOLLOWING EXCERPT PICKS UP IN THE YEAR 2284, WITH
CHARACTERS INTRODUCED IN THE FIRST BOOKS: SUPRAMATI,
WHO BEGAN LIFE AS BRITISH DR. RALPH MORGAN BUT WAS EN-
TICED BY THE ORIGINAL PRINCE SUPRAMATI, BORN IN EGYPT
AROUND 300 B.C., TO EXCHANGE DROPS OF BLOOD SO THAT THE
DOCTOR WOULD NOW LIVE FOR ETERNITY, PERMITTING SU-
PRAMATI TO DIE; DAKHIR, ONE OF HIS FIRST COMPANIONS IN THE
OCCULT; AND EBRAMAR, THEIR TEACHER AND GUIDE ACROSS THE
CENTURIES. THE NATIONALISM IMPLICIT IN KRYZHANOVSKAIA'S
VISION OF THE FUTURE IS AS OLD-FASHIONED AS THE DESCRIP-
TIONS OF TECHNOLOGY ARE FUTURISTIC.

In order to rest, Ebramar took his students to the same Himalayan palace where
Supramati had first seen his teacher and patron. Ebramar told them that they must
gradually become accustomed to temporal life, to the clothes they must wear in
Europe, to the general language—something like Esperanto—now spoken interna-
tionally; he told them that they had to prepare themselves so that they would not
stand out in the crowd, not call attention to themselves. The young people were
obviously disappointed by this program. They were no longer accustomed to the
bustle and noise. They felt so comfortable in solitude, in nature's bosom, absorbed
in the intellectual activity that had allowed them to forget about time. The realization that they had to leave this peaceful and elegant refuge lay heavy on them.

"Tell us, teacher, why it is mandatory that we return to vulgar humanity? We
would be so happy to stay here with you. The thought of joining the ignorant, de-

praved, and base crowd disgusts me," said Supramati as they sat on the terrace discussing the upcoming departure.

"To tell the truth, we left Europe so long ago that everything will have changed—the morals, the customs. We will have no idea how to behave," added Dakhir.

"You, Dakhir, must be more logical, seeing that you have already undergone similar experiences, falling from the fifteenth into the nineteenth century. You have always been able to orient yourself. Instead of reassuring Supramati, the youngest among us, you are feeding his anxieties," Ebramar answered disapprovingly. "Understand, my children, that the soul of a magician is elastic, that it must be able to bend and adapt itself to any situation. Moreover, it cannot stand distant from humanity. The role that has been assigned to us for the future requires that we always maintain some contacts and relations with the generations as they replace one another on earth. That is the fundamental law of our brotherhood, always maintained. Our members materialize in society as simple mortals, mix with the crowd, and emulate their physical and intellectual development. As long as you do this, I am confident that you will be able to fulfill your inescapable duty as conscientiously as you would if you were told to bring life to a desert island." Ebramar smiled.

"You're right, my teacher, and I understand the need to appear from time to time in society. I simply object to entering the fray on a daily basis," answered Supramati.

Dakhir blushed noticeably at Ebramar's remarks and sat quietly, hanging his head.

Seeing that Supramati was also red in the face and had lowered his head, Ebramar said cheerfully, "Now, my friends and pupils, why are you so depressed about your excursion to the world of transitory, temporal humanity? Let's look at the bright side. Most important is the moral aspect. The abhorrence you're experiencing derives from consciousness of your own scientific superiority, which places you far above the crowd. You don't want to have to mix with the crude and ignorant masses. But, my children, science is a relative matter.

"I know more than you, and before a layman, I am a demigod. Yet next to an archangel I am *nothing*, a blind and wretched atom. Comparison to the highest steps on the ladder of knowledge dampens our pride and pretentiousness quite effectively. But a human is created so that it is occasionally good for that person to stand on the bottom rung. It raises self-respect. People can then appreciate how insignificant they are, yet also take modest pleasure in their own essential worth. That satisfaction awaits you—even with our knowledge and the elixir of life.

"You will also appear to be demigods. You will be capable of performing 'miracles' and many good deeds in the process. No one will prevent your names from being recorded in the people's chronicles as doers of great deeds. These names, like you yourselves, will be immortal, so long as the planet does not harbor the insidious intention of destroying itself, and disappear into the great unknown with the names of all the heroes, the prides of all the different nationalities."

It was decided that they would go to a palace near Benares, where they would be met by a young man who had devoted his life to the lowest orders, who would guide them in their new assignment. He would function as their secretary, fulfilling all their commands, which a layman would not be able to understand. However, Ebramar deliberately did not want to say anything about the current date, the changes that had occurred on earth since they had left to pursue asceticism, or the place to which they would return.

"I won't say goodbye, because we will always be able to converse when necessary. Safe journey, my friends! Saddled horses and a retinue await you beyond the garden gate. You will travel in the old way as far as Benares. Here we have experienced few changes, but there you will fall under the power of the newest civilization."

Night had already fallen when they reached the palace, which looked exactly like the one they had just left. After a sumptuous dinner, such as they had not eaten in a long time, the secretary suggested that they move to the bedroom because it was time to change clothes.

Beneath his shirt, Supramati wore his magic star hanging on a blue ribbon; it shone like a tiny electric sun, and he had to hide it under a wide belt. He tied a black silk tie under his collar, stuck in it a sapphire tie pin given to him by Nivara,[1] and then looked at himself in the mirror.

The suit flattered him; it had been cut with taste and elegant simplicity. But he did not like his haircut. Nivara had cut it short in the back, leaving only the thick curls on the crown and sides of his head that fell on his forehead. Dakhir was also set.

"Your carriage is ready," announced the secretary.

Supramati looked around curiously. Apparently they were not going by train. Suddenly he saw a large star in the sky, approaching with dizzying speed.

"I hope we're not going on that star!" he said, laughing.

"Exactly. That's your airplane," answered the secretary with a smile.

A minute later the long cylindrical container, shaped like a cigar with two large round windows at either end, landed at the top of the platform. Nivara opened the door to a balustrade on the side of the cigar, and a small bridge attached with an iron ring was lowered from inside. The apparatus whirred and vibrated like an electric street lamp.

Dakhir and Supramati entered the ship, followed by Nivara and a Hindu servant with the baggage. They were met in the small, brightly lit aisle by a man dressed completely in black, who bowed low to the ground. He led them to a tiny room decorated with a gilded atlas, low, soft armchairs, and black lacquered tables. The airplane's interior furnishings were reminiscent of a train car with three compartments: a sitting room, a bedroom, and a room for the secretary, with luggage compartments in the back.

The bedroom, smaller than the hallway, held two low, narrow beds with a basin and toilet, all lacquered; the upholstery and wallpaper were done in white and light blue, edged in gold. Each room had a round window, covered at that moment with a silk shade.

In a moment, the bridge was drawn up, the door slammed, and a slight jolt indi-

---

1. Nivara was another of the priestly characters who lived in the Hindu-like world where the main protagonists had traveled to study the occult.

cated that the airplane was on its way. After a brief conversation, Dakhir suggested that they sleep.

"It's late and I'm tired. Obviously when we get to where we're supposed to, they'll wake us up."

But curiosity, eagerness, and nervousness prevented them from sleeping long. It had just started to get light when they entered the hallway, and Supramati raised the window shade. In the distance below he could see land—some buildings and an expanse of water—but the plane was going too fast for him to make out details. He realized that their space carriage had many fellow travelers; he could see a dark mass of airplanes of all sizes flying in all directions.

After breakfast, the friends examined all the technical details of the airship. On the whole, they very much liked this means of transportation; it had all the comforts, and was fast and not as tiring as railroad travel.

Day broke, and the sun shone so brightly that they had to lower the shades.

"Are we far from where we're supposed to land? Are we going to Paris?" asked Supramati, stretching out in an armchair.

"Oh, no. Paris no longer exists. It was destroyed by fire."

Supramati grew pale.

"What? A fire so great that it destroyed the whole city? It must've destroyed just one section."

"The city was burned to its foundations. It was a very complicated catastrophe. First, suffocating gases exploded from underground, poisoning the air. Then the land started cracking, and many buildings collapsed. Flames burst forth from the earth. All the gas pipes and electric lines caught fire. There was a sea of flames, devouring everything."

"I am taking your highnesses to Tsargrad, the former Constantinople," added Nivara, hoping, obviously, to erase the distressed looks on the travelers' faces. "We'll be there soon."

"Does Constantinople still belong to the Ottoman Empire?" asked Dakhir.

"No. The Muslims were driven to Asia long ago, where they united into a single state that remains very strong even today, despite being conquered by China, which also evolved and captured America, flooding it with a yellow horde.

"As for Tsargrad, it's now the capital of the Russian Empire, one of the most powerful states in the world, standing at the head of the great All-Slavic Union.

"Austria is no more; it disintegrated according to its various constituent nationalities. One part, the purely German, united with Germany, and the others, including the Hungarians, flowed into the Slavic sea."

The airship began to lower and dropped speed significantly. Now it was easy to see the picture as it came into focus below them. The Golden Horn had changed little. The sea was as calm and smooth as a mirror; the colossal city spread out along its banks. In many areas, fantastically high buildings towered over the others. An entire air flotilla of all sizes crowded around these structures, like bees around a hive.

In a few minutes, their plane landed on an expansive platform crowded with people. Here our travelers saw that they were on top of a huge building with an Eiffel tower; a long bridge connected the tower where they were located with other buildings of the same size. Passengers and porters scurried back and forth across this bridge.

Although Supramati, Dakhir, and the secretary were dressed just like everyone else, something about them attracted attention and many curious stares as they moved slowly across the platform and then took the elevator down into the waiting area. The descent ended in a large round hall with arched doors and more elevators behind them. The area between the doors contained plants, armchairs and sofas made of red leather, tables, and stands with books and journals; in the center of the hall was a pool with a silver shaft of water.

They exited through one of the many doors onto a wide, open platform, below which were numerous carriages that resembled automobiles but were much lighter and more elegant. Slowly and carefully, the carriage drove through long streets planted with trees and decorated with squares with fountains and flower beds; there was an abundance of greenery. The houses' exteriors had changed little; only the facades were trimmed in the whimsical excessiveness of the new style, which Supramati found unrefined and pretentious.

They crossed the intersection, and several pedestrians stopped, making way for their carriage. Supramati's attention was caught by two women and a man dressed—or, better put, undressed—in a most indecent manner, at least in the opinion of those who were used to the old attitudes about decorum.

The women were wearing diaphanous dresses which, although they reached down to their ankles, were so transparent that their bodies could be seen in detail. They wore colored silk belts with lace bags hanging on the side. On their feet they wore gold leather sandals. They had rings on their fingers, and leather gloves up to the elbow; a straw hat on a high head of hair and a parasol completed their wardrobe.

"They are members of the society 'Beauty and Nature,'" said the secretary. "According to their beliefs, the human body is nature's foremost creation and therefore cannot be indecent. Only hypocrisy and false modesty demand that it be covered. They say that if it is permissible to show the face, hands, and neck, then it is ludicrous to hide the rest, which is equally attractive, perfect, and functional. Nudity, like beauty, is 'sacred,' according to their beliefs, and because we now have complete freedom of opinion, no one pays attention to them and they are left alone."

"Are there many such apostles of holy nudity? Even in winter do they walk the streets naked?" Dakhir asked scornfully.

"There is an especially large number of them in France and Spain, but one meets them everywhere. The initial attempts to win citizenship for nudists were made in the twentieth century. At first there was strong opposition, but it gradually weakened as the disciples stuck fast to their convictions and steadily claimed their rights. At first they appeared on stage, in 'living pictures'; then they organized special circles, and when the era of unrestricted individual freedom came, they began to strut about on the streets. Everyone is used to them by now; they have their clubs, casinos, assemblies, theater, etc. In winter, when the weather is cold, they wear the usual dress; even in other places they remain true to their convictions."

They drove the length of the street along the Bosporus, which was planted with luxurious trees, and then turned into a courtyard paved with marble slabs, stopping at a columned doorway. Two servants came out to help them; the rest of the service personnel had gathered in the entrance hall and led them to the apartments on the first floor. Having dismissed the servants with a request that he be left alone to rest, Supramati examined his new, private accommodations: a bedroom, a study, a library, a hall, and a kitchen. It was all decorated in tsarist elegance, but he especially liked the bedroom. He anxiously grabbed the newspaper lying there and opened it up, finding the date: "14 July 2284."

The newspaper shook in his hands; his eyes fogged over. Suddenly feeling weak, he collapsed into an armchair. Leaning on his elbows, he put his head in his hands. Three centuries had passed, and he had seen nothing. His heart contracted, and an unfamiliar sense of desperation, fear, and loneliness filled his soul.

But the weakness was only temporary. The powerful will of the magus defeated it and returned him to his usual composure. Opening the paper, entitled *The Truth* (Istina), he began to read. Before meeting people, he wanted to orient himself in the new world. After finishing the paper, scrutinizing the most pressing issues of the day, Supramati began to leaf through the books and encyclopedias in his library. He was immersed in studying the new financial system when he was called to dinner.

Dakhir was already there and introduced him to his new personal secretary. Dinner, although vegetarian, was extraordinary. They chatted about various trivialities, and then the secretaries excused themselves, and the two friends moved into Supramati's apartment. They sat in the study, and Supramati quietly showed Dakhir the newspaper, pointing to the date.

"I know. We've aged three hundred years. I had the same paper in my room," he laughed. "I had more than one surprise of that sort. But I didn't come to talk about that. I'm planning to go away tomorrow . . . "

"What! You want to desert me?" interrupted Supramati.

"Yes. We'll enjoy ourselves each in his own way," explained the smiling Dakhir. "I discussed this with my secretary—a wonderful guy, by the way—and we decided to go to Graal's palace first, to visit a few friends. Then Nebo—my secretary—and I will travel to France and Spain, where I hope that we will meet up with you after you have grown bored with Tsargrad."

"Might you be going to the place where Paris used to be?" asked Supramati reflectively.

"No, that isn't so interesting to me. I have learned that both these countries are united in one European kingdom. I am especially eager to see how the Jews have established themselves—these peoples who have always destroyed every state structure, these breakers of all laws established to protect decent life. There's one bit of news that might pain you, if there's still an *Englishman* living beneath the cloak of a magus."

"Don't tell me that London suffered the same catastrophe that demolished Paris?" Supramati asked intently.

"Worse! An awful disaster ravaged a large part of England, which was then swallowed by the ocean."

Supramati grew pale; he shuddered, and braced himself against the chair. At that moment he had forgotten his immortality, his mastery of magic and science, the passed centuries; now he was simply Ralph Morgan, an English patriot, grief-stricken at the unparalleled calamity that had struck his motherland. A short silence ensued.

"Do you have any details of the disaster? Do you know when this happened?" he asked with his normal composure.

"About one hundred and eighty or two hundred years ago. I don't know the exact date. There was a terrible earthquake. The English part of the island broke off, and only the Scottish mountains remained, forming a small island. And imagine! Nebo told me that our old castle in Scotland, where you underwent your initiation, was left intact on its rocky slope. It needs only a few minor repairs," answered Dakhir.

"It's horrible, what happened on the earth during our absence, and I plan to devote myself to a serious historical study of all the changes. Of course, the earth's surface has already changed considerably. Whole continents have disappeared, and in comparison to the impending final destruction of the planet, these individual misfortunes are trivial. Still, the 'primordial person' lives so strongly in all of us that the devastation of England struck my heart, and I cannot reconcile myself to the thought that London, with its population of millions, with all its historical and scientific treasures, lies on the ocean floor!"

"You must get used to everything; this is simply preparation for another severe trial awaiting us, when our planet dies," said Dakhir with a sigh. "We will study contemporary history, and then tomorrow afternoon I'll depart. Also, we must not stay up too late, because we have to calm our nerves."

"Oh, yes! To sleep, to sleep! Every day I thank God that our immortality has not deprived us of this heavenly gift—*sleep*."

The Little Siberian Girl (Sibirochka)
Lidiia Charskaia (1910)

CHARSKAIA (1875–1937) WAS THE AUTHOR OF MORE THAN EIGHTY NOVELS, INCLUDING A BEST-SELLING SERIES ON HER GEORGIAN-RUSSIAN PRINCESS NINA DZHAVAKHA. SHE WAS AS EXTENSIVELY ADVERTISED BY HER PUBLISHERS AS SHE WAS

Adapted from L. A. Charskaya, *The Little Siberian*, trans. Hana Muskova Shaw (New York: Henry Holt, 1929), pp. 101–122.

SLIGHTED BY HIGH-CULTURE CRITICS. CHARSKAIA'S WORK WAS CLEARLY INTENDED FOR GIRLS. HER YOUNG AND INDEPENDENT HEROINES, WHO FOUND ADVENTURE IN RUSSIA AND EVEN MORE IN THE EXOTIC CAUCASUS, OFFERED THEM NEW MODELS COMBINING ACTION AND FEMININITY. SHE HELPED TO CREATE AND EXPAND THE RUSSIAN MARKET FOR CHILDREN'S LITERATURE, PROVIDING RUSSIAN WORKS WHERE THERE HAD BEEN ONLY TRANSLATIONS. HER HEROINES WERE USUALLY PRINCESSES AND VERY WELL OFF, YET HER READERSHIP WENT FAR BEYOND THE MIDDLE CLASS. DESPITE THE ACTIVE SUPPRESSION OF HER WORKS BY SOVIET AUTHORITIES, CHARSKAIA HAD A LARGE AND DEVOTED READERSHIP IN PROLETARIAN RUSSIA, AND EVEN TODAY ENJOYS FREQUENT REPRINTING.

CHAPTER XX: THE FALSE PRINCESS

Nick disappeared through the door, and his mother fell into disquieting thoughts. She recalled the events of five years before.

It was just the same sort of March evening; she was returning from the churchyard. She had just buried her husband, a tailor who had supported the family. The desolate widow was left with the children and no bread.

With her lived her ten-year-old son, Nick, and her four-year-old daughter, Sasha. All the way home from the cemetery, Anna Stepanovna was plagued by unhappy thoughts. What would she do? How would she feed the children? If her father had been with her, it would have been easier; he could have advised her. But her father was far away in Siberia, devoting himself to the education of a little girl whom, under strange circumstances, he had found in a forest. He often wrote about this little girl in his letters to Anna, begging her to accept the child as her own if he should die.

When her husband was alive, the family had been quite well-to-do. But now they had to go hungry. It was true that Anna Stepanovna's father had taught her to bear poverty, but those teachings were the last she wanted to think of now. All her thoughts were directed toward the children, whom she loved passionately. What would become of them now that their father was dead?

"I must find a job, as either a servant or a nurse," she told herself, "and put the children into an orphanage."

Just where a servant or a nurse might be needed, Anna did not know. But she knew that such advertisements were published in newspapers, so she bought one on her way home.

What a surprise she had when on the first page she read:

"An unhappy father who has just returned after spending four years in a sanitarium in a foreign country is seeking information about his little daughter, whom four years ago, in order to save her from the wolves, he left securely tied in a tree on the edge of a Siberian forest, and who subsequently disappeared without a trace." Descriptions of the little girl followed—of her clothing, and of the cross she had worn on a gold chain around her neck, with the inscription "God preserve His servant Alexandra." Accompanying this notice was the address of a very rich and noble gentleman who lived in the city.

Anna Stepanovna was excited when she read this announcement. She immediately concluded that the adopted granddaughter of her father was the little girl being sought by her father after four years. Her first thought was to go to the address given in the newspaper and inform the gentleman that his little daughter was living in Siberia with old Stepan Vikhrov, a bird-snarer of the forests. But then she had a new thought. It was a thought that was very daring and very wrong. "Supposing," she said to herself, "I should give to this rich man as his daughter my own daughter Sasha?" The plan flashed through her mind like lightning. "Sasha is as fair and soft as the real lady. Her name is the same. Sasha and Shura are both pet names for Alexandra, and my father calls her Sibirochka only because of the circumstances in which he found her. Sasha is also of the same age. Father will never come here with his little girl, and even if he should, no one would think of her as the lost girl. In this way Sasha will be forever happy. Now I just have to make my little girl believe that she isn't really my own daughter, but that she was brought here from Siberia, where she had lived with her adopted grandfather since she was a baby. I must also teach her to tell this to people for her own benefit. The rich and noble gentleman will surely reward me, and Sasha will be educated as a lady, and live in silk, luxury, and wealth. No one will ever find out the truth."

In this way Anna Stepanovna convinced herself.

Explaining her plan to her ten-year-old son and admonishing him never to say a word about it, she washed the little Sasha very carefully, dressing her as well as she could. She then took her to the address given in the paper. She was immediately taken to a young but very gray man.

As soon as she told him how her father had found the little girl tied to a tree in the Siberian forest, the man readily embraced the child with tears of happiness in his eyes.

He kissed the little girl repeatedly, saying, "It is she, it is she! She was just so slight and fair. My little girl; finally I have found you!" He wept in his joy.

"There can be no question about it," confirmed Anna in a most sincere tone. "My father brought her from Siberia three years ago. She even had the golden cross with the inscription 'God preserve His servant Alexandra.' But we sold the cross during some hard times. She lived with us for three years, and my husband and I never looked upon her as anything other than our own child. We cared for her and petted her no less than our own son. We wanted to publish a notice it in the paper, but we did not know how to, and to tell you the truth, we had become so fond of the little girl that we did not want to give her up."

"Oh," said the gentleman, "you could not have found me then. I have only recently returned from a foreign country, where I was trying to recover after the death of my wife and the loss of my little girl, who now has come back to me. I was very dangerously ill, and especially tortured by the thought that I had caused my child's destruction. But now I have her again, my dear, dear child!" Again he tenderly embraced Sasha Vikhrova, who looked at him curiously, not understanding what it was all about, and that he had accepted her as his lost daughter.

Then he richly rewarded the woman, asking her to come often to visit the girl, who would remain with him.

Pleased with the success of her plan, Anna returned home. She was all smiles. Her daughter Sasha would be a rich and noble lady, and she and her son Nick would never know poverty again.

But a secret fear remained in her heart. What if someone were to find out what she had done? What would happen if her father in Siberia were to learn about it? Troubled by these thoughts, she immediately wrote to her father to tell him that her daughter Sasha had died. She hoped that the exchange of the children would thus forever remain a secret. Now she would need to conceal from her neighbors the fact that she had money, which the noble gentleman had given her.

She finally decided that she would give her son for a time to the director of the Théâtre Variété, who was glad to accept the strong, good-looking boy. He put the child under the tutelage of his partner, the owner of the trained lions, an Englishman called Master Bull, who performed with his animals at the theater.

Under the tuition of Master Bull, Nick soon became a competent animal trainer who was paid as much as a man. He and his mother lived on this money, while the money they received from their "benefactor" his mother put away in a big trunk for better times.

"When our benefactor dies, we will take Sasha back, and then we will live a contented life," she often said to her son, sighing heavily.

Up to this time, Anna had been piling up money, living in a modest little room that she rented from the shoemaker at the end of the city. But the constant fear that her crime would one day be discovered wore upon her, making her increasingly irritable and nervous. She could not sleep at night; her conscience would not leave her in peace. Besides, she had developed an illness that she had inherited from her father. Anna Stepanovna began to cough and feel severe pains in her chest. She knew that she needed to trade her modest room for one that was larger and more comfortable, but she could not bring herself to do it. She was afraid that people might guess where she had gotten the money and give her away to her benefactor, who would disown Sasha and, still worse, have Anna jailed.

These thoughts tortured her unceasingly, reaching a crisis point whenever she beheld Sibirochka, the real Alexandra, whose place had been taken by Anna's own daughter.

In the midst of these troubled thoughts, the door suddenly burst open.

"Here we are; we have returned to you, Mother!" cried Nick. "Give us something to eat and shelter for these children tonight. Tomorrow I will take them as we arranged, where they will find good lodging and a square meal." He threw off his coat and stood there in his strange attire.

His mother struggled to maintain control as she prepared supper.

Andrei and Sibirochka, who had come in after Nick, remained near the door, uncertain about just what to do, and not seeming to understand why they had been brought back here.

CHAPTER XXI: A NEW ENEMY
Théâtre Variété

Each day, following the regular performance, we present an exhibition of trained lions, along with performances by a powerful Negro girl, rope climbers, clowns, and trapeze performers.

This attractive announcement, in colored letters, flew like a flag from a pole erected in front of the theater building.

As Andrei approached the entrance with his companions, he read this notice through quickly.

"What are you looking at?" asked Nick sharply, wrapping his coat around himself impatiently and glancing around angrily. "No one will pay you for that."

Nick was in a terrible mood. He had not slept much the preceding night, having given up his couch to the girl and gone with Andrei to a small room behind the kitchen. The spoiled boy did not like it a bit. Besides, he was afraid that the janitor, who had shown an interest in the newcomers, would come and ask questions about them.

"I can't wait until autumn, when Master Bull will leave Petrograd with his lions and the girl," muttered Nick to himself as he guided his companions to a dimly lighted room with a sign over the door announcing it as the office of the director.

"Oh, look here," said Nick, addressing a fat bald man who was engaged in a lively conversation with a tall, thin, red-haired man who wore a high hat and smoked a cigar. When he had the fat man's attention, he asked, "Ernest Ernestovich, can't you use this boy for a messenger?"

The two men turned around together.

"Ah, it's you, Nick," said the fat man. "You missed the morning rehearsal. Master Bull was very angry." Turning to his companion, he added, "Isn't that so, Master Bull?"

The red-haired man indifferently removed the cigar from his lips and said to Nick in broken Russian, "I take off from your salary. I punish for stand around the street when you should be in the rehearsal. But—"

His wandering glance suddenly fell upon Sibirochka. He stopped in mid-sentence, and his dull gray eyes lit up with curiosity and surprise.

"Where did this pretty girl come from?" he asked.

"I brought her with the hope that you would keep her," answered Nick, "along with this boy whom I wanted to recommend to Ernest Ernestovich."

"All right, I keep her. She make performance in cage with Caesar and Juno,"

Master Bull said through his yellow teeth, as he stroked the head of the embarrassed girl.

"And what do you know, my boy?" asked the director of the theater, smiling good-naturedly and patting Andrei on the shoulder as if to encourage him. "Do you know how to walk on a tightrope?"

"No," replied Andrei shortly.

"Are you an acrobat?"

"I don't know anything about that either."

"Can you dance?"

"No."

"Then what do you know?"

"I do not know anything now, but I will know everything that you teach me," said the boy courageously, fixing his sincere, honest eyes on the stout man.

"Ha ha ha!" laughed Ernest Ernestovich. "An interesting answer. I didn't expect that. I like you, boy, and we'll be friends if you aren't a good-for-nothing lazy loafer."

"Of course I'm not," answered Andrei, blushing.

"And how is that?" asked the director, raising his eyebrows.

"Because first of all I am honest," replied Andrei seriously and without embarrassment.

"Again an interesting answer," smiled the fat director. "Now, let's see; Master Bull is taking your sister, and I am taking you."

"She isn't my—" began Andrei, but Nick, who was standing beside him, pinched his hand with all his strength, and turning his back to the others, he whispered into the boy's ear, "Tell everyone that she is your sister."

"That would be a lie, and I do not lie," answered Andrei in the same tone but very firmly.

"I'll give you money for it," insisted Nick.

"Money or no money, you can't make me lie."

"You'd better be careful; you will make an enemy out of me," whispered Nick hotly.

"I'm not afraid."

"What are you boys whispering about?" the director interrupted them.

Flushing, Nick whispered again, "Don't give me away," and started to explain his absence to Master Bull.

For a while the director looked at Andrei.

"You are a good-looking, clever boy," he said, "and should be able to learn quickly. You will start out as a clown and entertain the public between the acts."

"I don't think I know how to amuse the public," said the boy quietly.

"That isn't difficult. You will act with our old clown, Durois, and he will show you what you should do and say. We will talk about your pay later. Agreed?"

"Entirely. I ask only that I not be separated from Sibirochka."

"From whom?" Ernest Ernestovich raised his eyebrows again.

"From this girl. Her name is Sibirochka."

"From his sister!" called Nick loudly.

"Is she your sister? What a pretty name."

"Yes, his sister," Nick repeated, before Andrei could reply.

"He isn't telling the truth," said Andrei in a quiet, firm voice. "Sibirochka is not a relative of mine."

"You are lying," laughed Nick. "Why are you trying to deny that she is your sister?"

"I am telling the truth."

"Don't quarrel, children," interrupted the director. "Whether or not she is your sister makes no difference to me. You will stay in my service and be taught by Durois. Master Bull will take Sibirochka into his care. Both of you will live with me. And now enough of talking. It is time to start the second part of the rehearsal." Sticking his head out the door, he called, "Ring for the second part!" Then, turning back to them, he added, "Nick, take the children on the stage."

"All right," answered Nick, with a bow. He turned sharply to Andrei. "Why are you standing there with your mouth open? Come on!" Then he whispered so that Andrei alone could hear him, "You dirty beast! You don't want my friendship. You made me out to be a liar in front of my boss. You will soon see what I will do to you."

With an angry glance from his black eyes at Andrei, Nick led the way.

CHAPTER XXII: CAESAR AND JUNO

The corridor with its small electric lights seemed endless to Andrei and Sibirochka as they walked along it for the first time behind Nick, who was grumbling something to himself. At the end of the passage was a door, through which came rays of light, loud voices, applause, and laughter.

"Go ahead; there is the stage," said their new acquaintance roughly. "Master Bull and Ernest Ernestovich will be here directly. But first take off those dirty, raggedy coats. You didn't intend to go like that, did you? I have my own business to take care of."

He disappeared as abruptly as if he had gone through a trapdoor.

Andrei and Sibirochka walked slowly on alone. After a few steps they reached the end of the corridor, which widened near the door, and stopped on the threshold.

The din from the stage beyond deafened them. On the boards, brightly illuminated by large electric lights, people were tumbling and turning somersaults. One group ran together, some climbing onto the shoulders and heads of others until they formed a high pyramid, with a stout man as the base, who was as strong as Hercules. On this man's shoulders stood another; on his head, a third, who used his outstretched hands to support a fourth, whose legs were in the air, and who was poised so lightly that his palms seemed hardly to touch those of the man below him. And at the very top, lightly moving and twisting in a curious sort of half-dance on the upturned soles of the fourth, was a small, attractive boy of twelve, with a carefree, animated face.

"Ah, that is Ivanov, a famous Russian acrobat, with his troupe," spoke a soft voice behind Andrei. "You must be new artists," he added. Andrei turned around and saw a slender girl a little older than Sibirochka, a pretty blonde as frail as a flower.

"I am Gerta, the daughter of the director," she continued, pressing Andrei's hand with a sweet, friendly smile, and kissing Sibirochka on her pale cheek.

"What a beautiful child!" she exclaimed, studying Sibirochka's golden curls and her large blue eyes that shone like stars. "A beautiful girl!" she repeated. "I must take you to Ella. You haven't seen her yet, have you? Don't be frightened by her. Ella's body is black, but her soul is as white as the morning dawn. Ella!" she called. "Ella, where are you?"

"Ella is here, mistress," someone answered in a soft, musical voice. Sibirochka stepped back a pace with an involuntary gasp.

Before them appeared a creature utterly strange to her, as black as soot, with shining white eyeballs in a totally black face, with short curly hair and a flat nose, and with thick, prominent bluish-red lips. The short but extremely muscular young Negress wore a yellow and black striped skirt and a white sailor blouse with a red collar. In her ears were large golden rings, and around her neck, which was as muscular as the rest of her body, were several strands of a coral necklace.

"This is my friend Ella. She calls me mistress, but we are friends. She speaks very little Russian. In fact, she knows only two sentences—'Ella is here, mistress,' and 'Ella loves you.' But she has a heart of gold, and she will be your friend. She was sent here from Africa last year. She is a Negress. Shake hands with her. Don't be afraid of her black hands."

Little Gerta looked so kindly at Andrei and Sibirochka that they did not have the courage to refuse her request, and they each, in turn, gave their hands to the Negress. Ella pressed Sibirochka's small hand very tenderly, but she shook Andrei's so vigorously that he winced. "Ella is a strong woman," explained Gerta to her new friends.

"She must be very strong," agreed Andrei ruefully. "I thought she wanted to break my fingers—or else put my shoulder out of joint," he added laughingly.

"She means that as friendship; but if she is angry, her strength can be very dangerous. Look at her: something is making her angry now," said Gerta quickly, turning around.

The Russian acrobats had finished their act and, bouncing on their feet like balls, surrounded Ella. The two eldest, strong, grown youths who looked to be twenty, stepped closer to her. "Listen, you black doll, sell me your corals; I want to give them to my sister," said one of them as he abruptly grasped the strands around Ella's neck.

"Sell them to me!" called the other. "I'll hang them on my nose," and he touched Ella's black ear.

Ella muttered something unintelligible and shook her head angrily.

The joking youths did not stop, and no matter how she defended herself, they pressed closer to her, insisting that she give them her jewels.

"What do you want them for?" laughed the older one. "They can't make a stupid black face like yours beautiful." He pulled harder on the string.

Then something unexpected happened. The string broke, and with it, Ella's patience. What followed, none of those present could have anticipated. With incredible swiftness, black Ella grasped the necks of her tormentors, one in each strong hand, and pounded their heads together so hard that the acrobats cried out in pain. With a last throaty growl, she threw first one to the floor, then the other on top of him, and then, as if her anger were satisfied, she sat calmly upon them, looking quietly around her with shining eyes. The two youths, cursing and yelling, writhed and twisted but could not seem to escape. Only the sound of the bell and the appearance of the director and Master Bull, followed by Nick, interrupted the scene.

Master Bull and Nick wore pink tights with green silk trunks covered with glittering spangles. The Englishman carried a long whip, and Nick held a piece of raw meat.

"Why has he got that? Why is he carrying the meat?" asked Sibirochka, turning to Gerta.

Gerta did not have time to answer. Almost immediately came a deafening roar, which seemed to shake the walls of the theater, a sound loud enough to make people go pale. A large door at one side, which until now had not been noticeable, was swung open, and through it the stage attendants wheeled a huge cage containing two enormous African lions.

"They are Caesar and Juno," said Gerta. "Aren't they beauties?"

Sibirochka hardly shared her opinion. She was terrified of their huge open jaws and their deafening roars.

But how surprised she was when as soon as the cage appeared on the stage, Nick ran to it, with Master Bull walking sedately after him, playing with his long whip.

Nick quickly lifted the iron door and entered the cage. Master Bull entered bravely behind him, and as if charmed, the animals ceased their terrifying roaring the instant the trainers were inside. Nick threw them each a piece of meat, and the animals commenced to eat ravenously.

CHAPTER XXIII: SIBIROCHKA GOES TO THE LIONS

"Miss Gerta, let me ask you to get the little actress, Miss Sibirochka, ready," said Master Bull in a tone that permitted of no argument. He showed his yellow teeth in a mirthless smile.

Andrei and Sibirochka heard these words two weeks after they had settled into the "Big House." The Big House, as they called it, stood on the very outskirts of Petrograd, at least ten blocks from the theater that Ernest Ernestovich had leased. In this house lived the director with the members of his company. With him were his daughter and aunt; the Russian acrobat Ivanov and his sons, Denis, Gleb, Peter, and Vadim; the old clown Durois and his grandson; the Negress Ella with her old mother; Master Bull, who employed Nick Vikhrov; and finally Andrei and Sibirochka.

The clown, Pierre Durois, who behind the scenes and at home was an irritable old man but on the stage was an inimitable jester, had immediately begun instructing Andrei in his not very difficult art. Since Andrei had not yet appeared on the stage, his chief duty was to care for Durois's six-year-old grandson, Robert, who was a real troublemaker and quarreler.

Gerta, the only daughter of the director, appeared as part of an act singing German songs, and she was also given another duty by her father: to watch over the little children who had been taken into the company, preparing them for their new occupation and, if necessary, encouraging and fortifying them for their task.

Gerta was a quiet, calm little girl of twelve, who could be as serious as an adult. She always appeared at just the right time. If small Robert Durois was bothering everyone, if his grandfather Pierre was out of sorts, if the Ivanov brothers were quarreling, if Ella got into a fit of temper, if Nick was being teased by his companions, Gerta was always the peacemaker, a comforting angel in the hard game of life. She was the good fairy of the troupe. At the same time, since the death of her mother, Gerta was the mistress of her house.

In the morning she was the first up, and with her aunt, she poured the tea and coffee and saw to breakfast for everyone. Then she arranged with the cook for dinner, after which she collected the children for rehearsal and made sure that those who were scheduled to perform made it into the carriages that were sent from the theater to get them.

In addition to the acrobats and lion performers, the director employed a group of singers who were quartered elsewhere. These were the ones with whom Gerta sang, and she spent the rest of her time studying the small parts suited to her age and voice.

At five o'clock the residents of the Big House returned for dinner, before heading back to the theater at eight for their separate performances, which followed the presentation of an operatic piece by the singers.

When they had returned for the night, Gerta saw to it that they were served tea and a cold supper, and only after twelve was she able to retire.

While everyone loved the girl, the Negress Ella fairly worshipped her. This half-wild girl, who had come so far to earn a living, regarded the calm, fair-haired Gerta as a creature from another world. For her beloved mistress, as she always called her, Ella was ready to scratch out the eyes of anyone who offended her.

Whomever Gerta loved, Ella also loved. From the first day Gerta had become attached to Sibirochka, and Ella looked upon the little girl with the same devotion she held for Gerta.

Such were the people in the environment to which Andrei and Sibirochka had come, and slowly they were becoming used to this strange life.

Sibirochka was taken at once under Gerta's care and shared Gerta's small pink room, which always was neat and cozy.

Andrei roomed with the clown Pierre and his little grandson; but the children saw each other in the theater and in the dining room, where the members spent much of their spare time.

"Miss Gerta," Master Bull said, "let me ask you to get the little actress, Miss Sibirochka, ready. She is about to enter the cage of Caesar and Juno for the first time."

At that moment the two girls were behind a wing, delightedly watching Ella, who, seemingly without effort, was attaching heavy weights to each of her strong fingers and waving them over her head as if they were feathers. The tone of Master Bull as he issued his command sounded severe to the girls, and he fixed them with a searching look from his dull, leaden eyes.

Sibirochka was nervous and excited, but she wasn't afraid of ordinary things. She would have gone in the dark into the densest taiga; but the lions' cage—that was something different. Whenever she thought of entering the cage and coming close to those terrible, wild, roaring beasts, her whole little body shuddered. Gerta had not allowed her to think too much about her approaching task and always tried to give her courage. . . .

The African Princess (Vampuka)

M. N. Volkonsky (1907)

THE AFRICAN PRINCESS, OR, AS IT WAS COMMONLY KNOWN, VAMPUKA, WAS THE CONSUMMATE CABARET PRODUCTION WHEN AFTER-HOURS THEATER BLOSSOMED AT THE TURN OF THE CENTURY. PRODUCED AT ST. PETERSBURG'S CROOKED MIRROR BY THE AVANT-GARDIST NIKOLAI EVREINOV, VAMPUKA AMUSED A CLIENTELE THAT COMBINED AMBITIOUS BOURGEOIS WHO CAME TO BE SEEN, AND THE CULTURAL AVANT-GARDE WHO CAME TO MOCK THEM.

EVREINOV'S CLEVER STAGING PLAYED TO AUDIENCES FAMILIAR ENOUGH WITH HIGH CULTURE TO ENJOY SPOOFING IT. VOLKONSKY WORKED ON THE PARODY FOR SEVERAL YEARS BEFORE IT CRYSTALLIZED AROUND THE NAME OF HIS AFRICAN HEROINE. HE WAS TELLING A FRIEND ABOUT A ROMANCE WITH THE REFRAIN "VAM PUK, VAM PUK" ("A BOUQUET FOR YOU"). THE CONFUSED VISITOR ASKED, "REALLY? IS VAMPUK A NAME?" THE DELIGHTED VOLKONSKY REALIZED THAT HE HAD THE PERFECT APPELLATION.

THE VAUDEVILLE WAS ACCOMPANIED BY MUSIC, PROVIDED BY DIFFERENT COMPOSERS FOR VARIOUS PRODUCTIONS. WRITTEN IN 1900, IT DID NOT APPEAR FOR ANOTHER SEVEN YEARS. VOLKON-

Russkaia teatral'naia parodiia XIX–nachala XX veka (Moscow: Iskusstvo, 1976).

SKY INTENDED TO WRITE A "GROTESQUE" OF DRAWING-ROOM RO-
MANCES, WHICH HE DID BY USING EUROPEANS TO CARICATURE
AFRICANS. STILL, THE FINAL CONQUEST, THE COSTUMES, AND
THE DANCES PROVIDED A RELEASE THAT WAS PROBABLY MORE
CHAUVINISTIC THAN ARTISTIC.

This comic opera in two acts is dedicated to Roberts and Chamberlain.[1]

CAST OF CHARACTERS

Strofokamil IV,[2] an Ethiopian king
Vampuka, an African princess
Merinos, Vampuka's unselfish protector
Lodyré, a young man wearing strategically
   placed feathers
a Page

the High Priest
Velim, the executioner of southeastern
   Ethiopia
Extras: Ethiopians, standard-bearers,
   priests, people, soldiers, doges,
   fishermen, senators, troubadors,
   major-domos, pages, and other
   members of the court, of both sexes.

The setting is a desert in full bloom with an indeterminate horizon.

The Crooked Mirror. Cast of *Vampuka*. The set depicts a desert in full bloom.

---

1. This dedication to fighters in the Boer War was intended as parody.
2. *Strofokamil* is an antiquated word for "ostrich."

ACT ONE

CHOIR OF ETHIOPIANS: We are, We are, We are Ethiopians;
    We're en-, We're en-, We're enemies of Europe.
    The beautiful Vampuka
    We're ordered to serve.
    Our chief wants to ask for her hand.
    We in Af-, we in Af-, we in Africa live,
    And Vam-, and Vam-, and Vampuka we will find!

(They leave; Vampuka and Merinos enter.)

MERINOS: Oh, beautiful Vampuka!
    The remains of your ill-fated father are now buried.
    He fought with the Ethiopians.

VAMPUKA (*crying*): I weep for the corpse,
    Buried here in the sand.
    I weep for my father,
    Killed before his time!

MERINOS: Oh, cry, Vampuka, cry!
    Fate is your executioner!

VAMPUKA: Tears are flowing in abundance,
    They are dimming my loving gaze,
    Ah, the thorns, not the roses
    That I have known until this time.

MERINOS: Oh, cry, Vampuka, cry!
    Fate is your executioner!

VAMPUKA: These aren't kind tears,
    I can find no comfort.
    Drained of my last strength,
    I am fainting! (*And she does so.*)

MERINOS: She has passed out! Oh, uncontrollable whirlwind!
    Thunderheads fill the sky, rain pours down,
    Hurry from place to place for cover.
    The sky above us is threatening a second deluge.
    Let the storm spill forth,
    Let the ice and snow on the unscalable, primeval
      heights
    Melt and turn into thundering streams;
    Let the sea, the rivers, the ocean itself
    Flow over the shore and rush down to us in the
      steppes
    In order to bring a drop of moisture to Vampuka!

(A pause, then he continues:)

The whirlwind is silent. A solemn still
Embraces the snowy mountaintops,
And the ocean is as before, waves lapping lazily,
Drowsily on the shore.
But I know—I'll dig out a spring
A five-minute walk from here,
I'll bring its icy waters.
On the wings of a hurricane,
I'll lament for her, faster than a fleet-footed
Wild doe—or the best racers,
I'll outdistance everyone in the race.
Oh, how I will run! Achilles himself
Will stay behind me, like a tortoise,
And I'll run faster than lightning;
Lightning, envying me, will stand still!

(He continues singing for a long time about how quickly he will run, then looks at Vampuka and, shaking his head, exits slowly.)

LODYRÉ (*runs in*):	What do I see? Vampuka Lying alone on the steppes. But my pledge of honor, She is coming to!
VAMPUKA (*jumping up*):	Is that you, Lodyré?
LODYRÉ:	It is I, Lodyré!
VAMPUKA:	Oh, drained of all strength, I suffered, loving . . .
LODYRÉ:	A kiss has resurrected you, My darling, you . . .

(The moon begins to shine on them.)

TOGETHER:	How wonderful to love, And be happy. The moon shines on us— How marvelous it is!

(They sit hurriedly on a stone and begin to sing.)

They chase after us,
We run, we hurry.
They hunt for us,
The terrible pursuit.
We run ever faster from them,
So as not to be caught.
They chase after us,

We run, we hurry,
We hurry, we run,
They chase after us . . .
We hu-rr-ry,
We run!

(They exit, and a group of Ethiopians run in, up to the footlights, and begin stamping in place.)

ETHIOPIANS: How they run away from us!
Hurry faster after them,
Ah, how they run away!
The chase after them quickens,
The hunt for them accelerates,
After them faster in pursuit . . .
Time is flying, don't waste a minute,
We run to overtake them!

ACT TWO

The setting is the same desert, but now with two thrones set up in the middle of it.

ETHIOPIANS: Strofokamil is very good to us,
We serve him,
And are happy to do so.
Long live Strofokamil!

(Strofokamil enters, leading Vampuka by the arm. They walk around the Ethiopians, who bow to them.)

VAMPUKA: Oh, earlier, when I was free to love whom I wanted,
I loved only Lodyré.
And now I must love
The detested Strofokamil.
I hate him,
This tormentor of mine.
He conquered the country
In order to make me a prisoner!

STROFOKAMIL: How I loved her,
The sun of my life.
Oh beautiful Vampuka,
My love is unrequited!

(Everyone exits. A page enters.)

PAGE (*sings, accompanying himself on a flute*):
>Oh, tell her,[3]
>You are my blossoms,
>I implore you to tell her
>That I love her . . .
>She pays no attention
>To any of my suffering,
>As if she doesn't know
>That I love her.

(He exits hurriedly. Strofokamil, Vampuka, and a retinue of Ethiopians enter.)

STROFOKAMIL:	And so we will continue our games. Call out the dancers and singers, and let them begin their songs and dances.

(He and Vampuka sit down on the thrones. The dancers come out and perform.)

CHORUS:
>Oh, how they dance,
>Until their energy is spent.
>Long live Strofokamil,
>For many days!

(The dancers, having finished, run off stage. A group of Ethiopian troubadors enter. Lodyré is among them, disguised and carrying a gusli.)

LODYRÉ (*sits down on a birch stump that has been brought out from the wings for him*):
>I'm a singer from the world,
>The world of daydreams.
>Request my lyre,
>Request tears.
>Ah, sacred love,
>Oh, my love,
>Together with heaven and happiness
>Are hell and blood!

STROFOKAMIL (*standing up*): I recognize you. You're my sworn enemy, Lodyré!

VAMPUKA AND LODYRÉ (*standing to the side of the stage by the prompter's box, with Strofokamil between them*): Oh, horror, we've been discovered,
>And Lodyré has been recognized
>Among the enemy retainers
>At the enemy's court.

STROFOKAMIL:	What are they saying,
>What are they whispering about?

---

3. This songs lampoons an aria from *Faust*.

VAMPUKA AND LODYRÉ:	So let him threaten
	    Us with the terrible executioner—
	    The executioner will marry us,
	    And we will die together!

STROFOKAMIL:	What are they saying, What are they whispering about?
THE HIGH PRIEST (*approaches from deep center stage*): I eavesdropped on them. You   must order the traitor executed immediately!
STROFOKAMIL:	Velim!
THE EXECUTIONER VELIM:	I am here, Your Majesty!
STROFOKAMIL:	Speak of the devil! Execute Lodyré for me now.
VELIM (*merrily*):	Bring me the axe!

(Pages bring out the axe.)

VAMPUKA:	Lodyré, you will die for me,
	    In the flower of your youth.
	    The executioner's axe
	    Will stain your jacket collar crimson.

LODYRÉ:	Let the executioner's axe
	    Stain my jacket collar crimson.
	    Your friend is happy to die
	    For you in the flower of his youth!

MERINOS (*appears unexpectedly*):	

	Why do they speak of death here?
	    Believe me truly
	    That death is not seemly for youth,
	    But rather happiness:
	    The young are accomplished only at that!

STROFOKAMIL:	Who are you, dressed like an aborigine, Interrupting our tranquility with your loud voice?

(Merinos strips off what was a costume of naked skin and now appears in European dress.)

ETHIOPIANS:	A European!
MERINOS:	Yes, I am a European, and I have conquered you!
ETHIOPIANS:	You have conquered us!
STROFOKAMIL:	I thank you, I didn't expect this![4]

(Merinos sentences Strofokamil to death and marries Lodyré and Vampuka.)

CURTAIN

---

4. This line is taken from the refrain of one of V. A. Sologub's improvised poems from the 1860s.

Gladiators of Our Times

N. N. Breshko-Breshkovsky (1909)

Breshko-Breshkovsky enjoyed a reputation in his day equal to that of his Socialist Revolutionary mother, Katherine, "grandmother of the Russian Revolution." The two had minimal contact after her exile to Siberia; raised by an uncle, Nikolai Nikolaevich began a career in Petersburg in the joint-stock department of a tobacco factory. By 1895, though, he was writing full-time. He specialized in describing the lives of athletes, especially wrestlers; he wrote the libretto for and played a part in an early silent film, *The Wrestler in the Black Mask*. The real-life models for his fictional characters were easily recognizable to readers familiar with the sports world. Specifically, Tampio in *Gladiators*, who also appears in other stories, bore a more than coincidental resemblance to Lurikh, the Estonian world champion and notorious ladies' man.

CHAPTER 1

They were seated in a loge. He had the air of a stolid, bored Petersburger who already knew it all and had wearied of it all. She, however, a thirty-five-year-old woman, was so full of curiosity that she gave the appearance of a schoolgirl. And no wonder. This summer theater, the crowd, the wrestling match she had come to see—all this was new for her. Ladies from her circle did not usually frequent such theaters.

The audience, some standing, some sitting, showed their impatience by clapping. The military band, in their gray coats with their big horns gleaming, walked single file into the orchestra pit.

"It's time to begin! Let's go!"

Isakova looked around. The boisterous crowd in the open pavilion resembled a thick, dark blanket. It looked as though the crowd would break the fence with one

Excerpts from N. N. Breshko-Breshkovskii, "Gladiatory nashikh dnei," in *V mire atletov* (St. Petersburg: Koreliakov, 1909), pp. 88–95, 128–132.

big push and pour into the theater, sweeping everyone away with them. The image terrified her.

"Jean,[1] is it always like this?"

"Always, my friend. You know, Liza, it's getting chilly, and maybe a little damp. I brought a warm coat and made an excellent—"

A new face appeared in their loge: the artist Liutsian Robertovich Moniushko. He was dressed with the elegance of someone who bought his clothes abroad, in a stylish derby and a long topcoat. Crisp, with a sharp chin and smoothly shaven cheeks, he smelled of "Coeur de Jannette."

"How kind of you, Liutsian Robertovich!" gushed Isakova.

"Did you bring your sketchbook?" Ivan Aleksandrovich greeted him less enthusiastically. He was thinking that if an artist were to start drawing in their loge, it would be, well, not quite proper.

"Naturally. My sketchbook is always with me. How could it be otherwise? I came here specifically to scrutinize. Russian artists don't like to do this, but in this case it's essential."

Isakova raised her mother-of-pearl binoculars to her eyes, her hand gloved in fine silk. Out of habit, she looked around for familiar faces. She saw none.

"These people aren't from our circle," she decided, feeling like an escapee from a schoolteacher's annoying surveillance. That made her happy.

A cavalry officer in a white cap entered the loge opposite theirs, where a vivid brunette in a large black hat was seated.

"Kirsanov! Jean, look! I don't think he's seen us."

"This isn't good. Look who he's with—a famous courtesan."

"Yes?" Elizaveta Stepanovna aimed her binoculars at the brunette.

The orchestra suddenly began to play a march. The curtain went up. Empty, covered with a green cloth, the stage looked like a giant card table. Around it sat the panel of jurors in a semicircle, newspaper correspondents covering the matches, and clean-shaven actors. In the middle, at center stage, stood the referee and judges. Right next to them stood the famous opera star Zhiznevsky in a bizarre cap. Even at age fifty he played the lisping schoolboy successfully in *Poor Sheep*.

"Zhiznevsky! Zhiznevsky!" The whisper reverberated around the seats.

On stage a student, broad-shouldered and thickset, with his chest puffed out and in a long frock coat, swaggered up to the footlights. The wrestlers in their colored tights marched around the circle, one after the other, with their strong, muscular legs. Then they lined up. Initially they all looked surprisingly alike to Isakova. In a clear, toneless voice, the student Gusev—all Petersburg knew him—announced:

"This international French style[2] championship, organized for wrestlers from around the world under the direction of Professor of Athletics Gansky, will feature the following names: World Champion Shi-ma-no-vich (Austria), World Champion A-u-er (Russia), Jerôme-Brisseau (France), World Champion Szam-po-walski (War-

---

1. A longtime affectation among Russian women was to use the French "Jean" (Zhan) for the Russian "Ivan."

2. "French" meant classical Greek style wrestling, as opposed to the free-for-all favored by Americans.

Georg Lurikh, wrestling champion and infamous ladies' man

saw)...." Gusev read off ten more names. They all stepped forward and bowed to the public. Most of them moved clumsily, not knowing what to do with their hands, bobbing their heads ridiculously. Others, who considered themselves ladies' men and to whom flowers were brought, moved with flirtatious elegance, semiclad men with great physiques.

A bronze figure in light blue tights stood out sharply among the white faces, hands, backs, and shoulders—the Tunisian Moor Hassan. The spectators' favorite, Hassan was met with great enthusiasm. With a naive, trusting smile, his teeth flashing, he bowed somewhat savagely, bending over low, touching his brown fingers to the floor, as if crouching, ready to leap.

The wrestlers walked off. The stage was empty again.

The student looked to his right and said, "Tampio!"

He looked to his left and announced, "Szampowalski!"

Two wrestlers came out from behind the curtain simultaneously: one was an exquisitely built light blond in almost foppish silk tights the color of rosy flesh; the other was a bald older wrestler in modest black tights. He was taller and heavier than Tampio.

Women's voices could be heard through the thunderous applause: "Tam-pio! Tam-pio!"

He received a bouquet. For a moment he held it behind his back, allowing the crowd to admire his body, posing in the style of the ancient Greeks. Then he handed it to the nearest correspondent and walked with Szampowalski toward the welcoming applause. The crowd showed less in excitement greeting the balding wrestler, who had an intelligent, expressive face. At one time he had been a fashionable European celebrity, but he was past his prime and now wrestled only with his right arm because his left was broken.

The teacher and the student stood together. Szampowalski had directed the first stage of Tampio's athletic career.

"Look, Elizaveta Stepanovna, at the lines on Tampio!" exclaimed Moniushko. "His chest, his legs! Regardez bien! See how he parades around. He looks just like a Greek discus thrower."

But Isakova was enthralled and did not need encouragement from Moniushko. "Ah, mon dieu, how fine he is!" she repeated, not taking her binoculars off him.

Ivan Aleksandrovich began to turn around; the realization of what was happening suddenly made him feel cold. He gave the artist a hostile stare, thinking—even the most proper people often imagine quite improperly—"What the hell do you think you're doing, trying to teach my wife about masculine charms?"

Teacher and pupil, worthy opponents, began to wrestle, cautiously at first. Spreading their legs and touching foreheads, they grasped each other's hands. As fast as lightning, Tampio spun his back to Szampowalski and grabbed his head in his hands, falling with him to the green carpet.

"Ah!" gasped Elizaveta Stepanovna.

"That's nothing," her husband soothed her. "It's one of the harmless holds, the 'tour de tête.' This is a friendly match."

The pretty brunette wasn't listening to the officer, who was whispering something to her. She was completely engrossed in the competition—or rather, in Tampio's body. It was rumored that she was attracted to him.

Agile for his forty-five years, Szampowalski twisted into an elastic "bridge." Tampio snapped this living arch. He tried to press the old wrestler's back to the floor. Tampio's face, nasty and white, distorted into a tormented grimace.

"Bravo, Tampio, bravo!"

"Pin him!" cried the gallery.

Thrusting out his chest, Gusev, every inch the seasoned veteran, did not miss their slightest movement. He held the bell at the ready. But Szampowalski twisted around to his chest. The crisis had passed. Angry at his failure, Tampio dug his elbow into the other man's neck.

"Jean, what's he doing? He's torturing him!" said his anxious wife.

"That hold is allowed."

Tampio wrestled beautifully, but there was something clownish in this beauty. He grimaced, grasped Szampowalski by the belt, threw himself on him with all his might, and spun him dizzily around until he turned pale.

Gusev looked at his large pocketwatch and rang the bell.

"Is that it? Is it over?" asked the disappointed Elizaveta Stepanovna, not understanding what was happening.

"It's been twenty minutes. Now there's a one-minute rest. Let's go home now," suggested Isakov.

"Home? No, Jean, let's stay longer. It's so interesting. If you want, if you're tired, I'll stay till the end with Liutsian Robertovich. He can take me home. Okay?"

"Naturally," replied the artist.

Isakov shrugged his shoulders and decided to play the victim.

Tampio and Szampowalski fought for an entire hour. Tampio astonished the whole theater with his amazing agility, putting his opponent in precarious positions, safely extricating himself at the worst moments, but for all his efforts he still could not defeat his teacher.

Another pair replaced this one. The curtain was not lowered until nearly 2 A.M.

"Thank God!" rejoiced Ivan Aleksandrovich.

Moniushko clapped his sketchbook shut, then carefully tied it up. They returned home in a rented landau. Dawn was breaking. Along the empty streets, dark houses slumbered like giant stone sarcophagi.

Ivan Aleksandrovich also slumbered, and even this he did properly, stolidly—as bureaucrats of the fourth rank are supposed to sleep.

"Can we go to the fights tomorrow, Jean?"

"Again?" he opened his eyes. "That's, well, indecent." He dozed off again.

If only he had seen the deprecating gaze his wife leveled at him. In seventeen years of married life, she had never looked at him like that. For the first time she thought with disgust about his thin, flat legs, like matchsticks, and about how flabby he was, and so scrawny that his bones stuck out.

[*Plot development in intervening chapters: Moniushko serves as something of an intermediary between wrestlers and society women because they can meet in his studio, where he paints portraits of both. Elizaveta Stepanovna becomes involved with the German wrestler Schmidt. When her husband gives her money to pay Moniushko for her portrait, she keeps it for her own use. Tampio exploits the attractions of many women, including Maria Semenovna, who forsakes more honorable suitors for the athlete's occasional attentions.*]

CHAPTER 9

Schmidt lived in a suite of dirty furnished rooms above a tavern. It was near the arena, just across the street. Other wrestlers also lived there. The "married" ones beat their girlfriends and then made up over a beer. From morning till evening the Germans carefully counted their income and expenditures. In the dimly lit corridors, the Turk droned savage, mournful songs in his incomprehensible language.

Like a good German, Schmidt was very orderly. He kept his clothes folded neatly in a leather suitcase, and once a week, on Saturday, he wrote his parents. A framed photo of them stood on the unsteady table: Papa in a suit with starched cuffs, the model of an honest burgher. He looked like the kind who, in friendly conversations over beer and cheap cigars, would proudly talk about how strong his Franz was, what a fine wrestler he was, and how much he earned.

Isakova's passion for Schmidt had completely overwhelmed her. It was an intoxication, a heavy, sensual daze. She went abroad when family honor, respectability, the conventions of polite society—when all this plunged into an abyss, crumbled, was driven away.

If two months ago Elizaveta Stepanovna had heard that one of her friends was dining openly with a wrestler on the veranda of one of the out-of-town resorts, and had entered the athlete's shady furnished rooms, she would have died of shame. And now she herself had rushed onto this precipice.

Rumors about Isakova's disgraceful affair were already spreading through society. In the ministry, Ivan Aleksandrovich was viewed with degrading, scornful pity.

There are affairs, and then there are affairs. It is no secret that society ladies are attracted to athletes. It depends on how the affair is carried out. If she shows disdain for the wrestler, looks upon him as a lackey or a gladiator-slave, sending her coach for him with the shades drawn, who cares? But to advertise this relationship by dining or walking together in public, well, that's more than indecent.

Isakova was a wellspring of money for Schmidt. Aware of the power he had over her, he quietly exploited her. And she slavishly brought him money, selling her clothes for practically nothing, pawning her diamonds, trying to economize from the monthly allowance Ivan Aleksandrovich gave her for housekeeping. He divided the money she gave him into thirds: part he sent home to the Fatherland, another part he saved, and the rest he spent on equipment.

Moniushko was correct in his suspicions about the payment for the portrait. Not allowing herself to think about the future—tomorrow no longer existed for her—Elizaveta Stepanovna had used it to buy Schmidt a diamond signet ring, hoping to warm the embraces that had recently cooled. Forcing a smile, she would slip bills into his billfold.

Liutsian Robertovich's letter stunned Isakov.

"Liza, what is this? He's asking me for money. Hasn't he already received it? You gave it to him. These artists are a dangerous lot. They appear so proper, so well mannered . . . "

The flustered, blushing face of his wife told him that the artist was not the guilty party.

"I . . . I don't understand. There's a lot that I don't understand lately. Money disappears into darkness, but where? I simply can't comprehend. This is truly scandalous. Our meals have gotten so much worse; they're prepared lazily, as if the people in the house are sick. And you, you dress sloppily and have stopped going to the hairdresser. You know I'm not stingy or petty; I never ask for accounts, but you have to agree—eight hundred rubles is a lot of money. Besides my salary, that's all I've got. Maybe you made some good use of it. Did the money go for something serious, important?"

She stood quietly, brandishing her silent weapon: tears.

"Why are you crying? There's some logic in your tears. I repeat, I want to know what you did with the money that you didn't give Moniushko."

Elizaveta Stepanovna pulled herself together.

"You ask me to account for every kopeck."

"That's not true. You're slandering me. In the first place, I don't ask for records, and in the second, eight hundred rubles isn't kopecks. If I had extra money, I wouldn't say a word; I'd just put it in an envelope to him. I'll have to do that anyway. But I'll have to take out a loan at a Jewish rate, put the noose around my neck. But I'll manage. It's a very expensive lesson, but a lesson I'll learn from the creditors themselves, and not with you as a go-between."

Elizaveta Stepanovna was crying, but in control of herself. She felt wronged, maligned. The most basic human sense of fairness had died in her; she blamed her husband for everything.

That evening, having further deteriorated, her eyes puffy and red from crying, she went to the matches. On the way there she was worried that Schmidt might not find her attractive. It was raining relentlessly. Happy couples sat at tables out on the veranda in their autumn coats; the unhappy ones, with umbrellas and raincoats, wandered dejectedly through the wet garden.

Schmidt, with a heavy, leaden gaze, was finishing off an enormous quantity of beer. White foam had settled on his red mustache. His dull gaze wandered back and forth between his new toy, the signet ring, and Elizaveta Stepanovna. She did not take her eyes off him. There was something humiliating, doglike, about her. She did not hear the melancholy Romanian orchestra; she did not notice when two clean-shaven young men in top hats looked at her and quickly turned away, exchanging glances.

Tampio sat at the next table drinking champagne with an elderly, heavily made up woman with a double chin. He laughed loudly, opening his mouth wide, showing off his large, white, predatory teeth. A waiter approached him. He bent over politely and whispered deferentially, "Mr. Tampio, a woman is asking to see you for a minute. She's standing over there."

Tampio squinted, trying to see in the dark, wet corner of the garden, which was covered by a thin sheen of the interminable rain. He saw Maria Semenovna. She stood there, motionless, like a living anchor.

His wrinkled, overly rouged escort jealously put her gold and pearl lorgnette to her baggy eyes.

Tampio yawned and straightened the wide, dark ribbon of his derby, which was tilted to the back of his head. "Tell her I'm busy. Some other time."

The waiter hesitated, hesitated, but could not disobey. Despite his subservient nature, and accustomed to such unpleasantries, he was not himself. To return with such a cruel answer to the lonely beauty waiting patiently in the rain, pleading, her voice shaking, asking him to call the wrestler "just for a minute" . . .

On stage a scantily clad woman with large breasts and bulging eyes was singing in a rasping, affected manner about a typewriter that some little old man had broken.

The singer was a success. The public laughed drunkenly, hoarsely, sending drinks over to the girl with the large breasts.

> [*Conclusion: Ivan Aleksandrovich goes abroad, with the intention of divorcing Eliza-veta Stepanovna upon his return. When the season ends, all the wrestlers disperse, without taking their female admirers with them. Moniushko's painting* Gladiators *is "the hit of the season."*]

Sanin
Mikhail Artsybashev (1908)

ARTSYBASHEV (1878–1927) CREATED SANIN TO EMBODY YOUNG ASPIRATIONS AND RESTLESSNESS IN POST-1905 RUSSIA. UNABLE TO LIVE IN RUSSIA AFTER RETURNING FROM A BRIEF EXILE IN PARIS, AND DISILLUSIONED WITH POLITICAL ACTIVITY, THE

Translated by Percy Pinkerton (New York: Viking Press, 1926).

YOUNG ADVENTURER TURNS TO LUST AND PERVERSION TO EX-
PEND HIS CREATIVE ENERGIES. WITHOUT AN OUTLET FOR HIS
TALENTS, HE EVENTUALLY WITHERS AND COMMITS SUICIDE. THE
NOVEL GAVE POPULAR READERS THE FIRST EXPOSURE TO THE
IDEAS OF FRIEDRICH NIETZSCHE, AND PEERS SUCH AS ANASTASIA
VERBITSKAIA APPRECIATED THE FRANK DISCUSSION OF SEXUAL-
ITY. YET MUCH OF ITS HUGE SUCCESS WAS ATTRIBUTED TO
TABOO-SHATTERING SCENES SUCH AS THE FOLLOWING FROM THE
THIRD CHAPTER, WHICH DEALS WITH THE SEDUCTION OF THE
HERO'S SISTER LIDA, AND SKETCHES A RANGE OF EROTIC PAS-
SIONS, FROM THE MEN'S SENTIMENTALITY OR ANIMAL LUST, TO
LIDA'S CAPRICIOUSNESS AND PASSIVITY. FOR A LARGE PART OF
THE INTELLIGENTSIA, *SANIN* REPRESENTED THE AMORALISM AND
PORNOGRAPHY THAT POLLUTED POPULAR CULTURE. FOR DE-
CADES, *SANINSHCHINA* AND *ARTSYBASHEVSHCHINA* WERE CODE
WORDS AMONG THE INTELLIGENTSIA, INCLUDING THE BOLSHE-
VIKS, FOR VALUELESS CULTURAL EXPLOITATION.

The tones of a piano rang out with silvery clearness through the green, humid garden. The moonlight became more and more intense and the shadows harder. Crossing the grass, Sanin sat down under a linden-tree and was about to light a cigarette. Then he suddenly stopped and remained motionless, as if spellbound by the evening calm, which was not disturbed by the sounds of the piano and of this youthfully sentimental voice. They rather served to make it more complete. "Lida Petrovna!" cried Novikov hurriedly, as if this particular moment must never be lost. "Well?" asked Lida mechanically, as she looked at the garden and the moon above it and the dark boughs that stood out sharply against its silver disc. "I have long waited—that is—I have been anxious to say something to you," Novikov stammered out. Sanin turned his head round to listen. "What about?" asked Lida, absently. Sarudin had finished his song and after a pause began to sing again. He thought that he had a voice of extraordinary beauty, and he much liked to hear it. Novikov felt himself growing red, and then pale. It was as if he were going to faint.

"I—look here—Lidia Petrovna—will you be my wife?" As he stammered out these words he felt all the while that he ought to have said something very different and that his own emotions should have been different also. Before he had got the words out he was certain that the answer would be "no"; and at the same time he had an impression that something utterly silly and ridiculous was about to occur. Lida asked mechanically, "Whose wife?" Then suddenly she blushed deeply, and rose, as if intending to speak. But she said nothing and turned aside in confusion. The moonlight fell full on her features. "I love you!" stammered Novikov.

For him, the moon no longer shone; the evening air seemed stifling; the earth, he thought, would open beneath his feet.

"I don't know how to make speeches—but—no matter, I love you very much!"

("Why, very much?" he thought to himself, "as if I were alluding to ice cream.") Lida played nervously with a little leaf that had fluttered down into her hands. What she had just heard embarrassed her, being both unexpected and futile; besides, it created a novel feeling of disagreeable restraint between herself and Novikov, whom from her childhood she had always looked upon as a relative, and whom she liked. "I really don't know what to say! I had never thought about it." Novikov felt a dull pain at his heart, as if it would stop beating. Very pale, he rose and seized his cap. "Good-bye," he said, not hearing the sound of his own voice. His quivering lips were twisted into a meaningless smile "Are you going? Good-bye!" said Lida, laughing nervously and proffering her hand. Novikov grasped it hastily, and without putting on his cap strode out across the grass, into the garden. In the shade he stood still and gripped his head with both hands. "My God! I am doomed to such luck as this! Shoot myself? No, that's all nonsense! Shoot myself, eh?" Wild, incoherent thoughts flashed through his brain. He felt that he was the most wretched and humiliated and ridiculous of mortals. Sanin at first wished to call out to him, but checking the impulse, he merely smiled. To him it was grotesque that Novikov should tear his hair and almost weep because a woman whose body he desired would not surrender herself to him. At the same time he was rather glad that his pretty sister did not care for Novikov. For some moments Lida remained motionless in the same place, and Sanin's curious gaze was riveted on her white silhouette in the moonlight. Sarudin now came from the lighted drawing room on to the veranda. Sanin distinctly heard the faint jingling of his spurs. In the drawing-room Tanarov was playing an old-fashioned, mournful waltz whose languorous cadences floated on the air. Approaching Lida, Sarudin gently and deftly placed his arm round her waist. Sanin could perceive that both figures became merged into one that swayed in the misty light. "Why so pensive?" murmured Sarudin, with shining eyes, as his lips touched Lida's dainty little ear. Lida was at once joyful and afraid. Now, as on all occasions when Sarudin embraced her, she felt a strange thrill. She knew that in intelligence and culture he was her inferior, and that she could never be dominated by him; yet at the same time she was aware of something delightful and alarming in letting herself be touched by this strong, handsome young man. She seemed to be gazing down into a mysterious, unfathomable abyss, and thinking, "I could hurl myself in, if I chose."

"We shall be seen," she murmured half audibly.

Though not encouraging his embrace, she yet did not shrink from it; such passive surrender excited him the more.

"One word, just one!" whispered Sarudin, as he crushed her closer to him, his veins throbbing with desire. "Will you come?"

Lida trembled. It was not the first time that he had asked her this question, and each time she had felt strange tremors that deprived her of her will.

"Why?" she asked in a low voice, as she gazed dreamily at the moon.

"Why? That I may have you near me, and see you, and talk to you. Oh! like this, it's torture! Yes, Lida, you're torturing me! Now, will you come?"

So saying, he strained her to him, passionately. His touch as that of glowing iron, sent a thrill through her limbs; it seemed as if she were enveloped in a mist, languorous, dreamy, oppressive. Her lithe, supple frame grew rigid and then swayed towards him, trembling with pleasure and yet with fear.

Around her all things had undergone a curious, sudden change. The moon was a moon no longer; it seemed close, close to the trellis-work of the veranda, as if it hung just above the luminous lawn. The garden was not the one that she knew, but another garden, sombre, mysterious, that, suddenly approaching, closed round her. Her brain reeled. She drew back, and with strange languor, freed herself from Sarudin's embrace.

"Yes," she murmured with difficulty. Her lips were white and parched.

With faltering steps she re-entered the house, conscious of something terrible yet alluring that inexorably drew her to the brink of an abyss.

"Nonsense!" she reflected. "It's not that at all. I am only joking. It just interests me, and it amuses me, too."

Thus did she seek to persuade herself, as she stood facing the darkened mirror in her room, wherein she only saw herself *en silhouette* against the glass door of the brightly lighted dining-room. Slowly she raised both arms above her head, and lazily stretched herself, watching meanwhile the sensuous movements of her supple body. Left to himself, Sarudin stood erect and shook his shapely limbs. His eyes were half closed, and, as he smiled, his teeth shone beneath his fair moustache. He was accustomed to having luck, and on this occasion he foresaw even greater enjoyment in the near future.

He imagined Lida in all her voluptuous beauty at the very moment of surrender. The passion of such a picture caused him physical pain. At first, when he paid court to her, and after that, when she had allowed him to embrace her and kiss her, Lida had always made him feel somewhat afraid. While he caressed her, there was something strange, unintelligible in her dark eyes, as though she secretly despised him. She seemed to him so clever, so absolutely unlike other women to whom he had always felt himself obviously superior, and so proud. He looked to receive a box on the ear for a kiss. The thought of possessing her was almost disquieting.

At times he believed that she was just playing with him and his position appeared simply foolish and absurd. But to-day, after this promise, uttered hesitatingly, in faltering tones such as he had heard other women use, he felt suddenly certain of his power and that victory was near. He knew that things would be just as he had desired them to be. And to this sense of voluptuous expectancy was added a touch of spite: this proud, pure, cultured girl should surrender to him, as all the others had surrendered; he would use her at his pleasure, as he had used the rest. Scenes libidinous and debasing rose up before him. Lida nude, with hair dishevelled and inscrutable eyes, became the central figure in a turbulent orgy of cruelty and lust. Suddenly he distinctly saw her lying on the ground; he heard the swish of the whip; he observed a blood-red stripe on the soft, nude, submissive body. His temples throbbed, he staggered backwards, sparks danced before his eyes. The thought of it all became physically intolerable. His hand shook as he lit a cigarette—again his strong limbs twitched convulsively, and he went indoors. Sanin, who had heard nothing yet who had seen and comprehended all, followed him, roused almost to a feeling of jealousy. "Brutes like that are always lucky," he thought to himself. "What the devil does it all mean? Lida and he?"

The Keys to Happiness
Anastasia Verbitskaia (1913)

ANASTASIA VERBITSKAIA IGNITED A CULTURAL FUROR WITH HER NOVEL *THE KEYS TO HAPPINESS*, PUBLISHED IN SIX VOLUMES BE-TWEEN 1908 AND 1913. SOMETHING OF A MILD-MANNERED FEMI-NIST BEFORE THE 1905 REVOLUTION, SHE LATER MADE A SPIR-ITED STAND AGAINST THE MALE CRITICS WHO DERIDED HER ROMANTIC ADVENTURES FEATURING STRONG HEROINES. *KEYS* WAS THE BEST-READ AND MOST CONTROVERSIAL NOVEL IN FIN DE SIÈCLE RUSSIA, AND THE FILM VERSION OF THE MOVIE BE-CAME THE COUNTRY'S FIRST BLOCKBUSTER. IT TELLS THE STORY OF MANYA ELTSOVA, A BRILLIANT DANCER WHO STRUGGLES WITH THE PHYSICAL PASSION SHE FEELS FOR SEVERAL MEN BE-CAUSE SHE WANTS TO OVERCOME CARNAL LUST AND DEDICATE HER LIFE INSTEAD TO ART. THE ILLEGITIMATE DAUGHTER OF AN INSANE WOMAN, MANYA HERSELF GIVES BIRTH OUT OF WED-LOCK, AND SHOWS SIGNS OF HAVING INHERITED HER MOTHER'S MADNESS. THE KEYS IN THE BOOK'S TITLE ELUDE HER BECAUSE SHE PROVES UNABLE TO CONTROL HER DESIRES. THE PASSAGE BELOW CAPTURES THE ESSENCE OF VERBITSKAIA'S CONTROVER-SIAL APPROACH TO SEX. THIS SCENE, IN WHICH MANYA'S THIRD AND MOST DESTRUCTIVE LOVER, THE REACTIONARY NELIDOV, TAKES HER AGAINST HER WILL, AROUSED MORE THAN NERVOUS

Anastasiia Verbitskaia, *Kliuchi schastia. Sovremennyi roman* (Moscow: I. N. Kushnerev, 1909–1913), vol. 2, pp. 34–38.

TITTERING; IT PROVIDED A VIVID REMINDER OF THE LACK OF CONTROL MOST RUSSIAN WOMEN ENJOYED OVER THEIR LIVES. YET THE OMINOUS NOTE UPON WHICH SHE BEGAN THIS AFFAIR WOULD HAUNT HER THE REST OF HER LIFE. WHEN SHE AND NELIDOV BOTH TAKE THEIR OWN LIVES AT THE END OF VOLUME SIX BECAUSE THEY CANNOT RECONCILE THEIR LOVE-HATE RELATIONSHIP, THEIR ACTIONS DEEPEN THE AMBIGUITY SURROUNDING THEIR FIRST ENCOUNTER: WAS IT RAPE, OR HAD MANYA WANTED TO BE DEVASTED BY DESIRE ALL ALONG?

Manya again fell silent. Once more she spent whole days sitting in the gazebo. But this was not the slow withering away of a fading soul. In the quiet and solitude, the regal white lily of her first love bloomed gloriously.

Everything that Jan had filled her slumbering soul with had been sleeping there till now, in the secret depths; all of Shteinbakh's dark passion, and the witchcraft of sensuality. All this awakened now with one look from him for whom her soul had been waiting.

There was no past. It had died. Life began only now. Jan and she . . . The jingle of a single chain. The very same happiness. The same radiance. But there was a black hole between the two of them—an abyss from which someone else's pale face looked back at her.

Manya stared at the road for hours and waited. Her eyes were like stars, big and thirsty, piercing the distance, calling, promising. And *he* came again. How could he not come, when her entire soul, every fiber of her body, called him and waited!

Nelidov arrived in a small carriage that he was driving himself. The spectacular autumn evening beckoned them to stroll. The sunset was blinding. Manya rushed out of the gazebo, into the courtyard, like a whirlwind. The barking dogs flung themselves at the carriage. Sonya flung open the window and looked down.

What happiness! They were alone. Manya quietly nodded her head. With blazing eyes and a bright smile, Nelidov greeted her, taking off his English riding cap.

"What a magnificent animal!" whispered Manya, rubbing the horse's neck. The horse snorted nervously and nipped at her scarlet sweater.

"Do you like horses?" asked Nelidov. His voice shook; his tone was strange, as if he were saying, "Do you love me?"

"Madly!" answered Manya. Her voice burned with recognition.

He understood. They stood there silently, heads down, bewildered. The deeper meaning of this trivial conversation was clear to both of them. He struggled to maintain control of himself. It was as if the ground were floating beneath him.

"Maybe you'd like to go for a drive?" he whispered through parched lips.

She heard the words. What was in them? His voice called her to the Unknown and the Inevitable. To fate's hidden paths.

"Yes!" She raised her eyelashes. Oh, what eyes! So many promises in them! Again they stood side by side, not moving, shaken. Both were pale and mute—not sure of what to do next, of how to proceed.

Sonya rescued them. She walked up and greeted the guest.

"Come have some tea! Petro will take the horse. They're putting on the samovar now."

"Pardon . . . Mademoiselle Eltsova wants to take a drive—that is, if your mother doesn't object?"

"Oh, of course. You'll be back in an hour? Where are you going, Manya? At least put on your sweater. Take my scarf!"

Like a sleepwalker, Manya slid out of the carriage and followed Sonya to the house.

When the carriage drove out of the gates of the estate, accompanied by the noisy barking of dogs, Sonya stood on the porch and watched after them. A subconscious uneasiness scratched at her heart, like a mouse.

The horse trotted quickly along the familiar road. The steppe embraced them in its green arms, grand and silent. They closed their mouths. The wind blew into their flushed faces and swirled up the dust on the road. They were both looking so fixedly into their own souls that for a long time they did not notice the silence. It was crowded in the carriage. They were sitting shoulder to shoulder, thigh to thigh. This touching inflamed Nelidov. His consciousness was growing foggy. His knees shook. He feared that she could feel it.

"Wait! Wait!" an internal voice said to him. "Just another minute—until we're in the woods."

The forest drifted up to meet them. Dark and cold, so heavy and somber—Likhoi Gai. The road gradually led into a ravine.

At last! Guided by a familiar hand, the horse walked onward. On one side, the forest. On the other, a steep clay wall.

Alone. With a sigh of exhaustion, Nelidov turned to Manya. He took her hands in his. How painful! A cry froze on her lips. Something caught in his throat. What could he say to her? He had never been so weak, such a slave to his desires. No matter! At this moment he was prepared to pay with his life.

She looked into his cruel eyes with a fear of happiness. A cry, a startling cry of joy and pain, suddenly burst out of her. She fell on his chest. Her impulse decided everything for both of them.

He kissed her in silence, greedily, rapaciously, like a wild animal. Crudely, roughly, almost primitively, he fondled her shoulders, breast, knees; with one stroke, his blind and powerful passion destroyed that which had separated them even yesterday, even today. What was this dark power controlling his behavior, when only a week ago he was unaware of this girl's existence? She was created for him. He had understood this from the first moment. Hadn't he been living like a monk for almost two years, waiting for this meeting? Had he not guarded his soul for this first love?

Manya was stupefied, overwhelmed. She lay weakly with her head on his shoulder, her eyes closed. Her hands fell helplessly on her knees, the rosy palms upward. She had not expected this. Had not wanted this. She was crushed by these passionate, coarse, foreign caresses. Something protested, crying out weakly, in her soul. Was this really necessary? Now? So soon?

He gathered her in his arms, like a hunter's prey, and walked into the forest. Like a slave she succumbed to his desires. She was submissive, impassive. It seemed to her that he wanted to crush her in his embraces. This was not love, but rather some kind of blind hatred. But what could she do! Even if he had suffocated her, she would not have lifted a finger to stop him.

It grew dark. He came to himself. Without a word, he extended his hand and led her to the road.

She waited; she trembled as she awaited his first words. But the silence lasted a long time. Manya's heart was scarcely beating. So cold! God, how cold! She shivered.

Suddenly he dropped the reins and clasped her shoulders. At last! cried her soul. She hid her face in his chest. Her burning tears fell like a spring rain, they were so heavy. She felt no shame or repentance. Her protests drowned in profound compassion. He was dear and close to her, as if she had known him for decades.

"Marie, Marie," he whispered and kissed her hot face, her wet temples. "Forgive me! I couldn't help myself. I don't know how it happened. Don't despise me. I'm ashamed of myself."

"No, no! Hush!" she cried furiously and put her fingers on his lips. He kissed them. More, still more . . . Unconsciously he bit them. His blood still boiled. He had not sated his agonizing desire. Oh, if only he could suspend everything else and be alone with her for another hour . . .

But night had fallen, and people were waiting for them.

He took her head in both his hands and kissed her lips. He pressed them so hard that he drew blood. Manya cried out in agony.

"Oh, forgive me! I'm losing my mind."

"Never mind, it's all right!" she said quickly and stroked his hand. Tears welled in her eyes.

The carriage stopped at the gates to the estate. Nelidov silently, hastily kissed Manya's hand. He had burned out completely. He was cold and did not even promise to return tomorrow. For a long time she listened to the sound of the wheels on the road.

Of course it was good that he was gone. After such moments can one really dine, carry on a banal conversation? If only he'd said one kind word, and not continued speaking to her so politely, so distantly. If only he'd given her one shy kiss, tender, as Jan and Shteinbakh kissed her.

Sonya's white figure suddenly emerged from the darkness.

"Manya, is that you? We've been waiting. You didn't— Why are you crying, dear?"

Throwing her arms around her friend's neck, Manya sobbed on her breast. She wept as passionately as a rich man who had been robbed in his sleep and awakened a beggar.

The Vanquished
A Conclusion to A. Verbitskaia's "Keys to Happiness"
Count Amori (1912)

THE MAN WHO WROTE *SECRETS OF THE JAPANESE COURT* OR *SLAVE TO PASSION* COULD HARDLY ACCUSE VERBITSKAIA OF POR-NOGRAPHY, BUT THE IRREPRESSIBLE IPPOLIT RAPGOF, WHO WROTE SERIAL NOVELS AND SCREENPLAYS (ONE INCLUDED IN THIS ANTHOLOGY) UNDER THE PSEUDONYM "COUNT AMORI," VOICED THE CONCERNS OF MANY CRITICS OVER MANYA ELTSO-VA'S SEXUAL AUTONOMY. HE MADE A COTTAGE INDUSTRY OF RE-WRITING *THE KEYS TO HAPPINESS;* THE PASSAGE BELOW AP-PEARED AFTER THE THIRD OF VERBITSKAIA'S SIX VOLUMES. HERE, HIS HERO IS SHTEINBAKH, THE SENSITIVE AND SENSUAL MALE WHO UNDERSTANDS TRUE FREEDOM AND MANYA BETTER THAN SHE DOES HERSELF. IT IS SHTEINBAKH RATHER THAN NELIDOV WHO DIES, AND MANYA ENDS UP IN AN INSANE ASYLUM. RAPGOF WROTE AT LEAST TWO OTHER SUCH NOVELS, SUCCESS-FUL ENOUGH TO HAVE FOOLED AT LEAST A FEW READERS.

(From Shteinbakh's diary) I sense that she hasn't forgotten Nelidov. Despite all her struggling for Freedom, for Beauty, she longs for shackles. She is like St. Vincent, weeping over her lost chains.[1] She thirsts for new torments, new degradations. She wants a powerful and rough force, callous and cruel, to make her fragile body an object of ridicule. This would bring her agonizingly sweet sufferings, and in this misery she would seek the renewal of her soul.

I read Jan's book again. It's strange, as though a veil has slid from my eyes. Only now can I see how deeply mistaken I was to accept his teachings as true, not to analyze what this idealist was preaching. How well I understand him now—he was a maniac for *freedom*. But can any person truly be free? Does it stand to reason that *everything* must be sacrificed to this freedom, in the name of infinitely fickle soulful fancies? "Secret, inviting voices draw us. Follow their alluring enticement. Re-

---

Pobezhdennye: Roman s poslesloviem grafa Amori (Okonchanie romana *Kliuchi schast'ia* A. Verbitskoi) (St. Petersburg: Gerol'd, 1912), pp. 5–11.

1. The word Rapgof uses here, *veriga,* refers to a special kind of chain used by ascetics as a form of penance.

nounce your family, your close friends, *your children;* don't be faint-hearted, and follow the voice of passion and dreams."

Thus spake Jan, and in this he saw *the path to freedom.*[2]

Oh, how mistaken he was! Tearing off the chains [*veriga*] of one masochistic relationship, he thought up new, more brutal ones for himself, in the name of new idols of thought. *Freedom*—the marvelous sound of dreams troubled my peace in my youth, those years when everything in me was exploding forward, forward, toward dimly perceptible ideals, when only in the world of sounds could I find a place to express the most elusive vibrations of my soul. For hours I would sit in a dark room, giving my entire being over to my best friend, my piano, and with it all sorrows and hopes for a bright future.

Much in my life was charmed, but even more was filled with disappointments. When I encountered ideal types among women, rarely did their internal and external selves correspond. I almost never met freedom-loving women. Only Manya tore herself up in the name of freedom. At least she was convinced that she was following the path to freedom, and that by taking this circuitous route she would reach that lofty tower from which the whole world is visible, and all the individual personalities would seem petty and insignificant.

But is freedom truly attainable? Even the utopians struggle vainly in their works to create freedom in principle. As long as people refuse to repudiate their bodies, don't stop feeding themselves, don't stop experiencing physical lust, as long as all of the body's demands do not seem to them expendable, people will not surrender the chains that bind their will. A person is to a large degree an animal. The need for food and the satisfaction of bodily functions remain questions of life. A normal person, under natural circumstances, will inevitably strive to satisfy his or her physical demands. The more complicated the organism's psyche, the sharper the intellectual and spiritual forces, the more refined the tastes. Cheap food and bad wine cannot satisfy me. A woman who has decided that she will try to arouse me must reckon with my mood. I can be cold as ice or burn like a flame. All depends on my mood. Happy are those men—I always envy them—who can sate their appetites as easily as animals do. I need to be in the right mood even to eat. I can feel instinctively when a woman is rebuffing my advances. It is very difficult for a woman to conceal her desires successfully. Her longings are obvious, palpable. But a few women try to suppress their desires while at the same time trying to excite men. Nothing irritates me more than this sort of game. Once I almost killed a Spanish woman who caressed me, kissed me with parted lips, pressed herself against me, but then quickly turned away when she felt the surge of passion within me. How often I see Manya bursting with desire for me, but thoughts about her Dream, about Freedom, intrude, and she reverts to her new self. Tears, or perhaps an expression of cold indifference, appear on her face. A glassy veil covers her eyes, and she moves away from me, far, far away.

---

2. Rapgof claims to be quoting from the first volume of Verbitskaia's *Keys*.

Do You Remember?

Director: Petr Chardynin; Script: Count Amori

Song lyrics and catalogue libretto for a silent film (1915)

THE FOLLOWING SCENARIO IS FOR ONE OF MANY SALON MELO-
DRAMAS OF THE AGE INSPIRED BY A POPULAR SONG (THIS ONE
WRITTEN BY A CLASSICAL COMPOSER, YULY BLEIKHMAN). THE
FILM PLOT, FULL OF HEAVY SENTIMENTALISM AND ENDING IN A
TRAGEDY CAUSED BY SEDUCTION AND INFIDELITY, WAS STAN-
DARD FOR THE TIME, AND WORKED FOR AUDIENCES UP TO THE
OCTOBER REVOLUTION. DIRECTED BY PETR CHARDYNIN, IT
STARRED VERA KORALLI, IVAN MOZZHUKHIN, AND CHARDYNIN
(AS THE WIFE, LOVER, AND HUSBAND RESPECTIVELY).

Ты помнишь-ли что обещала,	Do you remember what you promised,
Ты помнишь-ли былые дни,	Do you remember what we had,
Когда нас ласка опьяняла,	Intoxicated by caresses
В объятиях сладостной любви?	In the embraces of sweet love?
О возврати мне наслажденья!	Oh, return that rapture to me!
Лобзаний жаждет сердце вновь,	My heart desires your kiss anew.
О, пусть с восторгом упоенья	Oh, may the ecstasy of abandon
Вернется прежняя любовь!	Come back with the love we knew!
Ты помнишь-ли, когда, прощаясь,	Do you remember how we parted,
С тобою разставался я,	When I bade farewell to you,
От поцелуя отрываясь,	Tearing myself from your kisses,
Опять желал обнять тебя?	I wished to hold you once again?
О, возврати мне наслажденья!	Oh, preserve for us this rapture!
Лобзаний жаждет сердце вновь,	Your love's the dearest thing I know!
О, сохрани все упоенья!	Oh, return that rapture to me!
Мне дорога твоя любовь!	My heart desires your kiss anew,

The aging writer Lev Nalsky is madly in love with his young wife. His heart belongs only to her and their baby daughter, Netty. His whole life is devoted to these
two beings, and without them he knows no joy. Life holds no other attraction.

However, sometimes when his gaze comes to rest on his wife's youthful face, he

Zonophone, *Sbornik libretto dlia plastinok Zonofon: opery, operetki, romansy, piesni, razskazy i pr.* (Vilna: I. I.
Pirozhnikov, 1910–1912) 1:146; *Iz istorii kino,* 3 (Moscow, 1960): 91–93.

catches himself thinking that he is too old for her. Elena Nalsky laughs at this thought until the day she meets the violinist Yaron at an evening gathering. Several years before, Yaron and Elena had studied together in the conservatory, and he had courted her. Something like a strong attraction had developed. But with his sudden departure from the country, all had abated and faded. Elena, an inexperienced young girl, had accepted Nalsky's proposal. She became his wife; a daughter was born. It seemed as if Elena had forgotten her youthful romance. But suddenly all the details of these beautiful pages of her young life spring up before her. Seeing Elena sparkling with youth and beauty, Yaron is as attracted to her as before, and to the sounds of Bleikhman's romance "Do You Remember?" Elena reexperiences everything that once made her heart flutter.

Nalsky sees the sudden change in his wife and undergoes untold suffering, but he is too noble and loves Elena too much to spoil her mood with the slightest sound or word. When Elena comes home from Yaron's, full of the radiant happiness that mutual love can engender, Nalsky asks nary a question and does not shower her with reproaches. No, he only gives her freedom, the freedom of youth and beauty. Nalsky understands clearly that his days of happiness have passed, and he does not think he has the right to block Elena's road to happiness.

Summoned by a letter from Yaron, who awaits her in Petrograd, Elena departs on Christmas Eve. Netty spends the holy night of Christmas with her father. The child, not understanding the full tragedy of what has happened, takes joy as always in the Christmas tree and the holiday. But suddenly she falls quiet and presses against her father.

"What's wrong, Netty?" he asks.

"It's no fun without Mama," the girl whispers in response. United by their feelings for the woman who has left them, Nalsky and Netty say a prayer for her while the Christmas bells toll.

Meanwhile Elena, completely enslaved by the emotion gripping her, hurries toward her radiant, inevitable joy. A powerful, raging blizzard has covered all the rail lines. Before it has traveled twenty versts, the train is forced to stop at a small station. While the road is being cleared, Elena walks out on the platform and paces impatiently in anticipation of the moment the train will be cleared to go. The stationmaster graciously invites her to come in and warm herself. Elena accepts the invitation, and finds herself in a modest dining room where the simple, merry, sincere laughter of guests and children lighting a Christmas tree reigns.

A bell rings in the neighboring village. All bow their heads reverently.

"Merry Christmas," the host says, and he lovingly embraces his children and young wife.

The sight of this simple, guileless happiness acts so strongly on Elena that it is as if she is reborn. Where is she going? To what mirage? Did she really dare to leave her husband and child? She could have been just as happy as the elderly man and his young wife on this holy night. Elena's strained condition reaches its apogee: the poor woman is rent by sobbing. The sensitive-hearted stationmaster's wife understands the problem, and demands no explanation. Tenderly and gently she comforts Elena, without a question, without pressing her for explanations. And under the influence of her quiet tenderness, Elena calms down and resolves to return.

"The road is cleared, you can go on," announces the stationmaster as he enters.

But smiling through her tears, Elena shakes her head. No, she won't be going farther; she will return home.

It is almost dawn when Elena drives up to her house. Reconciled, radiant with joy, and loving her husband and child in a new way, she enters her husband's dark study, where he is sprawled on an armchair in the dying light of the fireplace. "The poor man, he's fallen asleep," whispers Elena; she'll wake him right away with a kiss. Elena leans over him, but instantly jumps back. Only weak breathing struggles from his chest. A revolver lies darkly on the floor. She picks it up mechanically, puts it on the table, and, still gripped by horror, notices a letter. It is Nalsky's farewell to his old mother. From these lines, filled with his selfless love for Elena, she discovers that even on the threshold of death, Nalsky feared wounding her with reproach.

The Wrath of Dionysus
E. A. Nagrodskaia (1910)

EUDOKIA NAGRODSKAIA (1866–1930) HAD A CAREER AS SENSATIONAL AS IT WAS BRIEF. SHE GREW UP IN INTELLECTUAL SURROUNDINGS: HER MOTHER, A. IA. PANAEVA, WAS A WELL-KNOWN SALON HOSTESS AND MISTRESS TO THE POET N. A. NEKRASOV, WITH WHOM NAGRODSKAIA'S FATHER, APOLLON GOLOVACHEV, WORKED AT THE INFLUENTIAL "THICK" JOURNAL *CONTEMPORARY* (*SOVREMENNIK*). NAGRODSKAIA WROTE BITS FOR THE AMUSEMENT OF HER FRIENDS, WHO PERSUADED HER TO PUBLISH HER FIRST NOVEL IN 1910. *THE WRATH OF DIONYSUS* WAS A SPECTACULAR SUCCESS, SELLING OUT TEN EDITIONS OVER THE NEXT SIX YEARS. LIKE VERBITSKAIA, NAGRODSKAIA BROUGHT UP TABOO TOPICS SUCH AS ILLICIT LOVE, FEMALE SEXUALITY, AND HOMOSEXUALITY, WHICH PROMPTED MANY TO CRY "PORNOGRA-

From *The Wrath of Dionysus* [*Gnev Dionisusa*], trans. and ed. Louise McReynolds (Bloomington and Indianapolis: Indiana University Press, 1997), pp. 180–189.

PHY!" NONE OF HER OTHER WORKS GENERATED SUCH AN IMPAS-
SIONED RESPONSE, PERHAPS BECAUSE THE CRITICS HAD ALREADY
DISMISSED HER. NAGRODSKAIA HAD BEGUN WRITING MOVIE LI-
BRETTOS WHEN THE REVOLUTION CAME. SHE AND HER HUSBAND
EMIGRATED TO NORTHERN FRANCE, WHERE SHE APPARENTLY
STOPPED WRITING.

THE FOLLOWING EXCERPT IS FROM THE BOOK'S CLIMAX, WHEN
LATCHINOV, A HOMOSEXUAL FRIEND OF TATA — OUR HEROINE
AND NARRATOR — TELLS HER HIS THEORY OF SEXUALITY. HIS HY-
POTHESIS EXPLAINS BOTH HER FEELINGS AND HER BEHAVIOR
WITH REMARKABLE CANDOR.

"This is our last siesta," I said to Latchinov. "Tomorrow I'll be taking mine alone.
Frankly, Alexander Vikentevich, this is terribly difficult for me. You're the only person to whom I don't have to lie. I've grown so accustomed to you, I value our friendship so. . . ."

Tears began streaming from my eyes.

"I don't know what we did to deserve your friendship. We put you through so
much aggravation, straining your nerves. Anyone else would have brushed us aside.
More than that, I think that Stark owes his life and his sanity to you. He loves you
so, admires you, is devoted to you."

"Tatiana Alexandrovna, stop talking about Stark. Let's talk about you in this last
hour that we'll have together alone."

"What's there to say about me, Alexander Vikentevich? As far as I'm concerned,
my life is over—I no longer think about myself. I will live for the child, and these
two people who, to my misfortune, love me. I believe no woman has ever found
herself in a situation like mine. My life has turned out very strange and unnatural."

Latchinov suddenly interrupted me. "Tatiana Alexandrovna, do you want me to
tell you now what I've long wanted to, my theory?"

"All right, Alexander Vikentevich."

"You just said that no other woman has found herself in this situation, in which
life turned out so peculiar, unnatural. But the point is, that you're a *woman*. Put
yourself in a man's place and the problem sorts itself out, everything becomes
normal.

"Really, tens—what am I saying?—hundreds, thousands of men live like that.
They undergo precisely what you have. Let's suppose for a minute that you're a
man, and we'll retell your story: you're married, living quietly and happily with an
unusually intelligent and kind wife. Your love is good, solid, 'conscious.' You devote
yourself completely to your art, and your wife doesn't bother you. She's a bit bour-

geois and can't always understand the demands of your artistic nature, but you know that she loves you faithfully—she lives for you, protects your tranquility, respects your occupation, your tastes and habits.

"Then suddenly you meet another woman—stunning, captivating, smart, passionate! This woman is in love with you, and she doesn't hide her feelings. She says things to you that your dear, meek little wife never would. She promises a world of delights. Her beauty is so extraordinary, her lust—infectious. What man could resist her? And you don't!

"You struggle with yourself, you suffer. You haven't stopped loving your wife, but 'the other woman' is everything—desire, beauty, poetry. But at the same time, she's a lovely despot who wants to possess you completely. Your body is not enough for her—she demands your soul. It doesn't matter that you've sacrificed your wife and family, she wants your art. You can't accept this. The tears begin, the scenes, all those things that men can't stand. You start growing cool to her. The tears and scenes double, triple. You're ready to break it all off, to run away, when suddenly a baby appears. You love it. Here the situation becomes different. Now you have to recognize that your love is stronger and more passionate than a man's would be in this situation.

"You yourself gave birth. For purely physiological reasons Stark could not have given birth for you. But if he could. . . .

"Yes, you love the baby. You pity it. This pity for the child and its mother supersedes all other feelings, and you decide to sacrifice both your art and your wife. But when you see your wife, the earlier emotions grip you with renewed intensity. What's more, you also see the possibility of devoting yourself to art again as before.

"Add to this that, because of extraneous circumstances, your wife has remained alone. You don't have the heart to break up with her, so you give up the other woman . . . and you do so cheerfully. This consoles you, except that you don't get custody of the baby. The attachment to the child keeps growing, and you realize that the peace and happiness of this child can only be bought at one price: getting back together with the mother, who is again alluring you with her beauty. To return to her means to kill your dear, devoted wife. Yet alienating her means sacrificing the child. You agonize, vacillate, and search for a compromise. . . . This story is banal, very common for tens of thousands of men."

"But I am a woman, Alexander Vikentevich," I said.

"No, Tatiana Alexandrovna, you are a *man*. You only have the body of a woman. You're feminine, soft, and gracious—but you're still a man. If one looks at you as a woman, your character appears quite original and complex. But as a man, you're plain and simple. A good man, poetic, with an amorous, sensitive disposition, but decent and kind—even though a little coarse, like all men. Have you ever paid attention to how you swear? My dear, you curse like a sailor. I'll never forget the time in Petersburg, during the white nights, we were walking along the embankment. You were in a melancholy, poetic mood. You were so sweet and tender. You recited to me, 'Look over there, at the end of the path; the shrubs are spread out in nighttime beauty; They've taken the shape of night fairies. . . .' At that moment a cabbie ran into us. 'Where do you think you're going, you oaf!' you hollered at him, and then continued softly, 'Beloved, you don't understand my melancholy.' How I wanted to burst out laughing! But you were so absorbed in the verse, the poetry around us, that I didn't want to destroy your mood.

"Remember how often in our long conversations we've discussed your masculine characteristics, how in childhood, when we all had terrible crushes, you only fell in love with women. You understand and appreciate feminine beauty and paint women as though spellbound. During our conversations in your studio, I listened closely; you evaluate women strictly from a man's perspective. Remember the French girl that your sculptor friend brought over? You watched her walk out and said, 'She's too made-up and no longer young, but I understand why he fell head-over-heels for her. There's something strangely attractive about her.' You should have been a lesbian."

"Alexander Vikentevich!"

"Calm down, my dear. The word frightens you, not the idea. You didn't become one simply because of your upbringing, circumstances, and gentility. Before you met Stark, your inclinations were still latent and didn't set you down this path. Besides, this never entered your head. You didn't know you had a 'secret.'

"Kismet led you to Stark. Here I find a truly remarkable coincidence, a kind of diabolical joke, because Stark is exactly among men what you are among women. Strong, courageous, he has more of a female nature than you do. There's nothing masculine in your appearance, whereas Stark's body, his manners are more refined and delicate than most men's. Most people consider femininity in a man unbecoming, but look at how everyone is attracted to Stark. Even people with completely opposite personalities like him. And his love for the child? Is this really a father's love? No, he's the mother, and a most passionate mother. Before he met you, overwhelmed by his ardent temperament, he chased one woman after another but then walked away angry, morally unsatiated. It might be strange that fate brought you together, but there's nothing surprising in how you threw yourselves at each other, despite all obstacles. It would have been more unusual if that had not happened. You would never have felt such passion for another man, nor he for another woman. You're a lucky woman, my dear."

I sat there just listening to Latchinov, recognizing the element of truth in what he said.

"But I could never be a lesbian, never!" I exclaimed.

"You're lucky that you never became aware of your secret, as it would have caused tremendous anguish. It would have pulled at you like wine does a drunkard. If you'd had to struggle with it, with your sense of morality, you would have fallen into despair. Your luck is that you never figured it out—and you met Stark. I repeat, you're a lucky woman."

"If your theory is correct, Alexander Vikentevich, then Stark didn't realize that he could have been happy with Baron Z."

"No, Tatiana Alexandrovna. There's a subtle difference. Women can love another woman, but men . . . it's not easy to explain this, but Baron Z. could have only aroused disgust and ridicule in Stark."

I said nothing.

"Such is my theory. Many people in this world have changed their sex. Some know this, others don't even suspect it. I don't know whether my theory is true or false, but if you accept it, you won't have to agonize trying to figure yourself out."

He stopped talking for a minute, then began again, smiling, "Maybe I have surprised you for now, but I feel terribly ill. I realize that this is the beginning of the end. I recently went to the doctor and demanded the truth about my health. Aesculapius said that if he performs the operation immediately, I'll live a long time. If not, I'll have only six months at most."

"Alexander Vikentevich! You agreed to the operation?!"

"No, my friend. The doctor has promised me an end without suffering, and I wouldn't give up the opportunity to terminate as quickly as possible this mess that we call life."

I wanted to talk, to beg him, but my voice betrayed me. I simply took his slender hands, with their beautiful rings, and squeezed them sadly. He looked at me with the same expression that I had seen only once before, that unforgettable night that Stark took the baby away. That night he held me on the bed, and said, "My poor dear. Pity them. I think they need you more than you realize. If not for them, I wouldn't have kept you here. I don't have poison or a revolver; I would have taken you to the rocks above the sea. But I know that your life is necessary for others."

At last I was able to speak. "Stay alive, if only for us. You've always lived for other people."

"My dear, I'm so tired that I just want peace. Don't call me back to life. I wanted to die back there, in Rome."

I lifted my head and, surprised and depressed, looked at his face, which still looked so sweet, yet melancholy. He gently stroked my head.

"Do you remember the day when Stark posed for you for the last time? How happy he was?"

I nodded.

"Well, that very day, when I got home, I wanted to kill myself."

"Why, why?" I asked him dejectedly.

He pensively stroked my head.

"My dearest friend! It's true, that among all my acquaintances, I've never loved any as I do you. I myself don't know why. You alone make me want to say things that I never thought I would tell anyone, ever. I attribute the fact that I want to talk to my illness, my weakness. My days are numbered, and I don't want to take anything earthly with me 'there.' For some reason, I believe that there's something 'there.' Of course, not heaven or hell, but I cannot believe that my thoughts, memory, and imagination will disappear with my body. That seems terribly stupid to me—that's the word I want, stupid.

"You see, Tata—let me call you that—I've become chatty, like all who are senile or dying. But I can't, I don't want to take with me the things that made me either happy or sad. I loved Stark madly, Tata, a thousand times more than you did. I see how surprised you are, but I want to tell you everything. You didn't know your 'secret,' but I've been aware of mine since childhood. I wanted to be 'pure,' and this was my torture. As a child, in my naive infatuations, like you I went for those of my own sex. But you switched your attraction to the opposite sex, while I always remained with men. When they sent me to one of the privileged boarding schools, and I saw the perversion among boys of my age, I shrank away in terror. I had good, intelligent parents; they gave me a moral upbringing, and therefore I recoiled from these boys. But much later, when I became an adult, I became horrified when I realized that female beauty had no effect on my emotions. Only the beautiful bodies of youths attracted me. I began trying to court women with a vengeance, involved myself in liaisons, lived with them, purchased them for a day. I was afraid of myself, ashamed of myself. It was the most horrible time of my life.

"I took these women like a disgusting medicine, which I hoped would cure me of my sickness, my shame. I experienced everything that a normal person would do if forced to engage in perversion. I tried to work, to go into government service. But work and service are productive only when they satisfy a thirst for money or ambition. I already had too much of the former and none of the latter.

"I threw myself into science, into art. But science was too easy for me and art . . . it spoke about love, and at times, sorrow. I tried physical labor. I lived in a Tolstoyan colony for two years.[1] I gave a third of my estate to the peasants. I tried to concentrate on my soul, but my body spoke louder and louder.

"At this point, my parents began to insist on marriage. They even found me a fiancée. One of my father's friends, Prince Ukolov, died ruined, heavily in debt. His daughter, Princess Varvara, was literally out on the street when my mother took her in. I refused this union point blank. Could I ruin the life of an innocent eighteen-year-old simply to please my parents? But this girl herself came to my study, where I'd retired following a row with mother, and said, 'I heard your conversation; I was eavesdropping. You don't love me, nor I you. You're afraid of destroying my life, but as far as I'm concerned, you could make me happy. I'm not especially pretty, and I'm poor. Who would marry me? A derelict? I want wealth and freedom. Your parents want to continue the line. Fine. We'll try to give them an heir. I think two would be sufficient, in case one dies. If they're girls, then we'll stipulate that when they marry, they'll keep your family name—at the least, they'll take a double surname. And then we won't bother each other.'

"Stunned, I looked at this slender girl, who appeared so chaste and innocent. 'You aren't mistaken,' she said quietly. 'I am completely virginal. But I'm not stupid. I know that I have to think about my future, and I've always wanted to be rich.'

"Then I told her that I don't like women in general. 'Are you really a . . . ?' She spoke the Greek word—although it didn't apply to me directly—with singular composure. 'Never mind. I know you can still have children.'

---

1. Several of Lev Tolstoi's more fanatical disciples established semi-utopian colonies, where members lived according to the master's ideals of Christian anarchism. Not surprisingly, these anti-statist colonies often ran afoul of the tsarist government.

"She gave me a thought: what if I have children and find through them a meaning to life? So I agreed. But this hope was never realized. My wife threw herself into social life with such reckless abandon, that after she gave birth prematurely to a stillborn baby, the doctor told her she could never again conceive. When I visited her after the birth, she told me, 'I've wronged you, Alexander. I didn't do my part properly, and it looks like I seduced you into a bad bargain. Can this be corrected? Can you impregnate another woman, and I'll simulate pregnancy and birth?'

'That would be a crime,' I answered her. 'Your conscientiousness is carrying you away. Let us accept the situation.'

"We lived together under the same roof for many years, meeting for dinner and to receive guests. We went to the theater and visited friends together. We enjoyed chatting in the evenings. She was dry, far from stupid, and I liked her malicious mind. You could call us a compatible pair.

"Did she have affairs? I don't know. No one ever said anything about her. But in society, I often met men to whom I felt a sudden attraction. What could I do? If I opened myself up to a woman, confessing my passion for her, and she did not want to return these feelings, she could still think about my rash declaration with a contemptuous smile, or perhaps even an involuntary sigh. But a young man? a proper youth? He would run from me with disgust and fear—at the very least with laughter, that same laughter Stark howled when remembering the baron.

"Tata, Tata, you're so lucky that you did not understand yourself when happenstance led you to Stark. Fate corrected this 'mistake' of nature; it didn't want to deprive you of the happy experience of shared passions."

Latchinov reflected for a moment, then continued.

"After my wife's unsuccessful pregnancy, I gave up and began to travel. And for the first time I met those creatures called 'queens.'[2] They repelled me more than women did. I wanted to love Ganymede,[3] Antinous,[4] but I saw before me caricatures of the women from whom I'd run away. This imitation, the women's dresses and wigs, revolted me; I wanted divine youth! What's more, I didn't want what they were proposing to me. I wanted to prostrate myself before a beautiful body, before the proud face of a demigod. I wanted to forget myself, caress my idol into oblivion, expecting only kisses and caresses from him. I wanted friendship, more sweet than love, and poetry in my devotion. . . .

"But these warped creatures, these painted dolls tried to sell me something else. They didn't understand the ancient cults, they knew only the vulgar customs of the Orient, inspired by the shortage of women. I fled from them with more disgust than I did from their female counterparts.

"Then I met an American, Johnny. He was also one of those miserable imperson-

---

2. The French word he uses is *chattes,* female cats.

3. Ganymede was a beautiful boy kidnapped by other gods to serve as Zeus's cupbearer and lover.

4. In another reference to the *Odyssey,* Antinous was one of Penelope's suitors when Odysseus was away fighting the Trojan War.

ators, but more clever than the others. He understood what I wanted and tricked me—or I fooled myself. He was an avaricious, capricious, intolerable creature, but I loved him for two years. He grew bored with me. He couldn't pretend forever that he enjoyed the cloistered life, with books, music. . . . In my naiveté I wanted to make him my companion, my friend. But he wanted to play cards, drink, and often told me that our love was 'too platonic,' that he liked a completely different sort. He stayed with me only because of the money, and I denied him nothing. Finally, Baron Z. seduced him and took him away from me.

"Stupidly—and I know how stupid it was, but I couldn't forget—years later, when I met Z., I used a card game as the pretext to challenge him to a duel.

"After Johnny left, I turned to doctors, then to a hypnotist. I don't know whether he did it or I hypnotized myself, but for a long time I lived peacefully with my books, paintings, and music. I traveled almost all the time. Suddenly, in your studio, I saw Stark and the torment began, worse this time than before . . . the wall . . . the futility. . . .

"Oh, Tata, it was horrible. Despair and joy at the same time. My pathetic happiness consisted of the fact that I could have him near me, be his one true friend. You left him, and he was lonely, depressed. You know how childlike his affections are. I stole touches, kind words, a smile. Sometimes I went into his bedroom, after he had already retired. I sat by his bed, and we had long, friendly conversations. On purpose, I would get him to speak about you, to see the fire in those fabulous eyes. Sometimes I was cruel enough to drive him to despair, so that then I would be able to caress his hands, kiss his forehead, hold him tight to me as he sobbed on my shoulder. Oh, I would feel so guilty the next morning, looking at his troubled face.

"During his illness, despite the fact that he was in grave danger, I was happy. Only then was I truly happy. Oblivious, he would lie in my arms for hours. I could kiss him as much as I wanted. I reveled in gazing at him for hours; there was only the night around us . . . and peace.

"Tata! My only and dearest friend! Forgive me. I got carried away and said too much. But you know that soon it will all be over—my endless love for him, and also my life."

Latchinov closed his eyes and sat there quietly. Troubled and feeling very sorry for him, I stroked his thin, pale hands.

The Countess-Actress
A Sensational Story of Our Times
Count Amori (1916)

COUNT AMORI'S FAVORITE TOPIC WAS THE PRIVATE—MOSTLY SEXUAL—LIVES OF THE UPPER CLASSES AND FOREIGN ROYALTY. WEARING HIS SARTORIAL TRADEMARK, A RED NECKTIE, HE WAS A PERMANENT FEATURE IN FILM STUDIOS AND COULD GRIND OUT SIMPLE PLOTS AS THE CAMERA WAS ROLLING.

ACTRESSES WERE A STAPLE OF BOULEVARD LITERATURE. THEY LIVED OUT THE SEXUAL FREEDOM AND SOCIAL MOBILITY THAT MADE THE MARGINS OF RUSSIAN SOCIETY SENSATIONAL READING. THEIR STATUS WAS ADDRESSED BY A TEARFUL LIGHT-FINGERED SONYA, WHO, LEARNING IN PRISON THAT HER DAUGHTERS HAD JOINED THE OPERETTA, SAID, "IF ONLY I'D BEEN THERE, THEY WOULD NEVER HAVE BECOME ACTRESSES!"

PROLOGUE

A woman, no longer young but still beautiful, nervously paced her boudoir in a luxurious robe. She wrung her hands, clasped her head several times, and kept running to the telephone. "Give me 727," she asked.

"The Prince isn't in? . . . Is this 727? O Lord, when will he be back ? Tell him to call the Fontanka. He knows where . . . "

Again she became anxious, and again she raced to the phone and called. "727? Still not in?"

She fell into despair. A horrible nightmare painted itself in her imagination.

How could she not worry? She had received shocking news: the secret she had kept like a conspirator had come into her enemies' possession.

Excerpted from [Graf Amori] *Grafinia–artistka. Sensatsionnaia byl' nashikh dnei* (Moscow: Moskovskoe izd., 1916), 3–23, 38–48, 53–64.

Countess Maria Leopoldovna was in dire agitation. A few times she began to cry, but she could muster only convulsive sobs. Not a single drop showed in her eyes, for the grief gripping her heart was too great for mere human tears.

THE FIRST CHOSEN

How unlucky the woman was.

Orphaned as a seven-year-old child, the oldest daughter from her father's first marriage, she was thrown out of the house. A distant relative who lived alone in the countryside put her up in the servants' wing out of the kindness of his heart.

How often the cold, hungry, and mistreated girl sought sympathy from the old priest's wife who lived near the village. Little Marusia found comfort there, and sometimes even some sweets. Marusia grew up. With her lively, pretty eyes, slender profile, snow-white teeth, and supple, shapely body, she cut a fine figure. The young beauty was not yet sixteen when she caught the attention of a neighboring landowner, a fussy old recluse and alcoholic.

She was sixteen, and he forty-seven. The young, graceful, foolishly affectionate girl tantalized the aging voluptuary's imagination. He paid frequent visits to the poor orphan's uncle, for whom she worked as a chambermaid or housekeeper. From time to time the guest brought Marusia a box of candy or other sweets.

One rainy autumn day, a troika drove into the modest village. Apollinarius Gennadievich Tsvetkov, as the reclusive alcoholic was called, leapt out, and with shaking steps the short, unattractive, tipsy gentleman trudged up the staircase. Marusia met him at the threshold.

"Uncle isn't home. He went to town for some wine."

"Well, all the better. You and I, Marusia, can drink some tea by ourselves."

The cordial girl ordered the samovar lit, and as it heated up, home-baked cookies, an assortment of preserves, and some leftovers from dinner appeared on the table.

Meanwhile, Apollinarius Gennadievich dozed in his armchair. Marusia woke him up and helped him to some tea.

"You're a fine girl," he said. "They take poor care of you. I would dress you to the nines."

Marusia looked at him in amazement.

"And so what, Marusia. I'm old, and ugly to boot, or else I'd take you for my wife. And what a wedding I'd throw. Everyone would shout that Tsvetkov had waited for the right wife and finally found her—one to astonish everybody."

Marusia was lost in thought and did not answer. Soon her uncle returned home. Tsvetkov returned to the topic of their conversation. When her uncle was in his cups, he promised her in marriage to Tsvetkov. Then they called her into the dining room.

"Well, Marusia. Look at the great fortune that's come your way. Not just anybody, but a nobleman, a landowner, a rich man has honored you with his proposal. You don't deserve such a groom. You've got no learning in you, no dowry."

"But what a beauty," put in Tsvetkov.

Marusia broke into tears, choked by emotion. Her uncle took her arms and pushed the young girl over to Tsvetkov's chair. Tsvetkov kissed her and caressed her. Wine was served.

"Kiss your fiancée," her uncle shouted, and stamped his foot.

And thus Maria Leopoldovna and Apollinarius Gennadievich were betrothed.

The priest's wife threw up her hands when she heard about the impending wedding: "What a sinner!" she yelled. "A real libertine. He's buried one wife, whom he led to the grave with his drinking, and now he wants to destroy a young soul, an orphan."

The priest's wife wept when she saw the unconcerned and smiling Marusia.

Poor Marusia did not realize that she was doomed. She was too young to understand what life was bringing her. Living in her uncle's house was so loathsome that any new setting seemed better than what she had experienced. She hated the house where she had borne so many insults and humiliations.

But she did not have to wait long for fresh disappointments. At first her husband, a drunkard, a man gone astray and with less wealth than people thought, tried to make his wife happy. He dressed her up. For the first time she wore decent clothes. He gave her baubles of gold and trifles with pretensions to opulence that awoke in her an unconscious longing for the good things in life.

Despite the straitened circumstances of her upbringing, the holy flame of beauty burned in Maria Leopoldovna. Little did she recognize her own exceptional beauty, but everything aesthetic, beautiful, and sublime beckoned her to an unknown distance.

LOVE AND THE STAGE

She did not live long in her husband's manor. They moved to a nearby provincial center, one of those backwater towns that are hard to distinguish from a respectable village. There was not even a theater. There were occasional amateur nights at the local club, and provincial troupes sometimes came through on tour. They organized plays and covered the town with colorful posters advertising the coming show. Once such a troupe played in the local club. Since the play, *A Ruined Life*, required the participation of many extras, the director raced about town asking local residents not to refuse him the favor of taking part. Apollinarius Gennadievich had been roaring drunk for three days. Hell ruled the roost. His young wife, convinced that all pleading and admonishment was useless, would flee the house on such days and wander aimlessly through the little town's empty streets. Walking by the local club, Maria Leopoldovna read the large announcement closely and was ready to move on when a clean-shaven stranger approached her.

"Excuse me, ma'am, for stopping you without being acquainted. It's just that we're a bit short-handed for today's show."

"But I'm not an actress. You've made a mistake," Maria Leopoldovna modestly observed.

"That means nothing. Your beauty and figure were created for the stage, and you could play a minor role like the young daughter magnificently."

The director began to explain what the play was about, and he so intrigued the young woman that she decided to fulfill his request.

Evening came. Tsvetkov was sleeping on the couch in his study. One of his drinking buddies was slumped asleep on the floor, and another had crawled out of the house.

The two drunkards were snoring loudly when the young woman glanced in at the disgusting spectacle, turned away with loathing, and ran into the bedroom.

She thought for a minute, and then resolved to get ready for her debut without waiting for her husband to wake up.

The unfamiliar surroundings, cynical remarks, face powder and rouge, eye makeup, tawdry costumes, and distinctive scent of cheap perfume mixed with vodka emanating not only from the men but from the women as well—taken together, all this caused Maria Leopoldovna some concern. The carpenters were working noisily on-stage; the assistant director egged them on with words and with punches, and curses hung in the air, punctuated by unambiguous asides directed at the female personnel. Maria Leopoldovna saw and understood it all. At one point she almost fled, but there was something alluring.

She vaguely realized that here was her chance to enter a new arena in life. This vague and mysterious thing enticed her, making her forget her surroundings.

When Maria Leopoldovna appeared on-stage wearing the modest and maidenly dress of a merchant's daughter and a simple ponytail, shyly lowered her gaze, and kissed her father's hand, a whisper went through the theater: "What a beauty. Take a look."

But she neither saw nor heard any of that. She was absorbed by her role and played it with true brilliance. Naturally, there were some purely technical defects, but her charming voice, her warm and sincere intonation, her gentle gestures, and her beauty had their effect. By the time the play was over, Maria Leopoldovna had become the object of everyone's attention.

The young actor playing the romantic lead fell instantly in love. He would not leave her for a moment, whispered unaccustomed compliments in her ear, and with his last few pennies treated his lady to as sumptuous a dinner as he could afford.

Several members of the audience approached her and introduced themselves, kissed her little hand, and lavished a profusion of compliments on her. Maria Leopoldovna smiled in confusion, but her heart was happy and content.

The actor was summoned to escort the new actress back to her residence. Along the way he continued whispering about the extraordinary impression she had made on him.

It was a warm September evening. They had long ago passed the house, but nothing could induce her to return to such humiliation and degradation.

Now, after the brightly lit theater, after intoxicating speeches full of sensuality and passion in a poetically moonlit setting, she feared her domestic situation, the presence of her dipsomaniac husband and his drunken buddy, and the obligations her husband's caresses might impose. They had already infused her with absolute disgust.

Of course she did not want to go home. So they went on, walking aimlessly, until finally the actor turned to her with the question: "But where do you live?"

"I don't want to go home yet. The weather is so nice."

The next morning she remembered only vaguely how she had gone to her companion's cheap hotel room, how he had kissed her, how the wine and intoxicating caresses had gone to her head. After that, everything merged vaguely in a magical dream in which she was on a high mountain surrounded by the bright light of a rising sun.

And when, awakening, she saw the young actor's curly head on her breast, Marusia sighed, fecklessly pushed him away, and quietly cried out.

He awoke—and again there were ardent speeches, whisperings of love, mad caresses.

The clock in the hotel corridor loudly struck nine.

Maria Leopoldovna jumped up and began to dress quickly.

The actor also jumped up. "Where are you going, Marusia?"

"What do you mean, where? Home."

"Don't. You yourself said yesterday that you don't love him, that he's a burden to you. Stay here."

But Maria Leopoldovna was not yet used to the thought of leaving her husband. Several impulses battled within her, and though she was fully conscious of her husband's intellectual poverty and moral depravity, she feared breaking her legal vows.

She performed again the next evening.

At home she found her husband still asleep. He had not even noticed her absence. She left him for her lover that day with the intention firm in her heart not to return home.

The entire troupe was leaving town that night after the show. The train would pass through the station at two in the morning.

Everyone already knew that Egorov, as the actor was called, and Marusia had become intimate. Some approved of the affair, but there were also those who whispered hateful things about Egorov in her ear.

She felt extremely confused, but she liked the actor—and said nothing.

The troupe traveled third-class. The car was packed. Nobody slept all night, and finally, as dawn was breaking, Egorov found Marusia a place on an upper berth.

The porters were already scurrying about the car when she awoke, and Egorov hurried her along.

"Moscow!" he shouted. "We're there."

For the first time since her forgotten childhood, she saw Moscow's golden crown.

They rented some dirty furnished rooms not far from the Nikolaevsk Station.

They embarked on the debauched life of bohemians. At night they drank and played cards, discussing grandiose plans. In the morning they slept till noon, dined on whatever came their way, and then in the evening the same gang began drinking and card-playing.

One morning Marusia awoke to a knock on the door.

Egorov had received an offer from Ryntovsky to act in a magic play. Overjoyed, he gave the messenger a tip.

"Marusia, get up. I'll introduce you to Ryntovsky. He's one of Moscow's celebrities. Try to make a good impression."

Marusia dressed without a murmur.

Ryntovsky took a liking to Marusia. He hired her for the role of the queen of beauty in a magic play.

When Marusia first saw herself in her sumptuous costume and magnificent coiffure crowned by a tiara of many-colored stones, she realized that she was truly pretty and that she was fated to play a role other than the mistress of some Egorov.

Ryntovsky was attracted to Marusia. It didn't take much effort for him to convince Egorov to yield the beautiful woman to him.

She listened through the dressing-room wall with horror as Egorov gave his servile agreement: he would persuade her to go over to the talented director.

So Marusia found herself in a new, unfamiliar, and brilliant setting. Ryntovsky occupied two suites in a high-class hotel, lived in great comfort, and did not spare expenses. His carriage was brought to him every day harnessed to a pair of sable horses, and the young beauty, dressed in a fashionable cloak and ostrich-plume hat, rode along Blacksmith Bridge, through Petrovsky Park and the adjoining areas. Ryntovsky went seriously to work on Marusia's unusual talent.

THE ACTRESS'S FIRST TRAGEDY

Meanwhile a peculiar drama was taking place in the small provincial town.

The husband sobered up and went looking for his wife. People mocked him and laughed at him. He scoured the whole town and finally turned to the local constable.

"Your wife left with the troupe of actors," the constable announced to the dismayed husband.

At first he wanted to chase after his wife, but by evening he was drunk. Thus began another week of drunkenness.

One day Ryntovsky was sharing a peaceful breakfast with young Marusia in his rooms when the door opened without warning and the stooped and drunken figure of Tsvetkov appeared on the threshold.

Maria Leopoldovna was so frightened that she clutched her heart and collapsed to the carpet. Ryntovsky roughly led her husband from the room. But Tsvetkov did not calm down. He turned to the police for assistance, and they dispatched a local patrolman to Ryntovsky's rooms.

Maria Leopoldovna gave such strange answers that even Ryntovsky was surprised.

The police left with the abandoned husband. That same evening, when Marusia, who had fallen ill, was lying in the room, an ambulance with a doctor and sanitarian drove up to the hotel building. They broke into the room with the help of the same patrolman, and an hour later the hysterical Maria Leopoldovna was in the municipal hospital's ward for the violently insane.

Ryntovsky returned and took energetic measures on her behalf.

But Tsvetkov, who was present for the whole terrible procedure, was frightened by what had been done. When he walked into the hospital room, he fell into such despair that he began to weep, and then to pray.

"You have punished me, Lord," he wailed, kneeling before the icon, "for my sinful, dissolute life. I have blackened my soul and clouded poor Marusia's mind."

The next morning, a submissive Tsvetkov knocked at the monastery gates. The Father Superior heard his confession and graciously allowed him to stay in the monastery as a novitiate.

When he discovered Marusia's fate, Ryntovsky became indignant.

He raced off in search of her husband, considering him solely responsible for what had happened. But soon he was convinced that Apollinarius Gennadievich had sought his peace in penitent retreat.

Maria Leopoldovna was on the verge of madness. Young and impressionable, she could not reconcile herself to being bound hand and foot for her alleged insanity. People truly deprived of reason wandered around her, staring at her curiously, and her every shriek of despair was greeted by a savage, cruel chuckle. Beaten and strait-jacketed patients could be heard wailing from all corners of the ward. Marusia herself was not spared, and her body was black and blue by the third day.

Beaten, terrorized by attendants' threats, lost in hopeless melancholy, the young actress succumbed to dull despair. She would not answer doctors' questions or accept food. When she grew quiet, they untied her hands. But horrible depression and three days of involuntary bed rest weakened her decisively.

Meanwhile, Ryntovsky left no stone unturned in the hospital administration; he demanded an immediate visit, threatened prosecution, but attained nothing.

Ryntovsky remembered that one of his greatest admirers, Senator Lazarev, was in Moscow. He turned to him in a moment of despair. The senator personally went to see that omnipotent ruler of all things, the Governor General Istomin, and finally, by administrative order, Maria Tsvetkova was brought to the province medical authorities for reexamination. Here the doctors gave the young actress proper care, agreeing that she was a hysteric, but finding no evidence of acute paranoia. They certified emotional exhaustion exacerbated by spiritual trials and overstimulation of the nervous system.

She was released by order of the provincial medical authorities and placed under the actor Ryntovsky's care.

Two months were needed to heal five days spent in the insane asylum.

She was only twenty years old, and how much grief, tragedy, humiliation and horror, she had seen. . . .

COUNT VORONOV

An enormous mansion, perhaps better called a palace, stood on Sergeev Street near the Tauride Gardens.

Here for more than a century the Counts Voronov had lived and flourished.

The once magnificently furnished palace, which even crowned heads had visited, had lost much of its splendor. The formerly renowned family, producer of men of state, had become spiritually impoverished. The children, grandchildren, and great-grandchildren inherited a glorious name, distinction, and millions, but the forebears' divine spark did not grace the descendants' brow.

Nature's law of gradual degeneration, the implacable law of unsuccessful inter-breeding and selection, was evident in a terrible decline. The inept descendants ceased to decorate the upper ranks of society's movers. They were spoken of with respect, but more because of their millions than because of personal merit.

One of the Voronov descendants, a healthy but unschooled young man whose mind was nourished solely by the occult sciences and pornography, spent his young years among the golden youth of high society.

While his father was alive, he had kept his son's obedience, and the son, though he took part in sundry and occasionally disgraceful binges, behaved quietly and modestly and avoided scandal.

A salon of aesthetes had been gathering in a Furstät Street residence for some time. Ladies pranced around in black cambric blouses, while the gentleman dressed exclusively in evening attire: men in tail-coats, officers in uniform. Of course, the latter were a very rare sight.

Most recently, only civilians had been coming.

The entertainments in that salon were extraordinary. Most of the men came with their ladies. But some also came as "orphans," without ladies. The gracious hostess Countess K. thoughtfully invited pretty young girls who knew how to conduct themselves in a decent salon. Acquaintances were struck up.

Even the female servants, young girls of fourteen to fifteen, raced barefoot across the carpets, wearing long black chemises that set their blossoming figures in bold relief.

The intoxicating atmosphere was one of lust constrained by decorum.

A gong sounded at the appointed hour, and the gathering streamed into a concert hall.

The hall was in semi-darkness. Risqué scenes were shown on-stage: Satyr and Nymph, Venus and Faun, and other such playlets. Then came the tableaux vivants. Both the risqué scenes and the tableaux vivants were performed in splendorous full nudity.

The curtain fell, and after the stimulating spectacle, the guests were invited into a circular hall. Sherbet, champagne, fruits, candies, and coffee with liqueurs were served.

The entire circular hall was carpeted with bear, tiger, and leopard pelts. They formed soft ottomans that ringed the room. The guests settled themselves, and finally the gong rang and the lights went out.

The air was filled with kisses, sighs, weak protests, and passionate moans. In an hour the gong rang again and the lights went on, illuminating the abashed faces and rumpled coiffures of the ladies. At that moment music began to play, and the gracious hostess invited her guests into the theater hall to watch a nude ballet per-formance of *A Midsummer Night's Dream*, which caused quite a sensation. Then the music struck up anew, and the guests went to the dining room, where merry conversation smoothed over the awkwardness. Champagne and music gave everything a certain luster, and everyone went home with a satisfied expression.

True, not everyone went straight home; some finished the evening in other establishments, but decorum was observed with delicacy.

The salon was frequented zealously by representatives of the fading and degenerate aristocracy.

There was yet another salon, of which we will not speak. It was also frequented by barons and counts with the following aim: to experience and taste everything in a ceaseless craving for newer and newer sensations.

MARRIAGE AND DISENCHANTMENT

The count married a beautiful Greek woman, the daughter of respectable parents. But he had been debauched by bachelor life. Hearth and home could not give him what the whirlpool of orgies available for a sack of gold could. His young wife, who had had a strict upbringing, and who was a cultured woman with refined traditions and elevated views, was soon convinced of the count's unsuitability for family life. He was perpetually seeking something special, some supersensation.

For a time the count was an ardent visitor of various occultists. He frequented a chiromancer's salon on Vereiskaia Street. At home, his family was in complete disarray. The countess lost patience and began to make harsh remarks to her husband. She could not stand by when the count, ignoring his own children, took a Latvian tyke named Franz under his wing. He took him along when he had his hair coifed, supplied him with expensive cologne, and gave him a room next to his own study that resembled a coquette's flirtoir more than the bedroom of a lackey's son who had been taken in as a favor.

And the upbringing he was given! He did little schoolwork, and he was fed little but candy, fruits, and other delicacies.

Nobody dared say a word about Franz. Once, to the immense satisfaction of the servants, the wife moved Franz's bedroom to the basement in her husband's absence. Upon his return, the husband raised such a ruckus, it was as if his closest relative had been insulted. It was obvious that the count cared more for the boy than for his own children.

Scandals of an abnormal character ensued.

Losing all patience, the countess turned to the highest medical authorities for help. Unbeknownst to the count, they examined him and found the typical symptoms of degeneration. A reception was scheduled, which was attended by government officials from France.

During the reception, the count caused a scandal for his wife that was hushed up only through the supreme efforts of an uncle, an old esteemed general. In rough, soldierly fashion, he subdued his nephew and led him out into the winter garden. There he left him, and during supper he smoothed over the sensation caused by the outburst, which made it all the way to the Parisian newspapers, as the esteemed French guest had been accompanied by reporters.

The next day, the countess paid a visit to the wife of a powerful dignitary and complained about her husband's abnormal behavior. On the advice of the dignitary himself, she resolved to send her husband to an insane asylum the next time something similar happened.

A rumor swept Petrograd that Count Voronov had lost his mind. Obviously, the wife was not ashamed to tell her closest friends of her husband's outbursts. And like a scandal sheet, the spicy news spread through the city with the speed of lightning. There soon was an opportunity for the high-strung count to display his unbridled rage.

He was horribly upset by the rumors reaching him.

He tried to discuss this matter with his wife. The discussions grew stormy. In a fit of anger, he swung a heavy china plate at his wife that almost wounded her.

His wife fled to her quarters, locked herself in, and called the dignitary's wife. She in turn called the municipal governor, and in half an hour an ambulance arrived, accompanied by the district doctor, and carrying muscular attendants and the police. The count, despite his active resistance, was taken off to a private hospital for the insane.

This created a sensation in the so-called highest spheres of society. The count's best friend, Count Saint-Fort, put his whole family to work. The affair caused a scandal, physicians and professors were called in, and despite the obvious indications of Count Voronov's instability, of his abnormal eccentricities, he was released from the hospital.

From that time on, the count concealed his wrath.

A virtual separation took place between the count and countess. The count began bringing his bachelor friends home without ceremony, and they spent their time so nicely with gypsy women, chansonettes, and dancing girls from various cabarets that he forgot that his position forbade him to advertise such a lifestyle.

It was at this time that the count met the actress Maria Leopoldovna at a palm-reader's. A gallant and handsome man, he caught the actress's attention.

The aura of his millions and grand title of course made an impression. The count drove the actress home in his automobile; flattered by the attention, Maria Leopoldovna invited him to "come visit."

From Prince Dolgov, her former lover and a distant relative of Count Voronov, she had heard many things about his eccentricities and his passion for mystery and mysticism.

Their meeting took place just when she was breaking up with the prince.

The count knew how to be gallant. Flowers, presents given as small tokens of affection, invitations to the opera and ballet, and dinners at fashionable restaurants rained down upon her.

Meanwhile, the countess left the country to live with her mother.

The count considered himself a bachelor and became intimate with the actress.

The countess wrote her husband rarely, and her letters concerned purely practical matters. She found respite from her husband's abnormal eccentricities among her close relatives. So it continued for several years, during which the count and Maria Leopoldovna grew very close.

Both the count and Maria Leopoldovna were fascinated by spiritualism. They found a medium in the person of Madame Akhalturova, a woman of dubious character who practiced palm-reading.

A MATCH MADE BY SPIRITS

An occult seance took place one evening. Madame Akhalturova went into a trance and began to mutter, a pencil found its way to her hand, and the spirit of the count's daughter began to speak on a sheet of paper put under the medium's hand. It spoke of the count's betrayal of her mother, and said that he would find happiness with a new life's companion, and that he would have a new heir.

The news made a powerful impression on the count. It was unclear whether the medium had influenced him, but from that moment he resolved to break with his hated wife.

Proper grounds for divorce were needed. But there were none.[1] The count went to various private investigation agencies, but came up with nothing, for the countess's conduct was spotless, and her whole life was dedicated to raising her children.

"How I would like to have the promised heir," the count once said.

This phrase found a place deep in Maria Leopoldovna's heart [despite the fact she could not bear children]. She sought the council of a psychographologist, and after some time the actress informed the love-stricken count in an intimate conversation that she felt motherhood stirring within her.

Her gambit proved successful. The count, hating his wife, sought only to justify himself, for he had long wanted to start a new family. The opportunity now presented itself, and he chivalrously did not wish his son to be born out of wedlock.

He sent an abrupt letter to his wife declaring that he wanted a divorce. She met his demand. He provided for his children and wife, and the divorce took place.

The actress advanced toward her goal. She had long wanted to establish a cozy family with a beloved man. She was attached to the count, although she could not forget her ardent love for Prince Dolgov.

The wedding took place. Slowly but surely, Maria Leopoldovna, the fledgling Countess Voronova, was forced to simulate pregnancy.

The new countess, however, found herself in unusual circumstances. The count was hiding his marriage to the actress from his family. He continued to occupy the palace, and Maria Leopoldovna remained in her old apartment on the Fontanka.

The count was not generous. As before, the actress was always in need of money; she pawned her diamonds and other things, and went, as they say, from bad to worse.

Once she made her husband a present of her black pearl earrings, which she had turned into cufflinks.

The count returned the favor with new, even bigger pearls.

---

1. Though family law had undergone considerable liberalization by 1916, divorces were still difficult to obtain. One option was to present the court with proof of moral turpitude.

But the count's bachelor friends, who had lost the sack of gold that paid for their good life and booze, felt a particular hatred for the countess.

They began to sulk. They worked to turn the count against his new wife, to tell him about her tempestuous life and affairs.

All that was in the past, but the count's vanity was set aflame, and he began to resent her past. The seeds of doubt had been planted, from which distrust grew. The count hid it from his new wife; he was as courteous as before, but there was something malignant hidden in his duplicity.

Someone's wife told a toady that the count had somehow "changed." He left the country during the supposed pregnancy and returned only for the due date. A ball was thrown by the Countess Menshikova. To everyone's surprise, the Countess Voronova took part in the dancing, and her husband did not even protest.

Nobody knew whether he believed in the supposed pregnancy or only pretended to. Most likely he had accepted his situation but hid spite in his heart. The anticipated birth took place in the absence of the count, who simulated joy at acquiring an heir.

So it continued for several months.

The bachelor friends found allies among the count's relatives, who were most dissatisfied with the prospect of so many millions falling to the new wife and heir.

They began to dig into it. They openly shared with the count their doubts about the propriety of the birth. The salons were filled with malicious gossip and hints about the dubious heir. The count began to receive anonymous notes and finally fell apart.

Although the vain Prince Dolgov did not seek to renew relations with his former beloved, he continued to observe her life from a distance. Just before her marriage to the count, he wrote Maria Leopoldovna a tender letter:

> Marusia, do not think I am governed by jealousy, but you have no idea what a cretin your count is. Ask his wife, and you will find out about his inclinations, which can only evoke a natural reaction of disgust. Look at him, at his eyes, at his prematurely swollen body, at his sluggish will, and you will understand that from such a man you can expect a ruined life and surprises you can't imagine.

She kept the missive for a long time, but fearing that it would fall into the hands of the count, who loved to go through her drawers, she finally destroyed it.

A COOLING OFF

The storm approached. The prince's predictions began to come true.

Once, arriving at her husband's palace on an urgent matter, she found him in his nightclothes, drinking tea with Franz in the dining room.

The old valet did not want to let her in at first, and even blocked her path. But the countess pushed him aside and went in anyway.

The count was befuddled, but Franz did not even get up and only nodded to her.

Then and there the countess knew that she was not the Countess Voronova, but an unwelcome guest.

From that moment the countess understood that there was something evil in her husband's affected courtesy.

The behavior of the servants, a less cultured element, reflected the count's real feelings. She understood this perfectly.

All the same, the count continued to visit his wife frequently. He conversed with her graciously, loved it when she sang gypsy songs, sometimes even spent the night, but at the same time he was consulting lawyers about how to expose her for falsifying a birth certificate with his name as father.

The child born to the marriage was baptized and registered under the count's name.

The lawyers, who enjoyed the prospect of such a job and a millionaire client, advised him to institute proceedings.

And the count resolved to.

After he had lodged his complaint with the procurator, the count continued to visit his wife, even spending the night, but he never revealed his hand. He visited her even when he knew she would be arrested the next day, and as he bade her farewell, he kissed her and embraced her in a most friendly fashion.

Eyewitnesses said that when the countess was put in the prison car by the detectives, someone's eye followed the nightmarish scene of the arrest through the lowered blinds of a carriage parked across the street.

Whose eye was it? It's not hard to guess.

The countess had barely been taken away when the count showed up at her apartment, demanded the key to the safe from the chambermaid, and began searching for the pearl earrings he had given the countess before their wedding. But they had been wisely hidden, and he left empty-handed.

The countess spent several months in jail, and the count would not make the twenty-five thousand dollars' bail. Somehow her friends collected the necessary sum and freed her from a premature death.

THE TRIAL AND CASE

The trial date arrived. But it was the count himself, not the countess-actress, who was tried. The matter was conducted behind closed doors, where the court of conscience heard things that would leave any decent man with a particularly malodorous residue of loathing.

The count treated the revelations not only calmly, but somehow naively.

It was no less naive for the count to accuse his wife of summoning false spirits through a medium. The spectators laughed and were amazed at his shortsightedness. But he continued to play the role of a seduced and handsome Joseph who had practically been raped by the perfidious woman.

But the court saw the matter differently. They understood where the true guilt lay. Nor did the prosecution witnesses help the count. True Russian conscience spoke in the person of the judges, who judged not by the letter of the law but according to Christian justice, and who were guided by sincere mercy.

With the spectators packed into the courtroom awaiting the judge's decision with bated breath, and the pale countess, barely breathing, convulsively pressed against the barrier, the jury foreman answered the question: "Is the countess guilty of fabricating a birth certificate with the intent of passing another child off as Count Voronov's?" with "Not guilty."

A sigh of relief sounded throughout the courtroom.

The countess's friends raced over to her. The former defendant's nerves gave out, and she melted in tears.

As the countess crossed the courtroom with a proud step, broken only by the grief she had endured, total strangers embraced and kissed her, weeping for joy.

The count did not even hear the verdict. He was standing by his automobile on Liteiny Prospect. One of his minions ran outside after the verdict was announced to convey the news. The count clutched his head and jumped into his automobile.

Ten minutes later, accompanied by an ovation, the Countess Voronova was seated in another automobile.

Thus ended a chapter of Maria Leopoldovna's story. A new life and new experiences now await her.

At the last moment fate took pity on her, and her acquittal was tantamount to convicting the count.

Something lies in store for the long-suffering woman. But its time has not yet come, and the prosecutor may yet appeal the verdict.

The Bloody Talisman
Nat Pinkerton, King of Detectives (1915)

BALANCING BANDIT ADVENTURE FICTION ON THE URBAN MARKET WERE DETECTIVE STORIES FEATURING PRIVATE SLEUTHS, SUCH AS SHERLOCK HOLMES, NICK CARTER, OR NAT PINKERTON, AND A VARIETY OF NEFARIOUS CRIMINALS. THOUGH THE DETEC-

Nat Pinkerton, korol' syshchikov. *Krovavyi talisman* (St. Petersburg: Razvlechenie, 1916?), pp 1–31.

TIVES THEMSELVES WERE MOSTLY IMPORTED, THE AUTHORS WERE USUALLY RUSSIANS CAPITALIZING ON THE POPULARITY OF FOREIGN TITLES AND LAX COPYRIGHT LAWS. DETECTIVE SERIALS WERE PUBLISHED IN NEWSPAPERS AND SEPARATELY, ENJOYING A HUGE READERSHIP THAT BOOMED AFTER 1905. RUSSIAN PINKERTONS DID NOT BETRAY THE ANTI-UNION BIAS OF THEIR AMERICAN COUNTERPART. ON OCCASION, HOWEVER, THEY REVEALED A SOLIDARITY THAT MANY RUSSIANS FELT WITH EURO-AMERICANS RELATIVE TO "ORIENTAL" PEOPLES.

CHAPTER I: THE CONSEQUENCES OF A DISCOVERY

On the evening of 20 December, 18—, a blond man with a beard, well-dressed and tall, walked along Mott Street, the main street of New York's Chinatown.

If you are not Chinese, it takes a certain daring to walk through this quarter at such a late hour. Streets that seem completely empty conceal danger around every corner.

More than once a white man has disappeared without a trace in Chinatown, and police searches almost always come up with nothing.

If the police do apprehend a suspicious son of the Middle Kingdom, then put him on trial and condemn him, it is impossible to be sure that the true perpetrator has been punished, because most Chinamen are as similar as two drops of water.

The blond man walking through Mott Street that night obviously was not thinking of the danger threatening him in that locale. True, he had heard that it was dangerous at night, that even the police avoid these streets, but he was relying on his courage and physical strength. He was built as powerfully as Hercules, and the noble features of his face revealed valor and manliness.

He walked deep in thought, not paying attention to the heads with slanted eyes that occasionally poked out of dark gateways and followed his progress. The street was absolutely quiet, and only the occasional sound of a passing tram could be heard from the Bowery.

The stranger stopped to light his cigar and was about to continue when a glittering object lying on the pavement suddenly caught his attention.

He bent down, picked it up, and walked over to the street lantern to examine his discovery. It was a medallion of pure gold, as big as a silver thaler, with calligraphy and several engravings of Chinese deities. The lost item had probably hung around its owner's neck by the silk string it was attached to.

Strangest of all, though, was that the medallion was covered in blood, which stained the blond man's fingers.

He could not understand the meaning of his find. Perhaps this valuable ornament had been lost by some Chinaman?

"I must," thought the finder, "hand this in at the nearest police station; let the loser get it back there."

He wrapped the golden medallion thoroughly in a piece of paper, put it in his side pocket, and prepared to set off.

But then something unexpected happened. A muffled bell rang from a gate to the right, and a second later a crowd of Chinamen poured out of the surrounding houses and advanced on him with daggers drawn.

Not one of the Chinamen said a word. The ominous silence was shattering.

At first the stranger was confused by the suddenness, but he quickly regained his composure. The crowd surrounded him, their daggers gleaming in his eyes, but still no one had touched him.

But then a gigantic Chinaman waved a thick staff, intending, apparently, to strike him, and someone's hands seized the blond man from behind.

He nimbly tore himself free from the traitorous embrace and hit the gigantic Chinaman so hard that he turned red from pain and tumbled to the pavement.

At that moment the stranger tore the staff from his grasp and began to flail away to the left and the right.

The crowd let out a roar and staggered back, which opened a passage that the blond man did not hesitate to use. He took off, still waving the staff, and leapt out of the ring of scoundrels, thinking it better to run away. With a savage yelp, the crowd chased after him.

Suddenly a piercing whistle was heard from the other end of the street, and several policemen appeared in the flickering light of the gas lanterns. The Chinese instantly scattered in all directions; the street was empty, and even the tall Chinaman had disappeared.

Eight policemen walked slowly along Mott Street, but they noticed nothing suspicious. That was how it always was; the police were used to it.

The policemen left, each of them glad in his heart that he had made it safely through that dangerous section of town.

After the attack, the stranger found himself in another section of town, the Bowery. He was breathing heavily, cursing the carelessness that had taken him along Mott Street at such a late hour.

He had been warned, but had only laughed, confident that he had nothing to fear from Chinamen.

But he had proved a dangerous opponent in battle, and probably many of the Chinese had returned home with bumps on their head. However, the incident had made a strong impression on him. He could still see before him those slanted eyes, those figures breathing hatred, and still it seemed to him that dagger blades were flashing before his face. He looked at the broken staff, made of dark, polished wood, which could easily smash any skull.

The blond quickly walked through the Bowery to Third Avenue, where on the corner of Fourteenth Street his accommodations, the Central Hotel, were located.

There was nobody on the streets, except the occasional figure of a policeman that soon disappeared into the fog. The stranger walked along the left side of Third Avenue, past basement shops with short stairways leading from the street.

Walking by one of them, he heard a strange whistle and suddenly felt a string noose around his neck. But, being on guard, he kept his cool and instantly grasped the noose with his left hand before it could be drawn tight.

Two Chinamen with long daggers in their hands ran straight at him from the basement.

The stranger again let the staff do its business, knocking the first Chinaman askance so that he tumbled head over heels down the staircase; the second received a good blow about his shoulders and turned to run.

The blond man sighed with relief and hastened his step. He did not even think of turning to the police for assistance, knowing that it would lead to naught.

Having saved himself from danger twice, he was deathly pale, his chest was heaving, and a cold sweat broke out on his brow.

Gradually calming down, he foresaw a sleepless night ahead of him, the result of such powerful physical and spiritual shocks. He felt beaten and tired, but when he lay down to sleep, he could not close his eyes.

After lying in bed for more than a quarter-hour, he got up, checked to see if the door was locked tight, then took out two revolvers and, checking the cartridges, put them on the nightstand.

He lay down again and waited. What exactly he was waiting for he could not say, but it seemed to him that the night's adventures were not yet over.

However, exhaustion overcame him: the stranger fell asleep. Terrible nightmares would not let him be, and he awoke around three in the morning covered in sweat.

At that moment he heard a strange rustling behind the wardrobe.

The room was not completely dark, as the weak light of the gas lanterns outside made its way through the blinds and allowed him to distinguish objects in his room.

The stranger grabbed his revolver and set his gaze on the wardrobe, which suddenly jolted slightly, and slowly, noiselessly, began to move forward.

Not knowing that in the wall behind the wardrobe there was a door to the next room, the blond man could not understand what this was. He clutched his head to make sure it was not a dream.

A passageway between the wall and wardrobe appeared, and through it crawled a lithe figure.

It stopped, evidently listening to something, then stole closer; the blond man saw a Chinaman sitting on the bed in the half-dark, staring at him.

He crouched as if preparing to spring, and a second figure appeared behind him.

The stranger was now in complete control of himself. The moment the first scoundrel leapt at him, he fired, and the Chinese collapsed right next to the bed.

A second bullet flew through the passage between the bed wardrobe and door, where the second Chinaman had vanished.

Everything fell quiet. The stranger quickly lit a candle.

The hotel was in turmoil. The shots had disturbed the guests; the owner ran up with several of his employees.

The stranger dressed and opened the door. He told them briefly what had happened and showed them the Chinaman lying on the floor, his skull pierced by a bullet.

He was a short, thickset man with a very cunning face; his right hand was still curled around the thin, sharp dagger with which he had intended to kill his victim.

Only now did the stranger see that behind the wardrobe there was a door into the next room. As it turned out, the Chinese had entered the hotel from the courtyard, scrambled up the fire escape to the third floor, and made their way into the empty room, easily crawling into the stranger's room.

The second Chinaman had probably managed to flee by the same route.

The hotel owner quickly informed the police, and around five in the morning Inspector MacConell appeared, accompanied by a stocky man with a smooth-shaven, energetic face. This was none other than the renowned New York detective Nat Pinkerton.

He had only just detained an important criminal and was still in conversation with MacConell when the latter received a report on the happenings in the Central Hotel.

Pinkerton took an interest in the "incident" and went with the inspector. It was he who discovered the route that the Chinamen had used to infiltrate the hotel.

The stranger expressed his joy at the opportunity to shake the hand of the renowned detective, about whom he had heard so much. The blond man introduced himself. He was Karl Nefeldt, a German businessman who had traveled to New York to establish trade agreements with several firms.

His efforts, however, had not been rewarded with success, and he intended to return to his homeland in a few days.

He described in detail how he had sat in a restaurant with some friends, admitted that they had warned him about visiting Chinatown, but precisely because of that, he had decided to take a walk along Mott Street. Then he told Pinkerton of his find and described all the adventures that he had come out of safe and sound, thanks to his own cool head.

The detective calmly heard him out.

"Would you be so kind, Mr. Nefeldt," he said, "as to show me the item you found on Mott Street?"

Nefeldt unwrapped the paper and handed the detective the golden medallion.

Pinkerton examined it attentively and then said slowly and deliberately, "I would advise you, Mr. Nefeldt, to leave as quickly as possible. An evil fate led you to find it! Your life is in danger. I swear that if you stay, those yellow-faced devils will do something bad to you!"

Nefeldt looked at the detective in amazement, not understanding that he had been condemned to death simply because he had discovered the golden medallion.

"I don't understand at all!" he muttered. "Is it my fault that I found this thing that, by the way, I was going to hand in at the police station!"

Here Inspector MacConell joined the conversation: "I must draw your attention, Mr. Nefeldt, to the fact that in all of New York, you will not find another man who knows Chinese customs and ways, the superstitions and extravagant habits of the Chinese and their language, as well as Mr. Pinkerton. He and his assistant Bob Ruland have many times rendered us valuable service in our battle with these yellow rascals. Believe Mr. Pinkerton and make haste to follow his advice!"

"I don't doubt," answered Karl Nefeldt, "that Mr. Pinkerton is better informed of these matters than I am, but I cannot understand why the Chinese want to kill me for finding that ornament."

"That's no ornament," the detective objected. "It's a talisman, on which a Chinese bonze has scratched his mad incantations. Many Chinese wear such talismans on their chests under their clothing. I think that this one belonged to a wealthy and important Chinese who was murdered yesterday. Fanatical Chinese priests sometimes invent insane horrors to satisfy the bloodthirsty instincts of the crowd, and in this case they have followed a similar plan: the bloodied talisman was taken from the chest of the murdered man and tossed on the pavement with the idea that whoever picked it up would be used as an offering and scapegoat for the murder of their compatriot. The Chinese, it stands to reason, subordinated themselves completely to the decision of their bonze, and so when you walked down Mott Street, they were watching from the doorways and gateways to see who would pick up the gold medallion. Unfortunately, it was you. However, they did not want to kill you immediately; otherwise this whole affair would not have happened, and you would have received countless stabs from their daggers. No, they only wanted to gag and carry you off to their heathen temple and sacrifice you to their gods. You're lucky you didn't lose your head. Otherwise, bitter experience would have convinced you how fanatical these people are!"

"But how did the Chinese find out what room I'm staying in?" remarked Nefeldt.

"Very simple!" answered Nat Pinkerton. "They followed you closely, and when you went into the hotel, the spies had only to see in which room a light went on. They attacked you, and because you shot one of them, on top of everything else you've brought their vengeance on you!"

"But I cannot leave right away!" exclaimed Nefeldt. "The steamer isn't leaving for three days!"

"In that case move to a more secluded hotel, and do everything to make sure your enemies do not find out! I can recommend the Hotel Victoria, on 27th Street. Move there. I'll visit you in the afternoon to find out if you were followed there too!"

Karl Nefeldt collected his baggage and left the Central Hotel by the back exit. By seven o'clock in the morning, he was in a room on the eighth floor of the Victoria.

CHAPTER II: CAUGHT ALL THE SAME

The Hotel Victoria was located in a busy area, and that had a calming effect on Nefeldt. The Chinese would not dare to come there.

He slept till noon, and soon Nat Pinkerton appeared at his door.

The detective was disguised as an old graybeard. Before entering the hotel, he had wandered around the building, but had noticed nothing suspicious.

One might think that the Chinese still had not discovered where Nefeldt was, but Pinkerton was not at all convinced, knowing the peculiarities of the yellow people and their craftiness.

He did not hide his fears from Nefeldt and advised him not to go out all day.

Nefeldt, of course, did not like that. He felt like he was under arrest, and being not at all cowardly, he did not lend much significance to Pinkerton's warnings. It was hardly possible that the Chinese could find him in such a huge city, where there were always thousands of people on the streets. And he was now staying far from Chinatown.

He went out after lunch to make a few business calls. Returning near evening, he had supper in the dining room on the second floor, then took the elevator back up to the eighth.

Back in his room he had a strange, gnawing feeling: an inexplicable fear weighed on his chest. He scolded himself for it, as he had never before known fear or horror.

Around ten o'clock he lay down in bed, again having readied his revolver to give any uninvited guest a loud greeting.

He lay awake until midnight, but then sleep overcame him, and he slept soundly until two, when he suddenly awoke in a sweat. He wanted to raise himself on the bed, but his body, as if made of lead, did not respond to his efforts. A sickly-sweet odor was suffocating him, and his head was spinning.

Somehow he realized that a new attempt was being made on him, but the terrible heaviness binding his limbs was stronger than he.

Nefeldt lost consciousness. He tried to get his revolver from the nightstand, but could not: his hand would not move.

A red mist covered his eyes. It seemed to him he saw a yellow face distorted by a malicious grin. With a heavy moan, he lost consciousness.

The two Chinamen who had stolen into the room lifted Nefeldt's body. They wrapped it in a piece of mottled cloth they had brought with them and carried it out to the corridor.

Then with silent steps they went two floors below and stopped by the door to a room in which, judging by the huge trunks, a commercial traveler with sample wares was staying.

The Chinese unlocked one of the trunks, all the while glancing over their shoulders to make sure they were not caught unawares. Their long, sharp daggers lay near them on the floor, and they would not have stopped at murder if someone had found them at their work.

Opening the trunk lid, they removed some of the samples and stowed the wrapped-up Nefeldt in such a way that he would not suffocate. Only later was he to die.

Then they carefully closed the lid and with a gloating grin looked at the trunk that held their victim.

For the time being, their task could be considered successfully completed. There was nothing more for them to do in the Hotel Victoria. Silently they slipped down the staircase. Nobody saw them. A waiter moaned in a second-floor corridor, with a large wound on his head dripping blood, and the porter lay bound by the front entrance.

The Chinamen cautiously opened the door and looked around the street. A third Chinese joined them from the porters' room.

The corner of 27th Street and Fifth Avenue was busy even at night, and the Chinese had to wait until they could walk out of the building unnoticed. As soon as a convenient moment presented itself, they leapt out and quickly disappeared.

Only after an hour had passed did one of the hotel employees come upon the bound porter and the wounded waiter. He immediately sounded the alarm.

When the porter was untied, he could not say what happened.

He had been sitting in the porters' room dozing when suddenly someone had struck him a terrible blow from behind. He had crumpled to the floor instantly. When he returned to his senses, he was lying bound and gagged. Everything was dark, but it seemed that someone was standing next to him. This person soon left, though.

The waiter said that as he was descending the stairs, someone grabbed him from behind and threw him to the floor. He had not even seen his opponent because he had been hit on the head.

The hotel owner telephoned the police. He could not explain the puzzling incident, but then he remembered that the day before the renowned detective Nat Pinkerton had visited the hotel and had asked to be summoned immediately if anything unusual happened.

The owner phoned the detective right away, and he quickly responded.

The detective listened to the incoherent story and asked, "Are all your guests in?"

"I couldn't wake everyone; that would cause a big misunderstanding!"

"All right! Go up to Room 55 on the eighth floor and see if Karl Nefeldt, a young blond German, is in. I have reason to think that misfortune has befallen him."

"I'll find out right away!"

The owner and several of his employees left for the eighth floor. The door to Room 55 was unlocked, and there was a stiflingly sweet odor.

The bed was empty, but one could see that the lodger had lain down on it, and on the nightstand the barrels of two loaded revolvers glistened.

"Aha, a crime has been committed!" exclaimed the owner excitedly. "Our guest seems to have disappeared without a trace! Not a word about this to anyone," he said to his employees, "or we'll incur terrible losses! I'll inform Mr. Pinkerton right away, and he surely will be able to explain this mystery and save that unfortunate man."

He returned to the telephone and informed the detective.

"We might have expected that," answered Pinkerton. "I'll be there in half an hour. Mr. Nefeldt has been taken from the hotel; he is now in the power of those scoundrels and will perish if the most energetic measures are not taken immediately!"

The hotel owner became even more worried. Wringing his hands, he ran back and forth through the room: if the incident was publicized, his hotel's reputation would be ruined. Merciful heavens, some scoundrels broke in during the night, and kidnapped a man, and nobody noticed? The poor man lost his head entirely. He would never have thought that such a thing could occur in a hotel full of people!

Half an hour later, Nat Pinkerton appeared together with his assistant Bob Ruland and quickly went up to the eighth floor. When they entered Room 55 and noticed the cloying odor, the detective immediately opened the window and said, "Now we know how the rascals overcame their victim! They filled the room with gas! It's a Chinese invention that's often used in China. Without a doubt, the Chinese following Nefeldt were here!"

Pinkerton went over to the open window and looked down.

"Strange!" he muttered. "I still don't understand how the slant-eyed devils managed to carry him out. They set it up cleverly!"

He went to the back of the hotel and examined the courtyard framed by tall apartment buildings; it was unthinkable that the Chinese could cross here unnoticed with their load. It was likewise improbable that they had gone out to the street, which was busy all night long. Besides, Chinatown was far from the hotel, which would probably have made transporting the prisoner very difficult.

Pinkerton thought for a while.

"I don't understand," he muttered. "Those Chinese put together a devilishly clever plan!"

He began to go over the room thoroughly, but found nothing, establishing only that the Chinamen had let the suffocating gas in through the door.

He found a pinch of white powder on the floor, which he took with him in a piece of paper, and a spot left by some acid. But he could not determine how the Chinese had left the building with their victim.

Since the porter was unconscious, the scoundrels could, it's true, have left by the front, but the detective considered that impossible.

"If they had not had such a load," he told Bob, "they could have gone out on the street and concealed themselves in an alleyway. After all, they know how to hide themselves in an instant! But they could not have walked very quickly carrying a large man. The alarm would have gone out in a moment if passersby had seen several Chinamen carrying a man at night, or even something of that size. That's what's complicating the story!"

The detective searched every floor, but he could find no clues. The criminals had planned everything carefully and walked barefoot through the hotel. The detective passed the trunks on the sixth floor. It did not even occur to him that Nefeldt might be in one of them.

The detective and the policeman who arrived right after him searched the hotel until morning.

Around seven o'clock, Inspector MacConell appeared, and he was equally baffled. He could not imagine that the Chinese had been able to carry their victim through the busy streets to Chinatown.

"You and I, Bob, must once again transform ourselves into slant-eyed sons of the Heavenly Kingdom!" Pinkerton finally said. "It would be base of me not to take every measure I can to free Nefeldt from the hands of his enemies. Let's off to Chinatown!"

Bob was compelled by the danger, and since he was as fluent in Chinese as his boss, he had no reason to fear being recognized.

Nat Pinkerton was still conversing with his assistant and the inspector by the entrance when somebody in a blue shirt drove up with a handcart. There was a savage expression on his face, and a scar stood out on his left cheek.

He politely doffed his cap and went in by the front entrance. Pinkerton looked at him and said, "Aha, an old acquaintance! How are you doing, Tom Bilsby?"

Bilsby shuddered, looked at the detective, and exclaimed, "Mister Pinkerton?"

"One and the same! I'm glad you remember me."

"Our acquaintance was not very pleasant," objected Bilsby as he looked gloomily at the detective.

"That's all in the past," replied Pinkerton. "I see that you're now a decent man and are earning your bread by honest labor."

"That's true; I transport freight and make enough to live."

"I'm glad," answered the detective. "I hope we won't meet again under circumstances as unpleasant as the last time."

The porter asked the worker what he needed. Bilsby gave him a calling card and said, "I was sent for one of the trunks in front of the room of a gentleman on the sixth floor."

On the calling card was written "Freddy Maxwell, representing the firm of Elfeston and Son, Boston." On the back was written in pencil "Please give the bearer of the card one of the trunks standing in front of my room, marked K. K. 100."

The porter went to his room, looked in a book, and announced, "Mr. Maxwell, No. 22 on the sixth floor!"

Bilsby went with one of the servants to get the trunk.

Pinkerton turned to his assistant and the inspector.

"I put that Tom Bilsby in prison, and they let him out only two years ago. In his time he was one of the most dangerous robbers, and I had to chase him for quite a while. To be honest, I don't believe he's gone entirely straight. That Bilsby is not one to earn his daily bread by heavy labor; he doesn't like to work at all. We'll have to put a tail on him."

"And what should I do?" asked Bob.

"Go to our spare apartment near Chinatown for the time being. Disguise yourself as a Chinaman there, but make sure your makeup is right. I have a feeling that we have a difficult fight ahead of us. And could you, Mr. MacConell, send at least fifty plainclothes policemen to the vicinity of Mott Street for the day, and have them respond to my first whistle. As you know, on such occasions in Chinatown you need a large detail, there are so many of those yellow devils, and at any moment a hundred of those scoundrels will materialize, armed."

The inspector promised to send the detail and bade the detective farewell.

Pinkerton concealed himself in a building across the street. In several minutes, a hunchbacked old man with a thin gray beard and blue glasses emerged.

Inspector MacConell, still in conversation with the hotel owner, saw the old man but did not for a moment think it was Nat Pinkerton.

Bilsby and the servant came down the staircase with the heavy trunk. They loaded it on the handcart.

Before leaving, Bilsby looked around cautiously. Evidently his conversation with Pinkerton had aroused his anxiety. But when he saw there was nothing suspicious around, he set off. Soon he was hidden in the crowd, but he didn't notice the gray old man in blue glasses following on his heels.

CHAPTER III: ON BILSBY'S TRAIL

Tom Bilsby drove the trunk along Fifth Avenue to Canal Street, then turned onto Mott Street, the main thoroughfare of Chinatown.

Nat Pinkerton did not fall behind. When he noticed which way Bilsby was headed, he grinned.

"Something's up!" he muttered. "It seems that Bilsby's errand is connected to the disappearance of Karl Nefeldt!"

The detective made it to Chinatown without attracting Bilsby's attention. Now he began to act like a foreigner in Chinatown for the first time; he looked around with curiosity and watched the Chinese with their braids and heavy footwear in amazement. However, he did not let Bilsby out of his sight, and it did not slip his attention that when Bilsby appeared with the trunk, several passing Chinamen made secret signs to each other that were absolutely incomprehensible to the uninitiated.

Finally Tom Bilsby turned onto Pell Street and slipped into a dark, narrow alleyway.

The detective could not follow him there, as he would have unavoidably given himself away, all the more so as he knew that in Chinatown every passerby is always followed by a hundred eyes.

Therefore he went farther down the street, turned back, and waited until Bilsby returned with the empty handcart. Bilsby was now in a big hurry, and evidently was glad to be done with his errand.

Nat Pinkerton followed him to the Bowery, and there approached two policemen, gave his name, and showed them his badge.

"Follow that hardy fellow with the empty cart!" he ordered. "When he's gone a bit beyond the Bowery, arrest him and take him to police headquarters to the inspector."

The policemen went on their way. Pinkerton quickly went to see MacConell at headquarters. MacConell did not recognize the old man at first and asked, "How were you let in to my office unannounced? I ordered that no one be allowed in!"

"Nobody at all?" asked the detective, changing his voice.

"Of course, how else! I'm busy with such important matters that I can't leave them for a moment!"

"But I was let straight in when I gave my name," declared the detective.

MacConell looked up at him in surprise.

"That's odd," he said. "With whom have I the honor of speaking?"

"It's odd that Mr. MacConell does not recognize old friends! My name is . . . "

"Nat Pinkerton!" exclaimed the inspector and jumped up from his seat. "You are an amazing fellow! I'm constantly coming to that conclusion! I remember now that you left the building opposite the Hotel Victoria looking like that."

Pinkerton sat down, removed his beard and glasses, and told the inspector about everything he had seen.

"The policemen will probably soon bring the prisoner in," he added, "and I think we will find out much of interest."

In fifteen minutes the policemen delivered Bilsby.

"He put up a desperate resistance," reported one of the police, "so we had to put the handcuffs on him."

At a signal from the inspector the policemen left, and Bilsby found himself face to face with the inspector and detective. He shuddered when he recognized Nat Pinkerton, since he did not expect to meet him here. But he guessed that the delivery of the trunk had led to his arrest.

"Just today I expressed the hope that we would never again meet under unpleasant circumstances," began Pinkerton. "But unfortunately I see that you're involved in foolishness again, and I had no choice but to order you brought in."

"I haven't done anything wrong!" responded Bilsby.

"We'll see about that! Tell me, please, how much were you paid to move the trunk?"

"Not a hell of a lot!" answered Bilsby. "The gentleman paid me one miserable dollar."

"Which gentleman?"

"The one who instructed me to take the trunk from the Hotel Victoria."

"What sort of gentleman?"

"A man of medium height, with a black beard."

"That's a lie. It was a Chinaman who told you to."

Bilsby stepped back in amazement and glanced around in confusion.

"Not true," he said in turn. "I would never do a job for a yellow-faced scoundrel!"

"Where did you take the trunk?"

"To 60 Broadway. Wait, that's not the right number; I don't remember it."

"Again a lie!" objected Pinkerton, "I know for sure that you delivered the trunk to Pell Street, to a narrow alley behind No. 18."

Bilsby became even more confused. Now he understood that the detective had managed to follow him.

"You see that nothing will come of your lies! Incidentally, I'll find out for myself how much you received for your work."

The detective went up to the prisoner and began to rummage through his pockets.

"The devil take you!" swore Bilsby. "What right do you have to do that?"

He tried to resist but could not evade the agile detective, who pulled a pack of bank notes containing five hundred dollars from his pocket.

"That's my savings!" shouted the angry Bilsby. "Don't you dare take it away from me!"

"Strange that you would carry such savings around with you," countered Pinkerton. "Admit that you received the money for delivering the trunk. And what was in it?"

"I have no idea," muttered Bilsby.

"Do you admit now that you delivered the trunk to Pell Street?"

"So be it," he growled.

"And who did you deliver it to there?"

"I handed it over at the back entrance."

"To whom—Chinamen?"

"I don't know; it was dark!"

"Don't lie!" the detective shouted at him. "You'll only make your punishment worse by lying. It seems to me you want to spend another few years behind bars."

"Hell's bells, how can you pick on me for just doing an errand?" roared Bilsby.

"Listen to me, Tom!" said the detective. "You can keep that five hundred dollars, and I'll try to make sure you get off light, if you'll be open with me. If you have only a bit of reason left in you, you'll understand the advantages."

"I don't have any wish to turn those yellow devils against me," muttered Tom.

"Nonsense," answered Pinkerton. "You're no coward! So tell me: who gave you Freddy Maxwell's calling card and hired you to deliver the trunk?"

"The Chinaman Lun Tsa-hang!"

"Where and when?"

"This morning in a Chinese restaurant on Mott Street."

"Had you known this Chinaman before?"

"We had occasion to be together."

Nat Pinkerton also knew Lun Tsa-hang, and was aware that he played a role something like an *ataman* among his compatriots. He was considered a prophet and wizard, and it was undoubtedly his idea to toss the bloody talisman out to find a sacrifice for the murdered Chinese rich man Hang-Po.

"He didn't tell you what was in the trunk?"

"No, and I wasn't interested in finding out."

"Lun Tsa-hang himself received the trunk at No. 18?"

"Yes, he and two other Chinamen, who took it down into a dark basement."

"This time I'll believe you, Tom! Mr. MacConell, would you be so kind as to hold this man under arrest until I clear this matter up, and then you may release him."

The inspector agreed, and Tom Bilsby had no objections. He was gladly prepared to spend a few days under arrest, as long as he didn't go to prison or lose his money.

They took him away. Nat Pinkerton said goodbye to the inspector and went to the apartment near Chinatown to disguise himself as a Chinese.

CHAPTER IV: AN EXECUTION THAT NEVER TOOK PLACE

Dressed as a Chinaman, Nat Pinkerton walked slowly along Mott Street. The Chinese he met along the way paid him no attention, which meant that the costume and makeup were a success.

The detective made his way forward with the heavy steps characteristic of sons of the Heavenly Kingdom. Turning onto Pell Street, he almost bumped into a Chinaman, whom he recognized as Bob Ruland.

They stopped and began to talk in a whisper.

"The German is in a basement reached by a staircase from the courtyard of 18 Pell Street," said Pinkerton. "I think that there's another prisoner there, too: the commercial traveler Freddy Maxwell. The Chinese forced him to write out the calling card that had the trunk brought over from the hotel. Nefeldt was most likely hidden in it."

"Excellent," answered Bob. "The policemen are already in place and will appear here at the first whistle. I think we should go down into the basement."

The disguised detectives moved slowly forward and turned into the dark alleyway of No. 18. A mass of Chinese were crowded together in the dilapidated building. There were tumbledown shacks built in the courtyard, and many of the yellow-faced rascals were living there too.

Walking along the passageway, the detectives heard the clomping of wooden shoes behind them. Three Chinese were following on their heels. One of them, with a dark expression on his face and a black beard, was dressed in a crimson-red outfit. His appearance did not instill trust.

Despite the darkness, Pinkerton recognized him. He'd had occasion to meet him previously. It was Lun Tsa-hang himself, the prophet and wizard, who enjoyed unlimited power over his compatriots.

He paid no attention to the Chinamen in front of him, and the detective calmly let him pass them. In the purest Chinese, Pinkerton asked one of the prophet's companions: "Will the captured dogs be executed soon?"

"Yes, their hour has come! Lun Tsa-hang himself will execute them, and the two sacrifices will free Hang-Po from the clutches of the evil spirit!"

"Lun Tsa-hang is a righteous judge! The blood of the executed will bring us good," the detective said quietly.

Then he went down the stairs leading to the basement and found himself in a passageway lit by a single paper lantern.

Ten steps took him to a doorway guarded by two Chinamen holding broad double-edged swords.

The sentries stepped aside when Lun Tsa-hang and his companions appeared. The door opened, and the detectives walked with the others into a new passageway that split into two branches.

Lun Tsa-hang went to the right and yelled to his two companions, "Bring me the first prisoner!"

They went off to the left. By an earlier agreement, the detectives split up and went in different directions: Bob followed the prophet, and Pinkerton his companions. Another door opened at the end of the corridor, and they entered a dimly lit room with a rug in the middle. It was also illuminated by a single paper lantern, and it was difficult to make out people's figures.

The prisoners, Freddy Maxwell and Karl Nefeldt, were sitting on the rug. Both were deathly pale. They closely resembled each other; both were blond and bearded.

Along the walls were two guards holding broad swords; their eyes never left the prisoners.

When the three Chinese entered, the prisoners shuddered. One of the Chinamen approached Maxwell and said, "The hour of vengeance is here! Get up and follow me."

Since the man spoke Chinese, Maxwell understood nothing and didn't move.

They grabbed him, stood him on his feet, and dragged him to the door. He put up a desperate resistance, but the swords and daggers they showed him forced him to submit. They dragged him away and slammed the door.

The guards again assumed a crouch. One of them looked in surprise at the detective who stayed behind.

"Don't you want to see the captive dog executed?" he asked.

"No," objected Pinkerton, "I want something else!"

"What's that?"

"This!" shouted Pinkerton in a choked voice and pounced like a tiger on the guard. He gave him a tremendous blow of the fist to the temple and the Chinaman collapsed without a sound. The second guard watched this scene in mute horror, but before he could get up and shout, he met the same fate.

Pinkerton quickly cut the ropes binding Nefeldt and whispered to him, "You're saved, Mr. Nefeldt! I'm not Chinese, I'm Nat Pinkerton!"

Nefeldt almost shouted for joy. He grabbed the revolver that the detective handed him.

"Let's go, Mr. Pinkerton! I'll thank you later. Right now let's get the rascals that dragged Mr. Maxwell and me here and taunted us so insolently."

"Let's go, let's go! There are policemen outside already; I'll go call them."

Pinkerton rushed ahead and opened the door to the staircase. He quickly dealt with the unsuspecting guards, collapsing them with heavy blows. Not a sound escaped them, and the path outside was clear; Pinkerton raced up and let out a piercing whistle. In a few seconds steps were heard, as the police detachment rushed into the alleyway from Pell Street.

—·—

The Chinaman Lun Tsa-hang, followed by Bob, also reached the door, which he opened. They entered a large, square room lit by a row of multicolored lanterns. There was a red carpet in the middle, and on it a broad, curved sword.

Fifty Chinese standing in a circle respectfully greeted the newcomer.

One of them lifted the sword, got to his knees, and handed it to the prophet. He took it and looked at those present, his eyes shining.

"Everything is ready! The first sacrifice will now be brought in, and Hang-Po's vengeance will be complete!"

Two Chinese then led in Freddy Maxwell and stood him in the middle of the carpet before the prophet.

Lun Tsa-hang fixed him with a piercing glance and said slowly, "The night before last, Hang-Po, one of our most esteemed compatriots, was murdered. His death demands a sacrifice, that his soul might be freed from the evil spirit! You shall be the first sacrifice, and must die!"

Freddy Maxwell understood nothing. The prophet made a sign to his assistants.

They threw themselves on Maxwell, untied him, and stripped him to the waist. Then they threw him to the carpet and bent his head to the floor. The unfortunate man understood that they intended to behead him in the Chinese way; he tried to put up resistance, which, of course, was quickly overcome.

His deathly pale face showed an iron resolution. He did not want the band of scoundrels to see his fear.

Until then, Bob had been watching the scene quietly, hoping that Pinkerton and the policemen would appear before the danger reached its peak. But the prophet had already raised his sword; the circle of Chinese was crowding in on the unfortunate man whose bared neck awaited the blow.

The final moment had come—the prisoner was to die! Bob made his decision. At the very second Lun Tsa-hang was going to cut off Maxwell's head, Pinkerton's assistant fired a shot, and the sword flew from the prophet's bloody hand.

A howl erupted. The entire yellow-faced band understood instantly that an enemy was among them. Daggers gleamed, and with a savage howl the Chinese threw themselves at Bob, who was standing next to Maxwell holding his revolvers.

At that moment the door opened, and Nat Pinkerton, Karl Nefeldt, and the police broke into the room. A battle began, one that ended in the total defeat of the Chinese. Ten were killed, including Lun Tsa-hang, and the remainder were placed under arrest.

So Karl Nefeldt and Freddy Maxwell were freed, and they did not know how to thank their savior. His energy and faultless logic had discovered their place of captivity and saved them from a horrible death at the last moment.

Nat Pinkerton celebrated a brilliant victory! It later came to light that he had been absolutely correct in his initial guess about the importance of the talisman found by Karl Nefeldt—it had been left on the street so that its finder could be made into a blood sacrifice.

With that, Nat Pinkerton proved once again that a detective needs not only a calling, but also a broad education. Coming up against other nationalities, one also needs a deep knowledge of their language, life, customs, and even their fanatical rituals.

The Headlands of Manchuria
(1906–1908)

HUMILIATING DEFEAT AT THE HANDS OF THE JAPANESE IN THE RUSSO-JAPANESE WAR OF 1905 REVERBERATED SILENTLY THROUGH RUSSIAN CULTURE FOR MANY YEARS. THIS REQUIEM, INTENDED FOR MILITARY BANDS BUT PLAYED ELSEWHERE AND

Zonophone, *Sbornik libretto dlia plastinok Zonofon: opery, operetki, romansy, piesni, razskazy i pr.* (Vilna: I. I. Pirozhnikov, 1910–1912) 2:257.

RECORDED SEVERAL TIMES, WAS ONE OF THE FEW TIMES THE DE-
FEAT WAS ADDRESSED DIRECTLY. DESPITE OVERWROUGHT RHET-
ORIC, THE IMAGES AND HAUNTING MELODY EXPRESSED THE
TRAGEDY OF THE WAR, AND THE DEEP WOUNDS IT LEFT. THE
SONG SURVIVED THE WAR IT DESCRIBED TO BE PLAYED BY LATER
GENERATIONS WHEN WAR TOOK THEIR LOVED ONES FROM THEM.

Страшно вокруг и ветер на сопках
   рыдает,
Порой из-за туч выплывает луна
И могилы солдат освещает.

Horror around, with the wind wailing
   over the headlands,
The moon peeks out from behind the
   clouds,
And shines on the graves of our
   soldiers.

Белеют кресты далеких героев,
   прекрасных,
И прошлого тени кружатся вокруг,
Твердят нам о жертвах напрасных.

Crosses shine white over our distant,
   fine heroes,
Shadows of the past are swirling around,
They say that our losses were senseless.

Средь будочной тьмы, житейской
   обыденной прозы,
Забыть до сих пор мы не можем войны
И льются горючие слезы.

Amid daily life, the bustle and prose of
   existence,
The war will not leave us, we cannot
   forget,
And bitter tears flow down our faces.

Плачет отец, плачет жена молодая
И плачет вся Русь, как один человек,
Злой рок судьбы проклиная.

A father laments, a young wife laments,
All Russia laments, its cries joining as
   one,
Cursing its destiny's cruel fate.

И слезы бегут, как волны далекого моря,
И сердце терзают тоска и печаль,
И бездна великого горя.

Tears flow like the waves of a faraway
   ocean,
Our hearts are rent by our sadness and
   woe,
And the unending burden of longing.

Героев тела давно уж в могилах истлели,
А мы им последний не отдали долг
И вечную память не пели.

Our heroes' remains have turned to
   dust in their coffins,
And still we have never paid our last
   respects
Or sung the last rites for their spirits.

Мир вашей душе. Вы погибли за Русь, за
   отчизну,
Но, верьте, еще мы за вас отомстим
И справим кровавую тризну.

Peace to your soul. You died for your
   homeland, for Russia.
Have faith, though, we'll take
   retribution for you,
And celebrate that bloody death rite.

The Heroic Feat of the Don Cossack Kuzma Firsovich Kriuchkov

(1914)

KRIUCHKOV WAS THE FIRST AND GREATEST OF RUSSIA'S WORLD WAR I HEROES. THE SIMPLE COSSACK TURNED CELEBRITY EMBODIED MANY VIRTUES ATTRIBUTED TO RUSSIAN SOLDIERS. LIKE THE AMERICAN SERGEANT YORK, HE REPRESENTED THE FOLKSY, UNEDUCATED COMMON SOLIDER. HIS STOIC COURAGE, ENDURANCE AND FORTITUDE, AND EPIC COOLNESS WERE PRAISED IN COUNTLESS FORMS, INCLUDING SONGS, MOVIES, POSTCARDS, AND NEWSPAPERS. ALWAYS A PATRIOT, HE WON THE HEARTS OF RUSSIANS, AND REMAINED IN THEM UNTIL THE WAR EFFORT FALTERED IN 1916, AND UNBLINKING PATRIOTISM BECAME A VIRTUE OF THE PAST.

A WOUNDED COSSACK'S STORY ABOUT THE FEAT OF KUZMA KRIUCHKOV

On the German border, which we had crossed at many points, our Cossack squadron was ordered to establish observation posts.

Our posts stretched for about ten versts. Farther to the east stood another squadron from our Cossack regiment, and to the west a third.

They were set at a respectable distance from one another.

That night—I remember as if it were now—the weather was wonderful. We were permitted to light a bonfire.

There were five Cossacks stationed at our post: Kuzma Firsovich Kriuchkov, from the district of Ust-Khopersk, hamlet of Kalmykov; Ivan Shchegolkov, Vasily Astakhov, Mikhail Ivankov, and Georgy Rogachev.

It was almost eleven in the evening when the Rogachev boy, Dmitry, who we call Mitka, came running up and announced that he had seen a spy hidden in a hollow in the distance.

Geroiskii podvig Donskogo kazaka Kuz'my Firsovicha Kriuchkova (Moscow: P. B. Beltsov, 1914).

These boys would even call an entire enemy reconnaisance squad a spy. It was always impossible to get from them exactly how many mounted or infantry soldiers there were.

After we heard about the spies, we stood post quietly all night. Nobody shut an eye, and not a fire was lit. Everyone waited. But the night was marvelous. The breeze lulled us to sleep. The aroma of freshly mown hay wafted toward us. It reminded me of a quiet Ukrainian night.

The sky shone clear, and in its color it was just like the Cossack sky.

I was lying on my back, watching the stars. My heart suddenly felt sad for some reason. I remembered my home village, my mother, my friends, the Don. I was so far away from where I was born. Maybe someday I'd get back there.

Yes, all sorts of things happen in a war. It's all God's will.

I was thinking about all those things, but my gloomy thoughts were quickly crowded out by some funny things I could remember.

A captured German officer was brought to us one day. Our squadron commander knew German well. He struck up a conversation and soon was laughing heartily.

Then sometime later, when we were relaxing one evening, he told us what had been so funny.

The German, you see, had been disparaging Russians. He said that they weren't real soldiers, that their style of fighting was barbaric, uncivilized.

"Mercy sakes," said the indignant German, "they hack away with one hand and shove their other fist into your teeth. I got two teeth knocked out. Is that how you fight a war?!"

The commander had a good chuckle as he told us about this guy's whining.

And how could he not? Germans practice their fancy fencing in some manège and forget that a battlefield is no fencing school. There you have to fight with whatever you've got—your hands and feet and teeth and whatever else comes in handy. It's war, so fight like it. You don't have time to be too fussy.

There was quiet all around, and as I remembered that episode, I laughed loudly.

"What are you laughing at?" Kuzma Kriuchkov called to me.

"It's terribly funny," I answered, reminding him of the episode with the German prisoner.

"Why should you look after them, they won't do it for us! If you fall into their mitts, they'll slice you to pieces," Kriuchkov remarked.

Kriuchkov and I really got talking.

Our Kuzma was a good-looking guy. He had light brown hair and a fine-featured face, and he was tall, agile, and muscular. He was considered the best horseman in our group.

It began to get light around three in the morning. We had some potatoes, so we kindled the fire and baked them in the coals. We salted the food, and it tasted delicious. Kriuchkov lay down to sleep. Astakhov stayed behind to stand guard, and Shchegolkov and Ivankov went to get hay for the horses.

Looking through my binoculars, I saw a line of horsemen making their way across a meadow to the west. German uniforms. They were hurrying, leading their horses by the reins. Once they'd crossed, they could hide themselves in a ditch.

I called to Astakhov, gave him the binoculars, and pointed out the German cavalrymen sneaking up on us.

Astakhov sent for Shchegolkov and Ivankov.

Kriuchkov held out all night, but toward sunrise sleep overcame him.

I woke him up. As soon as I said "Germans!" he leapt to his feet. Kriuchkov grabbed his binoculars too and began looking. He counted twenty-seven in all.

Suddenly Kriuchkov saw that they had mounted and were retreating across the hill that separated the hollow from the oat field.

Kriuchkov gave the order to saddle the horses. Within five minutes, we had ridden off after the Germans. Rogachev was ordered to report to our superiors.

We galloped off, and the Germans turned toward a stream to the south without seeing us. We chanced upon a front-line soldier who was making his way to our post.

We attached him to our squad for the time being. Kriuchkov, Ivankov, and I chased after the Germans, and Astakhov, Shchegolkov, and the front-line man set off to outflank them.

Kriuchkov, Ivankov, and I caught up with them in the bog. Without knowing we were there, the Germans suddenly turned and saw us. Their jaws dropped.

At first they were taken aback and were visibly scared of us Cossacks, but seeing that there were only three of us, they went on the attack. The distance between us was about two hundred steps. We dismounted and began shooting at them. They were frightened by our fire. We killed three immediately. The Germans began retreating off to the side. We remounted and raced off to catch them. At that moment Shchegolkov and Astakhov galloped up, and we all set off after the Germans.

We rode that way for about six versts. Seeing that they were not too far away, we dismounted again and began shooting. We took another two Germans out of commission.

The Germans were infuriated and went over to the attack. But as they were approaching, we killed their officer.

They caught up to us and began stabbing at Ivankov with their lances. Kriuchkov fought three Germans off, while the other Cossacks and I drew up in a circle to fight them off.

Oh, those Germans aren't much in hand-to-hand.

Shchegolkov knocked one off his horse, and began hacking another German who had swung a saber at him.

But only the German's helmet got dented. Then Ivankov struck him on the neck with his sword.

The head rolled right off his shoulders, and the horse carried the headless German off, sprinkling the ground with streams of blood.

Astakhov and Ivankov skirted the Germans to the right, and Shchegolkov to the left.

I was fending two Germans off with my lance. Six men were pursuing Ivankov and Astakhov, but they managed to hoodwink the Germans.

They rode off a high bank into the river and swam across to the flat bank. The Germans tried to do the same thing but flew head over heels. Their horses were not used to jumping from high places.

Three Germans chased after Shchegolkov. There was a moment when it looked like they would catch him, but praise be to God, Shchegolkov chased them off.

Seeing that chasing Ivankov, Astakhov, and Shchegolkov was useless, the Germans suddenly regrouped and went after Kriuchkov.

At first he fought with three of them, but when they were joined by another nine to become twelve, Kriuchkov evaded them and galloped off over all the ditches, putting thirty paces between them. But he was cut off on the flank by a German noncom, who swung at him with his sword. Kriuchkov fended the blow off deftly with his rifle. But as it slid down the barrel, the noncom's saber wounded three of Kriuchkov's fingers.

Blood spurted from the wound. Kriuchkov dropped his rifle, grabbed his sword, and cracked the noncom on the helmet. But the helmet only got dented a bit.

With a quick and unexpected stroke, Kriuchkov sliced the noncom's neck open. He grabbed his throat, blood gushed over his hands, and Kriuchkov went on his way, flying like an eagle among frightened birds.

Left without their superiors, the enemy were confused, and they panicked. Not knowing what to do, they took to their heels. There wasn't much they *could* do, since our guys hadn't been napping, and Kriuchkov hadn't been napping either.

The skirmish heated up again, and the yellow-bellied Prussians began sneaking off one by one, but bullets flew after them, and the cowards fell from their horses and stumbled like chickens with their heads cut off.

Two Prussians worked up their courage and went after Kriuchkov with their lances, trying to knock him out of his saddle, but Kriuchkov held his seat firmly.

Kriuchkov tore their lances from their hands and threw himself into the desperate battle. Now, that was a real skirmish! The enemy's lances snapped like feathers, and they themselves were no better than wet hens. Even when they seemed ready and bold, nothing came of it.

Several minutes passed—and from the twenty-seven Prussians who had fought four Don Cossacks, only three were left in the saddle, and they fled like cowardly rabbits in wild panic.

The rest were killed or wounded.

The three fugitives probably didn't survive, either, since we sent them off with well-aimed bullets, and Cossack bullets don't fly off just anywhere.

Despite the fact that Kriuchkov had received sixteen wounds and his hand was hacked by a saber, he had laid out eleven Germans and had stayed in the ranks till the end of the glorious battle.

For his heroic feat, Kuzma Firsovich Kriuchkov was awarded the St. George Cross. In addition, he received many expensive gifts.

Jackals

Sergei Sokolsky (1916)

Sergei Sokolsky,
self-caricature

SOKOLSKY WAS ONE OF THE MORE POPU-
LAR CLOWNS IN WARTIME PETROGRAD, A
PRACTITIONER OF THE "BAREFOOT," OR
HOBO, SCHOOL OF CLOWNING. CLOWN-
ING IN RUSSIA WAS A POETIC PROFES-
SION, AND SOKOLSKY'S SPECIALTY WAS
RECITING COUPLETS, POINTED RHYMES
FREQUENTLY USED FOR SOCIAL COMMEN-
TARY. CLOWNS, LIKE THEIR ANCESTORS
THE JESTERS, COULD OFTEN SAY THINGS
IN THE CIRCUS ARENA THAT WERE UNSPEAKABLE ELSEWHERE.
HERE WE SEE ONE OF THE FIRST SIGNS OF DISCONTENT WITH THE
FALTERING WAR EFFORT. SOKOLSKY ASSUMES THE STANCE OF A
PATRIOT AND CHRISTIAN TO CRITICIZE THE NEWLY WEALTHY;
AND HE REVEALS A DEEP-SEATED ANTIPATHY FOR BUSINESSMEN
AND JEWS, AN ATTITUDE THAT WOULD GROW STRONGER WITH
MANY RUSSIANS IN THE COMING YEARS.

A graying staff-captain appeared
To visit in my dressing room.
A vein was bandaged up in black,
His saddened face was paled by wounds.
We introduced ourselves. I'll say
Honestly: I felt delight
To hear the hero compliment
This modest poetaster's lines.
Our conversation warmed. I asked
Banally: "Soldier, are you tired?
Or are you used to always sitting, sleeping,
And eating under fire?"
He smiled. And then, wearily,

Sergei Sokol'skii, *Pliashushchaia lirika. Stikhotvoreniia i pesni* (Petrograd: Tsentral'naia tipografiia, 1916),
pp. 43–46.

He began to tell about his life.
He told how he had been
Struck by a bullet in a fight.
But having shown a reckless smile,
He said, "It's nothing that won't mend.
A soldier's greatest fear's not battle;
What scares and troubles him is when
He finds that he has been forgotten,
Lost out beyond his trench and earthworks.
Where in the night, amid the brush,
A predatory jackal lurks.
You lie there, powerless and sick,
And wait until that hound of graves
Finds you too among the corpses!
On such a night my hair went gray . . . "
He fell silent. And I could not
Answer him. I felt no bolder.
My agitation was too great:
What could a poet tell this soldier?
And so I still had no reply
When, brushing off his epaulets,
He said to me as we were parting:
"You're lucky! You've seen no jackals yet!"
The soldier left . . . and silvery
Rang the jingling of his spurs.
And in this actor's breast alone,
Our conversation was still heard.
"There are no jackals." Yes, it's true,
These beasts can roam our towns no more,
But those who, solely out of greed,
Opened up those rows of stores,
And took advantage of the war,
Inflating prices they demand,
To make a sinister bazaar
Of their own beloved land,
Scorning all the squalls of danger
That shake the motherland around,
Tell me: are they not jackals,
Those shopkeepers, those dirty louts?!
No, they're much worse—they're viler still!
A jackal can just blame his birth,
But after all, these are people,
They're businessmen,[1] from last to first.
Oh, businessman! Please, Hizzoner,

---

1. *Kommersanty.*

It's not for nothing that so long
You have rhymed with "prisoner"!
But please forgive my rudeness, sir.
I sorely fear you, you human beast,
So how could I not say it straight.
Though I believe, I firmly think
That we don't have so long to wait.
When all the battles have been fought,
Those evil men will not be here.
And on that blessed Easter Sunday
The Pharisees will disappear.
There won't be any Judases[2]
Extracting pennies from our home,
And from those Flesh-Day profligates
The last base spirit will be gone.
And patiently, we will be able
To start constructing our new life,
Standing up alone and praying
For those who've fallen in the strife.
All the hate will be forgotten,
And peace will come down from the skies,
With honesty and openness,
We'll tell each other "Christ is alive!"

---

2. Literally: Christ-sellers.

Rasputin's Nighttime Orgies (the Tsarist Miracle-Worker)
A Tale in One Act
V. V. Ramazanov (1917)

ONE OF THE FIRST SIGNS THAT THE FEBRUARY REVOLUTION OF 1917 HAD DEMOLISHED CENSORSHIP WAS THE PROLIFERATION OF CABARET THEATERS. CABARETS COULD REACT QUICKLY TO CURRENT EVENTS AND CHANGING REGULATIONS, RESPONDING WITH

Viktor V. Ramazanov, *Nochnye orgii Rasputina* (*tsarskii chudotvorets*). Byl' v 1-m d. Manuscript, n.p.d. 14 pp.

A FLOOD OF POLITICAL BURLESQUE AND SEMI-PORNOGRAPHIC TITILLATION. THE BOLSHEVIKS WERE A FAVORITE TARGET OF SATIRE, BUT THE TWO TASTES WERE BEST SATISFIED BY THE NOW-MYTHIC FIGURE OF GRIGORY RASPUTIN, WHO HAD MESMERIZED AND SUPPOSEDLY SEDUCED THE TRAITOROUS GERMAN-BORN TSARITSA, AND LED RUSSIA TO CATASTROPHE. THE SUBJECT HAD BEEN TABOO THROUGHOUT THE WAR, EVEN AFTER HIS MURDER IN DECEMBER 1916. THIS PIECE, WHICH OPENED MAY 11 IN THE NEVSKY FARCE THEATER, WAS JUST ONE OF MANY ON THE SUBJECT. USING BROAD HUMOR, IT COMBINES SEXUAL MYTHS OF RASPUTIN AND THE DECLINE OF THE ROMANOVS WITH THE ETHNIC AND CLASS POLITICS OF THE TIME.

Grishka Rasputin, wearing the long brown hair of a robust *muzhik,* a peasant jacket, tall boots, and a fur over a sewn Russian *sorochka* blouse. He's direct and abrupt, with a provincial accent.

Protopopov, his foppish friend[1]
Romanova (the tsaritsa Alexandra)
Vyrubova (her friend and reputed lover)[2]
Abdul and Faiz, Tatar lackeys

A room in the Villa Rodé, a chic restaurant on the outskirts of town. A piano, a door in the middle, and a small secret passage to the right. Nighttime. Lackeys are setting a sumptuous table, where bottles of madeira are already out.

ABDUL: Be careful, Faiz, you have to do your best today. You know who we're preparing this room for?

FAIZ: No, tell me.

ABDUL: You remember that big brawl here last Saturday night?

FAIZ: Ah, do you mean that big scandal?

ABDUL: Yeah, yeah. You remember that big, strong bearded guy who came? And those officers busted his chops when he started pawing our gypsy girl Shura?

FAIZ: 'Course I remember. It was that Grishka Rasputin.

ABDUL: Right, that's the one. He'll be here today with some friends.

FAIZ: Is it true what they say, that's he's some big bastard?

ABDUL: I heard that he used to be a big-time thief, a horse thief, but now he does

---

1. See *Anecdotes,* above.
2. Rumors vary, but the real gossip made her lover of the tsarevna. Alexandra found her a husband for a while, but in 1918 the Muraviev Commission made her submit to a doctor, who found her hymen intact.

his business with the ladies. He pinches their money, which they've skinned from the poor folk, and then they come here and squander it on drinks.

FAIZ: Is it true that he's her lover?

ABDUL: Who her?

FAIZ: The young majesty, the tsaritsa.

ABDUL: That's what the people say, so it must be true; you can't just make stuff like that up.

FAIZ: Isn't she ashamed with a *muzhik* . . .

ABDUL: That's how it is. Do you really think people like that have shame or a conscience?

FAIZ: You're right; if they felt any shame, they'd never do what they do to the people. (*A voice is heard from outside the door:*) Abdul, where are you? Come quickly!

ABDUL: Right away. (*He steps out, and returns immediately, letting in the guests: Rasputin in his fur, and behind him Romanova and Vyrubova, in black clothing with dark veils lowered. Behind them comes Protopopov.*)

ABDUL: This way, please.

RASPUTIN (*stopping in the middle of the room and speaking loudly*): Peace to this house . . . (*exclaiming loudly upon seeing the wine on the table*) Oho-o . . . my favorite madeira . . . (*blessing the table, using biblical language*) I bless this table and all hereon. My belly is great and abundant, and demands to be well met: be that to say, a profuse offering of wine. (*to the lackey*) Bring thou more madeira, and gladden my sight.

ABDUL (*running*): Right away, sir.

FAIZ (*to Rasputin*): Permit me to help you with your coat.

RASPUTIN (*roughly pushing him back*): Get away from me, riffraff. Your profane hands are unworthy of touching my holy garments. (*importantly*) Peaceable women, approach and be deemed worthy. (*He makes a gesture with both hands and keeps them stretched out. Romanova and Vyrubova throw back their veils together and kneel before Rasputin on both sides, kissing his hands.*)

ROMANOVA (*ecstatically*): You are our miracle worker.

VYRUBOVA (*similarly*): You are our prophet.

RASPUTIN: Amen. Rise and disrobe me.

ROMANOVA AND VYRUBOVA (*reciting in a prayerful hush*): Dear sire, our father. Our sunshine. You have penetrated our soul and tamed our spirit. (*Abdul enters carrying several uncorked bottles of madeira, while Faiz helps Romanova and Vyrubova take off their coats.*)

RASPUTIN: Well done. Okay, now git the hell outta here and wait till I call you. Got it?

ABDUL: As you wish. (*to Faiz*) Let's go, Faiz. (*They leave.*)

RASPUTIN: You blackguard, pour us out a goblet, or I won't be able to wait.

PROTOPOPOV: Ladies and gentlemen, you cannot imagine how happy I am that you have called me here. Despite the small size of our company, it is so pleasant to be among you that I cannot find words to express my ecstasy.

The Eruption of Commercial Culture in the Interrevolutionary Years

RASPUTIN: That's right, old chum. You could say our group is first-class. You just take a good look at who's here. (*importantly*) First of all, there's me. Can you understand what that "me" means? Answer me . . . (*articulating each syllable*) Un-der-stand? You can ask Sasha, you can ask Anna, they'll explain to you. Peaceable women, answer; do you feel me?

ROMANOVA (*ecstatically*): Oh, I feel it, sire . . . I feel it very much.

VYRUBOVA: We feel, great miracle worker. You bring light to Russia. You are the teacher of the people.

RASPUTIN: Enough of your explication; silence your tongue. Let us give fitting attention to the wine.

ROMANOVA: Sire, accept from mine own hands this cup of wine; drink it to your health and long life.

ALL (*drinking and singing*): Long life . . . long life, Father Grigory. (*The drunken carousing begins.*)

RASPUTIN: Pour some more. Splendid wine; I love this madeira more than anything in life. It goes to my member. Splendid. (*He drinks and bellows with pleasure.*)

PROTOPOPOV (*ecstatically*): My God, what beauty. What beauty . . . What could be better than our group. Oh, Grisha, what a talent you are. You're a Napoleon. You're an Alexander the Great. No, you're above them. (*turning to the ladies*) Isn't that right, Grisha's better?

ROMANOVA: Oh, much better. He is our god. Our idol. (*She kneels before Rasputin.*)

RASPUTIN: You're babbling, woman. (*quietly to her*) Did you forget that wimpy Nicky of yours? Oh, Sasha, no sense will ever come of him. He'll destroy you, and all of us, you mark my words.

ROMANOVA (*with feeling*): No, that will not be. Whatever I want will happen. If I want to, I can destroy everyone, him and all his ministers. . . . I'll squeeze all Russia in my hands. Wilhelm is strong, and he and I are allies; he trusts me, and I trust him. If I want, you, Grisha, will be the Russian tsar.

VYRUBOVA (*ecstatically*): And what a wonderful tsar he would be. How the people would love you, sire. (*She sits on Rasputin's lap and cuddles up to him.*)

RASPUTIN (*drunk, he roughly pushes her away*): Settle down a bit, you freak. Don't get pushy. Why are you crawling on me, woman?

VYRUBOVA (*languidly*): Oh, sire, look at me longer; I want to feel you.

RASPUTIN: Leave me alone, Anna. You want to feel too much. Wait your turn. The Lord has not cast his grace on thee today. Sasha, come here. Sit on my lap. The-r-e. It's hot as a steam bath in here; help me take off my vest. Hey, peaceable women, help me.

Romanova and Vyrubova help him off with his vest, and he remains in his shirt.

RASPUTIN: Oh you blackguard. Pour some more wine. (*He picks up the goblet.*) And now let's sing a song. (*He sings.*)

Let us drink to Sasha,
To our Sasha dear.

And if it's not Sasha,
There's another near.

He embraces Romanova, who strokes his beard.

ROMANOVA: Sire, my glorious sire.

PROTOPOPOV: No, what beauty . . . What talent. Such words. (*completely drunk*) Just think how intelligent those words are. "There's another near."

ROMANOVA (*pleading*): No, dear sire, don't; don't find another; I can't live without you—you are my life, my sunshine. Without you we'll all be destroyed. Be with us . . . Be with us . . . (*Hysterically, she falls to the ground and beats her breast.*)

VYRUBOVA (*pleading*): Sire, dear sire, please soothe the tsaritsa; the poor woman is suffering. You're a miracle worker, put an end to her suffering.

RASPUTIN: Sh-sh. Silence, Anna. Shut your trap. I tell you the truth, Satan dwells within her. Open the door on the right, Anna; I will expel the demon from the tsaritsa. (*Anna opens the door on the right, letting out Rasputin, who carries Romanova and, pushing her head through the doorway says:*) She won't go through the door. The demon has gotten deeply into the tsaritsa; we will need great strength to exorcise it. The Lord has given me an idea. (*He hides.*)

VYRUBOVA (*to Protopopov*): Do you feel the strength of this great man? Does Russia really have room for him? This is a genius for all the world, who has no equal.

PROTOPOPOV (*drunkenly*): I always said that Grishka would show us what's what. He's a talent. A huge talent. Did you know he has a great talent?

VYRUBOVA (*languidly*): Oh, I know—a huge one, a huge talent.

RASPUTIN (*entering without his belt on, breathing heavily*): Hey, blackguard, pour some wine. I'm beat; that demon had gotten deep into the tsaritsa. And still I defeated it; I Grigory, defeated and exorcised it. (*he shouts*) Sashka . . . come here! Do you hear, come here now . . . (*Romanova enters; she is in a happy mood and throws herself at Rasputin's feet.*)

ROMANOVA: Sire, dear sire, you are my healer . . . I thank you.

RASPUTIN: Get up. Do you see how the woman instantly perked up and her mood improved? It was all me . . . (*importantly*) Father Grigory . . . (*loudly*) Fall to my feet and I shall heal all the women and make them all merry. Laugh, ye all. Hey, Sashka, Anna, blackguard. Laugh, ye all, for knowledge and the joy of life are in laughter. (*All laugh with a stupid, drunken laughter.*)

PROTOPOPOV (*standing on the table, with great ceremony*): God, what a talent—what a great talent.

RASPUTIN: Hey, cook us up the "Dashing Merchant," and you, Sasha and Anna, help me sing, and then we can dance some. (*Protopopov plays the piano. Rasputin sings.*)

> A dashing merchant rode to the fair,
> A dashing merchant, fine young man.

ALL:
> Tra-la-la-la-la.
> A dashing merchant, fine young man.

After the second couplet, the music plays faster. Rasputin gives it his all, dancing in the middle of the room, with Romanova and Vyrubova dancing in accompaniment.

PROTOPOPOV (*shouting wildly in ecstasy*): What beauty . . . What piercing beauty . . . What a talent. There, now that's who should be tsar in Russia. Hurrah! hurrah!

CURTAIN

GLOSSARY

arshin: an old measurement equivalent to the ell, the distance from elbow to hand.

artel: a cooperative of workers, usually led by a *starosta,* or elder, who hired themselves out as a group, and traveled from worksite to worksite.

ataman: chief. Robber bands traditionally were organized by ranks, with titles taken from Cossack military terminology. The terms survived to the twentieth century.

balagan (plural *balagany*): a temporary but full-blown theater, usually erected for several months each holiday season.

bliny: thin pancakes eaten on the Mardi Gras (*maslenitsa*) feast.

bogatyr: roughly the equivalent of a courageous warrior or "knight" in Russian epics and fairy tales.

boyar (in Russian *boyarin,* plural *boyare*): a member of the pre-Petrine proto-nobility. Boyars were wealthy landowners who served both as the military elite and as advisors to the grand prince, and later the tsar. Neither their titles nor their land enjoyed the security of being hereditary, although in practice both were often passed along.

chuika: an old-fashioned knee-length cloth jacket worn as an outer garment by men.

desiatin: one desiatin is equal to 21 acres.

esaul (plural *esauly*): in the hierarchy of robber bands, esaul meant approximately captain or lieutenant, and was directly below ataman (see above).

Gostinyi dvor: a two-story building with long corridors lined by small shops (*lavki*), located in the commercial center of Petersburg.

gusli: an ancient minstrels' stringed instrument, similar to a psaltery.

kaftan: traditional long-sleeved robe with girdle.

kibitka: a nomad tent.

kumiss: fermented mare's milk, a Tatar and Central Asian beverage.

kvas: a popular drink fermented from bread, commonly available throughout Russia.

lubok (plural *lubki*): popular literature, either a graphic with text or, in later years, a short work of fiction printed on cheap paper for a lower-class audience.

mir: the peasant commune, which distributed land among villagers and decided various social issues.

muzhik (plural *muzhiki*): a peasant. The word implies a lack of culture and refinement.

Piter: a popular and affectionate abbreviation for St. Petersburg.

raeshnik (plural *raeshniki;* from **raek, a fairground peep show):** a rhyming verse form unique to the Russian fairground, and associated with popular culture, originating with peep-show barkers.

shuba: a large, heavy fur coat, especially as is needed for Russian winters.

sotnik: old administrative title roughly equivalent to bailiff.

starshina: the local elder.

tarantas: a springless two-wheeled carriage used mostly in the countryside.

trepak: an energetic and emotive folkdance.

valenki: felt boots traditional for peasants.

verst (Russian *versta*): an old Russian measurement equal to about two-thirds of a mile.

voevoda: a medieval provincial administrator, or sheriff.

SELECTED BIBLIOGRAPHY

Art and Culture in Nineteenth-Century Russia. Edited by Theofanis G. Stavrow. Bloomington: Indiana University Press, 1983.

Between Tsar and People: Educated Society and the Quest for Public Identity in Late Imperial Russia. Edited by Edith W. Clowes, Samuel D. Kassow, and James L. West. Princeton: Princeton University Press, 1991.

Bogdanov, Aleksandr. *Red Star: The First Bolshevik Utopia.* Edited by Loren R. Graham and Richard Stites. Translated by Charles Rougle. Bloomington: Indiana University Press, 1984.

Bradley, Joseph. *Muzhik and Muscovite: Urbanization in Late Imperial Russia.* Berkeley: University of California Press, 1985.

Brooks, Jeffrey. *When Russia Learned to Read: Literacy and Popular Literature, 1861–1917.* Princeton: Princeton University Press, 1985.

Brower, Daniel R. *The Russian City between Tradition and Modernity, 1850–1900.* Berkeley: University of California Press, 1990.

Buryshkin, P. A. *Moskva kupecheskaia.* New York: Chekhov, 1954.

Cultures in Flux: Lower-Class Values, Practices and Resistance in Late Imperial Russia. Edited by Stephen P. Frank and Mark D. Steinberg. Princeton: Princeton University Press, 1994.

Donskov, Andrew. *Mixail Lentovskij and the Russian Theatre.* East Lansing, Mich.: Russian Language Journal, 1985.

Eklof, Ben, and Stephen Frank, eds. *The World of the Russian Peasant: Post-emancipation Culture and Society.* Boston: Unwin Hyman, 1990.

Engelstein, Laura. *The Keys to Happiness: Sex and the Search for Modernity in Fin-de-siècle Russia.* Ithaca: Cornell University Press, 1992.

Fetzer, Leland, ed. and trans. *Pre-revolutionary Russian Science Fiction: Seven Utopias and a Dream.* Ann Arbor: Ardis, 1982.

Ginzburg. S. S. *Kinematografiia dorevoliutsionnoi Rossii.* Moscow: Iskusstvo, 1963.

Goulzadian, Anne. *L'empire du dernier tsar: 410 cartes postales, 1896–1917.* Paris: Editions Astrid, 1982.

Hilton, Alison. *Russian Folk Art.* Bloomington: Indiana University Press, 1995.

Ivanits, Linda J. *Russian Folk Belief.* Armonk: M. E. Sharpe, 1989.

Jahn, Hubertus. *Patriotic Culture in Russia during World War I.* Ithaca: Cornell University Press, 1995.

Johnson, Robert. *Peasant and Proletarian: The Working Class in Moscow in the Late Nineteenth Century.* New Brunswick, N.J.: Rutgers University Press, 1979.

Karlinsky, Simon. *Russian Drama from Its Beginnings to the Age of Pushkin.* Berkeley: University of California Press, 1985.

Kelly, Catriona. *Petrushka: The Russian Carnival Puppet Theatre.* Cambridge: Cambridge University Press, 1990.

Khanzhonkov, A. A. *Pervye gody russkoi kinematografii.* Moscow, 1937.

Kuznetsov, Evgenii. *Iz proshlogo russkoi estrady. Istoricheskie ocherki.* Moscow: Gosizdat, 1958.

Layton, Susan. *Russian Literature and Empire.* New York: Cambridge University Press, 1994.

Literature and Society in Imperial Russia, 1800–1914. Edited by William Mills Todd III. Stanford, Calif.: Stanford University Press, 1978.

McReynolds, Louise. *The News under Russia's Old Regime: The Development of a Mass-Circulation Press.* Princeton: Princeton University Press, 1991.

McReynolds, Louise, ed. *Russian Studies in History*. Special Issue on "Russian Nightlife, Fin-de-siècle," 31, no. 3 (Winter, 1992–93).

Mikhnevich, Vladimir. *Iazvy Peterburga: opyt istoriko-statisticheskogo izsledovaniia nravstvennosti stolichnogo naseleniia*. St. Petersburg: S. Sushchinskii, 1886.

Narodnaia graviura i fol'klor v. Rossii XVII–XIX vv. Moscow: Sovetskii khudozhnik, 1976.

Nekrylova, A. F. *Russkie narodnye gorodskie prazdniki, uveseleniia i zrelishcha: konets XVIII–nachalo XIX veka*. Leningrad: Iskusstvo, 1984.

Nest'ev, I. V. *Zvezdy russkoi estrady (Panina, Vial'tseva, Plevitskaia): ocherki o russkikh estradnykh pevitsakh nachala XX veka*. Moscow: Sovetskii kompozitor, 1970.

Neuberger, Joan. *Hooliganism: Crime, Culture and Power in St. Petersburg, 1900–1914*. Berkeley: University of California Press, 1993.

Orkestr imeni V. V. Andreeva. Leningrad: Muzyka, 1987.

Owens, Thomas. *Capitalism and Politics in Russia: A Social History of the Moscow Merchants*. Cambridge: Cambridge University Press, 1981.

Perrie, Maureen. "Folklore as Evidence of Peasant Mentalité: Social Attitudes and Values in Russian Popular Culture." *The Russian Review* 48 (1989): 119–143.

Peterburg i guberniia: istoriko-etnograficheskie issledovaniia. Edited by N. V. Iukhneva. Leningrad, 1989.

Petrovskaia, I. F. *Teatr i zritel' rossiiskikh stolits: 1885–1917*. Moscow: Iskusstvo, 1990.

Rom-Lebedev, I. I. *Ot tsyganskogo khora—k teatru 'Romen': zapiski moskovskogo tsygana*. Moscow: Iskusstvo, 1990.

Russia's Women: Accommodation, Resistance, Transformation. Edited by Barbara E. Clements, Barbara A. Engel, and Christine D. Worobec. Berkeley: University of California Press, 1991.

Segel, Harold B. *Turn-of-the-Century Cabaret: Paris, Barcelona, Berlin, Munich, Vienna, Cracow, Moscow, St. Petersburg, Zurich*. New York: Columbia University Press, 1987.

Silent Witnesses: Russian Films, 1908–1919. Edited by Yuri Tsivian. Edizioni Biblioteca dell'immagine, British Film Institute, 1989.

Steinberg, Mark. *Moral Communities: The Culture of Class Relations in the Russian Printing Industry, 1867–1907*. Berkeley: University of California Press, 1992.

Stites, Richard. *Soviet Popular Culture: Entertainment and Society in Russia since 1900*. Cambridge: Cambridge University Press, 1992.

Swift, Eugene Anthony. "Theater for the People: The Politics of Popular Culture in Urban Russia, 1861–1917." Ph.D. dissertation, University of California, Berkeley, 1992.

Thurston, Gary. "The Impact of Russian Popular Theatre, 1886–1915." *The Journal of Modern History* 55, no. 2 (June 1983): 239–243.

Tsivian, Yuri. *Early Cinema in Russia and Its Cultural Reception*. London: Routledge, 1994.

von Geldern, James. "Life In Between: Migration and Popular Culture in Late Imperial Russia." *The Russian Review* (July 1996), pp. 365–383.

Women and Society in Russia and the Soviet Union. Edited by Linda Edmondson. Cambridge: Cambridge University Press, 1992.

Wortman, Richard. *The Crisis of Russian Populism*. Cambridge: Cambridge University Press, 1967.

Zasosov, D. A., and Pyzin, V. I. *Iz zhizni Peterburga 1890–1910-x godov. Zapiski ochevidtsev*. Leningrad: Lenizdat, 1991.

Zelnik, Reginald E., ed. and trans. *A Radical Worker in Tsarist Russia: The Autobiography of Semen Ivanovich Kanatchikov*. Stanford: Stanford University Press, 1986.

Zorkaia, N. M. *Na rubezhe stoletii: u istokov massovogo iskusstva v Rossii 1900–1910*. Moscow: Nauka, 1976.

JAMES VON GELDERN is Associate Professor of Russian at Macalester College. He is author of *Bolshevik Festivals* and co-editor (with Richard Stites) of *Mass Culture in Soviet Russia: Tales, Poems, Songs, Movies, Plays, and Folklore, 1917–1953*.

LOUISE MCREYNOLDS is Associate Professor of History at the University of Hawai'i and author of *The News under Russia's Old Regime: The Development of a Mass-Circulation Press*. She is translator of the first English edition of Evdokia Nagrodskaia's novel *The Wrath of Dionysus*.